DISTRIBUTIONAL CHECKLIST OF NORTH AMERICAN BIRDS

He served his day; he recorded his convictions—and passed. In spite of the printed word, the commonplaces of his experience are buried in a practical oblivion, and the very high-lights of it are obscured. Another generation demands reappraisal, restatement—re-proving perhaps. And it rejoices—for an hour. In like manner, still another generation shall exclaim, "Why, it was not thus! It could not have been so! Behold! do we not know what *is*"—Patiently, little brothers! It was, and is, and ever shall be— *never the same.*

William Leon Dawson
The Birds of California, 1923

DISTRIBUTIONAL CHECKLIST OF NORTH AMERICAN BIRDS

VOLUME I: UNITED STATES AND CANADA

A compendium of annotated state and province checklists
providing status and abundance information for
all species of North American birds

by

David DeSante
and
Peter Pyle

Illustrated by

F. P. Bennett, Jr.
and
Keith Hansen

Artemisia Press

Lee Vining, California

DISTRIBUTIONAL CHECKLIST OF NORTH AMERICAN BIRDS
Copyright ©1986 by David DeSante and Peter Pyle. All rights reserved.

ISBN 0-932347-00-2
Library of Congress Catalog No. 85-71423

Cover designed and painted by F. P. Bennett, Jr., except Lewis' Woodpecker by Keith Hansen.

TEX typesetting and computing services by Zoological Data Processing, Socorro, New Mexico.

Printed in the United States of America by Braun-Brumfield, Inc., Ann Arbor, Michigan.

Special thanks to Paul de Fremery of Braun-Brumfield, and to Steve Bencze of TEXSource, Houston, Texas, Susan King and David Fuchs of Stanford University, Stanford, California, David Becker and Eddy Fries of New Mexico Tech, Socorro, New Mexico, and Cordell Green and Lydia Skinner of Kestrel Institute, Palo Alto, California.

Designed and produced by David DeSante for

> **Artemisia Press**
> P. O. Box 119
> Lee Vining, CA 93541

A Slate Creek Book.

To our parents,

>Gilbert and Irene DeSante
>
>and
>
>Robert and Leilani Pyle,

who instilled in us an appreciation for the natural world and a love of truth and beauty,

we gratefully dedicate this work.

Preface

The senior author originated the idea of this checklist some twelve years ago. He considered various formats, but deferred tackling the job because of two major problems. First, there existed no recent authoritative summary of the many taxonomic and nomenclatural changes that were continually being suggested, and he felt unqualified to make those decisions. Second, it seemed too overwhelming a task for one person.

All this changed in 1983. The American Ornithologists' Union announced a late summer publication date for the long-awaited Sixth Edition of their *Check-list of North American Birds*. Then, on February 14, in San Cristobal de las Casas, Mexico, DeSante shared his ideas with Peter Pyle and Steve Howell. Pyle possessed extensive and detailed knowledge of bird distribution in the United States and Canada, while Howell had recently accumulated similar knowledge of Mexican birds. By the end of a few hours of discussion, we decided to divide the *Checklist* into two volumes: Volume I to cover the United States and Canada, Volume II to cover Mexico, Central America and the West Indies. Pyle agreed to collaborate on Volume I and Howell on Volume II.

Our good fortune was soon augmented three more times: John W. Shipman of Zoological Data Processing took on the seemingly impossible job of keying in (and constantly revising and updating) this great mass of data, producing state and province checklists for review, and typesetting the book; artists F. P. Bennett Jr. and Keith Hansen agreed to contribute full-page black-and-white bird art to add warmth and life to the statistics; and David and Sally Gaines of Artemisia Press decided to publish the book.

We believe that we have created, with the generous assistance of over 150 of North America's foremost experts on bird distribution, a useful, accurate and complete compilation of the status and abundance of all of North America's bird species in all the states and provinces of the United States and Canada. We are confident that Hansen and Bennett's contribution represents one of the finest collections of black-and-white bird art ever published. We also trust that we have developed a convenient solution to the problem of keeping and updating personal state and province life lists.

Indeed we encourage the practice of keeping detailed lists, not only of birds recorded in the course of a lifetime, but also those recorded each year, each season and in each locality. We must caution, however, against the pitfall of allowing bird listing to become the goal and endpoint of birding activity. Instead, we urge everyone to become as well acquainted as possible with the lives and habits, the plumages and songs, the behavior and distribution, and even the individual personalities of our feathered fellow travelers with whom we share this small, fragile and beautiful planet. We urge all persons to consider themselves, not so much as bird listers, but as bird lovers.

We should always strive to conduct our birding activities under the maxim that "the welfare of the bird is our foremost concern." This will make us sensitive about our potential impact upon the habitats of the birds that we seek to observe. We will become sensitive as well about the extent of our interference into the nesting activities of birds and even into the privacy of their lives. If we could all keep this sensitivity in mind, there might be no more marshes trampled by hordes of birders, no more nests deserted under the pressure of too many prying eyes, no more territories deserted because of too many tape-recorded competitors. In our concern for the welfare of each individual bird, we might rise to the challenges that the growth of our population and technology—now both nearly out of control—present to the welfare of all birds everywhere. In so doing, we might learn to become wise and responsible stewards of our planet, as individuals living out our personal lives, and as members of society recognizing our responsibilities for the quality of life we leave for future generations of birds and humans alike.

For those bird lovers among us, however, who enjoy keeping track of what they have seen, we offer this checklist. Just for the record, the present compilation (through February 28, 1985) offers 28,031 potential "ticks", with many more, certainly, to be added in the years ahead. We wish you joy as you "tick" them all!

David DeSante
Peter Pyle

Bolinas, California
Vernal equinox, 1986

Contents

Preface . . . vii
List of illustrations . . . xiii
Introduction . . . 1
    Methods, accuracy and corrections . . . 2
    Scope . . . 3
        Geographic . . . 3
        Temporal . . . 3
    Taxonomy and nomenclature . . . 3
    Criteria for the acceptance of records . . . 4
        For the inclusion of species . . . 4
        For the confirmation of breeding . . . 6
    Format . . . 6
    Codes . . . 7
        Status codes . . . 7
        Suffixes to status codes . . . 11
        Abundance codes . . . 12
        Prefixes to abundance codes . . . 14
        The qualifier -q . . . 16
        Codes for continental North America, Canada, and the lower 48 states . . . 16
Acknowledgments . . . 17
Part I. Native populations . . . 19
    Gaviiformes: Loons . . . 21
        Gaviidae: Loons . . . 21
    Podicipediformes: Grebes . . . 21
        Podicipedidae: Grebes . . . 21
    Procellariiformes: Tube-nosed Swimmers . . . 21
        Diomedeidae: Albatrosses . . . 21
        Procellariidae: Shearwaters and Petrels . . . 29
        Hydrobatidae: Storm-Petrels . . . 37
    Pelecaniformes: Totipalmate Swimmers . . . 45
        Phaethontidae: Tropicbirds . . . 45
        Sulidae: Boobies and Gannets . . . 45
        Pelecanidae: Pelicans . . . 45
        Phalacrocoracidae: Cormorants . . . 45
        Anhingidae: Darters . . . 53
        Fregatidae: Frigatebirds . . . 53
    Ciconiiformes: Herons, Ibises, Storks and Allies . . . 53
        Ardeidae: Bitterns and Herons . . . 53
        Threskiornithidae: Ibises and Spoonbills . . . 61
            Threskiornithinae: Ibises . . . 61
            Plataleinae: Spoonbills . . . 61
        Ciconiidae: Storks . . . 61
    Phoenicopteriformes: Flamingos . . . 61
        Phoenicopteridae: Flamingos . . . 61
    Anseriformes: Screamers, Swans, Geese and Ducks . . . 61
        Anatidae: Swans, Geese and Ducks . . . 61
            Anserinae: Whistling-Ducks, Swans and Geese . . . 61
            Anatinae: Ducks . . . 69
    Falconiformes: Diurnal Birds of Prey . . . 85
        Cathartidae: American Vultures . . . 85
        Accipitridae: Kites, Eagles, Hawks and Allies . . . 85
            Pandioninae: Ospreys . . . 85
            Accipitrinae: Kites, Eagles, Hawks and Allies . . . 85
        Falconidae: Caracaras and Falcons . . . 93
    Galliformes: Gallinaceous Birds . . . 101

       Cracidae: Curassows and Guans 101
       Phasianidae: Partridges, Grouse, Turkeys and Quail 101
           Tetraoninae: Grouse 101
           Meleagridinae: Turkeys 101
           Odontophorinae: Quail 109
Gruiformes: Cranes, Rails and Allies 109
       Rallidae: Rails, Gallinules and Coots 109
           Rallinae: Rails, Gallinules and Coots 109
       Aramidae: Limpkins 117
       Gruidae: Cranes 117
           Gruinae: Typical Cranes 117
Charadriiformes: Shorebirds, Gulls, Auks and Allies 117
       Burhinidae: Thick-knees 117
       Charadriidae: Plovers and Lapwings 117
           Vanellinae: Lapwings 117
           Charadriinae: Plovers 117
       Haematopodidae: Oystercatchers 125
       Recurvirostridae: Stilts and Avocets 125
       Jacanidae: Jacanas 125
       Scolopacidae: Sandpipers, Phalaropes and Allies 125
           Scolopacinae: Sandpipers and Allies 125
           Phalaropodinae: Phalaropes 149
       Laridae: Skuas, Gulls, Terns and Skimmers 149
           Stercorariinae: Skuas and Jaegers 149
           Larinae: Gulls 149
           Sterninae: Terns 157
           Rynchopinae: Skimmers 165
       Alcidae: Auks, Murres and Puffins 165
Columbiformes: Sandgrouse, Pigeons and Doves 173
       Columbidae: Pigeons and Doves 173
Psittaciformes: Parrots and Allies 181
       Psittacidae: Lories, Parakeets, Macaws and Parrots 181
           Arinae: New World Parakeets, Macaws and Parrots 181
Cuculiformes: Cuckoos and Allies 181
       Cuculidae: Cuckoos, Roadrunners and Anis 181
           Cuculinae: Old World Cuckoos 181
           Coccyzinae: New World Cuckoos 181
           Neomorphinae: Ground-Cuckoos and Roadrunners 181
           Crotophaginae: Anis 189
Strigiformes: Owls 189
       Tytonidae: Barn-Owls 189
       Strigidae: Typical Owls 189
Caprimulgiformes: Goatsuckers, Oilbirds and Allies 197
       Caprimulgidae: Goatsuckers 197
           Chordeilinae: Nighthawks 197
           Caprimulginae: Nightjars 197
Apodiformes: Swifts and Hummingbirds 197
       Apodidae: Swifts 197
           Cypseloidinae: Cypseloidine Swifts 197
           Chaeturinae: Chaeturine Swifts 197
           Apodinae: Apodine Swifts 197
       Trochilidae: Hummingbirds 205
Trogoniformes: Trogons 213
       Trogonidae: Trogons 213
Coraciiformes: Kingfishers, Rollers, Hornbills and Allies 213
       Upupidae: Hoopoes 213
       Alcedinidae: Kingfishers 213
           Cerylinae: Typical Kingfishers 213
Piciformes: Puffbirds, Toucans, Woodpeckers and Allies 213
       Picidae: Woodpeckers and Allies 213
           Jynginae: Wrynecks 213

Contents • xi

Picinae: Woodpeckers	213
Passeriformes: Passerine Birds	221
Tyrannidae: Tyrant Flycatchers	221
Elaeniinae: Tyrannulets, Elaenias and Allies	221
Fluvicolinae: Fluvicoline Flycatchers	221
Tyranninae: Tyrannine Flycatchers	229
Tityrinae: Tityras and Becards	237
Alaudidae: Larks	237
Hirundinidae: Swallows	237
Hirundininae: Typical Swallows	237
Corvidae: Jays, Magpies and Crows	245
Paridae: Titmice	253
Remizidae: Penduline Tits and Verdins	253
Aegithalidae: Long-tailed Tits and Bushtits	253
Sittidae: Nuthatches	253
Sittinae: Typical Nuthatches	253
Certhiidae: Creepers	261
Certhiinae: Typical Creepers	261
Troglodytidae: Wrens	261
Cinclidae: Dippers	261
Muscicapidae: Muscicapids	261
Sylviinae: Old World Warblers, Kinglets and Gnatcatchers	261
Muscicapinae: Old World Flycatchers and Allies	269
Monarchinae: Monarch Flycatchers	269
Turdinae: Solitaires, Thrushes and Allies	269
Timaliinae: Babblers	277
Mimidae: Mockingbirds, Thrashers and Allies	277
Prunellidae: Accentors	285
Motacillidae: Wagtails and Pipits	285
Bombycillidae: Waxwings	285
Ptilogonatidae: Silky-flycatchers	293
Laniidae: Shrikes	293
Laniinae: Typical Shrikes	293
Sturnidae: Starlings and Allies	293
Sturninae: Starlings	293
Meliphagidae: Honeyeaters	293
Vireonidae: Vireos	293
Vireoninae: Typical Vireos	293
Emberizidae: Emberizids	301
Parulinae: Wood-Warblers	301
Coerebinae: Bananaquits	317
Thraupinae: Tanagers	317
Cardinalinae: Cardinals, Grosbeaks and Allies	325
Emberizinae: Emberizines	325
Icterinae: Icterines	349
Fringillidae: Fringilline and Carduelline Finches and Allies	357
Fringillinae: Fringilline Finches	357
Carduelinae: Carduelline Finches	357
Drepanidinae: Hawaiian Honeycreepers	365
Additional species	367
Part II. Introduced populations	375
Ciconiiformes: Herons, Ibises, Storks and Allies	377
Ardeidae: Bitterns and Herons	377
Anseriformes: Screamers, Swans, Geese and Ducks	377
Anatidae: Swans, Geese and Ducks	377
Anserinae: Whistling-Ducks, Swans and Geese	377
Anatinae: Ducks	377
Galliformes: Gallinaceous Birds	377
Cracidae: Curassows and Guans	377
Phasianidae: Partridges, Grouse, Turkeys and Quail	377

xii • *Distributional Checklist of North American Birds*

        Phasianinae: Partridges and Pheasants 377
        Tetraoninae: Grouse 385
        Meleagridinae: Turkeys 385
        Odontophorinae: Quail 385
Gruiformes: Cranes, Rails and Allies 385
    Gruidae: Cranes 385
        Gruinae: Typical Cranes 385
Columbiformes: Sandgrouse, Pigeons and Doves 385
    Pteroclididae: Sandgrouse 385
    Columbidae: Pigeons and Doves 385
Psittaciformes: Parrots and Allies 393
    Psittacidae: Lories, Parakeets, Macaws and Parrots 393
        Platycercinae: Australian Parakeets and Rosellas 393
        Psittacinae: Typical Parrots 393
        Arinae: New World Parakeets, Macaws and Parrots 393
Strigiformes: Owls 393
    Tytonidae: Barn-Owls 393
Apodiformes: Swifts and Hummingbirds 393
    Apodidae: Swifts 393
        Chaeturinae: Chaeturine Swifts 393
Passeriformes: Passerine Birds 393
    Alaudidae: Larks 393
    Paridae: Titmice 401
    Pycnonotidae: Bulbuls 401
    Muscicapidae: Muscicapids 401
        Sylviinae: Old World Warblers, Kinglets and Gnatcatchers 401
        Turdinae: Solitaires, Thrushes and Allies 401
        Timaliinae: Babblers 401
    Mimidae: Mockingbirds, Thrashers and Allies 401
    Sturnidae: Starlings and Allies 401
        Sturninae: Starlings 401
    Zosteropidae: White-eyes 409
    Emberizidae: Emberizids 409
        Cardinalinae: Cardinals, Grosbeaks and Allies 409
        Emberizinae: Emberizines 409
        Icterinae: Icterines 409
    Fringillidae: Fringilline and Carduelline Finches and Allies 409
        Carduelinae: Carduelline Finches 409
    Passeridae: Old World Sparrows 409
    Estrildidae: Estrildid Finches 409
        Estrildinae: Estrildine Finches 409
  Additional species 417
Bibliography 425
Biographical sketches 431
Addenda 433
Index 435

List of illustrations

Species are listed roughly from left to right and from top to bottom.

Species	Artist	Page
Tree Swallow	Keith Hansen	iii
Wood Duck	Keith Hansen	19
Red-throated Loon	Keith Hansen	20
Black-capped Petrel/Cory's Shearwater	Keith Hansen	28
Buller's Shearwater/Fork-tailed Storm-Petrel	Keith Hansen	36
Brown Pelican	F. P. Bennett, Jr.	44
Yellow-crowned Night-Heron/Anhinga	F. P. Bennett, Jr.	52
Wood Stork/White Ibis/Roseate Spoonbill	F. P. Bennett, Jr.	60
Emperor Goose	F. P. Bennett, Jr.	68
Ring-necked Duck	Keith Hansen	76
California Condor	Keith Hansen	84
Red-shouldered Hawk	Keith Hansen	92
Prairie Falcon/Sage Grouse	Keith Hansen	100
Black Rail	Keith Hansen	108
Lesser Golden-Plover	Keith Hansen	116
American Avocet/Black-necked Stilt	F. P. Bennett, Jr.	124
Spotted Sandpiper	Keith Hansen	132
Pectoral Sandpiper/Sharp-tailed Sandpiper	Keith Hansen	140
Wilson's Phalarope/American Woodcock	Keith Hansen	148
Great Black-backed Gull	F. P. Bennett, Jr.	156
White Tern	Keith Hansen	164
Marbled Murrelet	Keith Hansen	172
Passenger Pigeon	Keith Hansen	180
Great Horned Owl	F. P. Bennett, Jr.	188
Whip-poor-will	Keith Hansen	196
Magnificent Hummingbird/Blue-throated Hummingbird/White-eared Hummingbird	F. P. Bennett, Jr.	204
Green Kingfisher	F. P. Bennett, Jr.	212
Nuttall's Woodpecker/Ladder-backed Woodpecker/Red-cockaded Woodpecker	Keith Hansen	220
Say's Phoebe	F. P. Bennett, Jr.	228
Scissor-tailed Flycatcher	F. P. Bennett, Jr.	236
Gray Jay	Keith Hansen	244
Black-capped Chickadee/Boreal Chickadee	F. P. Bennett, Jr.	252
Carolina Wren	F. P. Bennett, Jr.	260
Bluethroat/Siberian Rubythroat	Keith Hansen	268
Wrentit/Wood Thrush	Keith Hansen	276
Sprague's Pipit	Keith Hansen	284
Northern Shrike	Keith Hansen	292
Northern Parula	F. P. Bennett, Jr.	300
American Redstart/Black-throated Blue Warbler	F. P. Bennett, Jr.	308
Red-faced Warbler/Olive Warbler/Painted Redstart	F. P. Bennett, Jr.	316
Dickcissel	F. P. Bennett, Jr.	324
Black-throated Sparrow	F. P. Bennett, Jr.	332
White-crowned Sparrow/White-throated Sparrow	F. P. Bennett, Jr.	340
Altamira Oriole	F. P. Bennett, Jr.	348
Lawrence's Goldfinch	Keith Hansen	356
Iiwi/Akiapolaau	Keith Hansen	364
Birdwatcher	F. P. Bennett, Jr.	366
Ring-necked Pheasant	Keith Hansen	375
Chukar	F. P. Bennett, Jr.	376
Rock Dove/Ringed Turtle-Dove	Keith Hansen	384
Red-crowned Parrot	F. P. Bennett, Jr.	392
European Starling	F. P. Bennett, Jr.	400
House Finch/House Sparrow	F. P. Bennett, Jr.	408
Wild Turkey/Yellow-headed Blackbird/Curve-billed Thrasher/Red-eyed Vireo/Yellow-rumped Warbler	Keith Hansen	416

Introduction

The purpose of this book is threefold. First, it provides a compendium of state and province bird lists developed according to identical criteria applied uniformly to each state of the United States and each province of Canada. There exists no similar compendium that will allow meaningful comparisons among the bird lists of the various states and provinces. We have chosen a matrix format to display this information so that the reader can see at a glance not only which species have been recorded in each state, but also in which states each species has been recorded.

The second purpose is to provide a convenient means for birdwatchers to keep all of their North American state and province life lists in a single volume and in such a manner that they can be updated easily and indefinitely into the future, even as new species are added to state and province lists.

The third, and perhaps most important, purpose is to provide complete, accurate and up-to-date status and abundance classifications, also developed according to identical and uniformly applied criteria, for every species in every state and province in North America. The classifications that we have used provide current breeding status as well as independent abundance codes for summer, winter, transient and vagrant status. It is our hope that this coded information can be used effectively to provide birders and travelers with an accurate indication of the current status, abundance and seasonality of every North American species in every state and province. These status and abundance classifications should also facilitate comparisons among the species in a given state or province, and among the states and provinces for a given species. Finally, we hope that this information will serve as a comprehensive and current reference data base to facilitate the monitoring of major changes in the status, abundance and seasonality of North American bird species that may occur in the future and that may have occurred in the past.

Among the most important discoveries by modern North American birders and field ornithologists is the fact that the ranges of birds are extremely dynamic. Consider, for example, the northward range expansions of several southeastern species of landbirds, including Northern Cardinal, Carolina Wren, Tufted Titmouse and Red-bellied Woodpecker, or the recent explosive population increases and associated range expansions of Cattle Egret and Great-tailed Grackle. While these may indeed represent extreme examples of the responses of individual species to favorable human-caused environmental changes, not all major range changes can be explained so easily. Consider the number of landbird species that have, in the past thirty years or so, become regular features of the avifauna of southeastern Arizona— Thick-billed Kingbird, Violet-crowned and Berylline hummingbirds, and Five-striped Sparrow, to name a few. And consider other species that were formerly thought to be southeastern Arizona specialties but have now moved north into California, Nevada and Utah—Whip-poor-will, Hepatic Tanager, Painted Redstart, Grace's Warbler and more.

It would seem that virtually all the areas of our continent have experienced recent major range changes in various members of their avifaunas: Elegant Tern along the Pacific Coast, Glossy Ibis along the Atlantic Coast, Western Meadowlark and Clay-colored Sparrow in the east, Barred Owl, Least Flycatcher and Blue Jay in the west, and gulls almost everywhere. If one projects these range expansions back into time at the same rate that they seem to be expanding today, one gets the distinct feeling that the ranges of many North American bird species may have been vastly different only a few hundred years ago. Of course, not all recent range changes have been expansive. Many contractions in range have also been prominent in the recent past including, for example, noticeable population declines and contractions in the eastern ranges of Red-cockaded Woodpecker, Bewick's Wren, Loggerhead Shrike, Bachman's Sparrow and Henslow's Sparrow.

The question that seems to be of overriding interest is whether or not range expansions and contractions have always been as rapid as they are today. Are these more remarkable examples of range changes merely the isolated responses of a few species or groups of species to certain human-caused habitat or environmental changes, or could we be witnessing in recent years a fundamental increase in the overall rate of range expansion for most species, a change fostered perhaps by a selective increase in the rate and extent of dispersal brought on by concomitant increases in the overall rate of habitat change? Are we in fact changing the fabric of life on earth into one of increasingly shorter-lived habitats, a fabric that would tend to favor opportunistic species characterized by, among other things, high dispersal rates? Such habitat changes, it can be argued, will tend to favor, within a given species, opportunistic individuals also characterized by high dispersal rates.

A corollary of this hypothesis is that the number of vagrant birds, those extreme examples of dispersal, would also be increasing. Certainly increasing numbers of vagrants are found each year all across our continent, but it is not yet clear that this increase in vagrants represents more than the result of the increased effort on the part of birders to find them. Only the controlled, detailed, long-term monitoring of certain select locations across the continent where vagrant birds tend to concentrate, such as Southeast Farallon Island off the coast of California, can provide the data to answer this last question. And only the detailed long-term monitoring of both the breeding and wintering distributions of all our North American birds will tell us whether or not the overall rate of range expansion is actually increasing.

We hope that the work presented here will serve as a starting point to shed light on this question. In effect, we have created a coarse geographical "grid" made up of the 63 politically defined and vastly unequal areas of the states and provinces of North America. Superimposed upon this array, for each North American bird species, is yet another coarse scale, this one consisting of five relative abundance classes plus "absent." It is our avowed intention to revise this work in regular ten-year intervals. We are certain that such revisions will document numerous changes in the status, abundance and seasonality of many avian species in many states and provinces. Considering the coarse nature of both our geographical and relative abundance scales, we are confident that such changes will be both dramatic and important. An analysis of the number of changes during each ten-year period, considered over five or ten of such periods, will provide quantitative information regarding the rate of range expansion or contraction on this continent.

A finer and more uniform geographical scale would, of course, provide increasingly accurate and more immediate results. It would also require considerably more detailed information. Perhaps the way to initiate such work would be at the county or quarter-latilong level within given states and provinces. If studies utilizing status and abundance codes similar to those presented in this work were compiled for about 50 to 100 units within a given state or province, and revised at regular ten-year intervals, a substantial increase in the detailed understanding of bird distribution, abundance and range changes would result. The creation of breeding bird atlases represents a major step in this direction and we strongly endorse all such projects. However, the breeding season alone does not provide the entire story—winter and migration seasons must be considered as well. It is our firm belief that enough serious birders exist with enough detailed knowledge of their local areas to make such compilations possible. And in this computer age, the storage, retrieval and editing of such databases should present no problem. We strongly urge birders in all states and provinces to initiate work on compendia of annotated county or quarter-latilong checklists similar in format to the state and province checklists presented here, and we would be happy to share our experiences with them.

Methods, accuracy and corrections

Our first step in preparing this checklist was to define, as precisely as possible, the classifications that we would use for both status and abundance. Interestingly, our classification scheme did not remain exactly as it was first developed. Rather, it evolved somewhat to accommodate the myriad of individual cases that we encountered as the project developed. In effect, the completion of this work can be viewed as the end product of a continual testing and refinement of our classification codes.

Once the initial classifications and codes were developed, Pyle set to work creating the first draft of the data set. This was based upon ranges outlined in the Fifth Edition of the *A.O.U. Check-list of North American Birds* (1957), and upon various regional books and monographs we had at our disposal. After the first draft was entered into a computer and proofed, it was checked for the occurrences of vagrants against the Sixth Edition of the *A.O.U. Check-list of North American Birds* (1983), which had just been released. After revisions and corrections to the computer files and a second round of proofreading, computer-generated state and province checklists were prepared showing status and abundance codes for each species.

Each checklist was sent to two or more people that we considered to be qualified to review that state or province list. Necessary qualifications for reviewers included an excellent working familiarity with the avifauna of that state or province including a detailed knowledge of bird distribution and abundance, complete and up-to-date knowledge of the individual records of rare and unusual birds in that region, and a thorough knowledge of the workings and decisions of any bird records committee that might exist for that state or province. Throughout the course of this work we have been continually impressed and delighted by the help we have received from the more than 150 people who kindly served as reviewers for this work. In all cases they demonstrated an outstanding expertise on the avifauna of their state or province, as well as an uncommon generosity in giving so freely of their time and knowledge. The names of all these reviewers are listed in the Acknowledgments.

Reviewers were asked to assure that the list of birds occurring in the state or province was complete and accurate, that all species that had ever bred in the state were correctly indicated, that all status codes were correct (in particular that all valid winter records were included), and that accurate abundance codes were provided for each species for each season or for each status given. In order to assure uniformity of response, all reviewers were supplied with detailed definitions for each code used.

After all the reviews were returned and entered in the database, new status and abundance codes were developed for each species in each state or province by comparing the suggested changes and comments provided by each of the reviewers to our initial codes, and by comparing the data for a given state or province with data from neighboring states and provinces. These data were all simultaneously compared to the range accounts in the Sixth Edition of the *A.O.U. Check-list* (1983), the range maps in several recent field guides (Peterson 1980, National Geographic Society 1983, and Robbins 1983), data contained in numerous other general and regional references cited in the Bibliography, and relevant data in the most recent seven volumes of *American Birds* (1979–1985). These new decisions were made with the utmost care and painstaking consideration, and in such a manner as to attempt to show continuity among neighboring states and provinces while still preserving the unique nature of the avifauna of each state and province.

As perhaps expected, there were a number of species in each state and province for which we were uncertain that we had chosen the most accurate codes. This was primarily caused by differences of opinion among reviewers, printed sources and information from adjacent states. For each state and province, therefore, we compiled a list of questioned species and sent this list back to the reviewers. This second review and the detailed comments provided by reviewers clarified most questions but, for virtually all states and provinces, a few questions still remained. These were sent back to the reviewers for yet a third (and sometimes a fourth or even fifth) review. After all this information was returned and entered in the database, a final pass was made through the entire data set to assure that all the final status and abundance codes were consistent with the data supplied by reviewers as well as with the final revised definitions for each code. Comprehensive status and abundance codes for continental North America as a whole, for Canada and for the "lower 48" states were developed at this time. This final coding and editing was completed by DeSante for all species except Anseriformes and Charadriiformes, which were completed by Pyle.

The final result of all this effort is a product that we believe represents an accurate assessment of the status and abundance of each North American bird species, meticulously reviewed by many of the leading regional authorities of North American bird distribution. We hasten to add, however, that we, the authors, take full and sole responsibility for all errors that remain in this work, including those of omission, commission and interpretation.

This work includes almost 1,000 bird species distributed over 63 states and provinces, a matrix of over 60,000 cells of which almost half are filled. With about five decisions required for each species, the number of individual decisions approaches 150,000. With such a large number of decisions, a few errors must exist. Some, no doubt, result from our misinterpretation of the information actually available to us; others result from the collective lack of knowledge of many of the finer details of North American bird distribution. Throughout the course of this work, we have continually been reminded how much more has yet to be learned about bird distribution on this continent. A detailed, comprehensive analysis of the interior occurrences of marine birds, for example, would provide a major advancement in the understanding of these species. Some of the gaps in our collective knowledge must certainly stem from the incomplete nature of our observations. Other gaps in knowledge must be caused by the fact that bird distribution is always changing.

Two of the avowed purposes of this work are to encourage the closing of these gaps in our understanding of the distribution and abundance of North American birds, and to document the process of avifaunal change on this continent. Toward the first goal, we actively encourage anyone who feels strongly that any particular status or abundance code is in error and should be changed in any way to inform us by writing to David DeSante, Box 219, Bolinas, CA 94924. Toward the second goal, we plan to provide a revised edition of this work after ten years have passed. In this way we hope to be able to monitor the dynamic nature of bird distribution in North America.

Scope

Geographic. The geographic coverage of this checklist is basically identical to that of the Sixth Edition of the *A.O.U. Check-list of North American Birds* (1983), except that the oceanic coverage is extended in our work to the standard 200 nautical mile (370 km) international fisheries zone, unless such oceanic localities lie outside the limits otherwise specified in the *A.O.U. Check-list*. Thus, "In the Bering Sea area, the boundary corresponds to that delimiting the United States from the U.S.S.R., which also corresponds to the International Date Line" (A.O.U., 1983).

The separation between Canada and Greenland (which is excluded), where they approach closer than 200 nautical miles, follows the midline of the various channels, straits and bays separating Ellesmere, Devon, Bylot and Baffin Islands from Greenland. We have extended the oceanic coverage to 200 nautical miles to include all of the waters that can be relatively easily reached on an extended weekend pelagic trip as well as virtually all of the waters lying above the various continental shelves.

This present volume, Volume I, excludes all of Mexico, Central America, the West Indies and Bermuda. These will be treated in Volume II. Included in Volume I, therefore, are all of the continental United States and Canada, their offshore islands and the Hawaiian Islands. The separation between the United States and the West Indies, where they approach closer than 200 nautical miles, is again along the midline of the seas separating Florida from Cuba and the Bahama Islands.

Treated separately in Volume I are all 50 states of the United States, the District of Columbia and the twelve provinces—actually ten provinces and two territories—of Canada. The two territories are Yukon Territory and the Northwest Territories. The Northwest Territories include the District of Mackenzie, the District of Keewatin, the District of Franklin, the Queen Elizabeth Islands and all of the water and islands in Hudson Bay and James Bay. Newfoundland is herein considered to include not only the Coast of Labrador and the Island of Newfoundland, as it does politically, but also the French islands of Saint-Pierre et Miquelon. In this way, all of North America except Greenland is included in our work.

The demarcation of the oceanic areas belonging to each state and province was accomplished according to standard methods that extend boundaries into the ocean along a line that is equidistant from points along the coastline of each state or province, that is, along a line that tends to be perpendicular to the shoreline at the boundary between the two states or provinces.

Temporal. The basic cutoff date for this work is February 28, 1985. We have made every effort to assure that all records of North American birds up to this date have been included. Status and abundance codes have been designed to reflect the *current* status and relative abundance of each species in each state or province. By current we mean the close of the decade 1975-1984 and, in particular, 1983 and 1984.

We include only modern historical records of live or freshly dead birds, in effect, only nineteenth and twentieth century records. We do not include any fossil records nor any records from archaeological sites (such as the middens of Native Americans) if the records were considered to have originated from earlier than 1800. All records older than 50 years (that is, prior to February 28, 1935), are treated with the prefix code *e*—extirpated.

Taxonomy and nomenclature

We have followed *exactly* the taxonomy, nomenclature (both English and scientific) and order of listing that was followed in the Sixth Edition of the *A.O.U. Check-list of*

4 • *Distributional Checklist of North American Birds*

North American Birds (1983) as modified by the *Thirty-fifth Supplement to the A.O.U. Check-List* (1985), even if we or any particular reviewers disagree strongly with it. Thus, we have included such species as Caribbean Coot (*Fulica caribaea*), Northwestern Crow (*Corvus caurinus*) and Hoary Redpoll (*Carduelis hornemanni*) even though many local authorities consider them to be conspecific with more widespread species. We have, however, only included as valid records the occurrences of Caribbean Coot from southern Florida. Individuals showing the phenotypic characters of Caribbean Coot have been documented from at least California, Texas, Tennessee and Michigan. We have not included any of these records.

Finally, we have also included the six new species recently split in the *Thirty-fifth Supplement to the A.O.U. Check-list* (1985) despite the fact that certain local authorities remain unconvinced that they all deserve full specific treatment. These six species are Pacific Loon (*Gavia pacifica*), Clark's Grebe (*Aechmophorus clarkii*), Red-naped Sapsucker (*Sphyrapicus nuchalis*), Kamao (*Myadestes myadestinus*), Amaui (*Myadestes oahensis*) and Olomao (*Myadestes lanaiensis*). In the case of the loons, we have assumed that all Arctic/Pacific type loons found in continental North America (including the Atlantic Coast) are Pacific Loons until proven otherwise.

Criteria for the acceptance of records

For the inclusion of species. Our criteria for including a species on a state or province list are as follows: (a) the existence (or, in a few cases, the former existence) of a specimen of the species, (b) the existence of an identifiable photograph of the species, (c) the existence of an identifiable audiospectrogram or tape recording of the vocalizations of the species, or (d) the existence of *one* or more sight records of the species documented by *written* descriptions by *one* or more persons. An additional criterion for every record included, whether based on a specimen, photograph, audiospectrogram, tape recording or documented sight record, is that the record be "accepted," that is, that a general authoritative consensus exists that the date, location and identification are correct beyond all reasonable doubt, and that the individual occurred naturally and not as the result of intentional or accidental introduction by humans.

Our criteria for the acceptance of an introduced species on a state or province list is that the species has become (or, in a few cases, *had* become) established in a wild condition, free from direct dependence upon humans, or that the species has occurred in the state or province as a result of transient, vagrant or winter resident individuals that originated from an established population. A species is accepted as established when it is documented that the species has (or had) bred successfully in a wild condition in the state or province for at least ten consecutive years, and the population has (or had) been reasonably stable or growing.

The key word in all of these criteria, "accepted," warrants further discussion. A number of states and provinces currently have official, established committees whose function is to review records of rare or unusual birds in that state or province in order to determine their authenticity and accuracy. We have attempted to follow *exactly* the decisions of such established records committees. In other states and provinces, no such established records committees yet exist and the acceptance or rejection of records has been based to a large extent upon the authority of the person or persons who have published the most recent comprehensive account or checklist of the birds of that state or province. In these cases we have attempted to follow more or less exactly the decisions rendered in such authoritative works provided that the works are generally accepted as being accurate and complete. In still other states and provinces, no recent comprehensive account or checklist has yet been published. In these cases, acceptance or rejection of records has been based on the general unwritten consensus of the more knowledgeable and expert ornithologists and birders of the area. We have relied heavily on the opinions of our reviewers in these cases.

Our work is intended not only to provide lists of species that are included on the "official" lists for each state and province, but also to facilitate comparisons of the avifaunas among all of the various states and provinces. As a result, a key requirement of our work is that *identical criteria for the inclusion of species must be applied uniformly to all states and provinces*. The fact is, however, that the various states and provinces themselves employ widely different criteria for the inclusion of species on their particular official state or province lists. Some states and provinces, for example, include only records documented by specimens, photographs or sound recordings on their "main" list; all species documented only by sight records, even by accepted sight records, are relegated to "hypothetical" or "provisional" status. Other states and provinces do include species documented by sight records but only after three or more accepted sight records have accumulated. In these cases, species documented by only one or two accepted sight records are given hypothetical or provisional status. In still other states and provinces, a single accepted sight record is sufficient to establish the species on the main state or province list provided that the written documentation for the sight record came independently from two, or in some cases three, observers. In these states and provinces, therefore, single-observer sight records, even if accepted, are relegated to hypothetical or provisional status.

While we understand and appreciate the reasons why various states and provinces have established different criteria for the inclusion of species on their official state or province lists, we must again stress the fact that the criteria that we have applied uniformly to all states and provinces for the inclusion of a species is the existence of *one* or more accepted sight records documented *in writing* by *one* or more observers. The result is that, for certain states and provinces, we have necessarily included species on our lists that are considered hypothetical or provisional on their official published lists.

The inclusion in our lists of such species is, *in all cases*, based upon fully documented and accepted records, and the lack of inclusion of these same species on the official main list for the state or province is, *in all cases*, based simply upon the fact that the particular state or province uses different criteria for inclusion than we do. We have used the qualifier -q for all such species in order to prevent confusion on the part of the reader between our lists and the official main list for each state and province as well as to acknowledge the different criteria for inclusion used by different states and provinces. This -q should always be interpreted as "qualified," that is, that the inclusion on our list and exclusion from other published lists results merely from the application of different criteria for inclusion. The -q should not be interpreted as "hypothetical," a word that implies to us that some doubt exists as to the accuracy or acceptance of the record.

We have been extremely conservative about our acceptance of records and have excluded all species and all seasonal records for which we felt any reasonable doubt existed. Furthermore, we have attempted to follow *exactly* all decisions reached by established records committees even if we or certain of our reviewers disagreed with any of those decisions. We urge all states and provinces to establish responsible, functioning records committees whose purpose is to review all records of rare and unusual species in their state or province, even including old sight and specimen records. Such work by dedicated individuals will prove to be of major importance in refining and clarifying our understanding of the distribution of North American birds.

The qualifier -q has also been used in a second manner. There currently exist (and probably always will exist), for many states and provinces, documented records that have not yet been reviewed by (or are still under the review of) established records committees, and for which no decision has yet been reached. We have included such records when we and the reviewers considered that acceptance was likely. Whenever we did include a species that was still under review we used the qualifier -q, again to indicate that a documented record exists (and, we believe, will be accepted), but that the species is not yet on the official main list of the state or province.

The criteria for inclusion of species on our lists is, therefore, essentially identical to the criteria for inclusion in the main list plus Appendix A of the *A.O.U. Check-list* (1983). Our list is not, however, identical to the main list plus Appendix A of the *A.O.U. Check-list*; there are several important differences. We and the Hawaiian reviewers believe that the written documentation that exists for Antarctic Giant-Petrel (*Macronectes giganteus*) is insufficient to establish this species on the Hawaiian (and North American) list. Furthermore, we believe that the written documentation that exists for the Hawaiian occurrences of Tahiti Petrel (*Pterodroma rostrata*) and Phoenix Petrel (*P. alba*) are insufficient to positively distinguish between the two species. We have, therefore, included all records of these two species as a species pair and placed them under the heading of Phoenix Petrel, the species that we feel is slightly more likely to occur near the Hawaiian Islands (see below under *Codes: Suffixes to status codes* for our use of species pair, -sp). This represents the only inclusion on the North American list solely on the basis of a species pair.

In contrast, we have included several species in our lists that were relegated to Appendix B, the "hypothetical list," of the *A.O.U. Check-list* (1983), either because new records or new information has been obtained, or because the criteria for inclusion on the appropriate state or province list differ from our criteria. Species included in our list for any of these reasons include: Soft-plumaged Petrel and Common Buzzard (added to Appendix B in the *Thirty-fifth Supplement to the A.O.U. Check-list*, 1985), Northern Hobby (added to the main list in the *Thirty-fifth Supplement*), Gray Swiftlet, Stonechat, Gray-sided Laughingthrush, Yellow-breasted Bunting, Eurasian Siskin, and European Greenfinch.

Comparisons between our work and the Sixth Edition of the *A.O.U. Check-list* (1983) for most individual state lists will also show a number of differences. In some cases species included in the *A.O.U. Check-list* are not included in our work while in other cases we include species that are not included in the *A.O.U. Check-list*. *In every case* where our list differed from the *A.O.U. Check-list*, we specifically questioned the species in our second round of review. In virtually every case questioned, the reviewers provided convincing evidence why certain records included in the *A.O.U. Check-list* were not accepted by the regional authorities, and why other records not included in the *A.O.U. Check-list* (most often because of oversight or because they were too recent) were valid and accepted. We followed the reviewers' advice in the great majority of these cases. Cape Petrel (*Daption capense*), which we do not include in this work, is one example. We believe that the origin of the Maine specimen and the identification of the California sightings are uncertain. Other examples are Elegant Quail (*Callipepla douglasii*) in Arizona and Helmeted Guineafowl (*Numida meleagris*) in Hawaii. We include neither of these species because we do not believe that they were ever actually established.

Some of the most difficult decisions regarding the acceptance or rejection of records are those that concern the possibility of ship-assisted passage or escape from captivity. It must be admitted that virtually all landbird species (and even some aquatic and marine species such as herons and boobies) that have appeared in North America after a probable ocean crossing may be suspected of having experienced at least some degree of ship-assisted passage. Because there is rarely a way to ascertain whether or not ship-assisted passage did occur, compilers of checklists are forced to make arbitrary decisions. Our policy has been to treat all such records as valid records provided that it seems possible that the species in question could have made the passage without resting or riding upon a ship, and that the timing and location of the occurrence, and the age, plumage, condition and behavior of the bird provide no indication that ship-assisted passage did occur. Notable records that we have rejected as having a substantial probability of ship assistance include Band-tailed Gull (*Larus belcheri*) in Florida, Black-tailed Gull in California and Maryland, and Great-tailed Grackle in Hawaii.

The problem of possible escapes from captivity is even more difficult, especially for waterfowl, flamingos, raptors, parrots and certain songbirds that are regularly kept in commercial or private aviaries throughout the continent. In some cases there is general agreement: to reject all records of species such as Red-breasted Goose (*Branta ruficollis*), Ruddy Shelduck (*Tadorna ferruginea*) and Common Shelduck (*Tadorna tadorna*) where detailed investigation shows most records to involve escapes, and to accept virtually all records of species such as Garganey and Brambling where repeated and seasonally consistent occurrences indicate genuine vagrancy. For other species, however, a pattern is not so clear and agreement is not so general.

Our policy for including records of possible escapes is based upon a synthesis of several factors. We tended to accept a record provided that (a) the age, plumage, condition, behavior and location of the bird provide no indication that it had escaped from captivity; (b) the timing and location of the occurrence is plausible given the normal range of the bird, the general direction, distance and timing of its migration, and the existing pattern of its vagrant records; and (c) genuine vagrancy provides a more probable explanation for the occurrence than escape from captivity when the population size of the species in the wild and its tendency to wander is compared to the status of the species in captivity and its tendency to escape. For example, a plausible model for vagrancy in the Greater Flamingo, a species that breeds in coastal estuaries and lagoons in Yucatan, the Greater Antilles and the Bahamas, includes records only in estuarine situations and only along the Gulf and Atlantic coasts. Inland and Pacific coastal records are assumed to have a substantial probability of being escapes and are therefore rejected. Similarly, a plausible model for vagrancy in the Barnacle Goose, a species that breeds in eastern Greenland, Svalbard (Spitsbergen) and Novaya Zemlya and that winters on western European coasts casually south to southern Europe and northern Africa, only includes records along the Atlantic coast of North America and only those as far south as North Carolina. We do, however, include all records of both of these species within their areas of acceptance provided that they fulfill the above three principles.

The application of these principles has led us to accept, for certain species, a few records that have been rejected by state or province record committees or other state or province authorities as possible escapes. Such records are always qualified by -q to clearly indicate the situation. On the other hand, the application of these same principles have led us to reject a number of records of various species, including two species contained in the *Thirty-fourth Supplement to the A.O.U. Check-list* (1982): Lesser White-fronted Goose (*Anser erythropus*) and Black-throated Magpie-Jay (*Calocitta colliei*), as well as a few species included in recent state checklists such as Antillean Crested Hummingbird (*Orthorhyncus cristatus*) in Texas and San Blas Jay (*Cyanocorax sanblasianus*) in Arizona. Other notable records that we have rejected as possible escapes include Scarlet Ibis in Nova Scotia, Falcated Teal in California, American Black Duck in Arizona, White-cheeked Pintail in Wisconsin and Illinois, Cinnamon Teal in Maryland, Black Vulture in the Yukon Territory and California, Common Black-Hawk in Minnesota, Zone-tailed Hawk in Nova Scotia, Crested Caracara in California, Wyoming, Wisconsin and Michigan, Green Violet-ear in California, Great Kiskadee in Saskatchewan, California and New Jersey, both Steller's and and Scrub jays in Illinois, Jackdaw in Florida, Gray Silky-flycatcher (*Ptilogonys cinereus*) in California and Arizona, and Yellow Grosbeak in California. Obviously, we do not expect everyone to agree with all of our decisions. Furthermore, we expect some of them to change as new information is uncovered and new records come to light. For example, the records mentioned above for Gray Silky-flycatcher may well have to be re-evaluated in light of a recent record in Texas in the fall of 1985, well after our cutoff date for records.

For the confirmation of breeding. Our criteria for establishing a species as a confirmed breeder in a state or province is that positive evidence of breeding has been obtained at least once. For the purposes of our lists, positive evidence of breeding is limited to the following: (a) observation of a nest with eggs or young, (b) observation of a nest being built or in attendance (exclusive of dummy nests or nests for roosting in the non-breeding season), (c) repeated observations of nesting material or food being carried to, or fecal sacs being carried away from, a likely nesting site, or (d) observations of fledglings, known to be locally hatched, being fed by an adult. We have used extreme caution in accepting evidence of breeding based upon this last criterion because certain species may move long distances from their nests (even up to 1800 km in Elegant Terns) and still retain and feed their fledglings.

A documented breeding attempt need not have been succesful, or even completed, to be considered positive evidence of breeding. The Yellow-throated Warbler, for example, is classified as a confirmed breeder in California based upon the fact that a pair began constructing a nest, though it was never completed. Furthermore, a species is given confirmed breeding status in a state or province even if only one individual of the species was involved in the breeding attempt (e.g., a lone female Curve-billed Thrasher in Wisconsin that laid infertile eggs for four consecutive seasons) or if a single individual was involved in an interspecific breeding attempt (e.g., Blue-throated Hummingbird in California, Scissor-tailed Flycatcher in California, and Black-headed Grosbeak in Oklahoma).

Format

A major purpose of this book is to provide information on two important aspects of bird distribution, status and abundance, for every species in every state and province of North America. The matrix format that we have chosen provides a convenient means of doing this. It has the added advantage that it presents all possible combinations of all species with all states and provinces and thus facilitates the updating of the state and province lists as new species are added to them. In order to overcome the space limitations caused by the use of the matrix format, we have encoded the status and abundance information. In the following section, we precisely define each of the codes that we use.

Species are listed according to the order presented in the *A.O.U. Check-list of North American Birds* (1983), and headings are provided for three systematic categories above the species level: order, family and subfamily. Accordingly, 24 or fewer species can be presented on a single page and six pages are necessary to present the complete matrix of 63 areas—the 50 U.S. states, the District of Columbia, and the ten provinces and two territories of Canada. Status and abundance codes are provided for each species for each state or province in which it has occurred. A place is also provided to "tick" each species in each state or province using an "X" or check-mark, or by recording the date of first encounter. For those who have the ability to write meticulously small (a perhaps inordinately common trait among birders and field ornithologists), both the date of first encounter and a meaningful abbreviation of the location of encounter can be squeezed into the space provided. In this way, users of this book can simultaneously keep all their state and province life lists in a single volume while having immediate access to status and abundance information.

Preceding the six pages of the state and province matrix is a page to be used for recording the date and location where each species was first encountered in North America, and a space to "tick" the species. This space could also be used for a number by those who prefer to number chronologically the species on their life lists. Also included on this first page are columns for continental North America (the entire area covered by this checklist excluding Hawaii), Canada and the "lower 48" states of the United States. Status and abundance codes are provided for each of these areas based on the same criteria used for the states and provinces. Space is also provided in these columns for life list data for these major areas.

The states and provinces are arranged through the matrix as follows: Hawaii, Alaska, the two Canadian territories and ten provinces from west to east, and the 50 U.S. states and D.C. roughly from northwest to southeast. We chose a geographical arrangement of states and provinces, rather than an alphabetical one, to facilitate comparison of geographically proximate areas. The exact arrangement that we chose came after experimentation with a number of alternatives, and seemed to be the most natural to work with.

This format was changed in only one case, that involving the page dealing with Hawaiian honeycreepers. Because all the species on this page have never been recorded outside of Hawaii (and most likely never will), we have eliminated the columns for continental North America, Canada and the lower 48 states and replaced them with a single column for Hawaii. We then eliminated the remaining six pages of unnecessary state and province matrices.

We have separated native populations from introduced populations, and treat them in Parts I and II of this book, respectively. We have done this in order to emphasize the fundamental difference in origin of the two groups of species, and because we believe that the dynamics of their range expansions and contractions deserve to be monitored separately. Note that our separation is between native and introduced *populations*, not species. Because of this, certain species are included in both lists, even sometimes for a single state or province. Indigenous populations of House Finches from western North America, for example, are included in Part I, Native Populations, while populations of this species in eastern North America and Hawaii are included in Part II, Introduced Populations. Northern Cardinals are, of course, included in Part I but are also included in Part II because of introduced populations in southern California and Hawaii. This species, therefore, occurs on the California lists in both parts of the book. Similarly, Canada Goose and Mallard, native winter residents in the southeastern United States, are also included in Part II for many southeastern states because of feral, permanent resident populations that have arisen from escaped or introduced birds. We encourage users to attempt to determine and record whether the birds they observe are derived from native or introduced populations.

At the end of Part I, Native Populations, data are provided for each state and province (and for North America as a whole, continental North America, Canada and the lower 48 states) giving the total count of native species that have been recorded, the total count of native species that have attempted to breed (including both confirmed breeders and assumed breeders; see below under "Suffixes to status codes", code †), and the total count of native species that have been recorded in winter. In all cases, these counts include extinct and extirpated species provided that they had occurred during the nineteenth or twentieth centuries. The cutoff date for all records in this checklist is February 28, 1985. Space is provided (to the left) for updating these counts as new species are recorded for each state and province without having to destroy the February 28, 1985, data. Space is also provided (above) for recording and updating life list totals for each state and province (and for North America as a whole, continental North America, Canada and the lower 48 states). Similar space is provided at the end of Part II, Introduced Populations, but the data here refer to the total counts of native and introduced species recorded in each state and province.

Finally, space is also provided at the ends of Parts I and II for the user to add new species to the North American list (and to the lists for each state and province) as they occur. Additions to the North American list and to the various state lists (since March 1, 1985) that have come to our attention are presented in the Addenda.

Codes

The information presented on the status and abundance of each species in each state and province has been encoded such that reasonably large amounts of information can be presented in a small space. The codes also provide precise definitions for the various status and abundance classifications, enabling them to be applied uniformly to all species in all states and provinces. The purpose of this section is to define and illustrate each of the codes that we use.

For the user's convenience, concise definitions of all of the codes used in this work are presented on both the front and back endpapers.

Status codes. The status codes, which are always shown in capital letters, basically apply to three major aspects of distribution: breeding, seasonality and whether or not the species is within its established range. For the most part, the various status codes can be quite objectively defined such that little uncertainty results regarding their usage. In those situations in which a species occurs with more than one status within a given state or province (as is usually the case), the appropriate status codes are always separated from each other by commas. In such cases, they are always arranged in the order in which they are presented in this discussion. The status codes are: *E*—extinct species that formerly bred, *E**—formerly non-breeding extinct species, *P*—permanent resident and breeder, *P**—non-breeding permanent resident, *S*—summer resident and breeder, *S**—non-breeding summer resident, *T*—transient, *V*—vagrant, *W*—winter resident or visitant, and *W+*—breeding winter resident.

E   *Extinct species that was formerly a confirmed breeder.* This code is used only when the entire species, including all extralimital populations, is officially established as being extinct. Only four species in continental North America have been officially classified as extinct by the A.O.U. (1983): Labrador Duck, Great Auk, Passenger Pigeon and Carolina Parakeet. An additional 14 species have been officially exterminated in the Hawaiian Islands. Four other species, Ivory-billed Woodpecker and Bachman's Warbler in continental North America, and Kauai Akialoa and Molokai Creeper in Hawaii, are also quite possibly extinct. However, reviewers in the appropriate areas as well as the A.O.U. (1983) did not feel comfortable in "officially establishing" these species as extinct and we are inclined to agree with this interpretation at this time. Whenever the status code *E* is used, it is always used alone without any other status code or suffix (except, in some cases, †, assumed breeder), and without any abundance code or prefix. Positive evidence of former breeding in the state or province exists for all species coded *E*.

E*   *Formerly non-breeding extinct species.* This code, like *E*, is used only when the entire species, including all extralimital populations, is officially established as being extinct. It indicates that the species formerly occurred in the state or province but that positive evidence of breeding does not exist. In most cases, such species were only transients, wanderers or winter residents in the state or province.

Winter occurrences for extinct species are not specifically indicated by the codes *E*, extinct breeding species, or *E**, extinct non-breeding species. Valid winter records can be assumed to exist, however, for all extinct species in all states and provinces where they have been recorded, except for Carolina Parakeet in Wisconsin and Michigan, and Passenger Pigeon in Canada and in all states north and west of Oklahoma, Missouri, Kentucky and Virginia, except for Indiana, Pennsylvania and Connecticut where apparently valid winter records do exist.

P   *Permanent resident and confirmed breeder.* This code is used for species that occur year-round in the state or province in numbers that are roughly similar, that is, that can be described by the same abundance code, in summer, winter and during the spring and fall migration periods. If the number of individuals of the species is substantially increased during any of these periods, that is, if either summer numbers, winter numbers or numbers during migration require the use of a higher abundance code than is used for the remainder of the year, then the status code *P* is not used. Such status codes would, for example, be coded *cS,fW* (common summer resident, fairly common winter resident), *fS,cW* (fairly common summer resident, common winter resident), or *fS,cT,fW* (fairly common summer resident, common transient, fairly common winter resident).

Three important points must be stressed regarding the use of *P*. First, this code provides no information whatsoever regarding the movement or lack of movement of *individual* birds. In California, for example, we use *P* for Brown Towhee, a species in which virtually all individuals appear to be completely sedentary, as well as for American Robin, a species in which virtually all individuals are likely migratory to some extent. We have made no attempt to distinguish sedentary species from wholly or partially migratory species in our use of the code *P*. The data necessary for making such distinctions simply do not exist for even the majority of bird populations in most states or provinces. One needs only to consider how recently the extensive migratory behavior of Blue Jays has become widely appreciated to realize how little we know about both local and long-distance movements of even our common year-round species.

Second, the code *P* must not be construed as providing any information at all regarding the geographic distribution of the species within the state or province. For example, a species could be a common summer resident that is virtually unknown in winter over one large portion of a state or province, and a common winter resident that is virtually unknown in summer over another large but entirely different area of the state or province, and would still be coded *cP* (common permanent resident) rather than *cS,cW* (common summer resident, common winter resident). Examples of such species include Common Loon in British Columbia, a common summer resident on interior lakes in the province and a common winter resident along the coast, Yellow-rumped Warbler in California, a common summer resident of higher elevations and a common winter resident throughout lower elevations of the state, and many species over continental North America as a whole.

Finally, the code *P* indicates that the species is a *confirmed breeder* in the state or province, that is, that positive evidence of breeding has been documented at least once.

P*   *Non-breeding permanent resident.* The code *P** is used for species that occur year-round with the same abundance in a state or province but for which no confirmed breeding is known. As in the use of *P*, the code *P** provides no information regarding the species' distribution and movements or lack of movements within the state or province, although *P**, especially when coupled with abundance codes of *r* (rare) or *x* (extremely rare), is often used to describe the occurrences of a few sedentary non-breeding individuals. Examples of this use of *P** include the occurrences of several apparently unmated Barred Owls that have resided in northern California for several years and the continuous residency of a lone Golden Eagle in Hawaii for many years. On the other hand, the code P* is also appropriate for describing a pattern of occurrences characterized by a scattering of records throughout the year with no clear-cut changes in abundance between non-breeding summer occurrences, transient occurrences, and winter occurrences.

S *Summer resident and confirmed breeder.* This code is used for species that occur during the summer in numbers that are substantially different than their numbers in winter, that is, that must be described by different abundance codes in summer and winter. It is, however, also used for species that are described by the same abundance code in summer and winter provided that their abundance in one of these seasons is modified by the prefix *i,* irregular, or *l,* limited, and their abundance in the other season is not so modified. The code *S* is also used for species that occur in roughly similar numbers in summer and winter but that are present in substantially greater numbers in either the spring or autumn migration periods. In this case, both a transient status and a winter status are also given. Examples include Gray Catbird in Louisiana, coded *uS,cT,uW* (uncommon summer resident, common transient, uncommon winter resident), and Swamp Sparrow in Delaware, coded *fS,cT,fW* (fairly common summer resident, common transient, fairly common winter resident).

Summer is always construed to mean the normal Northern Hemisphere breeding season for each individual species in each state or province, generally from about May to July in the more northerly latitudes and higher altitudes and from about April to July in the more southerly latitudes. For some species, however, including Anna's Hummingbird in California, certain wading birds in Florida, Mourning Dove in all extreme southern latitudes, and Great Horned Owl over much of the continent, the summer breeding season can begin as early as January and can be completed as early as May or can extend practically throughout the year.

The code *S* also indicates that the species is a *confirmed breeder* in the state or province, that is, that positive evidence of breeding has been documented at least once.

S* *Non-breeding summer resident.* This code is used for species in which non-breeding individuals are known (or, in the case of pelagic species, are highly suspected) to have established residency, even for a relatively brief time, during the summer season. The code *S** is only used when the species' non-breeding summer abundance in the state or province is substantially greater (that is, of a higher abundance code) than the species' breeding abundance in that same state or province. An exception to this rule occurs when the species' breeding abundance is modified by the prefix *i,* irregular, or *l,* limited, and the non-breeding summer abundance is not so modified. The code *S** is also used in this case. In general, *S** is used to describe four rather different situations.

(1) *S** is used to describe the regular summer occurrences of pelagic species, particularly Procellariiformes, that breed primarily in the Southern Hemisphere during our northern winter. *S** is only used in this manner, however, when it is established that the species is within its accepted "wintering" range where it is known to exhibit some, even small, degree of residency and that it is not merely passing through areas between its breeding and "wintering" ranges. In the latter case, the species is treated as a transient. Thus, Sooty and Greater shearwaters that occur off the south Atlantic states in May and June are treated as transients en route to their more northerly non-breeding summer ranges, but the smattering of records for both of these species later in the summer after the main movement has passed are considered to be valid non-breeding summer records. Similarly, the occurrences of Buller's Shearwaters off California from August to October are considered to be transients, that is, birds passing south along the Pacific coast toward their Southern Hemisphere breeding grounds. The large mid-summer buildup of Black-footed Albatrosses and Sooty and Pink-footed Shearwaters off the Pacific coast, however, are treated as valid non-breeding summer residents.

In addition, summer occurrences of pelagic species that are outside of their generally accepted transient and non-breeding ranges are classified as vagrants (*V*) rather than non-breeding summer residents (*S**). Thus, for example, until we know more about their ranges and movements, summer records of Red-billed Tropicbirds off the south Atlantic states and Wilson's Storm-Petrels off the California coast are considered to be vagrant occurrences.

(2) *S** is used to describe the regular, generally northward post-breeding movement of numerous marine and aquatic species that breed primarily in the tropics or along the southern fringe of temperate North America in late winter and early spring. Species coded *S** for this reason include many Pelecaniformes and Ciconiiformes as well as several Laridae such as Heermann's Gull and Elegant Tern along the Pacific Coast. *S** is only used in this manner, however, for post-breeding occurences that are within the generally accepted range of post-breeding movements for the species. Occurrences outside of this range, even during the summer months, are treated as vagrant occurrences.

(3) *S** is used to describe the regular non-breeding oversummering occurrences of numerous, primarily marine and aquatic, species on their established wintering grounds. Among those species that are most frequently classified *S** in this manner are loons, grebes, marine ducks, shorebirds and gulls. Because of the prevalence of hunter-caused cripples and wounded birds, however, all non-breeding summer records (as well as all nesting records) of geese and dabbling ducks in areas well south of their breeding ranges have been ignored. In general, for most species (especially shorebirds), a non-breeding summer resident status is provided only in areas where the species regularly winters. Summer records in areas where the species only occurs as a transient are generally assumed to be late spring or early fall transients.

(4) Finally, *S** is used to describe all other non-breeding summer occurrences outside of the normal breeding range, provided that the individuals involved are known to have remained in a single general locality for at least ten days during the species' normal breeding season, that is, during

the period of time when eggs or nestlings typically occur for that species. The code *S** can be applied in this manner to vagrant species (species whose normal ranges at all times of the year lie well outside of the state or province) as well as to species whose normal winter or transient ranges encompass the state or province. Thus, a Prairie Warbler summering in the mountains of eastern California, well outside of the species' normal range, is coded *xS**, as is an unmated male Hooded Warbler summering in Minnesota, slightly north of the species' usual range, or a White-throated Sparrow summering in Arkansas, well south of the species' normal breeding range but well within its normal wintering range. An American Tree Sparrow found dead in southern California on July 20, however, is not included as a valid non-breeding summer resident because the individual was not known to have been present for at least ten days in the same general locality. We treat it as a vagrant occurrence.

T   *Transient*. Transient status is provided for a species when its abundance during either spring or autumn migration periods (or both) is substantially greater than that at all other times of the year. Transient status is also provided, however, whenever a species' summer or winter abundance is modified by the prefix *i*, irregular, or *l*, limited, and its transient abundance is not so modified, provided that its transient abundance is greater than that for any other unmodified status. Finally, transient status is also provided if the abundance codes for all seasons are *x*, extremely rare. Thus, *xT,xW* is a valid code.

We have not separated spring and autumn occurrences either by status or by abundance. When a species occurs in different numbers in spring and fall, the abundance code given for its transient status represents its abundance in the season when it is more common. This, of course, also holds for those cases in which a species only occurs in one or the other of the two migration seasons. After a cursory examination of various states and provinces across the continent, we concluded that the number of species requiring substantially different spring and fall transient abundance codes, while significant, was rather small. We decided to leave that degree of detail to works concentrating on individual states and provinces.

Finally, transient status is only provided when it is believed that the state or province involved lies, at least partially, within the species' normal established migration route in either spring or autumn. Species that occur in a state or province only as a result of migrant individuals that are believed to be outside of the established migration routes of the species are coded *V*, vagrants.

V   *Vagrant*. The code *V* represents a special class of transient and is used *in place of* transient for those species whose established migration routes lie outside of the state or province under consideration. In general, we used recent standard works as guides in judging the limits of established migration routes—the range descriptions in A.O.U. (1983), the range maps in Peterson (1980), National Geographic Society (1983), Robbins et al. (1983), and Flint et al. (1984) for Siberian species. We also coupled the information from these references with our own estimates of the shortest great-circle routes roughly connecting the western and eastern edges of the breeding ranges to the corresponding western and eastern edges of the wintering ranges. We tended to be conservative in judging the edges of migration routes, thus classifying migrant individuals that are only slightly out of range, as well as individuals that are far out of range, as vagrants. We hope this will help promote the reporting of all potential vagrant individuals so that patterns of migration across the edges of migration routes as well as the occurrence patterns of far distant vagrants can be monitored and analyzed.

A number of species with fairly well-described principal ranges that also range widely over other large areas of the continent required troublesome decisions as to whether they should be classified as vagrants. These included various marine species, such as certain loons, grebes, scoters, phalaropes, jaegers and gulls, and certain Eurasian species, such as Eurasian Wigeon, in the interior of the continent. They also included certain landbird species, such as Townsend's Solitaire and Varied Thrush in the East, and Swamp Sparrow and Harris' Sparrow in the West, that not only occur widely as vagrants during the migration seasons but also winter widely and successfully well outside their traditional ranges. We also took a conservative approach with these species and usually listed them as vagrants, again with the hope of promoting the reporting, recording and analysis of their occurrence patterns.

We do not use the term vagrant to describe breeding or non-breeding summer resident occurrences nor to describe winter occurrences even though the individuals involved could be far outside their established breeding or wintering ranges. Such birds are indeed vagrants, but we prefer to describe their occurrences with the correct seasonal status (*P, P*, S, S** or *W*) because these records *are* the substance of range expansion, and monitoring range expansion is one of the major objectives of this work. Whenever one of the status codes *P, P*, S, S** or *W* is coupled with the use of *V* rather than *T*, the species is out of range at all seasons in that state or province. Of course, if the *P, P*, S, S** or *W* status code has an abundance modified by *l*, limited, and is coupled with *V*, the species should not be considered a vagrant in the limited area of the state or province to which the *l* applies, but is out of range elsewhere in the state or province.

The use of the code *V* differs from the use of *T* in that *V* is *always* used if there are occurrences during migration, regardless of the abundance associated with the migrant occurrences. In contrast, *T* is used only when the species' abundance during migration is greater than its summer and winter abundance. Thus, codes such as *rS*,xV* (rare non-breeding summer resident, extremely rare vagrant), *xV,rW* (extremely rare vagrant, rare winter resident), and *xS,xV,rW* (extremely rare summer resident and breeder, extremely rare vagrant, rare winter resident) are often used. The result is that a vagrant code and a vagrant abundance are presented for the great majority of out-of-range birds.

If the species is listed in such a manner that no vagrant or transient code is given, that is if the only status codes given are *P, P*, S, S** or *W*, the status codes themselves provide no direct information as to whether or not the state or province lies within or outside of the species' established range. Generally, if the species is listed with an abundance code of *x* (extremely rare), it is safe to assume that the species is indeed a vagrant and that no records exist during migration. An example is Curve-billed Thrasher in Wisconsin, *xP*, where a single female was present for over four years and laid infertile eggs in several summers. For abundance codes greater than *x*, one should generally assume that the species is within, or at least on the edge of, its established range, and that transient records may well exist, but that the species does not occur as a transient with an abundance greater than the highest given.

Finally, we make no distinction in the use of V between spring and autumn vagrant occurrences. The reasons for this have already been discussed above under status code *T*.

W *Winter resident or visitant.* This code is used for species that occur during the winter in numbers that are substantially different than their numbers in summer, that is, that must be described by different abundance codes in summer and winter. It is also used for species that are described by the same abundance code in summer and winter provided that their abundance in one of the seasons is modified by the prefix *i*, irregular, or *l*, limited, and their abundance in the other season is not so modified. The code *W* is also used for species that occur in roughly similar numbers in summer and winter but that are present in substantially greater numbers during migration. For such species, a transient status and a summer status are also given. Finally, the code *W* is also used to describe all valid winter occurrences of vagrant or out-of-range birds regardless of the status of the bird at other seasons. Thus, codes such as *xS,xW* (extremely rare summer resident and confirmed breeder, extremely rare winter resident or visitant) and *xV,xW* (extremely rare vagrant, extremely rare winter resident or visitant) can be used for out-of-range species.

For the purposes of this checklist, an individual bird must have been present during the winter season on or after January 1 in order to be considered a valid winter record. All December records of individuals that were not recorded on or after January 1 are considered transient or vagrant occurrences. With the exception of a couple of apparently wintering individuals that were intentionally collected during the last few days of December and which are coded *xW*, we have tried to adhere rigorously to this guideline.

The date January 1 was arbitrarily chosen as the date when the vast majority of extremely late fall stragglers will already have passed through. We hope the use of *W* will, therefore, be representative of the situation where individual birds are actually attempting to winter. We realize, of course, that the uniform application of this date over the entire continent will likely classify a few valid winter records as transients or vagrants in the more northern states and provinces, and classify a few late transients and vagrants as valid winter records in the southern states. The use of January 1 has, however, the added advantage that it effectively culls out the vast majority of Christmas Bird Count records, many of which seem to represent late stragglers, and some of which are questionable due to inadequate documentation.

No degree of residency is required for a species to be classified as *W*, winter resident or visitant. Thus, an individual that occurred on only a single date, say January 10, is considered a valid winter visitant and is coded *W*.

The separation between valid winter records and spring transient or vagrant records was arbitrarily determined for each species in each state or province as the earliest date when the first spring migrants could reasonably be expected to occur in that state or province. We tended to be conservative in classifying records from late February or March as valid winter records; more often we considered them early spring migrants or vagrants, for example, the February records of Sage Sparrow in Oregon and Washington. On the other hand, a Yellow-throated Warbler present March 15–28 in Arizona is considered a valid winter resident because it occurred nearly a full month earlier than the earliest spring vagrant warbler records in the West, and nicely fits the pattern expected from a departing winter resident that was discovered just before it left.

The documentation of winter records has received less attention in both regional and continent-wide checklists, and by the birding community in general, than the documentation of occurrence or breeding. We hope that this checklist will stimulate the reporting and documentation of winter records.

W+ *Confirmed breeder during the winter months.* This code is used for four Procellariiformes that breed in Hawaii during the Northern Hemisphere winter, roughly October to May, and are absent during the midsummer months. All four are Southern Hemisphere species or derived from Southern Hemisphere origins: Black-footed Albatross, Laysan Albatross, Bonin Petrel and Sooty Storm-Petrel.

Suffixes to status codes. The following suffixes are added to certain status codes in order to provide additional information relevant to this checklist.

† *Assumed breeder; undoubtedly breeds but positive evidence of breeding is lacking.* This code is used as a suffix to *E, P* or *S* to indicate that although the species is generally accepted as a breeding species in the state or province, positive evidence (as defined above under "Criteria for the acceptance of records") is lacking. We urge field ornithologists and birders in those states and provinces where this code has been used to make every effort to document breeding for these species.

1 *Re-introductions currently provide all or a major portion of the population.* This code can be used as a suffix to virtually any status code but is usually used with *P* or *S*. Code *1* is only used in states or provinces where native populations formerly existed or still exist with the indicated status. Thus it applies only to re-introductions, not to new introductions. It is also applicable in the case where a species formerly occurred in a state or province and now re-occurs as the result of a re-introduction into a *neighboring* state or province.

2 *Re-introductions currently augment the population to a small or unknown extent.* This code, like *1* above, can be used as a suffix to virtually any status code but is usually used with *P* or *S*. As in the case of *1* above, it applies only to re-introductions, not to new introductions.

-sp *Species pair.* This code, added as a suffix to any status code, indicates that the individuals recorded during the season in question were not positively identified to species, but were positively identified as belonging to one or the other of the species included in the species pair. If one of the species in the species pair has been positively documented in a given season for the state or province, all records of unidentified individuals of that species pair in other seasons are included under the heading of the documented species, but are given the suffix *-sp* (e.g., Black-backed Wagtail in Oregon, *xV-sp,xW*: one positively identified Black-backed Wagtail in winter and several birds on migration that may have been either Black-backed or White Wagtails). If both species of the pair have been documented for a state or province in one or another season, we placed unidentified individuals in undocumented seasons under the species that we felt was most appropriate for that season and used the suffix *-sp* (e.g., Black-backed Wagtail in California, *xV,xW-sp*: several positively identified Black-backed Wagtails and one White Wagtail during migration and several unidentified in winter that we consider more likely to be Black-backed). If neither of the species of the pair have been documented in any season, we placed the unidentified individuals under the heading of the species that we considered the most likely member of the pair to occur and used the suffix *-sp*.

We used the code for *-sp* for these species pairs: Pacific or Arctic Loon in Hawaii (we considered all individuals of this species pair that have occurred in continental North America to be Pacific Loons until proven otherwise); Western or Clark's Grebe in a number of eastern states; Black-browed or Yellow-nosed Albatross in North Carolina; Phoenix or Tahiti Petrel in Hawaii (listed under Phoenix Petrel, the species that we feel is slightly more likely to occur near the Hawaiian Islands, this is the only case of a "species" added to the North American list as the result of a species pair); Herald or Kermadec Petrel in Pennsylvania (we consider the individual photographed and initially reported as a Kermadec Petrel to be an unidentified member of this species pair and place the record under Herald Petrel as we believe it is the more likely species to appear in eastern North America); Black-vented or Townsend's or Manx Shearwater in Alaska (we believe the unidentified individuals of this species group could have been any of these species, but were most likely Black-vented); Magnificent or Great Frigatebird in Alaska; Glossy or White-faced Ibis in Kentucky and Tennessee and in winter in Mississippi; White-faced or Glossy Ibis in Manitoba and in winter in Mississippi; Short-billed or Long-billed Dowitcher in West Virginia (none have been positively identified to species yet but both probably occur); South Polar or Great Skua in Hawaii and Missouri; Least or Little Tern (*Sterna albifrons*) in Hawaii; Thick-billed or Common Murre in Manitoba; Groove-billed or Smooth-billed Ani in Manitoba and Iowa; Rufous or Allen's Hummingbird in several eastern states; Couch's or Tropical Kingbird in Alabama and Florida; White or Black-backed Wagtail in Canada (Yukon) and in migration in Washington, and Black-backed or White Wagtail in winter in Canada (British Columbia) and California and in migration in Oregon; Bishop's or undescribed Oo in Hawaii (we do not believe that the Oo sightings reported from Maui can be positively identified as Bishop's Oo—they could represent an undescribed species endemic to Maui); and Great-tailed or Boat-tailed Grackle in Minnesota and during migration in Nova Scotia. In all cases but two, both members of the species pair have been positively recorded somewhere in the area covered by this checklist. The exceptions are: Phoenix or Tahiti Petrel which we included from Hawaii, and from North America as a whole, as a species pair and listed under Phoenix Petrel; and Little Tern which we included in a species pair with Least Tern in Hawaii (interestingly, the Little Tern has recently been added to the Hawaiian list; see the Addenda).

In all of the cases where we have used the code *-sp*, there is reason to believe that both members of the species pair are possible in the state or province. We did not use *-sp* in cases where similar species were not eliminated but were considered to be extremely remote possibilities when compared to a more likely species or to a species with a history of occurrences in the general area. The occurrences of Ash-throated Flycatcher in the Northeast present a good illustration of this. In some cases (e.g., Québec), no specimen or photograph exists for Ash-throated Flycatcher that positively eliminates Nutting's Flycatcher (or perhaps other West Indian *Myiarchus* species as well). However, we did not list this species as *-sp* in these cases because Ash-throated Flycatcher is the only species of vagrant *Myiarchus* that has been documented from the Northeast, because it has been documented in many northeastern states and provinces, and because the possibility of other species seems far more remote than Ash-throated.

Abundance codes. In contrast to status codes, which can be defined fairly objectively, abundance codes must usually be defined rather subjectively. Our goal in this checklist has been to develop a system of abundance codes that reflects, as accurately as possible, the number of individual birds of each species that can be encountered by a diligent, experienced birding party within the species' established range and preferred major habitat type.

The concept of the preferred major habitat type is an important one. For the purposes of this checklist, we recognize only nine major habitat types based upon gross environmental considerations and upon major vegetational growth forms. These are: (1) open oceans; (2) the open water of bays and estuaries; (3) intertidal areas; (4) the open water of lakes and rivers; (5) marshes, swamps and other wetlands; (6) plains, grasslands, fields and pastures; (7) brushlands, scrublands and deserts; (8) woodlands and forests; and (9) urban and suburban environments. We do not consider any finer distinctions between habitats, such as any differences between coniferous, deciduous or riparian forests. Our system classifies a species as common within a state or province if it is common in only a single major habitat type, even if that major habitat type occupies a relatively small proportion of the total area of the state or province. Marsh Wrens, for example, are classified as "common" in some states because they can be encountered in substantial numbers in most of the state's widely scattered marshes, despite the fact that these marshes comprise only a small fraction of the area of the state. When a species occurs in several major habitat types within a state or province, it is generally given the abundance code of the major habitat type in which it is present with the greatest abundance.

The abundance codes presented in this work should only be used to compare the relative abundance of various species *within the same major habitat types*, and not to compare directly the relative abundances of various species in the state or province as a whole. This is simply because the various major habitat types typically comprise quite different proportions of any given state or province. Thus, for example, one cannot directly use these abundance codes to compare, over the state or province as a whole, the relative numbers of woodpeckers versus rails, sparrows versus sandpipers, or warblers versus shearwaters, without taking into consideration the relative areas of the various major habitat types preferred by these species.

The measures of relative abundance that we propose should not be interpreted as measures of either relative or absolute density or absolute abundance. This is because the numerical basis for our data, the number of birds encountered by an active, experienced birding party, depends not only upon the actual density of the birds present, but also upon their detectability and conspicuousness. Obviously, a much greater proportion of the individuals actually present in a given area will be encountered for large, noisy, unwary or otherwise more conspicuous species than for small, quiet or furtive species. The result is that a highly detectable species (such as Black-billed Magpie in the Great Basin) may be encountered in such numbers and with such a frequency as to be given a relative abundance of "common," while a species more difficult to detect (such as Gray Flycatcher in the same area) that may actually be present in greater numbers but encountered less frequently is given the relative abundance of "fairly common." We believe it is better to base our classifications of relative abundance on the actual number of encounters rather than on any arbitrary estimate of "true" abundance that is in turn based on unverified assumptions about the undetected proportion of the population.

Similarly, the number of encounters of nocturnal species (such as owls, caprimulgids and to some extent rails) cannot be directly compared to the numbers of encounters of diurnal species because typical birding activities involve comparatively little time at night. We have therefore based our relative abundance codes for nocturnal species on the numbers of encounters during extensive post-dusk and pre-dawn owling expeditions.

We readily admit that the relative abundance codes expressed in this work may not necessarily reflect reported estimates of relative or actual density obtained from spot-mapping methods of breeding bird censuses or from the many transect or fixed-point, variable-area or fixed-area censusing methods being developed and utilized at the present time. However, the data obtained from such methods apply only to small areas within specific habitats and at certain times of the year. While such density estimates may be useful for studying specific populations and communities, they are of little value for determining relative abundances of birds over areas as large as that of most states. The reason for this is that detailed habitat requirements for most species in most states have yet to be fully elucidated, if indeed useful and reliable detailed habitat mappings have even been developed. As a result, meaningful extrapolations from local density to large-scale abundance cannot be made. Furthermore, the actual accuracy and reliability of many of the more recently developed censusing methods remain a matter of scientific debate, while the subject of intra-habitat variability, including both inherent variability and that due to sampling, has barely been addressed.

In view of these considerations, we suggest that the straightforward tallying of the number of individuals encountered during whole (or partial) days of active birding may provide a simple and reasonably reproducible method for assessing the relative abundance of birds over relatively large areas. We encourage birders to record, as accurately as possible, the number of individual birds they encounter in their daily birding trips, along with an account of the timing and location of their birding activities, so that such data may become available to better describe the relative abundance of North American birds, not only at the state level, but also perhaps at the county or quarter-latilong level. It is our hope that the relative abundance codes utilized in this work will be found intuitive and useful for today's serious birder, and will remain so into the future. In this way, a major purpose of this work may be realized—the facilitation of the large-scale, long-term monitoring of the ranges, status and abundance of North American birds.

We have utilized a five-step scale for classifying and encoding relative abundance. This scale is designed to provide increasingly finer classifications for increasingly rarer species, and thus resembles a logarithmic scale. These codes are intended to represent the relative abundance of birds at the close of the decade, 1975-1984, specifically as typified by 1983 and 1984.

C   *Common or abundant.* Always or almost always encountered, usually in relatively large numbers.
Numbers themselves can vary from a few (on more than 90% of the days) to many (on more than 50% of the days). Common species can almost always be found in their proper range and habitat without any special searching. They are almost always widely, rather than locally, distributed. In this checklist, truly locally distributed species are virtually never described as common, even if they are quite common in those few optimal locations. No separation is made between common and truly abundant species, the latter being considered as those common species that effectively force themselves on the birder's attention by their large numbers.

f *Fairly common.* Usually encountered in small numbers but sometimes encountered in relatively large numbers in favored locations or situations. Numbers themselves can vary from a few (on 50%–90% of the days) to many (on 10%–50% of the days). Fairly common species can usually be found in small numbers in their proper range and habitat but sometimes require special searching. There are three fundamentally different distributions of individuals within a state or province that produce the code *f*: a species could be widely distributed over a substantial area (over 10%) of the state and be fairly common everywhere; a species could be locally distributed over a substantial area (over 10%) of the state but be common in those favored localities; or a species could be localized in distribution to some extent to an area of less than 10% of the state and be common there, but also occur regularly in reduced numbers elsewhere in the state. In each of these cases, the code *f,* fairly common, is used. Species that are limited to less than 10% of the state and are common there, but only occur as out-of-range vagrants or not at all in the remainder of the state, are given an abundance code of *c,* common, modified by the prefix *l,* limited (see below under "Prefixes to abundance codes").

u *Uncommon.* Not usually encountered unless a special search is made and even then typically encountered in only small numbers; rarely encountered in relatively large numbers. Numbers themselves vary from a few (on 10%–50% of the days) to many (on fewer than 10% of the days). As in the case of fairly common species, uncommon species can occur within a state or province as a result of three different distributions of individuals: a species could be widely distributed over a substantial area (over 10%) of the state and be uncommon everywhere; a species could be locally distributed over a substantial area (over 10%) of the state and be fairly common in those favored locations; or a species could be localized in distribution to an area of less than 10% of the state and be fairly common there but also occur regularly in reduced numbers elsewhere in the state.

r *Rare.* Generally not expected on any given day. Typically no more than a few are detected on fewer than 10% of the days. The actual number of occurences for a state or province in any given season (that is, for any given status code) can vary from as few as 11 recent records (for the past 50 years, that is, from March 1, 1935 to February 28, 1985) to as many as 30 (exceptionally 50) records per year in states such as California that have high observer effort and localized concentrations of vagrant birds.

x *Extremely rare.* Ten or fewer records for the past 50 years (March 1, 1935 to February 28, 1985) for the state or province in the given season (that is, for the given status code). In the case of rare and extremely rare abundance codes, a record is defined as the independent occurrence of a single bird or of a coherent group or flock of birds of any size. Note that the code *xV,xW* positively indicates at least two records, at least one in winter and at least one during migration. Similarly, the code *rV,rW* indicates at least 22 records, at least 11 during migration and another 11 or more during winter.

Breeding species that have declined in numbers to the point where only one or two pairs remain in a state or province (or even, as is apparently the case with the Kauai Oo, to a single individual) are *not* coded *x,* extremely rare. The code *x* is reserved for the case when only ten or fewer records are known for a species in the state or province in the season in question for the past 50 years. In general, birds given the abundance *x* can be considered vagrants or at least on the edge of the species' established range. An exception is the use of *xT* where fewer than ten records exist during migration for the past 50 years but the state or province is still considered to be within the established migration route for the species (e.g., Eskimo Curlew in Massachusetts and Bachman's Warbler in Florida).

The uses of codes rare, *r,* and extremely rare, *x,* are basically determined numerically and circumvent the use of such subjective and arbitrary terms as occasional, casual and accidental, terms that are widely employed in other works. We prefer instead to let the number of records themselves indicate the relative abundance of the species.

Prefixes to abundance codes. The following prefixes can be added to abundance codes to provide additional information about the temporal or spatial distribution of the species in the given season (that is, for the associated status code) in the state or province.

e *Extirpated.* This prefix code has two related uses. If it is used with only a status code, that is, without an abundance code, it means that the species formerly occurred with the indicated status, and the state or province was considered to have been within the established range of the species. It further implies that the species no longer exists in the state or province with that particular status, although populations of the species are still extant elsewhere in the world or even in that state or province at a different season or with a different status.

The codes *eP*, eS*, eT* and *eW* indicate that the species has not been observed in the state or province in that season or with that status *for at least 50 years,* that is, since at least February 28, 1935. In contrast, the codes *eP* and *eS* indicate a formerly regular within-range breeding species that *has not bred in the state or province for at least ten years,* that is, since 1974. We have shortened the criterion for the extirpation of a breeding population to ten years, rather than 50, in order to include appropriate information on major decreases that have recently occurred in the breeding ranges of several species. Examples include Bewick's Wren and Loggerhead Shrike in the Northeast, and Bachman's Sparrow in the northern part and Henslow's Sparrow in the eastern part of their ranges.

We only used *eP* and *eS* when the evidence was overwhelming that the species had not bred in the state or province during the past ten years. Although, for example, no nests have been found for Willow Flycatcher in Arizona for the past ten years, summering individuals have been present in the state and breeding might have occurred. We do not use *eS* for such cases; rather, we follow a conservative mode and use *rS* (or *lrS* if the birds are confined to a single small area of the state or province).

The use of the "extirpated" prefix *e* in conjunction with

an abundance code (usually *x*, sometimes *r*), means that the species formerly occurred as an out-of-range vagrant during the season given or with the status shown, but no records exist *for at least the past 50 years*, that is, since February 28, 1935. We do not use the code *eV*; instead, to provide information on the actual number of vagrant records older than 50 years, we use *exV* or *erV*. The appropriately modified abundance code *ex* or *er* can be used for out-of-range species with any status code, and the codes *exP* and *exS* indicate that the species has only bred ten or fewer times in the state or province and *not within the past 50 years*. An out-of-range species that has bred only ten or fewer times within the past 50 years is coded simply *xP* or *xS*. There is thus a fundamental difference in timing between the codes *exP* or *exS* and the codes *eP* or *eS*. The former two indicate no breeding records for at least the past 50 years for an out-of-range species, while the latter two indicate no breeding records for at least the past ten years for a formerly regular breeding species.

i   *Irregular*. This prefix code implies that the abundance of the species in that season or for that status code varies greatly from year to year in either a predictable (cyclic) or unpredictable (sporadic) manner. The abundance code that is given generally applies to typical numbers in a flight year, although the species may often occur in substantially smaller numbers (or be completely absent), and may occasionally occur in considerably larger numbers. The prefix *i* is generally used only with certain species whose abundance in a particular season is well established to be cyclic or sporadic. In such cases, *i* is generally used throughout most of the range of the species.

l   *Limited*. This prefix code indicates that the species occurs in a geographical area comprising about 10% or less of the terrestrial and aquatic (exclusive of marine and Great Lakes) area of the state or province during the indicated season. Such species are effectively limited in their distribution in the state or province. Note that limited is *not* used for species that are locally or patchily distributed over a larger area of the state or province. The distinction between a species that is locally distributed (for which we do not use *l*) and one with a limited distribution (for which we do use *l*) can, however, be rather arbitrary in some cases.

In general, species whose ranges encompass only a small corner or edge of a state or province, and that occur more widely in the adjoining states or provinces, are generally described as limited. Species whose ranges encompass only one or a few small isolated areas that are in relatively close proximity to one another—that is, a single contiguous area enclosing all these locations would in itself amount to less than 10% of the state or province—are also usually described as limited. Species whose ranges include only a few small areas that are rather widely distributed over the state or province, however, are not usually described as limited. Particularly troublesome in this regard were species limited to subalpine or alpine habitats (e.g., Gray-cheeked Thrush and Blackpoll Warbler in New England and White-tailed Ptarmigan, Water Pipit and Rosy Finch in western states). In general, if the alpine or subalpine habitat itself was effectively limited in the state or province, or if the species was limited to a portion (usually the higher parts) of the alpine or subalpine habitat, we then considered the species to be limited and used the prefix *l*. If, on the other hand, the alpine or subalpine habitat was relatively widespread (even if it comprised considerably less than 10% of the total area of the state or province) and the species was relatively widespread in the alpine or subalpine habitat, the species was not considered to be limited and the prefix *l* was not used.

Birds of marine and estuarine environments (including landbirds such as Mangrove Cuckoo, Black-whiskered Vireo, Sharp-tailed Sparrow and Seaside Sparrow) are *not* described as limited, despite the fact that estuarine habitat usually amounts to far less than 10% of the area of the state or province, unless it is established that they occur in only 10% or less of the marine or estuarine habitat available to them. Furthermore, because many colonially nesting waterbirds often actually breed at only a few small scattered locations within their breeding ranges, the breeding status of waterbirds are only described as limited if the area over which *breeding birds range during the breeding season* is limited to 10% or less of the marine or estuarine areas of the state or province available to them. As a result, most species of marine and estuarine habitats are *not* described as limited. Also, the status of marine and estuarine species in the interior of coastal states and provinces is not separately described in this work. This fine detail of avian distribution is left to the realm of state, provincial or other regional works.

In the interior of the continent, marine and estuarine species are often, but not always, attracted to the larger bodies of water, particularly to the Great Lakes and other large lakes and rivers. While such bodies may occupy less than 10% of the area of a state or province, the birds associated with them are treated similarly to marine and estuarine species in states with marine and estuarine habitat, that is, they are not usually considered to be limited in distribution. Thus, in Ohio, for example, we make no separation between records from Lake Erie and those from the remainder of the state. Such distinctions are again left for regional works.

Breeding ranges are typically more sharply defined than winter or transient ranges since breeding usually requires more constraints on habitat selection as well as the intimate presence of two individuals of opposite sex; hence, we have used the prefix code *l*, limited, most frequently with status codes *P* and *S* that indicate confirmed breeding. We have used *l* much less frequently with status codes *P**, *S** and *W*, and rarely with status code *T*. We do *not* use *l* with the status code *V* even if all known occurrences are within a limited area (10% or less) of the state or province. To use *l* with a vagrant status code would be to presuppose a certain pattern of occurrence that may not truly exist. For much the same reason, we do not use the prefix *l* with the abundance *x* even if all records are within a limited area. The first record of any species in a state or province must, by definition, be limited; in such cases the use of *l* is unnecessary. With few exceptions, species that are given the abundance code *x* are out-of-range vagrants at that season anyway.

Finally, if a species is described as limited to a small area of a state or province in a certain season or with a certain status, its status elsewhere in the state or province in the same or different seasons is also always given regardless of the abundance codes used. Thus, codes such as *lcS,rs*,fT* (common breeding summer resident in a limited area, rare non-breeding summer resident and fairly common transient elsewhere) and *lcT,rV* (common within-range transient in a limited area, rare out-of-range vagrant elsewhere) are regularly used in this work, especially in large states containing widely varied habitats such as Alaska, Texas, California and Arizona, and in many of the provinces and territories of Canada.

-q   **The qualifier** *-q*. We use the qualifier *-q* for those cases in which a species is included on this checklist on the basis of a generally accepted sight record (documented in writing), but is not included on the official list for that state or province because the criteria for acceptance on that list differ from our uniformly applied criteria. We also use *-q* when a species is included on this checklist on the basis of a sight record (documented in writing), photograph or sound recording that is still under review by an established records committee, and that we feel will almost certainly be accepted. Our use of *-q* should *not* be interpreted as "hypothetical," a term that implies to us some doubt as to the accuracy or acceptance of the record. The code should instead be interpreted as *qualified*, that is, that the inclusion on our checklist and the exclusion from any other official state or province lists results merely from the application of different criteria. For a more thorough discussion, see "Criteria for the acceptance of records" above.

Codes for continental North America, Canada and the lower 48 states. Status and abundance codes have been developed for continental North America as a whole, Canada (including the French islands of Saint-Pierre et Miquelon) and the "lower 48" or contiguous 48 United States by applying the same criteria used for individual states and provinces. Because these codes pertain to such large areas, however, there are a few minor differences in their usage. Many of these concern the application of the prefix *l*, limited, which is frequently used when considering areas as large as North America, Canada or the lower 48 states. In these cases, isolated breeding records that lie well outside a species' normally limited breeding range are specifically coded *xP* or *xS*. As a result, code groups involving the repetition of *P*, the repetition of *S* and the combination of *P* and *S* are often used. Curve-billed Thrasher in continental North America and the lower 48 is coded *lcP,xP,rV,rW* where the code *xP* represents several breeding attempts by a lone female in Wisconsin. Scissor-tailed Flycatcher in continental North America is coded *lcS,xS,rV,luW*; the *xS* represents isolated breeding attempts in California and South Carolina. Great Kiskadee in continental North America and the lower 48 is coded *lfP,xS,xV,xW*; the *xS* represents isolated breeding in Louisiana. Codes involving the repetition of *P** (such as *lcP*,xP**), *S** (such as *lcS*,xS**) and *W* (such as *lcW,xW*), however, are never used.

If a species is classified as limited in any particular season or for any status code over any of these continental or semi-continental areas, the abundance code given is always the highest abundance given to any individual state or province in the limited area in question. On the other hand, if a species occurs with a relatively high abundance in a limited area of any of these continental or semi-continental areas, but has also occurred more than ten times in that season or with that status outside of the limited area, it cannot be classified as limited for that season or status. In these cases, the species is given an abundance code reduced by one class from the highest abundance code given to any individual state or province in the limited area where it occurs with a relatively high abundance. Thus, a species can be coded *lc* in continental North America as a whole and *f* in the lower 48 states. Rufous-crowned Sparrow, for example, is coded *lcP,xS*,rV,xW* in continental North America and *fP* in the lower 48. Cassin's Kingbird is coded *lcS,xS*,rV,luW* in continental North America and *fS,luW* in the lower 48. Lesser Goldfinch is *fS,lcW* in continental North America and *fP* in the lower 48 states.

Similar considerations produce codes for a given species of *f* in continental North America and *c* in Canada or the lower 48. This is because a species can be common in more than 10% of Canada or the lower 48 but in less than 10% of North America as a whole. The North American code is therefore reduced by one abundance class. Bewick's Wren, for example, is coded *fP* in continental North America and *cP* in the lower 48. Cerulean Warbler is *uS* in North America and *fS* in the lower 48. Chipping Sparrow is *cS,fW* in North America and *cP* in the lower 48 states.

Finally, two other situations sometimes arise with these continental or semi-continental codes that can seem contradictory. The first case deals with species that have been given different abundance codes in summer and winter despite the fact that virtually all individuals of the species occur year-round in North America. Examples include Tundra Swan and Greater White-fronted Goose in continental North America, each coded *cS,fW*. This is because these species are extremely localized (but not truly limited) in winter so that their winter abundance code is reduced by one abundance class. Other examples include Gyrfalcon and Northern Hawk-Owl in continental North America, coded *uS,rW* and *fS,uW* respectively. Since these species have somewhat smaller summer than winter ranges, individuals tend to be more concentrated in summer and, thus, are more frequently and easily encountered. A higher summer abundance code is therefore appropriate.

The second case involves species with transient abundance codes in continental North America that are higher than both their summer and winter abundance codes. Gadwall, Brown Creeper and Palm Warbler, for example, are all coded *fS,cT,fW* in North America. This is because these species have relatively highly synchronized migration periods that tend to concentrate the population during migration, thus allowing individuals to be encountered more often than in summer or winter.

Acknowledgments

This project owes its greatest debt to those individuals in each state and province who reviewed our initial lists and then answered our seemingly endless additional requests for information. The energy, expertise and enthusiasm of these people, over 150 of them, along with their kind generosity in sharing their extensive knowledge and experience, have transformed this work from a simple compendium of annotated checklists to an accurate and authoritative compilation of the status and abundance of North America's birds. Any errors that remain are entirely our responsibility.

In many cases, these reviewers have written or are now writing definitive works on the avifauna of their state or province. In many other cases they have served or are now serving as seasonal Regional Editors and regional Christmas Bird Count Editors for *American Birds*. In all cases, they have demonstrated a truly expert knowledge of the birdlife of their state or province. This checklist would not have been possible without their help, and to each of them we extend a personal message of thanks and appreciation.

Our reviewers for Canada are: **Alberta**, Douglas M. Collister and Philip H. R. Stepney; **British Columbia**, R. Wayne Campbell and David Stirling; **Manitoba**, Rudolf F. Koes and Peter Taylor; **New Brunswick**, David S. Christie, Peter A. Pearce and Stuart Tingley; **Newfoundland** (including Labrador and Saint-Pierre et Miquelon), Bruce Mactavish and William A. Montevecchi, with help from Roger Etcheberry; **Northwest Territories**, Peter McLaren and Wayne Neily, with help from J. B. Gollop and Gavin Johnston; **Nova Scotia**, Ian A. McLaren and Eric Mills; **Ontario**, Clive E. Goodwin and Ron D. Weir, with help from Ross James; **Prince Edward Island**, Winifred Cairns and Geoffrey G. Hogan; **Québec**, Normand David and Michel Gosselin; **Saskatchewan**, J. B. Gollop and Wayne C. Harris, with help from Bob Godwin, Stuart Houston, Robert Kreba, Stan Shadick, Al Smith and Phil Taylor; **Yukon Territory**, Helmut Grünberg and Dave Mossop.

Our reviewers for the United States are: **Alabama**, Dan C. Holliman and Thomas A. Imhof; **Alaska**, Daniel D. Gibson and Theodore G. Tobish; **Arizona**, Gale Monson and David Stejskal; **Arkansas**, Douglas James and Joseph C. Neal; **California**, Guy McCaskie and Rich Stallcup, with help from Richard Erickson, Kimball Garrett and Don Roberson; **Colorado**, Charles A. Chase III and Peter Gent; **Connecticut**, Noble S. Proctor and Dennis Varza, with help from George A. Clark, Jr.; **Delaware**, Maurice V. Barnhill III and Gene K. Hess; **District of Columbia**, David Czaplak and Byron Swift; **Florida**, C. Wesley Biggs and Paul W. Sykes, Jr., with help from Howard P. Langridge; **Georgia**, J. Christopher Haney and Terry S. Moore; **Hawaii**, Peter V. Donaldson and Robert L. Pyle; **Idaho**, Daniel A. Stephens and Daniel M. Taylor; **Illinois**, H. David Bohlen and Vernon M. Kleen; **Indiana**, Kenneth J. Brock and Charles E. Keller; **Iowa**, Thomas H. Kent and Peter C. Petersen; **Kansas**, Roger L. Boyd and Charles A. Ely, with help from Marvin Schwilling and Max C. Thompson; **Kentucky**, Burt L. Monroe, Jr., Brainard Palmer-Ball, Jr. and Anne L. Stamm; **Louisiana**, J. Van Remsen and Thomas S. Schulenberg; **Maine**, Jody Despres, Will Russell and Peter D. Vickery, with help from Charles Duncan; **Maryland**, Danny Bystrak and Chandler S. Robbins, with help from Robert F. Ringler; **Massachusetts**, Richard A. Forster and Wayne R. Petersen, with help from Richard R. Veit; **Michigan**, Robert B. Payne and David J. Powell; **Minnesota**, Kim R. Eckert and Robert B. Janssen; **Mississippi**, Larry Gates and Judith Toups; **Missouri**, David A. Easterla, Mark B. Robbins and James D. Wilson; **Montana**, Chuck Carlson and Larry S. Thompson, with help from Don Skaar; **Nebraska**, Gary Lingle and Wayne J. Mollhoff; **Nevada**, C. S. Lawson and Vince Mowbray; **New Hampshire**, Dennis J. Abbott and Kimball C. Elkins; **New Jersey**, William J. Boyle, Jr. and Richard Kane; **New Mexico**, Dustin Huntington and Dale Zimmerman; **New York**, Douglas P. Kibbe and Robert O. Paxton; **North Carolina**, Richard J. Davis and Harry E. LeGrand, Jr.; **North Dakota**, Craig A. Faanes and Hal Kantrand; **Ohio**, Jean Hoffman and Bruce G. Peterjohn; **Oklahoma**, William A. Carter and Joseph A. Grzybowski, with help from Jack D. Tyler; **Oregon**, Jeff Gilligan and Steve Summers; **Pennsylvania**, Frank and Barbara Haas and Robert C. Leberman; **Rhode Island**, David Emerson and Richard Ferren; **South Carolina**, Dennis M. Forsythe and Harry E. LeGrand, Jr.; **South Dakota**, Bruce K. Harris and Dan Tallman; **Tennessee**, Charles P. Nicholson and James T. Tanner; **Texas**, John Arvin, Greg W. Lasley and Chuck Sexton; **Utah**, Steven Hedges and Ella D. Sorensen, with help from William H. Behle; **Vermont**, Walter G. Ellison and Douglas P. Kibbe; **Virginia**, Jackson M. Abbott and Fred R. Scott; **Washington**, Eugene S. Hunn and Dennis Paulson, with help from Phillip W. Mattocks, Jr.; **West Virginia**, A. R. Buckelew, Jr. and George A. Hall; **Wisconsin**, Samuel D. Robbins and Daryl D. Tessen, with help from Philip Ashman; **Wyoming**, Bob Oakleaf and Oliver K. Scott, with help from Helen Downing.

Part I

Native Populations

Order Gaviiformes: Loons
Family Gaviidae: Loons

	Date	Location	Cont. North America	Canada	Lower 48
Red-throated Loon *Gavia stellata*			cP	cP	rS*.cW
Arctic Loon *Gavia arctica*			lrS.xW	xW	
Pacific Loon *Gavia pacifica*			cP	cP	uS*.cW
Common Loon *Gavia immer*			cP	cP	lfS.uS*.cW
Yellow-billed Loon *Gavia adamsii*			uP	uS.rW	xS*.rW

Order Podicipediformes: Grebes
Family Podicipedidae: Grebes

	Date	Location	Cont. North America	Canada	Lower 48
Least Grebe *Tachybaptus dominicus*			lfP.xS.xV.xW		lfP.xS.xV.xW
Pied-billed Grebe *Podilymbus podiceps*			cP	cS.uW	cP
Horned Grebe *Podiceps auritus*			cP	cP	luS.cW
Red-necked Grebe *Podiceps grisegena*			fP	fP	luS.fW
Eared Grebe *Podiceps nigricollis*			cS.fW	cS.luW	cS.fW
Western Grebe *Aechmophorus occidentalis*			cP	fS.lcW	cP
Clark's Grebe *Aechmophorus clarkii*			uS.lfW	xS*.xV	uP

Order Procellariiformes: Tube-nosed Swimmers
Family Diomedeidae: Albatrosses

	Date	Location	Cont. North America	Canada	Lower 48
Wandering Albatross *Diomedea exulans*			xV		xV
Short-tailed Albatross *Diomedea albatrus*			eP*.xV	eS*.xV	eP*.xV
Black-footed Albatross *Diomedea nigripes*			fS*.uW	fS*.xW	fS*.uW
Laysan Albatross *Diomedea immutabilis*			uS*.rW	rS*.xW	lrS*.rW
Black-browed Albatross *Diomedea melanophris*			xV	xV	xV
Shy Albatross *Diomedea cauta*			xV		xV

Order Gaviiformes: Loons
Family Gaviidae: Loons

	Hawaii	Alaska	Yukon Terr.	Northwest Terr.	British Columbia	Alberta	Saskatchewan	Manitoba	Ontario
Red-throated Loon		cS,fW	lcS,uT	cS	luS,uS*,cW	xS,rT	lfS,rT	lfS,uT	luS,uT,rW
Arctic Loon		lrS,xW			xW				
Pacific Loon	xV-sp,xW-sp	cS,fW	cS	cS	luS,uS*,cW	lrS,rT	luS*,rT	lfS,rT	luS,xV
Common Loon		cS,fW	cS,xW	fS	cP	cS	cS,rW	cS,xW	cS,rW
Yellow-billed Loon		uP	lrS,rT	uS	xS*,rW	xV,xW	xV	xV-q	xV

Order Podicipediformes: Grebes
Family Podicipedidae: Grebes

	Hawaii	Alaska	Yukon Terr.	Northwest Terr.	British Columbia	Alberta	Saskatchewan	Manitoba	Ontario
Least Grebe									
Pied-billed Grebe	rV,xW	xS,rV,rW	xS*,xV	luS	fP	fS	cS,xW	cS	cS,rW
Horned Grebe	xW	cS,fW	cS,xW	fS	cP	cS,xW	cS,xW	fS,cT	uS,cT,rW
Red-necked Grebe		fP	fS,xW	fS	fP	fS,xW	fS,xW	fS	fS,rW
Eared Grebe	xW	xV-q		xV	fS,uW	fS	cS,xW	cS	rV
Western Grebe		xV,lrW	xV		luS,cW	fS	fS,xW	fS	rV-sp
Clark's Grebe						xV	xS*	xV	

Order Procellariiformes: Tube-nosed Swimmers
Family Diomedeidae: Albatrosses

	Hawaii	Alaska	Yukon Terr.	Northwest Terr.	British Columbia	Alberta	Saskatchewan	Manitoba	Ontario
Wandering Albatross									
Short-tailed Albatross	eP*,xW	eS*,xV			eS*,xV				
Black-footed Albatross	cW+	fS*			fS*,xW				
Laysan Albatross	cW+	fS*			rS*,xW				
Black-browed Albatross									
Shy Albatross									

Order Gaviiformes: Loons
Family Gaviidae: Loons

	Québec	Newfoundland	New Brunswick	Prince Edward I.	Nova Scotia	Washington	Oregon	California	Nevada	Idaho
Red-throated Loon	fS,xW	fS,uW	rS*,fT,uW	rS*,fT,rW	rS*,fT,uW	uS*,cW	rS*,cW	rS*,cW	rV,xW	rV
Arctic Loon										
Pacific Loon	lrS,xV	xV			xV,xW-q	uS*,cW	uS*,cW	uS*,cW	rV,xW	xV
Common Loon	cS,xW	cS,fW	fS,cT,fW	fS,cT,uW	fS,cT,fW	lrS,uS*,cW	eS,uS*,cW	eS,uS*,cW	xS*,fT,uW	rS,fT,rW
Yellow-billed Loon						rW	rW	xS*,rW	xW	

Order Podicipediformes: Grebes
Family Podicipedidae: Grebes

	Québec	Newfoundland	New Brunswick	Prince Edward I.	Nova Scotia	Washington	Oregon	California	Nevada	Idaho
Least Grebe								xS		
Pied-billed Grebe	cS,xW	rV,xW	fS,xW	fS	uS,rW	cP	cP	cP	cS,uW	fS,cT,rW
Horned Grebe	lrS,uT,xW	rV,xW	exS,xS*,fW	rS*,uT	rS*,fT,uW	lrS,rS*,cW	rS*,cW	rS*,cW	xS*,uT,rW	lrS,uT,rW
Red-necked Grebe	xS,uT,rW	xS*,uW	fT,uW	uT	fT,uW	luS,rS*,fW	xS,rS*,uW	rS*,uW	xV,xW	lrS,rV
Eared Grebe					xV-q	fS,cT,uW	fS,cT,uW	fS,cW	fS,cT,fW	fS,cT,xW
Western Grebe	xV-sp					cP	cP	fS,cW	cS,fW	cS,xW
Clark's Grebe						uS,xW	fS,rW	uS,fW	fS,uW	uS

Order Procellariiformes: Tube-nosed Swimmers
Family Diomedeidae: Albatrosses

	Québec	Newfoundland	New Brunswick	Prince Edward I.	Nova Scotia	Washington	Oregon	California	Nevada	Idaho
Wandering Albatross								xV		
Short-tailed Albatross						eS*	eP*,xV	eP*,xV		
Black-footed Albatross						fS*,rW	fS*,rW	fS*,uW		
Laysan Albatross						rS*,xW	xS*,rW	xS*,rW		
Black-browed Albatross					xV-q					
Shy Albatross						xV				

Order Gaviiformes: Loons
Family Gaviidae: Loons

	Montana	Wyoming	Utah	Colorado	Arizona	New Mexico	North Dakota	South Dakota	Nebraska	Kansas	Oklahoma
Red-throated Loon	xV,xW	xV	xV,xW	xV,xW	xV,xW	xV,xW	xV	xV	xV	xV	xV,xW-q
Arctic Loon											
Pacific Loon	xV	rV	xV	rV,xW	rV,xW	xV,xW	xV		xV	xV	xV-q
Common Loon	uS,fT,rW	lrS,rS*,fT,rW	rS*,fT,rW	rS*,fT,rW	rS*,uW	xS*,uW	lrS,uT	rS*,uT,xW	rS*,uT,xW	rS*,uT,xW	xS*,uT,rW
Yellow-billed Loon		xV		xV	xW						

Order Podicipediformes: Grebes
Family Podicipedidae: Grebes

	Montana	Wyoming	Utah	Colorado	Arizona	New Mexico	North Dakota	South Dakota	Nebraska	Kansas	Oklahoma
Least Grebe					xS†,xV,xW						
Pied-billed Grebe	cS,rW	fS,rW	cS,uW	fS,uW	fP	fP	cS	cS	cS,xW	fS,cT,rW	uS,cT,uW
Horned Grebe	uS,rW	fT	uT,rW	fT,rW	rW	rW	uS	lrS,uT	eS,uT,xW	uT,rW	uT,rW
Red-necked Grebe	rS,xW	xS,xV		rV	xV		uS	lrS,rV	xV	xV	xV,xW-q
Eared Grebe	cS,rW	cS,xW	cS,uW	cS,rW	uS,cT,fW	uS,cT,uW	cS	cS	cS	rS,fT,xW	xS*,fT,rW
Western Grebe	fS,xW	cS	cS,rW	cS,uW	luS,fW	luS,fT,uW	fS	fS,xW	fS	rS*,uT	uT,xW
Clark's Grebe	rV	uS†	fS,rW	uS,rW	lfS,fW	uW	xV				

Order Procellariiformes: Tube-nosed Swimmers
Family Diomedeidae: Albatrosses

	Montana	Wyoming	Utah	Colorado	Arizona	New Mexico	North Dakota	South Dakota	Nebraska	Kansas	Oklahoma
Wandering Albatross											
Short-tailed Albatross											
Black-footed Albatross											
Laysan Albatross					xV						
Black-browed Albatross											
Shy Albatross											

Gaviidae • 25

Order Gaviiformes: Loons
Family Gaviidae: Loons

	Texas	Minnesota	Iowa	Missouri	Arkansas	Louisiana	Wisconsin	Michigan	Illinois	Indiana	Ohio
Red-throated Loon	rV,rW	xS*,rT,xW	xV	xV	xV,xW	xV,xW	xS*,uT,xW	xS*,uT,xW	rT,xW	rT,xW	rT,xW
Arctic Loon											
Pacific Loon	xS*,xV,xW	xS*,rV	xV	xV			xV	xV	xV	xV	
Common Loon	rS*,fW	cS,xW	eS,xS*,uT,xW	xS*,uT,xW	uW	rS*,fW	uS,fT,rW	uS,fT,rW	eS,xS*,fT,rW	eS,rS*,fT,rW	eS,rS*,fT,rW
Yellow-billed Loon		xV									

Order Podicipediformes: Grebes
Family Podicipedidae: Grebes

	Texas	Minnesota	Iowa	Missouri	Arkansas	Louisiana	Wisconsin	Michigan	Illinois	Indiana	Ohio
Least Grebe	fP					xV					
Pied-billed Grebe	fS,cW	cS,rW	fS,cT,rW	uS,cT,uW	uS,cW	uS,cW	cS,rW	cS,rW	fS,cT,uW	fS,cT,uW	uS,cT,uW
Horned Grebe	uW	lfS,fT,rW	xS*,uT,xW	fT,rW	fT,uW	uW	lrS,fT,rW	rS*,fT,rW	eS,xS*,fT,rW	exS,fT,rW	fT,rW
Red-necked Grebe	rV,rW	fS,xW	xS*,rT	rV,xW	xV,xW	xV	luS,uT	xS,uT,xW	rT,xW	rT,xW	rT,xW
Eared Grebe	uS,cW	lfS,fT	lrS,uT	xS*,uT,xW	uT,rW	uW	xS,rV	rV,xW	xS,rV	rV,xW	rV
Western Grebe	rW	lfS,uT,xW	xS,rV	xS*,rV	rV,xW	xV,xW	rV-sp	rV,xW	rV	rV-q	xV
Clark's Grebe		xV							xV	xV	

Order Procellariiformes: Tube-nosed Swimmers
Family Diomedeidae: Albatrosses

	Texas	Minnesota	Iowa	Missouri	Arkansas	Louisiana	Wisconsin	Michigan	Illinois	Indiana	Ohio
Wandering Albatross											
Short-tailed Albatross											
Black-footed Albatross											
Laysan Albatross											
Black-browed Albatross											
Shy Albatross											

Order Gaviiformes: Loons
Family Gaviidae: Loons

	West Virginia	Kentucky	Tennessee	Mississippi	Alabama	Maine	New Hampshire	Vermont	Massachusetts	Rhode Island	Connecticut
Red-throated Loon	rV	xV	xV	xV,xW	rV,rW	rS*,fT,uW	xS*,fT,uW	rT	rS*,cT,uW	rS*,cT,uW	rS*,fT,uW
Arctic Loon											
Pacific Loon				xV	xV,xW-q	xV	xV		rV,rW	rV,xW	
Common Loon	xS*,uT,rW	xS*,uT,rW	xS*,uT,rW	rS*,fW	rS*,fW	fS,cT,fW	uS,cT,fW	uS,fT,rW	lrS,uS*,cT,fW	uS*,cT,fW	uS*,cT,fW
Yellow-billed Loon											

Order Podicipediformes: Grebes
Family Podicipedidae: Grebes

	West Virginia	Kentucky	Tennessee	Mississippi	Alabama	Maine	New Hampshire	Vermont	Massachusetts	Rhode Island	Connecticut
Least Grebe											
Pied-billed Grebe	rS,cT,rW	rS,cT,uW	rS,cT,fW	rS,cW	rS,cW	fS,rW	uS,fT,rW	uS,fT	uS,cT,uW	rS,cT,uW	uS,cT,uW
Horned Grebe	fT,rW	fT,rW	fT,uW	xS*,fW	xS*,fW	rS*,cT,fW	rS*,cT,fW	fT,rW	rS*,cT,fW	rS*,cT,fW	rS*,cT,fW
Red-necked Grebe	rV	rV,xW	rV,xW	xV,xW	xV,xW	rS*,fW	xS*,fW	uT,xW	fW	uW	uW
Eared Grebe		xV,xW	xV,xW	uW	uW	xV-q		xV	rV,rW	xV,xW	xV,xW
Western Grebe		xV-sp,xW-sp	xS-sp,xW-sp	xV-sp	xV-sp,xW-sp	xV,xW	xV-sp-q	xV-sp-q	rV,rW	xV-sp,xW-sp	xV,xW
Clark's Grebe											

Order Procellariiformes: Tube-nosed Swimmers
Family Diomedeidae: Albatrosses

	West Virginia	Kentucky	Tennessee	Mississippi	Alabama	Maine	New Hampshire	Vermont	Massachusetts	Rhode Island	Connecticut
Wandering Albatross											
Short-tailed Albatross											
Black-footed Albatross											
Laysan Albatross											
Black-browed Albatross						xV-q			xV		
Shy Albatross											

Order Gaviiformes: Loons
Family Gaviidae: Loons

	New York	Pennsylvania	New Jersey	Delaware	Maryland	Dist. of Columbia	Virginia	North Carolina	South Carolina	Georgia	Florida
Red-throated Loon	rS*,cT,uW	rT,xW	rS*,cT,uW	rS*,cT,fW	rS*,cT,fW	xT	rS*,cW	rS*,cW	fW	uW	uW
Arctic Loon											
Pacific Loon	xV,xW		xV,xW				xV-q				xV,xW
Common Loon	uS,cT,fW	eS,rS*,fT,uW	rS*,cT,fW	rS*,cT,fW	rS*,cT,fW	uT,xW	rS*,cW	rS*,cW	rS*,cW	rS*,fW	xS*,fW
Yellow-billed Loon	xV										

Order Podicipediformes: Grebes
Family Podicipedidae: Grebes

	New York	Pennsylvania	New Jersey	Delaware	Maryland	Dist. of Columbia	Virginia	North Carolina	South Carolina	Georgia	Florida
Least Grebe											xV
Pied-billed Grebe	uS,cT,uW	uS,cT,uW	rS,cT,uW	uS,cT,fW	rS,cT,fW	rS*,fT,uW	uS,cW	uS,cW	uS,cW	uS,cW	fS,cW
Horned Grebe	rS*,cT,fW	cT,uW	rS*,cT,fW	xS*,cT,fW	rS*,cT,fW	fT,xW	rS*,cW	rS*,cW	rS*,cW	rS*,cW	xS*,fW
Red-necked Grebe	uW	uT,rW	uW	rW	rW	rT,xW	rW	rW	rW	rW	rW
Eared Grebe	xV,xW	rV	xV,xW	xV	xV,xW		rV,xW	rV,rW	xW	xV	rW
Western Grebe	xV,xW	xV-sp	xV,xW	xV-sp,xW-sp	xV,xW		xV,xW	xV,xW	xV,xW		xV,xW
Clark's Grebe											

Order Procellariiformes: Tube-nosed Swimmers
Family Diomedeidae: Albatrosses

	New York	Pennsylvania	New Jersey	Delaware	Maryland	Dist. of Columbia	Virginia	North Carolina	South Carolina	Georgia	Florida
Wandering Albatross											
Short-tailed Albatross											
Black-footed Albatross											
Laysan Albatross											
Black-browed Albatross									xV-sp-q		xV
Shy Albatross											

	Date	Location	Cont. North America	Canada	Lower 48
Yellow-nosed Albatross					
Diomedea chlororhynchos			rV	xV	rV

Family Procellariidae: Shearwaters and Petrels

	Date	Location	Cont. North America	Canada	Lower 48
Northern Fulmar					
Fulmarus glacialis			cP	cP	iuS*,icW
Black-capped Petrel					
Pterodroma hasitata			lfS*,xV,luW	xV	uS*,luW
Bermuda Petrel					
Pterodroma cahow			xV		xV
Dark-rumped Petrel					
Pterodroma phaeopygia					
White-necked Petrel					
Pterodroma externa					
Phoenix Petrel					
Pterodroma alba					
Mottled Petrel					
Pterodroma inexpectata			uS*	xW	xV,xW
Solander's Petrel					
Pterodroma solandri			xV		xV
Soft-plumaged Petrel					
Pterodroma mollis			xV		xV
Murphy's Petrel					
Pterodroma ultima			xV		xV
Kermadec Petrel					
Pterodroma neglecta					
Herald Petrel					
Pterodroma arminjoniana			xV		xV
Cook's Petrel					
Pterodroma cookii			xS*,xV		xV
Bonin Petrel					
Pterodroma hypoleuca					
Black-winged Petrel					
Pterodroma nigripennis					
Stejneger's Petrel					
Pterodroma longirostris			xV		xV
Bulwer's Petrel					
Bulweria bulwerii			xV		xV
Jouanin's Petrel					
Bulweria fallax					
Streaked Shearwater					
Calonectris leucomelas			xV		xV
Cory's Shearwater					
Calonectris diomedea			fS*	uS*	fS*
Pink-footed Shearwater					
Puffinus creatopus			cS*,rW	fS*	cS*,rW

Distributional Checklist of North American Birds

Species	Hawaii	Alaska	Yukon Terr.	Northwest Terr.	British Columbia	Alberta	Saskatchewan	Manitoba	Ontario
Yellow-nosed Albatross									

Family Procellariidae: Shearwaters and Petrels

Species	Hawaii	Alaska	Yukon Terr.	Northwest Terr.	British Columbia	Alberta	Saskatchewan	Manitoba	Ontario
Northern Fulmar	xW	cP	xV	cS,uW	iuS*,icW				xV
Black-capped Petrel									xV
Bermuda Petrel									
Dark-rumped Petrel	uS								
White-necked Petrel	fS*,rW								
Phoenix Petrel	xV-sp								
Mottled Petrel	rT	uS*			xW				
Solander's Petrel									
Soft-plumaged Petrel									
Murphy's Petrel	xV								
Kermadec Petrel	rP*								
Herald Petrel	xV								
Cook's Petrel	xT	xS*							
Bonin Petrel	fW+								
Black-winged Petrel	fS*								
Stejneger's Petrel	xV								
Bulwer's Petrel	fS								
Jouanin's Petrel	xV								
Streaked Shearwater									
Cory's Shearwater									
Pink-footed Shearwater		rS*			fS*				

Diomedeidae • 31

	Québec	Newfoundland	New Brunswick	Prince Edward I.	Nova Scotia		Washington	Oregon	California	Nevada	Idaho
Yellow-nosed Albatross	exV		exV		xV-q						

Family Procellariidae: Shearwaters and Petrels

	Québec	Newfoundland	New Brunswick	Prince Edward I.	Nova Scotia		Washington	Oregon	California	Nevada	Idaho
Northern Fulmar	IuS*,xV	cP	rS*,iuW	rT	rS*,cW		iuS*,icW	iuS*,icW	iuS*,ifW		
Black-capped Petrel											
Bermuda Petrel											
Dark-rumped Petrel											
White-necked Petrel											
Phoenix Petrel											
Mottled Petrel							xW	xV,xW	xV,xW		
Solander's Petrel							xV		xV-q		
Soft-plumaged Petrel											
Murphy's Petrel								xV			
Kermadec Petrel											
Herald Petrel											
Cook's Petrel									xV		
Bonin Petrel											
Black-winged Petrel											
Stejneger's Petrel									xV		
Bulwer's Petrel											
Jouanin's Petrel											
Streaked Shearwater									xV		
Cory's Shearwater		rS*	xS*		uS*						
Pink-footed Shearwater							cS*	cS*	cS*,rW		

	Montana	Wyoming	Utah	Colorado	Arizona	New Mexico	North Dakota	South Dakota	Nebraska	Kansas	Oklahoma
Yellow-nosed Albatross											

Family Procellariidae: Shearwaters and Petrels

	Montana	Wyoming	Utah	Colorado	Arizona	New Mexico	North Dakota	South Dakota	Nebraska	Kansas	Oklahoma
Northern Fulmar											
Black-capped Petrel											
Bermuda Petrel											
Dark-rumped Petrel											
White-necked Petrel											
Phoenix Petrel											
Mottled Petrel											
Solander's Petrel											
Soft-plumaged Petrel											
Murphy's Petrel											
Kermadec Petrel											
Herald Petrel											
Cook's Petrel											
Bonin Petrel											
Black-winged Petrel											
Stejneger's Petrel											
Bulwer's Petrel											
Jouanin's Petrel											
Streaked Shearwater											
Cory's Shearwater											
Pink-footed Shearwater											

Diomedeidae • 33

	Texas	Minnesota	Iowa	Missouri	Arkansas	Louisiana	Wisconsin	Michigan	Illinois	Indiana	Ohio
Yellow-nosed Albatross	xV					xV					

Family Procellariidae: Shearwaters and Petrels

	Texas	Minnesota	Iowa	Missouri	Arkansas	Louisiana	Wisconsin	Michigan	Illinois	Indiana	Ohio
Northern Fulmar											
Black-capped Petrel											exV
Bermuda Petrel											
Dark-rumped Petrel											
White-necked Petrel											
Phoenix Petrel											
Mottled Petrel											
Solander's Petrel											
Soft-plumaged Petrel											
Murphy's Petrel											
Kermadec Petrel											
Herald Petrel											
Cook's Petrel											
Bonin Petrel											
Black-winged Petrel											
Stejneger's Petrel											
Bulwer's Petrel											
Jouanin's Petrel											
Streaked Shearwater											
Cory's Shearwater	rV										
Pink-footed Shearwater											

	West Virginia	Kentucky	Tennessee	Mississippi	Alabama	Maine	New Hampshire	Vermont	Massachusetts	Rhode Island	Connecticut
Yellow-nosed Albatross						xV	xV-q		xV	xV	

Family Procellariidae: Shearwaters and Petrels

	West Virginia	Kentucky	Tennessee	Mississippi	Alabama	Maine	New Hampshire	Vermont	Massachusetts	Rhode Island	Connecticut
Northern Fulmar						rS*,cW	ifW	xV	rS*,ifW	iuW	exV
Black-capped Petrel		exV				xV-q	exV				xV
Bermuda Petrel											
Dark-rumped Petrel											
White-necked Petrel											
Phoenix Petrel											
Mottled Petrel											
Solander's Petrel											
Soft-plumaged Petrel											
Murphy's Petrel											
Kermadec Petrel											
Herald Petrel											
Cook's Petrel											
Bonin Petrel											
Black-winged Petrel											
Stejneger's Petrel											
Bulwer's Petrel											
Jouanin's Petrel											
Streaked Shearwater											
Cory's Shearwater						xV-q	uS*	rS*	xV	fS*	fS*	xV
Pink-footed Shearwater											

	New York	Pennsylvania	New Jersey	Delaware	Maryland	Dist. of Columbia	Virginia	North Carolina	South Carolina	Georgia	Florida
Yellow-nosed Albatross	xV				xV		xV-q				xV

Family Procellariidae: Shearwaters and Petrels

	New York	Pennsylvania	New Jersey	Delaware	Maryland	Dist. of Columbia	Virginia	North Carolina	South Carolina	Georgia	Florida
Northern Fulmar	iuW		xS*,iuW	iuW	xS*,iuW		xS*,iuW	rV,xW		xW	
Black-capped Petrel	xV				xV-q		rS*	fS*,uW	uS*	uS*,rW	uS*
Bermuda Petrel							xV-q				
Dark-rumped Petrel											
White-necked Petrel											
Phoenix Petrel											
Mottled Petrel	exV										
Solander's Petrel											
Soft-plumaged Petrel								xV-q		xV	
Murphy's Petrel											
Kermadec Petrel											
Herald Petrel	xV	xV-sp						xV			
Cook's Petrel											
Bonin Petrel											
Black-winged Petrel											
Stejneger's Petrel											
Bulwer's Petrel											xV
Jouanin's Petrel											
Streaked Shearwater											
Cory's Shearwater	fS*		fS*	fS*	fS*		fS*	cS*	fS*	fS*	fS*
Pink-footed Shearwater											

	Date	Location	Cont. North America	Canada	Lower 48
Flesh-footed Shearwater *Puffinus carneipes*			uS*,xW	uS*	rS*,uT,xW
Greater Shearwater *Puffinus gravis*			cS*,xW	cS*,xW	fS*,cT,xW
Wedge-tailed Shearwater *Puffinus pacificus*					
Buller's Shearwater *Puffinus bulleri*			ifT,xW	uT	ifT,xW
Sooty Shearwater *Puffinus griseus*			cS*,uW	cS*,rW	cS*,uW
Short-tailed Shearwater *Puffinus tenuirostris*			cS*,uW	iuT,rW	uW
Christmas Shearwater *Puffinus nativitatis*					
Manx Shearwater *Puffinus puffinus*			luS,uS*,lrW	luS,uS*	xS,uS*,lrW
Black-vented Shearwater *Puffinus opisthomelas*			lrS*,xV,lifW	exV,exW	rS*,ifW
Townsend's Shearwater *Puffinus auricularis*					
Little Shearwater *Puffinus assimilis*			xV	exV	xV
Audubon's Shearwater *Puffinus lherminieri*			fS*,lrW	xV	fS*,lrW

Family Hydrobatidae: Storm-Petrels

	Date	Location	Cont. North America	Canada	Lower 48
Wilson's Storm-Petrel *Oceanites oceanicus*			cS*	fS*	cS*
White-faced Storm-Petrel *Pelagodroma marina*			rV		rV
British Storm-Petrel *Hydrobates pelagicus*			xV	xV	xV
Fork-tailed Storm-Petrel *Oceanodroma furcata*			cP	cP	fS,rW
Leach's Storm-Petrel *Oceanodroma leucorhoa*			cS,rW	cS,rW	fS,rW
Ashy Storm-Petrel *Oceanodroma homochroa*			lcS,rW		lcS,fS*,rW
Band-rumped Storm-Petrel *Oceanodroma castro*			luS*,rV	xV	luS*,rV
Wedge-rumped Storm-Petrel *Oceanodroma tethys*			xV,xW		xV,xW
Black Storm-Petrel *Oceanodroma melania*			lrS,lcS*,xV,xW		lrS,cS*,xW
Sooty Storm-Petrel *Oceanodroma tristrami*					

Species	Hawaii	Alaska	Yukon Terr.	Northwest Terr.	British Columbia	Alberta	Saskatch-ewan	Manitoba	Ontario
Flesh-footed Shearwater	xT	rS*			uS*				
Greater Shearwater				lrS*					
Wedge-tailed Shearwater	cS,xW								
Buller's Shearwater	xT	rT			uT				
Sooty Shearwater	fT	cS*			cS*,rW				
Short-tailed Shearwater	uT	cS*			iuT,rW				
Christmas Shearwater	uS								
Manx Shearwater									
Black-vented Shearwater		xV-sp-q			exV,exW				
Townsend's Shearwater	uS								
Little Shearwater	xW								
Audubon's Shearwater									xV

Family Hydrobatidae: Storm-Petrels

Species	Hawaii	Alaska	Yukon Terr.	Northwest Terr.	British Columbia	Alberta	Saskatch-ewan	Manitoba	Ontario
Wilson's Storm-Petrel	xV								xV
White-faced Storm-Petrel									
British Storm-Petrel									
Fork-tailed Storm-Petrel	xW	cP			cP				
Leach's Storm-Petrel	uW	cS,rW		exV	fS,rW				xV
Ashy Storm-Petrel									
Band-rumped Storm-Petrel	lrS								xV
Wedge-rumped Storm-Petrel									
Black Storm-Petrel									
Sooty Storm-Petrel	uW+								

Procellariidae • 39

	Québec	Newfoundland	New Brunswick	Prince Edward I.	Nova Scotia		Washington	Oregon	California	Nevada	Idaho
Flesh-footed Shearwater							rS*,uT	xS*,rT	xS*,rT,xW		
Greater Shearwater	uS*	cS*,xW	uS*	xS*	cS*				xW		
Wedge-tailed Shearwater											
Buller's Shearwater							uT,xW	uT	ifT,xW		
Sooty Shearwater	uS*	cS*	uS*	xS*	cS*		cS*,rW	cS*,rW	cS*,uW		
Short-tailed Shearwater							iuT,rW	rW	uW		
Christmas Shearwater											
Manx Shearwater	rS*	luS,uS*	uS*		uS*						
Black-vented Shearwater									rS*,ifW		
Townsend's Shearwater											
Little Shearwater					exV						
Audubon's Shearwater					xV						

Family Hydrobatidae: Storm-Petrels

	Québec	Newfoundland	New Brunswick	Prince Edward I.	Nova Scotia		Washington	Oregon	California	Nevada	Idaho
Wilson's Storm-Petrel	uS*	fS*	fS*	rS*	cS*		xV-q	xV	rV		
White-faced Storm-Petrel											
British Storm-Petrel					xV						
Fork-tailed Storm-Petrel							cS,rW	fS,rW	luS,rS*,rW		
Leach's Storm-Petrel	luS,xV	cS	lfS,uT	rS*	cS,xW		fS,rW	fS,rW	uS,lfS*,rW		
Ashy Storm-Petrel									lcS,fS*,rW		
Band-rumped Storm-Petrel									xV		
Wedge-rumped Storm-Petrel									xV,xW		
Black Storm-Petrel								xV	lrS,cS*,xW		
Sooty Storm-Petrel											

40 • Distributional Checklist of North American Birds

	Montana	Wyoming	Utah	Colorado	Arizona	New Mexico	North Dakota	South Dakota	Nebraska	Kansas	Oklahoma
Flesh-footed Shearwater											
Greater Shearwater											
Wedge-tailed Shearwater											
Buller's Shearwater											
Sooty Shearwater					xV						
Short-tailed Shearwater											
Christmas Shearwater											
Manx Shearwater											
Black-vented Shearwater											
Townsend's Shearwater											
Little Shearwater											
Audubon's Shearwater											

Family Hydrobatidae: Storm-Petrels

	Montana	Wyoming	Utah	Colorado	Arizona	New Mexico	North Dakota	South Dakota	Nebraska	Kansas	Oklahoma
Wilson's Storm-Petrel											
White-faced Storm-Petrel											
British Storm-Petrel											
Fork-tailed Storm-Petrel											
Leach's Storm-Petrel											
Ashy Storm-Petrel											
Band-rumped Storm-Petrel											
Wedge-rumped Storm-Petrel											
Black Storm-Petrel											
Sooty Storm-Petrel											

Procellariidae • 41

	Texas	Minnesota	Iowa	Missouri	Arkansas	Louisiana	Wisconsin	Michigan	Illinois	Indiana	Ohio
Flesh-footed Shearwater											
Greater Shearwater	xV					xV-q					
Wedge-tailed Shearwater											
Buller's Shearwater											
Sooty Shearwater	xV										
Short-tailed Shearwater											
Christmas Shearwater											
Manx Shearwater	xV										
Black-vented Shearwater											
Townsend's Shearwater											
Little Shearwater											
Audubon's Shearwater	rS*,xW					rS*					

Family Hydrobatidae: Storm-Petrels

	Texas	Minnesota	Iowa	Missouri	Arkansas	Louisiana	Wisconsin	Michigan	Illinois	Indiana	Ohio
Wilson's Storm-Petrel	xV					rS*					
White-faced Storm-Petrel											
British Storm-Petrel											
Fork-tailed Storm-Petrel											
Leach's Storm-Petrel	xV					xV					exV
Ashy Storm-Petrel											
Band-rumped Storm-Petrel	xV			xV						exV	
Wedge-rumped Storm-Petrel											
Black Storm-Petrel											
Sooty Storm-Petrel											

	West Virginia	Kentucky	Tennessee	Mississippi	Alabama	Maine	New Hampshire	Vermont	Massachusetts	Rhode Island	Connecticut
Flesh-footed Shearwater											
Greater Shearwater						rV	cS*	fS*	xV	cS*	fS*,cT	xV
Wedge-tailed Shearwater											
Buller's Shearwater											
Sooty Shearwater						xV-q	uS*,fT	uS*,fT		uS*,fT	rS*,fT	xV-q
Short-tailed Shearwater											
Christmas Shearwater											
Manx Shearwater							uS*	rS*		xS,uS*	uS*	xV-q
Black-vented Shearwater											
Townsend's Shearwater											
Little Shearwater						xV-q					
Audubon's Shearwater						xV	xV-q			rS*	xS*	

Family Hydrobatidae: Storm-Petrels

	West Virginia	Kentucky	Tennessee	Mississippi	Alabama	Maine	New Hampshire	Vermont	Massachusetts	Rhode Island	Connecticut
Wilson's Storm-Petrel				xV	uS*	cS*	cS*		cS*	cS*	rS*
White-faced Storm-Petrel									xV	xV	xV
British Storm-Petrel						xV-q					
Fork-tailed Storm-Petrel											
Leach's Storm-Petrel					xV	cS*,xW	xS*,uT	xV	lrS,uT	xS*,rT	xV
Ashy Storm-Petrel											
Band-rumped Storm-Petrel			xV						xV		
Wedge-rumped Storm-Petrel											
Black Storm-Petrel											
Sooty Storm-Petrel											

Procellariidae • 43

	New York	Pennsylvania	New Jersey	Delaware	Maryland	Dist. of Columbia	Virginia	North Carolina	South Carolina	Georgia	Florida
Flesh-footed Shearwater											
Greater Shearwater	fS*,cT	exV	fS*,cT	uS*,fT	uS*,fT		uS*,fT	uS*,fT	uS*,fT	uS*,fT	rS*,uT
Wedge-tailed Shearwater											
Buller's Shearwater			xV								
Sooty Shearwater	rS*,fT		rS*,fT	fT	fT		xS*,fT	uT	rT	xT	rT
Short-tailed Shearwater											
Christmas Shearwater											
Manx Shearwater	rS*,rT		rT		rT,xW		rT	rT,xW		xV,xW	xV,xW
Black-vented Shearwater											
Townsend's Shearwater											
Little Shearwater								xV-q	exV		
Audubon's Shearwater	rS*	xV	rS*	rS*	uS*		uS*	cS*	fS*	fS*,xW	cS*,rW

Family Hydrobatidae: Storm-Petrels

	New York	Pennsylvania	New Jersey	Delaware	Maryland	Dist. of Columbia	Virginia	North Carolina	South Carolina	Georgia	Florida
Wilson's Storm-Petrel	cS*	exV	cS*	cS*	cS*		cS*	cS*	fS*	fS*	fS*
White-faced Storm-Petrel	xV		xV	xV			xV-q	xV			
British Storm-Petrel											
Fork-tailed Storm-Petrel											
Leach's Storm-Petrel	xS*,rT	xV	rT	xT	xS*,rT	xV	xS*,rT	rS*,uT,xW	xS*,rT	xS*,rT	xS*,rT
Ashy Storm-Petrel											
Band-rumped Storm-Petrel		exV	xV	xV		exV		uS*	xS*	rS*	xV
Wedge-rumped Storm-Petrel											
Black Storm-Petrel											
Sooty Storm-Petrel											

Hydrobatidae • 45

	Date	Location	Cont. North America	Canada	Lower 48
Least Storm-Petrel *Oceanodroma microsoma*			lifS*,xV		ifS*

Order Pelecaniformes: Totipalmate Swimmers
Family Phaethontidae: Tropicbirds

White-tailed Tropicbird *Phaethon lepturus*			lrS*,rV	xV	rS*
Red-billed Tropicbird *Phaethon aethereus*			lrS*,rV		lrS*,rV
Red-tailed Tropicbird *Phaethon rubricauda*			xV		xV

Family Sulidae: Boobies and Gannets

Masked Booby *Sula dactylatra*			xS,luP*,rV,xW		xS,uS*,luW
Blue-footed Booby *Sula nebouxii*			lirS*,xV,xW		lirS*,xV,xW
Brown Booby *Sula leucogaster*			xP*,luS*,xV,xW	xV	xP*,luS*,xV,xW
Red-footed Booby *Sula sula*			lrS*,xV		lrS*,xV
Northern Gannet *Sula bassanus*			lcS,fS*,cT,fW	cS,rW	uS*,cW

Family Pelecanidae: Pelicans

American White Pelican *Pelecanus erythrorhynchos*			fP	fS,xW	fP
Brown Pelican *Pelecanus occidentalis*			lcS,cS*,fW	rV,exW	lcS,cS*,fW

Family Phalacrocoracidae: Cormorants

Great Cormorant *Phalacrocorax carbo*			lfS,fW	lfS,fW	lrS,fW
Double-crested Cormorant *Phalacrocorax auritus*			cP	cS,fW	fS,cW
Olivaceous Cormorant *Phalacrocorax olivaceus*			lcP,xS*,rV		lcP,xS*,rV
Brandt's Cormorant *Phalacrocorax penicillatus*			cP	luS,fW	cP
Pelagic Cormorant *Phalacrocorax pelagicus*			cP	cP	cP
Red-faced Cormorant *Phalacrocorax urile*			lcP		

	Hawaii	Alaska	Yukon Terr.	Northwest Terr.	British Columbia	Alberta	Saskatch- ewan	Manitoba	Ontario
Least Storm-Petrel									

Order Pelecaniformes: Totipalmate Swimmers
Family Phaethontidae: Tropicbirds

	Hawaii	Alaska	Yukon Terr.	Northwest Terr.	British Columbia	Alberta	Saskatch- ewan	Manitoba	Ontario
White-tailed Tropicbird	uP								
Red-billed Tropicbird	xV								
Red-tailed Tropicbird	fS,uW								

Family Sulidae: Boobies and Gannets

	Hawaii	Alaska	Yukon Terr.	Northwest Terr.	British Columbia	Alberta	Saskatch- ewan	Manitoba	Ontario
Masked Booby	fP								
Blue-footed Booby									
Brown Booby	fP								
Red-footed Booby	cP								
Northern Gannet					xV				rV

Family Pelecanidae: Pelicans

	Hawaii	Alaska	Yukon Terr.	Northwest Terr.	British Columbia	Alberta	Saskatch- ewan	Manitoba	Ontario
American White Pelican		xV	luS†,xV	luS,uT	uS	fS,xW	fS		lfS,xV
Brown Pelican					rV,exW				xV

Family Phalacrocoracidae: Cormorants

	Hawaii	Alaska	Yukon Terr.	Northwest Terr.	British Columbia	Alberta	Saskatch- ewan	Manitoba	Ontario
Great Cormorant				eS					xV,xW
Double-crested Cormorant		lfS,uW	xV	lrS,xV	lfS,cW	uS	fS,xW	fS	fS,rW
Olivaceous Cormorant									
Brandt's Cormorant		lrS			luS,fW				
Pelagic Cormorant	xV	cP			cP				
Red-faced Cormorant		cP							

Hydrobatidae • 47

	Québec	Newfoundland	New Brunswick	Prince Edward I.	Nova Scotia		Washington	Oregon	California	Nevada	Idaho
Least Storm-Petrel									ifS*	xV	

Order Pelecaniformes: Totipalmate Swimmers
Family Phaethontidae: Tropicbirds

	Québec	Newfoundland	New Brunswick	Prince Edward I.	Nova Scotia		Washington	Oregon	California	Nevada	Idaho
White-tailed Tropicbird					xV				xV		
Red-billed Tropicbird							xV		rS*		
Red-tailed Tropicbird									xV		

Family Sulidae: Boobies and Gannets

	Québec	Newfoundland	New Brunswick	Prince Edward I.	Nova Scotia		Washington	Oregon	California	Nevada	Idaho
Masked Booby									xW		
Blue-footed Booby							xV		irS*,xW	xS*,xW	
Brown Booby					xV				xP*,lirS*,xV	xS*	
Red-footed Booby									xV		
Northern Gannet	lcS,rV	cS,xW	eS,fS*,cT,xW	fS*,cT	eS,cS*,rW						

Family Pelecanidae: Pelicans

	Québec	Newfoundland	New Brunswick	Prince Edward I.	Nova Scotia		Washington	Oregon	California	Nevada	Idaho
American White Pelican	xV	xV	xV		xV		eS,uS*,xW	lfS,fT,xW	lfS,uS*,fW	lfS,fT,rW	lrS,uS*,fT,xW
Brown Pelican			xV-q		xV		iuS*	ifS*,xW	lrS,cS*,fW	lrS*	xV

Family Phalacrocoracidae: Cormorants

	Québec	Newfoundland	New Brunswick	Prince Edward I.	Nova Scotia		Washington	Oregon	California	Nevada	Idaho
Great Cormorant	lfS,uW	lfS,uW	eS,rS*,cT,fW	cS,fW	fS,cT,fW						
Double-crested Cormorant	cS,xW	fS	cS,xW	cS	cS,rW		cP	cP	fS,cW	fS,uW	fS,rW
Olivaceous Cormorant									xS*,xV	xV	
Brandt's Cormorant							fP	cP	cP		
Pelagic Cormorant							cP	cP	cP		
Red-faced Cormorant											

	Montana	Wyoming	Utah	Colorado	Arizona	New Mexico	North Dakota	South Dakota	Nebraska	Kansas	Oklahoma
Least Storm-Petrel					xV-q						

Order Pelecaniformes: Totipalmate Swimmers
Family Phaethontidae: Tropicbirds

	Montana	Wyoming	Utah	Colorado	Arizona	New Mexico	North Dakota	South Dakota	Nebraska	Kansas	Oklahoma
White-tailed Tropicbird					xV						
Red-billed Tropicbird					xV						
Red-tailed Tropicbird											

Family Sulidae: Boobies and Gannets

	Montana	Wyoming	Utah	Colorado	Arizona	New Mexico	North Dakota	South Dakota	Nebraska	Kansas	Oklahoma
Masked Booby											
Blue-footed Booby					lirS*,xV,xW						
Brown Booby					xP*,lirS*						
Red-footed Booby											
Northern Gannet								xV-q			

Family Pelecanidae: Pelicans

	Montana	Wyoming	Utah	Colorado	Arizona	New Mexico	North Dakota	South Dakota	Nebraska	Kansas	Oklahoma
American White Pelican	fS	luS,uS*,fT	lcS,fT,xW	lfS,uS*,fT,xW	rS*,uT,rW	xS*,uT,xW	fS	uS,fT,xW	uS*,fT	uS*,fT,xW	rS*,fT,uW
Brown Pelican		exV	xV	exV	lrS*,rV,xW	xV	xV	xV	xV	xV	xV

Family Phalacrocoracidae: Cormorants

	Montana	Wyoming	Utah	Colorado	Arizona	New Mexico	North Dakota	South Dakota	Nebraska	Kansas	Oklahoma
Great Cormorant											
Double-crested Cormorant	fS,xW	fS	fS,xW	fS,xW	luS,fW	uS,rW	fS	fS	fS	uS,fT,rW	uS,fT,uW
Olivaceous Cormorant				xV	lrP*,xV,xW	luP			xV	xS*	xS*,xV
Brandt's Cormorant											
Pelagic Cormorant											
Red-faced Cormorant											

Hydrobatidae • 49

	Texas	Minnesota	Iowa	Missouri	Arkansas	Louisiana	Wisconsin	Michigan	Illinois	Indiana	Ohio
Least Storm-Petrel											

Order Pelecaniformes: Totipalmate Swimmers
Family Phaethontidae: Tropicbirds

	Texas	Minnesota	Iowa	Missouri	Arkansas	Louisiana	Wisconsin	Michigan	Illinois	Indiana	Ohio
White-tailed Tropicbird	rV-q										
Red-billed Tropicbird											
Red-tailed Tropicbird											

Family Sulidae: Boobies and Gannets

	Texas	Minnesota	Iowa	Missouri	Arkansas	Louisiana	Wisconsin	Michigan	Illinois	Indiana	Ohio
Masked Booby	uS*,xW					rS*					
Blue-footed Booby	xV										
Brown Booby	rS*					xS*					
Red-footed Booby	xV					xV					
Northern Gannet	uW					uW		xV	xV	xV	rV,xW

Family Pelecanidae: Pelicans

	Texas	Minnesota	Iowa	Missouri	Arkansas	Louisiana	Wisconsin	Michigan	Illinois	Indiana	Ohio
American White Pelican	luS,uS*,cW	lfS,uS*,fT,xW	eS†,rS*,uT,xW	xS*,uT,xW	uT,xW	rS*,cW	rS*,uT	rV	xS*,rT,xW	rV	xS*,rV
Brown Pelican	lfS,uW		xV	xV	xV	lfS1,uW	xV	xV	xV	xV	

Family Phalacrocoracidae: Cormorants

	Texas	Minnesota	Iowa	Missouri	Arkansas	Louisiana	Wisconsin	Michigan	Illinois	Indiana	Ohio
Great Cormorant											
Double-crested Cormorant	luS,fS*,cW	fS,xW	rS,fT,rW	eS,rS*,fT,uW	eS,fW	uS,cW	fS	uS,fT,rW	lrS,uT,rW	eS,uT,rW	eS,rS*,uT,xW
Olivaceous Cormorant	cP					lcP		exV			
Brandt's Cormorant											
Pelagic Cormorant											
Red-faced Cormorant											

	West Virginia	Kentucky	Tennessee	Mississippi	Alabama	Maine	New Hampshire	Vermont	Massachusetts	Rhode Island	Connecticut
Least Storm-Petrel											

Order Pelecaniformes: Totipalmate Swimmers
Family Phaethontidae: Tropicbirds

	West Virginia	Kentucky	Tennessee	Mississippi	Alabama	Maine	New Hampshire	Vermont	Massachusetts	Rhode Island	Connecticut
White-tailed Tropicbird				xV-q	xV		xV	xV			
Red-billed Tropicbird										xV	
Red-tailed Tropicbird											

Family Sulidae: Boobies and Gannets

	West Virginia	Kentucky	Tennessee	Mississippi	Alabama	Maine	New Hampshire	Vermont	Massachusetts	Rhode Island	Connecticut
Masked Booby				xV	rS*.xW						
Blue-footed Booby											
Brown Booby					rS*.xW				xV		
Red-footed Booby											
Northern Gannet		xV		uW	xS*.fW	fS*.cT.rW	uS*.cT.uW	xV	rS*.cT.uW	rS*.cT.fW	rT

Family Pelecanidae: Pelicans

	West Virginia	Kentucky	Tennessee	Mississippi	Alabama	Maine	New Hampshire	Vermont	Massachusetts	Rhode Island	Connecticut
American White Pelican	xV	xV	rT	xS*.fW	rS*.fW	xV	xV-q	xV	rV.xW	xV	xV
Brown Pelican			xV	uP*	lrP.uP*	exV	exV		xV	xV	xV

Family Phalacrocoracidae: Cormorants

	West Virginia	Kentucky	Tennessee	Mississippi	Alabama	Maine	New Hampshire	Vermont	Massachusetts	Rhode Island	Connecticut
Great Cormorant	exV			xV.xW	rV.xW	lrS.cW	rS*.cW	xV	xS.cW	cW	fW
Double-crested Cormorant	xS*.uT.xW	xS.rS*.uT.rW	eS.uP*	rS.cW	uS*.cW	cS.rW	cS.xW	luS.uS*.fT	fS.cT.rW	fS.cT.uW	fS.cT.uW
Olivaceous Cormorant				xV							
Brandt's Cormorant											
Pelagic Cormorant											
Red-faced Cormorant											

Hydrobatidae • 51

	New York	Pennsylvania	New Jersey	Delaware	Maryland	Dist. of Columbia	Virginia	North Carolina	South Carolina	Georgia	Florida
Least Storm-Petrel											

Order Pelecaniformes: Totipalmate Swimmers
Family Phaethontidae: Tropicbirds

	New York	Pennsylvania	New Jersey	Delaware	Maryland	Dist. of Columbia	Virginia	North Carolina	South Carolina	Georgia	Florida
White-tailed Tropicbird	xV	xV					xV	rS*	rS*	rS*	rS*
Red-billed Tropicbird	xV		xV					xV		xV	xV
Red-tailed Tropicbird											

Family Sulidae: Boobies and Gannets

	New York	Pennsylvania	New Jersey	Delaware	Maryland	Dist. of Columbia	Virginia	North Carolina	South Carolina	Georgia	Florida
Masked Booby								xV	xV,xW	xV	xS,uS*,luW
Blue-footed Booby											
Brown Booby	xV		xV-q				xV	xV-q	xW	xV	uS*,xW
Red-footed Booby											rS*
Northern Gannet	rS*,cT,fW	xV,xW	rS*,cT,fW	cW	cW		cW	xS*,cW	fW	fW	fW

Family Pelecanidae: Pelicans

	New York	Pennsylvania	New Jersey	Delaware	Maryland	Dist. of Columbia	Virginia	North Carolina	South Carolina	Georgia	Florida
American White Pelican	rV	xS*,xV	rV,xW	xV	xV		xS*,rV,xW	rV,xW	rV,rW	rV,rW	rS*,fW
Brown Pelican	rV	xV	rV	xV,xW	rS*		uS*,xW	rS,fS*,uW	lfS,cS*,uW	cS*,fW	cP

Family Phalacrocoracidae: Cormorants

	New York	Pennsylvania	New Jersey	Delaware	Maryland	Dist. of Columbia	Virginia	North Carolina	South Carolina	Georgia	Florida
Great Cormorant	fW	xV,xW	fW	fW	uW	xV	uW	rW	rW	xW	rW
Double-crested Cormorant	luS,fS*,cT,uW	uS*,fT,rW	fS*,cT,uW	uS*,cT,fW	uS*,cT,fW	uS*,fT	luS,uS*,cW	lfS,fS*,cW	fS*,cW	fS,cW	cP
Olivaceous Cormorant											
Brandt's Cormorant											
Pelagic Cormorant											
Red-faced Cormorant											

Family Anhingidae: Darters

	Date	Location	Cont. North America	Canada	Lower 48
Anhinga *Anhinga anhinga*			lcS,xP*,rV,lfW	exV	cS,fW

Family Fregatidae: Frigatebirds

			Cont. North America	Canada	Lower 48
Magnificent Frigatebird *Fregata magnificens*			lfS,uS*,luW	xV	lfS,uS*,luW
Great Frigatebird *Fregata minor*			xV		xV
Lesser Frigatebird *Fregata ariel*			xV		xV

Order Ciconiiformes: Herons, Ibises, Storks and Allies
Family Ardeidae: Bitterns and Herons

			Cont. North America	Canada	Lower 48
American Bittern *Botaurus lentiginosus*			fP	fS,lrW	fP
Least Bittern *Ixobrychus exilis*			fS,luW	luS,xV	fS,luW
Great Blue Heron *Ardea herodias*			cP	cS,rW	cP
Great Egret *Casmerodius albus*			cS,fW	lrS,rS*,rV	cP
Chinese Egret *Egretta eulophotes*			xV		
Little Egret *Egretta garzetta*			xS*,xV		xS*,xV
Snowy Egret *Egretta thula*			cS,fW	rS*,rV	cP
Western Reef-Heron *Egretta gularis*			xV		xV
Little Blue Heron *Egretta caerulea*			cS,lcW	rS*,rV,xW	cS,fW
Tricolored Heron *Egretta tricolor*			lcP,xS,rS*,rV	xS*,rV	cS,fW
Reddish Egret *Egretta rufescens*			lfP,lrP*,rV	xV	lfP,lrP*,rV
Cattle Egret *Bubulcus ibis*			cS,fW	xS,rS*,rV,xW	cS,fW
Green-backed Heron *Butorides striatus*			cS,fW	lfS,rV,xW	cS,fW
Black-crowned Night-Heron *Nycticorax nycticorax*			fP	uS,lrW	cS,fW
Yellow-crowned Night-Heron *Nycticorax violaceus*			fS,lcW	rS*,rV	fP

Family Anhingidae: Darters

	Hawaii	Alaska	Yukon Terr.	Northwest Terr.	British Columbia	Alberta	Saskatchewan	Manitoba	Ontario
Anhinga									exV

Family Fregatidae: Frigatebirds

	Hawaii	Alaska	Yukon Terr.	Northwest Terr.	British Columbia	Alberta	Saskatchewan	Manitoba	Ontario
Magnificent Frigatebird		xV-sp-q			xV				
Great Frigatebird	cP								
Lesser Frigatebird	xS*,xV,xW								

Order Ciconiiformes: Herons, Ibises, Storks and Allies
Family Ardeidae: Bitterns and Herons

	Hawaii	Alaska	Yukon Terr.	Northwest Terr.	British Columbia	Alberta	Saskatchewan	Manitoba	Ontario
American Bittern		lrS		luS	uS,rW	fS	fS,xW	fS	fS,xW
Least Bittern					xV		exV	lrS	uS
Great Blue Heron	xV,xW	uS,rW	xS*	rS*	cS,uW	fS	fS	fS,xW	cS,rW
Great Egret	xV,xW	xV				xV	xV	xS,rS*	xS,rS*	lrS,uS*
Chinese Egret		xV							
Little Egret									
Snowy Egret	xV,xW	xV				xV	xV	rS*	rS*	rS*
Western Reef-Heron									
Little Blue Heron	xP*,xV					xW		xS*,xV	xS*,xV	rS*
Tricolored Heron							xV		xS*,rV	rV
Reddish Egret									
Cattle Egret		xV			xV	rV,xW	xV	xS,rS*	rS*	xS,uS*
Green-backed Heron	xP*	xV			lrS,xW	xV	xS*,xV	xS*,rV	fS
Black-crowned Night-Heron	fP	xV			rS*,xW	lrS,rS*	uS	uS	uS,xW
Yellow-crowned Night-Heron							xV-q	rS*	rS*

Family Anhingidae: Darters

	Québec	Newfoundland	New Brunswick	Prince Edward I.	Nova Scotia		Washington	Oregon	California	Nevada	Idaho
Anhinga									xP*		

Family Fregatidae: Frigatebirds

	Québec	Newfoundland	New Brunswick	Prince Edward I.	Nova Scotia		Washington	Oregon	California	Nevada	Idaho
Magnificent Frigatebird	exV				xV		xV	xV	rS*,xW	xS*	
Great Frigatebird											
Lesser Frigatebird											

Order Ciconiiformes: Herons, Ibises, Storks and Allies
Family Ardeidae: Bitterns and Herons

	Québec	Newfoundland	New Brunswick	Prince Edward I.	Nova Scotia		Washington	Oregon	California	Nevada	Idaho
American Bittern	fS	uS	fS,xW	uS	uS,xW		uP	fP	fP	uS,rW	uS
Least Bittern	lrS	xV	rS		rS			lrS	uS,rW	lrS	xS*
Great Blue Heron	cS,xW	rS*	cS,rW	cS,rW	cS,rW		cP	cP	cP	cS,fW	cS,uW
Great Egret	xS,rS*	rV	rS*	rS*	uS*		xS,rS*,xW	fS,uW	cP	lrS,uS*,xW	lrS,rS*,xW
Chinese Egret											
Little Egret	xS*	xV									
Snowy Egret	rS*	rV	rS*	xV	uS*		xS*,xV	luS,rS*,rW	cP	fS,xW	uS
Western Reef-Heron											
Little Blue Heron	rS*	rV	rS*	xV	uS*		xW		xS,rP*	xV	
Tricolored Heron	xS*,rV	xV	xV		xS*,xV			xV	xS*,rV,lrW	xV	
Reddish Egret					xV-q				lrP*,xV		
Cattle Egret	rS*	rV	rS*	xV	uS*		rV,xW	xV,uV,rW	cP	luS,uV,xW	xS,uV,xW
Green-backed Heron	lfS	rV	lrS,uS*	xV	uS*		uS,rW	fS,rW	fS,uW	uS,rW	rV
Black-crowned Night-Heron	luS,xV	xV	fS,xW	rS*	xS,uS*,xW		fS,rW	fS,uW	fP	uS,rW	fS,rW
Yellow-crowned Night-Heron	xS*	rV	xS*	xV	uS*				xS*,rV		

Family Anhingidae: Darters

	Montana	Wyoming	Utah	Colorado	Arizona	New Mexico	North Dakota	South Dakota	Nebraska	Kansas	Oklahoma
Anhinga				exV	exV	xV			xV	xV	lrS.rS*

Family Fregatidae: Frigatebirds

	Montana	Wyoming	Utah	Colorado	Arizona	New Mexico	North Dakota	South Dakota	Nebraska	Kansas	Oklahoma
Magnificent Frigatebird				lrS*.xV	xV					xV	xV
Great Frigatebird										xV	
Lesser Frigatebird											

Order Ciconiiformes: Herons, Ibises, Storks and Allies
Family Ardeidae: Bitterns and Herons

	Montana	Wyoming	Utah	Colorado	Arizona	New Mexico	North Dakota	South Dakota	Nebraska	Kansas	Oklahoma
American Bittern	fS.xW	uS	uS.rW	uS	eS.xS*.uW	uP	fS	fS	fS.xW	fS.xW	uS.rW
Least Bittern	xS*.xV	exV	eS.rV	lrS.rT	uS.rW	uS	rS	rS	uS	uS	uS
Great Blue Heron	cS.uW	cS.uW	cS.fW	cS.fW	fP	uS.fW	fS.cT	cS.xW	cS.uW	cS.fW	cP
Great Egret	rS*	xS*	rS*.xW	lrS.rS*	lcS.fS*.uW	xS.uS*.rW	uS*	luS.uS*	uS*	lrS.fS*	cS.xW
Chinese Egret											
Little Egret											
Snowy Egret	xS.rS*	uS	cS.xW	fS	rS.fS*.uW	uS.fS*.rW	rS*	lrS.rS*	eS.uS*	lrS.fS*	cS
Western Reef-Heron											
Little Blue Heron	xV	xV	xV	rS*	rS*	xS.rS*	xS.rS*	xS.rS*	uS*	luS.fS*	cS
Tricolored Heron		xV	xV	xV	rV	xS.rV	xS.xV	xV	xV	xS.xV	rV
Reddish Egret				exV	xV.xW						xV-q
Cattle Egret	rV	rV.xW	luS.uV	uS	fS*.uW	uS.rW	rS	rS	xS.rS*	uS.fS*	cS.xW
Green-backed Heron	xV	rV	luS.rV.xW	uS.xW	uS.rW	uS.rW	rS	uS	fS	cS	cS
Black-crowned Night-Heron	uS	uS.xW	fS.uW	fS.rW	uP	fS.uW	fS	fS	fS	fS.xW	fS.rW
Yellow-crowned Night-Heron	xV	xV		xS.rS*	xV	rS*.xW	xS*	rS*	lrS.uS*	uS	fS

Family Anhingidae: Darters

	Texas	Minnesota	Iowa	Missouri	Arkansas	Louisiana	Wisconsin	Michigan	Illinois	Indiana	Ohio
Anhinga	uS,cT,uW	xV	xV	exS,xS*,xV	luS	cS,uW	xV		eS*,xV	xV	exV

Family Fregatidae: Frigatebirds

	Texas	Minnesota	Iowa	Missouri	Arkansas	Louisiana	Wisconsin	Michigan	Illinois	Indiana	Ohio
Magnificent Frigatebird	xS,uS*,rW		exV-q	xV	xV	fS*	exV			xV	xV
Great Frigatebird											
Lesser Frigatebird											

Order Ciconiiformes: Herons, Ibises, Storks and Allies
Family Ardeidae: Bitterns and Herons

	Texas	Minnesota	Iowa	Missouri	Arkansas	Louisiana	Wisconsin	Michigan	Illinois	Indiana	Ohio
American Bittern	rS,fT,uW	fS	uS	rS,uT,rW	rS,uT,rW	rS,fT,uW	fS,rW	uS,xW	rS,uT,xW	rS,uT,xW	rS,uT,xW
Least Bittern	fS,rW	uS	rS,uT	uS	fS	fS,rW	uS	uS	uS	uS	uS
Great Blue Heron	cP	cS,xW	fS,cT,rW	cS,uW	cP	cP	cS,rW	cS,rW	cS,uW	cS,uW	cS,rW
Great Egret	cP	lfS,uS*	fS	fS,xW	uS,cS*,rW	cP	fS,xW	luS,fS*	fS,xW	eS,fS*,xW	luS,uS*,rW
Chinese Egret											
Little Egret											
Snowy Egret	cP	lrS,rS*	rS*	luS,uS*	luS,cS*	cP	lrS,rS*	rS*	lrS,rS*	rS*	lrS,rS*
Western Reef-Heron											
Little Blue Heron	cS,fW	lrS,rS*	xS,rS*	luS,fS*	fS	cS,fW	rS*	rS*	lfS,uS*	uS*	xS,uS*
Tricolored Heron	cP	xS*,xV		xS*,xV	xS,xV	cS,fW	xS*,rV	rV	xS*,rV	xS*,xV	xS*,xV
Reddish Egret	fP			xV		uS,rW					
Cattle Egret	cS,fW	rS	lrS,uS*	fS	cS,xW	cS,fW	rS,uS*	uS*	uS,fS*	uS*	lrS,uS*
Green-backed Heron	cS,uW	fS	fS	cS	cS	cS,uW	cS	cS	cS	cS,xW	cS
Black-crowned Night-Heron	cS,fW	fS,xW	uS	uS,fT,xW	uS,fT,rW	cS,fW	uS,xW	uS,xW	uS,fT,rW	rS,uT,rW	uS,rW
Yellow-crowned Night-Heron	fS,uW	lrS,rS*	rS	uS	fS	cS,rW	luS,rS*	lrS,rS*	uS	uS	rS

Family Anhingidae: Darters

	West Virginia	Kentucky	Tennessee	Mississippi	Alabama	Maine	New Hampshire	Vermont	Massachusetts	Rhode Island	Connecticut
Anhinga		xS.xV	xS.lrS*	uS.rW	uS.rW						

Family Fregatidae: Frigatebirds

	West Virginia	Kentucky	Tennessee	Mississippi	Alabama	Maine	New Hampshire	Vermont	Massachusetts	Rhode Island	Connecticut
Magnificent Frigatebird			uS*	uS*.xW	xV				xS*.xV	xV	xV
Great Frigatebird											
Lesser Frigatebird					xV						

Order Ciconiiformes: Herons, Ibises, Storks and Allies
Family Ardeidae: Bitterns and Herons

	West Virginia	Kentucky	Tennessee	Mississippi	Alabama	Maine	New Hampshire	Vermont	Massachusetts	Rhode Island	Connecticut
American Bittern	rS.uT.xW	xS.rS*.uT.xW	rS.uT.rW	uW	xS*.uW	fS	fS.xW	fS	uS.rW	rS.uT.rW	uS.rW
Least Bittern	luS.uT	rS.uT	fS	fS	fS.xW	uS	rS†	uS	rS	rS	uS
Great Blue Heron	rS*.fT.rW	rS.fT.uW	fS.cW	cP	cP	cS.uW	cS.rW	fS.cT.rW	uS.cT.fW	xS.uS*.cT.fW	uS.cT.fW
Great Egret	uS*	lrS.uS*.xW	uS.rW	cS.fW	cS.fW	uS*	rS*	rS*	lrS.uS*.xW	fS.xW	fS.xW
Chinese Egret											
Little Egret											
Snowy Egret	rS*	rS*	lrS.uS*	cS.fW	cS.fW	lfS.uS*	fS	xS.rS*	fS	fS.xW	fS.xW
Western Reef-Heron									xV		
Little Blue Heron	rS*	xS.uS*	lfS.uS*	cS.uW	cS.uW	lrS.uS*	uS*	rS*	lrS.uS*.xW	uS	uS
Tricolored Heron		xS*.rV	fS.uW	fS.uW	lrS.xV	rS*	xV	xS.rS*	rS*	xS.uS*	
Reddish Egret		xV		uS*.xW	lrS.uS*.xW				xV		xV-q
Cattle Egret	rS*	lrS.rS*.xW	rS.fS*.xW	cS.uW	cS.uW	lrS.uS*	rS*	lrS.rS*	lrS.uS*.xW	fS	uS
Green-backed Heron	fS	cS.xW	cS.xW	cS.rW	cS.rW	fS	fS	fS	fS.xW	fS.xW	cS
Black-crowned Night-Heron	lrS.uT.xW	uS.rW	uS.rW	uP	uP	fS	rS.fS*.xW	fS	fS.rW	fS.uW	fS.uW
Yellow-crowned Night-Heron	rS*	rS	uS	fS.rW	fS.rW	rS*	rS*	xS*	rS	rS	rS

Family Anhingidae: Darters

	New York	Pennsylvania	New Jersey	Delaware	Maryland	Dist. of Columbia	Virginia	North Carolina	South Carolina	Georgia	Florida
Anhinga			xS*,xV		xV		xV	lrS*,xW	uS,rW	fS,uW	cS,fW	cP

Family Fregatidae: Frigatebirds

	New York	Pennsylvania	New Jersey	Delaware	Maryland	Dist. of Columbia	Virginia	North Carolina	South Carolina	Georgia	Florida
Magnificent Frigatebird	xV	xV	xV	xV,xW	xV		xV	rS*	rS*	rS*	lfS,fS*,uW
Great Frigatebird											
Lesser Frigatebird											

Order Ciconiiformes: Herons, Ibises, Storks and Allies
Family Ardeidae: Bitterns and Herons

	New York	Pennsylvania	New Jersey	Delaware	Maryland	Dist. of Columbia	Virginia	North Carolina	South Carolina	Georgia	Florida
American Bittern	fS,rW	uS,rW	rS,uT,rW	rS†,uT,rW	rS,uT,rW	rT	rS,uW	rS,uW	rS,fW	rS*,fW	rS,fW
Least Bittern	uS	uS	uS	fS	uS,xW	eS,rT	uS	fS,xW	fS,xW	fS,xW	fS,uW
Great Blue Heron	cS,fW	cS,fW	fS,cT,fW	cS,fW	cS,fW	fS*,uW	cP	cP	cP	cP	cP
Great Egret	fS,rW	luS,fS*,rW	fS,rW	cS,xW	cS,rW	uS*	cS,uW	cS,fW	cS,fW	cP	cP
Chinese Egret											
Little Egret											
Snowy Egret	fS,xW	xS,uS*	cS,xW	cS,xW	cS,xW	uS*	cS,uW	cS,fW	cS,fW	cP	cP
Western Reef-Heron											
Little Blue Heron	fS	fS*	fS,xW	cS	cS,rW	uS*	cS,uW	cS,uW	cS,fW	cS,fW	cP
Tricolored Heron	luS,uS*,xW	rS*	uS,xW	fS,xW	fS,rW	xS*	cS,uW	cS,fW	cS,fW	cP	cP
Reddish Egret		xV					xV-q	xV	xV	xV,xW	uP
Cattle Egret	fS	lfS,fS*	fS,xW	cS	cS	uT	cS,xW	cS,rW	cS,rW	cS,uW	cP
Green-backed Heron	cS,xW	cS	cS,xW	cS	cS,xW	fS	cS,rW	cS,rW	cS,uW	cS,uW	cP
Black-crowned Night-Heron	fS,uW	uS,fT,uW	fS,uW	fS,uW	fS,uW	uP	cS,uW	cS,fW	cP	cP	cP
Yellow-crowned Night-Heron	uS	uS	uS	uS	uS	eS,rS*	fS,rW	fS,rW	fS,uW	cS,uW	cP

Family Threskiornithidae: Ibises and Spoonbills
Subfamily Threskiornithinae: Ibises

	Date	Location	Cont. North America	Canada	Lower 48
White Ibis *Eudocimus albus*			lcP,rS*,rV	xV	fP
Scarlet Ibis *Eudocimus ruber*			xV		xV
Glossy Ibis *Plegadis falcinellus*			lfP,rS*,rV	luS*,rV	fS,uW
White-faced Ibis *Plegadis chihi*			fS,lfW	xS,xS*,rV	fS,lfW

Subfamily Plataleinae: Spoonbills

	Date	Location	Cont. North America	Canada	Lower 48
Roseate Spoonbill *Ajaia ajaja*			lfP,lirS*,rV,xW		lfP,lirS*,rV,xW

Family Ciconiidae: Storks

	Date	Location	Cont. North America	Canada	Lower 48
Jabiru *Jabiru mycteria*			xV		xV
Wood Stork *Mycteria americana*			lfP,uS*,rV,xW	xV	lfP,uS*,rV,xW

Order Phoenicopteriformes: Flamingos
Family Phoenicopteridae: Flamingos

	Date	Location	Cont. North America	Canada	Lower 48
Greater Flamingo *Phoenicopterus ruber*			lrP*,rV,xW	xV	lrP*,rV,xW

Order Anseriformes: Screamers, Swans, Geese and Ducks
Family Anatidae: Swans, Geese and Ducks
Subfamily Anserinae: Whistling-Ducks, Swans and Geese

	Date	Location	Cont. North America	Canada	Lower 48
Fulvous Whistling-Duck *Dendrocygna bicolor*			lfP,rS*,rV	rV	lfP,rS*,rV
Black-bellied Whistling-Duck *Dendrocygna autumnalis*			lcS,xS,rV,luW		lcS,xS,rV,luW
Tundra Swan *Cygnus columbianus*			cS,fW	cS,lrW	fW
Whooper Swan *Cygnus cygnus*			luW,xV,xW		exV,xW
Trumpeter Swan *Cygnus buccinator*			uP2	luS,rT,lfW	luP1,luW
Bean Goose *Anser fabalis*			lrT,xV,xW	xV	xW
Pink-footed Goose *Anser brachyrhynchus*			xV	xV	

Family Threskiornithidae: Ibises and Spoonbills
Subfamily Threskiornithinae: Ibises

	Hawaii	Alaska	Yukon Terr.	Northwest Terr.	British Columbia	Alberta	Saskatchewan	Manitoba	Ontario
White Ibis									xV
Scarlet Ibis									
Glossy Ibis							xV-q		rV
White-faced Ibis	xP*,xV				xV	xS,xS*,xV	xS*,xV	xV-sp	

Subfamily Plataleinae: Spoonbills

	Hawaii	Alaska	Yukon Terr.	Northwest Terr.	British Columbia	Alberta	Saskatchewan	Manitoba	Ontario
Roseate Spoonbill									

Family Ciconiidae: Storks

	Hawaii	Alaska	Yukon Terr.	Northwest Terr.	British Columbia	Alberta	Saskatchewan	Manitoba	Ontario
Jabiru									
Wood Stork					xV				xV

Order Phoenicopteriformes: Flamingos
Family Phoenicopteridae: Flamingos

	Hawaii	Alaska	Yukon Terr.	Northwest Terr.	British Columbia	Alberta	Saskatchewan	Manitoba	Ontario
Greater Flamingo									

Order Anseriformes: Screamers, Swans, Geese and Ducks
Family Anatidae: Swans, Geese and Ducks
Subfamily Anserinae: Whistling-Ducks, Swans and Geese

	Hawaii	Alaska	Yukon Terr.	Northwest Terr.	British Columbia	Alberta	Saskatchewan	Manitoba	Ontario
Fulvous Whistling-Duck	xS,lrP*,xV								
Black-bellied Whistling-Duck					xV	xV			rV
Tundra Swan	xV	cS,luW	lcS,fT	cS	cT,rW	fT	xS,cT,xW	luS,cT	lrS,cT,rW
Whooper Swan		luW,xV							
Trumpeter Swan		fS,rW	lrS,uT	lrS	luS,fW	rS	lrS,xW	eS,rV	eS†
Bean Goose		lrT,xV							
Pink-footed Goose									

Family Threskiornithidae: Ibises and Spoonbills
Subfamily Threskiornithinae: Ibises

	Québec	Newfoundland	New Brunswick	Prince Edward I.	Nova Scotia
White Ibis	xV	xV	xV		xV
Scarlet Ibis					
Glossy Ibis	rV	rV	rS*	xV	uS*
White-faced Ibis					

	Washington	Oregon	California	Nevada	Idaho
White Ibis			xS*,xV		xV
Scarlet Ibis					
Glossy Ibis					
White-faced Ibis	xV,xW	luS,rS*,xW	uP	fS	lrS,uS*

Subfamily Plataleinae: Spoonbills

	Québec	Newfoundland	New Brunswick	Prince Edward I.	Nova Scotia
Roseate Spoonbill					

	Washington	Oregon	California	Nevada	Idaho
Roseate Spoonbill			irS*,xW	xV	

Family Ciconiidae: Storks

	Québec	Newfoundland	New Brunswick	Prince Edward I.	Nova Scotia
Jabiru					
Wood Stork			exV		

	Washington	Oregon	California	Nevada	Idaho
Jabiru					
Wood Stork			lfS*,xV,xW	xV	exV

Order Phoenicopteriformes: Flamingos
Family Phoenicopteridae: Flamingos

	Québec	Newfoundland	New Brunswick	Prince Edward I.	Nova Scotia
Greater Flamingo	xV	xV	xV		xV

	Washington	Oregon	California	Nevada	Idaho
Greater Flamingo					

Order Anseriformes: Screamers, Swans, Geese and Ducks
Family Anatidae: Swans, Geese and Ducks
Subfamily Anserinae: Whistling-Ducks, Swans and Geese

	Québec	Newfoundland	New Brunswick	Prince Edward I.	Nova Scotia
Fulvous Whistling-Duck	xV		xV	xV	xV
Black-bellied Whistling-Duck					
Tundra Swan	lrS,rT,xW	xV	xV	xV	rV,xW
Whooper Swan					
Trumpeter Swan	exV				
Bean Goose	xV				
Pink-footed Goose		xV			

	Washington	Oregon	California	Nevada	Idaho
Fulvous Whistling-Duck	xV	xV	lrS,rV,xW	exS,rV	
Black-bellied Whistling-Duck			xS*,xV		
Tundra Swan	fT,uW	fW	fW	fW	fT,xW
Whooper Swan			xW		
Trumpeter Swan	lrP1,uW	luP1,rW	rW	lrP1,rW	luP1,rT,luW
Bean Goose					
Pink-footed Goose					

Family Threskiornithidae: Ibises and Spoonbills
Subfamily Threskiornithinae: Ibises

	Montana	Wyoming	Utah	Colorado	Arizona	New Mexico	North Dakota	South Dakota	Nebraska	Kansas	Oklahoma
White Ibis		xV			xV	rV,xW	xV	xV	xV	xS*,xV	rS*
Scarlet Ibis											
Glossy Ibis											xV
White-faced Ibis	uS	uS	cS	uS,fT	rS*,fT,rW	xS,uS*,fT,xW	xS,rS*	rS	xS,uS*	luS,uS*	rS*,uT

Subfamily Plataleinae: Spoonbills

	Montana	Wyoming	Utah	Colorado	Arizona	New Mexico	North Dakota	South Dakota	Nebraska	Kansas	Oklahoma
Roseate Spoonbill			exV	xV	irS*	xV			xV	exV	rV

Family Ciconiidae: Storks

	Montana	Wyoming	Utah	Colorado	Arizona	New Mexico	North Dakota	South Dakota	Nebraska	Kansas	Oklahoma
Jabiru											xV
Wood Stork	exV	exV	xV	exV	luS*,xV	xS*,xV	xV	xV	exV	exV	rV

Order Phoenicopteriformes: Flamingos
Family Phoenicopteridae: Flamingos

	Montana	Wyoming	Utah	Colorado	Arizona	New Mexico	North Dakota	South Dakota	Nebraska	Kansas	Oklahoma
Greater Flamingo											

Order Anseriformes: Screamers, Swans, Geese and Ducks
Family Anatidae: Swans, Geese and Ducks
Subfamily Anserinae: Whistling-Ducks, Swans and Geese

	Montana	Wyoming	Utah	Colorado	Arizona	New Mexico	North Dakota	South Dakota	Nebraska	Kansas	Oklahoma
Fulvous Whistling-Duck		xV			xS*,rV,eW	xS*,xV	xV	xV		rV	xV-q
Black-bellied Whistling-Duck				xV	uS,rW	xV			xV	xV-q	
Tundra Swan	fT,rW	fT,rW	fT,uW	uT,rW	uW	rW	fT	fT	rT	rW	rW
Whooper Swan											
Trumpeter Swan	uS1,rW	luS1,rW	xS*1,eW	xV1		xW1	eS,xV	luP1,eT,xW	eS,luP1	eT,xW1	eW,xW1
Bean Goose									xW		
Pink-footed Goose											

Family Threskiornithidae: Ibises and Spoonbills
Subfamily Threskiornithinae: Ibises

	Texas	Minnesota	Iowa	Missouri	Arkansas	Louisiana	Wisconsin	Michigan	Illinois	Indiana	Ohio
White Ibis	fP			xS*.xV	rS*	fS.uW	xV-q	xV	xS*.xV	xV	xV
Scarlet Ibis	xV-q										
Glossy Ibis	xV	xV		xS*.rV	eS.rV	uP	xS*.rV	rV	rV	xV	xS*.rV
White-faced Ibis	cS.fW	exS.rV	rT	uT	uT	cS.fW	xV-q	xV	xV		xV

Subfamily Plataleinae: Spoonbills

	Texas	Minnesota	Iowa	Missouri	Arkansas	Louisiana	Wisconsin	Michigan	Illinois	Indiana	Ohio
Roseate Spoonbill	fS.uW		xV		xV	lfS.luW	exV		exV	xV	

Family Ciconiidae: Storks

	Texas	Minnesota	Iowa	Missouri	Arkansas	Louisiana	Wisconsin	Michigan	Illinois	Indiana	Ohio
Jabiru	xV										
Wood Stork	eS.ifS*.xW		xV	xV	rS*	eS.uS*.xW	xV	xV	xV	xV	xV

Order Phoenicopteriformes: Flamingos
Family Phoenicopteridae: Flamingos

	Texas	Minnesota	Iowa	Missouri	Arkansas	Louisiana	Wisconsin	Michigan	Illinois	Indiana	Ohio
Greater Flamingo	xV.xW										

Order Anseriformes: Screamers, Swans, Geese and Ducks
Family Anatidae: Swans, Geese and Ducks
Subfamily Anserinae: Whistling-Ducks, Swans and Geese

	Texas	Minnesota	Iowa	Missouri	Arkansas	Louisiana	Wisconsin	Michigan	Illinois	Indiana	Ohio
Fulvous Whistling-Duck	fS.rW	xV		xS*.xV	xV	fS.xW	xS*.xV	xV	xS*.xV	xV	
Black-bellied Whistling-Duck	lcS.xV.luW	xV-q	xV-q	xV	xV	xS*.xV	xV				
Tundra Swan	rW	fT.rW	rT	rT.xW	rT.xW	rW	cT.rW	cT.rW	uT.rW	uT.rW	uT.rW
Whooper Swan											
Trumpeter Swan	eW	eS.xS*.xV	eS	eS.xW1	eW	eW	eS†	eT	eS	eS	eT-q
Bean Goose				xW							
Pink-footed Goose											

Family Threskiornithidae: Ibises and Spoonbills
Subfamily Threskiornithinae: Ibises

	West Virginia	Kentucky	Tennessee	Mississippi	Alabama	Maine	New Hampshire	Vermont	Massachusetts	Rhode Island	Connecticut
White Ibis	xV	xV	rS*	fS,uW	fS,uW	xV	xV	xV-q	xV	xV	xV
Scarlet Ibis											
Glossy Ibis		xV-sp	rV-sp-q	rS*,rW-sp	uS,rW	luS,uS*	uS*	rS*	uS	uS	uS
White-faced Ibis				lrS*,xW-sp	lrS				xV		

Subfamily Plataleinae: Spoonbills

	West Virginia	Kentucky	Tennessee	Mississippi	Alabama	Maine	New Hampshire	Vermont	Massachusetts	Rhode Island	Connecticut
Roseate Spoonbill				xV	rV						

Family Ciconiidae: Storks

	West Virginia	Kentucky	Tennessee	Mississippi	Alabama	Maine	New Hampshire	Vermont	Massachusetts	Rhode Island	Connecticut
Jabiru											
Wood Stork	xV	rV,xW	rS*	rS*	eS†,uS*	exV	exV	xV	xS*,xV	exV	xV

Order Phoenicopteriformes: Flamingos
Family Phoenicopteridae: Flamingos

	West Virginia	Kentucky	Tennessee	Mississippi	Alabama	Maine	New Hampshire	Vermont	Massachusetts	Rhode Island	Connecticut
Greater Flamingo											

Order Anseriformes: Screamers, Swans, Geese and Ducks
Family Anatidae: Swans, Geese and Ducks
Subfamily Anserinae: Whistling-Ducks, Swans and Geese

	West Virginia	Kentucky	Tennessee	Mississippi	Alabama	Maine	New Hampshire	Vermont	Massachusetts	Rhode Island	Connecticut
Fulvous Whistling-Duck			xV	xV	lrS,xV,xW	xV			rV,xW	xS*,xV	xV-q
Black-bellied Whistling-Duck			xS								
Tundra Swan	fT	uT,xW	rW	xV	rW	rT,xW	rT	rT	rT,xW	rT,xW	rT,xW
Whooper Swan						exV					
Trumpeter Swan	eT	eW	eW								
Bean Goose											
Pink-footed Goose											

Family Threskiornithidae: Ibises and Spoonbills
Subfamily Threskiornithinae: Ibises

	New York	Pennsylvania	New Jersey	Delaware	Maryland	Dist. of Columbia	Virginia	North Carolina	South Carolina	Georgia	Florida
White Ibis	xV	xV	rS*	rS*	rS*		lrS,uS*,xW	cS,fW	cS,fW	cS,fW	cP
Scarlet Ibis											xV
Glossy Ibis	uS	uS*	fS,xW	fS,xW	fS,xW	xS*	fS,rW	fS,rW	fS,uW	fS,uW	fP
White-faced Ibis	xV			xV			xV				eS,xV

Subfamily Plataleinae: Spoonbills

	New York	Pennsylvania	New Jersey	Delaware	Maryland	Dist. of Columbia	Virginia	North Carolina	South Carolina	Georgia	Florida
Roseate Spoonbill		exV			xV			xV	xV	xS*,rV	fP

Family Ciconiidae: Storks

	New York	Pennsylvania	New Jersey	Delaware	Maryland	Dist. of Columbia	Virginia	North Carolina	South Carolina	Georgia	Florida
Jabiru											
Wood Stork	rV	xV	xV		xV	exV	rS*	rS*	lrS,uS*,xW	uS,rW	fP

Order Phoenicopteriformes: Flamingos
Family Phoenicopteridae: Flamingos

	New York	Pennsylvania	New Jersey	Delaware	Maryland	Dist. of Columbia	Virginia	North Carolina	South Carolina	Georgia	Florida
Greater Flamingo					xV-q		xV	xV-q	xS*,xV	xV	rP*

Order Anseriformes: Screamers, Swans, Geese and Ducks
Family Anatidae: Swans, Geese and Ducks
Subfamily Anserinae: Whistling-Ducks, Swans and Geese

	New York	Pennsylvania	New Jersey	Delaware	Maryland	Dist. of Columbia	Virginia	North Carolina	South Carolina	Georgia	Florida
Fulvous Whistling-Duck	rV	xV	rV	xW	xS*,rV,xW		rV,xW	rV,rW	xS*,uV,rW	uV,xW	fP
Black-bellied Whistling-Duck		xV									xV,rW
Tundra Swan	fT,rW	cT,uW	fT,uW	fT,uW	cW		uT,xW	cW	cW	uW	rW
Whooper Swan											
Trumpeter Swan				eT						eW	
Bean Goose											
Pink-footed Goose											

	Date	Location	Cont. North America	Canada	Lower 48
Greater White-fronted Goose *Anser albifrons*			cS,fW	cS,lrW	fW
Snow Goose *Chen caerulescens*			cP	cS,luW	cW
Ross' Goose *Chen rossii*			lcS,xS,uW	lcS,uT,xW	uW
Emperor Goose *Chen canagica*			luP,rV,rW	rV,xW	rV,rW
Brant *Branta bernicla*			lcS,xS,fW	cS,uW	cT,fW
Barnacle Goose *Branta leucopsis*			rV,xW	xV	xV,xW
Canada Goose *Branta canadensis*			cP2	cS,uW	fS2,cW
Hawaiian Goose *Nesochen sandvicensis*					

Subfamily Anatinae: Ducks

	Date	Location	Cont. North America	Canada	Lower 48
Muscovy Duck *Cairina moschata*			xV		xV
Wood Duck *Aix sponsa*			fP	uS,lrW	fP
Green-winged Teal *Anas crecca*			cP	cS,rW	fS,cW
Baikal Teal *Anas formosa*			rV,xW	xV	xV,xW
Falcated Teal *Anas falcata*			rV,xW	xV	xW
American Black Duck *Anas rubripes*			cP	cS,fW	fS,cW
Mottled Duck *Anas fulvigula*			lcP,rV		lcP,rV
Mallard *Anas platyrhynchos*			cP2	cS2,fW	cP2
Hawaiian Duck *Anas wyvilliana*					
Laysan Duck *Anas laysensis*					
Spot-billed Duck *Anas poecilorhyncha*			xP*,xV		
White-cheeked Pintail *Anas bahamensis*			rV,rW		rV,rW
Northern Pintail *Anas acuta*			cP	cS,uW	fS,cW
Garganey *Anas querquedula*			xS*,rV,xW	rV	rV,xW
Blue-winged Teal *Anas discors*			cS,fW	cS,lrW	fS,cT,fW

	Hawaii	Alaska	Yukon Terr.	Northwest Terr.	British Columbia	Alberta	Saskatchewan	Manitoba	Ontario
Gr. Wh.-fronted Goose	xV.xW	cS	lfS.fT	cS	uT.rW	fT	cT.xW	fT	rT
Snow Goose	xV.xW	luS.fT	lrS*.fT	cS	cT.uW	cT	cT.xW	lfS.cT.xW	lfS.cT.rW
Ross' Goose		xS.xV		lcS.fT	xV.xW	uT	fT	xS.rT	lrS.rT
Emperor Goose	xV.xW	uP			rV.xW				
Brant	xS*.rV.xW	cS.luW	lfS.rT	cS	cT.uW	xV	rV	rT	xS.uT.xW
Barnacle Goose				exV					
Canada Goose	xS*.rV.xW	cS.uW	cS	cS	cS.fW	cS.rW	cS.rW	cS.rW	cS.fW
Hawaiian Goose	luP1								

Subfamily Anatinae: Ducks

	Hawaii	Alaska	Yukon Terr.	Northwest Terr.	British Columbia	Alberta	Saskatchewan	Manitoba	Ontario
Muscovy Duck									
Wood Duck		xV				uS.rW	lrS.xW	uS	uS	uS.rW
Green-winged Teal	uW	cS.rW	cS	cS	cS.uW	cS.xW	cS.xW	cS	fS.cT.rW
Baikal Teal		rV			xV				
Falcated Teal		rV			xV				
American Black Duck		xV.xW	xV	lfS		rV.xW	uS.xW	uS	fS.uW
Mottled Duck									
Mallard	rW	cP	cS.rW	cS.xW	cP	cS.uW	cS.uW	cS.uW	cS.fW
Hawaiian Duck	lfP2								
Laysan Duck	luP								
Spot-billed Duck		xP*.xV							
White-cheeked Pintail									
Northern Pintail	fW	cS.uW	cS	cS	cS.fW	cS.xW	cS.rW	cS.rW	fS.cT.rW
Garganey	xV.rW	xS*.rV	xV		xV	xV		xV	
Blue-winged Teal	xS.rV.rW	uS	uS	uS	fS	fS	cS.xW	cS	cS.rW

	Québec	Newfound-land	New Brunswick	Prince Edward I.	Nova Scotia		Washington	Oregon	California	Nevada	Idaho
Gr. Wh.-fronted Goose	rV	rV	xV	xV	xV		uT,rW	fT,rW	cW	uT,xW	rT,xW
Snow Goose	lrS,fT	xV	rT	xV	rT		uT,lfW	cT,uW	cW	cT,fW	fT,rW
Ross' Goose	xV						rT,xW	uT,rW	fW	uT,rW	uT
Emperor Goose							rV,rW	rV,rW	rV,rW		
Brant	fT	rT	fT,luW	uT	fT,rW		cT,lcW	cT,fW	cT,fW	xV	xV
Barnacle Goose	xV	xV	xV		xV-q						
Canada Goose	cS,uW	cS,rW	luS1,cT,uW	uS1,cT,rW	cT,fW		fS2,cW	fS,cW	fS2,cW	uS,cW	fS,cT,fW
Hawaiian Goose											

Subfamily Anatinae: Ducks

	Québec	Newfound-land	New Brunswick	Prince Edward I.	Nova Scotia		Washington	Oregon	California	Nevada	Idaho
Muscovy Duck											
Wood Duck	uS,rW	rV	uS,xW	uS	rS2,xW		fS,rW	fS,uW	uP	uP	fS,rW
Green-winged Teal	uS,fT,xW	fS	fS,cT,rW	fS,cT,xW	fS,cT,rW		fS,cW	uS,cW	lfS,cW	uS,cT,fW	fS,cT,uW
Baikal Teal							exW-q	xV	xV,xW		
Falcated Teal							xW				
American Black Duck	cS,luW	cS,uW	cP	cS,fW	cP			xV	exW-q		xV
Mottled Duck											
Mallard	fS,luW	rS1,xW	uP1	uS1,rW	uP1		cP	cP	cP	cP	cP
Hawaiian Duck											
Laysan Duck											
Spot-billed Duck											
White-cheeked Pintail											
Northern Pintail	fS,cT,xW	fS,xW	fS,rW	uS,fT,rW	uS,fT,uW		fS,cW	fS,cW	fS,cW	fS,cT,fW	uS,cT,uW
Garganey	xV		xV	xV			xV	xV			
Blue-winged Teal	fS	uS	cS	fS	fS		fS	uS,xW	rS,uW	rS,uT,rW	uS,fT,xW

72 • Distributional Checklist of North American Birds

	Montana	Wyoming	Utah	Colorado	Arizona	New Mexico	North Dakota	South Dakota	Nebraska	Kansas	Oklahoma
Gr. Wh.-fronted Goose	uT,xW	rT	rT,xW	uT,xW	uT,rW	uT,xW	fT	fT	cT	cT,rW	cT,fW
Snow Goose	cT,rW	fT,xW	fT,xW	fT,rW	uW	fT,lcW	cT,xW	cT,rW	cT,rW	cT,uW	cT,fW
Ross' Goose	uT	rT	rT	rT	rW	rT,luW	rT	rT,xW	rT	rT,xW	rT,xW
Emperor Goose											
Brant	xV	xV	xV	xV	rV,xW	xV	rV	xV	xV	rV	xV,xW-q
Barnacle Goose											
Canada Goose	cS,fW	cS,fW	cP	fS,cW	cW	cW	uS2,cT,uW	uS2,cT,fW	rS2,cT,fW	uS1,cT,fW	cW
Hawaiian Goose											

Subfamily Anatinae: Ducks

	Montana	Wyoming	Utah	Colorado	Arizona	New Mexico	North Dakota	South Dakota	Nebraska	Kansas	Oklahoma
Muscovy Duck											
Wood Duck	uS,rW	uS,rW	rS,uT,rW	rS,uT,rW	rS,uT,rW	rT,lrW	fS	fS	lfS,uT,xW	fS,rW	uS,fT,uW
Green-winged Teal	cS,uW	cS,uW	uS,cT,fW	fS,cT,uW	lrS,cW	luS,cT,fW	fS,cT	uS,cT,rW	uS,cT,rW	lrS,cT,uW	cT,fW
Baikal Teal											
Falcated Teal											
American Black Duck	rV,xW	xV		rV		lrS,rT,xW	xV	rV,xW	xS,rW	rW	
Mottled Duck				xV					xV	lrS,rV	xV
Mallard	cS,fW	cS,fW	cP	fS,cW	fS,cW	fS,cW	cS,uW	cS,fW	cP	fS,cW	uS,cW
Hawaiian Duck											
Laysan Duck											
Spot-billed Duck											
White-cheeked Pintail											
Northern Pintail	cS,uW	cS,uW	cS,fW	fS,cT,fW	uS,cW	uS,cW	cS,xW	cS,rW	fS,cT,rW	uS,cT,uW	luS,cT,fW
Garganey	xV									xV	xV
Blue-winged Teal	cS,xW	cS	uS,fT,rW	fS,cT,rW	lrS,uT,rW	uS,fT,rW	cS	cS	cS	fS,cT,xW	uS,cT,rW

Anatidae • 73

	Texas	Minnesota	Iowa	Missouri	Arkansas	Louisiana	Wisconsin	Michigan	Illinois	Indiana	Ohio
Gr. Wh.-fronted Goose	cW	uT,xW	fT	fT,rW	fT,rW	fW	rT	rV	uT,xW	rT	rV
Snow Goose	cW	cT,xW	cT,rW	cT,rW	cT,fW	cW	cT,rW	cT,rW	cT,uW	cT,rW	fT,rW
Ross' Goose	uW	rT,xW	rT	rT,xW	xT,xW	rW	xT	xV	xT	xV-q	xV
Emperor Goose											
Brant	rV,xW	rT	xV	rV,xW		xV,xW	rT	rT,xW	rT,xW	rT,xW	rT,xW
Barnacle Goose											
Canada Goose	cW	cS2,uW	uS2,cT,fW	uS2,cW	rS1,cW	uW	fS2,cT,uW	cS2,fW	fS1,cW	cS2,fW	fS2,cT,fW
Hawaiian Goose											

Subfamily Anatinae: Ducks

	Texas	Minnesota	Iowa	Missouri	Arkansas	Louisiana	Wisconsin	Michigan	Illinois	Indiana	Ohio
Muscovy Duck	xV-q										
Wood Duck	cP	cS,rW	fS,cT,rW	cS,uW	cS,fW	cP	cS,rW	fS,rW	cS,rW	cS,rW	fS,rW
Green-winged Teal	xS,cW	uS,cT,rW	rS,cT,rW	cT,uW	cT,fW	cW	luS,cT,rW	uS,cT,rW	lrS,cT,uW	xS,cT,uW	lrS,cT,uW
Baikal Teal											
Falcated Teal											
American Black Duck	rW	uS,fT,rW	xS,uT,rW	uW	fW	uW	fS,uW	fS,uW	lrS,fW	uS,cT,fW	uS,cT,fW
Mottled Duck	cP					cP					
Mallard	uS,cW	cS,fW	cS,fW	fS,cW	rS1,cW	cW	cS,fW	cS,fW	fS2,cW	fS2,cW	fS2,cW
Hawaiian Duck											
Laysan Duck											
Spot-billed Duck											
White-cheeked Pintail	xW										
Northern Pintail	luS,cW	cS,rW	luS,cT,rW	cT,fW	cT,fW	xS,cW	luS,cT,rW	rS,cT,rW	xS,cT,uW	xS,cT,uW	lrS,cT,uW
Garganey					xV				xV		
Blue-winged Teal	uS,cT,fW	cS,xW	fS,cT,rW	uS,cT,rW	rS,cT,rW	fS,cT,fW	cS,xW	cS,xW	uS,cT,rW	uS,cT,xW	uS,cT,xW

74 • *Distributional Checklist of North American Birds*

	West Virginia	Kentucky	Tennessee	Mississippi	Alabama	Maine	New Hampshire	Vermont	Massachusetts	Rhode Island	Connecticut
Gr. Wh.-fronted Goose	xV	rT,xW	rT,xW	rW	rT,xW	xV		xV	rV,xW	xV	xV
Snow Goose	uT,rW	fT,luW	fT,uW	fW	fW	uT,xW	uT	fT	fT,xW	uT,rW	uT,rW
Ross' Goose					xV						
Emperor Goose											
Brant	xV		xV	xV	xV,xW	fT,rW	uT,rW	rT	fT,uW	fT,uW	uT,rW
Barnacle Goose									exV		xV-q
Canada Goose	cT,uW	rS1,cT,fW	uS1,cT,fW	cW	cW	uS1,cT,uW	cT,fW	cT,uW	fS1,cT,fW	cT,fW	cT,fW
Hawaiian Goose											

Subfamily Anatinae: Ducks

	West Virginia	Kentucky	Tennessee	Mississippi	Alabama	Maine	New Hampshire	Vermont	Massachusetts	Rhode Island	Connecticut
Muscovy Duck											
Wood Duck	fS,rW	uS,fT,uW	fS,uW	cP	cP	fS,xW	fS,rW	fS,xW	fS,rW	uS,fT,rW	fS2,rW
Green-winged Teal	xS,fT,rW	fT,uW	cT,fW	cW	cW	fS,cT,rW	uS,cT,rW	rS,cT,rW	uS,cT,uW	lrS,cT,uW	uS,cT,uW
Baikal Teal											
Falcated Teal											
American Black Duck	rS,cT,fW	cT,fW	cT,fW	fW	xS,fW	cP	fS,cT,fW	cS,fW	cP	cP	fS,cW
Mottled Duck				luP	luP						
Mallard	fS1,cT,fW	uS1,cW	cW	cW	cW	cS1,fW	cS2,fW	cS2,fW	cP2	cP1	cP2
Hawaiian Duck											
Laysan Duck											
Spot-billed Duck											
White-cheeked Pintail					xV						
Northern Pintail	fT,rW	xS,cT,uW	cT,fW	cT,fW	cW	xS*,uT,rW	xS*,uT,rW	rS,fT,rW	lrS,fT,uW	fT,uW	fT,uW
Garganey			xV		xV,xW-q				xV		
Blue-winged Teal	rS,fT,xW	xS,cT,xW	rS,cT,rW	rS,cT,uW	rS,cT,uW	cS	uS,fT	fS	uS,fT,xW	rS,fT,xW	uS,fT,xW

Anatidae • 75

	New York	Pennsylvania	New Jersey	Delaware	Maryland	Dist. of Columbia	Virginia	North Carolina	South Carolina	Georgia	Florida
Gr. Wh.-fronted Goose	rV,xW	rV,xW	rV,xW	rV,rW	rV,rW		rV,rW	rV,rW	rW	rW	rW
Snow Goose	cT,rW	cT,rW	cT,uW	cW	cW	rT	cW	cW	uW	uW	uW
Ross' Goose	xV		xV	xV	xV-q		xV,xW	xV,xW			
Emperor Goose											
Brant	fW	rT	cW	cW	IfW	xV,xW	fW	fW	rW	xW	rW
Barnacle Goose	xV			xV,xW				xV,xW-q			
Canada Goose	cT,fW	cT,fW	cW	cW	cW	fT,rW	cW	cW	fW	fW	uW
Hawaiian Goose											

Subfamily Anatinae: Ducks

	New York	Pennsylvania	New Jersey	Delaware	Maryland	Dist. of Columbia	Virginia	North Carolina	South Carolina	Georgia	Florida
Muscovy Duck											
Wood Duck	fS,rW	fS,rW	fS2,rW	fS,rW	fS,rW	fS,rW	fS,uW	fP	fP	fP	cP
Green-winged Teal	fS,cT,uW	luS,cT,uW	luS,cT,uW	xS,cT,fW	rS,cT,fW	fT,uW	xS,cT,fW	cW	cW	cW	cW
Baikal Teal											
Falcated Teal											
American Black Duck	cP	fS,cW	fS,cW	fS,cW	fS,cW	rS,uW	fS,cW	uS,cW	rS,cW	xS*,fW	uW
Mottled Duck											cP
Mallard	cP2	cP2	cP2	fS2,cT,fW	fS2,cW	cP1	lcS2,cW	cW	cW	cW	fW
Hawaiian Duck											
Laysan Duck											
Spot-billed Duck											
White-cheeked Pintail							xV				rV,rW
Northern Pintail	rS,cT,fW	rS*,cT,uW	cT,fW	cT,uW	xS,cT,fW	uW	xS,cW	cW	cW	cW	cW
Garganey				xV				xV-q			
Blue-winged Teal	fS,cT,xW	uS,cT,rW	fS,cT,rW	uS,cT,rW	uS,cT,rW	uT	uS,cT,rW	uS,cT,uW	rS,cT,fW	rS,cW	lrS,cW

	Date	Location	Cont. North America	Canada	Lower 48
Cinnamon Teal *Anas cyanoptera*			cS,uW	lfS,xS*,rV,xW	cS,uW
Northern Shoveler *Anas clypeata*			cP	cS,rW	fS,cW
Gadwall *Anas strepera*			fS,cT,fW	fS,rW	fS,cT,fW
Eurasian Wigeon *Anas penelope*			xS*,rW	xS*,rT,luW	rW
American Wigeon *Anas americana*			cP	cS,uW	fS,cW
Common Pochard *Aythya ferina*			rV		
Canvasback *Aythya valisineria*			fP	fS,uW	uS,fW
Redhead *Aythya americana*			fP	fS,rW	fP
Ring-necked Duck *Aythya collaris*			fP	fS,rW	uS,fW
Tufted Duck *Aythya fuligula*			xS*,luT,rV,rW	rV,xW	rV,rW
Greater Scaup *Aythya marila*			cP	cS,fW	rS*,cW
Lesser Scaup *Aythya affinis*			cP	cS,rW	uS,cW
Common Eider *Somateria mollissima*			cP	cP	lcS,rS*,fW
King Eider *Somateria spectabilis*			fP	fS,uW	xS*,rW
Spectacled Eider *Somateria fischeri*			luP,xV	xV	
Steller's Eider *Polysticta stelleri*			lfP,xS*,xV,xW	xS*,xV,xW	xV,xW
Labrador Duck *Camptorhynchus labradorius*			E†	E†	E*
Harlequin Duck *Histrionicus histrionicus*			fP	fP	luS,rS*,uW
Oldsquaw *Clangula hyemalis*			cP	cP	rS*,fW
Black Scoter *Melanitta nigra*			lcS,rS*,cW	lfS,rS*,cT,fW	rS*,cW
Surf Scoter *Melanitta perspicillata*			cP	cP	uS*,cW
White-winged Scoter *Melanitta fusca*			cP	cP	xS,uS*,cW
Common Goldeneye *Bucephala clangula*			cP	cS,fW	uS,cW
Barrow's Goldeneye *Bucephala islandica*			fP	fP	luS,uW

78 • *Distributional Checklist of North American Birds*

	Hawaii	Alaska	Yukon Terr.	Northwest Terr.	British Columbia	Alberta	Saskatchewan	Manitoba	Ontario
Cinnamon Teal	xV,xW	rV	xS*	xV	fS,xW	uS	luS†	xS*,rV	xS,rV
Northern Shoveler	cW	cS,rW	cS	fS	cS,uW	cS,xW	cS,xW	cS	lrS,fT,rW
Gadwall	xV,xW	uP	xV	lrS,xV	fS,uW	fS,xW	cS,rW	fS	uS,fT,rW
Eurasian Wigeon	rW	rS*,uT,rW	xV	xV	uW	xV	xV	rV	rV
American Wigeon	fW	cS,uW	cS	cS	cS,fW	cS,xW	cS,rW	cS,xW	fS,cT,rW
Common Pochard	xV	rV							
Canvasback	xV,xW	uS,lrW	fS	fS	uS,fW	fS,xW	cS,xW	fS	rS,fT,uW
Redhead	xV,xW	uS,xW	rT	luS	fS,rW	fS,xW	cS,xW	fS	rS,fT,uW
Ring-necked Duck	rW	uS,xW	fS	uS	fS,uW	fS	cS	fS,xW	fS,rW
Tufted Duck	rV,xW	xS*,luT,xV,xW			rV,xW				xV,xW
Greater Scaup	xV,xW	cS,fW	fS	cS	luS,rS*,cT,fW	uT	xS*,uT,xW	lfS,fT	luS,cT,uW
Lesser Scaup	uW	cS,lrW	cS	cS	cS,uW	cS,xW	cS,rW	cS,rW	uS,cT,rW
Common Eider		cP	lfS	cS,fW	xV		xV-q	lfS	luS,xW
King Eider		fP	lfS	fS	rW	xV	xV	lrS	luS,rV,rW
Spectacled Eider		uP		xV	xV				
Steller's Eider		fP		xS*,xV	xV,xW				
Labrador Duck									
Harlequin Duck	xV	fP	fS	luS	fP	luS,xW	rV	lrS*,rV	xS*,rV,rW
Oldsquaw	xV	cP	fS	cS,xW	lrS,fW	rT,xW	rT,xW	lcS,rT,xW	luS,cT,fW
Black Scoter	xV	cP	rS*	lfS	rS*,fW	rT	rT	luS*,rT	luS*,fT,rW
Surf Scoter	xV	cP	cS	cS	uS†,cW	lrS,uT	lfS,rT	xS,lfS*,rT	lrS,fT,rW
White-winged Scoter		cP	cS	cS	fS,cW	fS	fS,xW	uS	luS,fT,uW
Common Goldeneye		cS,fW	cS,rW	cS	cS,fW	cS,uW	cS,uW	cS,luW	fS,cT,fW
Barrow's Goldeneye		fP	cS,xW	luS†	fP	luS,xW	rV	rV	rV,rW

Anatidae • 79

	Québec	Newfoundland	New Brunswick	Prince Edward I.	Nova Scotia		Washington	Oregon	California	Nevada	Idaho
Cinnamon Teal	xV		xV				cS,xW	cS,rW	cS,fW	cS,uW	cS,xW
Northern Shoveler	luS,uT	xV	rS,uT,xW	rS,uT	lrS,rT,xW		fS,cW	fS,cW	fS,cW	uS,cT,fW	fS,cT,xW
Gadwall	luS,xW	xV	xS*,rT,xW	lrS	lrS,rT,xW		fP	fP	uS,fW	uS,cT,uW	fS,uW
Eurasian Wigeon	rT	rT	rT	xT	xS*,rT		rW	rW	rW	xV	rV
American Wigeon	luS,xW	luS,xW	uS,fT,xW	uS,xW	lrS,uT,rW		uS,cW	uS,cW	uS,cW	uS,cT,fW	uS,cT,uW
Common Pochard											
Canvasback	uT,xW	xV,xW	rT	xV	rT		uS,fW	uS,fW	lrS,rS*,fW	rS,fT,uW	uS,fT,rW
Redhead	luS,xW	xV	xS,rT	xV	lrS,rT		fS,rW	fS,uW	uS,fW	fS,rW	fS,rW
Ring-necked Duck	fS,xW	fS	fS,xW	fS	uS,fT,rW		uS,fW	luS,rS*,fW	lrS,rS*,fW	rS,fT,uW	rS,fT,rW
Tufted Duck	xV	xV,xW					xV,xW	xV,xW	xS*,xV,rW		
Greater Scaup	luS,cT,rW	luS,uT,rW	xS*,cT,uW	fT,uW	fT,uW		rS*,cW	rS*,cW	uS*,cW	uT,rW	rT,xW
Lesser Scaup	lrS,fT,xW	rT	xS*,uT,xW	rT,xW	uT,xW		uS,cW	luS,rS*,cW	lrS,uS*,cW	rS*,cT,fW	uS,cT,rW
Common Eider	lcS,rW	cP	cP	uS*,fT,uW	cP						
King Eider	lrS,rW	rS*,fW	xS*,rW	xT	rW		xV,xW	xV	xS*,xV,rW		
Spectacled Eider											
Steller's Eider	exV								xW		
Labrador Duck	E*	E†	E*		E*						
Harlequin Duck	rP	rS,uW	xS*,uW	xS*,uW	uW		uS,fW	rS,fW	lrS,rS*,uW	xV	rS
Oldsquaw	cS,fW	fS,cW	rS*,cW	rS*,cW	rS*,cW		xS*,fW	xS*,uW	xS*,rW	rT,xW	rT,xW
Black Scoter	uS,fT,xW	uS,fT,uW	rS*,cT,uW	rS*,cT,uW	rS*,cT,fW		rS*,fW	rS*,fW	rS*,uW	xV	xV
Surf Scoter	uS,fT,xW	uS,rW	rS*,cT,fW	rS*,fT,rW	rS*,cT,fW		uS*,cW	uS*,cW	uS*,cW	rV,xW	xV
White-winged Scoter	lrS,fT,xW	rS*,fT,uW	rS*,cT,fW	rS*,cT,uW	rS*,cT,fW		uS*,cW	uS*,cW	uS*,cW	rT,xW	rT
Common Goldeneye	fS,uW	cS,uW	fS,cW	rS,cT,fW	uS,cT,fW		lrS,xS*,cW	xS*,cW	rS*,cW	fW	xS*,fW
Barrow's Goldeneye	lrS,uW	lrS,rW	uW	uW	uW		uS,fW	luS,uW	eS,uW	uW	luS,fT,uW

80 • Distributional Checklist of North American Birds

	Montana	Wyoming	Utah	Colorado	Arizona	New Mexico	North Dakota	South Dakota	Nebraska	Kansas	Oklahoma
Cinnamon Teal	fS.xW	cS	cS.rW	cS.xW	fS.cT.uW	cS.rW	xS.rT	lrS.rT	lrS.uT	lrS.uT	lrS.uT
Northern Shoveler	cS.rW	cS.xW	cS.uW	fS.cT.uW	lrS*.cW	uS.cT.fW	cS	cS	fS.cT	uS.cT.xW	uS.cT.uW
Gadwall	cS.uW	cS.uW	fS.cT.uW	fS.cT.uW	uS.cT.fW	uS.cT.fW	cS.xW	cS.rW	fS.cT.rW	uS.cT.uW	uS.cW
Eurasian Wigeon	rV.xW	xV	xV.xW	xV	xV.xW		xV		xV	xV	xV-q
American Wigeon	cS.uW	cS.rW	rS.cT.uW	fS.cT.uW	lrS.cW	luS.cW	fS.cT.xW	fS.cT.xW	uS.cT.xW	lrS.cT.uW	cT.fW
Common Pochard											
Canvasback	uS.fT.rW	uS.fT.xW	rS.fT.uW	rS.fT.rW	rS*.fW	luS.fT.uW	fS.cT.xW	uS.fT.xW	rS.fT.xW	rS.fT.rW	xS*.fT.uW
Redhead	fS.rW	cS.rW	cS.uW	fS.cT.uW	luS.rS*.fW	luS.fT.uW	cS.xW	cS.rW	uS.fT.xW	rS.fT.rW	uS.fT.uW
Ring-necked Duck	uS.fT.rW	uS.fT	exS.fT.uW	rS.fT.uW	luS.rS*.fW	rS*.fW	uS.fT	rS.fT	lrS.fT	fT.rW	xS*.fT.uW
Tufted Duck		xV									
Greater Scaup	rT.xW	rT	rT.xW	rT.xW	rW	xV.xW	rT	rT	rT	rT.xW	rT.xW
Lesser Scaup	fS.cT.rW	fS.cT.xW	rS*.cT.fW	uS.cT.uW	rS*.cW	lrS.rS*.cT.fW	fS.cT.xW	luS.cT.xW	lrS.cT.rW	xS*.cT.uW	xS*.cT.uW
Common Eider							xV.xW		xV	exV	
King Eider										xV	
Spectacled Eider											
Steller's Eider											
Labrador Duck											
Harlequin Duck	uS	luS	exV-q	exS.xV		xW	xV		xV		
Oldsquaw	rT.xW	rT	rT.xW	rT	xS*.rW	rW	rT.xW	rT.xW	rT.xW	rW	rW
Black Scoter	xV	xV	xV	rV	xV	xV	rT	rT	xV	xV	xV-q
Surf Scoter	rV	rV	rV.xW	rV	rV	rV	rT	rT.xW	rV	rV	rV.xW
White-winged Scoter	rT.xW	rT	rT	rT	rT.xW	xS*.rV.xW	xS.rT	rT.xW	rT.xW	rT.xW	rW
Common Goldeneye	rS.fW	fW	fW	xS*.fW	uW	xS*.uW	lrS.fT.uW	fT.uW	fT.uW	fW	fW
Barrow's Goldeneye	rS.uW	uS.fW	uW	eS.rW	rV.lrW	xV.xW	xW	xV.xW	xW		xV

Anatidae • 81

	Texas	Minnesota	Iowa	Missouri	Arkansas	Louisiana	Wisconsin	Michigan	Illinois	Indiana	Ohio
Cinnamon Teal	rS,cT,uW	rV	rV	rV	xV	rV,xW	rV	xV	rV	xV	xV
Northern Shoveler	rS,cW	cS,xW	rS,cT,xW	lrS*,cT,rW	cT,uW	cW	rS,fT,rW	rS,fT,rW	lrS,cT,rW	rS,fT,rW	lrS,fT,rW
Gadwall	lrS,cW	fS,cT,rW	rS,cT,rW	cT,uW	cT,fW	cW	uS,fT,rW	uS,fT,rW	lrS*,fT,uW	fT,uW	lrS,fT,rW
Eurasian Wigeon	xV,rW	rV	xV	xV		xW	rV	rV	rV,xW	rV	rV
American Wigeon	lrS,cW	fS,cT,xW	lrS,cT,rW	cT,uW	cT,fW	cW	luS,cT,rW	rS,cT,rW	cT,uW	cT,uW	lrS,cT,rW
Common Pochard											
Canvasback	rS*,cW	fS,cT,xW	lrS,cT,rW	xS*,cT,uW	xS*,fT,uW	rS*,fW	rS,fT,rW	rS,fT,uW	xS,fT,uW	xS*,fT,uW	rS*,fT,uW
Redhead	lrS,rS*,cW	fS,cT,xW	luS,fT,rW	fT,rW	fT,uW	rS*,fW	rS,cT,rW	rS,cT,rW	rS,fT,rW	xS,fT,rW	lrS,fT,rW
Ring-necked Duck	rS*,cW	cS,xW	lrS,cT,rW	xS*,cT,uW	xS*,cT,fW	rS*,cW	uS,cT,rW	uS,cT,rW	xS*,cT,uW	xS,cT,uW	xS*,cT,rW
Tufted Duck								xV	xV,xW	xV-q	xV
Greater Scaup	xS*,rW	fT,xW	uT,rW	xS*,rT,xW	rT,xW	rW	xS*,fT,uW	rS*,fT,uW	xS*,fT,uW	xS*,fT,uW	xS*,fT,uW
Lesser Scaup	rS*,cW	uS,cT,rW	xS,cT,rW	rS*,cT,fW	rS*,cW	rS*,cW	rS,cT,uW	xS,rS*,cT,uW	xS,rS*,cT,fW	rS*,cT,fW	xS,rS*,cT,uW
Common Eider		xV	xV				xV	xV,xW	xV,xW		xV,xW
King Eider	xV-q	xV,xW	xV				rV,xW	rV,xW	xV,xW	xV,xW	rV,xW
Spectacled Eider											
Steller's Eider											
Labrador Duck											
Harlequin Duck	xV,xW-q	rV,xW	xV	xV			xS*,rV,xW	rV,rW	rV,xW	rV,rW	rV,xW
Oldsquaw	rW	uT,rW	rT,xW	rW	rW	rW	fT,uW	fT,uW	uW	uW	uT,rW
Black Scoter	rW	rT,xW	xT	rT,xW	xT	rW	rT,xW	uT,xW	rT,xW	rT,xW	uT,xW
Surf Scoter	rW	rT,xW	rT,xW	rT,xW	xT	rW	rT,xW	uT,xW	rT,xW	rT,xW	uT,xW
White-winged Scoter	rW	uT,xW	rT,xW	rT,xW	rT,xW	rW	uT,rW	uT,rW	uT,rW	uT,rW	uT,rW
Common Goldeneye	uW	uS,cT,uW	fW	fW	fW	uW	uS,cT,fW	uS,cT,fW	xS*,cT,fW	cT,fW	cT,fW
Barrow's Goldeneye	xV,xW	rV	xV	xV,xW			xV,xW	xV,xW	rV,xW	xV,xW	xW

	West Virginia	Kentucky	Tennessee	Mississippi	Alabama	Maine	New Hampshire	Vermont	Massachusetts	Rhode Island	Connecticut
Cinnamon Teal		xV	xV	xV	xV						
Northern Shoveler	fT,rW	fT,rW	cT,uW	cT,fW	xS,cW	lrS,uT	uT	eS,uT	xS,uT,xW	rT,xW	rT,xW
Gadwall	uT,rW	fT,uW	cT,fW	cW	xS,cW	lrS,rT	rT	rS,uT	rS,fT,rW	lrS2,fT,uW	rS,fT,uW
Eurasian Wigeon	xV	xV	xV	xV,xW	xW	rT	xT	xV	rT,xW	rT,xW	rT
American Wigeon	fT,rW	fT,uW	cT,fW	cW	cW	lrS,fT,xW	xS*,fT,rW	rS*,uT	xS,rS*,fT,rW	lrS*,cT,rW	lrS*,cT,uW
Common Pochard											
Canvasback	uT,rW	xS*,uT,rW	xS*,fT,uW	rS*,fW	rS*,fW	rT,xW	rT,xW	uT	rS*,fT,uW	xS*,fT,uW	xS*,fT,uW
Redhead	fT,uW	fT,uW	fT,uW	rS*,fW	rS*,fW	rT	rT	rT	xS*,uT,rW	uT,rW	uT,rW
Ring-necked Duck	xS*,cT,uW	xS*,cT,fW	rS*,cW	rS*,cW	rS*,cW	fS,rW	uS,fT,rW	eS,fT,rW	xS,fT,uW	xS*,fT,uW	xS*,fT,uW
Tufted Duck									rV,xW		xV,xW
Greater Scaup	rT,xW	uT,rW	uT,rW	xS*,uW	xS*,uW	rS*,cW	xS*,cT,fW	fT,rW	rS*,cW	rS*,cW	rS*,cW
Lesser Scaup	xS*,cT,rW	exS,rS*,cT,fW	rS*,cT,fW	rS*,cW	rS*,cW	uT,xW	xS*,uT,xW	fT,rW	xS*,fT,rW	xS*,fT,uW	xS*,fT,uW
Common Eider						cP	xS,uS*,cW	xV	xS,uS*,cW	rS*,fW	xS*,rW
King Eider	xV	xV	xV	xV	xV-q	rS*,uW	rW	xV	rS*,uW	rS*,uW	rW
Spectacled Eider											
Steller's Eider						exV			xV		
Labrador Duck						E*	E*		E*	E*	E*
Harlequin Duck	xW-q	xV	xW		xV,xW	uW	rW	xV,xW	uW	xS*,uW	xW
Oldsquaw	uT,rW	rW	rW	rW	rW	xS*,cW	xS*,cW	uT	xS*,cW	xS*,cW	xS*,cW
Black Scoter	xT	rT,xW	xT	rW	xS*,rW	rS*,cT,fW	rS*,cT,fW	uT	rS*,cT,fW	rS*,cT,fW	uT,rW
Surf Scoter	xT	rT,xW	rT,xW	rW	rW	rS*,cT,fW	xS*,cT,fW	uT	rS*,cT,fW	rS*,cT,fW	xS*,fT,uW
White-winged Scoter	uT,rW	rT,xW	rT,xW	rW	xS*,rW	rS*,cW	rS*,cW	uT	rS*,cW	rS*,cW	xS*,fW
Common Goldeneye	fW	fW	fW	fW	fW	fS,cT,fW	luS,xS*,cW	lfS,cT,fW	xS*,cW	xS*,cW	xS*,cW
Barrow's Goldeneye			xV,xW-q			uW	rW	rV,xW	uW	rW	rW

	New York	Pennsylvania	New Jersey	Delaware	Maryland	Dist. of Columbia	Virginia	North Carolina	South Carolina	Georgia	Florida
Cinnamon Teal	xV	xV	xV					xV,xW	xV,xW	xV,xW	xV,rW
Northern Shoveler	rS,fT,rW	rS,fT,rW	rS,fT,uW	xS,fT,uW	fT,uW	rT,xW	fW	fW	cW	cW	cW
Gadwall	rS,fT,uW	eS,fT,uW	uS,fT,uW	uS,fT,uW	rS,fW	rW	rS,fW	rS,fW	fW	fW	fW
Eurasian Wigeon	rT,xW	rT	rT,xW	rT,xW	rT,xW	xT	rW	rW	rW	xW	rW
American Wigeon	luS,cT,uW	xS,cT,uW	cT,uW	xS,cT,uW	xS*,cT,fW	fT,uW	cW	cW	cW	cW	cW
Common Pochard											
Canvasback	rS*,fT,uW	xS*,fT,uW	rS*,fW	xS*,fW	rS*,fW	xS*,fT,uW	rS*,fW	rS*,fW	rS*,fW	rS*,fW	rS*,fW
Redhead	lrS,uT,rW	xS,fT,uW	xS,uW	xS*,rW	xS*,uW	uW	xS*,uW	xS*,uW	xS*,uW	xS*,uW	rS*,fW
Ring-necked Duck	uS,fT,uW	exS,fT,uW	xS*,fT,uW	xS*,fT,uW	xS*,fT,uW	fT,uW	rS*,cT,fW	rS*,cW	rS*,cW	rS*,cW	rS*,fW
Tufted Duck	xV,xW		xW								
Greater Scaup	rS*,cW	xS*,fT,uW	rS*,cW	rS*,cW	rS*,fW	xS*,uW	xS*,fW	xS*,uW	xS*,uW	xS*,uW	xS*,uW
Lesser Scaup	xS,rS*,cT,uW	rS*,cT,fW	xS,rS*,cT,uW	rS*,cT,fW	rS*,cT,fW	fT,uW	rS*,cW	rS*,cW	rS*,cW	rS*,cW	rS*,cW
Common Eider	xS*,uW	xV	rW	rW	rW		xS*,rW	rW	rW		xW
King Eider	xS*,rW	rV,xW	xS*,rW	rW	xS*,rW		xS*,rW	rW	xW	xW	xW
Spectacled Eider											
Steller's Eider											
Labrador Duck	E*		E*		E*						
Harlequin Duck	uW	rV,xW	rW	rW	rW		xS*,rW	rW	xW	xW	xW
Oldsquaw	xS*,cW	uT,rW	xS*,cW	xS*,cW	xS*,cW	uT,rW	xS*,fW	uW	uW	rW	rW
Black Scoter	rS*,cT,fW	rT,xW	rS*,cT,fW	rS*,cT,fW	rS*,cW		rS*,cW	rS*,cW	rS*,cW	rS*,cW	xS*,uW
Surf Scoter	rS*,cT,fW	uT,rW	rS*,cT,fW	rS*,cW	rS*,cW	xT	rS*,cW	rS*,cW	rS*,fW	xS*,uW	xS*,uW
White-winged Scoter	rS*,cW	uT,rW	rS*,cW	rS*,cW	rS*,cW		rW	rS*,cW	xS*,uW	xS*,uW	xS*,uW	xS*,rW
Common Goldeneye	luS,xS*,cW	xS*,cT,fW	xS*,cW	xS*,cW	xS*,cW	uW	xS*,cW	xS*,fW	uW	uW	uW
Barrow's Goldeneye	rW	xW	xW				xW				

	Date	Location	Cont. North America	Canada	Lower 48
Bufflehead *Bucephala albeola*			cP	cS.fW	luS.rS*.cW
Smew *Mergellus albellus*			xV.lrW	xV.xW	xV.xW
Hooded Merganser *Lophodytes cucullatus*			uP	uS.rW	uS.fW
Common Merganser *Mergus merganser*			fP	fS.uW	fP
Red-breasted Merganser *Mergus serrator*			cP	cS.fW	luS.rS*.cW
Ruddy Duck *Oxyura jamaicensis*			cP	cS.rW	fS.cW
Masked Duck *Oxyura dominica*			lrP.lrP*.xV.xW		lrP.lrP*.xV.xW

Order Falconiformes: Diurnal Birds of Prey
Family Cathartidae: American Vultures

	Date	Location	Cont. North America	Canada	Lower 48
Black Vulture *Coragyps atratus*			fP	rV.xW	cP
Turkey Vulture *Cathartes aura*			cP	uS.lrW	cP
California Condor *Gymnogyps californianus*			lrP		lrP

Family Accipitridae: Kites, Eagles, Hawks and Allies
Subfamily Pandioninae: Ospreys

	Date	Location	Cont. North America	Canada	Lower 48
Osprey *Pandion haliaetus*			fS.uW	fS	fS.uW

Subfamily Accipitrinae: Kites, Eagles, Hawks and Allies

	Date	Location	Cont. North America	Canada	Lower 48
Hook-billed Kite *Chondrohierax uncinatus*			lrP		lrP
American Swallow-tailed Kite *Elanoides forficatus*			lfS.xS*.rV	xV	lfS.xS*.rV
Black-shouldered Kite *Elanus caeruleus*			lcP.xS.rV.xW		lcP.xS.rV.xW
Snail Kite *Rostrhamus sociabilis*			luP.xV		luP.xV
Mississippi Kite *Ictinia mississippiensis*			lfS.xS*.rV.xW	xV	fS.xW
Bald Eagle *Haliaeetus leucocephalus*			fP	fP	uS.fW
White-tailed Eagle *Haliaeetus albicilla*			lrP.exS*.xV.xW	exS*	exV.xW
Steller's Sea-Eagle *Haliaeetus pelagicus*			xV		

86 • *Distributional Checklist of North American Birds*

	Hawaii	Alaska	Yukon Terr.	Northwest Terr.	British Columbia	Alberta	Saskatchewan	Manitoba	Ontario
Bufflehead	rW	cS,fW	cS	lfS	cS,fW	cS,xW	cS,xW	fS,cT,xW	uS,cT,fW
Smew		xV,lrW			xV,xW			xV-q	xV
Hooded Merganser	xW	luS,lrW	xS*	xS*	uP	lrS,rT,xW	uS,xW	uS	fS,rW
Common Merganser		fS,rW	fS,rW	fS	cS,uW	fS,rW	fS,rW	fS,rW	fP
Red-breasted Merganser	xV	cS,fW	fS,xW	cS	uS,cW	uS,xW	fS,xW	fS	uS,cT,fW
Ruddy Duck	xV,xW	lrS,xW	xV	lrS	cS,uW	fS,xW	cS,rW	fS,cT	lrS,uT,rW
Masked Duck									

Order Falconiformes: Diurnal Birds of Prey
Family Cathartidae: American Vultures

	Hawaii	Alaska	Yukon Terr.	Northwest Terr.	British Columbia	Alberta	Saskatchewan	Manitoba	Ontario
Black Vulture									xV,xW
Turkey Vulture		xV			uS,lrW	uS	uS	uS	fS,xW
California Condor									

Family Accipitridae: Kites, Eagles, Hawks and Allies
Subfamily Pandioninae: Ospreys

	Hawaii	Alaska	Yukon Terr.	Northwest Terr.	British Columbia	Alberta	Saskatchewan	Manitoba	Ontario
Osprey	rV,xW	uS	uS	uS	fS	uS	uS	uS	fS

Subfamily Accipitrinae: Kites, Eagles, Hawks and Allies

	Hawaii	Alaska	Yukon Terr.	Northwest Terr.	British Columbia	Alberta	Saskatchewan	Manitoba	Ontario
Hook-billed Kite									
Am. Swallow-tld. Kite							xV-q		xV
Black-shouldered Kite									
Snail Kite									
Mississippi Kite									xV
Bald Eagle		cP	fS,rW	uS,xW	fS,cW	uS,fT,rW	fS,rW	uS,rW	rS,uT,rW
White-tailed Eagle		lrP,xV			exS*				
Steller's Sea-Eagle	xV	xV							

	Québec	Newfound-land	New Brunswick	Prince Edward I.	Nova Scotia		Washington	Oregon	California	Nevada	Idaho
Bufflehead	lrS,uT,rW	rW	xS*,cT,fW	uT,rW	fT,uW		uS,cW	uS,cW	lrS,rS*,cW	rS*,fW	rS,fT,uW
Smew		xW					xV-q		xW		
Hooded Merganser	uS,rW	rV,xW	uS,xW	xS,rV,xW	rS,xW		uP	rS,uW	xS,uW	rW	rS,uT,rW
Common Merganser	fS,uW	fS,uW	fS,cW	uS,cW	fS,cT,fW		fP	uS,fW	uS,fW	uS,fW	fS,cT,fW
Red-breasted Merganser	fS,uW	cS,fW	fS,cW	cS,fW	fS,cT,fW		rS*,cW	rS*,cW	uS*,cW	xS*,fT,uW	fT,rW
Ruddy Duck	lrS	rV,xW	xS*,rT	xS*,rT	xS,rT,xW		fS,cW	fS,cW	fS,cW	fS,cT,fW	fS,cT,rW
Masked Duck											

Order Falconiformes: Diurnal Birds of Prey
Family Cathartidae: American Vultures

	Québec	Newfound-land	New Brunswick	Prince Edward I.	Nova Scotia		Washington	Oregon	California	Nevada	Idaho
Black Vulture	xV		rV	xV	xV,exW						
Turkey Vulture	luS*,xV,xW	xV	rS*,xW	xV	rP*		fS,rW	cS,rW	cP	cS,xW	fS,xW
California Condor							eP*	eP*	lrP	exV	

Family Accipitridae: Kites, Eagles, Hawks and Allies
Subfamily Pandioninae: Ospreys

	Québec	Newfound-land	New Brunswick	Prince Edward I.	Nova Scotia		Washington	Oregon	California	Nevada	Idaho
Osprey	fS	fS	fS,cT	fS	fS		fS,xW	fS,rW	uS,fT,uW	rS,uT,xW	fS,xW

Subfamily Accipitrinae: Kites, Eagles, Hawks and Allies

	Québec	Newfound-land	New Brunswick	Prince Edward I.	Nova Scotia		Washington	Oregon	California	Nevada	Idaho
Hook-billed Kite											
Am. Swallow-tld. Kite	xV				exV						
Black-shouldered Kite							lrP	uP	cP	rV	xV
Snail Kite											
Mississippi Kite									xS*,rV	xV	
Bald Eagle	rP	uP	uP	uP	uP		uS,fW	uS,fW	rS,uW	eS,fW	rS,fW
White-tailed Eagle											
Steller's Sea-Eagle											

88 • *Distributional Checklist of North American Birds*

	Montana	Wyoming	Utah	Colorado	Arizona	New Mexico	North Dakota	South Dakota	Nebraska	Kansas	Oklahoma
Bufflehead	rS,fT,uW	rS,fT,uW	xS*,fW	rS*,fT,uW	xS*,fW	xS*,uW	luS,cT,xW	fT,xW	fT,rW	fT,rW	fT,uW
Smew											
Hooded Merganser	rS,uT,rW	rS*,uT,rW	uT,rW	lrS,rW	rW	xS,rW	rS,uT	rS,uT,xW	rS,uT,rW	rS,uW	lrS,uW
Common Merganser	cS,fW	cS,fW	xS,cW	fS,cW	uS,fW	uS,fW	eS,fT,rW	xS,fT,uW	lrS,cT,fW	cW	cW
Red-breasted Merganser	uT,xW	fT	xS*,fT,rW	fT,rW	rS*,fT,uW	xS*,uW	xS*,uT,xW	xS*,uT,xW	uT,xW	uT,rW	uT,rW
Ruddy Duck	cS,xW	cS,xW	cS,fW	fS,cT,uW	uS,cW	uS,fW	cS	cS,xW	uS,cT,rW	rS,cT,uW	rS,cT,fW
Masked Duck											

Order Falconiformes: Diurnal Birds of Prey
Family Cathartidae: American Vultures

	Montana	Wyoming	Utah	Colorado	Arizona	New Mexico	North Dakota	South Dakota	Nebraska	Kansas	Oklahoma
Black Vulture					luP				xV	exS	fS,uW
Turkey Vulture	fS,xW	fS	fS	fS	fS,uW	cS,rW	uS	fS	fS,xW	cS,rW	cS,uW
California Condor					exP*						

Family Accipitridae: Kites, Eagles, Hawks and Allies
Subfamily Pandioninae: Ospreys

	Montana	Wyoming	Utah	Colorado	Arizona	New Mexico	North Dakota	South Dakota	Nebraska	Kansas	Oklahoma
Osprey	fS,xW	fS	uS,xW	uS,xW	rS,uT,rW	rS,uT,rW	xS,rS*,uT	rS*,uT	eS,rS*,uT	rS*,fT	xS*,fT

Subfamily Accipitrinae: Kites, Eagles, Hawks and Allies

	Montana	Wyoming	Utah	Colorado	Arizona	New Mexico	North Dakota	South Dakota	Nebraska	Kansas	Oklahoma
Hook-billed Kite											
Am. Swallow-tld. Kite				xV	xV-q	xV	xV	exS*	eS	eS,xV	eS,xV
Black-shouldered Kite		xV			rP	xS*,xV		xV	xV		xS,xV
Snail Kite											
Mississippi Kite				luS,xV	luS,rT	uS		exV	rV	fS	fS
Bald Eagle	uS,fT,uW	rS,fW	lrS,fW	lrS,fW	lrS,uW	eS,rS*,uW	lrS,uT,rW	eS,uW	lrS,fW	eS,uW	lrS,uW
White-tailed Eagle											
Steller's Sea-Eagle											

	Texas	Minnesota	Iowa	Missouri	Arkansas	Louisiana	Wisconsin	Michigan	Illinois	Indiana	Ohio
Bufflehead	xS*,fW	xS,cT,rW	xS,fT,rW	xS*,fT,rW	fW	xS*,fW	xS*,cT,uW	rS*,cT,uW	xS*,fT,uW	xS*,fT,uW	xS*,fT,uW
Smew											
Hooded Merganser	xS,uW	fS,rW	rS,uT,rW	rS,uW	rS,fW	lrS,fW	uS,fT,rW	uS,fT,rW	rS,fT,uW	rS,fT,uW	rS,fT,uW
Common Merganser	uW	fS,cT,uW	cT,fW	xS*,cW	uW	rW	uS,cT,fW	fS,cT,fW	xS*,fW	fW	fW
Red-breasted Merganser	rS*,fW	fS,cT,rW	xS*,uT,rW	xS*,uT,rW	xS*,fT,uW	rS*,fW	uS,cT,uW	uS,cT,uW	xS*,cT,uW	xS*,cT,uW	rS*,cT,uW
Ruddy Duck	uS,cW	fS,cT,xW	uS,cT,xW	xS*,cT,uW	rS*,cW	rS*,cW	rS,cT,rW	rS,cT,rW	rS,cT,rW	lrS,cT,uW	lrS,cT,rW
Masked Duck	lrP,xV					xV,xW	exV				

Order Falconiformes: Diurnal Birds of Prey
Family Cathartidae: American Vultures

	Texas	Minnesota	Iowa	Missouri	Arkansas	Louisiana	Wisconsin	Michigan	Illinois	Indiana	Ohio
Black Vulture	cP		xV	luS,lrW	cP	cP	xV		luS,exV,lrW	luS,lrW	luS,lrW
Turkey Vulture	cP	uS,fT	fS,xW	cS,uW	cP	cP	fS	fS	cS,rW	cS,rW	cS,lrW
California Condor											

Family Accipitridae: Kites, Eagles, Hawks and Allies
Subfamily Pandioninae: Ospreys

	Texas	Minnesota	Iowa	Missouri	Arkansas	Louisiana	Wisconsin	Michigan	Illinois	Indiana	Ohio
Osprey	lrS,fT,uW	fS,xW	rS*,fT,xW	rS*,fT,xW	xS,fT	uS,fT,rW	uS,fT	uS,fT	eS,rS*,fT	xS,rS*,fT	rS*,fT,xW

Subfamily Accipitrinae: Kites, Eagles, Hawks and Allies

	Texas	Minnesota	Iowa	Missouri	Arkansas	Louisiana	Wisconsin	Michigan	Illinois	Indiana	Ohio
Hook-billed Kite	lrP										
Am. Swallow-tld. Kite	eS,rT	eS,xV	eS	eS,xV	eS	uS	eS,xV	exV	eS,xV	eS,xV	eS,xV
Black-shouldered Kite	fP	xV		xV	xV	xS,rV	xS*			xV	
Snail Kite	xV										
Mississippi Kite	uS,fT,xW	xV	exS	luS,xV	fS	fS	xV	xV-q	luS,xV	exS	xV
Bald Eagle	lrS,uW	uS,fT,uW	lrS,fW	lrS,fW	lrS,uW	rP	uP	uS,rW	lrS,uT,fW	eS,uT,rW	lrS,uT,rW
White-tailed Eagle											
Steller's Sea-Eagle											

90 • Distributional Checklist of North American Birds

	West Virginia	Kentucky	Tennessee	Mississippi	Alabama	Maine	New Hampshire	Vermont	Massachusetts	Rhode Island	Connecticut
Bufflehead	fT,rW	fT,uW	fT,uW	xS*,fW	xS*,fW	rS*,cT,fW	xS*,cT,fW	fT,rW	rS*,cW	xS*,cW	xS*,cW
Smew										xW	
Hooded Merganser	rS,fT,uW	xS,fT,uW	rS,fW	rS,fW	rS,fW	uS,fT,rW	fS,rW	fS,rW	uS,fT,uW	uS,fT,uW	uS,fT,uW
Common Merganser	fT,uW	uW	uW	rW	rW	fS,cW	fP	fP	lrS,fW	fW	rS,fW
Red-breasted Merganser	fT,rW	xS*,fT,rW	xS*,fT,uW	rS*,fW	rS*,fW	uS,cW	rS*,cW	xS,fT,uW	lrS,uS*,cW	xS,uS*,cW	uS*,cW
Ruddy Duck	fT,rW	xS*,fT,rW	xS*,fT,uW	rS*,cW	rS*,cW	xS*,rW	xS*,rT,xW	uT	lrS,fT,uW	eS,fT,uW	xS*,fT,uW
Masked Duck		xV	xV		xV-q				exV		

Order Falconiformes: Diurnal Birds of Prey
Family Cathartidae: American Vultures

	West Virginia	Kentucky	Tennessee	Mississippi	Alabama	Maine	New Hampshire	Vermont	Massachusetts	Rhode Island	Connecticut
Black Vulture	fS,uW	fS,uW	fP	cP	cP	rV	exV-q	xV	rV,xW	xV	rV
Turkey Vulture	cS,uW	cS,uW	cS,fW	cP	cP	uS	fS	fS,rW	uS,fT,rW	fS,rW	fS,rW
California Condor											

Family Accipitridae: Kites, Eagles, Hawks and Allies
Subfamily Pandioninae: Ospreys

	West Virginia	Kentucky	Tennessee	Mississippi	Alabama	Maine	New Hampshire	Vermont	Massachusetts	Rhode Island	Connecticut
Osprey	rS,fT	xS,fT,xW	rS,fT	uS,fT,rW	uS,fT,rW	fS,cT	rS,fT	rS,fT	uS,cT	fS,cT,xW	fS,cT,xW

Subfamily Accipitrinae: Kites, Eagles, Hawks and Allies

	West Virginia	Kentucky	Tennessee	Mississippi	Alabama	Maine	New Hampshire	Vermont	Massachusetts	Rhode Island	Connecticut
Hook-billed Kite											
Am. Swallow-tld. Kite	exV	eS	eS†,xV	uS	uS		xV	xV	xV	xV	xV
Black-shouldered Kite				xP	xV				exV		
Snail Kite											
Mississippi Kite		xS,luS*,xV	lfS	fS	fS		xV-q		xS*,xV		
Bald Eagle	lrS,uT,rW	lrS,uW	eS,uW	lrS,uW	lrS,uW	uP	eS,uP*	eS,rP*	eS,rS*,uW	eS†,rS*,uW	eS,rS*,uW
White-tailed Eagle									exV,xW		
Steller's Sea-Eagle											

Anatidae • 91

	New York	Pennsylvania	New Jersey	Delaware	Maryland	Dist. of Columbia	Virginia	North Carolina	South Carolina	Georgia	Florida
Bufflehead	rS*,cW	rS*,cW	rS*,cW	xS*,cW	rS*,cW	uW	rS*,cW	rS*,cW	xS*,cW	xS*,fW	xS*,fW
Smew	xW										
Hooded Merganser	fS,uW	uS,fT,uW	rS,fT,uW	fT,uW	rS,fT,uW	rW	rS,fW	rS,fW	rS,fW	rS,fW	lrS,uW
Common Merganser	uS,fW	xS,fW	xS,fW	fT,uW	fW	fW	xS,fW	exS,uW	rW	rW	rW
Red-breasted Merganser	rS,cT,fW	xS,fW	xS,cW	rS*,cW	rS*,cT,fW	fW	rS*,cW	rS*,cW	rS*,cW	rS*,cW	rS*,cW
Ruddy Duck	rS,uW	rS,fT,uW	lrS,rS*,fW	xS*,cT,fW	xS*,cT,fW	uW	rS*,cW	rS*,cW	xS,rS*,cW	rS*,cW	xS,cW
Masked Duck		xV			exV			xW		xV	rP*

Order Falconiformes: Diurnal Birds of Prey
Family Cathartidae: American Vultures

	New York	Pennsylvania	New Jersey	Delaware	Maryland	Dist. of Columbia	Virginia	North Carolina	South Carolina	Georgia	Florida
Black Vulture	rV	uP	uP	uP	fP	fP	fP	fP	cP	cP	cP
Turkey Vulture	fS,rW	cS,fW	cS,fW	cP	cP	cP	cP	cP	cP	cP	cP
California Condor											

Family Accipitridae: Kites, Eagles, Hawks and Allies
Subfamily Pandioninae: Ospreys

	New York	Pennsylvania	New Jersey	Delaware	Maryland	Dist. of Columbia	Virginia	North Carolina	South Carolina	Georgia	Florida
Osprey	fS,cT,xW	xS,rS*,fT	fS2,cT,xW	fS,cT	fS,cT,xW	rS*,uT	fS,cT,rW	fS,cT,rW	fS,cT,uW	fS,cT,uW	fS,cT,fW

Subfamily Accipitrinae: Kites, Eagles, Hawks and Allies

	New York	Pennsylvania	New Jersey	Delaware	Maryland	Dist. of Columbia	Virginia	North Carolina	South Carolina	Georgia	Florida
Hook-billed Kite											
Am. Swallow-tld. Kite	rV	xV	xS*,rV	xV	xV		xV	rV	rS	uS	fS
Black-shouldered Kite	xV							xV-q	xV,xW	xV	eS,rV
Snail Kite											luP,xV
Mississippi Kite	xV	exV	xS*,rV	xV			xV	lrS*	uS	fS	fS
Bald Eagle	rS,uW	lrS,rS*,uW	lrS,rS*,uW	rS,uW	uP	eS,uW	luS,uP*	lrS,uP*	lrS,rS*,uW	lrS,rS*,uW	fP
White-tailed Eagle											
Steller's Sea-Eagle											

Accipitridae • 93

	Date	Location	Cont. North America	Canada	Lower 48
Northern Harrier *Circus cyaneus*			cP	cS,rW	cP
Sharp-shinned Hawk *Accipiter striatus*			fS,cT,fW	fS,uW	uS,cT,fW
Cooper's Hawk *Accipiter cooperii*			uP	uS,rW	uP
Northern Goshawk *Accipiter gentilis*			uP	uP	uP
Common Black-Hawk *Buteogallus anthracinus*			luS,rV,lrW		luS,rV,lrW
Harris' Hawk *Parabuteo unicinctus*			lfP,xS,xV,rW		lfP,xS,xV,rW
Gray Hawk *Buteo nitidus*			luS,xV,lrW		luS,xV,lrW
Roadside Hawk *Buteo magnirostris*			xV,xW		xV,xW
Red-shouldered Hawk *Buteo lineatus*			fP	luS,xV,lrW	cP
Broad-winged Hawk *Buteo platypterus*			fS,cT,luW	cS	fS,cT,luW
Short-tailed Hawk *Buteo brachyurus*			luP,xV,xW		luP,xV,xW
Swainson's Hawk *Buteo swainsoni*			cS,lrW	cS,xW	cS,lrW
White-tailed Hawk *Buteo albicaudatus*			lfP,exS*,xV,xW		lfP,exS*,xV,xW
Zone-tailed Hawk *Buteo albonotatus*			luS,xS,rV,lrW		luS,xS,rV,lrW
Hawaiian Hawk *Buteo solitarius*					
Red-tailed Hawk *Buteo jamaicensis*			cP	cS,uW	cP
Common Buzzard *Buteo buteo*			xV		
Ferruginous Hawk *Buteo regalis*			fP	lfS	fP
Rough-legged Hawk *Buteo lagopus*			icP	icS,ifW	icW
Golden Eagle *Aquila chrysaetos*			fP	fS,uW	fP

Family Falconidae: Caracaras and Falcons

	Date	Location	Cont. North America	Canada	Lower 48
Crested Caracara *Polyborus plancus*			luP,xS,rV,xW		luP,xS,rV,xW
Eurasian Kestrel *Falco tinnunculus*			xV	xV	xV
American Kestrel *Falco sparverius*			cP	cS,rW	cP

94 • *Distributional Checklist of North American Birds*

	Hawaii	Alaska	Yukon Terr.	Northwest Terr.	British Columbia	Alberta	Saskatchewan	Manitoba	Ontario
Northern Harrier	xV	fS.rW	cS.xW	fS	cS.uW	cS.rW	cS.xW	cS.xW	cS.rW
Sharp-shinned Hawk		fS.uW	fS	uS	fS.uW	fS.xW	fS.rW	fS	fS.cT.rW
Cooper's Hawk					uS.luW	uS.xW	uS.xW	uS	rS.uT.rW
Northern Goshawk		fP	fS.uW	fS.rW	uP	uP	uP	uP	uP
Common Black-Hawk									
Harris' Hawk									
Gray Hawk									
Roadside Hawk									
Red-shouldered Hawk									
Broad-winged Hawk					xV		xV-q	xV	uS.rW
Short-tailed Hawk				xV	lrS*.xV	uS	fS	fS	cS
Swainson's Hawk		lrS	luS	lrS.xV	uS	cS	cS.xW	luS	xV
White-tailed Hawk									
Zone-tailed Hawk									
Hawaiian Hawk	fP								
Red-tailed Hawk		fS.xW	cS.xW	uS	cS.fW	cS.rW	cS.rW	cS.rW	cS.fW
Common Buzzard		xV-q							
Ferruginous Hawk					xS	uS	fS	lrS.rV	
Rough-legged Hawk		icS.xW	icS.xW	icS.xW	ifW	cT.iuW	cT.iuW	luS.cT.iuW	lrS.fT.ifW
Golden Eagle	xP*	fS.uW	fS.rW	uS.xW	fS.uW	uS.fT.uW	uP	rP	rP

Family Falconidae: Caracaras and Falcons

	Hawaii	Alaska	Yukon Terr.	Northwest Terr.	British Columbia	Alberta	Saskatchewan	Manitoba	Ontario
Crested Caracara									
Eurasian Kestrel		xV				xV			
American Kestrel		cS.xW	cS	fS	cS.uW	cS.xW	cS.xW	cS.rW	cS.uW

Accipitridae

	Québec	Newfoundland	New Brunswick	Prince Edward I.	Nova Scotia		Washington	Oregon	California	Nevada	Idaho
Northern Harrier	fS.rW	uS	fS.rW	fS	fS.rW		cP	cP	fS.cW	cP	cS.fW
Sharp-shinned Hawk	fS.rW	uS.fT.luW	fS.cT.uW	uS.fT.uW	fS.cT.uW		uS.fW	uS.fW	uS.cW	uS.fW	uS.fT.uW
Cooper's Hawk	lrS.xW	xV.xW	xS.rT.xW		eS.rT.xW		uP	uS.fW	uS.fW	uS.fT.uW	uP
Northern Goshawk	uP	uP	uP	rP	uP		uP	uP	uP	uP	uP
Common Black-Hawk										xS*.xV	
Harris' Hawk									lrP1	xV	
Gray Hawk											
Roadside Hawk											
Red-shouldered Hawk	luS.xW		rS		xS*.rT.xW		xW	exS.lrP*.rV.xW	fP		lrP
Broad-winged Hawk	fS		fS		uS.fT		xV-q	xV	rV.rW	xV	xV
Short-tailed Hawk											
Swainson's Hawk	xV				xV-q		uS	uS	uS.xW	fS	fS
White-tailed Hawk											
Zone-tailed Hawk									xS.rV.xW	xV	
Hawaiian Hawk											
Red-tailed Hawk	fS.rW	xS.xV.xW	fS.uW	uS.rW	uS.fW		cP	cP	cP	cP	cS.fW
Common Buzzard											
Ferruginous Hawk							rS.xW	uS.rW	xS*.uW	fS.uW	fS.rW
Rough-legged Hawk	ifS.fT.iuW	ifS.iuW	fT.ifW	fT.ifW	xS.iuW		ifW	ifW	ifW	icW	cT.ifW
Golden Eagle	rP	rS.xW	xS*.rW	exT	xS*.rW		uP	uP	uP	fP	fP

Family Falconidae: Caracaras and Falcons

	Québec	Newfoundland	New Brunswick	Prince Edward I.	Nova Scotia		Washington	Oregon	California	Nevada	Idaho
Crested Caracara											
Eurasian Kestrel											
American Kestrel	cS.rW	luS.xW	cS.rW	cS.rW	cS.uW		cP	cP	cP	cS.fW	cS.fW

	Montana	Wyoming	Utah	Colorado	Arizona	New Mexico	North Dakota	South Dakota	Nebraska	Kansas	Oklahoma
Northern Harrier	cS,uW	cS,uW	cS,fW	fS,cT,fW	xS,rS*,cW	uS,cW	fS,cT,rW	fS,cT,uW	uS,cT,fW	uS,cW	uS,cW
Sharp-shinned Hawk	uS,fT,uW	uS,fT,uW	uS,fW	uS,fT,uW	uS,cW	uS,fW	xS,fT,rW	rS,fT,rW	rS,fT,uW	lrS,fT,uW	eS,fT,uW
Cooper's Hawk	uS,rW	uP	uS,fT,uW	uP	uS,fW	uS,fW	rS,uT,rW	rS,uT,rW	rS,uT,rW	rS,uT,rW	rS,uW
Northern Goshawk	uP	uP	uP	uP	rP	rP	xS,uW	lrS,iuW	iuW	irW	irW
Common Black-Hawk			xS,rV	xV	uS	lrS					
Harris' Hawk					luP	luP			exV	xS,exV	xV,rW
Gray Hawk					luS,xW	xV					
Roadside Hawk											
Red-shouldered Hawk	xV		xV,xW	rV,xW	xS,xV,xW	xV	xV	xV	xS,rT,xW	uS,rW	fP
Broad-winged Hawk	rV	rV	rV	xS,rV	rV,xW	rV	luS,uT	xS,uT	lrS,uT	luS,uT	uS,fT
Short-tailed Hawk											
Swainson's Hawk	cS	cS	fS	fS,cT	fS	fS,cT	cS	cS	fS,cT	fS,cT	fS,cT
White-tailed Hawk					exS*,xW	xV					
Zone-tailed Hawk			xV-q		uS,xW	uS,xW					
Hawaiian Hawk											
Red-tailed Hawk	cS,uW	cS,fW	cP	cP	cP	cP	cS,rW	cS,uW	cP	cP	cP
Common Buzzard											
Ferruginous Hawk	fS,xW	fS,rW	fS,uW	fS,uW	uS,fW	uS,fW	fS	uS,rW	uS,rW	luS,uW	lrS,uW
Rough-legged Hawk	cT,ifW	icW	icW	icW	iuW	iuW	cT,iuW	cT,ifW	icW	ifW	iuW
Golden Eagle	fP	fP	fP	fP	uP	uP	uS,rW	uP	uP	lrS,uW	luS,uW

Family Falconidae: Caracaras and Falcons

	Montana	Wyoming	Utah	Colorado	Arizona	New Mexico	North Dakota	South Dakota	Nebraska	Kansas	Oklahoma
Crested Caracara					luP,rV,xW	xS,xV,xW					xV-q
Eurasian Kestrel											
American Kestrel	cS,uW	cS,uW	cS,fW	cS,fW	cP	cP	cS,rW	cS,uW	cS,fW	cP	uS,cW

	Texas	Minnesota	Iowa	Missouri	Arkansas	Louisiana	Wisconsin	Michigan	Illinois	Indiana	Ohio
Northern Harrier	uS,cW	fS,cT,rW	rS,cT,uW	rS,cT,fW	rS,cW	xS*,cW	fS,cT,rW	uS,fT,rW	rS,cT,fW	rS,fT,uW	rS,fT,uW
Sharp-shinned Hawk	lrS,fT,uW	uS,cT,rW	xS,fT,uW	xS,fT,uW	eS,rS*,fT,uW	fT,uW	uS,cT,rW	uS,cT,rW	xS,fT,uW	rS,fT,uW	rS,fT,uW
Cooper's Hawk	rS,uW	uS,rW	rS,uT,rW	rS,uW	eS,rS*,uW	rS,uW	uS,rW	rS,uT,rW	rS,uW	rS,uW	rS,uW
Northern Goshawk	irW	uP	iuW	irW	xV,xW	xV	uP	uP	iuW	iuW	irW
Common Black-Hawk	lrP,rV										
Harris' Hawk	fP										exV
Gray Hawk	lrP,xV										
Roadside Hawk	xV,xW										
Red-shouldered Hawk	cP	uS,rW	uS,rW	fP	fP	cP	uS,rW	uS,rW	uP	uP	uP
Broad-winged Hawk	uS,cT,xW	cS	uS,cT,xW	fS,cT	fS,cT	fS,cT	cS	fS,cT	uS,cT	uS,cT	uS,cT
Short-tailed Hawk	xV,xW-q										
Swainson's Hawk	fS,cT,xW	fS	lrS,rT	eS,xS*,rT	xS*,rT	rT	rT	rV	lrS,rT	xV-q	xV
White-tailed Hawk	lfP,xV					exV					
Zone-tailed Hawk	rS,xW					xV					
Hawaiian Hawk											
Red-tailed Hawk	cP	cS,uW	cP	cP	cP	fS,cW	cS,fW	cS,fW	fS,cW	fS,cW	fS,cW
Common Buzzard											
Ferruginous Hawk	lrS,fW	rV,xW	rV	rV,xW	xV	xV,xW	xV,xW	xV,xW-q	rV,xW	xV,xW	
Rough-legged Hawk	iuW	fT,ifW	ifW	ifW	irW	irW	fT,ifW	fT,ifW	ifW	ifW	ifW
Golden Eagle	luS,uW	rW	rW	rW	rW	rW	rW	rW	rW	rT,xW	rT,xW

Family Falconidae: Caracaras and Falcons

	Texas	Minnesota	Iowa	Missouri	Arkansas	Louisiana	Wisconsin	Michigan	Illinois	Indiana	Ohio
Crested Caracara	uP					lrP					
Eurasian Kestrel											
American Kestrel	uS,cW	cS,uW	fS,cT,fW	fS,cW	fS,cW	uS,cW	cS,uW	cS,uW	fS,cW	fS,cT,fW	fS,cT,fW

98 • *Distributional Checklist of North American Birds*

	West Virginia	Kentucky	Tennessee	Mississippi	Alabama	Maine	New Hampshire	Vermont	Massachusetts	Rhode Island	Connecticut
Northern Harrier	rS,fT,uW	eS,xS*,fW	rS*,fW	xS*,fW	xS*,fW	fS,cT,rW	uS,fT,xW	uS,fT,rW	uS,cT,uW	IuS,cT,fW	eS,rS*,cT,fW
Sharp-shinned Hawk	uS,cT,uW	rS,fT,uW	rS,fW	rS*,fT,uW	rS,fW	fS,cT,uW	uS,cT,uW	uS,cT,rW	rS,cT,uW	rS,cT,uW	rS,cT,uW
Cooper's Hawk	uS,fT,uW	rS,uW	rS,uW	rS,uW	rS,uW	rS,uT,rW	rS,uT,rW	uS,rW	rS,uT,rW	rS,uT,rW	rS,uT,rW
Northern Goshawk	xS,uW	irW	irW		xV,xW	uP	uP	uP	uP	rS,uW	uP
Common Black-Hawk											
Harris' Hawk				xV							
Gray Hawk											
Roadside Hawk											
Red-shouldered Hawk	fS,uW	uP	fP	cP	cP	uS,rW	uS,rW	uS,xW	uS,rW	uS,rW	uP
Broad-winged Hawk	fS,cT	uS,cT	fS,cT	fS,cT	fS,cT,xW	fS	fS,cT	fS,cT	fS,cT	fS,cT	fS,cT
Short-tailed Hawk											
Swainson's Hawk	exV		xV-q	xV	rV,xW	xV	xV-q	xV	rV,xW	xV	xV-q
White-tailed Hawk											
Zone-tailed Hawk											
Hawaiian Hawk											
Red-tailed Hawk	fS,cT,fW	fS,cW	fS,cW	fS,cW	fS,cW	fS,uW	fS,uW	fS,uW	fP	fS,cW	fS,cW
Common Buzzard											
Ferruginous Hawk				xV							
Rough-legged Hawk	ifW	iuW	iuW	xV,xW	irW	fT,ifW	ifW	ifW	ifW	iuW	ifW
Golden Eagle	lrS,rW	xS*,rW	xS*,rW	xV,xW	rW	xS,rW	xS*,rT	rT,xW	rW	rW	rT,xW

Family Falconidae: Caracaras and Falcons

	West Virginia	Kentucky	Tennessee	Mississippi	Alabama	Maine	New Hampshire	Vermont	Massachusetts	Rhode Island	Connecticut
Crested Caracara				xV							
Eurasian Kestrel										exV	
American Kestrel	fS,cW	fS,cW	fS,cW	uS,cW	fS,cW	cS,uW	cS,uW	cS,uW	fS,cT,uW	fS,cT,fW	cS,fW

Accipitridae • 99

	New York	Pennsylvania	New Jersey	Delaware	Maryland	Dist. of Columbia	Virginia	North Carolina	South Carolina	Georgia	Florida
Northern Harrier	fS.cT.uW	uS.cT.uW	uS.cT.fW	rS.cT.fW	rS.cT.fW	uT.rW	luS.rS*.cW	lrS.rS*.cW	rS*.cW	rS*.cW	eS.rS*.cW
Sharp-shinned Hawk	uS.cT.uW	uS.cT.fW	rS.cT.fW	xS*.cT.fW	rS.cT.fW	fT.uW	uS.cT.fW	rS.cT.fW	lrS.cT.fW	lrS.cT.fW	cT.fW
Cooper's Hawk	uP	uS.fT.uW	rS.fT.uW	rS.uW	rS.uW	uT.rW	rS.uW	rS.uW	rS.uW	rS.uW	xS.uW
Northern Goshawk	uP	rS.uW	rS.uT.rW	rW	xS.rW	rT.xW	rW	xS*.rW		xW	xV
Common Black-Hawk											
Harris' Hawk											
Gray Hawk											
Roadside Hawk											
Red-shouldered Hawk	uS.rW	uS.fT.uW	uS.fT.uW	uS.fT.uW	fP	uP	fP	fP	fP	cP	cP
Broad-winged Hawk	fS.cT.xW	fS.cT.xW	fS.cT	fS.cT	uS.cT	uS.fT	fS.cT.xW	fS	uS.fT	uS.fT	luS.fT.uW
Short-tailed Hawk											uP
Swainson's Hawk	xV	xV	rV		xV-q		xV	xV-q	xV		uV.rW
White-tailed Hawk											
Zone-tailed Hawk											
Hawaiian Hawk											
Red-tailed Hawk	cS.fW	cP	fS.cW	fS.cW	fS.cW	fW	cP	cP	fS.cW	fS.cW	fS.cW
Common Buzzard											
Ferruginous Hawk			xV-q				xV-q				xV.xW
Rough-legged Hawk	fT.ifW	ifW	ifW	iuW	iuW	rT.xW	iuW	irW	irW	irW	rV.rW
Golden Eagle	lrS.rW	lrS*.uT.rW	rW	rW	rW		xS*.rW	lrS*.rW	rW	rW	rW

Family Falconidae: Caracaras and Falcons

	New York	Pennsylvania	New Jersey	Delaware	Maryland	Dist. of Columbia	Virginia	North Carolina	South Carolina	Georgia	Florida
Crested Caracara										xV	uP
Eurasian Kestrel			xV								
American Kestrel	cS.fW	fS.cW	fS.cT.fW	uS.cW	uS.cW	uS.fT.uW	fS.cW	uS.cW	uS.cW	uS.cW	uS.cW

	Date	Location	Cont. North America	Canada	Lower 48
Merlin *Falco columbarius*			uP	fS,rW	rS,uW
Aplomado Falcon *Falco femoralis*			eP,xV,xW		eP,xV,xW
Northern Hobby *Falco subbuteo*			xV		
Peregrine Falcon *Falco peregrinus*			rP2	rP	rS2,uT,rW
Gyrfalcon *Falco rusticolus*			uS,rW	uS,rW	irW
Prairie Falcon *Falco mexicanus*			uP	luS,lrW	fP

Order Galliformes: Gallinaceous Birds
Family Cracidae: Curassows and Guans

Plain Chachalaca *Ortalis vetula*			lcP		lcP

Family Phasianidae: Partridges, Grouse, Turkeys and Quail
Subfamily Tetraoninae: Grouse

Spruce Grouse *Dendragapus canadensis*			fP	fP	luP
Blue Grouse *Dendragapus obscurus*			fP	fP	fP
Willow Ptarmigan *Lagopus lagopus*			cP	cP	xV,eW
Rock Ptarmigan *Lagopus mutus*			fP	fP	
White-tailed Ptarmigan *Lagopus leucurus*			lfP	lfP	lfP
Ruffed Grouse *Bonasa umbellus*			cP	cP	fP
Sage Grouse *Centrocercus urophasianus*			lfP	luP	fP
Greater Prairie-Chicken *Tympanuchus cupido*			lfP2	eP	lfP2
Lesser Prairie-Chicken *Tympanuchus pallidicinctus*			luP		luP
Sharp-tailed Grouse *Tympanuchus phasianellus*			cP	cP	fP

Subfamily Meleagridinae: Turkeys

Wild Turkey *Meleagris gallopavo*			fP2	lrP1	fP2

102 • Distributional Checklist of North American Birds

	Hawaii	Alaska	Yukon Terr.	Northwest Terr.	British Columbia	Alberta	Saskatchewan	Manitoba	Ontario
Merlin		uS,rW	uS	uS	uS,fT,uW	fS,rW	fS,rW	uS,rW	uS,rW
Aplomado Falcon									
Northern Hobby		xV							
Peregrine Falcon	rV,xW	uS,rW	uS	rS	uP	rS2,rT,xW	eS†,rT,xW	eS,rP*	eS,rT,xW
Gyrfalcon		uP	uP	uS,rW	lrS,irW	irW	irW	irW	irW
Prairie Falcon					uS,rW	uS,rW	uS,rW	rP*	

Order Galliformes: Gallinaceous Birds
Family Cracidae: Curassows and Guans

	Hawaii	Alaska	Yukon Terr.	Northwest Terr.	British Columbia	Alberta	Saskatchewan	Manitoba	Ontario
Plain Chachalaca									

Family Phasianidae: Partridges, Grouse, Turkeys and Quail
Subfamily Tetraoninae: Grouse

	Hawaii	Alaska	Yukon Terr.	Northwest Terr.	British Columbia	Alberta	Saskatchewan	Manitoba	Ontario
Spruce Grouse		fP	fP	fP	fP	fP	fP	uP	uP
Blue Grouse		lfP	uP		fP	luP			
Willow Ptarmigan		cP	cP	cP	uS,ifW	luS,iuW	ifW	luS,ifW	luS,ifW
Rock Ptarmigan		fP	fP	fP	uP		xW	uW	lrW
White-tailed Ptarmigan		uP	fP	luP	fP	luP			
Ruffed Grouse		fP	fP	fP	cP	cP	cP	fP	fP
Sage Grouse					eP	luP	luP		
Greater Prairie-Chicken						eP	eP	eP	eP
Lesser Prairie-Chicken									
Sharp-tailed Grouse		fP	uP	fP	uP	fP	cP	cP	uP

Subfamily Meleagridinae: Turkeys

	Hawaii	Alaska	Yukon Terr.	Northwest Terr.	British Columbia	Alberta	Saskatchewan	Manitoba	Ontario
Wild Turkey									lrP1

Falconidae • 103

	Québec	Newfound-land	New Brunswick	Prince Edward I.	Nova Scotia		Washington	Oregon	California	Nevada	Idaho
Merlin	uS.rW	fS.rW	rS.fT.rW	rS.uT.xW	rS.fT.uW		rS.fT.uW	xS.uW	uW	uW	rS.uT.rW
Aplomado Falcon											
Northern Hobby											
Peregrine Falcon	lrS2.rT.xW	lrS.uT.xW	rS1.uT.xW	uT	eS.uT.xW		rS.uW	rS.uW	rS2.uW	xS.rT.xW	rS1.rT.xW
Gyrfalcon	luS.irW	luS.uW	irW	rT.xW	irW		irW	xV.xW	xV.xW		irW
Prairie Falcon							uP	uP	uP	fP	fS.uW

Order Galliformes: Gallinaceous Birds
Family Cracidae: Curassows and Guans

Plain Chachalaca											

Family Phasianidae: Partridges, Grouse, Turkeys and Quail
Subfamily Tetraoninae: Grouse

Spruce Grouse	fP	fP2	uP	eP	uP		rP	lrP			uP
Blue Grouse							fP	fP	uP	uP	fP
Willow Ptarmigan	fP	fP			xV						
Rock Ptarmigan	fP	fP			exV						
White-tailed Ptarmigan							luP				xP*
Ruffed Grouse	fP2	fP2	fP	fP	fP		fP	fP	lrP		fP
Sage Grouse							uP	uP	luP	uP	fP
Greater Prairie-Chicken											
Lesser Prairie-Chicken											
Sharp-tailed Grouse	luP						uP	eP	eP	eP	uP

Subfamily Meleagridinae: Turkeys

Wild Turkey											

104 • *Distributional Checklist of North American Birds*

	Montana	Wyoming	Utah	Colorado	Arizona	New Mexico	North Dakota	South Dakota	Nebraska	Kansas	Oklahoma
Merlin	uS,rW	rS,uT,rW	uW	uW	uW	uW	lrS,uT,rW	lrS,uT,rW	lrS,uT,rW	uT,rW	uT,rW
Aplomado Falcon					eP,xV	exS,xV					
Northern Hobby											
Peregrine Falcon	rP	rS1,rT,xW	rP	rS2,rT,xW	rS2,rW	rP	eS,rT,xW	eS,rT,xW	eS,rT,xW	eS,rT,xW	rW
Gyrfalcon	irW	irW	xV,xW	xV,xW			irW	irW	xW	xW	xV,xW
Prairie Falcon	fS,uW	fS,uW	fP	fP	uS,fW	uS,fW	uS,rW	uP	luS,uW	rS*,uW	luS,uW

Order Galliformes: Gallinaceous Birds
Family Cracidae: Curassows and Guans

Plain Chachalaca											

Family Phasianidae: Partridges, Grouse, Turkeys and Quail
Subfamily Tetraoninae: Grouse

	Montana	Wyoming	Utah	Colorado	Arizona	New Mexico	North Dakota	South Dakota	Nebraska	Kansas	Oklahoma
Spruce Grouse	uP										
Blue Grouse	fP	fP	uP	fP	uP2	uP		eP			
Willow Ptarmigan	exW							exV			
Rock Ptarmigan											
White-tailed Ptarmigan	luP	lrP†		fP		luP1					
Ruffed Grouse	fP	fP	uP				lfP	luP	eP	rP1	
Sage Grouse	uP	cP	uP	fP		eP	luP	luP	lrP		eP
Greater Prairie-Chicken	eP	xP*		luP			uP	uP	fP	fP2	luP2
Lesser Prairie-Chicken				luP		luP			eP	luP	luP
Sharp-tailed Grouse	fP	fP	luP	uP		eP	cP	fP	fP	lrP1	eP

Subfamily Meleagridinae: Turkeys

	Montana	Wyoming	Utah	Colorado	Arizona	New Mexico	North Dakota	South Dakota	Nebraska	Kansas	Oklahoma
Wild Turkey				uP1	uP2	uP2		uP1	fP1	fP2	fP2

Falconidae • 105

	Texas	Minnesota	Iowa	Missouri	Arkansas	Louisiana	Wisconsin	Michigan	Illinois	Indiana	Ohio
Merlin	uW	luS.uT.rW	eS.rT.xW	uT.rW	uT.rW	uW	lrS.uT.xW	lrS.uT.rW	rT.xW	rT.xW	eS.rT.xW
Aplomado Falcon	eS.xV.xW										
Northern Hobby											
Peregrine Falcon	lrS.uT.rW	eS.rT.xW	eS.rW	eS.rW	eS.rT.xW	eS.uT.rW	eS.rT.xW	eS.rT.xW	eS.rT.xW	eS.rT.xW	eS†.rT.xW
Gyrfalcon		irW		xV			irW	irW	irW		xV.xW
Prairie Falcon	lrS.uW	rV.xW	rV.xW	exS.rV.xW	xW		xV-q	xV	rV.xW	xW	xW

Order Galliformes: Gallinaceous Birds
Family Cracidae: Curassows and Guans

	Texas	Minnesota	Iowa	Missouri	Arkansas	Louisiana	Wisconsin	Michigan	Illinois	Indiana	Ohio
Plain Chachalaca	lcP										

Family Phasianidae: Partridges, Grouse, Turkeys and Quail
Subfamily Tetraoninae: Grouse

	Texas	Minnesota	Iowa	Missouri	Arkansas	Louisiana	Wisconsin	Michigan	Illinois	Indiana	Ohio
Spruce Grouse		luP					lrP	uP			
Blue Grouse											
Willow Ptarmigan		xV					exV	eW-q			
Rock Ptarmigan											
White-tailed Ptarmigan											
Ruffed Grouse		fP	lfP2	lrP1	lrP1		fP	fP	lrP1	luP	uP
Sage Grouse											
Greater Prairie-Chicken	lrP2	uP2	eP.xV.xW	luP	eP	eP	luP2	lrP1	lrP	eP	eP
Lesser Prairie-Chicken	luP										
Sharp-tailed Grouse	eP	uP	eP†				uP	uP2	eP		

Subfamily Meleagridinae: Turkeys

	Texas	Minnesota	Iowa	Missouri	Arkansas	Louisiana	Wisconsin	Michigan	Illinois	Indiana	Ohio
Wild Turkey	fP2		uP1	uP2	fP	uP2	uP1	uP1	uP1	uP1	uP1

	West Virginia	Kentucky	Tennessee	Mississippi	Alabama	Maine	New Hampshire	Vermont	Massachusetts	Rhode Island	Connecticut
Merlin	rT	rT,xW	rT,xW	rW	uW	rS*,fT,rW	uT,xW	uT,rW	uT,rW	uT,rW	uT,rW
Aplomado Falcon											
Northern Hobby											
Peregrine Falcon	eS,rT	eS,rT,xW	eS,rW	uT,rW	eS,uT,rW	lrS1,uT,rW	rS1,uT,xW	eS,rT,xW	eS,uT,rW	xS,uT,rW	eS,uT,rW
Gyrfalcon						irW	irW	irW	irW	irW	irW
Prairie Falcon			xV-q		xW						

Order Galliformes: Gallinaceous Birds
Family Cracidae: Curassows and Guans

Plain Chachalaca											

Family Phasianidae: Partridges, Grouse, Turkeys and Quail
Subfamily Tetraoninae: Grouse

	West Virginia	Kentucky	Tennessee	Mississippi	Alabama	Maine	New Hampshire	Vermont	Massachusetts	Rhode Island	Connecticut
Spruce Grouse						uP	luP	lrP			
Blue Grouse											
Willow Ptarmigan						xV					
Rock Ptarmigan											
White-tailed Ptarmigan											
Ruffed Grouse	fP	uP	luP			lrP1	cP	cP	cP	fP	fP	fP
Sage Grouse											
Greater Prairie-Chicken		eP	eP						eP	eP	eP
Lesser Prairie-Chicken											
Sharp-tailed Grouse											

Subfamily Meleagridinae: Turkeys

Wild Turkey	fP	uP2	uP	fP	fP	luP1	luP1	uP1	uP1	lrP1	uP1

Falconidae • 107

	New York	Pennsylvania	New Jersey	Delaware	Maryland	Dist. of Columbia	Virginia	North Carolina	South Carolina	Georgia	Florida
Merlin	xS*,uT,rW	xS*,uT,rW	uT,rW	uT,rW	uT,rW	rT,xW	uW	uW	uW	uW	uW
Aplomado Falcon											
Northern Hobby											
Peregrine Falcon	rS1,uT,rW	eS,uT,rW	lrS1,uT,rW	uT,rW	rS1,uT,rW	rT,xW	lrS1,uW	eS,uW	eS,uT,rW	eS,uW	uW
Gyrfalcon	irW	irW	irW	xV			xW				
Prairie Falcon								xV-q	xV	xV,xW	

Order Galliformes: Gallinaceous Birds
Family Cracidae: Curassows and Guans

Plain Chachalaca											

Family Phasianidae: Partridges, Grouse, Turkeys and Quail
Subfamily Tetraoninae: Grouse

	New York	Pennsylvania	New Jersey	Delaware	Maryland	Dist. of Columbia	Virginia	North Carolina	South Carolina	Georgia	Florida
Spruce Grouse	luP										
Blue Grouse											
Willow Ptarmigan											
Rock Ptarmigan											
White-tailed Ptarmigan											
Ruffed Grouse	fP	fP	uP		fP	eP	lfP	fP	luP	luP	
Sage Grouse											
Greater Prairie-Chicken	eP	eP	eP		eP	eP					
Lesser Prairie-Chicken											
Sharp-tailed Grouse											

Subfamily Meleagridinae: Turkeys

	New York	Pennsylvania	New Jersey	Delaware	Maryland	Dist. of Columbia	Virginia	North Carolina	South Carolina	Georgia	Florida
Wild Turkey	uP1	uP2	uP1	eP	uP2	eP,rP*2	uP	uP	uP	fP	fP

Phasianidae • 109

Subfamily Odontophorinae: Quail

	Date	Location	Cont. North America	Canada	Lower 48
Montezuma Quail *Cyrtonyx montezumae*			luP		luP
Northern Bobwhite *Colinus virginianus*			cP2	luP2	cP2
Scaled Quail *Callipepla squamata*			lcP		lcP
Gambel's Quail *Callipepla gambelii*			lcP		lcP
California Quail *Callipepla californica*			lcP2		lcP2
Mountain Quail *Oreortyx pictus*			lfP		lfP

Order Gruiformes: Cranes, Rails and Allies
Family Rallidae: Rails, Gallinules and Coots
Subfamily Rallinae: Rails, Gallinules and Coots

	Date	Location	Cont. North America	Canada	Lower 48
Yellow Rail *Coturnicops noveboracensis*			uS,luW	uS	luS,rT,luW
Black Rail *Laterallus jamaicensis*			luS,rT,luW		uS,luW
Corn Crake *Crex crex*			erV	exV	erV
Clapper Rail *Rallus longirostris*			cP	rV	cP
King Rail *Rallus elegans*			uP	lrS,xV,xW	fP
Virginia Rail *Rallus limicola*			fS,uW	fS,lrW	fP
Sora *Porzana carolina*			fS,uW	cS,lrW	fS,cT,fW
Hawaiian Rail *Porzana sandwichensis*					
Laysan Rail *Porzana palmeri*					
Paint-billed Crake *Neocrex erythrops*			xV,xW		xV,xW
Spotted Rail *Pardirallus maculatus*			xV		xV
Purple Gallinule *Porphyrula martinica*			lfP,xS,rV	xS*,rV,xW	uS,lfW
Common Moorhen *Gallinula chloropus*			fP	luS,rV,xW	fP
Eurasian Coot *Fulica atra*			xV	exV	
American Coot *Fulica americana*			cP	cS,uW	cP
Caribbean Coot *Fulica caribaea*			rV,rW		rV,rW

Subfamily Odontophorinae: Quail

	Hawaii	Alaska	Yukon Terr.	Northwest Terr.	British Columbia	Alberta	Saskatchewan	Manitoba	Ontario
Montezuma Quail									
Northern Bobwhite									IuP2
Scaled Quail									
Gambel's Quail									
California Quail									
Mountain Quail									

Order Gruiformes: Cranes, Rails and Allies
Family Rallidae: Rails, Gallinules and Coots
Subfamily Rallinae: Rails, Gallinules and Coots

	Hawaii	Alaska	Yukon Terr.	Northwest Terr.	British Columbia	Alberta	Saskatchewan	Manitoba	Ontario
Yellow Rail		xV-q			lrS	rS	rS	uS	uS
Black Rail									
Corn Crake				exV					
Clapper Rail									
King Rail								exV	lrS,xV,xW
Virginia Rail				xV	luS,lrW	uS	fS	fS	fS,lrW
Sora		lrS	rS	fS	fS,lrW	fS	cS	cS	fS,xW
Hawaiian Rail	E†								
Laysan Rail	E								
Paint-billed Crake									
Spotted Rail									
Purple Gallinule									xS*,rV
Common Moorhen	fP				xV			xV	uS,xW
Eurasian Coot		xV							
American Coot	cP	lrS,rV,xW	rS	luS,xV	cS,fW	cS,rW	cS,rW	cS	fS,rW
Caribbean Coot									

Subfamily Odontophorinae: Quail

	Québec	Newfoundland	New Brunswick	Prince Edward I.	Nova Scotia	Washington	Oregon	California	Nevada	Idaho
Montezuma Quail										
Northern Bobwhite										
Scaled Quail										
Gambel's Quail									cP	lcP
California Quail				/			cP1	cP2		
Mountain Quail						uP2	fP	fP	luP	uP

Order Gruiformes: Cranes, Rails and Allies
Family Rallidae: Rails, Gallinules and Coots
Subfamily Rallinae: Rails, Gallinules and Coots

	Québec	Newfoundland	New Brunswick	Prince Edward I.	Nova Scotia	Washington	Oregon	California	Nevada	Idaho
Yellow Rail	rS	xV	rS		xS*,rV	xV	lrS,exW	eP,xV,xW	xV	xV
Black Rail							uP			
Corn Crake		exV			exV					
Clapper Rail		xV	xV	xV	rV			uP		
King Rail	xV	xV	xV							
Virginia Rail	lfS	xS,xV	uS	uS†	uS,rW	fS,uW	fP	fP	uS,fT,uW	fS,xW
Sora	fS	luS,xW	uS	uS	uS,xW	fS,rW	fS,rW	fP	fS,rW	fS,xW
Hawaiian Rail										
Laysan Rail										
Paint-billed Crake										
Spotted Rail										
Purple Gallinule	xV	rV,xW	rV,xW		rV,xW			xV	xV	
Common Moorhen	luS,xV	rV	lrS,rV	xV	xS,rV		xV	fP	luS,lrW	xV
Eurasian Coot		exV								
American Coot	luS,xV,xW	rV,xW	luS,xW	xS,rT	luS,uT,rW	cP	cP	cP	cS,fW	fS,cT,fW
Caribbean Coot										

Subfamily Odontophorinae: Quail

	Montana	Wyoming	Utah	Colorado	Arizona	New Mexico	North Dakota	South Dakota	Nebraska	Kansas	Oklahoma
Montezuma Quail					uP	uP					
Northern Bobwhite		luP1		fP1	lrP1	luP2		uP2	fP2	cP2	cP2
Scaled Quail				fP	lfP	cP				lfP	lfP
Gambel's Quail			cP	fP	cP	cP2					
California Quail											
Mountain Quail											

Order Gruiformes: Cranes, Rails and Allies
Family Rallidae: Rails, Gallinules and Coots
Subfamily Rallinae: Rails, Gallinules and Coots

	Montana	Wyoming	Utah	Colorado	Arizona	New Mexico	North Dakota	South Dakota	Nebraska	Kansas	Oklahoma
Yellow Rail	xS*,xV	xV		xV	exV	xV	rS	xS*,xT	xS*,rT	xT	xT
Black Rail				xV	lfS,xV,lrW	xV	xV-q		xS,xT	rS	xS,xT
Corn Crake											
Clapper Rail					lfS,lrW				xV		
King Rail				xV			xS*	xS	rS	uS	rS,xW
Virginia Rail	fS,xW	fS,xW	fS,uW	fS,rW	uS,fW	uS,fT,uW	fS	uS,fT,xW	uS,fT	uS,fT,xW	uS,fT,rW
Sora	fS,xW	fS	fS,rW	fS,rW	fP	fS,uW	cS	cS	fS	luS,fT	rS*,fT,xW
Hawaiian Rail											
Laysan Rail											
Paint-billed Crake											
Spotted Rail											
Purple Gallinule			xV	xV	xS*,rV	xS*,xV			xV	xV	lrS
Common Moorhen	xV	xV	luS,lrW	xV	fP	fS,uW	xV-q	xV	lrS	luS	uS
Eurasian Coot											
American Coot	cS,rW	cS,uW	cS,fW	cS,fW	cP	cP	cS,xW	cS,rW	cS,rW	fS,cT,uW	uS,cT,fW
Caribbean Coot											

Subfamily Odontophorinae: Quail

	Texas	Minnesota	Iowa	Missouri	Arkansas	Louisiana	Wisconsin	Michigan	Illinois	Indiana	Ohio
Montezuma Quail	lrP										
Northern Bobwhite	cP2	lrP2	fP2	cP	cP	cP	uP2	uP2	fP2	fP2	uP2
Scaled Quail	cP										
Gambel's Quail	lfP										
California Quail											
Mountain Quail											

Order Gruiformes: Cranes, Rails and Allies
Family Rallidae: Rails, Gallinules and Coots
Subfamily Rallinae: Rails, Gallinules and Coots

	Texas	Minnesota	Iowa	Missouri	Arkansas	Louisiana	Wisconsin	Michigan	Illinois	Indiana	Ohio
Yellow Rail	uW	uS	rT	rT	xT,xW	rT,xW	rS	rS	eS,rT	rT	eS,rT
Black Rail	lrS,uW	xS*,xV	xV	xS,xT	xT	rW	xV-q	xV	xS,rT	xS*,rT	xS*,rT
Corn Crake											
Clapper Rail	cP					cP					
King Rail	fP	rS	rS	rS,uT,xW	uS,rW	cP	rS	rS,xW	uS,xW	uS,xW	rS,xW
Virginia Rail	rS,fW	fS,xW	fS	xS,fT	xS,fT,uW	lrS,fW	fS,rW	fS,rW	uS,fT,xW	uS,fT,xW	uS,fT,xW
Sora	rS,cT,fW	cS,xW	fS,cT	xS,cT,xW	fT,rW	cT,fW	fS,xW	fS,xW	uS,cT,xW	uS,fT,xW	uS,fT,xW
Hawaiian Rail											
Laysan Rail											
Paint-billed Crake	xW										
Spotted Rail	xV										
Purple Gallinule	fS,xW	xV	xV	xS*,rV,xW	luS,xV	fS,rW	rV	xV	xS,rV	xV	xS,rV,xW
Common Moorhen	cP	rS,exW	rS	uS	uS,lrW	cP	uS	uS,xW	uS	uS	uS
Eurasian Coot											
American Coot	fS,cW	cS,rW	fS,cT,rW	uS,cT,uW	uS,cW	uS,cW	cS,uW	cS,uW	uS,cT,uW	uS,cT,uW	uS,cT,uW
Caribbean Coot											

Subfamily Odontophorinae: Quail

	West Virginia	Kentucky	Tennessee	Mississippi	Alabama	Maine	New Hampshire	Vermont	Massachusetts	Rhode Island	Connecticut
Montezuma Quail											
Northern Bobwhite	fP	cP2	cP	cP	cP		eP	lrP1	uP2	uP2	uP2
Scaled Quail											
Gambel's Quail											
California Quail											
Mountain Quail											

Order Gruiformes: Cranes, Rails and Allies
Family Rallidae: Rails, Gallinules and Coots
Subfamily Rallinae: Rails, Gallinules and Coots

	West Virginia	Kentucky	Tennessee	Mississippi	Alabama	Maine	New Hampshire	Vermont	Massachusetts	Rhode Island	Connecticut
Yellow Rail	xT	xT	rT	xT,xW	rW	rT	xT	xT	rT,xW	rT	rT
Black Rail			xS,xT	xT	xS*,rT				xV	xS*,xV	eS,xS*,xV
Corn Crake						exV				exV	exV
Clapper Rail				cP	cP	rV	xS*,rV,xW	xV	lrS,rW	uS,rW	fS,rW
King Rail	lrS,rT	rS	uS,rW	uS,fW	uS,fW	rV	xS*,rV	xV	lrS,rT	xS,rT,xW	luS,rT
Virginia Rail	lrS,uT,xW	rS*,fT,xW	rS,fT,rW	uW	xS,uW	fS,rW	fS	fS	fS,rW	uS,fT,uW	fS,uW
Sora	lrS,uT,xW	fT	fT,rW	cT,uW	cT,uW	fS	uS,fT	uS,fT,xW	uS,fT,rW	rS,fT,rW	uS,fT,rW
Hawaiian Rail											
Laysan Rail											
Paint-billed Crake											
Spotted Rail											
Purple Gallinule	xV	xV,xW	xS,rV	uS	lfS,rV	rV,xW	xV		rV,xW	xV	rV
Common Moorhen	luS,rT	xS,rT	rS	cS,fW	cS,fW	rS	rS	uS	uS,rW	eS,uT,xW	rS,uT,xW
Eurasian Coot											
American Coot	rS,fT,uW	rS,cT,uW	rS,cW	rS,cW	rS,cW	rS,uT,rW	uT,rW	rS,uT	rS,cT,rW	rS*,cT,uW	rS*,cT,uW
Caribbean Coot											

Subfamily Odontophorinae: Quail

	New York	Pennsylvania	New Jersey	Delaware	Maryland	Dist. of Columbia	Virginia	North Carolina	South Carolina	Georgia	Florida
Montezuma Quail											
Northern Bobwhite	luP2	uP2	fP2	cP	cP	uP	cP	cP	cP	cP	fP
Scaled Quail											
Gambel's Quail											
California Quail											
Mountain Quail											

Order Gruiformes: Cranes, Rails and Allies
Family Rallidae: Rails, Gallinules and Coots
Subfamily Rallinae: Rails, Gallinules and Coots

	New York	Pennsylvania	New Jersey	Delaware	Maryland	Dist. of Columbia	Virginia	North Carolina	South Carolina	Georgia	Florida
Yellow Rail	rT	rT	rT	xT	rT	exT	rT,xW	rW	rW	rW	rW
Black Rail	lrS,xV,xW	xV	rS	luS	uS,xW	exS*	uS,xW	uS,rW	uS,xW	uS,rW	uP
Corn Crake	exV	exV	exV		exV						
Clapper Rail	fS,rW	xV	fS,rW	cS,rW	fS,uW	exV	cS,fW	cP	cP	cP	cP
King Rail	luS,rT,xW	luS,rT,xW	uS,rW	uS,rW	fS,uW	xT	fS,uW	fP	fP	fP	cP
Virginia Rail	fS,rW	fS,rW	fS,uW	uS,fT,uW	fP	rT	uS,fW	luS,fW	fW	lrS,fW	xS,fW
Sora	fS,xW	fS	fS,rW	xS,fT,uW	xS,fT,rW	uT	xS,cT,uW	cT,fW	xS*,cT,fW	cT,fW	cT,fW
Hawaiian Rail											
Laysan Rail											
Paint-billed Crake							xV				
Spotted Rail		xV									
Purple Gallinule	rV	xS*,rV	rV	xS,xV	xS,rV	exV	rS	rS	uS	uS	fP
Common Moorhen	uS,xW	uS	fS,rW	fS	fS,xW	rS	fS,rW	fS,uW	cS,fW	cS,fW	cP
Eurasian Coot											
American Coot	fS,cT,uW	uS,cT,uW	uS,cT,fW	uS,cW	rS,uS*,cW	fW	rS,uS*,cW	xS,uS*,cW	xS,uS*,cW	xS,uS*,cW	uS,cW
Caribbean Coot											rV,rW

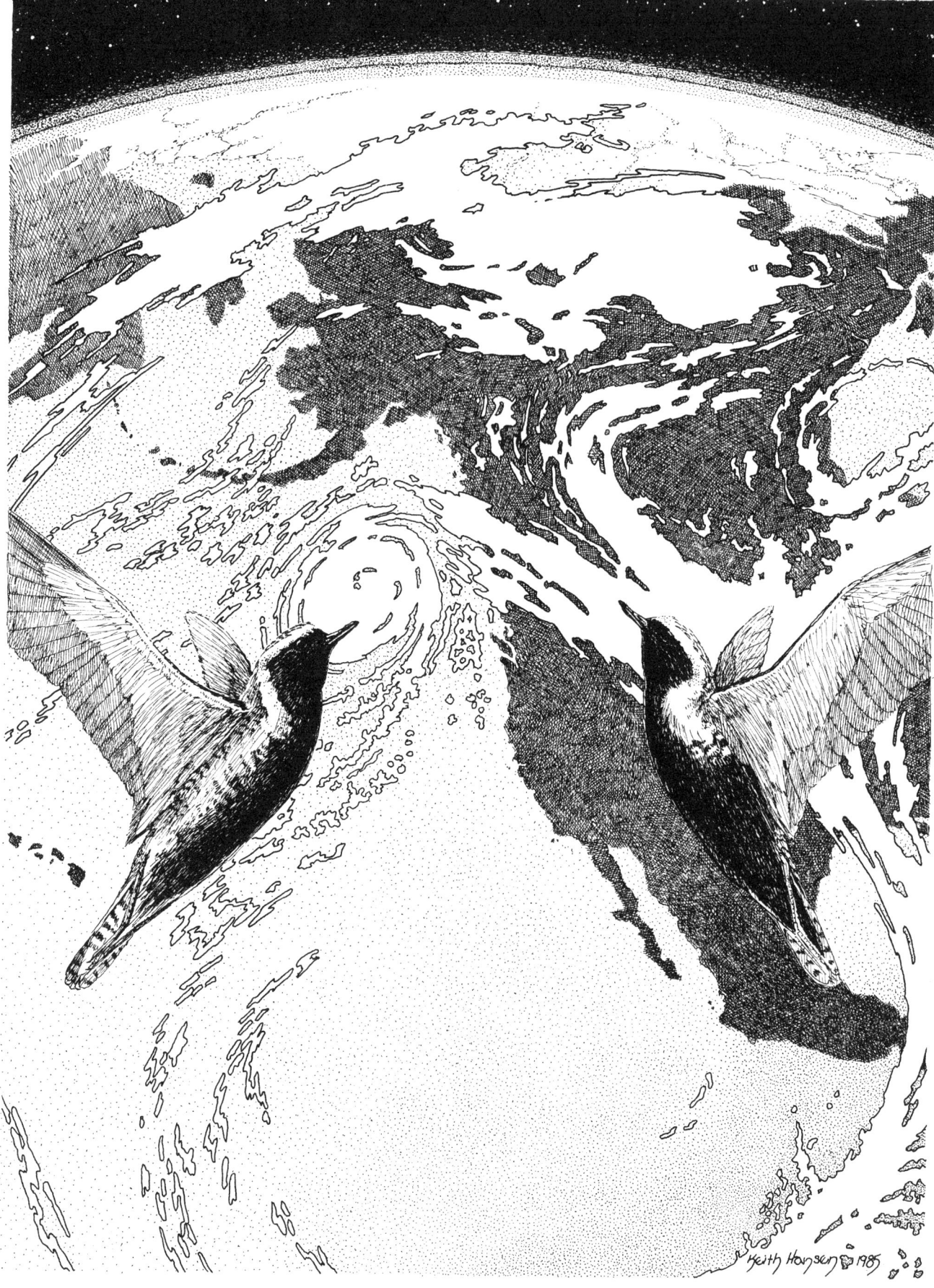

Family Aramidae: Limpkins

	Date	Location	Cont. North America	Canada	Lower 48
Limpkin *Aramus guarauna*			lfP,rV	xV	lfP,rV

Family Gruidae: Cranes
Subfamily Gruinae: Typical Cranes

Sandhill Crane *Grus canadensis*			cS,fW	cS,xW	uS,cT,fW
Common Crane *Grus grus*			xV	xV	xV
Whooping Crane *Grus americana*			lrS,rT,lrW	lrS,rT	eS,xS*,rT,lrW

Order Charadriiformes: Shorebirds, Gulls, Auks and Allies
Family Burhinidae: Thick-knees

Double-striped Thick-knee *Burhinus bistriatus*			xV		xV

Family Charadriidae: Plovers and Lapwings
Subfamily Vanellinae: Lapwings

Northern Lapwing *Vanellus vanellus*			rV,rW	rV,rW	xV

Subfamily Charadriinae: Plovers

Black-bellied Plover *Pluvialis squatarola*			lcS,uS*,cW	cS,luW	uS*,cW
Greater Golden-Plover *Pluvialis apricaria*			xV	xV	
Lesser Golden-Plover *Pluvialis dominica*			cS,lrW	cS	fT,lrW
Mongolian Plover *Charadrius mongolus*			lrS,xV	xV	xV
Snowy Plover *Charadrius alexandrinus*			uP	xV	uP
Wilson's Plover *Charadrius wilsonia*			lfS,xS,rV,luW	xV	fS,uW
Common Ringed Plover *Charadrius hiaticula*			lfS,xS,lrT,xV	lfS,xV	
Semipalmated Plover *Charadrius semipalmatus*			cS,fW	cS,xW	xS,rS*,cT,fW
Piping Plover *Charadrius melodus*			uS,lfW	uS	uS,fW
Little Ringed Plover *Charadrius dubius*			xV		

Family Aramidae: Limpkins

	Hawaii		Alaska	Yukon Terr.	Northwest Terr.	British Columbia	Alberta	Saskatchewan	Manitoba	Ontario
Limpkin										

Family Gruidae: Cranes
Subfamily Gruinae: Typical Cranes

	Hawaii		Alaska	Yukon Terr.	Northwest Terr.	British Columbia	Alberta	Saskatchewan	Manitoba	Ontario
Sandhill Crane	exV		cS	fS,lcT	cS	uS,fT,xW	rS,cT	uS,cT	uS,fT	luS,rT,xW
Common Crane			xV				xV			
Whooping Crane				xV	lrS	xV	lrS,rT	eS,xS*,rT	eS,rT	eT

Order Charadriiformes: Shorebirds, Gulls, Auks and Allies
Family Burhinidae: Thick-knees

	Hawaii		Alaska	Yukon Terr.	Northwest Terr.	British Columbia	Alberta	Saskatchewan	Manitoba	Ontario
Double-striped Thick-knee										

Family Charadriidae: Plovers and Lapwings
Subfamily Vanellinae: Lapwings

	Hawaii		Alaska	Yukon Terr.	Northwest Terr.	British Columbia	Alberta	Saskatchewan	Manitoba	Ontario
Northern Lapwing				exV						

Subfamily Charadriinae: Plovers

	Hawaii		Alaska	Yukon Terr.	Northwest Terr.	British Columbia	Alberta	Saskatchewan	Manitoba	Ontario
Black-bellied Plover	xS*,uW		uS,fT	lrS†,fT	cS	cT,uW	fT	fT	fT	fT,xW
Greater Golden-Plover			xV-q							
Lesser Golden-Plover	uS*,cW		cS	cS	cS	luS,uT	fT	fT	luS,fT	lrS,fT
Mongolian Plover	xV		lrS,xV							xV
Snowy Plover							xV	xV	xV	
Wilson's Plover										
Common Ringed Plover			xS,lrT		lfS					
Semipalmated Plover	rW		cS	cS	cS	uS,cT,xW	lrS,uT	luS,fT	lfS,cT	lfS,cT
Piping Plover						xV	rS	uS	uS	luS,rT
Little Ringed Plover			xV							

Family Aramidae: Limpkins

	Québec	Newfound-land	New Brunswick	Prince Edward I.	Nova Scotia	Washington	Oregon	California	Nevada	Idaho
Limpkin					xV-q					

Family Gruidae: Cranes
Subfamily Gruinae: Typical Cranes

	Québec	Newfound-land	New Brunswick	Prince Edward I.	Nova Scotia	Washington	Oregon	California	Nevada	Idaho
Sandhill Crane	lrS,xV	xS*,xV	xV	xV	xP*,rV	xS,fT,xW	luS,fT,uW	luS,fW	luS,fT,rW	luS,fT
Common Crane										
Whooping Crane										eT

Order Charadriiformes: Shorebirds, Gulls, Auks and Allies
Family Burhinidae: Thick-knees

	Québec	Newfound-land	New Brunswick	Prince Edward I.	Nova Scotia	Washington	Oregon	California	Nevada	Idaho
Double-striped Thick-knee										

Family Charadriidae: Plovers and Lapwings
Subfamily Vanellinae: Lapwings

	Québec	Newfound-land	New Brunswick	Prince Edward I.	Nova Scotia	Washington	Oregon	California	Nevada	Idaho
Northern Lapwing	xV,xW	rV,rW	xV,xW	xV	xV					

Subfamily Charadriinae: Plovers

	Québec	Newfound-land	New Brunswick	Prince Edward I.	Nova Scotia	Washington	Oregon	California	Nevada	Idaho
Black-bellied Plover	fT	fT	cT	cT	cT,xW	xS*,cT,fW	rS*,cT,fW	uS*,cW	uT	uT
Greater Golden-Plover		xV								
Lesser Golden-Plover	uT	uT	uT	uT	uT	uT	uT,xW	uT,rW	xT	rT
Mongolian Plover							xV	xV		
Snowy Plover						lrS,xW	fS,uW	fP	uS	xV
Wilson's Plover					xV			xS,xS*,xV		
Common Ringed Plover		xV								
Semipalmated Plover	fS,cT	fS,cT	lrS,cT	uS,cT	uS,cT	xS,cT,rW	xS*,cT,uW	rS*,cT,fW	uT	uT
Piping Plover	lrS	rS	uS	uS	uS			xV,xW		
Little Ringed Plover										

Family Aramidae: Limpkins

	Montana	Wyoming	Utah	Colorado	Arizona	New Mexico	North Dakota	South Dakota	Nebraska	Kansas	Oklahoma
Limpkin											

Family Gruidae: Cranes
Subfamily Gruinae: Typical Cranes

	Montana	Wyoming	Utah	Colorado	Arizona	New Mexico	North Dakota	South Dakota	Nebraska	Kansas	Oklahoma
Sandhill Crane	uS,cT	fS,cT	rS,fT,xW	luS,cT,rW	exS*,rT,lfW	cW	lrS,cT	eS,cT	eS,cT	cT,xW	cT,uW
Common Crane						xV			xV		
Whooping Crane	rT	xT		xT		eT	eS,rT	rT	rT	rT	rT

Order Charadriiformes: Shorebirds, Gulls, Auks and Allies
Family Burhinidae: Thick-knees

	Montana	Wyoming	Utah	Colorado	Arizona	New Mexico	North Dakota	South Dakota	Nebraska	Kansas	Oklahoma
Double-striped Thick-knee											

Family Charadriidae: Plovers and Lapwings
Subfamily Vanellinae: Lapwings

	Montana	Wyoming	Utah	Colorado	Arizona	New Mexico	North Dakota	South Dakota	Nebraska	Kansas	Oklahoma
Northern Lapwing											

Subfamily Charadriinae: Plovers

	Montana	Wyoming	Utah	Colorado	Arizona	New Mexico	North Dakota	South Dakota	Nebraska	Kansas	Oklahoma
Black-bellied Plover	uT	uT	uT	uT	uT,xW	rT	fT	uT	uT	uT	uT
Greater Golden-Plover											
Lesser Golden-Plover	rT	rT	rT,xW	rT	rT	xT	fT	fT	fT	uT	uT
Mongolian Plover											
Snowy Plover	xS*,xV	xV	uS	rS	rS,uT,xW	rS,uT,xW			xV	uS	uS
Wilson's Plover											xV
Common Ringed Plover											
Semipalmated Plover	uT	uT	uT	uT	uT	uT	fT	fT	uT	uT	uT
Piping Plover	lrS,xT	xS*,rT		xS,rT		xV	uS	uS	uS	uT	uT
Little Ringed Plover											

Family Aramidae: Limpkins

	Texas	Minnesota	Iowa	Missouri	Arkansas	Louisiana	Wisconsin	Michigan	Illinois	Indiana	Ohio
Limpkin	xV,xW-q										

Family Gruidae: Cranes
Subfamily Gruinae: Typical Cranes

	Texas	Minnesota	Iowa	Missouri	Arkansas	Louisiana	Wisconsin	Michigan	Illinois	Indiana	Ohio
Sandhill Crane	eS,cW	uS,fT	eS,rT,xW	rT,xW	rT,xW	eP,rT,luW	uS,xW	uS,xW	lrS,uT,xW	xS,uT,xW	eS,rT,xW
Common Crane	xV-q										
Whooping Crane	eS,xS*,rT,lrW	eS,xT	eS,xT	xT	eT	eP,xW	eT		eS†,xV	eT	

Order Charadriiformes: Shorebirds, Gulls, Auks and Allies
Family Burhinidae: Thick-knees

	Texas	Minnesota	Iowa	Missouri	Arkansas	Louisiana	Wisconsin	Michigan	Illinois	Indiana	Ohio
Double-striped Thick-knee	xV										

Family Charadriidae: Plovers and Lapwings
Subfamily Vanellinae: Lapwings

	Texas	Minnesota	Iowa	Missouri	Arkansas	Louisiana	Wisconsin	Michigan	Illinois	Indiana	Ohio
Northern Lapwing											

Subfamily Charadriinae: Plovers

	Texas	Minnesota	Iowa	Missouri	Arkansas	Louisiana	Wisconsin	Michigan	Illinois	Indiana	Ohio
Black-bellied Plover	uS*,cW	fT	uT	uT	uT,xW	uS*,cW	fT	fT	fT	fT	fT
Greater Golden-Plover											
Lesser Golden-Plover	fT,xW	fT	fT	fT	fT	fT	fT	fT	fT	fT	fT
Mongolian Plover						xV					
Snowy Plover	uP	xV		xV	xV	xS,rW	xV			xV-q	
Wilson's Plover	cS,uW	xV				cS,rW					xV
Common Ringed Plover											
Semipalmated Plover	rS*,cT,fW	fT	fT	fT	fT	rS*,cT,fW	fT	cT	fT	fT	fT
Piping Plover	rS*,fW	uS	lrS,rT	rT	uT	rS*,fW	rS	rS	lrS,rT	eS,rT	eS,rT
Little Ringed Plover											

Family Aramidae: Limpkins

	West Virginia	Kentucky	Tennessee	Mississippi	Alabama	Maine	New Hampshire	Vermont	Massachusetts	Rhode Island	Connecticut
Limpkin			xV	xV							

Family Gruidae: Cranes
Subfamily Gruinae: Typical Cranes

	West Virginia	Kentucky	Tennessee	Mississippi	Alabama	Maine	New Hampshire	Vermont	Massachusetts	Rhode Island	Connecticut
Sandhill Crane	xT	uT,xW	uT,rW	lrP,xT	eP,rW	rV	xV	xV	rV,xW	xV	rV,xW
Common Crane											
Whooping Crane			eT	exV	eW						eT

Order Charadriiformes: Shorebirds, Gulls, Auks and Allies
Family Burhinidae: Thick-knees

	West Virginia	Kentucky	Tennessee	Mississippi	Alabama	Maine	New Hampshire	Vermont	Massachusetts	Rhode Island	Connecticut
Double-striped Thick-knee											

Family Charadriidae: Plovers and Lapwings
Subfamily Vanellinae: Lapwings

	West Virginia	Kentucky	Tennessee	Mississippi	Alabama	Maine	New Hampshire	Vermont	Massachusetts	Rhode Island	Connecticut
Northern Lapwing					exV					exV	

Subfamily Charadriinae: Plovers

	West Virginia	Kentucky	Tennessee	Mississippi	Alabama	Maine	New Hampshire	Vermont	Massachusetts	Rhode Island	Connecticut
Black-bellied Plover	uT	uT	uT	uS*,cW	uS*,cW	cT,rW	cT,xW	fT	xS*,cT,rW	xS*,cT,rW	cT,rW
Greater Golden-Plover											
Lesser Golden-Plover	uT	fT	fT	fT,xW	uT	uT	uT	uT	uT	uT	uT
Mongolian Plover											
Snowy Plover			xV	rP	rP						
Wilson's Plover				fS	uS	xV		xV	rV	xV	rV
Common Ringed Plover											
Semipalmated Plover	uT	uT	uT	rS*,fT,uW	rS*,fT,uW	cT	cT	fT	cT	cT	cT
Piping Plover		rT	rT	xS*,fT,uW	xS*,fT,uW	uS	rT	exV	uS	rS,uT	rS,uT
Little Ringed Plover											

Family Aramidae: Limpkins

	New York	Pennsylvania	New Jersey	Delaware	Maryland	Dist. of Columbia	Virginia	North Carolina	South Carolina	Georgia	Florida
Limpkin					xV		xV	xV-q	xV	lrP	fP

Family Gruidae: Cranes
Subfamily Gruinae: Typical Cranes

	New York	Pennsylvania	New Jersey	Delaware	Maryland	Dist. of Columbia	Virginia	North Carolina	South Carolina	Georgia	Florida
Sandhill Crane	rV	xS*,rV,xW	rV,xW	xV,xW	xV		xV,xW	rT,xW	rW	lrS,uT,rW	uS,fW
Common Crane											
Whooping Crane	eT	eT	eT-q						eT	eW	eW

Order Charadriiformes: Shorebirds, Gulls, Auks and Allies
Family Burhinidae: Thick-knees

	New York	Pennsylvania	New Jersey	Delaware	Maryland	Dist. of Columbia	Virginia	North Carolina	South Carolina	Georgia	Florida
Double-striped Thick-knee											

Family Charadriidae: Plovers and Lapwings
Subfamily Vanellinae: Lapwings

	New York	Pennsylvania	New Jersey	Delaware	Maryland	Dist. of Columbia	Virginia	North Carolina	South Carolina	Georgia	Florida
Northern Lapwing	xV								exV	xV	

Subfamily Charadriinae: Plovers

	New York	Pennsylvania	New Jersey	Delaware	Maryland	Dist. of Columbia	Virginia	North Carolina	South Carolina	Georgia	Florida
Black-bellied Plover	rS*,cT,uW	fT,rW	rS*,cT,uW	rS*,cT,fW	rS*,cT,fW	uT,xW	uS*,cW	uS*,cW	uS*,cW	uS*,cW	uS*,cW
Greater Golden-Plover											
Lesser Golden-Plover	uT	uT	uT	uT	uT	uT	uT	uT	rT,xW	rT	rT
Mongolian Plover											
Snowy Plover		exV									uP
Wilson's Plover	rV	xV	eS,rV		lrS		luS,rT	fS,xW	fS,rW	cS,uW	cS,fW
Common Ringed Plover											
Semipalmated Plover	cT,xW	fT	cT,xW	cT	cT,rW	uT	xS*,cT,uW	rS*,cT,fW	uS*,cW	uS*,cW	uS*,cW
Piping Plover	rS,uT	eS,rT	uS,xW	uS	uS,rW	xT	uS,rW	uP	xS*,fW	rS*,fW	rS*,fW
Little Ringed Plover											

	Date	Location	Cont. North America	Canada	Lower 48
Killdeer *Charadrius vociferus*			cP	cS,rW	cP
Mountain Plover *Charadrius montanus*			luS,xS*,rV,luW	xS,xV	uS,luW
Eurasian Dotterel *Charadrius morinellus*			lrS,xV		xV

Family Haematopodidae: Oystercatchers

	Date	Location	Cont. North America	Canada	Lower 48
American Oystercatcher *Haematopus palliatus*			cP	xS*,xV	cP
Black Oystercatcher *Haematopus bachmani*			fP	fP	fP

Family Recurvirostridae: Stilts and Avocets

	Date	Location	Cont. North America	Canada	Lower 48
Black-winged Stilt *Himantopus himantopus*			xV		
Black-necked Stilt *Himantopus mexicanus*			cS,lcW	xS,xS*,rV	cS,fW
American Avocet *Recurvirostra americana*			cS,lcW	fS	cS,fW

Family Jacanidae: Jacanas

	Date	Location	Cont. North America	Canada	Lower 48
Northern Jacana *Jacana spinosa*			lrP		lrP

Family Scolopacidae: Sandpipers, Phalaropes and Allies
Subfamily Scolopacinae: Sandpipers and Allies

	Date	Location	Cont. North America	Canada	Lower 48
Common Greenshank *Tringa nebularia*			lrT,xW	xW	
Greater Yellowlegs *Tringa melanoleuca*			cS,fW	cS,lrW	rS*,cT,fW
Lesser Yellowlegs *Tringa flavipes*			cS,uW	cS,xW	xS,rS*,cT,fW
Marsh Sandpiper *Tringa stagnatilis*			xV		
Spotted Redshank *Tringa erythropus*			lrT,rV	xV	rV
Wood Sandpiper *Tringa glareola*			lrS,luT,exV		exV
Green Sandpiper *Tringa ochropus*			xV		
Solitary Sandpiper *Tringa solitaria*			fS,lrW	fS	xS,fT,lrW
Willet *Catoptrophorus semipalmatus*			cP	fS	cP

Species	Hawaii	Alaska	Yukon Terr.	Northwest Terr.	British Columbia	Alberta	Saskatchewan	Manitoba	Ontario
Killdeer	xP*,xV,xW	uS,lrW	lfS	lfS	cS,uW	cS,xW	cS,xW	cS	cS,rW
Mountain Plover						xS	xV-q		
Eurasian Dotterel	xV	lrS							

Family Haematopodidae: Oystercatchers

Species	Hawaii	Alaska	Yukon Terr.	Northwest Terr.	British Columbia	Alberta	Saskatchewan	Manitoba	Ontario
American Oystercatcher									xS*
Black Oystercatcher		fP			fP				

Family Recurvirostridae: Stilts and Avocets

Species	Hawaii	Alaska	Yukon Terr.	Northwest Terr.	British Columbia	Alberta	Saskatchewan	Manitoba	Ontario
Black-winged Stilt		xV							
Black-necked Stilt	fP				rV	xS,xV	xV-q	xS*,xV	xV
American Avocet		xV		eS	lrS,xV	fS	cS	lfS	xS,rT

Family Jacanidae: Jacanas

Species	Hawaii	Alaska	Yukon Terr.	Northwest Terr.	British Columbia	Alberta	Saskatchewan	Manitoba	Ontario
Northern Jacana									

Family Scolopacidae: Sandpipers, Phalaropes and Allies
Subfamily Scolopacinae: Sandpipers and Allies

Species	Hawaii	Alaska	Yukon Terr.	Northwest Terr.	British Columbia	Alberta	Saskatchewan	Manitoba	Ontario
Common Greenshank		lrT							
Greater Yellowlegs	xV,xW	lfS	rS	lrS*,xV	fS,rW	fS	cS	cS	fS,cT,xW
Lesser Yellowlegs	rV,xW	cS	cS	cS	fS,xW	cS	cS	cS	fS,cT
Marsh Sandpiper		xV							
Spotted Redshank		lrT				xV			xV
Wood Sandpiper	xV	lrS,xV,luT							
Green Sandpiper		xV							
Solitary Sandpiper	xV	fS	cS	fS	fS	fS	fS	fS	fS
Willet	xV,xW	xV	xV	xS*,rT,xW	fS	cS	lfS	rV	

Charadriidae • 127

	Québec	Newfound-land	New Brunswick	Prince Edward I.	Nova Scotia
Killdeer	cS,xW	lrS,xW	fS,xW	uS	uS,rW
Mountain Plover					
Eurasian Dotterel					

	Washing-ton	Oregon	California	Nevada	Idaho
Killdeer	cS,fW	cP	cP	cS,uW	cS,uW
Mountain Plover	xV	xV,xW	uW	rT	xV
Eurasian Dotterel	xV		xV		

Family Haematopodidae: Oystercatchers

	Québec	Newfound-land	New Brunswick	Prince Edward I.	Nova Scotia
American Oystercatcher	xV		exV		xV
Black Oystercatcher					

	Washing-ton	Oregon	California	Nevada	Idaho
American Oystercatcher			xP*,xV,xW		xV
Black Oystercatcher	fP	fP	fP		

Family Recurvirostridae: Stilts and Avocets

	Québec	Newfound-land	New Brunswick	Prince Edward I.	Nova Scotia
Black-winged Stilt					
Black-necked Stilt		xV	xV		xV
American Avocet	xV		xV		xV

	Washing-ton	Oregon	California	Nevada	Idaho
Black-winged Stilt					
Black-necked Stilt	luS	uS	cP	cS	uS
American Avocet	fS	cS	cP	fS,cT,xW	fS,cT

Family Jacanidae: Jacanas

	Québec	Newfound-land	New Brunswick	Prince Edward I.	Nova Scotia
Northern Jacana					

	Washing-ton	Oregon	California	Nevada	Idaho
Northern Jacana					

Family Scolopacidae: Sandpipers, Phalaropes and Allies
Subfamily Scolopacinae: Sandpipers and Allies

	Québec	Newfound-land	New Brunswick	Prince Edward I.	Nova Scotia
Common Greenshank		xW			
Greater Yellowlegs	fS,cT	cS	rS*,cT	uS†,cT	lrS,cT
Lesser Yellowlegs	lrS,fT	rT	cT	fT	cT
Marsh Sandpiper					
Spotted Redshank		xV			
Wood Sandpiper					
Green Sandpiper					
Solitary Sandpiper	uS	uS	uT	uT	uT
Willet	rV	rV	lfS,uT	uS	fS

	Washing-ton	Oregon	California	Nevada	Idaho
Common Greenshank					
Greater Yellowlegs	cT,rW	xS*,cT,uW	rS*,cT,fW	fT,xW	fT
Lesser Yellowlegs	fT,xW	fT,rW	xS*,fT,uW	fT,xW	fT
Marsh Sandpiper					
Spotted Redshank		xV	xV	xV	
Wood Sandpiper					
Green Sandpiper					
Solitary Sandpiper	uT	xS,uT	uT,xW	uT	uT
Willet	rW	fS,rW	fS,cW	uS,fT	fS

128 • Distributional Checklist of North American Birds

	Montana	Wyoming	Utah	Colorado	Arizona	New Mexico	North Dakota	South Dakota	Nebraska	Kansas	Oklahoma
Killdeer	cS,rW	cS,xW	cS,uW	cS,uW	cP	cS,fW	cS,xW	cS,rW	cS,rW	cS,uW	cS,uW
Mountain Plover	uS	fS	rT	uS	rT,luW	uS	eS	eS,xS*	lrS	eS	lrS,xV
Eurasian Dotterel											

Family Haematopodidae: Oystercatchers

	Montana	Wyoming	Utah	Colorado	Arizona	New Mexico	North Dakota	South Dakota	Nebraska	Kansas	Oklahoma
American Oystercatcher							xV				
Black Oystercatcher											

Family Recurvirostridae: Stilts and Avocets

	Montana	Wyoming	Utah	Colorado	Arizona	New Mexico	North Dakota	South Dakota	Nebraska	Kansas	Oklahoma
Black-winged Stilt											
Black-necked Stilt	irS,rV	luS,uT	cS	uS	uS,cT,rW	rS,uT	xV	xV	xV	lrS,rT	rT
American Avocet	cS	cS	cS,xW	cS	uS,cT,rW	uS,cT,xW	cS	fS	uS,fT	fS	fS

Family Jacanidae: Jacanas

	Montana	Wyoming	Utah	Colorado	Arizona	New Mexico	North Dakota	South Dakota	Nebraska	Kansas	Oklahoma
Northern Jacana											

Family Scolopacidae: Sandpipers, Phalaropes and Allies
Subfamily Scolopacinae: Sandpipers and Allies

	Montana	Wyoming	Utah	Colorado	Arizona	New Mexico	North Dakota	South Dakota	Nebraska	Kansas	Oklahoma
Common Greenshank											
Greater Yellowlegs	fT	fT	fT,xW	fT,xW	fT,uW	fT,rW	fT	fT	fT	fT	fT,xW
Lesser Yellowlegs	cT	cT	fT,xW	cT	fT,xW	fT,xW	cT	cT	cT	cT	cT
Marsh Sandpiper											
Spotted Redshank											
Wood Sandpiper											
Green Sandpiper											
Solitary Sandpiper	fT	fT	uT	fT	uT	uT	fT	fT	fT	fT	fT
Willet	cS	fS	fS	lrS,fT	fT	uT	fS	fS	luS,fT	fT	uT

Charadriidae • 129

	Texas	Minnesota	Iowa	Missouri	Arkansas	Louisiana	Wisconsin	Michigan	Illinois	Indiana	Ohio
Killdeer	cP	cS.xW	cS.rW	cS.uW	cS.fW	cP	cS.xW	cS.rW	cS.uW	cS.uW	cS.uW
Mountain Plover	lrS.rT.lrW		xV	xV	xV						
Eurasian Dotterel											

Family Haematopodidae: Oystercatchers

	Texas	Minnesota	Iowa	Missouri	Arkansas	Louisiana	Wisconsin	Michigan	Illinois	Indiana	Ohio
American Oystercatcher	uP					luP					
Black Oystercatcher											

Family Recurvirostridae: Stilts and Avocets

	Texas	Minnesota	Iowa	Missouri	Arkansas	Louisiana	Wisconsin	Michigan	Illinois	Indiana	Ohio
Black-winged Stilt											
Black-necked Stilt	cS.uW		xV	xV	xT	cS.uW	xV	xV-q	xV	xV-q	xV
American Avocet	fS.cW	rS.uT	rT	uT	uT	rS*.fW	xS.rT	rT	rT	rT	rT

Family Jacanidae: Jacanas

	Texas	Minnesota	Iowa	Missouri	Arkansas	Louisiana	Wisconsin	Michigan	Illinois	Indiana	Ohio
Northern Jacana	lrP										

Family Scolopacidae: Sandpipers, Phalaropes and Allies
Subfamily Scolopacinae: Sandpipers and Allies

	Texas	Minnesota	Iowa	Missouri	Arkansas	Louisiana	Wisconsin	Michigan	Illinois	Indiana	Ohio
Common Greenshank											
Greater Yellowlegs	rS*.cW	fT	fT	fT	fT.rW	rS*.cW	fT	fT	fT	fT	fT
Lesser Yellowlegs	rS*.cT.fW	cT	cT	cT	cT.rW	rS*.cT.fW	xS.cT	cT	cT	cT	cT
Marsh Sandpiper											
Spotted Redshank	xV-q						xV-q				xV
Wood Sandpiper											
Green Sandpiper											
Solitary Sandpiper	fT.rW	xS.fT	fT	fT	fT	fT.xW	fT	fT	fT	fT	fT
Willet	cP	eS.rS*.uT	eS.uT	uT	uT	cP	uT	uT	uT	uT	rT

130 • *Distributional Checklist of North American Birds*

	West Virginia	Kentucky	Tennessee	Mississippi	Alabama	Maine	New Hampshire	Vermont	Massachusetts	Rhode Island	Connecticut
Killdeer	cS,uW	cS,fW	cP	cP	cP	cS,rW	cS,rW	cS	cS,rW	fS,cT,rW	cS,uW
Mountain Plover					xV,xW				exV		
Eurasian Dotterel											

Family Haematopodidae: Oystercatchers

	West Virginia	Kentucky	Tennessee	Mississippi	Alabama	Maine	New Hampshire	Vermont	Massachusetts	Rhode Island	Connecticut
American Oystercatcher			xP*	luP	eS*,xV				luS	uS	luS
Black Oystercatcher											

Family Recurvirostridae: Stilts and Avocets

	West Virginia	Kentucky	Tennessee	Mississippi	Alabama	Maine	New Hampshire	Vermont	Massachusetts	Rhode Island	Connecticut
Black-winged Stilt											
Black-necked Stilt		xV	xS,xV	luS,uT,rW	luS,uT,xW	xV	exV	exV	xS*,xV	xS*,xV	xV
American Avocet	xT	rT	rT	rS*,uW	rS*,uW	xV	xV	xV	rV	rV	rV

Family Jacanidae: Jacanas

	West Virginia	Kentucky	Tennessee	Mississippi	Alabama	Maine	New Hampshire	Vermont	Massachusetts	Rhode Island	Connecticut
Northern Jacana											

Family Scolopacidae: Sandpipers, Phalaropes and Allies
Subfamily Scolopacinae: Sandpipers and Allies

	West Virginia	Kentucky	Tennessee	Mississippi	Alabama	Maine	New Hampshire	Vermont	Massachusetts	Rhode Island	Connecticut
Common Greenshank											
Greater Yellowlegs	fT	fT	fT,xW	rS*,cT,uW	rS*,cT,uW	cT	cT	fT	cT,rW	cT,rW	cT,rW
Lesser Yellowlegs	fT	fT	fT	rS*,cT,uW	rS*,cT,uW	cT	fT	fT	cT	cT,xW	cT
Marsh Sandpiper											
Spotted Redshank										xV	xV	xV
Wood Sandpiper											
Green Sandpiper											
Solitary Sandpiper	fT	fT	fT	fT	fT	fT	fT	fT	fT	uT	fT
Willet	xV	rT	uT	cP	cP	uS	rT	xV	uS	uT	rS,uT

	New York	Pennsylvania	New Jersey	Delaware	Maryland	Dist. of Columbia	Virginia	North Carolina	South Carolina	Georgia	Florida
Killdeer	cS,uW	cS,fW	cS,fW	cS,fW	cS,fW	fP	cP	cP	cP	cP	cP
Mountain Plover							xV			xV,xW	xV
Eurasian Dotterel											

Family Haematopodidae: Oystercatchers

	New York	Pennsylvania	New Jersey	Delaware	Maryland	Dist. of Columbia	Virginia	North Carolina	South Carolina	Georgia	Florida
American Oystercatcher	luS,xW	exV	fS,rW	uS	fS,rW		cP	cP	fS,cW	fS,cW	luS,fW
Black Oystercatcher											

Family Recurvirostridae: Stilts and Avocets

	New York	Pennsylvania	New Jersey	Delaware	Maryland	Dist. of Columbia	Virginia	North Carolina	South Carolina	Georgia	Florida
Black-winged Stilt											
Black-necked Stilt	rV	xV	exS,rS*	luS	rT		lrS,rT	uS	uS	rS	fS,uW
American Avocet	rT	rT	rS*,uT	rS*,uT	rT		rS*,uT,lrW	xS,rS*,uT,luW	rS*,uW	rS*,uW	rS*,uW

Family Jacanidae: Jacanas

	New York	Pennsylvania	New Jersey	Delaware	Maryland	Dist. of Columbia	Virginia	North Carolina	South Carolina	Georgia	Florida
Northern Jacana											

Family Scolopacidae: Sandpipers, Phalaropes and Allies
Subfamily Scolopacinae: Sandpipers and Allies

	New York	Pennsylvania	New Jersey	Delaware	Maryland	Dist. of Columbia	Virginia	North Carolina	South Carolina	Georgia	Florida
Common Greenshank											
Greater Yellowlegs	cT,rW	fT,rW	cT,rW	cT,rW	xS*,cT,uW	uT	xS*,cT,uW	rS*,cT,fW	rS*,cT,fW	rS*,cT,fW	rS*,cW
Lesser Yellowlegs	cT,xW	cT	cT,rW	cT,rW	cT,rW	fT	xS*,cT,uW	xS*,cT,uW	xS*,cT,uW	rS*,cT,fW	rS*,cW
Marsh Sandpiper											
Spotted Redshank	xV	xV	xV								
Wood Sandpiper	exV										
Green Sandpiper											
Solitary Sandpiper	fT	fT	fT	uT	fT	fT	fT	fT	fT	fT,xW	fT,rW
Willet	fS,xW	rV	cS,xW	fS,xW	cS,xW	xV	cS,rW	cS,fW	cS,fW	cP	cP

Scolopacidae • 133

	Date		Location	Cont. North America	Canada	Lower 48
Wandering Tattler *Heteroscelus incanus*				lcS,rS*,fT,luW	luS,xS*,fT	rS*,fT,uW
Gray-tailed Tattler *Heteroscelus brevipes*				lrT,xV		xV
Common Sandpiper *Actitis hypoleucos*				xS,lrT		
Spotted Sandpiper *Actitis macularia*				cS,fW	cS,lrW	cS,fW
Terek Sandpiper *Xenus cinereus*				rV		
Upland Sandpiper *Bartramia longicauda*				fS	fS	fS
Eskimo Curlew *Numenius borealis*				eS,rT	eS,xT	rT
Little Curlew *Numenius minutus*				xV		xV
Whimbrel *Numenius phaeopus*				fS,uW	fS,xW	rS*,fT,uW
Bristle-thighed Curlew *Numenius tahitiensis*				lrS,xV	xV	xV
Slender-billed Curlew *Numenius tenuirostris*				exV	exV	
Far Eastern Curlew *Numenius madagascariensis*				rV	xV	
Eurasian Curlew *Numenius arquata*				xV,xW	xV	xV,xW
Long-billed Curlew *Numenius americanus*				fS,lfW	uS,xW	fS,uW
Black-tailed Godwit *Limosa limosa*				rV,xW	xV	xV,xW
Hudsonian Godwit *Limosa haemastica*				luS,uT	luS,uT	uT
Bar-tailed Godwit *Limosa lapponica*				lfS,xS*,rV,xW	xV	xS*,rV,xW
Marbled Godwit *Limosa fedoa*				fP	fS,xW	lfS,rS*,fW
Ruddy Turnstone *Arenaria interpres*				lcS,rS*,cT,fW	cS,rW	rS*,cT,fW
Black Turnstone *Arenaria melanocephala*				lcS,rS*,cW	rS*,cW	rS*,cW
Surfbird *Aphriza virgata*				lfS,xS*,fW	luS,uW	xS*,fW
Great Knot *Calidris tenuirostris*				rV		
Red Knot *Calidris canutus*				lcS,rS*,fT,uW	lcS,fT,xW	rS*,cT,uW
Sanderling *Calidris alba*				lcS,uS*,cW	lcS,cT,uW	uS*,cW

	Hawaii	Alaska	Yukon Terr.	Northwest Terr.	British Columbia	Alberta	Saskatchewan	Manitoba	Ontario
Wandering Tattler	rS*,fW	cS	uS	xS*	luS,fT	xV		xV	xV
Gray-tailed Tattler	xV	lrT							
Common Sandpiper		xS,lrT							
Spotted Sandpiper	xV	cS,xW	cS	cS	cS,rW	cS	cS	cS	cS,xW
Terek Sandpiper		rV							
Upland Sandpiper		lfS	fS	luS	luS,rT	uS	fS	fS	uS
Eskimo Curlew		eS†		eS		eT	xT-q	xT	xT
Little Curlew									
Whimbrel	xV	fS	uS	fS	fT,xW	rT	rT	lfS,rT	luS,uT
Bristle-thighed Curlew	rS*,uW	lrS			xV				
Slender-billed Curlew									exV
Far Eastern Curlew		rV			xV				
Eurasian Curlew									
Long-billed Curlew		xV-q		xV	uS,xW	uS	fS	eS,xV	
Black-tailed Godwit		rV							
Hudsonian Godwit		uS	rT	luS	xV	rT	uT	luS,uT	lrS,uT
Bar-tailed Godwit	rT	lfS		xV	xV		xV-q		
Marbled Godwit	xV	lrS†,rT	xV	lrS	rT,xW	fS	cS	fS	lrS,rT
Ruddy Turnstone	uS*,cW	cS	lrS,uT	cS	uT,rW	uT	uT	fT	fT,xW
Black Turnstone		cS,uW	xV	xV	rS*,cW				
Surfbird		fS,uW	luS		uW	xV			
Great Knot		rV							
Red Knot	xV	luS,cT	xT	cS	uT,xW	uT	uT	uT	fT,xW
Sanderling	rS*,fW	lfS,fT,rW	rT	cS	cT,uW	fT	cT	cT	cT

Scolopacidae • 135

	Québec	Newfoundland	New Brunswick	Prince Edward I.	Nova Scotia	Washington	Oregon	California	Nevada	Idaho
Wandering Tattler						fT	fT,xW	rS*,fT,uW		
Gray-tailed Tattler						xV		xV		
Common Sandpiper										
Spotted Sandpiper	cS	cS	cS	cS	cS	cS,uW	cS,uW	fP	fS,cT,xW	cS
Terek Sandpiper										
Upland Sandpiper	luS	xV	luS,rT	xS,rT	xS*,rT	lrS,xV	lrS,xS*,xV	rV	xV	rS
Eskimo Curlew	eT	eT	eT	eT	eT					
Little Curlew								xV		
Whimbrel	fT	fT	fT	fT	fT	fT,rW	xS*,fT,rW	rS*,fT,uW	rT	xT
Bristle-thighed Curlew						xV-q	xV			
Slender-billed Curlew										
Far Eastern Curlew										
Eurasian Curlew					xV-q					
Long-billed Curlew			xV		exV	uS,rW	uS,fT,rW	luS,rS*,fW	fS	fS
Black-tailed Godwit	xV	xV								
Hudsonian Godwit	uT	rT	uT	uT	uT	xV	xV	xV	xV	exV
Bar-tailed Godwit		xV				rV	xV	xV,xW		
Marbled Godwit	rT	xV	xV	xV	rV	uT,xW	uT,xW	uS*,cW	fT	uT
Ruddy Turnstone	fT	fT	cT,xW	fT	cT,rW	fT,rW	xS*,fT,uW	rS*,fT,uW	xT	xT
Black Turnstone						rS*,cW	rS*,cW	rS*,cW		
Surfbird						cW	xS*,fW	xS*,fT,uW		
Great Knot										
Red Knot	fT	uT	fT	fT	fT,xW	fT,xW	fT,rW	rS*,fW	rT	xT
Sanderling	cT	fT,xW	cT,xW	cT	cT,rW	uS*,cW	uS*,cW	uS*,cW	rT	rT

	Montana	Wyoming	Utah	Colorado	Arizona	New Mexico	North Dakota	South Dakota	Nebraska	Kansas	Oklahoma
Wandering Tattler			xV		xV						
Gray-tailed Tattler											
Common Sandpiper											
Spotted Sandpiper	cS	cS	cS,xW	fS,cT	fS,cT,fW	uS,cT,uW	fS,cT	fS,cT	fS,cT	uS,cT	xS,cT,xW
Terek Sandpiper											
Upland Sandpiper	fS	uS	xV	uS	xV	xS*,uT	fS	fS	cS	cS	uS,fT
Eskimo Curlew				exT			eT	eT	eT	eT	eT
Little Curlew											
Whimbrel	rT	rT	rT	rT	rT	xT	xT	xT	rT	rT	rT
Bristle-thighed Curlew											
Slender-billed Curlew											
Far Eastern Curlew											
Eurasian Curlew											
Long-billed Curlew	fS	fS	fS	uS,fT	xS*,fT,rW	uS,rW	luS,rT	uS	uS	lrS,uT	luS,uT
Black-tailed Godwit											
Hudsonian Godwit	rT	xT	xV	rT	xV	xV	uT	uT	uT	uT	uT
Bar-tailed Godwit											
Marbled Godwit	uS,fT	fT	fT	xS,fT	fT,xW	uT	fS	lfS,uT	uT	uT	uT
Ruddy Turnstone	rT	rT	xT	rT	rT	xT	rT	rT	rT	rT	rT
Black Turnstone	xV										
Surfbird											
Great Knot											
Red Knot	rT	rT	rT	rT	rT	rT	rT	xT	rT	rT	rT
Sanderling	uT	uT	uT,xW	uT	uT	rT	uT	uT	uT	uT	uT

Scolopacidae • 137

	Texas	Minnesota	Iowa	Missouri	Arkansas	Louisiana	Wisconsin	Michigan	Illinois	Indiana	Ohio
Wandering Tattler											
Gray-tailed Tattler											
Common Sandpiper											
Spotted Sandpiper	eS,rS*,cT,fW	cS	fS,cT	fS,cT	rS,cT,xW	xS*,cT,uW	cS	cS	fS,cT	fS,cT	fS,cT
Terek Sandpiper											
Upland Sandpiper	eS,rS*,fT	fS	uS	uS,fT	uT	fT	uS	uS	uS	uS	uS
Eskimo Curlew	rT	eT	eT	eT	eT	eT	eT	eT	eT	eT	eT
Little Curlew											
Whimbrel	rS*,fT,rW	rT	rT	rT	xT	rS*,uT,rW	uT	uT	rT	rT	rT
Bristle-thighed Curlew											
Slender-billed Curlew											
Far Eastern Curlew											
Eurasian Curlew											
Long-billed Curlew	luS,rS*,fW	eS,rV	eS	rT	xT	uW	eS,xV		eS,xV	xV	xV
Black-tailed Godwit											
Hudsonian Godwit	uT	uT	uT	uT	uT	uT	uT	rT	rT	xT	rT
Bar-tailed Godwit	xV-q										
Marbled Godwit	fW	lfS,rT	eS,rT	rT	xT	xS*,uW	eS,rT	rT	rT	rT	rT
Ruddy Turnstone	rS*,fW	uT	rT	rT	rT	rS*,fW	fT	fT	uT	uT,xW	uT
Black Turnstone							xV				
Surfbird	xV										
Great Knot											
Red Knot	fT,uW	rT	xT	rT	rT	fT,uW	uT	uT	rT	rT	rT
Sanderling	uS*,cW	uT	rT	uT	uT	uS*,cW	fT	fT,xW	uT	uT	uT

	West Virginia	Kentucky	Tennessee	Mississippi	Alabama	Maine	New Hampshire	Vermont	Massachusetts	Rhode Island	Connecticut
Wandering Tattler									xV		
Gray-tailed Tattler											
Common Sandpiper											
Spotted Sandpiper	fS,cT	rS,cT	rS,cT,xW	xS,cT,rW	xS,cT,rW	cS	cS	cS	fS,cT	fS,cT	cS
Terek Sandpiper											
Upland Sandpiper	uS	xS,uT	uT	uT	uT	uS	rS	uS	rS,uT	rS	rS,uT
Eskimo Curlew						eT		eT	xT	eT	eT
Little Curlew											
Whimbrel		xT	xT	uT,xW	uT,rW	fT	uT	rT	fT	fT	fT
Bristle-thighed Curlew											
Slender-billed Curlew											
Far Eastern Curlew											
Eurasian Curlew									xV,xW		
Long-billed Curlew		eT		rT,xW	rT,xW	xV	exV		xV	xV	exV-q
Black-tailed Godwit									xV		
Hudsonian Godwit	xV	xV	xV	xV	rV	uT	rT	xT	uT	rT	rT
Bar-tailed Godwit						xV			xS*,xV		
Marbled Godwit		xT	rT	uT,rW	uT,rW	rV	rV		rV,xW	rV	rV
Ruddy Turnstone	rT	uT	uT	rS*,fW	rS*,fW	cT,rW	fT,xW	uT	cT,rW	cT,rW	cT,uW
Black Turnstone											
Surfbird											
Great Knot											
Red Knot		xT	rT	fT,uW	fT,uW	fT	uT	rT	cT,rW	cT,rW	fT,rW
Sanderling	xT	rT	rT	uS*,cW	uS*,cW	cT,rW	cT,rW	fT	rS*,cT,uW	xS*,cT,uW	xS*,cT,uW

Scolopacidae • 139

	New York	Pennsylvania	New Jersey	Delaware	Maryland	Dist. of Columbia	Virginia	North Carolina	South Carolina	Georgia	Florida
Wandering Tattler											
Gray-tailed Tattler											
Common Sandpiper											
Spotted Sandpiper	cS.xW	fS.cT.xW	fS.cT	rS*.cT	rS.cT.xW	rS.fT	uS.cT.xW	rS.cT.rW	xS.cT.uW	rS*.cT.fW	rS*.cW
Terek Sandpiper											
Upland Sandpiper	uS	uS	rS.uT	rT	rS.uT	rT	lrS.uT	uT	rT	uT	uT
Eskimo Curlew	eT	eT	xT		eT				xT		
Little Curlew											
Whimbrel	uT.xW	uT	fT	uT.xW	uT.xW	xT	fT.rW	xS*.fT.rW	xS*.fT.rW	rS*.fT.uW	rS*.fT.uW
Bristle-thighed Curlew											
Slender-billed Curlew											
Far Eastern Curlew											
Eurasian Curlew	exV										
Long-billed Curlew	xV	exV			xV	exV	xV	rV.xW	rW	rW	rW
Black-tailed Godwit		xV	xV					xW			xV
Hudsonian Godwit	rT	rT	uT	rT	rT	xT	uT	uT	xV	xV	rV
Bar-tailed Godwit	xV		rV				xV-q	xV			xV
Marbled Godwit	rT.xW	rT	rT	rT	rT.xW		uT.rW	xS*.fT.uW	rS*.fW	rS*.fW	rS*.fW
Ruddy Turnstone	xS*.cT.uW	uT.rW	xS*.cT.uW	xS*.cT.uW	rS*.cT.fW	xT	rS*.cT.fW	uS*.cW	uS*.cW	uS*.cW	uS*.cW
Black Turnstone											
Surfbird		xV									xV
Great Knot											
Red Knot	fT.rW	uT	cT.rW	fT.rW	fT.rW	xT	cT.uW	cT.uW	cT.uW	cT.uW	fT.uW
Sanderling	rS*.cT.uW	fT.xW	rS*.cT.fW	rS*.cT.fW	rS*.cT.fW	rT	uS*.cW	uS*.cW	uS*.cW	uS*.cW	uS*.cW

Scolopacidae • 141

		Date	Location	Cont. North America	Canada	Lower 48
Semipalmated Sandpiper *Calidris pusilla*				cS,lrW	cS	cT,lrW
Western Sandpiper *Calidris mauri*				lcS,rS*,cW	fT,lrW	rS*,cW
Rufous-necked Stint *Calidris ruficollis*				luS,rV	xV	rV
Little Stint *Calidris minuta*				rV	xV	xV
Temminck's Stint *Calidris temminckii*				lrT,xV	xV	xV
Long-toed Stint *Calidris subminuta*				lrT,xV		xV
Least Sandpiper *Calidris minutilla*				cS,fW	cS,lrW	xS,cT,fW
White-rumped Sandpiper *Calidris fuscicollis*				lcS,fT,xW	lcS,fT	fT,xW
Baird's Sandpiper *Calidris bairdii*				cS,xW	cS	cT,xW
Pectoral Sandpiper *Calidris melanotos*				lcS,cT,xW	lcS,cT,xW	cT,xW
Sharp-tailed Sandpiper *Calidris acuminata*				lfT,rV,xW	rV	rV,xW
Purple Sandpiper *Calidris maritima*				lfS,xS*,fW	lfS,fW	xS*,fW
Rock Sandpiper *Calidris ptilocnemis*				lcS,fW	fW	uW
Dunlin *Calidris alpina*				cP	cS,fW	rS*,cW
Curlew Sandpiper *Calidris ferruginea*				lrS,rV	rV	rV
Stilt Sandpiper *Calidris himantopus*				lfS,fT,luW	lfS,fT	fT,luW
Spoonbill Sandpiper *Eurynorhynchus pygmeus*				xV	xV	
Broad-billed Sandpiper *Limicola falcinellus*				xV		
Buff-breasted Sandpiper *Tryngites subruficollis*				luS,uT	luS,uT	uT
Ruff *Philomachus pugnax*				xS,lrT,rV,rW	rV,xW	rV,rW
Short-billed Dowitcher *Limnodromus griseus*				cS,fW	fS,cT,xW	rS*,cT,fW
Long-billed Dowitcher *Limnodromus scolopaceus*				lcS,rS*,cT,fW	lfS,cT,lrW	rS*,cT,fW
Jack Snipe *Lymnocryptes minimus*				xV	exV	xV
Common Snipe *Gallinago gallinago*				cP	cS,uW	fS,cW

	Hawaii	Alaska	Yukon Terr.	Northwest Terr.	British Columbia	Alberta	Saskatchewan	Manitoba	Ontario
Semipalmated Sandpiper	xV,xW	cS	lcS,cT	cS	uT	cT	cT	lcS,cT	lcS,cT
Western Sandpiper	rV,xW	cS,xW	rT	rT	cT,rW	rT	xT-q	rT	uT
Rufous-necked Stint	xV	luS,xV			xV				
Little Stint	xV	rV							xV
Temminck's Stint		lrT			xV				
Long-toed Stint	xV	lrT							
Least Sandpiper	rV,xW	cS	cS	cS	lfS,cT,rW	cT	luS,cT	lcS,cT	lfS,cT
White-rumped Sandpiper		luS,xV	xT	cS	rT	uT	fT	fT	fT
Baird's Sandpiper	rV,xW	fS	luS,rT	cS	fT	cT	cT	fT	uT
Pectoral Sandpiper	uT,xW	cS	lcS,cT	cS	fT	fT	cT	luS†,cT	lfS,cT,xW
Sharp-tailed Sandpiper	uT,xW	fT	xV	xV	rV	xV	xV-q		xV
Purple Sandpiper				fS				xV	rV,xW
Rock Sandpiper		cP			fW				
Dunlin	uW	cS,rW	luS†,rT	cS	cT,fW	uT	uT	lfS,fT	lfS,cT,xW
Curlew Sandpiper	xV	lrS,rV			xV	xV		xV	rV
Stilt Sandpiper		fS	lfS,uT	fS	rT	uT	fT	lfS,fT	luS,fT
Spoonbill Sandpiper		xV			xV				
Broad-billed Sandpiper		xV							
Buff-breasted Sandpiper	xV	uS	lrS,rT	uS	rT	uT	uT	uT	rT
Ruff	rT,xW	xS,lrT,xV			rV	xV	xV	xV	rV
Short-billed Dowitcher	xV	cS	luS	luS	lrS,fT,xW	uS,fT	uS†,fT	fS	lrS,fT
Long-billed Dowitcher	uW	cS	lfS†,fT	lfS,uT	cT,rW	fT	fT	fT	rT
Jack Snipe		xV							
Common Snipe	xV,rW	cS,rW	cS	cS	cS,fW	cS,xW	cS,xW	cS	cS,rW

Scolopacidae • 143

	Québec	Newfoundland	New Brunswick	Prince Edward I.	Nova Scotia	Washington	Oregon	California	Nevada	Idaho
Semipalmated Sandpiper	fS,cT	cS	cT	cT	cT	rV	rV	rV	xV	rV
Western Sandpiper	rT		rT	rT	rT	xS*,cT,uW	xS*,cT,fW	rS*,cW	cT,xW	fT
Rufous-necked Stint							xV	xV		
Little Stint			xV		xV					
Temminck's Stint						xV-q				
Long-toed Stint							xV			
Least Sandpiper	fS,cT	cS	xS,cT	cT	luS,cT	cT,uW	cT,uW	rS*,cW	cT,rW	cT
White-rumped Sandpiper	fT	fT	fT	fT	fT	xV		xV		xV
Baird's Sandpiper	rT	rT	rT	rT	rT	fT	uT	uT	uT	fT
Pectoral Sandpiper	fT	uT	fT	uT	fT	fT	fT	fT,xW	uT	uT
Sharp-tailed Sandpiper						rV	rV	rV,xW	xV	
Purple Sandpiper	fT,xW	fW	fW	uT,rW	cW					
Rock Sandpiper						fW	uW	uW		
Dunlin	fT	uT	cT,xW	fT	cT,rW	xS*,cW	xS*,cW	xS*,cW	uT,xW	rT
Curlew Sandpiper	xV		xV	xV	xV	xV	xV	xV		
Stilt Sandpiper	rT		rT	xV	uT	rT	rT	rT,luW	rT	rT
Spoonbill Sandpiper										
Broad-billed Sandpiper										
Buff-breasted Sandpiper	rT	rT	rT	xT	rT	rV	rV	rV		xV
Ruff	rV	xV,xW	xV	xV	rV	rV	xV,xW	rV,rW		
Short-billed Dowitcher	fS	lfS,uT	cT	fT	cT	cT	cT	uS*,cT,fW	rT	rT
Long-billed Dowitcher	xT		rT		rT	cT,rW	xS*,cT,uW	rS*,cW	cT,rW	cT
Jack Snipe		exV							xV	
Common Snipe	fS,xW	cS,xW	cS,xW	fS,xW	fS,rW	cP	cP	fS,cW	fS,cT,fW	cS,uW

	Montana	Wyoming	Utah	Colorado	Arizona	New Mexico	North Dakota	South Dakota	Nebraska	Kansas	Oklahoma
Semipalmated Sandpiper	fT	fT	rV	fT	rV	rT	cT	cT	cT	cT	fT
Western Sandpiper	uT	fT	cT,xW	fT	cT,rW	cT,xW	rT	rT	uT	fT	cT
Rufous-necked Stint											
Little Stint											
Temminck's Stint											
Long-toed Stint											
Least Sandpiper	cT	cT	cT,xW	cT	xS*,cT,fW	cT,uW	cT	cT	cT	cT,xW	cT,uW
White-rumped Sandpiper	xT	rT		rT	xV	rT	cT	cT	cT	cT	fT
Baird's Sandpiper	cT	cT	fT	cT	fT	fT	cT	cT	cT	cT	cT
Pectoral Sandpiper	fT	uT	uT	uT	uT	uT	cT	cT	cT	cT	cT
Sharp-tailed Sandpiper				xV	xV						
Purple Sandpiper											xV
Rock Sandpiper											
Dunlin	uT	rT	uT	rT	uT,rW	rT,xW	fT	fT	uT,xW	uT	uT,xW
Curlew Sandpiper	xV						xV			xV	
Stilt Sandpiper	uT	uT	rT	uT	uT	uT	fT	fT	fT	fT	fT
Spoonbill Sandpiper											
Broad-billed Sandpiper											
Buff-breasted Sandpiper	xT	xV		rV		xV	uT	rT	uT	uT	uT
Ruff				xV	xW		xV			xV	
Short-billed Dowitcher	rT	rT	rT	rT	rT,xW	rT	uT	rT	rT	rT	rT
Long-billed Dowitcher	cT	cT	cT,xW	fT	xS*,cT,uW	cT,rW	fT	fT	fT	fT	fT
Jack Snipe											
Common Snipe	fS,cT,uW	fS,cT,uW	fS,cT,fW	fS,cT,fW	lrS,cT,fW	lrSt,cT,fW	fS,cT,xW	uS,cT,rW	luS,cT,rW	cT,rW	cT,uW

Scolopacidae • 145

	Texas	Minnesota	Iowa	Missouri	Arkansas	Louisiana	Wisconsin	Michigan	Illinois	Indiana	Ohio
Semipalmated Sandpiper	cT	cT	cT	cT	cT	cT	cT	cT	cT	cT	cT
Western Sandpiper	rS*,cW	uT	rT	uT	fT,xW	rS*,cW	uT	uT	uT	uT	uT
Rufous-necked Stint											xV
Little Stint											
Temminck's Stint											
Long-toed Stint											
Least Sandpiper	rS*,cW	cT	cT	cT,xW	cT,uW	rS*,cW	cT	cT	cT,xW	cT	cT,xW
White-rumped Sandpiper	fT,xW	fT	uT	fT	uT	fT	uT	uT	uT	uT	uT
Baird's Sandpiper	cT	fT	uT	fT	uT	uT	uT	uT	uT	uT	uT,xW
Pectoral Sandpiper	cT,xW	cT	cT	cT	cT	cT	cT	cT	cT	cT	cT
Sharp-tailed Sandpiper			xV						xV		xV
Purple Sandpiper	xV,rW	xV		xV	xV	xV,xW	rV,xW	rV,xW	rV,xW	rV,xW	rV,xW
Rock Sandpiper											
Dunlin	xS*,fW	fT	fT	fT,xW	uT,xW	xS*,cW	cT	cT	fT	fT	cT,rW
Curlew Sandpiper	xV					xV	xV	xV	xV	xV	xV
Stilt Sandpiper	fT,uW	fT	fT	fT	fT	fT	fT	uT	fT	uT	uT
Spoonbill Sandpiper											
Broad-billed Sandpiper											
Buff-breasted Sandpiper	uT	uT	rT	uT	uT	uT	uT	uT	uT	uT	uT
Ruff	rV,xW	rV	xV	xV	xV	xV	rV	rV	rV	xV	rV
Short-billed Dowitcher	rS*,cT,fW	uT	uT	uT	uT	xS*,cT,uW	fT	fT	fT	fT	fT
Long-billed Dowitcher	rS*,cW	fT	fT	fT	fT	rS*,fW	uT	uT	uT	uT	uT
Jack Snipe											
Common Snipe	cW	fS,cT,xW	lrS,cT,rW	cT,uW	cW	cW	fS,cT,rW	fS,cT,rW	luS,cT,uW	exS,cT,rW	lrS,cT,rW

146 • Distributional Checklist of North American Birds

	West Virginia	Kentucky	Tennessee	Mississippi	Alabama	Maine	New Hampshire	Vermont	Massachusetts	Rhode Island	Connecticut
Semipalmated Sandpiper	fT	fT	cT	cT	cT	cT	cT	cT	cT	cT	cT
Western Sandpiper	rT	uT,xW	uT,rW	rS*,cW	rS*,cW	uT	uT	rT	uT,xW	uT,xW	fT,xW
Rufous-necked Stint						xV			xV		xV-q
Little Stint									xV		
Temminck's Stint											
Long-toed Stint											
Least Sandpiper	fT	cT,rW	cT,uW	xS*,cT,fW	xS*,cT,fW	cT	cT	cT	xS,cT,xW	cT,xW	cT,xW
White-rumped Sandpiper	rT	uT	uT	uT	uT	fT	uT	uT	fT	uT	uT
Baird's Sandpiper	rT	uT	uT	uT	rT	rT	rT	rT	rT	rT	rT
Pectoral Sandpiper	fT	cT	cT	cT	cT,xW	fT	fT	fT	fT	fT	fT
Sharp-tailed Sandpiper									xV		xV-q
Purple Sandpiper		xV	xV-q			xS*,cW	fW	xV	fW	fW	lfW
Rock Sandpiper											
Dunlin	rT	uT,xW	uT,rW	xS*,cW	xS*,cW	cT,rW	cT,uW	fT	cT,uW	cT,uW	cT,uW
Curlew Sandpiper					xV-q	xV	xV		rV	xV	rV
Stilt Sandpiper	rT	uT	uT	uT	uT	uT	uT	rT	uT	uT	uT
Spoonbill Sandpiper											
Broad-billed Sandpiper											
Buff-breasted Sandpiper	xT	rT	rT	rT	rT	rT	rT	rT	rT	uT	uT
Ruff		xV	xV	xV	rV	xV	xV-q	rV	rV	rV	
Short-billed Dowitcher	rT-sp	uT	uT	xS*,fT,uW	xS*,fT,uW	cT,xW	cT	fT	cT	cT	cT
Long-billed Dowitcher		rT	uT	uT,rW	uT,rW	rT	rT	rT	uT,rW	uT,rW	uT,xW
Jack Snipe											
Common Snipe	lrS,fT,rW	cT,fW	cT,fW	cW	cW	fS,cT,rW	fS,rW	fS,xW	luS,fT,rW	fT,rW	fT,rW

Scolopacidae • 147

	New York	Pennsylvania	New Jersey	Delaware	Maryland	Dist. of Columbia	Virginia	North Carolina	South Carolina	Georgia	Florida
Semipalmated Sandpiper	cT	cT	cT	cT	cT	fT	cT	cT	cT	cT	cT,rW
Western Sandpiper	fT,rW	uT	fT,rW	cT,rW	fT,rW	uT	xS*,cT,uW	xS*,cT,uW	xS*,cT,uW	xS*,cW	rS*,cW
Rufous-necked Stint				xV							
Little Stint	xV			xV							
Temminck's Stint							xV-q				
Long-toed Stint											
Least Sandpiper	cT,xW	cT,xW	cT,xW	cT,xW	cT,rW	fT	cT,rW	cT,uW	xS*,cT,fW	xS*,cT,fW	rS*,cW
White-rumped Sandpiper	uT	uT	uT	uT	uT	rT	uT	uT	uT	uT	uT
Baird's Sandpiper	rT	rT	rT	xT	rT	rT	rT	rT	rT	xT	rT
Pectoral Sandpiper	fT	fT	fT	fT	fT	fT	cT	cT	cT	cT,xW	cT,xW
Sharp-tailed Sandpiper	xV						xV				xV
Purple Sandpiper	xS*,fW	rV,xW	xS*,fW	fW	xS*,fW		xS*,uW	uW	uW	rW	rW
Rock Sandpiper											
Dunlin	cT,fW	cT,rW	xS*,cT,fW	cT,fW	cT,fW	uT,xW	xS*,cW	xS*,cW	xS*,cW	xS*,cW	xS*,fW
Curlew Sandpiper	rV	xV	rV	rV			rV	rV			rV
Stilt Sandpiper	fT	uT	fT	fT	fT	rT	fT	fT	uT	uT	uT,rW
Spoonbill Sandpiper											
Broad-billed Sandpiper											
Buff-breasted Sandpiper	uT	uT	uT	rT	uT	rT	uT	uT	rT	rT	rT
Ruff	rV,xW	rV	rV	rV	xV,xW	xV	rV	rV	xV	xV	rV,xW
Short-billed Dowitcher	cT	fT	cT,xW	cT	cT,xW	uT	cT,rW	rS*,cT,fW	rS*,cT,fW	rS*,cT,fW	rS*,cW
Long-billed Dowitcher	uT,rW	rT	uT,rW	uT	uT,xW	rT	uT,rW	uT,rW	uT,rW	uW	uW
Jack Snipe											
Common Snipe	fS,cT,rW	luS,cT,rW	lrS,cT,uW	cT,rW	cT,uW	uT,rW	cT,fW	cT,fW	cW	cW	cW

Scolopacidae • 149

	Date	Location	Cont. North America	Canada	Lower 48
Pin-tailed Snipe *Gallinago stenura*			xV		
Eurasian Woodcock *Scolopax rusticola*			xV	exV	xV
American Woodcock *Scolopax minor*			fP	fS,xW	fP

Subfamily Phalaropodinae: Phalaropes

Wilson's Phalarope *Phalaropus tricolor*			cS,lrW	cS	cS,lrW
Red-necked Phalarope *Phalaropus lobatus*			cS,luW	cS	cT,luW
Red Phalarope *Phalaropus fulicaria*			lcS,uW	cS,xW	cT,uW

Family Laridae: Skuas, Gulls, Terns and Skimmers
Subfamily Stercorariinae: Skuas and Jaegers

Pomarine Jaeger *Stercorarius pomarinus*			lcS,rS*,fT,uW	fS	rS*,fT,uW
Parasitic Jaeger *Stercorarius parasiticus*			cS,rW	cS,xW	rS*,fT,rW
Long-tailed Jaeger *Stercorarius longicaudus*			cS	cS	rT
Great Skua *Catharacta skua*			luS*,rW	uS*,rW	lrS*,rW
South Polar Skua *Catharacta maccormicki*			uS*	uS*	uS*

Subfamily Larinae: Gulls

Laughing Gull *Larus atricilla*			cS,fW	lrS,rS*,rV	cP
Franklin's Gull *Larus pipixcan*			cS,rW	cS,xW	uS,cT,rW
Little Gull *Larus minutus*			lrS,xS*,rW	lrS,rT,lrW	lrS,xS*,rW
Common Black-headed Gull *Larus ridibundus*			xS,xS*,uT,rW	xS,uT,rW	xS,xS*,uT,rW
Bonaparte's Gull *Larus philadelphia*			cS,fW	cS,rW	xS,rS*,cW
Heermann's Gull *Larus heermanni*			xS,cS*,lfW	luS*	xS,cS*,fW
Black-tailed Gull *Larus crassirostris*			xV		
Mew Gull *Larus canus*			cP	cP	rS*,cW
Ring-billed Gull *Larus delawarensis*			cP	cS,rW	fS,cW

	Hawaii	Alaska	Yukon Terr.	Northwest Terr.	British Columbia	Alberta	Saskatchewan	Manitoba	Ontario
Pin-tailed Snipe	xV	xV-q							
Eurasian Woodcock									
American Woodcock							xV-q	lfS	fS,xW

Subfamily Phalaropodinae: Phalaropes

	Hawaii	Alaska	Yukon Terr.	Northwest Terr.	British Columbia	Alberta	Saskatchewan	Manitoba	Ontario
Wilson's Phalarope	rV	rV	lrS	xS*	fS	fS	cS	cS	luS,rT
Red-necked Phalarope	xV	cS	cS	cS	luS,cT	fT	luS,cT	lfS,fT	lfS,uT
Red Phalarope	uT,xW	cS	luS	cS	fT	xV	xV	rT	rT,xW

Family Laridae: Skuas, Gulls, Terns and Skimmers
Subfamily Stercorariinae: Skuas and Jaegers

	Hawaii	Alaska	Yukon Terr.	Northwest Terr.	British Columbia	Alberta	Saskatchewan	Manitoba	Ontario
Pomarine Jaeger	rW	cS	luS*,rT	fS	fT	xV-q	xV	lrS*,rT	lrS*,rT
Parasitic Jaeger		cS	lfS,fT	cS	cT	rT	rT	lfS,rT	luS,uT,xW
Long-tailed Jaeger		cS	lcS	cS	uT	rT	xV	luS*,rT	lrS*,rT
Great Skua				rS*					
South Polar Skua	xT-sp	xS*				uS*			

Subfamily Larinae: Gulls

	Hawaii	Alaska	Yukon Terr.	Northwest Terr.	British Columbia	Alberta	Saskatchewan	Manitoba	Ontario
Laughing Gull	rV,rW						xV-q	xS*,xV	rS*
Franklin's Gull	xV	xV		xV	rT,xW	cS	cS	cS	rT,xW
Little Gull		xV-q	xV	xV	rV		xV	xS,rV	lrS,rW
Com. Black-head. Gull	xV	uT			xV			xV	rV,xW
Bonaparte's Gull	xV,rW	cS,xW	cS	cS	fS,cT,rW	fS	cS	cS	cS,rW
Heermann's Gull					uS*				
Black-tailed Gull		xV							
Mew Gull		cS,fW	cS	cS	fS,cW	lrS†,uT	uS	xS,xV	xV
Ring-billed Gull	xV,rW	xS*,rV,xW	xV	luS,xV	lrS,uT,rW	cS	cS,xW	cS	cS,uW

	Québec	Newfoundland	New Brunswick	Prince Edward I.	Nova Scotia		Washington	Oregon	California	Nevada	Idaho
Pin-tailed Snipe											
Eurasian Woodcock	exV	exV									
American Woodcock	lfS	lrS,xW	fS	uS	uS,xW						

Subfamily Phalaropodinae: Phalaropes

	Québec	Newfoundland	New Brunswick	Prince Edward I.	Nova Scotia		Washington	Oregon	California	Nevada	Idaho
Wilson's Phalarope	luS,xV	xV	xS*,rV	xV	xS*,rV		fS	fS	fS,cT,rW	fS,cT	fS,cT
Red-necked Phalarope	fS	uS	cT	rT	cT		cT	cT	cT,luW	fT	fT
Red Phalarope	lfS,uT	rS†,cT	cT	xT	cT		fT	fT,xW	cT,uW	xV	xV

Family Laridae: Skuas, Gulls, Terns and Skimmers
Subfamily Stercorariinae: Skuas and Jaegers

	Québec	Newfoundland	New Brunswick	Prince Edward I.	Nova Scotia		Washington	Oregon	California	Nevada	Idaho
Pomarine Jaeger	luS,rT	uS*,fT	rT	xT	fT		fT,xW	fT,xW	rS*,fT,uW		xV
Parasitic Jaeger	luS,uT	lfS,uS*,fT	uT	xT	cT		cT	fT,xW	xS*,fT,rW	xV	xV
Long-tailed Jaeger	lfS,rT	rS*,uT	xT		rT		uT	rT	rT	xV	xV
Great Skua	xV	uS*,rW	xW		rS*,uW						
South Polar Skua		xS*					uS*	uS*	rS*,uT		

Subfamily Larinae: Gulls

	Québec	Newfoundland	New Brunswick	Prince Edward I.	Nova Scotia		Washington	Oregon	California	Nevada	Idaho
Laughing Gull	xS*,rV	rV	lrS,rS*	xV	eS,rS*		xV	xV	eS,luS*,rV,xW	xV	
Franklin's Gull	rV	xV	rV		xV		rT,xW	luS,rT,xW	xS*,uT,rW	xS,uT	uS
Little Gull	xS,rT	rT,xW	rT,xW	rT	xT		rV,xW	xV	rV,xW		xV
Com. Black-head. Gull	xS,rT	xS,uT,luW	rW	rT,xW	uT,rW		xV-q	xV	xV,xW		
Bonaparte's Gull	lrS,fT	rT,xW	rS*,cT,rW	fT	rS*,cT,rW		rS*,cT,fW	rS*,cT,fW	rS*,cW	uT,xW	uT
Heermann's Gull							fS*,xW	cS*,xW	xS,cS*,fW	xV	
Black-tailed Gull											
Mew Gull	xV	xV,xW	xV		xV		rS*,cW	rS*,cW	rS*,cW	rV,xW	xV
Ring-billed Gull	cS,xW	fS,xW	cS,rW	fS,rW	uS*,fT,rW		cS,fW	cS,fW	lfS,uS*,cW	rS*,cT,fW	cS,uW

152 • Distributional Checklist of North American Birds

	Montana	Wyoming	Utah	Colorado	Arizona	New Mexico	North Dakota	South Dakota	Nebraska	Kansas	Oklahoma
Pin-tailed Snipe											
Eurasian Woodcock											
American Woodcock	xV	xV		xV		xV	lrS	luS	luS	uS	uS,rW

Subfamily Phalaropodinae: Phalaropes

	Montana	Wyoming	Utah	Colorado	Arizona	New Mexico	North Dakota	South Dakota	Nebraska	Kansas	Oklahoma
Wilson's Phalarope	cS	cS	fS,cT,xW	fS,cT	lrS,cT,xW	lrS,cT	cS	cS	cS	uS,cT	cT
Red-necked Phalarope	fT	uT	fT	uT	fT	uT	cT	fT,xW	uT	uT	rT
Red Phalarope	xV		xV	rV	rV,xW	xV	xV	xV	xV	rV	xV

Family Laridae: Skuas, Gulls, Terns and Skimmers
Subfamily Stercorariinae: Skuas and Jaegers

	Montana	Wyoming	Utah	Colorado	Arizona	New Mexico	North Dakota	South Dakota	Nebraska	Kansas	Oklahoma
Pomarine Jaeger		xV		xV	xV	xV		xV	xV	xV	xV
Parasitic Jaeger	rV	rV	xV	rV	rV	xV,xW-q	xV		xV	xV	xV
Long-tailed Jaeger	xV		xV	xV	xV	xV	xV	xV	xV	xV	
Great Skua											
South Polar Skua											

Subfamily Larinae: Gulls

	Montana	Wyoming	Utah	Colorado	Arizona	New Mexico	North Dakota	South Dakota	Nebraska	Kansas	Oklahoma
Laughing Gull	xV			rV	xV	xV	xV-q	xV	xV	xV	rV
Franklin's Gull	uS,fT	uS*,fT	lcS,rS*,fT	rS*,cT	uT	uT	fS,cT,xW	fS,cT	luS,rS*,cT	cT	cT
Little Gull				xV						xV	xW-q
Com. Black-head. Gull										xV	xV-q
Bonaparte's Gull	uT	uT	uT	uT	uT,rW	uT,xW	fT	uT	uT,xW	uT,rW	uW
Heermann's Gull		xV			rV,xW	xV					xW
Black-tailed Gull											
Mew Gull	xV	exV	xW	xV,xW	xV,xW	xW					
Ring-billed Gull	cS,rW	uS,cT,xW	rS*,cW	exS,rS*,cT,fW	uS*,cW	rS*,cT,uW	cS,xW	lfS,cT,xW	cT,rW	xS*,cT,uW	rS*,cT,fW

Scolopacidae • 153

	Texas	Minnesota	Iowa	Missouri	Arkansas	Louisiana	Wisconsin	Michigan	Illinois	Indiana	Ohio
Pin-tailed Snipe											
Eurasian Woodcock											xV
American Woodcock	lrS,uW	cS	fS	fS,rW	uS,fT,uW	uS,fW	cS	cS,xW	fS,rW	fS,xW	uS,fT,xW

Subfamily Phalaropodinae: Phalaropes

	Texas	Minnesota	Iowa	Missouri	Arkansas	Louisiana	Wisconsin	Michigan	Illinois	Indiana	Ohio
Wilson's Phalarope	xS,cT,xW	uS,fT	lrS,fT	fT	uT	uT,xW	uS,fT	xS,uT	lrS,uT	xS,uT	xS,uT
Red-necked Phalarope	rT	uT	rT	rT	rT	xT	uT	uT	rT	rT	rT
Red Phalarope	rV,xW	xV		xV	xV	xV	rT	rT	rT	rT	rT,xW

Family Laridae: Skuas, Gulls, Terns and Skimmers
Subfamily Stercorariinae: Skuas and Jaegers

	Texas	Minnesota	Iowa	Missouri	Arkansas	Louisiana	Wisconsin	Michigan	Illinois	Indiana	Ohio
Pomarine Jaeger	xS*,rW	rV		xV	xV	rT,xW	xV	rV,xW	xV	xV-q	xV
Parasitic Jaeger	xS*,rW	rT	xV	xV	xV	rT,xW	rT	uT	rT	rT	rT
Long-tailed Jaeger	xV	xV	exV	xV	xV	xV	xV	rV	exV	xV	xV
Great Skua											
South Polar Skua				xV-sp							

Subfamily Larinae: Gulls

	Texas	Minnesota	Iowa	Missouri	Arkansas	Louisiana	Wisconsin	Michigan	Illinois	Indiana	Ohio
Laughing Gull	cP	xS*,xV	xV	rV,xW	rV	cP	xS*,xV	rS*	rS*	rS*	xS,rS*
Franklin's Gull	cT,rW	fS	lrS,rS*,fT	fT,xW	fT	uT	rS*,uT	uT	uT	uT	rT
Little Gull	xV,xW	rV		xV		xV,xW	lrS,rT,xW	xS,rT,xW	rT,xW	rT,xW	rW
Com. Black-head. Gull	xW			xV			xS*,xV	rV,xW	xV,xW	xV-q	rV,xW
Bonaparte's Gull	fW	rS*,cT,rW	fT,xW	fT,rW	fT,uW	fW	xS,rS*,cT,rW	eS,rS*,cT,rW	rS*,cT,uW	rS*,cT,uW	rS*,cT,uW
Heermann's Gull	xV							xV			xW
Black-tailed Gull											
Mew Gull		xV	xV						xV		xV
Ring-billed Gull	uS*,cW	fS,cT,xW	xS*,cT,uW	rS*,cT,fW	rS*,cT,fW	uS*,cW	cS,uW	cS,uW	lfS,uS*,cT,fW	uS*,cT,fW	lfS,uS*,cT,fW

154 • Distributional Checklist of North American Birds

	West Virginia	Kentucky	Tennessee	Mississippi	Alabama	Maine	New Hampshire	Vermont	Massachusetts	Rhode Island	Connecticut
Pin-tailed Snipe											
Eurasian Woodcock											
American Woodcock	fS,rW	uS,fT,rW	uS,fT,uW	uS,fW	uS,fW	cS,xW	cS,xW	cS,xW	fS,rW	fS,rW	fS,rW

Subfamily Phalaropodinae: Phalaropes

	West Virginia	Kentucky	Tennessee	Mississippi	Alabama	Maine	New Hampshire	Vermont	Massachusetts	Rhode Island	Connecticut
Wilson's Phalarope	xT	uT	uT	uT	uT,xW	rV	rV	rV	xS,rT	rT	rT
Red-necked Phalarope	xV	xV	xV	rT	rT	cT	cT	rV	fT	fT	xV
Red Phalarope	xV	xV	xV	xV	rV,xW	cT	fT	rV	fT	fT	xV

Family Laridae: Skuas, Gulls, Terns and Skimmers
Subfamily Stercorariinae: Skuas and Jaegers

	West Virginia	Kentucky	Tennessee	Mississippi	Alabama	Maine	New Hampshire	Vermont	Massachusetts	Rhode Island	Connecticut
Pomarine Jaeger				rT,xW	rW	fT	fT		fT,xW	fT	xV-q
Parasitic Jaeger	xV			rT,xW	rW	cT	cT	rT	cT	fT	xT
Long-tailed Jaeger			xV		xV-q	rT	xT	xV	rT	rT	exV
Great Skua						rS*,uW			xS*,rW	xW	
South Polar Skua						rS*	xS*		rS*	rS*	xV

Subfamily Larinae: Gulls

	West Virginia	Kentucky	Tennessee	Mississippi	Alabama	Maine	New Hampshire	Vermont	Massachusetts	Rhode Island	Connecticut
Laughing Gull	xV	rV,xW	rV	cP	cP	uS	uS*	xS*,xV	fS,xW	cS*,xW	fS*,xW
Franklin's Gull		rT	rT	rT,xW	rT,xW	xV	xV	xV-q	rV	xV	xV
Little Gull				xV		rT,xW	rT	xT	uT,rW	uT,rW	rW
Com. Black-head. Gull				xV,xW		uW	rW		xS,uW	uW	uT,rW
Bonaparte's Gull	uT	fT,rW	fT,uW	fW	fW	xS,rS*,cT,rW	rS*,cT,uW	rS*,uT	rS*,cT,uW	xS*,cT,fW	xS*,cT,fW
Heermann's Gull											
Black-tailed Gull											
Mew Gull						xV-q			rV,xW	xV	xV,xW
Ring-billed Gull	cT,fW	rS*,cW	rS*,cW	uS*,cW	uS*,cW	xS,uS*,cT,uW	fS,cT,uW	cS,uW	uS*,cT,fW	uS*,cT,fW	uS*,cT,fW

Scolopacidae • 155

	New York	Pennsylvania	New Jersey	Delaware	Maryland	Dist. of Columbia	Virginia	North Carolina	South Carolina	Georgia	Florida
Pin-tailed Snipe											
Eurasian Woodcock		exV	xV				exV				
American Woodcock	fS,rW	fS,rW	fS,rW	fS,rW	fS,uW	xS,rT,xW	fP	fP	uS,fW	uS,fW	uS,fW

Subfamily Phalaropodinae: Phalaropes

	New York	Pennsylvania	New Jersey	Delaware	Maryland	Dist. of Columbia	Virginia	North Carolina	South Carolina	Georgia	Florida
Wilson's Phalarope	xS*,rT	rT	rT	rT	rT	xT	uT	uT	rT	rT	uT,xW
Red-necked Phalarope	fT	rV	fT	fT	fT	xV	fT	fT	fT	uT,rW	uT,xW
Red Phalarope	uT,xW	rV,xW	uT	fT	fT,xW	exV	fT,xW	fT,rW	fT,uW	fT,uW	fT,uW

Family Laridae: Skuas, Gulls, Terns and Skimmers
Subfamily Stercorariinae: Skuas and Jaegers

	New York	Pennsylvania	New Jersey	Delaware	Maryland	Dist. of Columbia	Virginia	North Carolina	South Carolina	Georgia	Florida
Pomarine Jaeger	fT,xW	xV	fT,xW	fT	fT,xW		xS*,uT,rW	xS*,uT,rW	xS*,uT,rW	xS*,uT,rW	rS*,uW
Parasitic Jaeger	fT,xW	rT	fT,xW	fT	fT,xW	exV	uT,rW	uT,rW	uT,rW	xS*,uW	xS*,uW
Long-tailed Jaeger	rT		rT		xT		xT	rT	xT	xT	rT
Great Skua	rW		uW	rW	uW		rW	xW			
South Polar Skua	xS*		rS*		xS*-q		xS*-q	rS*	xS*	xS*	xS*

Subfamily Larinae: Gulls

	New York	Pennsylvania	New Jersey	Delaware	Maryland	Dist. of Columbia	Virginia	North Carolina	South Carolina	Georgia	Florida
Laughing Gull	cS,rW	uT,xW	cS,rW	cS,rW	cS,rW	cS*	cS,rW	cS,uW	cS,uW	cS,fW	cP
Franklin's Gull	rV	rV	xV,xW		rV	xV	xV	xV	xV	xV	rV,rW
Little Gull	uT,rW	rT,xW	xS*,uT,rW	uT,rW	rW		xS*,rW	rW			xV,xW
Com. Black-head. Gull	uT,rW	xV	uW	rW	rW		xS*,rW	rW	xW		xV,xW
Bonaparte's Gull	rS*,cT,fW	fT,uW	xS*,cT,fW	xS*,cT,fW	xS*,cT,fW	fT,rW	xS*,cW	cW	cW	cW	xS*,fW
Heermann's Gull											
Black-tailed Gull											
Mew Gull			xV,xW-q	xV			xV-q	xV-q			
Ring-billed Gull	fS,cT,fW	luS,uS*,cT,fW	uS*,cT,fW	uS*,cW	uS*,cW	uS*,cW	uS*,cW	uS*,cW	uS*,cW	uS*,cW	uS*,cW

Laridae • 157

	Date	Location	Cont. North America	Canada	Lower 48
California Gull *Larus californicus*			cS,fW	cS,lrW	fS,cT,fW
Herring Gull *Larus argentatus*			cP	cP	cP
Thayer's Gull *Larus thayeri*			lfS,rS*,fW	lfS,rS*,fT,lfW	rS*,fW
Iceland Gull *Larus glaucoides*			lcS,rS*,fW	lcS,rS*,fW	rS*,uW
Lesser Black-backed Gull *Larus fuscus*			xS*,rW	xS*,rT,lrW	xS*,rW
Slaty-backed Gull *Larus schistisagus*			lrS*,xV,xW	xV	xW
Yellow-footed Gull *Larus livens*			lcS*,lrW		lcS*,lrW
Western Gull *Larus occidentalis*			cP	lrS,luW	cP
Glaucous-winged Gull *Larus glaucescens*			cP	cP	lcS,uS*,cW
Glaucous Gull *Larus hyperboreus*			cS,fW	cS,fW	rS*,uW
Great Black-backed Gull *Larus marinus*			cP	cP	cP
Black-legged Kittiwake *Rissa tridactyla*			cS,fW	fP	rS*,fW
Red-legged Kittiwake *Rissa brevirostris*			lfS,xV,lrW	exV	xV,xW
Ross' Gull *Rhodostethia rosea*			lrS,lfT,xV,xW	lrS,luT,xV	xV,xW
Sabine's Gull *Xema sabini*			fS,xW	fS	uT,xW
Ivory Gull *Pagophila eburnea*			luS,rS*,uW	luS,xS*,uW	rV,rW

Subfamily Sterninae: Terns

	Date	Location	Cont. North America	Canada	Lower 48
Gull-billed Tern *Sterna nilotica*			fS,luW	xV	fS,uW
Caspian Tern *Sterna caspia*			fS,uW	uS	fP
Royal Tern *Sterna maxima*			cS,fW	xV	cP
Elegant Tern *Sterna elegans*			luS,fS*,xW	xS*	luS,cS*,xW
Sandwich Tern *Sterna sandvicensis*			fS,luW	exV	fS,rW
Roseate Tern *Sterna dougallii*			lfS,uT,lrW	luS	lfS,uT,lrW
Common Tern *Sterna hirundo*			cS,rW	cS	cS,rW

	Hawaii	Alaska	Yukon Terr.	Northwest Terr.	British Columbia	Alberta	Saskatchewan	Manitoba	Ontario
California Gull	xV,xW	rS*	xS*	lfS	uS,fT,rW	cS	cS	luS,rT	xS,xV
Herring Gull	xV,xW	fP	cS	cS	fP	lfS,uT	fS,xW	cS	cP
Thayer's Gull		xS*,fT,uW	xT	fS	xS*,fW	xT	xV	lrS*,rT	lrS*,rW
Iceland Gull		xV-q	xV	lcS	xV,xW	xV	xV-q	lrS*,rT	rS*,uW
Les. Black-back. Gull				xV			xV-q	xV	rV,xW
Slaty-backed Gull	xV	rS*,xW				xV			
Yellow-footed Gull									
Western Gull	xW	xV			lrS,uW				
Glaucous-winged Gull	rV,rW	cP	xV		cP	xV			
Glaucous Gull	xV,xW	cP	lcS	cS,rW	xS*,uW	xV	rV,xW	luS*,rT	rS*,uW
Gr. Black-backed Gull				xS*,rV			xV-q	xS*,rV	luS,rS*,uW
Black-legged Kittiwake	xV,xW	cS,uW	xV	lcS,fS*	iuS*,fT,uW	xV		xV	uT,xW
Red-legged Kittiwake		lfS,rW	exV						
Ross' Gull		lfT		lrS,uT	xV			lrS	xV
Sabine's Gull		fS	xV	fS	uT	xV	rV	rV	rV
Ivory Gull		rS*,uT,rW	xV	luS,uW	xV	xV-q	xV-q	rV,xW	xV,xW

Subfamily Sterninae: Terns

	Hawaii	Alaska	Yukon Terr.	Northwest Terr.	British Columbia	Alberta	Saskatchewan	Manitoba	Ontario
Gull-billed Tern									
Caspian Tern	xP*,xV	xS*,rV			lrS	rT	lrS,rT	luS,rT	fS	fS
Royal Tern									xV
Elegant Tern					xS*				
Sandwich Tern									exV
Roseate Tern									
Common Tern	xS*,xV	lrT		lfS	fT	cS	cS	cS	cS

	Québec	Newfoundland	New Brunswick	Prince Edward I.	Nova Scotia
California Gull					
Herring Gull	cS,uW	cS,fW	cP	cP	cP
Thayer's Gull	rT,xW	xS*,xV,rW			
Iceland Gull	lrS,rS*,fW	rS*,cW	rS*,fW	xS*,fW	rS*,fW
Les. Black-back. Gull	rT,xW	xS*,rT,xW	xT	xW	rW
Slaty-backed Gull					
Yellow-footed Gull					
Western Gull					
Glaucous-winged Gull					
Glaucous Gull	lfS,rS*,uW	lfS,rS*,fW	rS*,uW	xS*,uW	xS*,uW
Gr. Black-backed Gull	cS,fW	cS,fW	cP	cS,fW	cP
Black-legged Kittiwake	fS,xW	cS,fW	uS*,cW	uS*,fT,uW	lfS,uS*,cW
Red-legged Kittiwake					
Ross' Gull		xV			
Sabine's Gull	rV	rT	xT		xT
Ivory Gull	rW	xS*,uW	xW	xV	xW

Subfamily Sterninae: Terns

	Québec	Newfoundland	New Brunswick	Prince Edward I.	Nova Scotia
Gull-billed Tern		xV			xV
Caspian Tern	lrS,rT	luS	rT	rT	rT
Royal Tern		xV			xV
Elegant Tern					
Sandwich Tern					
Roseate Tern	lrS		xS		uS
Common Tern	cS	cS	cS	cS	cS

	Washington	Oregon	California	Nevada	Idaho
California Gull	fS,cT,uW	fS,cT,fW	fS,cW	lfS,rS*,cT,uW	cS,rW
Herring Gull	rS*,fT,uW	rS*,fW	rS*,fW	xS*,uW	xS*,uW
Thayer's Gull	xS*,fT,uW	xS*,fW	xS*,fW	rV,xW	xW
Iceland Gull			xW-q		xV
Les. Black-back. Gull			xW		
Slaty-backed Gull					
Yellow-footed Gull			lcS*,lrW		
Western Gull	cP	cP	cP	xV,xW	xV
Glaucous-winged Gull	cP	lfS,fS*,cW	uS*,cW	rV	xV
Glaucous Gull	rW	rW	rW	xV,xW	xV,xW
Gr. Black-backed Gull					
Black-legged Kittiwake	iuS*,fW	irS*,fW	irS*,fW	rV,xW	xV
Red-legged Kittiwake	xW	xV,xW		xV	
Ross' Gull					
Sabine's Gull	uT	uT	fT	rV	xV
Ivory Gull	xV-q				

	Washington	Oregon	California	Nevada	Idaho
Gull-billed Tern			lfS,xW		
Caspian Tern	uS	fS	fS,uW	luS,uT	uS
Royal Tern			xS,uS*,fW		
Elegant Tern	irS*	irS*	luS,cS*,xW		
Sandwich Tern			xS*,xV		
Roseate Tern					
Common Tern	lrS,fT	fT	fT,rW	uT	rT

	Montana	Wyoming	Utah	Colorado	Arizona	New Mexico	North Dakota	South Dakota	Nebraska	Kansas	Oklahoma
California Gull	cS,rW	fS,rW	lcS,rS*,cT,fW	lfS,rS*,uW	rS*,fT,uW	xS*,rT,xW	fS,xW	lrS,uT	rV	xV	xV
Herring Gull	xS,fT,xW	uT,xW	xS*,uW	xS*,uW	xS*,rW	rT,xW	xS*,fT,rW	xS*,fT,rW	rS*,fT,uW	rS*,fT,uW	rS*,fW
Thayer's Gull	xV		xV,rW	xV,xW	xV,xW	xV,xW	xV,xW	xV	xV	xW	xV,xW-q
Iceland Gull	xV,xW							xV		xV		xW-q
Les. Black-back. Gull				xV							xW
Slaty-backed Gull											
Yellow-footed Gull											
Western Gull					xV						
Glaucous-winged Gull			xV,xW	xV	xV						exW
Glaucous Gull	xV,xW	xV	xV,xW	xV,xW		xV,xW	rT,xW	rT,xW	xW	rW	rW
Gr. Black-backed Gull	xW			xW					xV		
Black-legged Kittiwake	xV	xV	xV	rV	rV,xW	xV	xV,xW	xV	xV	rV	xV
Red-legged Kittiwake											
Ross' Gull				xV							
Sabine's Gull	xV	rV	rV	rV	rV	rV,xW	xV	xV	xV	rV	rV
Ivory Gull	xV			xV							

Subfamily Sterninae: Terns

	Montana	Wyoming	Utah	Colorado	Arizona	New Mexico	North Dakota	South Dakota	Nebraska	Kansas	Oklahoma
Gull-billed Tern					xV						
Caspian Tern	xS,rT	uS	luS,uT	rT	uT,xW	rT	lrS,uT	rT	rT	rT	rT
Royal Tern											
Elegant Tern											
Sandwich Tern											
Roseate Tern											xV-q
Common Tern	fS	xS*,rT	rT	rT	uT	rT	fS	luS,uT	uT	uT	rT

Laridae • 161

	Texas	Minnesota	Iowa	Missouri	Arkansas	Louisiana	Wisconsin	Michigan	Illinois	Indiana	Ohio
California Gull	rV,rW	rV		xV				xV	xV,xW	xV	xV,xW
Herring Gull	uS*,cW	fS,cT,uW	rS*,fT,uW	rS*,fT,uW	rS*,fT,uW	uS*,cW	cS,fW	cS,fW	luS,fS*,cW	fS*,cW	lfS,fS*,cW
Thayer's Gull	xV,xW	rW		rW		xV,xW	xT,xW	rW	rW	rW	rW
Iceland Gull	xW-q	rW		xW			rW	rW	rW	rW	rW
Les. Black-back. Gull	rV,rW	xV	xV	xV		xV,xW	xV	xV	xV,xW	xV,xW	rV,xW
Slaty-backed Gull				xW					xW		
Yellow-footed Gull											
Western Gull									xV		
Glaucous-winged Gull											
Glaucous Gull	rW	rW	rW	rW	xT	rW	xS*,rW	xS*,rW	rW	rW	rW
Gr. Black-backed Gull	xV,xW	xV,xW	xV	xV,xW		xV,xW	xS*,rW	xS*,uW	rW	rW	uS*,fW
Black-legged Kittiwake	xV,rW	xV	xV	rV,rW		xS*,xV,xW	rV,xW	uT,xW	rV,xW	rV,xW	rT,xW
Red-legged Kittiwake											
Ross' Gull		xV							xV		
Sabine's Gull	rV	xV	xV	xV	xV	xV	xV	rV	rV,xW	rV	rV
Ivory Gull		xV,xW					xV	xV,xW-q			xW

Subfamily Sterninae: Terns

	Texas	Minnesota	Iowa	Missouri	Arkansas	Louisiana	Wisconsin	Michigan	Illinois	Indiana	Ohio
Gull-billed Tern	fS,uW					fS,uW					
Caspian Tern	fS,cW	xS,rS*,fT	uT	uT	uT	fS,cW	luS,fT	fS	rS*,uT	rS*,uT	rS*,fT
Royal Tern	cP					cP					
Elegant Tern	exV										
Sandwich Tern	fS,rW					fS,rW					
Roseate Tern	xV						xV	xV-q		xV	
Common Tern	eS,rS*,cT,rW	fS	uT	uT	uT	lrS,fT,rW	fS	fS,cT	lrS,rS*,fT	eS,rS*,fT	luS,rS*,cT

162 • Distributional Checklist of North American Birds

	West Virginia	Kentucky	Tennessee	Mississippi	Alabama	Maine	New Hampshire	Vermont	Massachusetts	Rhode Island	Connecticut
California Gull		xV									
Herring Gull	xS*,uT,rW	rS*,fW	rS*,fW	uS*,cW	uS*,cW	cP	cP	fP	cP	cP	cP
Thayer's Gull		rW				xW		xV-q	xS*,xV,rW	xW	
Iceland Gull		xW	xW-q			rS*,fW	rS*,fW	rW	rS*,fW	xS*,uW	xS*,uW
Les. Black-back. Gull		xV,xW		xV,xW	xV	rT,xW	xT	xW	xS*,rW	xS*,rW	rW
Slaty-backed Gull											
Yellow-footed Gull											
Western Gull											
Glaucous-winged Gull											
Glaucous Gull		rW	xT	xT,xW	rW	rS*,uW	xS*,uW	xS*,uW	xS*,uW	xS*,uW	xS*,uW
Gr. Black-backed Gull	xW-q	xV,xW	xV,xW-q	xV	xV,xW	cP	cP	xS,rS*,fW	cP	cP	cP
Black-legged Kittiwake	xV	xV	xV	xV,xW	xV,xW	rS*,cW	cW	xV	rS*,cW	rS*,cW	rT,xW
Red-legged Kittiwake											
Ross' Gull										xW	xV
Sabine's Gull		xV		xV	xV	rT	xT		rT	xT	
Ivory Gull						xV,xW	xW	xV-q	xW		

Subfamily Sterninae: Terns

	West Virginia	Kentucky	Tennessee	Mississippi	Alabama	Maine	New Hampshire	Vermont	Massachusetts	Rhode Island	Connecticut
Gull-billed Tern				fS,xW	fS,rW	xV			rS*	rS*	rS*-q
Caspian Tern	rT	uT	uT	uS,fW	uS,fW	rT	rT	rT	uT	uT	uT
Royal Tern				cP	cP	rV	xV		rS*	rS*	rS*
Elegant Tern											
Sandwich Tern				fS,xW	fS,rW	xV-q			rV	xV	
Roseate Tern				xV	xV	uS	eS,rT		uS,fT	lrS,uS*,fT	luS,uT
Common Tern	rT	rT	uT	rS,fT,rW	lrS,uT,rW	cS	fS,cT	uS,cT	cS	cS	cS

	New York	Pennsylvania	New Jersey	Delaware	Maryland	Dist. of Columbia	Virginia	North Carolina	South Carolina	Georgia	Florida
California Gull	xV,xW						xV-q				
Herring Gull	cP	fS*,cW	cP	cP	cP	uS*,cW	cP	fS,cW	fS*,cW	fS*,cW	uS*,fW
Thayer's Gull	xV,rW	xV	xW	xV	xW-q		xV,xW-q	xV-q			xW
Iceland Gull	xS*,uW	rW	xS*,uW	xS*,rW	rW	rW	xS*,rW	rW	xW	xW	rW
Les. Black-back. Gull	xS*,rW	rW	rW	rW	xS*,rW	uW	xS*,uW	xS*,uW	rW	rW	rW
Slaty-backed Gull											
Yellow-footed Gull											
Western Gull											
Glaucous-winged Gull											
Glaucous Gull	xS*,uW	rW	xS*,uW	rW	rW	xW	xS*,rW	rW	rW	rW	rW
Gr. Black-backed Gull	cP	rS*,fW	fS,cW	uS*,cW	lrS,uS*,cW	uS*,cW	lrS,uS*,cW	lrS,uS*,cW	xS*,uW	xS*,uW	xS*,uW
Black-legged Kittiwake	xS*,cW	rV,xW	fW	fW	fW		fW	fW	fW	fW	uW
Red-legged Kittiwake											
Ross' Gull											
Sabine's Gull	rT	xV	rT	xT	xT		xT-q	xT		xT	xT
Ivory Gull	xV,xW		xW	xW			xV-q				

Subfamily Sterninae: Terns

	New York	Pennsylvania	New Jersey	Delaware	Maryland	Dist. of Columbia	Virginia	North Carolina	South Carolina	Georgia	Florida
Gull-billed Tern	lrS,rS*		lrS,rS*	rS	rS	xV	uS	fS	fS,xW	fS,xW	fS,uW
Caspian Tern	lfS,uT	eS,lrS*,fT	xS,rS*,uT	rS*,fT	uS*,fT	fT	lrS,rS*,fT	lrS,rS*,fT,rW	lrS,rS*,fT,uW	rS*,fT,uW	uS,fW
Royal Tern	lrS,rS*	xV	uS*	fS*	cS	xV	cS,rW	cS,fW	cS,fW	cS,fW	fS,cW
Elegant Tern											
Sandwich Tern	rV		rV	xS*	xS,rS*		luS,rS*	fS	fS	fS*,xW	fS,uW
Roseate Tern	luS,uT	xV	lrS,rT	rT	eS,xT		eS,rT	xS,rT	rT		luS,rW
Common Tern	cS	eS,fT	cS	cS	cS,xW	rT	cS,xW	cS,rW	luS,uS*,cT,rW	rS*,cT,rW	eS,cT,rW

Laridae • 165

	Date	Location	Cont. North America	Canada	Lower 48
Arctic Tern *Sterna paradisaea*			cS	cS	lfS.uT
Forster's Tern *Sterna forsteri*			fS.cW	fS	fS.cW
Least Tern *Sterna antillarum*			cS.xW	xV	cS.xW
Aleutian Tern *Sterna aleutica*			lfS		
Gray-backed Tern *Sterna lunata*					
Bridled Tern *Sterna anaethetus*			lcS*.xV.lrW	xV.xW	fS*.lrW
Sooty Tern *Sterna fuscata*			lcS.xS.rS*.rV	xV	lcS.xS.rS*.rV
Large-billed Tern *Phaetusa simplex*			xV		xV
White-winged Tern *Chlidonias leucopterus*			xS*.rV	xS*.xV	rV
Black Tern *Chlidonias niger*			cS.xW	cS	fS.cT.xW
Brown Noddy *Anous stolidus*			lcS.lrS*.rV		lcS.rS*.rV
Black Noddy *Anous minutus*			lrS*.xV		lrS*.xV
Blue-gray Noddy *Procelsterna cerulea*					
White Tern *Gygis alba*					

Subfamily Rynchopinae: Skimmers

	Date	Location	Cont. North America	Canada	Lower 48
Black Skimmer *Rynchops niger*			cS.fW	rV	cP

Family Alcidae: Auks, Murres and Puffins

	Date	Location	Cont. North America	Canada	Lower 48
Dovekie *Alle alle*			lrS.cS*.ifW	lrS.cS*.ifW	xS*.iuW
Common Murre *Uria aalge*			cP	cP	cP
Thick-billed Murre *Uria lomvia*			cS.ifW	cS.ifW	xS*.rV.lifW
Razorbill *Alca torda*			lfS.iuW	fS.ifW	luS.xS.iuW
Great Auk *Pinguinus impennis*			E	E	E*
Black Guillemot *Cepphus grylle*			cS.fW	cS.fW	lfP.xV
Pigeon Guillemot *Cepphus columba*			cP	cP	cS.fW

	Hawaii	Alaska	Yukon Terr.	Northwest Terr.	British Columbia	Alberta	Saskatch- ewan	Manitoba	Ontario
Arctic Tern	xV	cS	cS	cS	lfS.uT	xV	lfS.xV	lcS.rV	lfS.rV
Forster's Tern		exV			lrS.rT	uS	fS	fS	lrS.uT
Least Tern	rV-sp.xW-sp						xV-q		xV
Aleutian Tern		fS							
Gray-backed Tern	luS								
Bridled Tern									
Sooty Tern	cS.uW								xV
Large-billed Tern									
White-winged Tern		xV							
Black Tern	xV.xW	exS.xV	xV	luS	fS	cS	cS	cS	cS
Brown Noddy	cS.fW								
Black Noddy	fP								
Blue-gray Noddy	luS								
White Tern	fS.uW								

Subfamily Rynchopinae: Skimmers

	Hawaii	Alaska	Yukon Terr.	Northwest Terr.	British Columbia	Alberta	Saskatch- ewan	Manitoba	Ontario
Black Skimmer									xV

Family Alcidae: Auks, Murres and Puffins

	Hawaii	Alaska	Yukon Terr.	Northwest Terr.	British Columbia	Alberta	Saskatch- ewan	Manitoba	Ontario
Dovekie		lrSt		lrS.cS*.rW				xV	xV
Common Murre		cP			cP				
Thick-billed Murre		cS.fW	xV	cS.rW	lrS.rW			xV-sp	xV
Razorbill				lrS					xV.xW
Great Auk									
Black Guillemot		fP	luS	cS.uW				rV.xW	lrP.xV
Pigeon Guillemot		cP			cP				

Laridae • 167

	Québec	Newfoundland	New Brunswick	Prince Edward I.	Nova Scotia	Washington	Oregon	California	Nevada	Idaho
Arctic Tern	cS	cS	cS	uS	cS	lrS,uT	uT	fT		xV
Forster's Tern	rV	xV	xV		xV	fS	fS	cP	luS,fT	fS
Least Tern		xV			xV	xV	xV	uS	xV	xV
Aleutian Tern										
Gray-backed Tern										
Bridled Tern		xV,xW								
Sooty Tern					xV			xV		
Large-billed Tern										
White-winged Tern			xS*,xV							
Black Tern	fS	rV	lfS,rT	xV	xS,rT	fS	fS	fS,xW	fS	uS,fT
Brown Noddy										
Black Noddy										
Blue-gray Noddy										
White Tern										

Subfamily Rynchopinae: Skimmers

	Québec	Newfoundland	New Brunswick	Prince Edward I.	Nova Scotia	Washington	Oregon	California	Nevada	Idaho
Black Skimmer	xV	xV	xV		rV			lfP,rV		

Family Alcidae: Auks, Murres and Puffins

	Québec	Newfoundland	New Brunswick	Prince Edward I.	Nova Scotia	Washington	Oregon	California	Nevada	Idaho
Dovekie	xV,luW	rS*,icW	xS*,fT,ifW	rT	fT,ifW					
Common Murre	lcS,xW	cS,uW	xS,uS*,rW	rT	eS,uS*,fT,uW	cP	cP	cP		
Thick-billed Murre	lcS,luW	uS,ifW	xS*,ifW	rT	fT,ifW	xV,xW	xV,xW	rV,xW		
Razorbill	lcS	fS,rW	fS,ifW		fS,ifW					
Great Auk	E*	E	E*		E*					
Black Guillemot	fP	cP	fP	fS,rW	fP					
Pigeon Guillemot						cS,fW	cS,fW	fS,uW		

	Montana	Wyoming	Utah	Colorado	Arizona	New Mexico	North Dakota	South Dakota	Nebraska	Kansas	Oklahoma
Arctic Tern				xV	xV		xV-q				
Forster's Tern	rS.uT	luS.fT	cS	uS.fT	fT	uT	fS	fS	uS.fT	luS.fT	fT
Least Tern	xV	exV	xV-q	lrS.xV	xS*.rV	lrS	luS.xV	uS	rS.uT	rS.uT	rS.uT
Aleutian Tern											
Gray-backed Tern											
Bridled Tern											
Sooty Tern											
Large-billed Tern											
White-winged Tern											
Black Tern	fS.cT	uS.fT	fS	uS.fT	rS*.fT	rS*.uT	cS	cS	uS.cT	uS.cT	rS*.cT
Brown Noddy											
Black Noddy											
Blue-gray Noddy											
White Tern											

Subfamily Rynchopinae: Skimmers

	Montana	Wyoming	Utah	Colorado	Arizona	New Mexico	North Dakota	South Dakota	Nebraska	Kansas	Oklahoma
Black Skimmer					xV	xV				xV	xV

Family Alcidae: Auks, Murres and Puffins

	Montana	Wyoming	Utah	Colorado	Arizona	New Mexico	North Dakota	South Dakota	Nebraska	Kansas	Oklahoma
Dovekie											
Common Murre											
Thick-billed Murre											
Razorbill											
Great Auk											
Black Guillemot											
Pigeon Guillemot											

Laridae • 169

	Texas	Minnesota	Iowa	Missouri	Arkansas	Louisiana	Wisconsin	Michigan	Illinois	Indiana	Ohio
Arctic Tern	xV	xV					xV	xV-q			xV
Forster's Tern	cP	fS	luS,fT	fT	fT,xW	cP	uS,fT	uS,fT	lrS,uS*,fT	eS,uS*,fT	uS*,fT
Least Tern	cS,xW	xV	lrS,xV	lrS,xV	rS,uT	cS	xV	xV	luS,rS*	rS*	rS*
Aleutian Tern											
Gray-backed Tern											
Bridled Tern	xV-q						xV				
Sooty Tern	lrS,rS*				xV	lrS,rS*	xV				
Large-billed Tern									xV		xV
White-winged Tern							exV			xV-q	
Black Tern	rS*,cT,xW	cS	fS,cT	eS,xS*,cT	cT	cT	cS	fS,cT	uS,cT	uS,cT	lrS,fT
Brown Noddy	xV					xV					
Black Noddy	xV										
Blue-gray Noddy											
White Tern											

Subfamily Rynchopinae: Skimmers

	Texas	Minnesota	Iowa	Missouri	Arkansas	Louisiana	Wisconsin	Michigan	Illinois	Indiana	Ohio
Black Skimmer	cP				xV	cP				xV-q	

Family Alcidae: Auks, Murres and Puffins

	Texas	Minnesota	Iowa	Missouri	Arkansas	Louisiana	Wisconsin	Michigan	Illinois	Indiana	Ohio
Dovekie		xV					xV,exW	xV			
Common Murre											
Thick-billed Murre			exV					xV		exV	exV
Razorbill											
Great Auk											
Black Guillemot											
Pigeon Guillemot											

170 • Distributional Checklist of North American Birds

	West Virginia	Kentucky	Tennessee	Mississippi	Alabama	Maine	New Hampshire	Vermont	Massachusetts	Rhode Island	Connecticut
Arctic Tern						fS	eS,uT	xV	luS,rT	xT	xV-q
Forster's Tern	xT-q	uT,xW	fT	uS*,cW	cP	rT	rT		uT	uT	uT
Least Tern	xV	luS,xV	lfS,rV	cS	cS,xW	rS	rS		cS	cS	cS
Aleutian Tern											
Gray-backed Tern											
Bridled Tern				xV	rS*				xV	xV,xW	
Sooty Tern	xV		xV	xS*	rS*	xV	xV	xV	rV	xV	xV
Large-billed Tern											
White-winged Tern										xV	
Black Tern	uT	exS,fT	fT	fT	fT,xW	luS,rT	rT	lfS,rT	uT	uT	uT
Brown Noddy				xV	xV				xV	xV	
Black Noddy											
Blue-gray Noddy											
White Tern											

Subfamily Rynchopinae: Skimmers

	West Virginia	Kentucky	Tennessee	Mississippi	Alabama	Maine	New Hampshire	Vermont	Massachusetts	Rhode Island	Connecticut
Black Skimmer			exV	cS,fW	cS,fW	rV	xV		xS,rS*	uS*	lrS,uS*

Family Alcidae: Auks, Murres and Puffins

	West Virginia	Kentucky	Tennessee	Mississippi	Alabama	Maine	New Hampshire	Vermont	Massachusetts	Rhode Island	Connecticut
Dovekie						fT,ifW	fT,ifW	xV	uT,ifW	xS*,uT,ifW	rV
Common Murre						xS*,uT,ifW	uT,iuW	xV	iuW	iuW	
Thick-billed Murre						xS*,ifW	ifW	exV	ifW	irW	rV,xW
Razorbill						luS,ifW	ifW		ifW	xS,iuW	rV,xW-q
Great Auk						E*	E*		E*		
Black Guillemot						fP	rS*,fW	xV	fW	rW	rW
Pigeon Guillemot											

	New York	Pennsyl-vania	New Jersey	Delaware	Maryland	Dist. of Columbia	Virginia	North Carolina	South Carolina	Georgia	Florida
Arctic Tern	rT	xV	rT	xT	xT-q		xT	rT	xT	rT	rT
Forster's Tern	xS,fT,xW	fT	fS,xW	rS*,cT,rW	lfS,rS*,cT,rW	fT	fS,cT,uW	fS,cW	exS,rS*,cW	rS*,cW	rS*,cW
Least Tern	cS	rV	fS,cT	cS	cS	xV	cS	cS	cS	cS	cS,xW
Aleutian Tern											
Gray-backed Tern											
Bridled Tern	xV		xV		xV		rS*	fS*	fS*	fS*,xW	cS*,rW
Sooty Tern	rV	xV	rV	xV	xV	xV	rV	xS,uS*	uS*	uS*	lcS,rS*
Large-billed Tern											
White-winged Tern		xV-q	xV			xV			xV		
Black Tern	fS	lrS,fT	uT	uT	uT	rT	fT	fT	fT	fT	fT,xW
Brown Noddy	xV		xV-q					rS*	rS*		lcS,rS*
Black Noddy											lrS*
Blue-gray Noddy											
White Tern											

Subfamily Rynchopinae: Skimmers

	New York	Pennsyl-vania	New Jersey	Delaware	Maryland	Dist. of Columbia	Virginia	North Carolina	South Carolina	Georgia	Florida
Black Skimmer	uS,rW	xV	uS,rW	fS	fS,xW	xV	cS,rW	cS,uW	cS,fW	cS,fW	cP

Family Alcidae: Auks, Murres and Puffins

	New York	Pennsyl-vania	New Jersey	Delaware	Maryland	Dist. of Columbia	Virginia	North Carolina	South Carolina	Georgia	Florida
Dovekie	iuW	xV	iuW	iuW	iuW		irW	irW	irW	xW	irW
Common Murre	irW		xW		xV						
Thick-billed Murre	irW	exV,exW	irW	xW	xV	exV,exW	xW	xW	exV		xV
Razorbill	iuW	exV	iuW	iuW	iuW		irW	irW	xW	xW	xV,xW
Great Auk			E*						E*		
Black Guillemot	xW	xV	xW							xV	
Pigeon Guillemot											

Alcidae • 173

	Date	Location	Cont. North America	Canada	Lower 48
Marbled Murrelet *Brachyramphus marmoratus*			cP	cP	fP
Kittlitz's Murrelet *Brachyramphus brevirostris*			luS.xV.lrW		xV.xW
Xantus' Murrelet *Synthliboramphus hypoleucus*			luS.rS*.lrW	xS*	luS.uS*.lrW
Craveri's Murrelet *Synthliboramphus craveri*			liuS*.xW		iuS*.xW
Ancient Murrelet *Synthliboramphus antiquus*			lfS.rS*.fW	lfS.fW	lrS.rS*.uW
Cassin's Auklet *Ptychoramphus aleuticus*			fP	fS.uW	fP
Parakeet Auklet *Cyclorrhynchus psittacula*			lfS.rV.luW	xV	rV.xW
Least Auklet *Aethia pusilla*			lcS.xV.luW	exV	xV
Whiskered Auklet *Aethia pygmaea*			lfS.lrW		
Crested Auklet *Aethia cristatella*			lcS.xV.lfW	exV	xV
Rhinoceros Auklet *Cerorhinca monocerata*			fP	fS.uW	uS.fW
Tufted Puffin *Fratercula cirrhata*			fS.uW	uS.rW	uS.rW
Atlantic Puffin *Fratercula arctica*			lcS.xV.luW	fS.rW	luS.lfT.irW
Horned Puffin *Fratercula corniculata*			lcP.rS*.rV.rW	lrS.xS*.rV.xW	rS*.rV.rW

Order Columbiformes: Sandgrouse, Pigeons and Doves
Family Columbidae: Pigeons and Doves

	Date	Location	Cont. North America	Canada	Lower 48
Scaly-naped Pigeon *Columba squamosa*			xV		xV
White-crowned Pigeon *Columba leucocephala*			lcS.lfW		lcS.lfW
Red-billed Pigeon *Columba flavirostris*			luS.lrW		luS.lrW
Band-tailed Pigeon *Columba fasciata*			lcS.rV.lfW	lcS.rV.luW	cS.fW
White-winged Dove *Zenaida asiatica*			lcS.xS*.rV.lrW	xV	lcS.xS*.rV.lrW
Zenaida Dove *Zenaida aurita*			eP.rV		eP.rV
Mourning Dove *Zenaida macroura*			cP	cS.rW	cP

Species	Hawaii	Alaska	Yukon Terr.	Northwest Terr.	British Columbia	Alberta	Saskatchewan	Manitoba	Ontario
Marbled Murrelet		cP			cP				
Kittlitz's Murrelet		uS,rW							
Xantus' Murrelet					xS*				
Craveri's Murrelet									
Ancient Murrelet		fP	xV		lfS,fW	xV		xV	exV
Cassin's Auklet		cS,rW			fS,uW				
Parakeet Auklet	irW	fS,uW			xV				
Least Auklet		cS,uW	exV						
Whiskered Auklet		lfS,rW							
Crested Auklet		cS,fW			exV				
Rhinoceros Auklet		fS,uW			fS,uW				
Tufted Puffin	xV	cS,fW			uS,rW				
Atlantic Puffin				luS*					
Horned Puffin	rV	cP		xV	lrS,xS*,rV,xW				

Order Columbiformes: Sandgrouse, Pigeons and Doves
Family Columbidae: Pigeons and Doves

Species	Hawaii	Alaska	Yukon Terr.	Northwest Terr.	British Columbia	Alberta	Saskatchewan	Manitoba	Ontario
Scaly-naped Pigeon									
White-crowned Pigeon									
Red-billed Pigeon									
Band-tailed Pigeon		luS*,xV			cS,uW	rV	xV	xV	xV
White-winged Dove		xV				exV			xV
Zenaida Dove									
Mourning Dove		rV,xW	rV	rV	cS,rW	cS,xW	cS,rW	cS,rW	cS,uW

Alcidae • 175

	Québec	Newfoundland	New Brunswick	Prince Edward I.	Nova Scotia		Washington	Oregon	California	Nevada	Idaho
Marbled Murrelet	xV						fP	fP	fP		
Kittlitz's Murrelet							xW		xV		
Xantus' Murrelet							rS*	xS*	luS,uS*,rW		
Craveri's Murrelet									iuS*,xW		
Ancient Murrelet	exV						lrS,uW	xS*,uW	rS*,uW	xV	xV
Cassin's Auklet							fS,uW	fP	fP		
Parakeet Auklet							xV,xW	xV	xV,xW		
Least Auklet									xV		
Whiskered Auklet											
Crested Auklet								xV			
Rhinoceros Auklet							fP	uS,fW	uS,fW		
Tufted Puffin							uS,rW	uS,rW	uS,rW		
Atlantic Puffin	fS,xW	cS,luW	lfS,uT,rW	xW	lfS,fT,uW						
Horned Puffin							xS*,xV,xW	xS*,rV,rW	xS*,rV,rW		

Order Columbiformes: Sandgrouse, Pigeons and Doves
Family Columbidae: Pigeons and Doves

	Québec	Newfoundland	New Brunswick	Prince Edward I.	Nova Scotia		Washington	Oregon	California	Nevada	Idaho
Scaly-naped Pigeon											
White-crowned Pigeon											
Red-billed Pigeon											
Band-tailed Pigeon			xV,xW		xV		cS,uW	cS,uW	cP	lcS,rW	xS*,rV
White-winged Dove		xV	xV		xV		xV	xV	lcS,rV,rW	lcS	
Zenaida Dove											
Mourning Dove	lfS,rV,rW	xS*,uV,xW	uP	uS,rW	rS,uW		cS,uW	cS,fW	cP	cS,fW	cS,uW

	Montana	Wyoming	Utah	Colorado	Arizona	New Mexico	North Dakota	South Dakota	Nebraska	Kansas	Oklahoma
Marbled Murrelet				xV							
Kittlitz's Murrelet											
Xantus' Murrelet											
Craveri's Murrelet											
Ancient Murrelet	xV	xV	xV	xV					xV		
Cassin's Auklet											
Parakeet Auklet											
Least Auklet											
Whiskered Auklet											
Crested Auklet											
Rhinoceros Auklet											
Tufted Puffin											
Atlantic Puffin											
Horned Puffin											

Order Columbiformes: Sandgrouse, Pigeons and Doves
Family Columbidae: Pigeons and Doves

	Montana	Wyoming	Utah	Colorado	Arizona	New Mexico	North Dakota	South Dakota	Nebraska	Kansas	Oklahoma
Scaly-naped Pigeon											
White-crowned Pigeon											
Red-billed Pigeon											
Band-tailed Pigeon	rV	rV	uS.rW	fS	fS	cS.rW	xV-q	xV		xV	xV
White-winged Dove	xV	xV	lrS	rV,xW	cS.rW	fS.rW					xS*.xV-q
Zenaida Dove											
Mourning Dove	cS.rW	cS.rW	cS.uW	cS.uW	cP	cS.fW	cS.rW	cS.uW	cS.uW	cS.uW	cS.fW

Alcidae • 177

	Texas	Minnesota	Iowa	Missouri	Arkansas	Louisiana	Wisconsin	Michigan	Illinois	Indiana	Ohio
Marbled Murrelet					xV					xV	
Kittlitz's Murrelet										xW-q	
Xantus' Murrelet											
Craveri's Murrelet											
Ancient Murrelet		xV				xV	xV	xV	xV	xV	xV
Cassin's Auklet											
Parakeet Auklet											
Least Auklet											
Whiskered Auklet											
Crested Auklet											
Rhinoceros Auklet											
Tufted Puffin											
Atlantic Puffin										xV	
Horned Puffin											

Order Columbiformes: Sandgrouse, Pigeons and Doves
Family Columbidae: Pigeons and Doves

	Texas	Minnesota	Iowa	Missouri	Arkansas	Louisiana	Wisconsin	Michigan	Illinois	Indiana	Ohio
Scaly-naped Pigeon											
White-crowned Pigeon											
Red-billed Pigeon	luS.lrW										
Band-tailed Pigeon	lfP.xV	xV			xW	xV.xW		xV		xW	
White-winged Dove	cS.rW					rS.uV.rW					
Zenaida Dove											
Mourning Dove	cP	cS.uW	cS.fW	cP	cP	cP	cS.fW	cS.fW	cP	cP	cP

	West Virginia	Kentucky	Tennessee	Mississippi	Alabama	Maine	New Hampshire	Vermont	Massachusetts	Rhode Island	Connecticut
Marbled Murrelet									xV		
Kittlitz's Murrelet											
Xantus' Murrelet											
Craveri's Murrelet											
Ancient Murrelet											
Cassin's Auklet											
Parakeet Auklet											
Least Auklet											
Whiskered Auklet											
Crested Auklet											
Rhinoceros Auklet											
Tufted Puffin											
Atlantic Puffin						IuS,fT,uW	rT,iuW	xV	rT,iuW	irW	xV
Horned Puffin											

Order Columbiformes: Sandgrouse, Pigeons and Doves
Family Columbidae: Pigeons and Doves

	West Virginia	Kentucky	Tennessee	Mississippi	Alabama	Maine	New Hampshire	Vermont	Massachusetts	Rhode Island	Connecticut
Scaly-naped Pigeon											
White-crowned Pigeon											
Red-billed Pigeon											
Band-tailed Pigeon		xV	xV-q	xV	xV-q	xV	xV				xV,xW-q
White-winged Dove				xS*,rV,rW	rV,xW	xV			xV		xV-q
Zenaida Dove											
Mourning Dove	cP	cP	cP	cP	cP	cS,fW	cS,fW	cS,fW	cP	cP	cP

Alcidae • 179

	New York	Pennsyl-vania	New Jersey	Delaware	Maryland	Dist. of Columbia	Virginia	North Carolina	South Carolina	Georgia	Florida
Marbled Murrelet											
Kittlitz's Murrelet											
Xantus' Murrelet											
Craveri's Murrelet											
Ancient Murrelet											
Cassin's Auklet											
Parakeet Auklet											
Least Auklet											
Whiskered Auklet											
Crested Auklet											
Rhinoceros Auklet											
Tufted Puffin											
Atlantic Puffin	irW	exV	irW	irW	irW		xW				
Horned Puffin											

Order Columbiformes: Sandgrouse, Pigeons and Doves
Family Columbidae: Pigeons and Doves

	New York	Pennsyl-vania	New Jersey	Delaware	Maryland	Dist. of Columbia	Virginia	North Carolina	South Carolina	Georgia	Florida
Scaly-naped Pigeon											xV
White-crowned Pigeon											lcS,xV,lfW
Red-billed Pigeon											
Band-tailed Pigeon			xV-q					xV-q			xV
White-winged Dove	xV		xV		xV-q		xV-q	xV	xV	xV	rV,xW
Zenaida Dove											eP,rV
Mourning Dove	cS,fW	cP	cP	cP	cP	cP	cP	cP	cP	cP	cP

	Date	Location	Cont. North America	Canada	Lower 48
Passenger Pigeon *Ectopistes migratorius*			E	E	E
Inca Dove *Columbina inca*			lcP,xS,rV,xW		lcP,xS,rV,xW
Common Ground-Dove *Columbina passerina*			lfP,rV,xW	xV	fP
Ruddy Ground-Dove *Columbina talpacoti*			xV,xW		xV,xW
White-tipped Dove *Leptotila verreauxi*			lcP		lcP
Key West Quail-Dove *Geotrygon chrysia*			eP,xP*,xV		eP,xP*,xV
Ruddy Quail-Dove *Geotrygon montana*			xV		xV

Order Psittaciformes: Parrots and Allies
Family Psittacidae: Lories, Parakeets, Macaws and Parrots
Subfamily Arinae: New World Parakeets, Macaws and Parrots

	Date	Location	Cont. North America	Canada	Lower 48
Carolina Parakeet *Conuropsis carolinensis*			E		E
Green Parakeet *Aratinga holochlora*			xV,xW		xV,xW
Thick-billed Parrot *Rhynchopsitta pachyrhyncha*			eP*,xV		eP*,xV
Red-crowned Parrot *Amazona viridigenalis*			rV,rW		rV,rW
Yellow-headed Parrot *Amazona oratrix*			xV,xW		xV,xW

Order Cuculiformes: Cuckoos and Allies
Family Cuculidae: Cuckoos, Roadrunners and Anis
Subfamily Cuculinae: Old World Cuckoos

	Date	Location	Cont. North America	Canada	Lower 48
Common Cuckoo *Cuculus canorus*			rV		xV
Oriental Cuckoo *Cuculus saturatus*			xV		

Subfamily Coccyzinae: New World Cuckoos

	Date	Location	Cont. North America	Canada	Lower 48
Black-billed Cuckoo *Coccyzus erythropthalmus*			fS	ifS	fS
Yellow-billed Cuckoo *Coccyzus americanus*			cS	lfS,uV	cS
Mangrove Cuckoo *Coccyzus minor*			luS,xV,lrW		luS,xV,lrW

Subfamily Neomorphinae: Ground-Cuckoos and Roadrunners

	Date	Location	Cont. North America	Canada	Lower 48
Greater Roadrunner *Geococcyx californianus*			fP		fP

Distributional Checklist of North American Birds

	Hawaii	Alaska	Yukon Terr.	Northwest Terr.	British Columbia	Alberta	Saskatch-ewan	Manitoba	Ontario
Passenger Pigeon				E*	E*	E*	E	E	E
Inca Dove									
Common Ground-Dove									xV
Ruddy Ground-Dove									
White-tipped Dove									
Key West Quail-Dove									
Ruddy Quail-Dove									

Order Psittaciformes: Parrots and Allies
Family Psittacidae: Lories, Parakeets, Macaws and Parrots
Subfamily Arinae: New World Parakeets, Macaws and Parrots

	Hawaii	Alaska	Yukon Terr.	Northwest Terr.	British Columbia	Alberta	Saskatch-ewan	Manitoba	Ontario
Carolina Parakeet									
Green Parakeet									
Thick-billed Parrot									
Red-crowned Parrot									
Yellow-headed Parrot									

Order Cuculiformes: Cuckoos and Allies
Family Cuculidae: Cuckoos, Roadrunners and Anis
Subfamily Cuculinae: Old World Cuckoos

	Hawaii	Alaska	Yukon Terr.	Northwest Terr.	British Columbia	Alberta	Saskatch-ewan	Manitoba	Ontario
Common Cuckoo		rV							
Oriental Cuckoo		xV							

Subfamily Coccyzinae: New World Cuckoos

	Hawaii	Alaska	Yukon Terr.	Northwest Terr.	British Columbia	Alberta	Saskatch-ewan	Manitoba	Ontario
Black-billed Cuckoo					xS*,xV	iuS	ifS	ifS	fS
Yellow-billed Cuckoo					eS†	xV	xV-q	xS,xV	IfS
Mangrove Cuckoo									

Subfamily Neomorphinae: Ground-Cuckoos and Roadrunners

	Hawaii	Alaska	Yukon Terr.	Northwest Terr.	British Columbia	Alberta	Saskatch-ewan	Manitoba	Ontario
Greater Roadrunner									

Columbidae • 183

	Québec	Newfoundland	New Brunswick	Prince Edward I.	Nova Scotia	Washington	Oregon	California	Nevada	Idaho
Passenger Pigeon	E	E*	E	E†	E				E*	E*
Inca Dove								IuP	IrP	
Common Ground-Dove					xV-q			fP	IrP*	
Ruddy Ground-Dove								xV-q		
White-tipped Dove										
Key West Quail-Dove										
Ruddy Quail-Dove										

Order Psittaciformes: Parrots and Allies
Family Psittacidae: Lories, Parakeets, Macaws and Parrots
Subfamily Arinae: New World Parakeets, Macaws and Parrots

	Québec	Newfoundland	New Brunswick	Prince Edward I.	Nova Scotia	Washington	Oregon	California	Nevada	Idaho
Carolina Parakeet										
Green Parakeet										
Thick-billed Parrot										
Red-crowned Parrot										
Yellow-headed Parrot										

Order Cuculiformes: Cuckoos and Allies
Family Cuculidae: Cuckoos, Roadrunners and Anis
Subfamily Cuculinae: Old World Cuckoos

	Québec	Newfoundland	New Brunswick	Prince Edward I.	Nova Scotia	Washington	Oregon	California	Nevada	Idaho
Common Cuckoo										
Oriental Cuckoo										

Subfamily Coccyzinae: New World Cuckoos

	Québec	Newfoundland	New Brunswick	Prince Edward I.	Nova Scotia	Washington	Oregon	California	Nevada	Idaho
Black-billed Cuckoo	iuS	rV	iuS	rS	iuS	xV	xV	xV		rS*,xV
Yellow-billed Cuckoo	IrS	rV	xS*,uV	rV	uV	eS,xS*,xV	eS,xS*,rV	rS	xS,rT	exS,xS*,xV
Mangrove Cuckoo										

Subfamily Neomorphinae: Ground-Cuckoos and Roadrunners

	Québec	Newfoundland	New Brunswick	Prince Edward I.	Nova Scotia	Washington	Oregon	California	Nevada	Idaho
Greater Roadrunner								fP	uP	

	Montana	Wyoming	Utah	Colorado	Arizona	New Mexico	North Dakota	South Dakota	Nebraska	Kansas	Oklahoma
Passenger Pigeon	E*	E*					E	E	E	E	E
Inca Dove			xV		cP	lfP				xV,xW	xS*,xV,xW
Common Ground-Dove		xV	xV		cS,uW	lrS,rW		xV	xV	rV	rV
Ruddy Ground-Dove					xV-q	xV					
White-tipped Dove											
Key West Quail-Dove											
Ruddy Quail-Dove											

Order Psittaciformes: Parrots and Allies
Family Psittacidae: Lories, Parakeets, Macaws and Parrots
Subfamily Arinae: New World Parakeets, Macaws and Parrots

	Montana	Wyoming	Utah	Colorado	Arizona	New Mexico	North Dakota	South Dakota	Nebraska	Kansas	Oklahoma
Carolina Parakeet								E*	E†	E	E
Green Parakeet											
Thick-billed Parrot					eP*,xV	exV					
Red-crowned Parrot											
Yellow-headed Parrot											

Order Cuculiformes: Cuckoos and Allies
Family Cuculidae: Cuckoos, Roadrunners and Anis
Subfamily Cuculinae: Old World Cuckoos

	Montana	Wyoming	Utah	Colorado	Arizona	New Mexico	North Dakota	South Dakota	Nebraska	Kansas	Oklahoma
Common Cuckoo											
Oriental Cuckoo											

Subfamily Coccyzinae: New World Cuckoos

	Montana	Wyoming	Utah	Colorado	Arizona	New Mexico	North Dakota	South Dakota	Nebraska	Kansas	Oklahoma
Black-billed Cuckoo	uS	uS	xV	rS	xV	xV	fS	fS	uS	uS	uS
Yellow-billed Cuckoo	rS†	uS	rS	uS	fS	uS	rS	fS	fS	cS	cS
Mangrove Cuckoo											

Subfamily Neomorphinae: Ground-Cuckoos and Roadrunners

	Montana	Wyoming	Utah	Colorado	Arizona	New Mexico	North Dakota	South Dakota	Nebraska	Kansas	Oklahoma
Greater Roadrunner			uP	fP	cP	fP				luP	fP

	Texas	Minnesota	Iowa	Missouri	Arkansas	Louisiana	Wisconsin	Michigan	Illinois	Indiana	Ohio
Passenger Pigeon	E	E	E	E	E	E*	E	E	E	E	E
Inca Dove	cP				xV	xS,rV,xW					
Common Ground-Dove	fP			xV,xW	rV,xW	uP	xV	xV	xV	xV	
Ruddy Ground-Dove	xV,xW										
White-tipped Dove	lcP,xV										
Key West Quail-Dove											
Ruddy Quail-Dove											

Order Psittaciformes: Parrots and Allies
Family Psittacidae: Lories, Parakeets, Macaws and Parrots
Subfamily Arinae: New World Parakeets, Macaws and Parrots

	Texas	Minnesota	Iowa	Missouri	Arkansas	Louisiana	Wisconsin	Michigan	Illinois	Indiana	Ohio
Carolina Parakeet	E		E*	E	E	E	E*	E*-q	E†	E†	E†
Green Parakeet	xV,xW-q										
Thick-billed Parrot											
Red-crowned Parrot	rV,rW-q										
Yellow-headed Parrot	xV,xW-q										

Order Cuculiformes: Cuckoos and Allies
Family Cuculidae: Cuckoos, Roadrunners and Anis
Subfamily Cuculinae: Old World Cuckoos

	Texas	Minnesota	Iowa	Missouri	Arkansas	Louisiana	Wisconsin	Michigan	Illinois	Indiana	Ohio
Common Cuckoo											
Oriental Cuckoo											

Subfamily Coccyzinae: New World Cuckoos

	Texas	Minnesota	Iowa	Missouri	Arkansas	Louisiana	Wisconsin	Michigan	Illinois	Indiana	Ohio
Black-billed Cuckoo	lrS,uT	fS	uS,fT	uS,fT	lrS,fT	fT	fS	fS	uS,fT	uS,fT	uS,fT
Yellow-billed Cuckoo	cS	fS	fS	cS	cS	cS	fS	fS	cS	fS	fS
Mangrove Cuckoo	xV,xW										

Subfamily Neomorphinae: Ground-Cuckoos and Roadrunners

	Texas	Minnesota	Iowa	Missouri	Arkansas	Louisiana	Wisconsin	Michigan	Illinois	Indiana	Ohio
Greater Roadrunner	fP			lrP	uP	uP					

	West Virginia	Kentucky	Tennessee	Mississippi	Alabama	Maine	New Hampshire	Vermont	Massachusetts	Rhode Island	Connecticut
Passenger Pigeon	E	E	E	E	E	E	E	E	E	E	E
Inca Dove											
Common Ground-Dove			xV-q	luP*	uP				xV		
Ruddy Ground-Dove											
White-tipped Dove											
Key West Quail-Dove											
Ruddy Quail-Dove											

Order Psittaciformes: Parrots and Allies
Family Psittacidae: Lories, Parakeets, Macaws and Parrots
Subfamily Arinae: New World Parakeets, Macaws and Parrots

	West Virginia	Kentucky	Tennessee	Mississippi	Alabama	Maine	New Hampshire	Vermont	Massachusetts	Rhode Island	Connecticut
Carolina Parakeet	E†	E	E	E	E						
Green Parakeet											
Thick-billed Parrot											
Red-crowned Parrot											
Yellow-headed Parrot											

Order Cuculiformes: Cuckoos and Allies
Family Cuculidae: Cuckoos, Roadrunners and Anis
Subfamily Cuculinae: Old World Cuckoos

	West Virginia	Kentucky	Tennessee	Mississippi	Alabama	Maine	New Hampshire	Vermont	Massachusetts	Rhode Island	Connecticut
Common Cuckoo									xV		
Oriental Cuckoo											

Subfamily Coccyzinae: New World Cuckoos

	West Virginia	Kentucky	Tennessee	Mississippi	Alabama	Maine	New Hampshire	Vermont	Massachusetts	Rhode Island	Connecticut
Black-billed Cuckoo	uS,fT	rS,fT	rS,fT	fT	lrS,fT	ifS	ifS	fS	fS	ifS	fS
Yellow-billed Cuckoo	fS	cS	cS	cS	cS	iuS	iuS	iuS	ifS	ifS	fS
Mangrove Cuckoo											

Subfamily Neomorphinae: Ground-Cuckoos and Roadrunners

	West Virginia	Kentucky	Tennessee	Mississippi	Alabama	Maine	New Hampshire	Vermont	Massachusetts	Rhode Island	Connecticut
Greater Roadrunner											

	New York	Pennsylvania	New Jersey	Delaware	Maryland	Dist. of Columbia	Virginia	North Carolina	South Carolina	Georgia	Florida
Passenger Pigeon	E	E	E	E	E	E	E	E	E	E	E*
Inca Dove											
Common Ground-Dove	xV	xV,xW	xV	xW	xV	exV	rV	luP	fP	fP	cP
Ruddy Ground-Dove											
White-tipped Dove											
Key West Quail-Dove											eP,xP*,xV
Ruddy Quail-Dove											xV

Order Psittaciformes: Parrots and Allies
Family Psittacidae: Lories, Parakeets, Macaws and Parrots
Subfamily Arinae: New World Parakeets, Macaws and Parrots

	New York	Pennsylvania	New Jersey	Delaware	Maryland	Dist. of Columbia	Virginia	North Carolina	South Carolina	Georgia	Florida
Carolina Parakeet	E*	E*	E*		E*			E	E	E	E
Green Parakeet											
Thick-billed Parrot											
Red-crowned Parrot											
Yellow-headed Parrot											

Order Cuculiformes: Cuckoos and Allies
Family Cuculidae: Cuckoos, Roadrunners and Anis
Subfamily Cuculinae: Old World Cuckoos

	New York	Pennsylvania	New Jersey	Delaware	Maryland	Dist. of Columbia	Virginia	North Carolina	South Carolina	Georgia	Florida
Common Cuckoo											
Oriental Cuckoo											

Subfamily Coccyzinae: New World Cuckoos

	New York	Pennsylvania	New Jersey	Delaware	Maryland	Dist. of Columbia	Virginia	North Carolina	South Carolina	Georgia	Florida
Black-billed Cuckoo	fS	uS,fT	uS	rS,uT	uS	uT	uS	luS,uT	lrS,uT	lrS,uT	uT
Yellow-billed Cuckoo	fS	fS	fS	fS	cS	rS,fT	cS	cS	cS	cS	cS
Mangrove Cuckoo											uS,lrW

Subfamily Neomorphinae: Ground-Cuckoos and Roadrunners

	New York	Pennsylvania	New Jersey	Delaware	Maryland	Dist. of Columbia	Virginia	North Carolina	South Carolina	Georgia	Florida
Greater Roadrunner											

Subfamily Crotophaginae: Anis

		Date	Location	Cont. North America	Canada	Lower 48
Smooth-billed Ani *Crotophaga ani*				lfP,xV		lfP,xV
Groove-billed Ani *Crotophaga sulcirostris*				lfS,xS,rV,lrW	xV	lfS,xS,rV,lrW

Order Strigiformes: Owls
Family Tytonidae: Barn-Owls

Common Barn-Owl *Tyto alba*				fP	luP,rV,xW	fP

Family Strigidae: Typical Owls

Oriental Scops-Owl *Otus sunia*				xV		
Flammulated Owl *Otus flammeolus*				uS,xW	lrS	uS,xW
Eastern Screech-Owl *Otus asio*				cP	lfP,xS,xV,xW	cP
Western Screech-Owl *Otus kennicottii*				fP	lfP	fP
Whiskered Screech-Owl *Otus trichopsis*				lcP,xV		lcP,xV
Great Horned Owl *Bubo virginianus*				cP	cP	cP
Snowy Owl *Nyctea scandiaca*				icP	icP	iuW
Northern Hawk-Owl *Surnia ulula*				fS,uW	fS,uW	xS,irW
Northern Pygmy-Owl *Glaucidium gnoma*				uP	luP	fP
Ferruginous Pygmy-Owl *Glaucidium brasilianum*				lrP		lrP
Elf Owl *Micrathene whitneyi*				lcS,xW		lcS,xW
Burrowing Owl *Athene cunicularia*				fS,lfW	lfS,xV,lrW	fP
Spotted Owl *Strix occidentalis*				luP	lrP	uP
Barred Owl *Strix varia*				cP	uP	cP
Great Gray Owl *Strix nebulosa*				uS,iuW	uS,iuW	lrS,irW
Long-eared Owl *Asio otus*				uP	uS,rW	uP
Short-eared Owl *Asio flammeus*				ifS,uW	icS,uW	ifS,fW

Subfamily Crotophaginae: Anis

	Hawaii	Alaska	Yukon Terr.	Northwest Terr.	British Columbia	Alberta	Saskatch-ewan	Manitoba	Ontario
Smooth-billed Ani									
Groove-billed Ani								xV-sp-q	xV

Order Strigiformes: Owls
Family Tytonidae: Barn-Owls

	Hawaii	Alaska	Yukon Terr.	Northwest Terr.	British Columbia	Alberta	Saskatch-ewan	Manitoba	Ontario
Common Barn-Owl					luP	xV-q	xV	xV,exW	lrP,xV

Family Strigidae: Typical Owls

	Hawaii	Alaska	Yukon Terr.	Northwest Terr.	British Columbia	Alberta	Saskatch-ewan	Manitoba	Ontario
Oriental Scops-Owl		xV							
Flammulated Owl					lrS				
Eastern Screech-Owl						xS,xV,xW	lrP†	luP	fP
Western Screech-Owl		lrP			fP				
Whiskered Screech-Owl									
Great Horned Owl		cP	cP	fS,uW	cP	cP	cP	cP	cP
Snowy Owl		icP	lifS,iuW	icS,ifW	icW	icW	icW	lirS,icW	icW
Northern Hawk-Owl		fP	fP	fS,uW	uP	uP	uP	uP	uP
Northern Pygmy-Owl		lrW			uP	luP			
Ferruginous Pygmy-Owl									
Elf Owl									
Burrowing Owl					luS,lrW	luS	fS	luS	xV
Spotted Owl					lrP				
Barred Owl									
Great Gray Owl		xS*,xV	xP*	xS*	uP	uP	uP	uP	uP
Long-eared Owl		uP	uP	uS,iuW	uP	uS,iuW	uS,iuW	uS,iuW	rS,iuW
Short-eared Owl		xV	xV	lrS	uS,rW	uS,xW	uS,rW	uS,xW	uP
	uP	icS,xW	icS	icS	ifS,fW	ifS,rW	ifS,rW	ifS,rW	uP

Subfamily Crotophaginae: Anis

	Québec	Newfoundland	New Brunswick	Prince Edward I.	Nova Scotia	Washington	Oregon	California	Nevada	Idaho
Smooth-billed Ani										
Groove-billed Ani								xV	xV	

Order Strigiformes: Owls
Family Tytonidae: Barn-Owls

	Québec	Newfoundland	New Brunswick	Prince Edward I.	Nova Scotia	Washington	Oregon	California	Nevada	Idaho
Common Barn-Owl	rV	xV	xV,xW		xV	uP	fP	fP	fS,uW	fS,uW

Family Strigidae: Typical Owls

	Québec	Newfoundland	New Brunswick	Prince Edward I.	Nova Scotia	Washington	Oregon	California	Nevada	Idaho
Oriental Scops-Owl										
Flammulated Owl						uS	uS	uS,xW	uS	rS
Eastern Screech-Owl	luP		xV		exV					
Western Screech-Owl						fP	fP	fP	fP	uP
Whiskered Screech-Owl										
Great Horned Owl	fP	uP	fP	uP	uP	cP	cP	cP	cP	cP
Snowy Owl	liuS,ifW	liuS,iuW	xS*,iuW	iuW	xS*,iuW	iuW	irW	irW	xW	iuW
Northern Hawk-Owl	uP	rP	xS,irW	xW	xP	xV,exW	xV			irW
Northern Pygmy-Owl						uP	fP	fP	uP	uP
Ferruginous Pygmy-Owl										
Elf Owl								lrS	xS	
Burrowing Owl	xV		xV			fS,rW	fS,rW	fP	fS,rW	fS,xW
Spotted Owl						uP	uP	uP		
Barred Owl	uP		fP	uP	uP	rP	rP	xP*		rP
Great Gray Owl	xS*,iuW	xV,xW	xV,xW		xV	xV,xW	rP	lrP	xW	rP
Long-eared Owl	uS,rW	xV,xW	rP	rS	rP	uP	uP	uS,fW	uP	uP
Short-eared Owl	uS,rW	uS,xW	uS,rW	uS,rW	uS,rW	ifS,fW	uS,fW	uS,fW	uS,fW	ifS,fW

Subfamily Crotophaginae: Anis

	Montana	Wyoming	Utah	Colorado	Arizona	New Mexico	North Dakota	South Dakota	Nebraska	Kansas	Oklahoma
Smooth-billed Ani											
Groove-billed Ani				xV	rV.xW	xS*.xV		xV	xV	xV	rV

Order Strigiformes: Owls
Family Tytonidae: Barn-Owls

	Montana	Wyoming	Utah	Colorado	Arizona	New Mexico	North Dakota	South Dakota	Nebraska	Kansas	Oklahoma
Common Barn-Owl	xS*.xV	uS.rW	fS.uW	fS.rW	fP	fP	xS.xV	rS	rP	uP	uP

Family Strigidae: Typical Owls

	Montana	Wyoming	Utah	Colorado	Arizona	New Mexico	North Dakota	South Dakota	Nebraska	Kansas	Oklahoma
Oriental Scops-Owl											
Flammulated Owl	xV	xV	uS	uS	fS.xW	uS					
Eastern Screech-Owl	uP	uP		uP			uP	uP	fP	fP	fP
Western Screech-Owl	rP†	fP	fP	fP	cP	cP					luP
Whiskered Screech-Owl					lcP	xV					
Great Horned Owl	cP	cP	cP	cP	cP	cP	cP	cP	cP	cP	cP
Snowy Owl	ifW	irW	xV.xW	irW			iuW	iuW	irW	irW	irW
Northern Hawk-Owl	irW	xV					xV.xW	xW	xV		
Northern Pygmy-Owl	uP	uP	uP	uP	fP	fP					
Ferruginous Pygmy-Owl					lrP						
Elf Owl					cS	lfS					
Burrowing Owl	fS	fS	fS	fS	fS.uW	fS.uW	fS	fS	fS	fS.xW	fS.uW
Spotted Owl			rP	xP*	uP	rP					
Barred Owl	uP	xV		xV			lrP*	eP.xP*	luP	fP	cP
Great Gray Owl	uP	lrP.xW	xV				xV.xW		xV.xW		
Long-eared Owl	uS.rW	uP	uP	uP	rS.uW	rS.uW	uS.rW	uS.rW	uP	uP	uP
Short-eared Owl	ifS.uW	ifS.uW	ifS.fW	uS.fW	rW	rW	ifS.rW	ifS.uW	uS.fT.uW	luS.fT.uW	eS.uW

Subfamily Crotophaginae: Anis

	Texas	Minnesota	Iowa	Missouri	Arkansas	Louisiana	Wisconsin	Michigan	Illinois	Indiana	Ohio
Smooth-billed Ani											
Groove-billed Ani	fS.rW	xV	xV-sp	xV	xV	xS.rW	rV	xV	xV	xV	xV

Order Strigiformes: Owls
Family Tytonidae: Barn-Owls

	Texas	Minnesota	Iowa	Missouri	Arkansas	Louisiana	Wisconsin	Michigan	Illinois	Indiana	Ohio
Common Barn-Owl	fP	xS.rV.xW	rP2	rP	uP	fP	rP	rP	rP	rP	rP

Family Strigidae: Typical Owls

	Texas	Minnesota	Iowa	Missouri	Arkansas	Louisiana	Wisconsin	Michigan	Illinois	Indiana	Ohio
Oriental Scops-Owl											
Flammulated Owl	luS.xV					xW					
Eastern Screech-Owl	cP	fP	fP	fP	cP	cP	fP	fP	cP	cP	fP
Western Screech-Owl	lfP										
Whiskered Screech-Owl											
Great Horned Owl	cP	cP	cP	cP	cP	fP	cP	cP	cP	cP	cP
Snowy Owl	xV.xW	ifW	irW	irW	xW	xW	iuW	iuW	irW	irW	irW
Northern Hawk-Owl		xS.iuW	xW				irW	exS.irW	xV.xW		xV.xW
Northern Pygmy-Owl	xV										
Ferruginous Pygmy-Owl	lrP										
Elf Owl	lfS.xW										
Burrowing Owl	fP	lrS.rT	xS.rT	xS.rT.xW	rT.xW	xS*.uW	xV	xV	xS*.rV	xS*.xV	xV
Spotted Owl	lrP										
Barred Owl	cP	fP	fP	cP	cP	cP	fP	fP	cP	fP	fP
Great Gray Owl		luS.iuW	xW				xS.irW	xS.irW		xW	xV
Long-eared Owl	lrS.rW	uS.rW	rS.uW	xS.uW	xS.rW	rW	uP	uP	rS.uW	rS.uW	lrS.uW
Short-eared Owl	uW	uS.rW	rS.uT.rW	xS*.uW	uW	rW	rS.uW	rS.uT.rW	rS.uW	rS.uW	lrS.uW

Subfamily Crotophaginae: Anis

	West Virginia	Kentucky	Tennessee	Mississippi	Alabama	Maine	New Hampshire	Vermont	Massachu- setts	Rhode Island	Connec- ticut
Smooth-billed Ani											
Groove-billed Ani		xV	xV	rV.xW	rV.xW						

Order Strigiformes: Owls
Family Tytonidae: Barn-Owls

	West Virginia	Kentucky	Tennessee	Mississippi	Alabama	Maine	New Hampshire	Vermont	Massachu- setts	Rhode Island	Connec- ticut
Common Barn-Owl	uP	uP	uP	fP	uP	xS.xV	xS	lrP	rP	uP	rP

Family Strigidae: Typical Owls

	West Virginia	Kentucky	Tennessee	Mississippi	Alabama	Maine	New Hampshire	Vermont	Massachu- setts	Rhode Island	Connec- ticut
Oriental Scops-Owl											
Flammulated Owl											
Eastern Screech-Owl	cP	cP	cP	cP	cP	lrP*	rP	uP	fP	fP	cP
Western Screech-Owl											
Whiskered Screech-Owl											
Great Horned Owl	cP	cP	cP	fP	fP	fP	fP	fP	fP	fP	fP
Snowy Owl	irW	irW	irW	xV	xV.xW	iuW	iuW	iuW	iuW	iuW	iuW
Northern Hawk-Owl						irW	irW	irW	exV.xW	exV	exV.xW
Northern Pygmy-Owl											
Ferruginous Pygmy-Owl											
Elf Owl											
Burrowing Owl			xV.rW	rV.xW		xV		xS*.xV	xV	xV	
Spotted Owl											
Barred Owl	fP	fP	cP	cP	cP	fP	fP	fP	fP	fP	fP
Great Gray Owl						irW	irW	irW	irW	exV.xW	xW
Long-eared Owl	xS.rW	rW	rW	xT.xW	rW	rP	rP	rP	rP	rS.uW	rS.uW
Short-eared Owl	rW	uW	uW	rW	uW	rS*.uT.rW	uT.rW	xS.uW	lrS.uW	uW	uW

Subfamily Crotophaginae: Anis

	New York	Pennsylvania	New Jersey	Delaware	Maryland	Dist. of Columbia	Virginia	North Carolina	South Carolina	Georgia	Florida
Smooth-billed Ani			xV						xV	xV	fP
Groove-billed Ani					xV		xV		xV,xW		rV,rW

Order Strigiformes: Owls
Family Tytonidae: Barn-Owls

	New York	Pennsylvania	New Jersey	Delaware	Maryland	Dist. of Columbia	Virginia	North Carolina	South Carolina	Georgia	Florida
Common Barn-Owl	uP	uP	uP	uP	uP	rP	uP	uP	uP	uP	fP

Family Strigidae: Typical Owls

	New York	Pennsylvania	New Jersey	Delaware	Maryland	Dist. of Columbia	Virginia	North Carolina	South Carolina	Georgia	Florida
Oriental Scops-Owl											
Flammulated Owl											xV
Eastern Screech-Owl	fP	fP	fP	cP	cP	fP	cP	cP	cP	cP	cP
Western Screech-Owl											
Whiskered Screech-Owl											
Great Horned Owl	cP	cP	cP	cP	cP	uP	cP	fP	fP	fP	fP
Snowy Owl	iuW	iuW	iuW	irW	irW	xV,xW	irW	irW	irW	xV,xW	
Northern Hawk-Owl	irW	xV,xW	xV,xW								
Northern Pygmy-Owl											
Ferruginous Pygmy-Owl											
Elf Owl											
Burrowing Owl	xV				xV		xV	xS*,xW	xV		fP
Spotted Owl											
Barred Owl	fP	fP	fP	uP	cP	uP	cP	cP	cP	cP	cP
Great Gray Owl	irW	xV,xW	xW-q								
Long-eared Owl	uP	rS,uW	rS,uW	uW	xS,uW	rW	lrS,rW	xS*,rW	rW	rW	xV
Short-eared Owl	uP	rS,uW	lrS,uW	uW	xS,uW	rW	xS,uW	uW	uW	uW	rW

Strigidae • 197

	Date	Location	Cont. North America	Canada	Lower 48
Boreal Owl *Aegolius funereus*			uS,iuW	uS,iuW	lrP,irW
Northern Saw-whet Owl *Aegolius acadicus*			uP	uS,rW	uP

Order Caprimulgiformes: Goatsuckers, Oilbirds and Allies
Family Caprimulgidae: Goatsuckers
Subfamily Chordeilinae: Nighthawks

Lesser Nighthawk *Chordeiles acutipennis*			lcS,rV,lrW	xV	lcS,rV,lrW
Common Nighthawk *Chordeiles minor*			cS,lrW	fS	cS,lrW
Antillean Nighthawk *Chordeiles gundlachii*			luS,xS*		luS,xS*

Subfamily Caprimulginae: Nightjars

Common Pauraque *Nyctidromus albicollis*			lfP		lfP
Common Poorwill *Phalaenoptilus nuttallii*			fS,luW	luS,xS*,xV	cS,luW
Chuck-will's-widow *Caprimulgus carolinensis*			cS,lrW	lrS,xV	cS,lrW
Buff-collared Nightjar *Caprimulgus ridgwayi*			lrS†		lrS†
Whip-poor-will *Caprimulgus vociferus*			fS,luW	fS	fS,rW
Jungle Nightjar *Caprimulgus indicus*			xV		

Order Apodiformes: Swifts and Hummingbirds
Family Apodidae: Swifts
Subfamily Cypseloidinae: Cypseloidine Swifts

Black Swift *Cypseloides niger*			luS,rT	luS,xV	luS,rT
White-collared Swift *Streptoprocne zonaris*			xV,xW		xV,xW

Subfamily Chaeturinae: Chaeturine Swifts

Chimney Swift *Chaetura pelagica*			cS	fS	cS
Vaux's Swift *Chaetura vauxi*			lfS,rV,lrW	lfS	lfS,fT,lrW
White-throated Needletail *Hirundapus caudacutus*			xV		

Subfamily Apodinae: Apodine Swifts

Common Swift *Apus apus*			xV		

	Hawaii		Alaska		Yukon Terr.	Northwest Terr.	British Columbia	Alberta	Saskatch-ewan	Manitoba	Ontario
Boreal Owl			fP		fP	uS,iuW	uP	uS,iuW	uS,iuW	uS,iuW	rS,irW
N. Saw-whet Owl			uP				uP	uS,rW	uS,rW	uS,rW	uS,fT,rW

Order Caprimulgiformes: Goatsuckers, Oilbirds and Allies
Family Caprimulgidae: Goatsuckers
Subfamily Chordeilinae: Nighthawks

	Hawaii		Alaska		Yukon Terr.	Northwest Terr.	British Columbia	Alberta	Saskatch-ewan	Manitoba	Ontario
Lesser Nighthawk											xV
Common Nighthawk			lrT,xV		fS	lfS,xV	fS	fS	fS,cT	fS	fS,cT
Antillean Nighthawk											

Subfamily Caprimulginae: Nightjars

	Hawaii		Alaska		Yukon Terr.	Northwest Terr.	British Columbia	Alberta	Saskatch-ewan	Manitoba	Ontario
Common Pauraque											
Common Poorwill							luS	xS*	lrS	xV-q	xV
Ch.-will's-widow											lrS
Buff-collared Nightjar											
Whip-poor-will			xV					xV-q	luS,xV	fS	cS
Jungle Nightjar			xV								

Order Apodiformes: Swifts and Hummingbirds
Family Apodidae: Swifts
Subfamily Cypseloidinae: Cypseloidine Swifts

	Hawaii		Alaska		Yukon Terr.	Northwest Terr.	British Columbia	Alberta	Saskatch-ewan	Manitoba	Ontario
Black Swift			luS				uS	luS	xV-q		
White-collared Swift											

Subfamily Chaeturinae: Chaeturine Swifts

	Hawaii		Alaska		Yukon Terr.	Northwest Terr.	British Columbia	Alberta	Saskatch-ewan	Manitoba	Ontario
Chimney Swift			xV			xV		xS	lrS	fS	cS
Vaux's Swift			lfS				fS	xV			
White-throated Needletail			xV								

Subfamily Apodinae: Apodine Swifts

	Hawaii		Alaska		Yukon Terr.	Northwest Terr.	British Columbia	Alberta	Saskatch-ewan	Manitoba	Ontario
Common Swift			xV								

	Québec	Newfoundland	New Brunswick	Prince Edward I.	Nova Scotia		Washington	Oregon	California	Nevada	Idaho
Boreal Owl	rS,irW	uP	eS,xW	xW	xV,xW		xW	exV			rP
N. Saw-whet Owl	uS,rW	xV,xW	fS,uW	rP	uP		uP	uP	uS,fW	uP	uP

Order Caprimulgiformes: Goatsuckers, Oilbirds and Allies
Family Caprimulgidae: Goatsuckers
Subfamily Chordeilinae: Nighthawks

	Québec	Newfoundland	New Brunswick	Prince Edward I.	Nova Scotia		Washington	Oregon	California	Nevada	Idaho
Lesser Nighthawk									cS,rW	cS	
Common Nighthawk	fS	rS	fS	uS	uS		cS	cS	fS	cS	cS
Antillean Nighthawk											

Subfamily Caprimulginae: Nightjars

	Québec	Newfoundland	New Brunswick	Prince Edward I.	Nova Scotia		Washington	Oregon	California	Nevada	Idaho
Common Pauraque											
Common Poorwill							fS	fS	fS,uW	cS	fS
Ch.-will's-widow	xV		exV		xV				xV		
Buff-collared Nightjar											
Whip-poor-will	luS,xV	xV	uS	xV	rS				lrS†,xV,xW	lrS†	
Jungle Nightjar											

Order Apodiformes: Swifts and Hummingbirds
Family Apodidae: Swifts
Subfamily Cypseloidinae: Cypseloidine Swifts

	Québec	Newfoundland	New Brunswick	Prince Edward I.	Nova Scotia		Washington	Oregon	California	Nevada	Idaho
Black Swift							uS	rS*,uT	uS	xT	xT
White-collared Swift									xV		

Subfamily Chaeturinae: Chaeturine Swifts

	Québec	Newfoundland	New Brunswick	Prince Edward I.	Nova Scotia		Washington	Oregon	California	Nevada	Idaho
Chimney Swift	fS	rS*,uV	fS	uS†	fS				xS,rV		
Vaux's Swift							cS	cS	fS,rW	uT	uS
White-throated Needletail											

Subfamily Apodinae: Apodine Swifts

	Québec	Newfoundland	New Brunswick	Prince Edward I.	Nova Scotia		Washington	Oregon	California	Nevada	Idaho
Common Swift											

200 • *Distributional Checklist of North American Birds*

	Montana	Wyoming	Utah	Colorado	Arizona	New Mexico	North Dakota	South Dakota	Nebraska	Kansas	Oklahoma
Boreal Owl	lrP,xV	lrP†,xV,xW		uP			xV,xW		xV		
N. Saw-whet Owl	uP	uP	uP	uP	rS,irW	rS,irW	lrS†,uT,rW	lrS,rW	lrS*,rW	xS,rW	xV,xW

Order Caprimulgiformes: Goatsuckers, Oilbirds and Allies
Family Caprimulgidae: Goatsuckers
Subfamily Chordeilinae: Nighthawks

	Montana	Wyoming	Utah	Colorado	Arizona	New Mexico	North Dakota	South Dakota	Nebraska	Kansas	Oklahoma
Lesser Nighthawk			lfS	exV	cS,xW	cS					xV
Common Nighthawk	fS,cT	cS	cS	cS	cS	cS	fS,cT	fS,cT	cS	cS	cS
Antillean Nighthawk											

Subfamily Caprimulginae: Nightjars

	Montana	Wyoming	Utah	Colorado	Arizona	New Mexico	North Dakota	South Dakota	Nebraska	Kansas	Oklahoma
Common Pauraque											
Common Poorwill	fS	fS	cS	fS	cS,uW	cS,rW	luS†	lfS	fS	fS	fS
Ch.-will's-widow								xV	lrS	lfS	cS
Buff-collared Nightjar					rS†	xS*					
Whip-poor-will				xV	fS,xW	uS	eS†,xT	luS,rT	luS,uT	luS,uT	uS
Jungle Nightjar											

Order Apodiformes: Swifts and Hummingbirds
Family Apodidae: Swifts
Subfamily Cypseloidinae: Cypseloidine Swifts

	Montana	Wyoming	Utah	Colorado	Arizona	New Mexico	North Dakota	South Dakota	Nebraska	Kansas	Oklahoma
Black Swift	luS,xT	xT	lrS,xT	rS	rT-q	lrS*,rT					
White-collared Swift											

Subfamily Chaeturinae: Chaeturine Swifts

	Montana	Wyoming	Utah	Colorado	Arizona	New Mexico	North Dakota	South Dakota	Nebraska	Kansas	Oklahoma
Chimney Swift	uS	rS†	xV	uS	lrS*,xV	lrS*,rT	fS	cS	cS	cS	cS
Vaux's Swift	uS		xT		fT						
White-throated Needletail											

Subfamily Apodinae: Apodine Swifts

	Montana	Wyoming	Utah	Colorado	Arizona	New Mexico	North Dakota	South Dakota	Nebraska	Kansas	Oklahoma
Common Swift											

Strigidae • 201

	Texas	Minnesota	Iowa	Missouri	Arkansas	Louisiana	Wisconsin	Michigan	Illinois	Indiana	Ohio
Boreal Owl		IrP,irW					rV,rW	iuW	exV,exW		
N. Saw-whet Owl	xS,irW	uS,fT,rW	xS*,rW	xS,rW	xV,xW	xV,xW	uS,fT,uW	uS,fT,uW	xS,uW	xS,uW	xS,uT,rW

Order Caprimulgiformes: Goatsuckers, Oilbirds and Allies
Family Caprimulgidae: Goatsuckers
Subfamily Chordeilinae: Nighthawks

	Texas	Minnesota	Iowa	Missouri	Arkansas	Louisiana	Wisconsin	Michigan	Illinois	Indiana	Ohio
Lesser Nighthawk	cS,xW						rV				
Common Nighthawk	cS,xW	fS,cT	fS,cT	fS,cT	fS,cT	fS,cT	fS,cT	fS,cT	fS,cT	fS,cT	fS,cT
Antillean Nighthawk						xS*					

Subfamily Caprimulginae: Nightjars

	Texas	Minnesota	Iowa	Missouri	Arkansas	Louisiana	Wisconsin	Michigan	Illinois	Indiana	Ohio
Common Pauraque	lfP										
Common Poorwill	fS,uW	xV		xV							
Ch.-will's-widow	cS	xS*	lrS	fS	cS	cS,rW	lrS*	lrS*,xV	uS	uS	lrS
Buff-collared Nightjar											
Whip-poor-will	lfS,fT,xW	fS	fS	fS	fS	fT,rW	cS	cS	fS	fS	fS
Jungle Nightjar											

Order Apodiformes: Swifts and Hummingbirds
Family Apodidae: Swifts
Subfamily Cypseloidinae: Cypseloidine Swifts

	Texas	Minnesota	Iowa	Missouri	Arkansas	Louisiana	Wisconsin	Michigan	Illinois	Indiana	Ohio
Black Swift	xV-q								xV		
White-collared Swift	xV										

Subfamily Chaeturinae: Chaeturine Swifts

	Texas	Minnesota	Iowa	Missouri	Arkansas	Louisiana	Wisconsin	Michigan	Illinois	Indiana	Ohio
Chimney Swift	cS	cS	cS	cS	cS	cS	cS	cS	cS	cS	cS
Vaux's Swift	xV,xW-q					xV,rW					
White-throated Needletail											

Subfamily Apodinae: Apodine Swifts

	Texas	Minnesota	Iowa	Missouri	Arkansas	Louisiana	Wisconsin	Michigan	Illinois	Indiana	Ohio
Common Swift											

	West Virginia	Kentucky	Tennessee	Mississippi	Alabama	Maine	New Hampshire	Vermont	Massachusetts	Rhode Island	Connecticut
Boreal Owl						irW	irW	exV,xW	xV,xW	exV,exW	exW
N. Saw-whet Owl	lrS,uW	rW	lrS†,rW	xW	xV	fP	fP	fP	rS,fT,uW	xS,uT,rW	rS,uW

Order Caprimulgiformes: Goatsuckers, Oilbirds and Allies
Family Caprimulgidae: Goatsuckers
Subfamily Chordeilinae: Nighthawks

	West Virginia	Kentucky	Tennessee	Mississippi	Alabama	Maine	New Hampshire	Vermont	Massachusetts	Rhode Island	Connecticut
Lesser Nighthawk				xV	xV,xW						
Common Nighthawk	fS,cT	fS,cT	fS,cT	fS,cT	fS,cT,xW	fS,cT	fS,cT	fS,cT	uS,cT	uS,cT	fS,cT
Antillean Nighthawk											

Subfamily Caprimulginae: Nightjars

	West Virginia	Kentucky	Tennessee	Mississippi	Alabama	Maine	New Hampshire	Vermont	Massachusetts	Rhode Island	Connecticut
Common Pauraque											
Common Poorwill											
Ch.-will's-widow	lrS	fS	cS	cS	cS,rW	xV	xV		lrS†	xV	xS
Buff-collared Nightjar											
Whip-poor-will	fS	cS	cS	luS†,fT,rW	fS,rW	fS	uS	uS	uS	fS	fS
Jungle Nightjar											

Order Apodiformes: Swifts and Hummingbirds
Family Apodidae: Swifts
Subfamily Cypseloidinae: Cypseloidine Swifts

	West Virginia	Kentucky	Tennessee	Mississippi	Alabama	Maine	New Hampshire	Vermont	Massachusetts	Rhode Island	Connecticut
Black Swift											
White-collared Swift											

Subfamily Chaeturinae: Chaeturine Swifts

	West Virginia	Kentucky	Tennessee	Mississippi	Alabama	Maine	New Hampshire	Vermont	Massachusetts	Rhode Island	Connecticut
Chimney Swift	cS	cS	cS	cS	cS	cS	cS	cS	cS	cS	cS
Vaux's Swift											
White-throated Needletail											

Subfamily Apodinae: Apodine Swifts

	West Virginia	Kentucky	Tennessee	Mississippi	Alabama	Maine	New Hampshire	Vermont	Massachusetts	Rhode Island	Connecticut
Common Swift											

Strigidae • 203

	New York	Pennsylvania	New Jersey	Delaware	Maryland	Dist. of Columbia	Virginia	North Carolina	South Carolina	Georgia	Florida
Boreal Owl	irW	xV	xV				xW-q				
N. Saw-whet Owl	uS,fT,uW	rS,uW	lrS,uW	uT,rW	lrS,uW	uW	lrS*,uW	lrS,rW	irW	irW	xV

Order Caprimulgiformes: Goatsuckers, Oilbirds and Allies
Family Caprimulgidae: Goatsuckers
Subfamily Chordeilinae: Nighthawks

	New York	Pennsylvania	New Jersey	Delaware	Maryland	Dist. of Columbia	Virginia	North Carolina	South Carolina	Georgia	Florida
Lesser Nighthawk											rV,xW
Common Nighthawk	fS,cT	fS,cT	uS,cT	uS,cT	fS,cT	fS,cT	fS,cT	fS,cT	fS,cT	fS,cT	fS,cT,rW
Antillean Nighthawk											luS

Subfamily Caprimulginae: Nightjars

	New York	Pennsylvania	New Jersey	Delaware	Maryland	Dist. of Columbia	Virginia	North Carolina	South Carolina	Georgia	Florida
Common Pauraque											
Common Poorwill											
Ch.-will's-widow	lrS	rV	luS	fS	fS	xT	cS,xW	cS	cS	cS	cS,rW
Buff-collared Nightjar											
Whip-poor-will	fS	fS	fS	fS	fS	uT	cS	cS,rW	fS,rW	fS,rW	fT,uW
Jungle Nightjar											

Order Apodiformes: Swifts and Hummingbirds
Family Apodidae: Swifts
Subfamily Cypseloidinae: Cypseloidine Swifts

	New York	Pennsylvania	New Jersey	Delaware	Maryland	Dist. of Columbia	Virginia	North Carolina	South Carolina	Georgia	Florida
Black Swift											xV
White-collared Swift											xW

Subfamily Chaeturinae: Chaeturine Swifts

	New York	Pennsylvania	New Jersey	Delaware	Maryland	Dist. of Columbia	Virginia	North Carolina	South Carolina	Georgia	Florida
Chimney Swift	cS	cS	cS	cS	cS	cS	cS	cS	cS	cS	cS
Vaux's Swift											xV,xW
White-throated Needletail											

Subfamily Apodinae: Apodine Swifts

	New York	Pennsylvania	New Jersey	Delaware	Maryland	Dist. of Columbia	Virginia	North Carolina	South Carolina	Georgia	Florida
Common Swift											

	Date	Location	Cont. North America	Canada	Lower 48
Fork-tailed Swift *Apus pacificus*			xV		
White-throated Swift *Aeronautes saxatalis*			fS,lfW	luS,xV	cS,lfW
Antillean Palm Swift *Tachornis phoenicobia*			xV		xV

Family Trochilidae: Hummingbirds

	Date	Location	Cont. North America	Canada	Lower 48
Green Violet-ear *Colibri thalassinus*			xS*,xV		xS*,xV
Cuban Emerald *Chlorostilbon ricordii*			xV		xV
Broad-billed Hummingbird *Cynanthus latirostris*			lcS,rV,lrW		lcS,rV,lrW
White-eared Hummingbird *Hylocharis leucotis*			lrS*,xV		lrS*,xV
Berylline Hummingbird *Amazilia beryllina*			lrS		lrS
Rufous-tailed Hummingbird *Amazilia tzacatl*			exV		exV
Buff-bellied Hummingbird *Amazilia yucatanensis*			lfS,rV,luW		lfS,rV,luW
Violet-crowned Hummingbird *Amazilia violiceps*			luS,xV,xW		luS,xV,xW
Blue-throated Hummingbird *Lampornis clemenciae*			luS,xS,rS*,xV,lrW		luS,xS,rS*,xV,lrW
Magnificent Hummingbird *Eugenes fulgens*			lfS,xS*,xV,lrW		lfS,xS*,xV,lrW
Plain-capped Starthroat *Heliomaster constantii*			xV		xV
Bahama Woodstar *Calliphlox evelynae*			xV		xV
Lucifer Hummingbird *Calothorax lucifer*			luS,xS*,xV		luS,xS*,xV
Ruby-throated Hummingbird *Archilochus colubris*			fS,luW	fS	fS,rW
Black-chinned Hummingbird *Archilochus alexandri*			fS,lrW	luS,xV	fS,lrW
Anna's Hummingbird *Calypte anna*			lcP,xS,xS*,rV,rW	lrP,xS*,xV	lcP,xS,rV,rW
Costa's Hummingbird *Calypte costae*			lcS,xS*,xV,luW	xV	lcS,xS*,xV,luW
Calliope Hummingbird *Stellula calliope*			lfS,fT	luS,xV	fS
Bumblebee Hummingbird *Atthis heloisa*			exV		exV
Broad-tailed Hummingbird *Selasphorus platycercus*			lcS,rV,xW		cS,xW

Distributional Checklist of North American Birds

	Hawaii	Alaska	Yukon Terr.	Northwest Terr.	British Columbia	Alberta	Saskatchewan	Manitoba	Ontario
Fork-tailed Swift		xV							
White-throated Swift						luS	xV-q		
Antillean Palm Swift									

Family Trochilidae: Hummingbirds

	Hawaii	Alaska	Yukon Terr.	Northwest Terr.	British Columbia	Alberta	Saskatchewan	Manitoba	Ontario
Green Violet-ear									
Cuban Emerald									
Broad-billed Hummingbird									
White-eared Hummingbird									
Berylline Hummingbird									
Rufous-tailed Hummingbird									
Buff-bellied Hummingbird									
Violet-crowned Hummingbird									
Blue-throated Hummingbird									
Magnificent Hummingbird									
Plain-capped Starthroat									
Bahama Woodstar									
Lucifer Hummingbird									
Ruby-throated Hummingbird		xV		xV	xV	uS	fS	fS	fS
Black-chinned Hummingbird					luS	xV	xV-q		
Anna's Hummingbird		rV.xW			lrP	xV	xS*-q		
Costa's Hummingbird					xV				
Calliope Hummingbird		xV-q				uS	luS	xV	
Bumblebee Hummingbird									
Broad-tailed Hummingbird									

	Québec	Newfoundland	New Brunswick	Prince Edward I.	Nova Scotia	Washington	Oregon	California	Nevada	Idaho
Fork-tailed Swift										
White-throated Swift						uS	uS	fP	cS.lrW	fS
Antillean Palm Swift										

Family Trochilidae: Hummingbirds

	Québec	Newfoundland	New Brunswick	Prince Edward I.	Nova Scotia	Washington	Oregon	California	Nevada	Idaho
Green Violet-ear										
Cuban Emerald										
Broad-billed Hummingbird								rV.rW		
White-eared Hummingbird										
Berylline Hummingbird										
Rufous-tailed Hummingbird										
Buff-bellied Hummingbird										
Violet-crowned Hummingbird								xV		
Blue-throated Hummingbird								xS		
Magnificent Hummingbird								xV-q	xV	
Plain-capped Starthroat										
Bahama Woodstar										
Lucifer Hummingbird										
Ruby-throated Hummingbird	fS	xS.rV	fS	fS	fS					
Black-chinned Hummingbird						uS	uS	fS.xW	uS	uS
Anna's Hummingbird						luP	fP	cP	rV.xW	xV.xW
Costa's Hummingbird							xS*.xV.xW	cS.uW	luS	
Calliope Hummingbird						fS	fS	uS.fT	uS.fT	fS
Bumblebee Hummingbird										
Broad-tailed Hummingbird							rS*	luS.xV.xW	cS	uS

	Montana	Wyoming	Utah	Colorado	Arizona	New Mexico	North Dakota	South Dakota	Nebraska	Kansas	Oklahoma
Fork-tailed Swift											
White-throated Swift	fS	fS	cS,xW	fS	cS,fW	cS,lrW		lfS	lfS	xV	xV-q
Antillean Palm Swift											

Family Trochilidae: Hummingbirds

	Montana	Wyoming	Utah	Colorado	Arizona	New Mexico	North Dakota	South Dakota	Nebraska	Kansas	Oklahoma
Green Violet-ear											
Cuban Emerald											
Broad-billed Hummingbird			xV		cS,rW	luS,xV					
White-eared Hummingbird					lrS*	xS*					
Berylline Hummingbird					lrS						
Rufous-tailed Hummingbird											
Buff-bellied Hummingbird											
Violet-crowned Hummingbird					luS,xV,xW	lrS					
Blue-throated Hummingbird		xV-q		xS*,xV	luS,xV,lrW	rS*					
Magnificent Hummingbird		xS*,xV	xV	rS	fS,lrW	uS†,xW				xS*,xV	
Plain-capped Starthroat					xV						
Bahama Woodstar											
Lucifer Hummingbird					lrS	xS*,xV					
Ruby-throated Hummingbird	xS,xV	xV				xV	luS,uT	xS,uT	luS,uT	uS,fT	uS,fT
Black-chinned Hummingbird	rS	uS*	fS	fS	cS	cS					lrS
Anna's Hummingbird	xV,xW	xV		xV	uS,fW	rT,xW					xW
Costa's Hummingbird			luS,xW		cS,luW	lrS*					
Calliope Hummingbird	uS	fS	uS,fT	uT	fT	fT			xV	xV	xV
Bumblebee Hummingbird					exV						
Broad-tailed Hummingbird	xS*,xV	cS	cS	cS	cS	cS			xV	xV	xV	xV-q

Apodidae • 209

	Texas	Minnesota	Iowa	Missouri	Arkansas	Louisiana	Wisconsin	Michigan	Illinois	Indiana	Ohio
Fork-tailed Swift											
White-throated Swift	lfS,rV,luW					xV		xS*,exV			
Antillean Palm Swift											

Family Trochilidae: Hummingbirds

	Texas	Minnesota	Iowa	Missouri	Arkansas	Louisiana	Wisconsin	Michigan	Illinois	Indiana	Ohio
Green Violet-ear	xS*,xV				xV						
Cuban Emerald											
Broad-billed Hummingbird	lrS,xV,xW										
White-eared Hummingbird	xV										
Berylline Hummingbird											
Rufous-tailed Hummingbird	exV										
Buff-bellied Hummingbird	lfS,uW					rV,rW					
Violet-crowned Hummingbird											
Blue-throated Hummingbird	lfS,xV										
Magnificent Hummingbird	lrS,xV										
Plain-capped Starthroat											
Bahama Woodstar											
Lucifer Hummingbird	luS,xV										
Ruby-throated Hummingbird	fS,cT,rW	fS	uS,fT	fS	fS	fS,cT,rW	fS	fS	fS	fS	fS
Black-chinned Hummingbird	cS,rW					rV,rW					
Anna's Hummingbird	xS,rW					xV					
Costa's Hummingbird	xV,xW										
Calliope Hummingbird	rT					xV					
Bumblebee Hummingbird											
Broad-tailed Hummingbird	lfS,uT,xW					xV,xW					

	West Virginia	Kentucky	Tennessee	Mississippi	Alabama	Maine	New Hampshire	Vermont	Massachusetts	Rhode Island	Connecticut
Fork-tailed Swift											
White-throated Swift											
Antillean Palm Swift											

Family Trochilidae: Hummingbirds

	West Virginia	Kentucky	Tennessee	Mississippi	Alabama	Maine	New Hampshire	Vermont	Massachusetts	Rhode Island	Connecticut
Green Violet-ear											
Cuban Emerald											
Broad-billed Hummingbird											
White-eared Hummingbird											
Berylline Hummingbird											
Rufous-tailed Hummingbird											
Buff-bellied Hummingbird											
Violet-crowned Hummingbird											
Blue-throated Hummingbird											
Magnificent Hummingbird											
Plain-capped Starthroat											
Bahama Woodstar											
Lucifer Hummingbird											
Ruby-throated Hummingbird	fS	fS	fS	fS.cT.xW	fS.cT.rW	fS	fS	fS	uS.fT	uS.fT	uS.fT
Black-chinned Hummingbird					xV.xW				xV		
Anna's Hummingbird											
Costa's Hummingbird											
Calliope Hummingbird											
Bumblebee Hummingbird											
Broad-tailed Hummingbird											

	New York	Pennsylvania	New Jersey	Delaware	Maryland	Dist. of Columbia	Virginia	North Carolina	South Carolina	Georgia	Florida
Fork-tailed Swift											
White-throated Swift											
Antillean Palm Swift											xV

Family Trochilidae: Hummingbirds

	New York	Pennsylvania	New Jersey	Delaware	Maryland	Dist. of Columbia	Virginia	North Carolina	South Carolina	Georgia	Florida
Green Violet-ear											
Cuban Emerald											xV
Broad-billed Hummingbird											
White-eared Hummingbird											
Berylline Hummingbird											
Rufous-tailed Hummingbird											
Buff-bellied Hummingbird											
Violet-crowned Hummingbird											
Blue-throated Hummingbird											
Magnificent Hummingbird											
Plain-capped Starthroat											
Bahama Woodstar											xV
Lucifer Hummingbird											
Ruby-throated Hummingbird	fS	fS	uS.fT	uS.fT	fS	rS.uT	fS.xW	fS.rW	fS.rW	fS.rW	fS.cT.uW
Black-chinned Hummingbird											xV.xW
Anna's Hummingbird											
Costa's Hummingbird											
Calliope Hummingbird											
Bumblebee Hummingbird											
Broad-tailed Hummingbird											

	Date	Location	Cont. North America	Canada	Lower 48
Rufous Hummingbird *Selasphorus rufus*			lcS,xS,cT,luW	lcS,rV,xW	lcS,xS,cT,rW
Allen's Hummingbird *Selasphorus sasin*			lcS,xV,lfW		lcS,xV,lfW

Order Trogoniformes: Trogons
Family Trogonidae: Trogons

Elegant Trogon *Trogon elegans*			lfS,xV,lrW		lfS,xV,lrW
Eared Trogon *Euptilotis neoxenus*			xV		xV

Order Coraciiformes: Kingfishers, Rollers, Hornbills and Allies
Family Upupidae: Hoopoes

Hoopoe *Upupa epops*			xV		

Family Alcedinidae: Kingfishers
Subfamily Cerylinae: Typical Kingfishers

Ringed Kingfisher *Ceryle torquata*			luP		luP
Belted Kingfisher *Ceryle alcyon*			fP	cS,uW	fS,cW
Green Kingfisher *Chloroceryle americana*			luP,rV,rW		luP,rV,rW

Order Piciformes: Puffbirds, Toucans, Woodpeckers and Allies
Family Picidae: Woodpeckers and Allies
Subfamily Jynginae: Wrynecks

Eurasian Wryneck *Jynx torquilla*			xV		

Subfamily Picinae: Woodpeckers

Lewis' Woodpecker *Melanerpes lewis*			uS,iuW	luS,rV,lrW	uS,iuW
Red-headed Woodpecker *Melanerpes erythrocephalus*			fP	fS,lrW	cS,fW
Acorn Woodpecker *Melanerpes formicivorus*			lcP,xV,xW		lcP,xV,xW
Gila Woodpecker *Melanerpes uropygialis*			lcP		lcP
Golden-fronted Woodpecker *Melanerpes aurifrons*			lcP,xV,xW		lcP,xV,xW
Red-bellied Woodpecker *Melanerpes carolinus*			cP	luP,xS,rV,rW	cP

	Hawaii	Alaska	Yukon Terr.	Northwest Terr.	British Columbia	Alberta	Saskatchewan	Manitoba	Ontario
Rufous Hummingbird		cS	lrS*		cS,xW	lfS,rV	xV	xV	xV
Allen's Hummingbird									

Order Trogoniformes: Trogons
Family Trogonidae: Trogons

	Hawaii	Alaska	Yukon Terr.	Northwest Terr.	British Columbia	Alberta	Saskatchewan	Manitoba	Ontario
Elegant Trogon									
Eared Trogon									

Order Coraciiformes: Kingfishers, Rollers, Hornbills and Allies
Family Upupidae: Hoopoes

	Hawaii	Alaska	Yukon Terr.	Northwest Terr.	British Columbia	Alberta	Saskatchewan	Manitoba	Ontario
Hoopoe		xV							

Family Alcedinidae: Kingfishers
Subfamily Cerylinae: Typical Kingfishers

	Hawaii	Alaska	Yukon Terr.	Northwest Terr.	British Columbia	Alberta	Saskatchewan	Manitoba	Ontario
Ringed Kingfisher									
Belted Kingfisher	xV,xW	cS,uW	cS	fS	cS,fW	fS	fS,xW	fS	cS,uW
Green Kingfisher									

Order Piciformes: Puffbirds, Toucans, Woodpeckers and Allies
Family Picidae: Woodpeckers and Allies
Subfamily Jynginae: Wrynecks

	Hawaii	Alaska	Yukon Terr.	Northwest Terr.	British Columbia	Alberta	Saskatchewan	Manitoba	Ontario
Eurasian Wryneck		xV							

Subfamily Picinae: Woodpeckers

	Hawaii	Alaska	Yukon Terr.	Northwest Terr.	British Columbia	Alberta	Saskatchewan	Manitoba	Ontario
Lewis' Woodpecker					uS,rW	lrS,xV	rV	rV,xW	xW
Red-headed Woodpecker					xV	xS*,xV	lrS,xV	fS,rW	fS,rW
Acorn Woodpecker									
Gila Woodpecker									
Golden-fronted Woodpecker									
Red-bellied Woodpecker								xV	xS,rV,rW	luP

Trochilidae • 215

	Québec	Newfoundland	New Brunswick	Prince Edward I.	Nova Scotia	Washington	Oregon	California	Nevada	Idaho
Rufous Hummingbird					xV-q	cS	cS	xS,cT,rW	cT	fS
Allen's Hummingbird						exV	lfS	lcS,cT,lfW	xV	

Order Trogoniformes: Trogons
Family Trogonidae: Trogons

Elegant Trogon										
Eared Trogon										

Order Coraciiformes: Kingfishers, Rollers, Hornbills and Allies
Family Upupidae: Hoopoes

Hoopoe										

Family Alcedinidae: Kingfishers
Subfamily Cerylinae: Typical Kingfishers

Ringed Kingfisher										
Belted Kingfisher	cS,xW	fS,rW	cS,rW	cS,rW	cS,rW	cP	cP	cP	fP	fS,uW
Green Kingfisher										

Order Piciformes: Puffbirds, Toucans, Woodpeckers and Allies
Family Picidae: Woodpeckers and Allies
Subfamily Jynginae: Wrynecks

Eurasian Wryneck										

Subfamily Picinae: Woodpeckers

	Québec	Newfoundland	New Brunswick	Prince Edward I.	Nova Scotia	Washington	Oregon	California	Nevada	Idaho
Lewis' Woodpecker						uS,rW	uP	rS,iuW	uP	fS,rW
Red-headed Woodpecker	luS,xW	xV	exS,xS*,rV,xW		rV			xV		xV
Acorn Woodpecker						xV	fP	cP	xV	
Gila Woodpecker								lfP	exP	
Golden-fronted Woodpecker										
Red-bellied Woodpecker	rV,xW				xW					

	Montana	Wyoming	Utah	Colorado	Arizona	New Mexico	North Dakota	South Dakota	Nebraska	Kansas	Oklahoma
Rufous Hummingbird	fS	luS,fT	cT	fT	cT,xW	cT		xV	rV	xV	rV,xW
Allen's Hummingbird					uT						

Order Trogoniformes: Trogons
Family Trogonidae: Trogons

	Montana	Wyoming	Utah	Colorado	Arizona	New Mexico	North Dakota	South Dakota	Nebraska	Kansas	Oklahoma
Elegant Trogon					lfS,lrW	xS*,xV					
Eared Trogon					xV	xV					

Order Coraciiformes: Kingfishers, Rollers, Hornbills and Allies
Family Upupidae: Hoopoes

	Montana	Wyoming	Utah	Colorado	Arizona	New Mexico	North Dakota	South Dakota	Nebraska	Kansas	Oklahoma
Hoopoe											

Family Alcedinidae: Kingfishers
Subfamily Cerylinae: Typical Kingfishers

	Montana	Wyoming	Utah	Colorado	Arizona	New Mexico	North Dakota	South Dakota	Nebraska	Kansas	Oklahoma
Ringed Kingfisher											
Belted Kingfisher	fS,uW	cS,uW	fP	fS,uW	rS,fW	luS,fT,uW	fS,rW	fS,rW	fS,rW	fS,uW	fS,uW
Green Kingfisher					rV,rW						

Order Piciformes: Puffbirds, Toucans, Woodpeckers and Allies
Family Picidae: Woodpeckers and Allies
Subfamily Jynginae: Wrynecks

	Montana	Wyoming	Utah	Colorado	Arizona	New Mexico	North Dakota	South Dakota	Nebraska	Kansas	Oklahoma
Eurasian Wryneck											

Subfamily Picinae: Woodpeckers

	Montana	Wyoming	Utah	Colorado	Arizona	New Mexico	North Dakota	South Dakota	Nebraska	Kansas	Oklahoma
Lewis' Woodpecker	uS,rW	uS	uS,rW	uS,iuW	uS,iuW	uS,iuW	xV	luS,xV	lrS,rT,xW	xT	lrS,rT,xW
Red-headed Woodpecker	fS,xW	fS	xS*,xV	fS	exV,xW	uS,rW	fS,xW	cS,rW	cS,rW	cS,uW	fP
Acorn Woodpecker		xV			cP	cP					xW
Gila Woodpecker					cP	luP					
Golden-fronted Woodpecker						xV,xW					lrP
Red-bellied Woodpecker	xV				lrS,rV,xW		xV,xW	lrP	luP	lfP	cP	cP

	Texas	Minnesota	Iowa	Missouri	Arkansas	Louisiana	Wisconsin	Michigan	Illinois	Indiana	Ohio
Rufous Hummingbird	fT,uW	xV	xV-sp	xV	xV,xW	rV,rW	xV-q	xV-q		xV-sp	
Allen's Hummingbird	xV,xW					xV,xW					

Order Trogoniformes: Trogons
Family Trogonidae: Trogons

	Texas	Minnesota	Iowa	Missouri	Arkansas	Louisiana	Wisconsin	Michigan	Illinois	Indiana	Ohio
Elegant Trogon	xV,xW										
Eared Trogon											

Order Coraciiformes: Kingfishers, Rollers, Hornbills and Allies
Family Upupidae: Hoopoes

	Texas	Minnesota	Iowa	Missouri	Arkansas	Louisiana	Wisconsin	Michigan	Illinois	Indiana	Ohio
Hoopoe											

Family Alcedinidae: Kingfishers
Subfamily Cerylinae: Typical Kingfishers

	Texas	Minnesota	Iowa	Missouri	Arkansas	Louisiana	Wisconsin	Michigan	Illinois	Indiana	Ohio
Ringed Kingfisher	luP,xV										
Belted Kingfisher	fS,cW	fS,rW	fS,rW	fP	fP	fS,cW	fS,rW	fS,uW	fP	fS,uW	fS,uW
Green Kingfisher	uP										

Order Piciformes: Puffbirds, Toucans, Woodpeckers and Allies
Family Picidae: Woodpeckers and Allies
Subfamily Jynginae: Wrynecks

	Texas	Minnesota	Iowa	Missouri	Arkansas	Louisiana	Wisconsin	Michigan	Illinois	Indiana	Ohio
Eurasian Wryneck											

Subfamily Picinae: Woodpeckers

	Texas	Minnesota	Iowa	Missouri	Arkansas	Louisiana	Wisconsin	Michigan	Illinois	Indiana	Ohio
Lewis' Woodpecker	rW	xW	xW	xW	xV		xW				
Red-headed Woodpecker	fP	cS,uW	cS,uW	cS,fW	fP	fP	cS,uW	fS,uW	cS,fW	fS,uW	fS,uW
Acorn Woodpecker	lcP,xV,xW										
Gila Woodpecker											
Golden-fronted Woodpecker	cP										
Red-bellied Woodpecker	cP	fP	fP	cP	cP	cP	fP	fP	cP	fP	fP

Order Trogoniformes: Trogons
Family Trogonidae: Trogons

	West Virginia	Kentucky	Tennessee	Mississippi	Alabama	Maine	New Hampshire	Vermont	Massachusetts	Rhode Island	Connecticut
Rufous Hummingbird				rV,xW	rV,xW	xV-q	xV		xV		xV-sp-q
Allen's Hummingbird											
Elegant Trogon											
Eared Trogon											

Order Coraciiformes: Kingfishers, Rollers, Hornbills and Allies
Family Upupidae: Hoopoes

	West Virginia	Kentucky	Tennessee	Mississippi	Alabama	Maine	New Hampshire	Vermont	Massachusetts	Rhode Island	Connecticut
Hoopoe											

Family Alcedinidae: Kingfishers
Subfamily Cerylinae: Typical Kingfishers

	West Virginia	Kentucky	Tennessee	Mississippi	Alabama	Maine	New Hampshire	Vermont	Massachusetts	Rhode Island	Connecticut
Ringed Kingfisher											
Belted Kingfisher	fS,uW	fP	fP	fS,cW	fS,cW	cS,rW	fS,rW	fS,rW	fS,uW	fS,uW	fS,uW
Green Kingfisher											

Order Piciformes: Puffbirds, Toucans, Woodpeckers and Allies
Family Picidae: Woodpeckers and Allies
Subfamily Jynginae: Wrynecks

	West Virginia	Kentucky	Tennessee	Mississippi	Alabama	Maine	New Hampshire	Vermont	Massachusetts	Rhode Island	Connecticut
Eurasian Wryneck											

Subfamily Picinae: Woodpeckers

	West Virginia	Kentucky	Tennessee	Mississippi	Alabama	Maine	New Hampshire	Vermont	Massachusetts	Rhode Island	Connecticut
Lewis' Woodpecker									xV	exV	
Red-headed Woodpecker	uP	fP	fP	fP	fP	eS,rV	rS,xW	rS,xW	rS,uT,rW	xS,rW	rP
Acorn Woodpecker											
Gila Woodpecker											
Golden-fronted Woodpecker											
Red-bellied Woodpecker	fP	cP	cP	cP	cP	rV	xV,xW	xV,xW	lrP,rV,rW	rV,rW	uP

	New York	Pennsylvania	New Jersey	Delaware	Maryland	Dist. of Columbia	Virginia	North Carolina	South Carolina	Georgia	Florida
Rufous Hummingbird	xV-sp	xV		xV	xV	xV-sp	xV,xW	xV-sp	xV,xW	xV,xW	rV,rW
Allen's Hummingbird											

Order Trogoniformes: Trogons
Family Trogonidae: Trogons

	New York	Pennsylvania	New Jersey	Delaware	Maryland	Dist. of Columbia	Virginia	North Carolina	South Carolina	Georgia	Florida
Elegant Trogon											
Eared Trogon											

Order Coraciiformes: Kingfishers, Rollers, Hornbills and Allies
Family Upupidae: Hoopoes

	New York	Pennsylvania	New Jersey	Delaware	Maryland	Dist. of Columbia	Virginia	North Carolina	South Carolina	Georgia	Florida
Hoopoe											

Family Alcedinidae: Kingfishers
Subfamily Cerylinae: Typical Kingfishers

	New York	Pennsylvania	New Jersey	Delaware	Maryland	Dist. of Columbia	Virginia	North Carolina	South Carolina	Georgia	Florida
Ringed Kingfisher											
Belted Kingfisher	fS,uW	fS,uW	fS,uW	fP	fP	uP	fS,cW	fS,cW	fS,cW	fS,cW	uS,cW
Green Kingfisher											

Order Piciformes: Puffbirds, Toucans, Woodpeckers and Allies
Family Picidae: Woodpeckers and Allies
Subfamily Jynginae: Wrynecks

	New York	Pennsylvania	New Jersey	Delaware	Maryland	Dist. of Columbia	Virginia	North Carolina	South Carolina	Georgia	Florida
Eurasian Wryneck											

Subfamily Picinae: Woodpeckers

	New York	Pennsylvania	New Jersey	Delaware	Maryland	Dist. of Columbia	Virginia	North Carolina	South Carolina	Georgia	Florida
Lewis' Woodpecker											
Red-headed Woodpecker	uS,rW	uS,rW	rS,uT,rW	uP	uP	xS,rW	uP	uP	fP	fP	fP
Acorn Woodpecker											
Gila Woodpecker											
Golden-fronted Woodpecker											xV
Red-bellied Woodpecker	fP	fP	fP	fP	cP	cP	cP	cP	cP	cP	cP

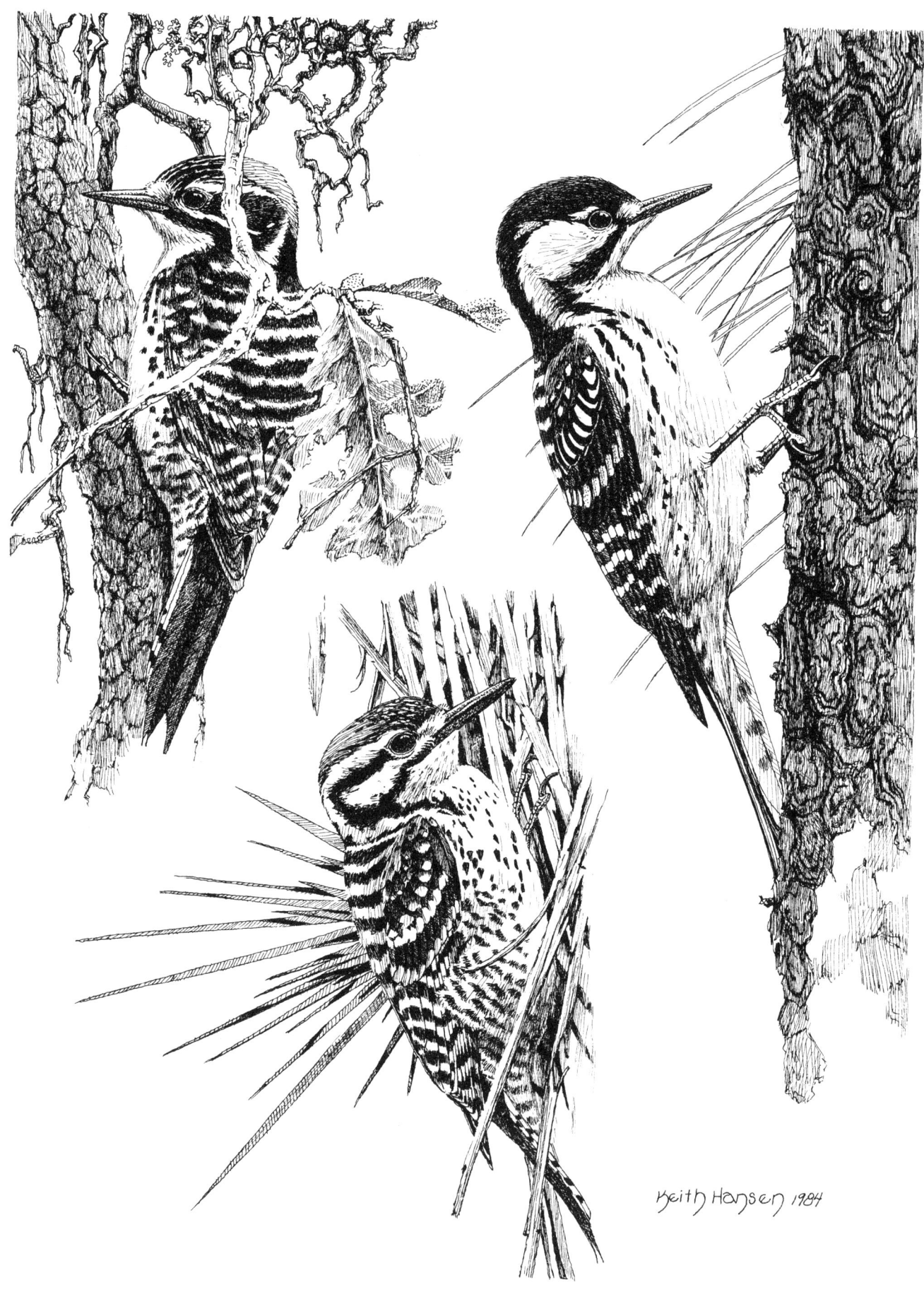

	Date	Location	Cont. North America	Canada	Lower 48
Yellow-bellied Sapsucker *Sphyrapicus varius*			fP	fS,lrW	fP
Red-naped Sapsucker *Sphyrapicus nuchalis*			fS,lcP	lfS,xS*,xW	fP
Red-breasted Sapsucker *Sphyrapicus ruber*			lfP,xS*,xV	lfP,xV	lfP,xS*,xV
Williamson's Sapsucker *Sphyrapicus thyroideus*			uS,luW	luS,xV	uS,rW
Ladder-backed Woodpecker *Picoides scalaris*			lcP		fP
Nuttall's Woodpecker *Picoides nuttallii*			lcP		lcP
Downy Woodpecker *Picoides pubescens*			cP	fP	cP
Hairy Woodpecker *Picoides villosus*			fP	fP	fP
Strickland's Woodpecker *Picoides stricklandi*			lfP		lfP
Red-cockaded Woodpecker *Picoides borealis*			luP,xV		uP
White-headed Woodpecker *Picoides albolarvatus*			lfP,xV	lrP	lfP,xV
Three-toed Woodpecker *Picoides tridactylus*			fP	fP	uP
Black-backed Woodpecker *Picoides arcticus*			uP	uP	uP
Northern Flicker *Colaptes auratus*			cP	cS,uW	cP
Pileated Woodpecker *Dryocopus pileatus*			fP	uP	fP
Ivory-billed Woodpecker *Campephilus principalis*			eP,lrP*		eP,lrP*

Order Passeriformes: Passerine Birds
Family Tyrannidae: Tyrant Flycatchers
Subfamily Elaeniinae: Tyrannulets, Elaenias and Allies

Northern Beardless-Tyrannulet *Camptostoma imberbe*			lfS,lrW		lfS,lrW
Greenish Elaenia *Myiopagis viridicata*			xV		xV
Caribbean Elaenia *Elaenia martinica*			xV		xV

Subfamily Fluvicolinae: Fluvicoline Flycatchers

Olive-sided Flycatcher *Contopus borealis*			fS,xW	fS	fS,xW
Greater Pewee *Contopus pertinax*			lfS,xV,lrW		lfS,xV,lrW

Distributional Checklist of North American Birds

	Hawaii	Alaska	Yukon Terr.	Northwest Terr.	British Columbia	Alberta	Saskatchewan	Manitoba	Ontario
Yellow-bellied Sapsucker		lrS.xV	lfS	fS	fS.xW	fS	cS.xW	cS	fS.rW
Red-naped Sapsucker					fS.xW	luS	xS*		
Red-breasted Sapsucker		lfS.xV			fS.lfW			xV-q	
Williamson's Sapsucker					luS	xV	xV		
Ladder-backed Woodpecker									
Nuttall's Woodpecker									
Downy Woodpecker		fP	luP	lfS.luW	fP	fP	fP	fP	cP
Hairy Woodpecker		fP	uP	fS.lfW	cP	fP	fP	fP	fP
Strickland's Woodpecker									
Red-cockaded Woodpecker									
White-headed Woodpecker									
Three-toed Woodpecker		fP	fP	fP	uP	uP	uP	uP	uP
Black-backed Woodpecker		rP	luP	uP	uP	uP	uP	uP	uP
Northern Flicker		cS.rW	cS.xW	cS	cS.fW	cS.rW	cS.rW	cS.rW	cS.uW
Pileated Woodpecker			lrP*	luS.xW	uP	uP	uP	uP	uP
Ivory-billed Woodpecker		xV-q							

Order Passeriformes: Passerine Birds
Family Tyrannidae: Tyrant Flycatchers
Subfamily Elaeniinae: Tyrannulets, Elaenias and Allies

Northern Beard.-Tyran.									
Greenish Elaenia									
Caribbean Elaenia									

Subfamily Fluvicolinae: Fluvicoline Flycatchers

Olive-sided Flycatcher		fS	fS	uS	fS	fS	fS	fS	fS
Greater Pewee									

Picidae • 223

	Québec	Newfoundland	New Brunswick	Prince Edward I.	Nova Scotia	Washington	Oregon	California	Nevada	Idaho
Yellow-bellied Sapsucker	fS,xW	rS,xW	cS	uS	fS					
Red-naped Sapsucker						fS,xW	fS,rW	luS,fW	uS,fT,rW	fS
Red-breasted Sapsucker						fP	fP	fP	lrP	
Williamson's Sapsucker						uS,xW	uS,rW	uS,rW	uS,rW	uS
Ladder-backed Woodpecker								fP	lfP	
Nuttall's Woodpecker							exV	cP		
Downy Woodpecker	fP	fP	cP	fP	fP	fP	fP	fP	fP	fP
Hairy Woodpecker	fP	fP	cP	fP	fP	cP	cP	cP	fP	fP
Strickland's Woodpecker										
Red-cockaded Woodpecker										
White-headed Woodpecker						uP	fP	fP	luP	uP
Three-toed Woodpecker	uP	uP	rP	rT	xW	uP	rP		luP	uP
Black-backed Woodpecker	uP	uP	uP	rP	uP	uP	uP	uP	exV,exW	rP
Northern Flicker	cS,lrW	fS,lrW	cS,rW	cS,xW	cS,rW	cP	cP	cP	cP	cP
Pileated Woodpecker	uP	xV	uP	eP	uP	uP	uP	uP		uP
Ivory-billed Woodpecker										

Order Passeriformes: Passerine Birds
Family Tyrannidae: Tyrant Flycatchers
Subfamily Elaeniinae: Tyrannulets, Elaenias and Allies

	Québec	Newfoundland	New Brunswick	Prince Edward I.	Nova Scotia	Washington	Oregon	California	Nevada	Idaho
Northern Beard.-Tyran.										
Greenish Elaenia										
Caribbean Elaenia										

Subfamily Fluvicolinae: Fluvicoline Flycatchers

	Québec	Newfoundland	New Brunswick	Prince Edward I.	Nova Scotia	Washington	Oregon	California	Nevada	Idaho
Olive-sided Flycatcher	fS	fS	fS	uS	fS	fS	fS	fS,xW	uS,fT	fS
Greater Pewee								xV,rW		

224 • Distributional Checklist of North American Birds

	Montana	Wyoming	Utah	Colorado	Arizona	New Mexico	North Dakota	South Dakota	Nebraska	Kansas	Oklahoma
Yellow-bellied Sapsucker	xV	xV		rV,rW	rV,rW	rV,rW	lfS,uT	luS,uT,xW	uT,xW	uT,rW	uW
Red-naped Sapsucker	fS,xW	fS	fS,rW	fS,rW	uS,cW	fP			xV	xV	lrT
Red-breasted Sapsucker			xV-q		xS*,rW						
Williamson's Sapsucker	uS	uS	uS,xW	uS	uP	uP			xV	xV	xV	xV
Ladder-backed Woodpecker			lfP	uP	cP	fP				lrP	luP
Nuttall's Woodpecker											
Downy Woodpecker	fP	fP	fP	fP	uP	fP	fP	cP	cP	cP	cP
Hairy Woodpecker	fP	fP	fP	fP	fP	fP	fP	fP	fP	fP	fP
Strickland's Woodpecker					fP	lrP					
Red-cockaded Woodpecker											lrP
White-headed Woodpecker	xV	exV									
Three-toed Woodpecker	uP	uP	uP	uP	uP	uP	xV,xW	lrP	xW		
Black-backed Woodpecker	uP	rP					xV,xW	luP	xW		
Northern Flicker	cS,uW	cP	cP	cP	cP	cP	cS,rW	cS,uW	cS,fW	cP	fS,cW
Pileated Woodpecker	uP	xV					lrP	xV	eP,xP*	luP	fP
Ivory-billed Woodpecker											eP

Order Passeriformes: Passerine Birds
Family Tyrannidae: Tyrant Flycatchers
Subfamily Elaeniinae: Tyrannulets, Elaenias and Allies

	Montana	Wyoming	Utah	Colorado	Arizona	New Mexico	North Dakota	South Dakota	Nebraska	Kansas	Oklahoma
Northern Beard.-Tyran.					lfS,xV,lrW	luS					
Greenish Elaenia											
Caribbean Elaenia											

Subfamily Fluvicolinae: Fluvicoline Flycatchers

	Montana	Wyoming	Utah	Colorado	Arizona	New Mexico	North Dakota	South Dakota	Nebraska	Kansas	Oklahoma
Olive-sided Flycatcher	fS	fS	fS	fS	fS	uS,fT	xS*,uT	xS*,uT	uT	uT	uT
Greater Pewee					fS,rW	luS					

Picidae • 225

	Texas	Minnesota	Iowa	Missouri	Arkansas	Louisiana	Wisconsin	Michigan	Illinois	Indiana	Ohio
Yellow-bellied Sapsucker	fW	fS,rW	lrS,fT,rW	exS,fT,uW	cW	cW	fS,rW	uS,fT,rW	lrS,fT,uW	lrS,fT,rW	lrS,fT,rW
Red-naped Sapsucker	lrS,uW								xV		
Red-breasted Sapsucker											
Williamson's Sapsucker	rW	xV				xV					
Ladder-backed Woodpecker	fP										
Nuttall's Woodpecker											
Downy Woodpecker	cP	cP	cP	cP	cP	cP	cP	cP	cP	cP	cP
Hairy Woodpecker	fP	fP	fP	fP	fP	fP	fP	fP	fP	fP	fP
Strickland's Woodpecker											
Red-cockaded Woodpecker	lrP			eP	uP	uP					xV
White-headed Woodpecker											
Three-toed Woodpecker		lrS,rW	xV				rV,rW	xS,rW			
Black-backed Woodpecker		uP	xV,exW				rP	uP	irW	xV,xW	xV,xW
Northern Flicker	fS,cW	cS,uW	cS,fW	cP	cP	cP	cS,uW	cS,uW	cS,fW	cS,fW	cS,fW
Pileated Woodpecker	fP	uP	uP	uP	fP	fP	uP	uP	uP	uP	uP
Ivory-billed Woodpecker	eP,lrP*			eP	eP	eP,lrP*			eP†	eP	

Order Passeriformes: Passerine Birds
Family Tyrannidae: Tyrant Flycatchers
Subfamily Elaeniinae: Tyrannulets, Elaenias and Allies

	Texas	Minnesota	Iowa	Missouri	Arkansas	Louisiana	Wisconsin	Michigan	Illinois	Indiana	Ohio
Northern Beard.-Tyran.	luS,lrW										
Greenish Elaenia	xV										
Caribbean Elaenia											

Subfamily Fluvicolinae: Fluvicoline Flycatchers

	Texas	Minnesota	Iowa	Missouri	Arkansas	Louisiana	Wisconsin	Michigan	Illinois	Indiana	Ohio
Olive-sided Flycatcher	lrS,fT	uS	uT	uT	uT	uT	uS	uS	uT	uT	exS,uT
Greater Pewee	xV										

	West Virginia	Kentucky	Tennessee	Mississippi	Alabama	Maine	New Hampshire	Vermont	Massachusetts	Rhode Island	Connecticut
Yellow-bellied Sapsucker	rS,fT,rW	fT,uW	lrS,fW	cW	cW	cS,xW	cS	cS	fS,xW	fT,rW	luS,fT,rW
Red-naped Sapsucker											
Red-breasted Sapsucker											
Williamson's Sapsucker											
Ladder-backed Woodpecker											
Nuttall's Woodpecker											
Downy Woodpecker	cP	cP	cP	cP	cP	cP	cP	cP	cP	cP	cP
Hairy Woodpecker	fP	fP	fP	fP	fP	cP	cP	cP	fP	fP	fP
Strickland's Woodpecker											
Red-cockaded Woodpecker		luP	rP	uP	uP						
White-headed Woodpecker											
Three-toed Woodpecker						rP	rP	lrS,rW	xV,xW		
Black-backed Woodpecker	xV-q					uP	uP	uP	irW	xV,xW	irW
Northern Flicker	cS,fW	cP	cP	cP	cP	cS,rW	cS,rW	cS,rW	cS,uW	cS,fW	cS,fW
Pileated Woodpecker	fP	fP	fP	fP	fP	uP	uP	uP	uP	rP	uP
Ivory-billed Woodpecker		eP	eP	eP	eP						

Order Passeriformes: Passerine Birds
Family Tyrannidae: Tyrant Flycatchers
Subfamily Elaeniinae: Tyrannulets, Elaenias and Allies

Northern Beard.-Tyran.											
Greenish Elaenia											
Caribbean Elaenia											

Subfamily Fluvicolinae: Fluvicoline Flycatchers

Olive-sided Flycatcher	rS	uT	lrS,uT	uT	rT	uS	uS	uS	lrS,uT	uT	uT
Greater Pewee											

	New York	Pennsylvania	New Jersey	Delaware	Maryland	Dist. of Columbia	Virginia	North Carolina	South Carolina	Georgia	Florida
Yellow-bellied Sapsucker	fS,rW	uS,fT,rW	fT,uW	fT,rW	xS,fT,uW	fT,uW	lrS,fW	lrS,fW	fW	xS,fW	fW
Red-naped Sapsucker											
Red-breasted Sapsucker											
Williamson's Sapsucker											
Ladder-backed Woodpecker											
Nuttall's Woodpecker											
Downy Woodpecker	cP	cP	cP	cP	cP	cP	cP	cP	cP	cP	cP
Hairy Woodpecker	fP	fP	fP	fP	fP	fP	fP	fP	fP	fP	fP
Strickland's Woodpecker											
Red-cockaded Woodpecker		exV	xV		lrP,xV		lrP	uP	uP	uP	uP
White-headed Woodpecker											
Three-toed Woodpecker	lrP,xV,xW	xV,xW		xV							
Black-backed Woodpecker	luP,irW	irW	xW	xV							
Northern Flicker	cS,fW	cS,fW	cP	cP	cP	cP	cP	cP	cP	cP	cP
Pileated Woodpecker	uP	uP	uP	uP	fP	fP	fP	fP	fP	fP	fP
Ivory-billed Woodpecker								eP	eP	eP	eP

Order Passeriformes: Passerine Birds
Family Tyrannidae: Tyrant Flycatchers
Subfamily Elaeniinae: Tyrannulets, Elaenias and Allies

	New York	Pennsylvania	New Jersey	Delaware	Maryland	Dist. of Columbia	Virginia	North Carolina	South Carolina	Georgia	Florida
Northern Beard.-Tyran.											
Greenish Elaenia											
Caribbean Elaenia												xV

Subfamily Fluvicolinae: Fluvicoline Flycatchers

	New York	Pennsylvania	New Jersey	Delaware	Maryland	Dist. of Columbia	Virginia	North Carolina	South Carolina	Georgia	Florida
Olive-sided Flycatcher	uS	rS,uT	uT	rT	xS,uT	rT	lrS,rT	lrS,rT	xT	rT	rT
Greater Pewee											

Tyrannidae • **229**

	Date	Location	Cont. North America	Canada	Lower 48
Western Wood-Pewee _Contopus sordidulus_			cS	cS	cS
Eastern Wood-Pewee _Contopus virens_			cS	fS	cS
Yellow-bellied Flycatcher _Empidonax flaviventris_			fS	fS	lfS.uT
Acadian Flycatcher _Empidonax virescens_			cS	lrS.xS*.xV	cS
Alder Flycatcher _Empidonax alnorum_			fS	cS	fS
Willow Flycatcher _Empidonax traillii_			fS.xW	lfS.xS.xV	fS.xW
Least Flycatcher _Empidonax minimus_			cS.lrW	cS	fS.cT.lrW
Hammond's Flycatcher _Empidonax hammondii_			fS.lrW	fS	fS.lrW
Dusky Flycatcher _Empidonax oberholseri_			fS.lrW	lfS	fS.lrW
Gray Flycatcher _Empidonax wrightii_			lfS.xV.luW	xV	fS.luW
Western Flycatcher _Empidonax difficilis_			fS.lrW	lfS	cS.lrW
Buff-breasted Flycatcher _Empidonax fulvifrons_			lrS.xV		lrS.xV
Black Phoebe _Sayornis nigricans_			lcP.xS.xV	xV	fP
Eastern Phoebe _Sayornis phoebe_			fP	fS.lrW	fP
Say's Phoebe _Sayornis saya_			fS.uW	fS	fS.uW
Vermilion Flycatcher _Pyrocephalus rubinus_			lfS.xS.rV.luW	xV	lfS.xS.uW

Subfamily Tyranninae: Tyrannine Flycatchers

	Date	Location	Cont. North America	Canada	Lower 48
Dusky-capped Flycatcher _Myiarchus tuberculifer_			lcS.xS*.rV.xW		lcS.xS*.rV.xW
Ash-throated Flycatcher _Myiarchus cinerascens_			fS.lrW	rV	cS.lrW
Nutting's Flycatcher _Myiarchus nuttingi_			xW		xW
Great Crested Flycatcher _Myiarchus crinitus_			cS.luW	fS	cS.luW
Brown-crested Flycatcher _Myiarchus tyrannulus_			luS.rV.lrW	xV	luS.rV.lrW
La Sagra's Flycatcher _Myiarchus sagrae_			xV.xW		xV.xW
Great Kiskadee _Pitangus sulphuratus_			lfP.xS.xV.xW		lfP.xS.xV.xW

	Hawaii	Alaska	Yukon Terr.	Northwest Terr.	British Columbia	Alberta	Saskatchewan	Manitoba	Ontario
Western Wood-Pewee		fS	cS	lfS	cS	cS	fS	rS	xV
Eastern Wood-Pewee							rS*	fS	cS
Yellow-bellied Flycatcher		xV	xV	lfS	luS	uS	uS	uS	fS
Acadian Flycatcher						xV			lrS
Alder Flycatcher		cS	cS	cS	fS	fS	fS	fS	fS
Willow Flycatcher					fS	luS	luS	lrS*	fS
Least Flycatcher		xS*,xV	fS	fS	fS	cS	cS	cS	cS
Hammond's Flycatcher		fS	luS	luS†	fS	luS			
Dusky Flycatcher		xV	luS		fS	luS	lfS†		
Gray Flycatcher									xV
Western Flycatcher		lfS			fS	luS			
Buff-breasted Flycatcher									
Black Phoebe					xV				
Eastern Phoebe			xV	uS	uS	fS	fS	fS	fS,xW
Say's Phoebe		uS	fS	uS	fS	fS	fS	lrS	xV
Vermilion Flycatcher									xV

Subfamily Tyranninae: Tyrannine Flycatchers

	Hawaii	Alaska	Yukon Terr.	Northwest Terr.	British Columbia	Alberta	Saskatchewan	Manitoba	Ontario
Dusky-capped Flycatcher									
Ash-throated Flycatcher					rV				xV
Nutting's Flycatcher									
Great Crested Flycatcher					xV	lrS,xV	fS	fS	cS
Brown-crested Flycatcher					xV				
La Sagra's Flycatcher									
Great Kiskadee									

Tyrannidae • 231

	Québec	Newfoundland	New Brunswick	Prince Edward I.	Nova Scotia		Washington	Oregon	California	Nevada	Idaho
Western Wood-Pewee							cS	cS	cS	cS	cS
Eastern Wood-Pewee	fS	rS*,rV	fS	fS	fS				xS*,xV		
Yellow-bellied Flycatcher	fS	cS	fS	uS	fS				xV		
Acadian Flycatcher	xS*,exV										
Alder Flycatcher	fS	fS	cS	fS	cS						
Willow Flycatcher	luS*		xV		xS		fS	fS	uS,fT,xW	fS	fS
Least Flycatcher	cS	rS*,rV	cS	fS	cS		rS†	lrS,xV	xS,rV,xW	xV	xS*,rT
Hammond's Flycatcher							fS	fS	fS,cT,xW	fS,cT	fS
Dusky Flycatcher							cS	fS	cS,xW	fS	fS
Gray Flycatcher							rS	uS	luS,uT,rW	fS	luS
Western Flycatcher							cS	cS	cS,rW	fS,cT	uS
Buff-breasted Flycatcher											
Black Phoebe							xV-q	luP	cP	cS,lfW	
Eastern Phoebe	lfS,xW	xV	uS	xS*,xV	rS,uT				rV,rW	xV,xW	xV
Say's Phoebe	xV				xV		fS,xW	fS,rW	fP	fS,lfW	fS,xW
Vermilion Flycatcher									lrP,xV,xW	luS,lrW	

Subfamily Tyranninae: Tyrannine Flycatchers

	Québec	Newfoundland	New Brunswick	Prince Edward I.	Nova Scotia		Washington	Oregon	California	Nevada	Idaho
Dusky-capped Flycatcher									xV,xW	xV	
Ash-throated Flycatcher	xV						luS	uS	fS,rW	cS	luS
Nutting's Flycatcher											
Great Crested Flycatcher	lfS	xV	uS		lrS,uT				rV		
Brown-crested Flycatcher									luS,xV	luS	
La Sagra's Flycatcher											
Great Kiskadee											

	Montana	Wyoming	Utah	Colorado	Arizona	New Mexico	North Dakota	South Dakota	Nebraska	Kansas	Oklahoma
Western Wood-Pewee	cS	cS	cS	cS	cS	cS	luS†	lfS	lfS,uT	lrS,uT	fS
Eastern Wood-Pewee	xV	xV		rV	xV	xV	fS	fS	fS	fS	fS
Yellow-bellied Flycatcher					xV	xV	xS,uT	uT	uT	uT	uT
Acadian Flycatcher					exV		xV	exV	lrS,rT	luS,rT	uS
Alder Flycatcher	xV			xV			luS,uT	rT	rT	rT	rT
Willow Flycatcher	fS	fS	fS	fS	rS,fT	uS,fT	fS	fS	uS	lrS,uT	rS,uT
Least Flycatcher	fS	fS		uT	xV	luT	cS	fS	luS,fT	fT	fT
Hammond's Flycatcher	uS	uS	uS	fS	xS,cT,rW	luS,uT,xW			xV	xV	xV
Dusky Flycatcher	fS	fS	fS	fS	lfS,fT,rW	uS,fT,xW		luS		lrT	lrT
Gray Flycatcher		fS	fS	uS	fS,uW	uS				xV	
Western Flycatcher	uS	fS	fS	fS	cS,rW	cS		luS	lrS	xV	xV
Buff-breasted Flycatcher					lrS	eS					
Black Phoebe			fS,luW	xS,xV	cP	fP					
Eastern Phoebe	xT	xS*,rT	xV	lrS,rT	rV,rW	lrS,rW	fS	fS	fS	fS	fS,rW
Say's Phoebe	fS	fS	fS,luW	fS,xW	fP	fS,uW	uS	fS	fS	fS,xW	luS,rT,xW
Vermilion Flycatcher			lrS	xS,rV	cS,fW	fS,rW	xV-q	xV	xV	xV	rS

Subfamily Tyranninae: Tyrannine Flycatchers

	Montana	Wyoming	Utah	Colorado	Arizona	New Mexico	North Dakota	South Dakota	Nebraska	Kansas	Oklahoma
Dusky-capped Flycatcher				exV	lcS,xV	luS					xV-q
Ash-throated Flycatcher	xV	luS,rT	cS	fS	cS,rW	cS				rV	luS
Nutting's Flycatcher					xW						
Great Crested Flycatcher	xV	xV		xS*,rV	xV	rV	uS	fS	fS	cS	cS
Brown-crested Flycatcher			lrS		cS	luS					
La Sagra's Flycatcher											
Great Kiskadee					xV,xW	xV					

	Texas	Minnesota	Iowa	Missouri	Arkansas	Louisiana	Wisconsin	Michigan	Illinois	Indiana	Ohio
Western Wood-Pewee	lcS,uT	xS,xV	xV			xV	xV-q		xV		
Eastern Wood-Pewee	cS	cS	cS	cS	cS	cS	cS	cS	cS	cS	cS
Yellow-bellied Flycatcher	fT	fS	uT	uT	uT	fT	uS,fT	uS,fT	fT	fT	uT
Acadian Flycatcher	fS,cT	luS,rT	uS	fS	cS	cS	uS	uS	fS	fS	cS
Alder Flycatcher	fT	fS	xS*,uT	xS*,uT	uT	fT	fS	fS	fT	lrS*,fT	lrS,uT
Willow Flycatcher	rS,fT	fS	fS	uS	rS,uT	xS,fT	fS	fS	fS	fS	fS
Least Flycatcher	cT,xW	cS	rS,cT	exS,cT	cT	cT	cS	fS,cT	rS,cT	rS,cT	rS,cT
Hammond's Flycatcher	luT,xV					xV,xW					
Dusky Flycatcher	luT,xV,xW										
Gray Flycatcher	luT										
Western Flycatcher	lfS										
Buff-breasted Flycatcher	xV-q										
Black Phoebe	fP	xV									
Eastern Phoebe	fS,cW	fS	fS,xW	fS,rW	fS,uW	lrS,cW	fS,xW	fS	fS,rW	fS,rW	fS,rW
Say's Phoebe	fS,uW	xS*,xV	lrS,xV	xV,xW	xV	xV,xW	xV	xV	xV,xW	xV-q	
Vermilion Flycatcher	xS*,rV,xW	xV	xV	xV	rV,rW	rW	xV-q	xV-q	xV		xV

Subfamily Tyranninae: Tyrannine Flycatchers

	Texas	Minnesota	Iowa	Missouri	Arkansas	Louisiana	Wisconsin	Michigan	Illinois	Indiana	Ohio
Dusky-capped Flycatcher	xS*,rV,xW										
Ash-throated Flycatcher	cS,rW					rV,xW			xV		
Nutting's Flycatcher											
Great Crested Flycatcher	cS	cS	cS	cS	cS	cS	cS	cS	cS	cS	cS
Brown-crested Flycatcher	cS,xW					xV,xW					
La Sagra's Flycatcher											
Great Kiskadee	lfP,xV					xS,xV,xW					

	West Virginia	Kentucky	Tennessee	Mississippi	Alabama	Maine	New Hampshire	Vermont	Massachusetts	Rhode Island	Connecticut
Western Wood-Pewee				xV					xV		
Eastern Wood-Pewee	cS	cS	cS	cS	cS	cS	cS	cS	cS	fS.cT	cS
Yellow-bellied Flycatcher	uT	uT	uT	uT	rT	fS	fS	uS.fT	rS*.uT	uT	uT
Acadian Flycatcher	cS	cS	cS	cS	cS	xS*.rV	xS*	exS.xV	rS	lrS.rT	uS
Alder Flycatcher	uS	uT	lrS.uT	uT	rT	cS	fS	fS	uS	uT	rS.uT
Willow Flycatcher	uS	uS	uS	uT	uT	rS	uS	uS	fS	uS	fS
Least Flycatcher	fS	xS*.cT	lrS.cT	cT	uT	cS	cS	cS	fS	uS.fT	fS
Hammond's Flycatcher											
Dusky Flycatcher											
Gray Flycatcher									xV		
Western Flycatcher											
Buff-breasted Flycatcher											
Black Phoebe											
Eastern Phoebe	fS.xW	fS.rW	fS.uW	lfS.cW	fS.cW	fS	fS	fS	fS.rW	fS.rW	fS.xW
Say's Phoebe		xV		xV	xV	xV			rV.xW	xV.xW	xV-q
Vermilion Flycatcher	xV-q	xV	xV	rV.rW	rV.rW				xV		

Subfamily Tyranninae: Tyrannine Flycatchers

	West Virginia	Kentucky	Tennessee	Mississippi	Alabama	Maine	New Hampshire	Vermont	Massachusetts	Rhode Island	Connecticut
Dusky-capped Flycatcher											
Ash-throated Flycatcher					rV.xW	xV			xV	xV	xV-q
Nutting's Flycatcher											
Great Crested Flycatcher	cS	cS	cS	cS	cS	fS	fS	fS	fS	cS	cS
Brown-crested Flycatcher											
La Sagra's Flycatcher					xV						
Great Kiskadee											

Tyrannidae • 235

	New York	Pennsylvania	New Jersey	Delaware	Maryland	Dist. of Columbia	Virginia	North Carolina	South Carolina	Georgia	Florida
Western Wood-Pewee					xV						
Eastern Wood-Pewee	cS	cS	cS	cS	cS	uS,fT	cS	cS	cS	cS	fS
Yellow-bellied Flycatcher	uS,fT	lrS,fT	uT	rT	uT	uT	lrS,uT	rT	rT	rT	rT
Acadian Flycatcher	uS	cS	fS	cS	cS	fS	cS	cS	cS	cS	fS
Alder Flycatcher	fS	uS	lrS,uT	uT	luS,uT	rT	luS,uT	lrS,rT	rT	rT	rT
Willow Flycatcher	fS	fS	fS	uS	uS	xS*,uT	uS	luS,uT	uT	lrS,uT	uT
Least Flycatcher	cS	fS,cT	uS	xS*,uT	luS,fT	uT	luS,fT	lfS,uT	uT	lrS,uT	uT,rW
Hammond's Flycatcher		xV									
Dusky Flycatcher		xV									
Gray Flycatcher											
Western Flycatcher											
Buff-breasted Flycatcher											
Black Phoebe											xV
Eastern Phoebe	fS,rW	fS,rW	fS,xW	fS,xW	fS,rW	fS,xW	fS,uW	fP	uS,fW	uS,fW	cW
Say's Phoebe	rV	xV,xW	xV,xW				xW	xV-q	xV,xW	xV	xV,xW
Vermilion Flycatcher							xV-q	xV,xW	xV,xW		rV,rW

Subfamily Tyranninae: Tyrannine Flycatchers

	New York	Pennsylvania	New Jersey	Delaware	Maryland	Dist. of Columbia	Virginia	North Carolina	South Carolina	Georgia	Florida
Dusky-capped Flycatcher											
Ash-throated Flycatcher	xV		xW		xV		xV,xW	xV-q			xV,xW
Nutting's Flycatcher											
Great Crested Flycatcher	cS	cS	cS	cS	cS	fS	cS,xW	cS	cS	cS	cS,uW
Brown-crested Flycatcher											rV,rW
La Sagra's Flycatcher											xV,xW
Great Kiskadee											xV

Tyrannidae • 237

		Date	Location	Cont. North America	Canada	Lower 48
Sulphur-bellied Flycatcher *Myiodynastes luteiventris*				lfS.xS.rV		lfS.xS.rV
Variegated Flycatcher *Empidonomus varius*				xV		xV
Tropical Kingbird *Tyrannus melancholicus*				luS.rV.lrW	xV.exW	luS.rV.lrW
Couch's Kingbird *Tyrannus couchii*				lcS.rV.luW		lcS.rV.luW
Cassin's Kingbird *Tyrannus vociferans*				lcS.xS*.rV.luW	xV	fS.luW
Thick-billed Kingbird *Tyrannus crassirostris*				lfS.rV.xW	xV	lfS.rV.xW
Western Kingbird *Tyrannus verticalis*				cS.luW	cS	cS.rW
Eastern Kingbird *Tyrannus tyrannus*				cS.xW	cS	cS.xW
Gray Kingbird *Tyrannus dominicensis*				lcS.rV.lrW	xV	lcS.rV.lrW
Loggerhead Kingbird *Tyrannus caudifasciatus*				xV.xW		xV.xW
Scissor-tailed Flycatcher *Tyrannus forficatus*				lcS.xS.rV.luW	rV	fS.luW
Fork-tailed Flycatcher *Tyrannus savana*				rV.xW	xV	rV.xW

Subfamily Tityrinae: Tityras and Becards

Rose-throated Becard *Pachyramphus aglaiae*				luS.xV.lrW		luS.xV.lrW

Family Alaudidae: Larks

Eurasian Skylark *Alauda arvensis*				xS*.lrT.xW		xW
Horned Lark *Eremophila alpestris*				cP	cS.uW	cP

Family Hirundinidae: Swallows
Subfamily Hirundininae: Typical Swallows

Purple Martin *Progne subis*				cS.xW	fS	cS.xW
Cuban Martin *Progne cryptoleuca*				xV		xV
Gray-breasted Martin *Progne chalybea*				exV		exV
Southern Martin *Progne elegans*				exV		exV
Brown-chested Martin *Phaeoprogne tapera*				xV		xV
Tree Swallow *Tachycineta bicolor*				cS.uW	cS	cS.fW

	Hawaii	Alaska	Yukon Terr.	Northwest Terr.	British Columbia	Alberta	Saskatchewan	Manitoba	Ontario
Sulphur-bellied Flycatcher									
Variegated Flycatcher									
Tropical Kingbird		xV-q			xV,exW				
Couch's Kingbird									
Cassin's Kingbird									xV
Thick-billed Kingbird					xV				
Western Kingbird		xV		xV	cS	fS	cS	cS	lrS†,rT
Eastern Kingbird		rS*,rV	xS	luS	cS	cS	cS	cS	cS
Gray Kingbird					exV				xV
Loggerhead Kingbird									
Scissor-tailed Flycatcher		xV-q			xV	xV	xV	rV	rV
Fork-tailed Flycatcher									xV

Subfamily Tityrinae: Tityras and Becards

	Hawaii	Alaska	Yukon Terr.	Northwest Terr.	British Columbia	Alberta	Saskatchewan	Manitoba	Ontario
Rose-throated Becard									

Family Alaudidae: Larks

	Hawaii	Alaska	Yukon Terr.	Northwest Terr.	British Columbia	Alberta	Saskatchewan	Manitoba	Ontario
Eurasian Skylark	xV	xS*,lrT							
Horned Lark		cS	cS,xW	cS	fS,cT,uW	cS,uW	cS,fW	cS,luW	cS,fW

Family Hirundinidae: Swallows
Subfamily Hirundininae: Typical Swallows

	Hawaii	Alaska	Yukon Terr.	Northwest Terr.	British Columbia	Alberta	Saskatchewan	Manitoba	Ontario
Purple Martin		xV	xV	xV	luS	fS	fS	fS	fS
Cuban Martin									
Gray-breasted Martin									
Southern Martin									
Brown-chested Martin									
Tree Swallow		fS	fS	fS	cS	cS	cS	cS	cS

	Québec	Newfound-land	New Brunswick	Prince Edward I.	Nova Scotia	Washington	Oregon	California	Nevada	Idaho
Sulphur-bellied Flycatcher								xV		
Variegated Flycatcher										
Tropical Kingbird						xV	rV	rV,rW	xV	
Couch's Kingbird										
Cassin's Kingbird							xV	fS,luW	lfS	xS*
Thick-billed Kingbird								xV,xW		
Western Kingbird	rV	rV	rV		rV	cS	cS	cS,xW	cS	cS
Eastern Kingbird	cS	rS*,uV	cS	fS	fS,cT	cS	fS	xS,rV	uS	fS
Gray Kingbird			xV-q		xV-q					
Loggerhead Kingbird										
Scissor-tailed Flycatcher	xV		xV		xV	xV	xV	xS,rV,xW	rV	xV
Fork-tailed Flycatcher	xV		xV		xV					

Subfamily Tityrinae: Tityras and Becards

	Québec	Newfound-land	New Brunswick	Prince Edward I.	Nova Scotia	Washington	Oregon	California	Nevada	Idaho
Rose-throated Becard										

Family Alaudidae: Larks

	Québec	Newfound-land	New Brunswick	Prince Edward I.	Nova Scotia	Washington	Oregon	California	Nevada	Idaho
Eurasian Skylark								xW		
Horned Lark	cS,rW	fS,rW	fS,uW	fS,rW	uS,fT,uW	cP	cP	cP	cP	cP

Family Hirundinidae: Swallows
Subfamily Hirundininae: Typical Swallows

	Québec	Newfound-land	New Brunswick	Prince Edward I.	Nova Scotia	Washington	Oregon	California	Nevada	Idaho
Purple Martin	lfS	rV	fS	xS*,xV	luS	luS	uS	uS	rT	xV
Cuban Martin										
Gray-breasted Martin										
Southern Martin										
Brown-chested Martin										
Tree Swallow	cS	cS	cS	cS	cS	cS	cS,rW	cS,fW	fS,cT,lfW	cS

240 • *Distributional Checklist of North American Birds*

	Montana	Wyoming	Utah	Colorado	Arizona	New Mexico	North Dakota	South Dakota	Nebraska	Kansas	Oklahoma
Sulphur-bellied Flycatcher					lfS	xV					
Variegated Flycatcher											
Tropical Kingbird					luS.xV	xV					
Couch's Kingbird											
Cassin's Kingbird	lrS	uS	fS	fS	cS	cS		xV	xS*.xV	lrS*.xV	luS.xV
Thick-billed Kingbird					lfS.xV.xW	luS					
Western Kingbird	cS	cS	cS	cS	cS	cS.xW	cS	cS	cS	cS	cS
Eastern Kingbird	cS	cS	fS	fS	lrS*.rT	fS	cS	cS	cS	cS	cS
Gray Kingbird											
Loggerhead Kingbird											
Scissor-tailed Flycatcher	xV	xV	xV	luS.rV	xS*.rV	luS.rV	cS.fW	xV	luS.rV	cS	cS
Fork-tailed Flycatcher											

Subfamily Tityrinae: Tityras and Becards

	Montana	Wyoming	Utah	Colorado	Arizona	New Mexico	North Dakota	South Dakota	Nebraska	Kansas	Oklahoma
Rose-throated Becard					luS						

Family Alaudidae: Larks

	Montana	Wyoming	Utah	Colorado	Arizona	New Mexico	North Dakota	South Dakota	Nebraska	Kansas	Oklahoma
Eurasian Skylark											
Horned Lark	cP	cP	cP	cP	cP	cP	cS.fW	cP	cP	cP	cP

Family Hirundinidae: Swallows
Subfamily Hirundininae: Typical Swallows

	Montana	Wyoming	Utah	Colorado	Arizona	New Mexico	North Dakota	South Dakota	Nebraska	Kansas	Oklahoma
Purple Martin	exS*.rT	exS.rT	uS	lrS.rT	uS	uS	fS	fS	fS	fS	fS
Cuban Martin											
Gray-breasted Martin											
Southern Martin											
Brown-chested Martin											
Tree Swallow	cS	cS	fS.cT	cS	lrS.cT.fW	rS.cT.rW	fS.cT	fS.cT	luS.cT	lrS.cT	lrS.fT.xW

Species	Texas	Minnesota	Iowa	Missouri	Arkansas	Louisiana	Wisconsin	Michigan	Illinois	Indiana	Ohio
Sulphur-bellied Flycatcher	xS.xV-q					xV					
Variegated Flycatcher											
Tropical Kingbird	xV					xV					
Couch's Kingbird	lcS.xV.luW					xV					
Cassin's Kingbird	lcS.rV.xW				xV	xV	xV-q				
Thick-billed Kingbird	xV										
Western Kingbird	cS.xW	cS	lfS.uT	luS.uT	xS.rT	uT.xW	rS	lrS.rT	xS.rT.xW	rT	exS.rT
Eastern Kingbird	cS	cS	cS	cS	cS	cS	cS	cS	cS	cS	cS
Gray Kingbird	xV					xV		xV			
Loggerhead Kingbird											
Scissor-tailed Flycatcher	cS.rW	rV	xS.rV	luS.rT	fS	lfS.uT.rW	xS*.xV	rV	rV	xS.rV	xV
Fork-tailed Flycatcher	xV.xW						xV	xV			

Subfamily Tityrinae: Tityras and Becards

Species	Texas	Minnesota	Iowa	Missouri	Arkansas	Louisiana	Wisconsin	Michigan	Illinois	Indiana	Ohio
Rose-throated Becard	lrP.xV										

Family Alaudidae: Larks

Species	Texas	Minnesota	Iowa	Missouri	Arkansas	Louisiana	Wisconsin	Michigan	Illinois	Indiana	Ohio
Eurasian Skylark											
Horned Lark	cP	cS.uW	cS.fW	cP	fP	lrS.uW	cS.fW	cS.fW	cP	cP	cP

Family Hirundinidae: Swallows
Subfamily Hirundininae: Typical Swallows

Species	Texas	Minnesota	Iowa	Missouri	Arkansas	Louisiana	Wisconsin	Michigan	Illinois	Indiana	Ohio
Purple Martin	cS	cS	fS	cS	fS.cT	cS.xW	cS	fS	cS	fS	fS
Cuban Martin											
Gray-breasted Martin	exV										
Southern Martin											
Brown-chested Martin											
Tree Swallow	exS.cT.fW	cS	fS.cT	uS.cT	rS.cT	lrS.cT.fW	cS	cS	fS.cT	fS.cT	fS.cT

	West Virginia	Kentucky	Tennessee	Mississippi	Alabama	Maine	New Hampshire	Vermont	Massachusetts	Rhode Island	Connecticut
Sulphur-bellied Flycatcher				xV	xV				xV		
Variegated Flycatcher			xV			xV					
Tropical Kingbird						exV					
Couch's Kingbird					xV-sp-q						
Cassin's Kingbird									xV		
Thick-billed Kingbird											
Western Kingbird		xT	rT	rT.xW	rT.xW	rV	rV	xV-q	rV.xW	rV	rV
Eastern Kingbird	cS	cS	cS	cS	cS	cS	cS	cS	cS	cS	cS
Gray Kingbird				lrS	lrS.xV				exV		xV
Loggerhead Kingbird											
Scissor-tailed Flycatcher		xV	xS.rV	xS.rT	xS*.rT.xW	rV	xV		rV	xV	xV
Fork-tailed Flycatcher		exV				xV		xV	xV		

Subfamily Tityrinae: Tityras and Becards

	West Virginia	Kentucky	Tennessee	Mississippi	Alabama	Maine	New Hampshire	Vermont	Massachusetts	Rhode Island	Connecticut
Rose-throated Becard											

Family Alaudidae: Larks

	West Virginia	Kentucky	Tennessee	Mississippi	Alabama	Maine	New Hampshire	Vermont	Massachusetts	Rhode Island	Connecticut
Eurasian Skylark											
Horned Lark	uS.fW	uS.fW	uS.fW	luS.uW	luS.uW	uS.fT.uW	uS.cT.fW	uS.cT.uW	uS.cW	uS.cW	uS.cW

Family Hirundinidae: Swallows
Subfamily Hirundininae: Typical Swallows

	West Virginia	Kentucky	Tennessee	Mississippi	Alabama	Maine	New Hampshire	Vermont	Massachusetts	Rhode Island	Connecticut
Purple Martin	fS	cS	cS	cS	cS	uS	uS	uS	uS	uS	uS
Cuban Martin											
Gray-breasted Martin											
Southern Martin											
Brown-chested Martin									xV		
Tree Swallow	fS.cT	uS.cT.xW	rS.cT	xS*.cT.fW	cT.fW	cS	cS	cS	cS.rW	fS.cT.rW	cS

	New York	Pennsylvania	New Jersey	Delaware	Maryland	Dist. of Columbia	Virginia	North Carolina	South Carolina	Georgia	Florida
Sulphur-bellied Flycatcher											
Variegated Flycatcher											
Tropical Kingbird											
Couch's Kingbird												rV-sp
Cassin's Kingbird							xV-q				
Thick-billed Kingbird											
Western Kingbird	rV,xW	rV	rV,xW	xV	rV	xV	rV,xW	uT,xW	uT,xW	uT,rW	fT,uW
Eastern Kingbird	cS	cS	cS	cS	cS	fS,cT	cS	cS	cS	cS	cS,xW
Gray Kingbird	xV		xV		xV		xV	rV	lrS	lrS	cS,rW
Loggerhead Kingbird											xV,xW
Scissor-tailed Flycatcher	rV	rV	rV	xV	xV-q		xV,xW	rV	xS,rV,xW	rV,xW	uW
Fork-tailed Flycatcher	xV	xV	fS,xW		xV-q				xV		xV

Subfamily Tityrinae: Tityras and Becards

Rose-throated Becard											

Family Alaudidae: Larks

Eurasian Skylark											
Horned Lark	fS,cW	uS,cT,fW	uS,fW	uS,fW	uS,fW	uT,rW	uS,fW	uS,fW	luS,uW	lrS,uW	rW

Family Hirundinidae: Swallows
Subfamily Hirundininae: Typical Swallows

Purple Martin	fS	fS	fS,xW	fS	fS	rS,fT	cS	cS	cS	cS	cS,xW
Cuban Martin											xV
Gray-breasted Martin											
Southern Martin											exV
Brown-chested Martin											
Tree Swallow	cS,rW	cS	fS,cT,rW	fS,cT,xW	fS,cT,rW	fT	luS,cT,iuW	lrS,cT,ifW	cT,fW	cT,fW	cW

Hirundinidae • 245

		Date	Location	Cont. North America	Canada	Lower 48
Violet-green Swallow *Tachycineta thalassina*				cS.luW	cS	cS.luW
Bahama Swallow *Tachycineta cyaneoviridis*				xS*.rV.xW		xS*.rV.xW
Northern Rough-winged Swallow *Stelgidopteryx serripennis*				fS.cT.luW	fS.xW	fS.cT.luW
Bank Swallow *Riparia riparia*				cS.lrW	cS	fS.cT.lrW
Cliff Swallow *Hirundo pyrrhonota*				cS.xW	cS	cS.xW
Cave Swallow *Hirundo fulva*				lfS.xS.rV	xV	lfS.xS.rV
Barn Swallow *Hirundo rustica*				cS.lrW	cS.xW	cS.lrW
Common House-Martin *Delichon urbica*				xV		

Family Corvidae: Jays, Magpies and Crows

Gray Jay *Perisoreus canadensis*				cP	cP	fP
Steller's Jay *Cyanocitta stelleri*				cP	lcP.xV.xW	cP
Blue Jay *Cyanocitta cristata*				cP	cP	cP
Green Jay *Cyanocorax yncas*				lcP		lcP
Brown Jay *Cyanocorax morio*				lrP		lrP
Scrub Jay *Aphelocoma coerulescens*				fP	xV	cP
Gray-breasted Jay *Aphelocoma ultramarina*				lcP.exV.xW		lcP.exV.xW
Pinyon Jay *Gymnorhinus cyanocephalus*				lfP.xV.iuW	exV	fP
Clark's Nutcracker *Nucifraga columbiana*				fP	lfP.xV	fP
Black-billed Magpie *Pica pica*				cP	cP	cP
Yellow-billed Magpie *Pica nuttalli*				lcP		lcP
Jackdaw *Corvus monedula*				xP*.xV.xW	xP*.xV.xW	xP*.xV
American Crow *Corvus brachyrhynchos*				cP	cS.fW	cP
Northwestern Crow *Corvus caurinus*				lcP.exV.exW	lcP	lcP.exV.exW
Mexican Crow *Corvus imparatus*				lfW		lfW

246 • Distributional Checklist of North American Birds

	Hawaii	Alaska	Yukon Terr.	Northwest Terr.	British Columbia	Alberta	Saskatch-ewan	Manitoba	Ontario
Violet-green Swallow		cS	cS	luS	cS	fS	lrS	xV	
Bahama Swallow									
N. Rough-winged Swallow		lrS,rV	xS		fS	fS	uS	luS	fS,xW
Bank Swallow		cS	cS	fS	cS	cS	cS	cS	cS
Cliff Swallow		cS	cS	cS	cS	cS	cS	cS	fS
Cave Swallow									
Barn Swallow	xV,xW	fS	fS	uS	cS	cS	cS	cS	cS,xW
Common House-Martin		xV							

Family Corvidae: Jays, Magpies and Crows

	Hawaii	Alaska	Yukon Terr.	Northwest Terr.	British Columbia	Alberta	Saskatch-ewan	Manitoba	Ontario
Gray Jay		cP	cP	cP	cP	cP	cP	cP	cP
Steller's Jay		cP	xV		cP	luP,xV,xW	xV		
Blue Jay					lrS,rW	fP	cP	cP	cP
Green Jay									
Brown Jay									
Scrub Jay					xV				
Gray-breasted Jay									
Pinyon Jay							exV-q		
Clark's Nutcracker		xV	xV	xV	fP	lfP,rW	xV	xV	xV
Black-billed Magpie		cP	cP	rV,xW	cP	cP	cP	fP	lrP,rV,xW
Yellow-billed Magpie									
Jackdaw									
American Crow			xV	luS	cP	cS,rW	cS,rW	cS,rW	cS,fW
Northwestern Crow		fP			cP				
Mexican Crow									

	Québec	Newfoundland	New Brunswick	Prince Edward I.	Nova Scotia		Washington	Oregon	California	Nevada	Idaho
Violet-green Swallow					xV-q		cS	cS	cS,uW	cS	cS
Bahama Swallow											
N. Rough-winged Swallow	luS	xV	rS		rV		fS	fS	cS,rW	cS,xW	fS
Bank Swallow	cS	uS	cS	cS	cS		fS	fS	uS,rW	uS,fT	fS
Cliff Swallow	fS	xS*,rV	fS	rS	uS		cS	cS	cS,xW	cS	cS
Cave Swallow					xV						
Barn Swallow	cS	luS	cS	cS	cS		cS	cS,xW	cS,rW	cS	cS
Common House-Martin											

Family Corvidae: Jays, Magpies and Crows

	Québec	Newfoundland	New Brunswick	Prince Edward I.	Nova Scotia		Washington	Oregon	California	Nevada	Idaho
Gray Jay	cP	cP	fP	uP	uP		fP	fP	luP	xV	fP
Steller's Jay	exV						cP	cP	cP	cP	cP
Blue Jay	cP	fS,uW	cP	cP	cP		irW	xS,irW	xV,xW	xV	xS*,irW
Green Jay											
Brown Jay											
Scrub Jay							luP	cP	cP	cP	luP
Gray-breasted Jay											
Pinyon Jay							xV	uP	uP	cP	luP
Clark's Nutcracker							fP	fP	fP	fP	fP
Black-billed Magpie	xV	xV	xV		xV		cP	cP	lcP	cP	cP
Yellow-billed Magpie									cP		
Jackdaw	xV	xP*			xV,xW						
American Crow	cS,uW	cS,fW	cS,fW	cP	cP		cP	cP	cP	fP	cP
Northwestern Crow							cP	exV,exW			
Mexican Crow											

248 • *Distributional Checklist of North American Birds*

	Montana	Wyoming	Utah	Colorado	Arizona	New Mexico	North Dakota	South Dakota	Nebraska	Kansas	Oklahoma
Violet-green Swallow	cS	cS	cS	cS	cS,xW	cS	lrS†,rV	lcS	lfS,lcT	rV	xV-q
Bahama Swallow											
N. Rough-winged Swallow	fS	fS	cS	fS	cS,rW	cS	fS	fS,cT	fS,cT	fS,cT	cS
Bank Swallow	cS	fS	uS,fT	uS,fT	fT	uS,fT	fS	fS	fS	fS	uS,fT
Cliff Swallow	cS	cS	cS	cS	cS,xW	cS	cS	cS	cS	cS	cS
Cave Swallow					xS	lfS					
Barn Swallow	cS	cS	cS	cS	fS,cT	fS,cT	cS	cS	cS	cS	cS
Common House-Martin											

Family Corvidae: Jays, Magpies and Crows

	Montana	Wyoming	Utah	Colorado	Arizona	New Mexico	North Dakota	South Dakota	Nebraska	Kansas	Oklahoma
Gray Jay	cP	fP	fP	fP	lfP	lfP	eP,irW	lfP,irW	irW		xV-q
Steller's Jay	cP	cP	cP	cP	cP	cP		xV	xV,xW	xV,xW	xV,lirW
Blue Jay	uP	fP	rV,rW	fP	xV	luP	cP	cP	cP	cP	cP
Green Jay											
Brown Jay											
Scrub Jay		luP,rP*	cP	fP	cP	cP			xV	xV,xW	luP
Gray-breasted Jay					cP	lcP				exV,xW	
Pinyon Jay	fP	fP	fP	fP	cP	fP		lfP,iuW	lfP,iuW	irW	luP,irW
Clark's Nutcracker	fP	fP	fP	fP	fP	fP	irW	irW	irW	irW	xV,xW
Black-billed Magpie	cP	cP	cP	cP	lfP,xV	fP	cP	fP	fP	fP	luP
Yellow-billed Magpie											
Jackdaw											
American Crow	cS,uW	fP	uS,fW	fS,cW	fP	fP	cS,uW	cS,uW	cS,fW	cP	cP
Northwestern Crow											
Mexican Crow											

Hirundinidae • 249

	Texas	Minnesota	Iowa	Missouri	Arkansas	Louisiana	Wisconsin	Michigan	Illinois	Indiana	Ohio
Violet-green Swallow	lcS,rV	xV							exV		
Bahama Swallow											
N. Rough-winged Swallow	fS,cT,uW	fS,cT	fS,cT	cS	cS	cS,rW	fS,cT	fS,cT	fS,cT	fS,cT	fS,cT
Bank Swallow	uS,cT,xW	cS	fS	fS	uS,fT	fT,xW	cS	cS	fS,cT	fS,cT	fS,cT
Cliff Swallow	cS	cS	fS	fS	fS	lrS,uT	fS	uS,fT	uS,fT	uS,fT	uS
Cave Swallow	fS										
Barn Swallow	cS,xW	cS	cS	cS	cS	uS,cT	cS	cS	cS	cS	cS
Common House-Martin											

Family Corvidae: Jays, Magpies and Crows

	Texas	Minnesota	Iowa	Missouri	Arkansas	Louisiana	Wisconsin	Michigan	Illinois	Indiana	Ohio
Gray Jay		lcP,iuW	xV,xW				luS,iuW	uS,iuW			
Steller's Jay	lcP,rV,xW										
Blue Jay	cP	cP	cP	cP	cP	cP	cP	cP	cP	cP	cP
Green Jay	lcP										
Brown Jay	lrP										
Scrub Jay	cP										
Gray-breasted Jay	lcP										
Pinyon Jay	xS*,iuW		xW								
Clark's Nutcracker	xS*,iuW	rV,xW	xV	xV,xW	xV		xV,xW	xV-q			
Black-billed Magpie	lrW	luS,uW	xP,xV,xW	xV,xW			rV,xW	rV,xW	xV,xW	xV,xW	xV,xW
Yellow-billed Magpie											
Jackdaw											
American Crow	cP	cS,fW	cP	cP	cP	cP	cP	cS,fW	cP	cP	cP
Northwestern Crow											
Mexican Crow	lfW										

	West Virginia	Kentucky	Tennessee	Mississippi	Alabama	Maine	New Hampshire	Vermont	Massachusetts	Rhode Island	Connecticut
Violet-green Swallow							xV-q				
Bahama Swallow											
N. Rough-winged Swallow	fS.cT	fS.cT	fS.cT	fS.cT.xW	fS.cT.xW	uS	uS	uS	uS	uS	fS
Bank Swallow	uS.fT	rS.fT	rS.fT	fT	lrS.fT	fS	fS	fS	fS	uS.fT	uS.fT
Cliff Swallow	uS	uS	uS	lrS.fT	uS.fT	fS	fS	fS	uS	rS.uT	rS.uT
Cave Swallow						xV-q					
Barn Swallow	cS	cS.xW	cS	fS.cT	cS.xW	cS	cS	cS	cS	cS	cS
Common House-Martin											

Family Corvidae: Jays, Magpies and Crows

	West Virginia	Kentucky	Tennessee	Mississippi	Alabama	Maine	New Hampshire	Vermont	Massachusetts	Rhode Island	Connecticut
Gray Jay						fP	uP	luP	irW		xV.xW-q
Steller's Jay											
Blue Jay	cP	cP	cP	cP	cP	cP	cP	cP	cP	cP	cP
Green Jay											
Brown Jay											
Scrub Jay											
Gray-breasted Jay											
Pinyon Jay											
Clark's Nutcracker											
Black-billed Magpie						xV			xV.xW-q		xV-q
Yellow-billed Magpie											
Jackdaw									xP*	xV	
American Crow	cP	cP	cP	cP	cP	cP	cS.fW	cS.fW	cP	cP	cP
Northwestern Crow											
Mexican Crow											

	New York	Pennsylvania	New Jersey	Delaware	Maryland	Dist. of Columbia	Virginia	North Carolina	South Carolina	Georgia	Florida
Violet-green Swallow											xV
Bahama Swallow											xS*,rV,xW
N. Rough-winged Swallow	fS,cT	fS,cT	fS	fS	fS	fS	fS	fS	fS,xW	fS,cT,xW	fS,cT,uW
Bank Swallow	fS	fS	fS	uS	uS,fT	uT	luS,fT	lrS,uT	xS,uT	uT	uT
Cliff Swallow	fS	uS,fT	rS,uT	rT	uS	rT	uS	luS,uT	luS,uT	luS,uT	lrS,rT
Cave Swallow											rV
Barn Swallow	cS	cS	cS	cS	cS	cS	cS,xW	cS	cS	fS,cT,xW	luS,cT,rW
Common House-Martin											

Family Corvidae: Jays, Magpies and Crows

	New York	Pennsylvania	New Jersey	Delaware	Maryland	Dist. of Columbia	Virginia	North Carolina	South Carolina	Georgia	Florida
Gray Jay	lrS,iuW	xV,xW									
Steller's Jay											
Blue Jay	cP	cP	cP	cP	cP	cP	cP	cP	cP	cP	cP
Green Jay											
Brown Jay											
Scrub Jay										xV	fP
Gray-breasted Jay											
Pinyon Jay											
Clark's Nutcracker											
Black-billed Magpie	xV,xW		xV				xV,xW	xW-q			
Yellow-billed Magpie											
Jackdaw											
American Crow	cP	cP	cP	cP	cP	cP	cP	cP	cP	cP	cP
Northwestern Crow											
Mexican Crow											

Hirundinidae • 251

	Date	Location	Cont. North America	Canada	Lower 48
Fish Crow *Corvus ossifragus*			lcP,xS*,rV	xV	cP
Hawaiian Crow *Corvus hawaiiensis*					
Chihuahuan Raven *Corvus cryptoleucus*			lcP		lcP
Common Raven *Corvus corax*			cP	cP	cP

Family Paridae: Titmice

	Date	Location	Cont. North America	Canada	Lower 48
Black-capped Chickadee *Parus atricapillus*			cP	cP	cP
Carolina Chickadee *Parus carolinensis*			cP	xV	cP
Mexican Chickadee *Parus sclateri*			lcP		lcP
Mountain Chickadee *Parus gambeli*			cP	lcP,rW	cP
Siberian Tit *Parus cinctus*			lrP	lrP	
Boreal Chickadee *Parus hudsonicus*			cP	cP	lfP,irW
Chestnut-backed Chickadee *Parus rufescens*			lcP,xV	lcP,xV	lcP
Bridled Titmouse *Parus wollweberi*			lcP,xV		lcP,xV
Plain Titmouse *Parus inornatus*			lfP		fP
Tufted Titmouse *Parus bicolor*			cP	lrP,xS*,xV,xW	cP

Family Remizidae: Penduline Tits and Verdins

	Date	Location	Cont. North America	Canada	Lower 48
Verdin *Auriparus flaviceps*			lcP		lcP

Family Aegithalidae: Long-tailed Tits and Bushtits

	Date	Location	Cont. North America	Canada	Lower 48
Bushtit *Psaltriparus minimus*			fP	lfP	cP

Family Sittidae: Nuthatches
Subfamily Sittinae: Typical Nuthatches

	Date	Location	Cont. North America	Canada	Lower 48
Red-breasted Nuthatch *Sitta canadensis*			cS,ifW	cS,ifW	cS,ifW
White-breasted Nuthatch *Sitta carolinensis*			fP	uP	fP

254 • Distributional Checklist of North American Birds

	Hawaii	Alaska	Yukon Terr.	Northwest Terr.	British Columbia	Alberta	Saskatch-ewan	Manitoba	Ontario
Fish Crow									
Hawaiian Crow	lrP								
Chihuahuan Raven									xV
Common Raven		cP	cP	cP	cP	cP	cP	cP	cP

Family Paridae: Titmice

	Hawaii	Alaska	Yukon Terr.	Northwest Terr.	British Columbia	Alberta	Saskatch-ewan	Manitoba	Ontario
Black-capped Chickadee		cP	cP	lfS.luW	cP	cP	cP	cP	cP
Carolina Chickadee									xV
Mexican Chickadee									
Mountain Chickadee					cP	lfP,rW	xW-q		
Siberian Tit		xV,xW	lrSt,xW						
Boreal Chickadee		rP	rP†	lrP					
Chestnut-backed Chickadee		cP	cP	cP	uP	fP	cP	fP	fS.icW
Bridled Titmouse		cP			cP	xV			
Plain Titmouse									
Tufted Titmouse									lrP

Family Remizidae: Penduline Tits and Verdins

	Hawaii	Alaska	Yukon Terr.	Northwest Terr.	British Columbia	Alberta	Saskatch-ewan	Manitoba	Ontario
Verdin									

Family Aegithalidae: Long-tailed Tits and Bushtits

	Hawaii	Alaska	Yukon Terr.	Northwest Terr.	British Columbia	Alberta	Saskatch-ewan	Manitoba	Ontario
Bushtit					lfP				

Family Sittidae: Nuthatches
Subfamily Sittinae: Typical Nuthatches

	Hawaii	Alaska	Yukon Terr.	Northwest Terr.	British Columbia	Alberta	Saskatch-ewan	Manitoba	Ontario
Red-breasted Nuthatch		rS.ifT.rW	uS.xW	lfS.rW	cP	fS.uW	fS.uW	cS.uW	cS.ifW
White-breasted Nuthatch					uP	uP	uP	fP	fP

	Québec	Newfoundland	New Brunswick	Prince Edward I.	Nova Scotia		Washington	Oregon	California	Nevada	Idaho
Fish Crow					xV-q						
Hawaiian Crow											
Chihuahuan Raven											
Common Raven	cP	cP	cP	cP	cP		cP	cP	cP	cP	fP

Family Paridae: Titmice

	Québec	Newfoundland	New Brunswick	Prince Edward I.	Nova Scotia		Washington	Oregon	California	Nevada	Idaho
Black-capped Chickadee	cP	cP	cP	cP	cP		cP	cP	luP	luP	cP
Carolina Chickadee											
Mexican Chickadee											
Mountain Chickadee							cP	cP	cP	cP	cP
Siberian Tit											
Boreal Chickadee	fP	cP	cP	fP	fP		luP				xV
Chestnut-backed Chickadee							cP	cP	cP		uP
Bridled Titmouse											
Plain Titmouse								lfP	cP	fP	luP
Tufted Titmouse	xV,lrW		xS*,xV,xW								

Family Remizidae: Penduline Tits and Verdins

Verdin									fP	fP	

Family Aegithalidae: Long-tailed Tits and Bushtits

Bushtit							cP	cP	cP	fP	luP

Family Sittidae: Nuthatches
Subfamily Sittinae: Typical Nuthatches

	Québec	Newfoundland	New Brunswick	Prince Edward I.	Nova Scotia		Washington	Oregon	California	Nevada	Idaho
Red-breasted Nuthatch	fS,ifW	uS,rW	fS,ifW	fP	cP		cP	cS,icW	cS,icW	fS,ifW	cP
White-breasted Nuthatch	lfP		fP	uP†	uP		fP	fP	fP	fP	fP

256 • Distributional Checklist of North American Birds

	Montana	Wyoming	Utah	Colorado	Arizona	New Mexico	North Dakota	South Dakota	Nebraska	Kansas	Oklahoma
Fish Crow											luP
Hawaiian Crow											
Chihuahuan Raven				uP	cP	cP			lrS	luS,rW	lfP
Common Raven	fP	cP	cP	cP	fP	fP	eP,irW	eP,xV	eP,xV	eP,xV,xW	lfP

Family Paridae: Titmice

	Montana	Wyoming	Utah	Colorado	Arizona	New Mexico	North Dakota	South Dakota	Nebraska	Kansas	Oklahoma
Black-capped Chickadee	cP	cP	cP	cP	rV,xW	lfP	cP	cP	cP	cP	xV,xW
Carolina Chickadee									xV	lcP	cP
Mexican Chickadee					lcP	luP					
Mountain Chickadee	cP	cP	cP	cP	cP	cP		xV	xW	lrP†	luT,xW
Siberian Tit											
Boreal Chickadee	luP	xV					irW	xV	xW		
Chestnut-backed Chickadee	luP										
Bridled Titmouse					cP	lfP					
Plain Titmouse		lfP,rV	fP	fP	fP	fP					luP
Tufted Titmouse								exS,xV,xW	lfP	cP	cP

Family Remizidae: Penduline Tits and Verdins

	Montana	Wyoming	Utah	Colorado	Arizona	New Mexico	North Dakota	South Dakota	Nebraska	Kansas	Oklahoma
Verdin			luP		cP	fP					lrP

Family Aegithalidae: Long-tailed Tits and Bushtits

	Montana	Wyoming	Utah	Colorado	Arizona	New Mexico	North Dakota	South Dakota	Nebraska	Kansas	Oklahoma
Bushtit		luP	fP	uP	cP	cP				xV	lfP

Family Sittidae: Nuthatches
Subfamily Sittinae: Typical Nuthatches

	Montana	Wyoming	Utah	Colorado	Arizona	New Mexico	North Dakota	South Dakota	Nebraska	Kansas	Oklahoma
Red-breasted Nuthatch	cP	cP	fS,ifW	fS,ifW	fS,ifW	fS,ifW	lrS,ifW	lfS,ifW	lrS,ifW	xS,ifW	iuW
White-breasted Nuthatch	uP	fP	fP	fP	fP	fP	uP	fP	uP	uP	uP

	Texas	Minnesota	Iowa	Missouri	Arkansas	Louisiana	Wisconsin	Michigan	Illinois	Indiana	Ohio
Fish Crow	luP			luS,lrW	luP	cP			luS		
Hawaiian Crow											
Chihuahuan Raven	cP										
Common Raven	fP	cP	ePt,xV	eP			fP	fP	eP	eP,xV	eP,xW

Family Paridae: Titmice

	Texas	Minnesota	Iowa	Missouri	Arkansas	Louisiana	Wisconsin	Michigan	Illinois	Indiana	Ohio
Black-capped Chickadee	xV,xW-q	cP	cP	cP			cP	cP	cP	cP	cP
Carolina Chickadee	cP			cP	cP	cP		xV	cP	cP	cP
Mexican Chickadee											
Mountain Chickadee	lfP,xW										
Siberian Tit											
Boreal Chickadee		fP	xV,xW				lrP,irW	uP	xV,xW	xV,xW	rV
Chestnut-backed Chickadee											
Bridled Titmouse	xV-q										
Plain Titmouse	luP										
Tufted Titmouse	cP	luP	cP	cP	cP	cP	fP	fP	cP	cP	cP

Family Remizidae: Penduline Tits and Verdins

	Texas	Minnesota	Iowa	Missouri	Arkansas	Louisiana	Wisconsin	Michigan	Illinois	Indiana	Ohio
Verdin	fP										

Family Aegithalidae: Long-tailed Tits and Bushtits

	Texas	Minnesota	Iowa	Missouri	Arkansas	Louisiana	Wisconsin	Michigan	Illinois	Indiana	Ohio
Bushtit	fP										

Family Sittidae: Nuthatches
Subfamily Sittinae: Typical Nuthatches

	Texas	Minnesota	Iowa	Missouri	Arkansas	Louisiana	Wisconsin	Michigan	Illinois	Indiana	Ohio
Red-breasted Nuthatch	iuW	fS,icW	xS,ifW	xS,ifW	ifW	iuW	fS,icW	fS,icW	xS,ifW	xS,ifW	rS,ifW
White-breasted Nuthatch	uP	cP	cP	cP	fP	fP	cP	cP	cP	cP	cP

	West Virginia	Kentucky	Tennessee	Mississippi	Alabama	Maine	New Hampshire	Vermont	Massachusetts	Rhode Island	Connecticut
Fish Crow	luP	luS*	luP	cP	cP	xV-q	xS*,rV	exV	luP	uP	uP
Hawaiian Crow											
Chihuahuan Raven											
Common Raven	fP	luP	luP		eP	cP	fP	fP	rP	exV	xV

Family Paridae: Titmice

	West Virginia	Kentucky	Tennessee	Mississippi	Alabama	Maine	New Hampshire	Vermont	Massachusetts	Rhode Island	Connecticut
Black-capped Chickadee	cP	xW	lfP			cP	cP	cP	cP	cP	cP
Carolina Chickadee	cP	cP	cP	cP	cP						
Mexican Chickadee											
Mountain Chickadee											
Siberian Tit											
Boreal Chickadee	xV					cP	uP	luP,iuW	iuW	irW	irW
Chestnut-backed Chickadee											
Bridled Titmouse											
Plain Titmouse											
Tufted Titmouse	cP	cP	cP	cP	cP	uP	uP	uP	fP	fP	cP

Family Remizidae: Penduline Tits and Verdins

	West Virginia	Kentucky	Tennessee	Mississippi	Alabama	Maine	New Hampshire	Vermont	Massachusetts	Rhode Island	Connecticut
Verdin											

Family Aegithalidae: Long-tailed Tits and Bushtits

	West Virginia	Kentucky	Tennessee	Mississippi	Alabama	Maine	New Hampshire	Vermont	Massachusetts	Rhode Island	Connecticut
Bushtit											

Family Sittidae: Nuthatches
Subfamily Sittinae: Typical Nuthatches

	West Virginia	Kentucky	Tennessee	Mississippi	Alabama	Maine	New Hampshire	Vermont	Massachusetts	Rhode Island	Connecticut
Red-breasted Nuthatch	uS,icW	xS*,ifW	lfS,ifW	iuW	ifW	cS,icW	cS,icW	fS,icW	fS,icW	rS,ifW	rS,ifW
White-breasted Nuthatch	fP	fP	fP	fP	fP	fP	fP	fP	cP	fP	cP

Corvidae • 259

	New York	Pennsylvania	New Jersey	Delaware	Maryland	Dist. of Columbia	Virginia	North Carolina	South Carolina	Georgia	Florida
Fish Crow	uP	uP	fP	fP	fP	cP	cP	cP	cP	cP	cP
Hawaiian Crow											
Chihuahuan Raven											
Common Raven	luS,uW	uP	rV	xV	luP	xV,xW	lfP	uP	eP,lrP*	luP	

Family Paridae: Titmice

	New York	Pennsylvania	New Jersey	Delaware	Maryland	Dist. of Columbia	Virginia	North Carolina	South Carolina	Georgia	Florida
Black-capped Chickadee	cP	cP	cP	ifW	lcP,ifW	irW	lcP,iuW	lfP			
Carolina Chickadee		lcP	cP	cP	cP	cP	cP	cP	cP	cP	cP
Mexican Chickadee											
Mountain Chickadee											
Siberian Tit											
Boreal Chickadee	lfP,iuW	irW	irW	xV	xW		xV,xW				
Chestnut-backed Chickadee											
Bridled Titmouse											
Plain Titmouse											
Tufted Titmouse	cP	cP	cP	cP	cP	cP	cP	cP	cP	cP	cP

Family Remizidae: Penduline Tits and Verdins

	New York	Pennsylvania	New Jersey	Delaware	Maryland	Dist. of Columbia	Virginia	North Carolina	South Carolina	Georgia	Florida
Verdin											

Family Aegithalidae: Long-tailed Tits and Bushtits

	New York	Pennsylvania	New Jersey	Delaware	Maryland	Dist. of Columbia	Virginia	North Carolina	South Carolina	Georgia	Florida
Bushtit											

Family Sittidae: Nuthatches
Subfamily Sittinae: Typical Nuthatches

	New York	Pennsylvania	New Jersey	Delaware	Maryland	Dist. of Columbia	Virginia	North Carolina	South Carolina	Georgia	Florida
Red-breasted Nuthatch	fS,icW	uS,icW	lrS,ifW	ifW	xS*,ifW	ifW	lfS,ifW	lfS,ifW	iuW	iuW	iuW
White-breasted Nuthatch	cP	cP	fP	fP	fP	fP	fP	fP	fP	fP	fP

Sittidae • 261

	Date	Location	Cont. North America	Canada	Lower 48
Pygmy Nuthatch *Sitta pygmaea*			lcP,xV,rW	luP,xV	cP
Brown-headed Nuthatch *Sitta pusilla*			lcP,xV,xW		cP

Family Certhiidae: Creepers
Subfamily Certhiinae: Typical Creepers

Brown Creeper *Certhia americana*			fS,cT,fW	fS,uW	fS,cT,fW

Family Troglodytidae: Wrens

Cactus Wren *Campylorhynchus brunneicapillus*			lcP		lcP
Rock Wren *Salpinctes obsoletus*			fS,uW	luS,xS*,xV	fP
Canyon Wren *Catherpes mexicanus*			fP	lrP,xV	fP
Carolina Wren *Thryothorus ludovicianus*			cP	liuP,xV,xW	cP
Bewick's Wren *Thryomanes bewickii*			fP	lfP,xS,rV	cP
House Wren *Troglodytes aedon*			cS,fW	cS,xW	cS,fW
Winter Wren *Troglodytes troglodytes*			fP	fS,uW	fP
Sedge Wren *Cistothorus platensis*			uP	uS,xW	uS,fW
Marsh Wren *Cistothorus palustris*			cP	fS,luW	cP

Family Cinclidae: Dippers

American Dipper *Cinclus mexicanus*			fP	fP	fP

Family Muscicapidae: Muscicapids
Subfamily Sylviinae: Old World Warblers, Kinglets and Gnatcatchers

Middendorff's Grasshopper-Warbler *Locustella ochotensis*			xV		
Lanceolated Warbler *Locustella lanceolata*			xS*,xV		
Millerbird *Acrocephalus familiaris*					
Wood Warbler *Phylloscopus sibilatrix*			xV		
Dusky Warbler *Phylloscopus fuscatus*			xV		xV

	Hawaii	Alaska	Yukon Terr.	Northwest Terr.	British Columbia	Alberta	Saskatchewan	Manitoba	Ontario
Pygmy Nuthatch					luP	xV			
Brown-headed Nuthatch									

Family Certhiidae: Creepers
Subfamily Certhiinae: Typical Creepers

	Hawaii	Alaska	Yukon Terr.	Northwest Terr.	British Columbia	Alberta	Saskatchewan	Manitoba	Ontario
Brown Creeper		uP	xV		fP	uP	uS,rW	fS,rW	fS,cT,uW

Family Troglodytidae: Wrens

	Hawaii	Alaska	Yukon Terr.	Northwest Terr.	British Columbia	Alberta	Saskatchewan	Manitoba	Ontario
Cactus Wren									
Rock Wren					xV	uS	uS	fS	xS*,xV	xV
Canyon Wren					lrP		xV-q			
Carolina Wren									xV	liuP
Bewick's Wren					lfP					xS,rV
House Wren						cS	cS	cS	cS	cS,xW
Winter Wren			fP	xV	xS*	fP	uS,xW	uS†	fS	fS,rW
Sedge Wren							lrS	uS	fS	uS,xW
Marsh Wren					fS,luW	fS	fS	cS	fS,rW

Family Cinclidae: Dippers

	Hawaii	Alaska	Yukon Terr.	Northwest Terr.	British Columbia	Alberta	Saskatchewan	Manitoba	Ontario
American Dipper		fP	fP	lrP*	fP	lfP,xV,xW	xV,xW-q		

Family Muscicapidae: Muscicapids
Subfamily Sylviinae: Old World Warblers, Kinglets and Gnatcatchers

	Hawaii	Alaska	Yukon Terr.	Northwest Terr.	British Columbia	Alberta	Saskatchewan	Manitoba	Ontario
Middendorff's Grass-Warb.		xV							
Lanceolated Warbler		xS*,xV							
Millerbird	luP								
Wood Warbler		xV							
Dusky Warbler		xV							

Sittidae • 263

	Québec	Newfoundland	New Brunswick	Prince Edward I.	Nova Scotia
Pygmy Nuthatch					
Brown-headed Nuthatch					

	Washington	Oregon	California	Nevada	Idaho
Pygmy Nuthatch	uP	cP	cP	fP	fP
Brown-headed Nuthatch					

Family Certhiidae: Creepers
Subfamily Certhiinae: Typical Creepers

	Québec	Newfoundland	New Brunswick	Prince Edward I.	Nova Scotia
Brown Creeper	fS,luW	uS,rW	uP	uP	fP

	Washington	Oregon	California	Nevada	Idaho
Brown Creeper	fP	fP	fP	fP	fP

Family Troglodytidae: Wrens

	Québec	Newfoundland	New Brunswick	Prince Edward I.	Nova Scotia
Cactus Wren					
Rock Wren					xV
Canyon Wren					
Carolina Wren	IirP		xV,xW		xV-q
Bewick's Wren					
House Wren	fS	xV	rS	xS*,xV	xS*,rT
Winter Wren	fS,rW	uS,xW	cS,rW	uS	fS,rW
Sedge Wren	lrS		lrS*	xV	xS*,rV
Marsh Wren	lfS		lrS		xS*,rT

	Washington	Oregon	California	Nevada	Idaho
Cactus Wren				fP	lcP
Rock Wren	fS	fS,rW	fP	cS,uW	fS,xW
Canyon Wren	uP	fP	fP	fP	uP
Carolina Wren					
Bewick's Wren	cP	cP	cP	cP	xP*,xV
House Wren	cS	cS	cS,fW	cS,lrW	cS
Winter Wren	cP	cP	cP	rW	fS,uW
Sedge Wren			xV		
Marsh Wren	cS,uW	cS,fW	cP	fP	fS,rW

Family Cinclidae: Dippers

	Québec	Newfoundland	New Brunswick	Prince Edward I.	Nova Scotia
American Dipper					

	Washington	Oregon	California	Nevada	Idaho
American Dipper	fP	fP	fP	uP	fP

Family Muscicapidae: Muscicapids
Subfamily Sylviinae: Old World Warblers, Kinglets and Gnatcatchers

	Québec	Newfoundland	New Brunswick	Prince Edward I.	Nova Scotia
Middendorff's Grass.-Warb.					
Lanceolated Warbler					
Millerbird					
Wood Warbler					
Dusky Warbler					

	Washington	Oregon	California	Nevada	Idaho
Middendorff's Grass.-Warb.					
Lanceolated Warbler					
Millerbird					
Wood Warbler					
Dusky Warbler			xV		

	Montana	Wyoming	Utah	Colorado	Arizona	New Mexico	North Dakota	South Dakota	Nebraska	Kansas	Oklahoma
Pygmy Nuthatch	uP	uP	fP	fP	cP	cP		lrP,xV	lrP,xV	xW	xV,lrW
Brown-headed Nuthatch											lrP

Family Certhiidae: Creepers
Subfamily Certhiinae: Typical Creepers

	Montana	Wyoming	Utah	Colorado	Arizona	New Mexico	North Dakota	South Dakota	Nebraska	Kansas	Oklahoma
Brown Creeper	uP	fP	fP	fP	fP	fP	lrS†,uW	luS,uW	lrS,fW	fW	fW

Family Troglodytidae: Wrens

	Montana	Wyoming	Utah	Colorado	Arizona	New Mexico	North Dakota	South Dakota	Nebraska	Kansas	Oklahoma
Cactus Wren			lfP		cP	cP					
Rock Wren	fS,xW	fS,xW	cS,uW	fS,uW	cP	cS,fW	uS	fS,xW	fS	fS,rW	fS,uW
Canyon Wren	uS,rW	uS,rW	fP	fS,uW	fP	fP		lfS,luW	xV		luP
Carolina Wren		xV		rV		xV,xW		xV	luP	uP	fP
Bewick's Wren		lfS,rV,xW	fP	uP	cP	cP		xV	lrS	fS,uW	fP
House Wren	cS	cS	cS,xW	cS	cP	cP	cS	cS	cS	cS,xW	uS,cT,rW
Winter Wren	uP	exS,xS*,rT,xW	uW	rW	rW	rW	rT,xW	rT,xW	uT,rW	uT,rW	uW
Sedge Wren	xS*,xV	exV		xS*,xV		xV,xW	fS	fS	uS	lrS,uT	xS,uT,xW
Marsh Wren	fS,rW	fS,xW	cS,uW	fS,uW	lfS,cW	luS,cW	fS	fS,xW	fS,rW	luS,uT,rW	uW

Family Cinclidae: Dippers

	Montana	Wyoming	Utah	Colorado	Arizona	New Mexico	North Dakota	South Dakota	Nebraska	Kansas	Oklahoma
American Dipper	fP	fP	fP	fP	fP	uP		luP	xV		

Family Muscicapidae: Muscicapids
Subfamily Sylviinae: Old World Warblers, Kinglets and Gnatcatchers

	Montana	Wyoming	Utah	Colorado	Arizona	New Mexico	North Dakota	South Dakota	Nebraska	Kansas	Oklahoma
Middendorff's Grass.-Warb.											
Lanceolated Warbler											
Millerbird											
Wood Warbler											
Dusky Warbler											

	Texas	Minnesota	Iowa	Missouri	Arkansas	Louisiana	Wisconsin	Michigan	Illinois	Indiana	Ohio
Pygmy Nuthatch	lfP,xV		xW								
Brown-headed Nuthatch	fP			eP	uP	cP	xW				

Family Certhiidae: Creepers
Subfamily Certhiinae: Typical Creepers

	Texas	Minnesota	Iowa	Missouri	Arkansas	Louisiana	Wisconsin	Michigan	Illinois	Indiana	Ohio
Brown Creeper	luS,fW	fS,cT,uW	rS,cT,fW	exS,cT,fW	xS*,fW	fW	uS,cT,uW	uS,cT,uW	rS,cT,fW	xS,cT,fW	lrS,cT,fW

Family Troglodytidae: Wrens

	Texas	Minnesota	Iowa	Missouri	Arkansas	Louisiana	Wisconsin	Michigan	Illinois	Indiana	Ohio
Cactus Wren	cP										
Rock Wren	fP	xS,xV	exS,xV	xS*,xV,xW	xV,xW	xW		xV	xV,xW	xV	xV
Canyon Wren	fP										
Carolina Wren	cP	eS,xS*,rV,xW	iuP	fP	cP	cP	irP	irP	fP	fP	fP
Bewick's Wren	cP	eS,xS*,rV	rS	uS,rW	uP	uW	eS,rV	eS,rV,xW	rS,xW	rS,exW	lrS,rV,xW
House Wren	luS,cW	cS	cS	cS,xW	luS,cT,uW	cT,fW	cS	cS	cS,xW	cS	cS
Winter Wren	uW	fS,rW	xS,uT,rW	fW	fW	uW	uS,fT,rW	fS,rW	fT,uW	xS*,fT,uW	lrS,fT,uW
Sedge Wren	fW	fS,xW	fS	uS,xW	liuS,uW	cW	fS	uS,xW	uS,xW	rS,uT,xW	irS,uT
Marsh Wren	lfS,cW	cS,xW	fS,xW	uS,rW	fT,rW	fS,cW	fS,xW	fS,xW	fS,rW	fS,xW	fS,rW

Family Cinclidae: Dippers

	Texas	Minnesota	Iowa	Missouri	Arkansas	Louisiana	Wisconsin	Michigan	Illinois	Indiana	Ohio
American Dipper	xV	xV,xW									

Family Muscicapidae: Muscicapids
Subfamily Sylviinae: Old World Warblers, Kinglets and Gnatcatchers

	Texas	Minnesota	Iowa	Missouri	Arkansas	Louisiana	Wisconsin	Michigan	Illinois	Indiana	Ohio
Middendorff's Grass.-Warb.											
Lanceolated Warbler											
Millerbird											
Wood Warbler											
Dusky Warbler											

	West Virginia	Kentucky	Tennessee	Mississippi	Alabama	Maine	New Hampshire	Vermont	Massachusetts	Rhode Island	Connecticut
Pygmy Nuthatch											
Brown-headed Nuthatch			luP	cP	cP						

Family Certhiidae: Creepers
Subfamily Certhiinae: Typical Creepers

	West Virginia	Kentucky	Tennessee	Mississippi	Alabama	Maine	New Hampshire	Vermont	Massachusetts	Rhode Island	Connecticut
Brown Creeper	uS,fW	fW	luS,fW	fW	fW	fS,uW	fS,uW	fS,uW	uS,fT,uW	uS,fT,uW	uS,cT,fW

Family Troglodytidae: Wrens

	West Virginia	Kentucky	Tennessee	Mississippi	Alabama	Maine	New Hampshire	Vermont	Massachusetts	Rhode Island	Connecticut
Cactus Wren											
Rock Wren		xV	xV		xV,xW				xW		
Canyon Wren											
Carolina Wren	cP	cP	cP	cP	cP	xS*,rT,lrW	irP*	xS,irP*	iuP	uS,fW	fP
Bewick's Wren	rS	rP	uP	lrS,rW	lrS,rW	xV-q	xS,xV	xV	xV	xV	
House Wren	cS	fS,cT,xW	uS,cT,rW	cT,fW	xS,cT,fW	uS	fS	fS	cS,xW	fS,xW	cS,xW
Winter Wren	fP	xS*,fW	lfS,fW	uW	fW	fS,rW	fS,rW	fS,rW	uS,fT,uW	rS,fT,uW	rS,fT,uW
Sedge Wren	rS,uT	rS,uT,xW	xS*,uW	fW	xS,fW	eS,rS*	eS,rS*	rS	irS,rT,xW	eS†,rT	xS,rT
Marsh Wren	rS	uT	uT,rW	cP	cP	fS	fS,xW	fS	fS,rW	fS,rW	cS,rW

Family Cinclidae: Dippers

	West Virginia	Kentucky	Tennessee	Mississippi	Alabama	Maine	New Hampshire	Vermont	Massachusetts	Rhode Island	Connecticut
American Dipper											

Family Muscicapidae: Muscicapids
Subfamily Sylviinae: Old World Warblers, Kinglets and Gnatcatchers

	West Virginia	Kentucky	Tennessee	Mississippi	Alabama	Maine	New Hampshire	Vermont	Massachusetts	Rhode Island	Connecticut
Middendorff's Grass.-Warb.											
Lanceolated Warbler											
Millerbird											
Wood Warbler											
Dusky Warbler											

	New York	Pennsylvania	New Jersey	Delaware	Maryland	Dist. of Columbia	Virginia	North Carolina	South Carolina	Georgia	Florida
Pygmy Nuthatch											
Brown-headed Nuthatch	xV	exV		uP	uP		fP	cP	cP	cP	cP

Family Certhiidae: Creepers
Subfamily Certhiinae: Typical Creepers

	New York	Pennsylvania	New Jersey	Delaware	Maryland	Dist. of Columbia	Virginia	North Carolina	South Carolina	Georgia	Florida
Brown Creeper	fS,cT,fW	uS,cT,fW	uS,cT,fW	xS*,fW	uS,fW	xS*,fW	uS,fW	luS,fW	fW	fW	uW

Family Troglodytidae: Wrens

	New York	Pennsylvania	New Jersey	Delaware	Maryland	Dist. of Columbia	Virginia	North Carolina	South Carolina	Georgia	Florida
Cactus Wren											
Rock Wren											xW
Canyon Wren											
Carolina Wren	ifP	fP	fP	fP	cP	cP	cP	cP	cP	cP	cP
Bewick's Wren	eS,rV	lrS,xV,xW	xV	xV	lrS	exV	lrP	lrS,rW	eS,rW	lrS,rW	rW
House Wren	cS,rW	cS,xW	cS,xW	cS,rW	cS,rW	fS	cS,uW	fS,cT,fW	luS,fW	luS,fW	fW
Winter Wren	fS,uW	uS,fW	rS,fT,uW	fT,rW	lrS,fW	uW	lfS,fW	lfS,fW	fW	lrS,fW	uW
Sedge Wren	uS	rS,uT	lrS,rT,xW	rS,xW	lrS,rW	xT	rS,uW	rS*,fW	fW	fW	fW
Marsh Wren	fS,rW	fS,rW	cS,uW	cS,rW	cS,uW	rS,uT	cS,uW	cP	cP	cP	cP

Family Cinclidae: Dippers

	New York	Pennsylvania	New Jersey	Delaware	Maryland	Dist. of Columbia	Virginia	North Carolina	South Carolina	Georgia	Florida
American Dipper											

Family Muscicapidae: Muscicapids
Subfamily Sylviinae: Old World Warblers, Kinglets and Gnatcatchers

	New York	Pennsylvania	New Jersey	Delaware	Maryland	Dist. of Columbia	Virginia	North Carolina	South Carolina	Georgia	Florida
Middendorff's Grass.-Warb.											
Lanceolated Warbler											
Millerbird											
Wood Warbler											
Dusky Warbler											

	Date	Location	Cont. North America	Canada	Lower 48
Arctic Warbler *Phylloscopus borealis*			lfS.xV	xV	
Golden-crowned Kinglet *Regulus satrapa*			cP	cS.uW	fS.cW
Ruby-crowned Kinglet *Regulus calendula*			cP	cS.luW	fS.cW
Blue-gray Gnatcatcher *Polioptila caerulea*			cS.fW	luS.rV	cS.fW
Black-tailed Gnatcatcher *Polioptila melanura*			lfP		lfP
Black-capped Gnatcatcher *Polioptila nigriceps*			lrS.xV		lrS.xV

Subfamily Muscicapinae: Old World Flycatchers and Allies

	Date	Location	Cont. North America	Canada	Lower 48
Red-breasted Flycatcher *Ficedula parva*			xV		
Siberian Flycatcher *Muscicapa sibirica*			xV		
Gray-spotted Flycatcher *Muscicapa griseisticta*			rV		

Subfamily Monarchinae: Monarch Flycatchers

	Date	Location	Cont. North America	Canada	Lower 48
Elepaio *Chasiempis sandwichensis*					

Subfamily Turdinae: Solitaires, Thrushes and Allies

	Date	Location	Cont. North America	Canada	Lower 48
Siberian Rubythroat *Luscinia calliope*			rV	xV	
Bluethroat *Luscinia svecica*			luS.xS*	xS*	
Red-flanked Bluetail *Tarsiger cyanurus*			xV		
Northern Wheatear *Oenanthe oenanthe*			lfS.rV.xW	uS.xW	rV
Stonechat *Saxicola torquata*			xV	xV	
Eastern Bluebird *Sialia sialis*			fP	fS.lrW	cP
Western Bluebird *Sialia mexicana*			fS.uW	luS.xV.lrW	fP
Mountain Bluebird *Sialia currucoides*			cS.fW	fS.lrW	cS.fW
Townsend's Solitaire *Myadestes townsendi*			fP	fS.rW	fP
Kamao *Myadestes myadestinus*					
Amaui *Myadestes oahensis*					
Olomao *Myadestes lanaiensis*					

	Hawaii	Alaska	Yukon Terr.	Northwest Terr.	British Columbia	Alberta	Saskatchewan	Manitoba	Ontario
Arctic Warbler		fS			xV				
Golden-crowned Kinglet		fS,uW	luS	lrS*	cS,fW	fS,uW	uS,rW	fS,rW	cS,uW
Ruby-crowned Kinglet		cS,xW	cS	fS	cS,uW	cS	cS,xW	cS	cS,rW
Blue-gray Gnatcatcher					xV	xV-q		xV-q	luS
Black-tailed Gnatcatcher									
Black-capped Gnatcatcher									

Subfamily Muscicapinae: Old World Flycatchers and Allies

	Hawaii	Alaska	Yukon Terr.	Northwest Terr.	British Columbia	Alberta	Saskatchewan	Manitoba	Ontario
Red-breasted Flycatcher		xV							
Siberian Flycatcher		xV							
Gray-spotted Flycatcher		rV							

Subfamily Monarchinae: Monarch Flycatchers

	Hawaii	Alaska	Yukon Terr.	Northwest Terr.	British Columbia	Alberta	Saskatchewan	Manitoba	Ontario
Elepaio	fP								

Subfamily Turdinae: Solitaires, Thrushes and Allies

	Hawaii	Alaska	Yukon Terr.	Northwest Terr.	British Columbia	Alberta	Saskatchewan	Manitoba	Ontario
Siberian Rubythroat		rV							xV
Bluethroat		luS	xS*						
Red-flanked Bluetail		xV							
Northern Wheatear		fS	uS	uS	xV			xV-q	rV
Stonechat		xV-q							
Eastern Bluebird						xV	uS	uS	fS,rW
Western Bluebird					uS,rW	xS	xV-q		
Mountain Bluebird		lrS,rT	fS	rV	fS,rW	fS	cS,xW	fS	xV,xW
Townsend's Solitaire		fS,xW	fS	lfS	fS,uW	lfS,rW	xS,rW	rV,xW	rV,xW
Kamao	luP†								
Amaui	E†								
Olomao	lrP†								

	Québec	Newfoundland	New Brunswick	Prince Edward I.	Nova Scotia	Washington	Oregon	California	Nevada	Idaho
Arctic Warbler										
Golden-crowned Kinglet	fS,rW	fS,uW	cS,fW	cS,fW	cS,fW	cP	cP	cP	fP	fP
Ruby-crowned Kinglet	cS,xW	cS,xW	cS,xW	fS,cT,xW	fS,cT,xW	fS,cT,fW	uS,cW	uS,cW	fS,cT,fW	cS,fW
Blue-gray Gnatcatcher	lrS	xV	rV	xV	rV	xV,xW	luS	fP	fS,lrW	luS
Black-tailed Gnatcatcher							fP		lfP	
Black-capped Gnatcatcher										

Subfamily Muscicapinae: Old World Flycatchers and Allies

	Québec	Newfoundland	New Brunswick	Prince Edward I.	Nova Scotia	Washington	Oregon	California	Nevada	Idaho
Red-breasted Flycatcher										
Siberian Flycatcher										
Gray-spotted Flycatcher										

Subfamily Monarchinae: Monarch Flycatchers

	Québec	Newfoundland	New Brunswick	Prince Edward I.	Nova Scotia	Washington	Oregon	California	Nevada	Idaho
Elepaio										

Subfamily Turdinae: Solitaires, Thrushes and Allies

	Québec	Newfoundland	New Brunswick	Prince Edward I.	Nova Scotia	Washington	Oregon	California	Nevada	Idaho
Siberian Rubythroat										
Bluethroat										
Red-flanked Bluetail										
Northern Wheatear	lrS,rT	lrS,rT	xV		rV,xW		xV	xV		
Stonechat			xV							
Eastern Bluebird	uS		uS	xS*	eS,rT					
Western Bluebird						fS,rW	fP	fP	fP	uS,xW
Mountain Bluebird	xV					fS,rW	cS,uW	fP	cS,fW	cS,rW
Townsend's Solitaire	xV,xW	xW	xV,xW		xV	fS,uW	fP	uS,fW	fP	fS,ifW
Kamao										
Amaui										
Olomao										

	Montana	Wyoming	Utah	Colorado	Arizona	New Mexico	North Dakota	South Dakota	Nebraska	Kansas	Oklahoma
Arctic Warbler											
Golden-crowned Kinglet	fS.uW	fS.uW	fP	fP	fP	uS.fW	fT.rW	luS.fT.rW	fT.uW	fT.uW	fW
Ruby-crowned Kinglet	cS.xW	cS	cS.fW	fS.cT.uW	fS.cW	fS.cW	fT	lrS.fT	fT.rW	cT.rW	cT.fW
Blue-gray Gnatcatcher	xV	uS	fS.xW	fS.xW	fP	uS	xV	xS*.xV	uS	fS	cS.xW
Black-tailed Gnatcatcher			xP		fP	uP					
Black-capped Gnatcatcher					lrS						

Subfamily Muscicapinae: Old World Flycatchers and Allies

	Montana	Wyoming	Utah	Colorado	Arizona	New Mexico	North Dakota	South Dakota	Nebraska	Kansas	Oklahoma
Red-breasted Flycatcher											
Siberian Flycatcher											
Gray-spotted Flycatcher											

Subfamily Monarchinae: Monarch Flycatchers

	Montana	Wyoming	Utah	Colorado	Arizona	New Mexico	North Dakota	South Dakota	Nebraska	Kansas	Oklahoma
Elepaio											

Subfamily Turdinae: Solitaires, Thrushes and Allies

	Montana	Wyoming	Utah	Colorado	Arizona	New Mexico	North Dakota	South Dakota	Nebraska	Kansas	Oklahoma
Siberian Rubythroat											
Bluethroat											
Red-flanked Bluetail											
Northern Wheatear									xV		
Stonechat											
Eastern Bluebird	lrS.rT	uS		uS.xW	luP	lrS.uW	uS	uS.xW	fS.rW	fS.uW	cS.fW
Western Bluebird	uS	uS	fP	fS.uW	cP	cP	xV-q		xV		xV.xW
Mountain Bluebird	cS.rW	cS.rW	cS.uW	cS.fW	cP	cP	lfS.uT	lfS.uT	lfS.fT.rW	fW	xS.fW
Townsend's Solitaire	fS.uW	fP	fP	fP	fS.cW	fS.cW	rW	lfS.uT.rW	lrS.uT.rW	uW	uW
Kamao											
Amaui											
Olomao											

Muscicapidae • 273

	Texas	Minnesota	Iowa	Missouri	Arkansas	Louisiana	Wisconsin	Michigan	Illinois	Indiana	Ohio
Arctic Warbler											
Golden-crowned Kinglet	ifW	fS.cT.uW	cT.uW	cT.fW	cW	fW	rS.cT.uW	uS.cT.uW	cT.fW	xS.cT.fW	cT.fW
Ruby-crowned Kinglet	cW	fS.cT.xW	cT.xW	cT.uW	cW	cW	rS.cT.rW	uS.cT.rW	cT.uW	cT.uW	cT.rW
Blue-gray Gnatcatcher	fS.cW	ifS	fS	fS	cS.xW	cS.fW	fS	uS	fS	fS	fS
Black-tailed Gnatcatcher	IfP										
Black-capped Gnatcatcher	xV-q										

Subfamily Muscicapinae: Old World Flycatchers and Allies

	Texas	Minnesota	Iowa	Missouri	Arkansas	Louisiana	Wisconsin	Michigan	Illinois	Indiana	Ohio
Red-breasted Flycatcher											
Siberian Flycatcher											
Gray-spotted Flycatcher											

Subfamily Monarchinae: Monarch Flycatchers

	Texas	Minnesota	Iowa	Missouri	Arkansas	Louisiana	Wisconsin	Michigan	Illinois	Indiana	Ohio
Elepaio											

Subfamily Turdinae: Solitaires, Thrushes and Allies

	Texas	Minnesota	Iowa	Missouri	Arkansas	Louisiana	Wisconsin	Michigan	Illinois	Indiana	Ohio
Siberian Rubythroat											
Bluethroat											
Red-flanked Bluetail											
Northern Wheatear		xV					xV	xV-q	xV		
Stonechat											
Eastern Bluebird	fS.cW	fS.xW	uS.fT.rW	fS.uW	cP	cP	fS.rW	fS.rW	fS.uW	fS.uW	fS.uW
Western Bluebird	lfS.fW										
Mountain Bluebird	lrS*.ifW	rV.xW	xV.xW	xV.xW		xV.xW	xV.xW	xV-q	xV.xW		
Townsend's Solitaire	uW	rV.rW	rV.rW	rV.rW	xV		rV.xW	xV.rW	xV.xW		xV.xW
Kamao											
Amaui											
Olomao											

	West Virginia	Kentucky	Tennessee	Mississippi	Alabama	Maine	New Hampshire	Vermont	Massachusetts	Rhode Island	Connecticut
Arctic Warbler											
Golden-crowned Kinglet	lfS,cT,fW	cT,fW	lfS,cW	cW	cW	cS,fW	fS,cT,fW	fS,cT,uW	uS,cT,fW	lrS,cT,fW	luS,cT,fW
Ruby-crowned Kinglet	cT,rW	cT,uW	cT,fW	cW	cW	cS,rW	fS,cT,rW	uS,cT	lrS,cT,rW	cT,rW	xS,cT,rW
Blue-gray Gnatcatcher	cS	cS	cS,xW	cS,uW	cS,uW	lrS,uT	uS	uS	uS,fT	uS	fS
Black-tailed Gnatcatcher											
Black-capped Gnatcatcher											

Subfamily Muscicapinae: Old World Flycatchers and Allies

	West Virginia	Kentucky	Tennessee	Mississippi	Alabama	Maine	New Hampshire	Vermont	Massachusetts	Rhode Island	Connecticut
Red-breasted Flycatcher											
Siberian Flycatcher											
Gray-spotted Flycatcher											

Subfamily Monarchinae: Monarch Flycatchers

	West Virginia	Kentucky	Tennessee	Mississippi	Alabama	Maine	New Hampshire	Vermont	Massachusetts	Rhode Island	Connecticut
Elepaio											

Subfamily Turdinae: Solitaires, Thrushes and Allies

	West Virginia	Kentucky	Tennessee	Mississippi	Alabama	Maine	New Hampshire	Vermont	Massachusetts	Rhode Island	Connecticut
Siberian Rubythroat											
Bluethroat											
Red-flanked Bluetail											
Northern Wheatear						rV	xV	xV	rV	xV	rV
Stonechat											
Eastern Bluebird	fS,uW	cS,fW	cS,fW	cP	cP	uS	uS,xW	uS,xW	uS,rW	uP	fS,uW
Western Bluebird											
Mountain Bluebird		xW		xV					xV		
Townsend's Solitaire						xV-q	xV		xV,xW	xW	xV-q
Kamao											
Amaui											
Olomao											

	New York	Pennsylvania	New Jersey	Delaware	Maryland	Dist. of Columbia	Virginia	North Carolina	South Carolina	Georgia	Florida
Arctic Warbler											
Golden-crowned Kinglet	fS,cT,fW	uS,cT,fW	IrS,cT,fW	cT,fW	IrS,cT,fW	cT,fW	IfS,cW	IfS,cW	cW	cW	uW
Ruby-crowned Kinglet	IuS,cT,rW	cT,rW	cT,rW	cT,rW	cT,uW	cT,uW	cT,fW	cW	cW	cW	cW
Blue-gray Gnatcatcher	fS	fS	cS,xW	fS,xW	cS,xW	rS,fT	cS,rW	cS,rW	cS,uW	cS,uW	fS,cW
Black-tailed Gnatcatcher											
Black-capped Gnatcatcher											

Subfamily Muscicapinae: Old World Flycatchers and Allies

	New York	Pennsylvania	New Jersey	Delaware	Maryland	Dist. of Columbia	Virginia	North Carolina	South Carolina	Georgia	Florida
Red-breasted Flycatcher											
Siberian Flycatcher											
Gray-spotted Flycatcher											

Subfamily Monarchinae: Monarch Flycatchers

	New York	Pennsylvania	New Jersey	Delaware	Maryland	Dist. of Columbia	Virginia	North Carolina	South Carolina	Georgia	Florida
Elepaio											

Subfamily Turdinae: Solitaires, Thrushes and Allies

	New York	Pennsylvania	New Jersey	Delaware	Maryland	Dist. of Columbia	Virginia	North Carolina	South Carolina	Georgia	Florida
Siberian Rubythroat											
Bluethroat											
Red-flanked Bluetail											
Northern Wheatear	rV	exV	rV	xV			xV	xV-q	xV		xV
Stonechat											
Eastern Bluebird	fS,uW	fS,uW	fS,uW	fP	fP	rT	fP	cP	cP	cP	cP
Western Bluebird											
Mountain Bluebird	xV,xW	xV,xW	xV								
Townsend's Solitaire	xV	xV	xV								
Kamao											
Amaui											
Olomao											

		Date	Location	Cont. North America	Canada	Lower 48
Omao *Myadestes obscurus*						
Puaiohi *Myadestes palmeri*						
Veery *Catharus fuscescens*				cS,xW	cS	fS,xW
Gray-cheeked Thrush *Catharus minimus*				cS	cS	lfS,fT
Swainson's Thrush *Catharus ustulatus*				cS,rW	cS,xW	fS,cT,rW
Hermit Thrush *Catharus guttatus*				cS,fW	cS,luW	cS,fW
Wood Thrush *Hylocichla mustelina*				cS,lrW	lfS,xS,rV	cS,lrW
Eurasian Blackbird *Turdus merula*				xV	xV	
Eye-browed Thrush *Turdus obscurus*				rV		
Dusky Thrush *Turdus naumanni*				rV		
Fieldfare *Turdus pilaris*				xV,xW	xV,xW	xV,xW
Redwing *Turdus iliacus*				xS*,xV,xW	xS*,xV	xW
Clay-colored Robin *Turdus grayi*				lrP		lrP
Rufous-backed Robin *Turdus rufopalliatus*				rV,rW		rV,rW
American Robin *Turdus migratorius*				cP	cS,uW	cP
Varied Thrush *Ixoreus naevius*				fS,lfW	fS,rW	lfP,rV,rW
Aztec Thrush *Ridgwayia pinicola*				xS*,xV,xW		xS*,xV,xW

Subfamily Timaliinae: Babblers

Wrentit *Chamaea fasciata*				lcP		lcP

Family Mimidae: Mockingbirds, Thrashers and Allies

Gray Catbird *Dumetella carolinensis*				cS,uW	cS,lrW	cS,fW
Northern Mockingbird *Mimus polyglottos*				cP	rP,uV	cP
Bahama Mockingbird *Mimus gundlachii*				xV		xV
Sage Thrasher *Oreoscoptes montanus*				fS,luW	luS,xV	fS,uW

	Hawaii	Alaska	Yukon Terr.	Northwest Terr.	British Columbia	Alberta	Saskatchewan	Manitoba	Ontario
Omao	fP								
Puaiohi	lrP								
Veery						fS	fS	cS	cS	cS
Gray-cheeked Thrush		cS	cS	cS	uS	xS,lrS*,uT	luS,fT	fS	luS,fT
Swainson's Thrush		cS	cS	cS	cS,xW	cS	cS	cS	cS
Hermit Thrush		cS	fS	lfS	cS,uW	cS	cS	cS	cS,rW
Wood Thrush							xV	xS,rV	fS
Eurasian Blackbird									xV
Eye-browed Thrush		rV							
Dusky Thrush		rV							
Fieldfare		xV			xV				xV,xW
Redwing									
Clay-colored Robin									
Rufous-backed Robin									
American Robin		cS,rW	cS,xW	cS	cS,fW	cS,rW	cS,uW	cS,uW	cS,uW
Varied Thrush		fS,rW	fS	lfS	fS,uW	lfS,uT,xW	rV	rV,rW	rV,rW
Aztec Thrush									

Subfamily Timaliinae: Babblers

	Hawaii	Alaska	Yukon Terr.	Northwest Terr.	British Columbia	Alberta	Saskatchewan	Manitoba	Ontario
Wrentit									

Family Mimidae: Mockingbirds, Thrashers and Allies

	Hawaii	Alaska	Yukon Terr.	Northwest Terr.	British Columbia	Alberta	Saskatchewan	Manitoba	Ontario
Gray Catbird					fS,xW	fS	cS	cS	cS,rW
Northern Mockingbird		xS*,xV		xV	xS,rS*,rV,xW	xS,rS*,rV,xW	xS,rS*,rV,xW	xS,rP*	lrS,uV,rW
Bahama Mockingbird									
Sage Thrasher					luS	xV	lrS	xV	xV

Muscicapidae • 279

	Québec	Newfoundland	New Brunswick	Prince Edward I.	Nova Scotia	Washington	Oregon	California	Nevada	Idaho
Omao										
Puaiohi										
Veery	cS	luS	cS	uS	fS	fS	uS	xV	lrS,xV	fS
Gray-cheeked Thrush	cS	cS	lfS,uT	uT	lrS,uT		xV	xV	xV	xV
Swainson's Thrush	cS	cS	cS	fS	fS	cS	cS	cS	uS	cS
Hermit Thrush	cS,xW	cS,xW	cS,xW	cS	cS,rW	cS,uW	cS,fW	cP	cS,rW	cS,xW
Wood Thrush	lfS		uS		xS,rV		xV	xV,xW	xV	xV
Eurasian Blackbird	xV									
Eye-browed Thrush										
Dusky Thrush										
Fieldfare	xW	xW			xV-q					
Redwing		xS*,xV								
Clay-colored Robin										
Rufous-backed Robin								xV,xW		
American Robin	cS,uW	cS,rW	cS,uW	cS,rW	cS,uW	cP	cP	cP	cS,fW	cS,fW
Varied Thrush	xV,xW		xV,xW		xV	fP	fP	luS,ifW	luT,rV,rW	fS,rW
Aztec Thrush										

Subfamily Timaliinae: Babblers

	Québec	Newfoundland	New Brunswick	Prince Edward I.	Nova Scotia	Washington	Oregon	California	Nevada	Idaho
Wrentit							fP	cP		

Family Mimidae: Mockingbirds, Thrashers and Allies

	Québec	Newfoundland	New Brunswick	Prince Edward I.	Nova Scotia	Washington	Oregon	California	Nevada	Idaho
Gray Catbird	fS,xW	rS*,rV	cS	uS	fS	fS	uS	rV,xW	lrS,rV,xW	fS
Northern Mockingbird	lrS,rV,xW	rS,rV,xW	rP	xV	rS,uV,rW	rP*	rP*	cP	cS,uW	rP*
Bahama Mockingbird										
Sage Thrasher						fS	fS,xW	lfS,uW	fS,luW	fS

280 • Distributional Checklist of North American Birds

	Montana	Wyoming	Utah	Colorado	Arizona	New Mexico	North Dakota	South Dakota	Nebraska	Kansas	Oklahoma
Omao											
Puaiohi											
Veery	fS	fS	rS	uS	lrS	xS*,lrT	fS	luS,uT	uT	uT	uT
Gray-cheeked Thrush	rV	rV		rV	exV	xV	fT	uT	uT	uT	uT
Swainson's Thrush	cS	fS,cT	fS	fS,cT,xW	lrS,uT	uS	xS*,cT	lfS,cT	lrS,cT,xW	cT	cT
Hermit Thrush	fS	fS,xW	cS,xW	fS,xW	cP	fP	fT,xW	lrS,fT,rW	fT,rW	fT,rW	fT,rW
Wood Thrush	xS*,xV	rV	xV	rV	rV,xW	xV	lrS	uS	fS	fS	uS
Eurasian Blackbird											
Eye-browed Thrush											
Dusky Thrush											
Fieldfare											
Redwing											
Clay-colored Robin											
Rufous-backed Robin					rV,rW						
American Robin	cS,uW	cS,uW	cS,fW	cS,fW	cP	cP	cS,uW	cS,uW	cS,uW	cS,fW	fS,cW
Varied Thrush	fS,rW	rV,xW	rV,rW	rV,rW	rV,rW	xV	rV,rW	xV,xW	xV,xW	xV	xW
Aztec Thrush					xS*,xV						

Subfamily Timaliinae: Babblers

Wrentit											

Family Mimidae: Mockingbirds, Thrashers and Allies

	Montana	Wyoming	Utah	Colorado	Arizona	New Mexico	North Dakota	South Dakota	Nebraska	Kansas	Oklahoma
Gray Catbird	cS	fS,xW	uS	fS,xW	luS,rV,xW	luS,rT,xW	cS	cS	cS	cS,xW	uS,cT,rW
Northern Mockingbird	rS,xW	uS,rW	fS,uW	fS,uW	cP	cS,fW	xS,rS*,rV	rP	fS,rW	cS,uW	cS,fW
Bahama Mockingbird											
Sage Thrasher	uS	fS	fS	fS,xW	lfS,uW	fS,uW	lrS*,rT	xS,xT	lrS*,rT	xS,rT	eS,uT,rW

Muscicapidae • 281

	Texas	Minnesota	Iowa	Missouri	Arkansas	Louisiana	Wisconsin	Michigan	Illinois	Indiana	Ohio
Omao											
Puaiohi											
Veery	uT,xW	cS	rS,uT	uT	uT	fT	cS	fS	uS,fT	uS,fT	uS,fT
Gray-cheeked Thrush	fT	fT	fT	fT	fT	fT	fT	fT	fT	fT	fT
Swainson's Thrush	cT,xW	fS,cT	cT	cT	cT	cT	uS,cT	fS,cT	cT	cT,xW	cT
Hermit Thrush	lfS,cW	fS,cT,rW	fT,rW	fT,rW	fT,rW	cW	fS,cT,rW	fS,cT,rW	cT,uW	cT,rW	lrS,cT,rW
Wood Thrush	cS,xW	cS	fS	cS	cS	cS,xW	cS	cS	cS	cS	cS
Eurasian Blackbird											
Eye-browed Thrush											
Dusky Thrush											
Fieldfare											
Redwing											
Clay-colored Robin	lrP,xV										
Rufous-backed Robin	xV										
American Robin	fS,cW	cS,uW	cS,uW	cS,fW	cP	cP	cS,uW	cS,uW	cS,fW	cS,uW	cS,uW
Varied Thrush	xV,rW	rV,rW	rV,rW	xW		xV	rV,rW	rV,rW	rV,rW	xV,xW	rW
Aztec Thrush	xV,xW										

Subfamily Timaliinae: Babblers

	Texas	Minnesota	Iowa	Missouri	Arkansas	Louisiana	Wisconsin	Michigan	Illinois	Indiana	Ohio
Wrentit											

Family Mimidae: Mockingbirds, Thrashers and Allies

	Texas	Minnesota	Iowa	Missouri	Arkansas	Louisiana	Wisconsin	Michigan	Illinois	Indiana	Ohio
Gray Catbird	fS,cT,rW	cS,xW	cS,xW	cS,rW	fS,cT,rW	uS,cT,uW	cS,rW	cS,xW	cS,rW	cS,rW	cS,rW
Northern Mockingbird	cP	xS,rP*	uS,rW	cS,fW	cP	cP	uS,rW	uS,rW	cS,fW	cS,fW	fS,uW
Bahama Mockingbird											
Sage Thrasher	lrS*,fW	xV	xW	xW	xV	xV,xW	xV,xW		xV,xW		

	West Virginia	Kentucky	Tennessee	Mississippi	Alabama	Maine	New Hampshire	Vermont	Massachusetts	Rhode Island	Connecticut
Omao											
Puaiohi											
Veery	fS	lfS,fT	lfS,fT	fT	xS*,fT	cS	cS	cS	fS,cT	fS	fS,cT
Gray-cheeked Thrush	fT	fT	fT	fT	fT	lfS,uT	lfS,uT	luS,uT	eS,uT	uT	uT
Swainson's Thrush	luS,cT	cT	cT	cT,xW	cT	cS	cS	fS,cT	lrS,cT	fT	xS,cT,xW
Hermit Thrush	uS,cT,rW	cT,uW	cT,fW	cT,fW	cT,fW	cS,xW	fS,cT,rW	fS,cT,xW	fS,rW	fS,uW	uS,fT,uW
Wood Thrush	cS	cS	cS	cS	cS	cS	cS	cS	cS	cS	cS
Eurasian Blackbird											
Eye-browed Thrush											
Dusky Thrush											
Fieldfare											exV
Redwing											
Clay-colored Robin											
Rufous-backed Robin											
American Robin	cS,fW	cS,fW	cP	cP	cP	cS,uW	cS,uW	cS,uW	cS,uW	cS,uW	cS,uW
Varied Thrush						rV,rW	rV,rW	xV,xW	xV,rW	xW	rV,rW
Aztec Thrush											

Subfamily Timaliinae: Babblers

Wrentit											

Family Mimidae: Mockingbirds, Thrashers and Allies

	West Virginia	Kentucky	Tennessee	Mississippi	Alabama	Maine	New Hampshire	Vermont	Massachusetts	Rhode Island	Connecticut
Gray Catbird	cS,rW	cS,xW	cS,rW	fS,cT,uW	fS,cT,uW	cS,rW	cS,xW	cS,xW	cS,rW	cS,rW	cS,rW
Northern Mockingbird	cS,fW	cP	cP	cP	cP	uP	fP	uP	fP	fP	cP
Bahama Mockingbird											
Sage Thrasher					xV				xV		

Muscicapidae • 283

	New York	Pennsylvania	New Jersey	Delaware	Maryland	Dist. of Columbia	Virginia	North Carolina	South Carolina	Georgia	Florida
Omao											
Puaiohi											
Veery	cS	fS	fS,cT	fS	fS	fS	fS	lcS,fT	fT	luS,fT	fT
Gray-cheeked Thrush	luS,uT	uT	uT	uT	uT	uT	uT	uT	uT	fT	fT
Swainson's Thrush	fS,cT,xW	uS,cT,xW	cT	fT	eS,cT	cT	lrS,cT,xW	cT	fT	fT	fT,xW
Hermit Thrush	fS,cT,rW	fS,cT,rW	luS,fT,uW	fT,uW	luS,fW	fT,uW	luS,fW	lrS*,fW	fW	fW	fW
Wood Thrush	cS,xW	cS,xW	cS	cS	cS	fS	cS,xW	cS	cS	cS	fS,rW
Eurasian Blackbird											
Eye-browed Thrush											
Dusky Thrush											
Fieldfare	xW			xV							
Redwing	xW										
Clay-colored Robin											
Rufous-backed Robin											
American Robin	cS,uW	cS,uW	cS,uW	cS,fW	cS,fW	cS,uW	cP	cP	cP	cP	fS,cW
Varied Thrush	rV,rW	xV,xW	rV,rW		xV,xW		xV,xW			xV,xW	xV
Aztec Thrush											

Subfamily Timaliinae: Babblers

Wrentit											

Family Mimidae: Mockingbirds, Thrashers and Allies

	New York	Pennsylvania	New Jersey	Delaware	Maryland	Dist. of Columbia	Virginia	North Carolina	South Carolina	Georgia	Florida
Gray Catbird	cS,rW	cS,rW	cS,rW	fS,rW	cS,uW	cS,rW	cS,uW	cS,fW	cS,fW	fS,cT,fW	lrS,cW
Northern Mockingbird	fP	cP	cP	cP	cP	cP	cP	cP	cP	cP	cP
Bahama Mockingbird											xV
Sage Thrasher	xV		xV		xV-q		xV	xV			xV,xW

Mimidae • 285

		Date	Location	Cont. North America	Canada	Lower 48
Brown Thrasher *Toxostoma rufum*				cS,fW	fS,rW	cP
Long-billed Thrasher *Toxostoma longirostre*				lfP,xV		lfP,xV
Bendire's Thrasher *Toxostoma bendirei*				lfS,rV,luW	xV	lfS,rV,luW
Curve-billed Thrasher *Toxostoma curvirostre*				lcP,xP,rV,rW		lcP,xP,rV,rW
California Thrasher *Toxostoma redivivum*				lfP,xP*		lfP,xP*
Crissal Thrasher *Toxostoma crissale*				lfP		lfP
Le Conte's Thrasher *Toxostoma lecontei*				luP		luP

Family Prunellidae: Accentors

Siberian Accentor *Prunella montanella*				xV		xV

Family Motacillidae: Wagtails and Pipits

Yellow Wagtail *Motacilla flava*				lfS,xV	luS	xV
Gray Wagtail *Motacilla cinerea*				rV	xV	
White Wagtail *Motacilla alba*				luS,xV,xW	xV-sp	xV,xW
Black-backed Wagtail *Motacilla lugens*				xS,rV,xW	xV,xW-sp	xV,xW
Brown Tree-Pipit *Anthus trivialis*				xV		
Olive Tree-Pipit *Anthus hodgsoni*				rV		xV
Pechora Pipit *Anthus gustavi*				xV		
Red-throated Pipit *Anthus cervinus*				luS,rV	xV	rV
Water Pipit *Anthus spinoletta*				cP	cS,lrW	fS,cW
Sprague's Pipit *Anthus spragueii*				lfS,uT,luW	fS	lfS,uW

Family Bombycillidae: Waxwings

Bohemian Waxwing *Bombycilla garrulus*				fS,icW	fS,icW	lrS,ifW
Cedar Waxwing *Bombycilla cedrorum*				cS,icW	cS,iuW	fS,cT,icW

	Hawaii	Alaska	Yukon Terr.	Northwest Terr.	British Columbia	Alberta	Saskatchewan	Manitoba	Ontario
Brown Thrasher		xV	xV	xV	xV.xW	fS	cS.xW	fS.rW	fS.rW
Long-billed Thrasher									
Bendire's Thrasher							xV-q	xV-q	
Curve-billed Thrasher									
California Thrasher									
Crissal Thrasher									
Le Conte's Thrasher									

Family Prunellidae: Accentors

	Hawaii	Alaska							
Siberian Accentor		xV							

Family Motacillidae: Wagtails and Pipits

	Hawaii	Alaska	Yukon Terr.	Northwest Terr.	British Columbia	Alberta	Saskatchewan	Manitoba	Ontario
Yellow Wagtail		fS	luS	lrS					
Gray Wagtail		rV			xV				
White Wagtail		luS.xV	xV-sp						
Black-backed Wagtail		xS.rV					xV.xW-sp		
Brown Tree-Pipit		xV							
Olive Tree-Pipit	xV	rV							
Pechora Pipit		xV							
Red-throated Pipit	xV	luS.rV	xV						
Water Pipit	xV	cS.xW	cS	cS	cS.lrW	lfS.cT	fT	lcS.fT	lfS.fT.xW
Sprague's Pipit						fS	cS	uS	xS*

Family Bombycillidae: Waxwings

	Hawaii	Alaska	Yukon Terr.	Northwest Terr.	British Columbia	Alberta	Saskatchewan	Manitoba	Ontario
Bohemian Waxwing		fS.iuW	fS.iuW	fS.irW	fS.icW	fS.icW	uS.icW	fS.cT.ifW	lrS*.ifW
Cedar Waxwing		luS		xV	cS.iuW	cS.irW	cS.iuW	cS.iuW	cS.iuW

	Québec	Newfoundland	New Brunswick	Prince Edward I.	Nova Scotia		Washington	Oregon	California	Nevada	Idaho
Brown Thrasher	luS,xW	xV,xW	rS,xW	xS*,rV	uV,rW			xV,xW	xS*,rV,rW	rV,xW	xV
Long-billed Thrasher											
Bendire's Thrasher									lrS,rV,rW	lrS	
Curve-billed Thrasher									xV,rW	lrS*,xW	
California Thrasher								xP*	fP		
Crissal Thrasher									lfP	lfP	
Le Conte's Thrasher									uP	luP	

Family Prunellidae: Accentors

	Québec	Newfoundland	New Brunswick	Prince Edward I.	Nova Scotia		Washington	Oregon	California	Nevada	Idaho
Siberian Accentor							xV				

Family Motacillidae: Wagtails and Pipits

	Québec	Newfoundland	New Brunswick	Prince Edward I.	Nova Scotia		Washington	Oregon	California	Nevada	Idaho
Yellow Wagtail									xV		
Gray Wagtail											
White Wagtail							xV-sp,xW		xV		
Black-backed Wagtail								xV-sp,xW	xV,xW-sp		
Brown Tree-Pipit											
Olive Tree-Pipit										xV	
Pechora Pipit											
Red-throated Pipit							xV		rV		
Water Pipit	cS	fS,xW	xS*,fT	uT	fT,rW		fS,cT,uW	lfS,cW	luS,cW	luS,cW	rS,cT,rW
Sprague's Pipit									rV,xW	xV	

Family Bombycillidae: Waxwings

	Québec	Newfoundland	New Brunswick	Prince Edward I.	Nova Scotia		Washington	Oregon	California	Nevada	Idaho
Bohemian Waxwing	xS*,iuW	irW	iuW	irW	iuW		lrS,ifW	iuW	irW	iuW	lrS,icW
Cedar Waxwing	cS,iuW	uS,irW	cS,irW	fS,irW	cS,irW		cS,iuW	cS,icW	uS,icW	uS*,cT,icW	fS,ifW

	Montana	Wyoming	Utah	Colorado	Arizona	New Mexico	North Dakota	South Dakota	Nebraska	Kansas	Oklahoma
Brown Thrasher	fS,xW	fS,xW	xS*,rV,xW	uS,rW	rV,rW	lrS,rW	cS,xW	cS,rW	cS,rW	cS,rW	fS,uW
Long-billed Thrasher				xV							
Bendire's Thrasher			rS	xS	fS,uW	uS,lrW					
Curve-billed Thrasher				uS,rW	cP	fP			xV,xW	xV	xS,xV,xW	luP
California Thrasher											
Crissal Thrasher			luP		fP	uP					
Le Conte's Thrasher			xP*		luP						

Family Prunellidae: Accentors

Siberian Accentor											

Family Motacillidae: Wagtails and Pipits

	Montana	Wyoming	Utah	Colorado	Arizona	New Mexico	North Dakota	South Dakota	Nebraska	Kansas	Oklahoma
Yellow Wagtail											
Gray Wagtail											
White Wagtail											
Black-backed Wagtail											
Brown Tree-Pipit											
Olive Tree-Pipit											
Pechora Pipit											
Red-throated Pipit											
Water Pipit	fS,cT,xW	fS,cT,rW	fS,cT,fW	fS,cT,rW	lfS,cW	luS,cW	fT	fT	fT,rW	fT,rW	fT,uW
Sprague's Pipit	uS	rT		rT	rW	rW	fS	uS	uT	uT,lrW	fT,rW

Family Bombycillidae: Waxwings

	Montana	Wyoming	Utah	Colorado	Arizona	New Mexico	North Dakota	South Dakota	Nebraska	Kansas	Oklahoma
Bohemian Waxwing	lrS,icW	icW	ifW	icW	irW	iuW	icW	icW	iuW	iuW	irW
Cedar Waxwing	fS,cT,iuW	fS,ifW	uS,fT,ifW	uS,fT,ifW	cT,icW	rS*,cT,icW	cS,iuW	fS,cT,ifW	uS,cT,ifW	rS,cT,ifW	xS,cT,icW

	Texas	Minnesota	Iowa	Missouri	Arkansas	Louisiana	Wisconsin	Michigan	Illinois	Indiana	Ohio
Brown Thrasher	fS,cW	cS,rW	cS,rW	cS,uW	cS,fW	fS,cW	cS,rW	fS,rW	cS,uW	cS,rW	cS,rW
Long-billed Thrasher	fP										
Bendire's Thrasher											
Curve-billed Thrasher	cP	xV	xV,xW				xV	xP			
California Thrasher											
Crissal Thrasher	IuP										
Le Conte's Thrasher											

Family Prunellidae: Accentors

	Texas	Minnesota	Iowa	Missouri	Arkansas	Louisiana	Wisconsin	Michigan	Illinois	Indiana	Ohio
Siberian Accentor											

Family Motacillidae: Wagtails and Pipits

	Texas	Minnesota	Iowa	Missouri	Arkansas	Louisiana	Wisconsin	Michigan	Illinois	Indiana	Ohio
Yellow Wagtail											
Gray Wagtail											
White Wagtail											
Black-backed Wagtail											
Brown Tree-Pipit											
Olive Tree-Pipit											
Pechora Pipit											
Red-throated Pipit											
Water Pipit	cW	fT,xW	fT	fT,xW	fW	cW	fT	fT,xW	fT	fT	fT,xW
Sprague's Pipit	fT,uW	lrS,rT	xT	rT	rW	uW	xV-q	xV	rT,xW	xV-q	xV

Family Bombycillidae: Waxwings

	Texas	Minnesota	Iowa	Missouri	Arkansas	Louisiana	Wisconsin	Michigan	Illinois	Indiana	Ohio
Bohemian Waxwing	irW	xS*,ifW	irW	irW	xW		iuW	iuW	irW	irW	irW
Cedar Waxwing	xS*,cT,icW	cS,ifW	fS,cT,ifW	rS,cT,ifW	xS,cT,icW	cT,icW	cS,ifW	fS,cT,ifW	uS,cT,ifW	uS,cT,ifW	fS,cT,ifW

Distributional Checklist of North American Birds

	West Virginia	Kentucky	Tennessee	Mississippi	Alabama	Maine	New Hampshire	Vermont	Massachusetts	Rhode Island	Connecticut
Brown Thrasher	cS,rW	cS,uW	cS,fW	cP	cP	fS,rW	fS,rW	fS,xW	fS,rW	fS,rW	fS,rW
Long-billed Thrasher											
Bendire's Thrasher											
Curve-billed Thrasher											
California Thrasher											
Crissal Thrasher											
Le Conte's Thrasher											

Family Prunellidae: Accentors

Siberian Accentor											

Family Motacillidae: Wagtails and Pipits

	West Virginia	Kentucky	Tennessee	Mississippi	Alabama	Maine	New Hampshire	Vermont	Massachusetts	Rhode Island	Connecticut
Yellow Wagtail											
Gray Wagtail											
White Wagtail											
Black-backed Wagtail											
Brown Tree-Pipit											
Olive Tree-Pipit											
Pechora Pipit											
Red-throated Pipit											
Water Pipit	fT,rW	fT,rW	fW	cW	cW	lrS,fT	fT	fT	fT,rW	fT,rW	fT,rW
Sprague's Pipit			lrT	xV,lrW	rV,xW	xV-q					

Family Bombycillidae: Waxwings

	West Virginia	Kentucky	Tennessee	Mississippi	Alabama	Maine	New Hampshire	Vermont	Massachusetts	Rhode Island	Connecticut
Bohemian Waxwing	xW					iuW	iuW	iuW	irW	xV	xV,xW-q
Cedar Waxwing	fS,cT,ifW	uS,cT,ifW	uS,cT,ifW	cT,icW	luS,cT,icW	cS,irW	cS,iuW	cS,ifW	fS,cT,ifW	fS,cT,ifW	uS,cT,ifW

Mimidae • 291

	New York	Pennsylvania	New Jersey	Delaware	Maryland	Dist. of Columbia	Virginia	North Carolina	South Carolina	Georgia	Florida
Brown Thrasher	fS,rW	cS,rW	fS,rW	fS,rW	cS,uW	fS,uW	cS,uW	cS,fW	cP	cP	fS,cW
Long-billed Thrasher											
Bendire's Thrasher											
Curve-billed Thrasher												xS*
California Thrasher											
Crissal Thrasher											
Le Conte's Thrasher											

Family Prunellidae: Accentors

Siberian Accentor											

Family Motacillidae: Wagtails and Pipits

	New York	Pennsylvania	New Jersey	Delaware	Maryland	Dist. of Columbia	Virginia	North Carolina	South Carolina	Georgia	Florida
Yellow Wagtail											
Gray Wagtail											
White Wagtail											
Black-backed Wagtail								xV			
Brown Tree-Pipit											
Olive Tree-Pipit											
Pechora Pipit											
Red-throated Pipit											
Water Pipit	fT,rW	fT,rW	fT,rW	uT,rW	fT,uW	uT,rW	cT,fW	cT,fW	cW	cW	cW*
Sprague's Pipit		xV					xV-q	xV	xV,xW	xV,xW	rV,xW

Family Bombycillidae: Waxwings

	New York	Pennsylvania	New Jersey	Delaware	Maryland	Dist. of Columbia	Virginia	North Carolina	South Carolina	Georgia	Florida
Bohemian Waxwing	iuW	irW	xV,xW			xW	xV-q				
Cedar Waxwing	cS,ifW	cS,ifW	uS,cT,ifW	uS,cT,ifW	fS,cT,ifW	cT,ifW	uS,cT,ifW	IuS,icW	xS,icW	IuS,icW	icW

Keith Hansen 1984

Family Ptilogonatidae: Silky-flycatchers

	Date	Location	Cont. North America	Canada	Lower 48
Phainopepla *Phainopepla nitens*			lcP,rV,xW	xW	lcP,rV,xW

Family Laniidae: Shrikes
Subfamily Laniinae: Typical Shrikes

	Date	Location	Cont. North America	Canada	Lower 48
Brown Shrike *Lanius cristatus*			xV		xV
Northern Shrike *Lanius excubitor*			uS,ifW	uS,ifW	ifW
Loggerhead Shrike *Lanius ludovicianus*			fP	uS,lrW	fP

Family Sturnidae: Starlings and Allies
Subfamily Sturninae: Starlings

	Date	Location	Cont. North America	Canada	Lower 48
European Starling *Sturnus vulgaris*			exV	exV	

Family Meliphagidae: Honeyeaters

	Date	Location	Cont. North America	Canada	Lower 48
Kauai Oo *Moho braccatus*					
Oahu Oo *Moho apicalis*					
Bishop's Oo *Moho bishopi*					
Hawaii Oo *Moho nobilis*					
Kioea *Chaetoptila angustipluma*					

Family Vireonidae: Vireos
Subfamily Vireoninae: Typical Vireos

	Date	Location	Cont. North America	Canada	Lower 48
White-eyed Vireo *Vireo griseus*			cS,luW	lrS,rV	cS,uW
Thick-billed Vireo *Vireo crassirostris*			xV,xW		xV,xW
Bell's Vireo *Vireo bellii*			fS,lrW	rV	fS,lrW
Black-capped Vireo *Vireo atricapillus*			lfS,xV		lfS,xV
Gray Vireo *Vireo vicinior*			luS,xS*,xV,lrW		uS,lrW
Solitary Vireo *Vireo solitarius*			fS,uW	fS	fS,uW
Yellow-throated Vireo *Vireo flavifrons*			fS,lrW	luS,xS*,rV	fS,lrW

Family Ptilogonatidae: Silky-flycatchers

	Hawaii	Alaska	Yukon Terr.	Northwest Terr.	British Columbia	Alberta	Saskatch-ewan	Manitoba	Ontario
Phainopepla									xW

Family Laniidae: Shrikes
Subfamily Laniinae: Typical Shrikes

	Hawaii	Alaska	Yukon Terr.	Northwest Terr.	British Columbia	Alberta	Saskatch-ewan	Manitoba	Ontario
Brown Shrike		xV							
Northern Shrike		uS,iuW	uS,irW	uS	luS,ifW	luS,iuW	lrS*,uT,iuW	uS,ifW	lrS,ifW
Loggerhead Shrike					xS*,rT,xW	fS	fS,xW	rS	rP

Family Sturnidae: Starlings and Allies
Subfamily Sturninae: Starlings

	Hawaii	Alaska	Yukon Terr.	Northwest Terr.	British Columbia	Alberta	Saskatch-ewan	Manitoba	Ontario
European Starling									

Family Meliphagidae: Honeyeaters

	Hawaii	Alaska	Yukon Terr.	Northwest Terr.	British Columbia	Alberta	Saskatch-ewan	Manitoba	Ontario
Kauai Oo	lrP								
Oahu Oo	E†								
Bishop's Oo	lrP†-sp								
Hawaii Oo	E†								
Kioea	E†								

Family Vireonidae: Vireos
Subfamily Vireoninae: Typical Vireos

	Hawaii	Alaska	Yukon Terr.	Northwest Terr.	British Columbia	Alberta	Saskatch-ewan	Manitoba	Ontario
White-eyed Vireo								xV	lrS
Thick-billed Vireo									
Bell's Vireo									rV
Black-capped Vireo									
Gray Vireo									
Solitary Vireo			xV	lfS	cS	fS	fS	fS	fS
Yellow-throated Vireo							xS*,xV	luS	luS

Family Ptilogonatidae: Silky-flycatchers

	Québec	Newfound-land	New Brunswick	Prince Edward I.	Nova Scotia		Washington	Oregon	California	Nevada	Idaho
Phainopepla								xV	fP	lfP	

Family Laniidae: Shrikes
Subfamily Laniinae: Typical Shrikes

Brown Shrike									xV-q		
Northern Shrike	uS.ifW	luS.rW	iuW	rW	iuW		ifW	ifW	iuW	ifW	ifW
Loggerhead Shrike	lrS.xW		xS.rV	xS*.xV	xS.rV		fS.rW	fS.rW	cP	cS.fW	fS.rW

Family Sturnidae: Starlings and Allies
Subfamily Sturninae: Starlings

European Starling		exV									

Family Meliphagidae: Honeyeaters

Kauai Oo											
Oahu Oo											
Bishop's Oo											
Hawaii Oo											
Kioea											

Family Vireonidae: Vireos
Subfamily Vireoninae: Typical Vireos

White-eyed Vireo	xV	xV	xV		rV		xV-q		xS*.xV		
Thick-billed Vireo											
Bell's Vireo								xV	rS.xW	lrS	xV
Black-capped Vireo											
Gray Vireo									lrS	uS	
Solitary Vireo	fS	luS	fS	fS	uS		cS	cS	fS.cT.rW	fS	fS
Yellow-throated Vireo	lrS	xV	rV		rV				rV.xW	xV	

Family Ptilogonatidae: Silky-flycatchers

	Montana	Wyoming	Utah	Colorado	Arizona	New Mexico	North Dakota	South Dakota	Nebraska	Kansas	Oklahoma
Phainopepla			luS.lrW	xV	cP	uP			xW		xW-q

Family Laniidae: Shrikes
Subfamily Laniinae: Typical Shrikes

	Montana	Wyoming	Utah	Colorado	Arizona	New Mexico	North Dakota	South Dakota	Nebraska	Kansas	Oklahoma
Brown Shrike											
Northern Shrike	ifW	ifW	ifW	ifW	iuW	iuW	ifW	ifW	ifW	iuW	irW
Loggerhead Shrike	fS.xW	fS	cS.fW	cS.uW	cP	fS.cW	uS	fS	fS.rW	fS.uW	fP

Family Sturnidae: Starlings and Allies
Subfamily Sturninae: Starlings

	Montana	Wyoming	Utah	Colorado	Arizona	New Mexico	North Dakota	South Dakota	Nebraska	Kansas	Oklahoma
European Starling											

Family Meliphagidae: Honeyeaters

	Montana	Wyoming	Utah	Colorado	Arizona	New Mexico	North Dakota	South Dakota	Nebraska	Kansas	Oklahoma
Kauai Oo											
Oahu Oo											
Bishop's Oo											
Hawaii Oo											
Kioea											

Family Vireonidae: Vireos
Subfamily Vireoninae: Typical Vireos

	Montana	Wyoming	Utah	Colorado	Arizona	New Mexico	North Dakota	South Dakota	Nebraska	Kansas	Oklahoma
White-eyed Vireo			xV	xV	xV	xV	xV	xV	lrS	uS	fS
Thick-billed Vireo											
Bell's Vireo		xV	lrS.xV	luS.xV	fS.xW	fS	lrS	fS	fS	fS	fS
Black-capped Vireo					xV	xV			eS*	eS	lrS
Gray Vireo		xS*	uS	uS	uS.lrW	uS					exS.xV
Solitary Vireo	fS	fS	fS	fS	cS.uW	cS.rW	lrS†.uT	lfS.uT	luS.uT	uT	uT
Yellow-throated Vireo			xV	xV-q	rV	rV	xV	uS	lrS	luS	lrS.uT	uS

Family Ptilogonatidae: Silky-flycatchers

	Texas	Minnesota	Iowa	Missouri	Arkansas	Louisiana	Wisconsin	Michigan	Illinois	Indiana	Ohio
Phainopepla	IuP.rV										

Family Laniidae: Shrikes
Subfamily Laniinae: Typical Shrikes

	Texas	Minnesota	Iowa	Missouri	Arkansas	Louisiana	Wisconsin	Michigan	Illinois	Indiana	Ohio
Brown Shrike											
Northern Shrike	irW	ifW	iuW	irW			iuW	iuW	irW	irW	irW
Loggerhead Shrike	fS.cW	uS	uS.rW	fS.uW	uS.fW	fS.cW	uS.xW	rP	fS.uW	uS.rW	rP

Family Sturnidae: Starlings and Allies
Subfamily Sturninae: Starlings

	Texas	Minnesota	Iowa	Missouri	Arkansas	Louisiana	Wisconsin	Michigan	Illinois	Indiana	Ohio
European Starling											

Family Meliphagidae: Honeyeaters

	Texas	Minnesota	Iowa	Missouri	Arkansas	Louisiana	Wisconsin	Michigan	Illinois	Indiana	Ohio
Kauai Oo											
Oahu Oo											
Bishop's Oo											
Hawaii Oo											
Kioea											

Family Vireonidae: Vireos
Subfamily Vireoninae: Typical Vireos

	Texas	Minnesota	Iowa	Missouri	Arkansas	Louisiana	Wisconsin	Michigan	Illinois	Indiana	Ohio
White-eyed Vireo	cS.uW	xV	rS	fS	cS.xW	cS.uW	lrS	luS.xV	fS	fS	fS
Thick-billed Vireo											
Bell's Vireo	fS.cT.xW	lrS.rV	uS	fS	uS	lrS.rT.xW	luS	lrS	uS	rS	xS.rT
Black-capped Vireo	lfS.rT										
Gray Vireo	luS.xW						xV				
Solitary Vireo	lfS.fW	fS	fT	fT.xW	fT.rW	fW	uS.fT	uS.fT	xS.fT	xS.fT	rS.fT
Yellow-throated Vireo	fS.xW	fS	uS.fT	fS	fS	fS.xW	fS	fS	fS	fS	fS

Family Ptilogonatidae: Silky-flycatchers

	West Virginia	Kentucky	Tennessee	Mississippi	Alabama	Maine	New Hampshire	Vermont	Massachusetts	Rhode Island	Connecticut
Phainopepla									xV	xV	

Family Laniidae: Shrikes
Subfamily Laniinae: Typical Shrikes

	West Virginia	Kentucky	Tennessee	Mississippi	Alabama	Maine	New Hampshire	Vermont	Massachusetts	Rhode Island	Connecticut
Brown Shrike											
Northern Shrike	xV,xW	exW	xV			ifW	ifW	ifW	iuW	irW	iuW
Loggerhead Shrike	rP	uP	uP	uS,fW	uP	eS,rS*,rV	eS,rV	lrS,rV	eS,rT,xW	rW	eS,rW

Family Sturnidae: Starlings and Allies
Subfamily Sturninae: Starlings

	West Virginia	Kentucky	Tennessee	Mississippi	Alabama	Maine	New Hampshire	Vermont	Massachusetts	Rhode Island	Connecticut
European Starling											

Family Meliphagidae: Honeyeaters

	West Virginia	Kentucky	Tennessee	Mississippi	Alabama	Maine	New Hampshire	Vermont	Massachusetts	Rhode Island	Connecticut
Kauai Oo											
Oahu Oo											
Bishop's Oo											
Hawaii Oo											
Kioea											

Family Vireonidae: Vireos
Subfamily Vireoninae: Typical Vireos

	West Virginia	Kentucky	Tennessee	Mississippi	Alabama	Maine	New Hampshire	Vermont	Massachusetts	Rhode Island	Connecticut
White-eyed Vireo	fS	cS	cS,xW	cS,uW	cS,uW	rV	rV	rV	luS,uT	uS	fS
Thick-billed Vireo											
Bell's Vireo		xS,xT	xS,xT	rT	rV			exV			
Black-capped Vireo				xV							
Gray Vireo											
Solitary Vireo	fS	lfS,fT	lfS,fT	fT,uW	lrS†,fT,uW	fS	fS	fS	uS	uS	luS,uT
Yellow-throated Vireo	fS	fS	fS	fS	fS,xW	uS	uS	uS	uS	uS	uS

Family Ptilogonatidae: Silky-flycatchers

	New York	Pennsylvania	New Jersey	Delaware	Maryland	Dist. of Columbia	Virginia	North Carolina	South Carolina	Georgia	Florida
Phainopepla											

Family Laniidae: Shrikes
Subfamily Laniinae: Typical Shrikes

	New York	Pennsylvania	New Jersey	Delaware	Maryland	Dist. of Columbia	Virginia	North Carolina	South Carolina	Georgia	Florida
Brown Shrike											
Northern Shrike	ifW	irW	irW	xV.xW	xV.xW		xV.xW	xV			
Loggerhead Shrike	rP	eS.rW	exS.rW	xS*.rW	rP	eS.rT.xW	uP	uP	uP	uP	fP

Family Sturnidae: Starlings and Allies
Subfamily Sturninae: Starlings

	New York	Pennsylvania	New Jersey	Delaware	Maryland	Dist. of Columbia	Virginia	North Carolina	South Carolina	Georgia	Florida
European Starling											

Family Meliphagidae: Honeyeaters

	New York	Pennsylvania	New Jersey	Delaware	Maryland	Dist. of Columbia	Virginia	North Carolina	South Carolina	Georgia	Florida
Kauai Oo											
Oahu Oo											
Bishop's Oo											
Hawaii Oo											
Kioea											

Family Vireonidae: Vireos
Subfamily Vireoninae: Typical Vireos

	New York	Pennsylvania	New Jersey	Delaware	Maryland	Dist. of Columbia	Virginia	North Carolina	South Carolina	Georgia	Florida
White-eyed Vireo	luS.xV	fS	cS	fS	cS.xW	rS.fT	cS.rW	cS.rW	cS.uW	cS.uW	cS.fW
Thick-billed Vireo											xV.xW
Bell's Vireo	xV		xV				xV-q	xV-q		xV	rV.rW
Black-capped Vireo											
Gray Vireo											
Solitary Vireo	fS	uS.fT	luS.fT.xW	uT	luS.fT	uT	fS.xW	fS.uW	luS.fT.uW	uS.fT.uW	fW
Yellow-throated Vireo	uS	fS	fS	fS	fS	rS.uT	fS	fS	fS	fS.xW	fS.rW

	Date	Location	Cont. North America	Canada	Lower 48
Hutton's Vireo *Vireo huttoni*			lfP,xV	luP	lfP,xV
Warbling Vireo *Vireo gilvus*			cS,xW	cS	cS,xW
Philadelphia Vireo *Vireo philadelphicus*			uS,xW	fS	luS,uT,xW
Red-eyed Vireo *Vireo olivaceus*			cS	cS	cS
Black-whiskered Vireo *Vireo altiloquus*			lcS,xS*,rV		lcS,xS*,rV
Yucatan Vireo *Vireo magister*			xV		xV

Family Emberizidae: Emberizids
Subfamily Parulinae: Wood-Warblers

	Date	Location	Cont. North America	Canada	Lower 48
Bachman's Warbler *Vermivora bachmani*			eS,lrS*,xV,exW		eS,lrS*,rT,exW
Blue-winged Warbler *Vermivora pinus*			uS,xW	luS,rV	fS,xW
Golden-winged Warbler *Vermivora chrysoptera*			luS,uT	luS,xV	uS
Tennessee Warbler *Vermivora peregrina*			cS,lrW	cS	lcS,cT,lrW
Orange-crowned Warbler *Vermivora celata*			cS,fW	fS,cT,lrW	fS,cT,fW
Nashville Warbler *Vermivora ruficapilla*			cS,luW	cS,xW	fS,cT,luW
Virginia's Warbler *Vermivora virginiae*			lcS,rV,xW	xV	fS,xW
Colima Warbler *Vermivora crissalis*			lfS,xV		lfS,xV
Lucy's Warbler *Vermivora luciae*			lcS,rV,xW		lcS,rV,xW
Northern Parula *Parula americana*			cS,lfW	fS	cS,lfW
Tropical Parula *Parula pitiayumi*			lrP,xS*,xV		lrP,xS*,xV
Crescent-chested Warbler *Parula superciliosa*			xS,xV		xS,xV
Yellow Warbler *Dendroica petechia*			cS,luW	cS,xW	cS,luW
Chestnut-sided Warbler *Dendroica pensylvanica*			cS,lrW	cS	fS,cT,lrW
Magnolia Warbler *Dendroica magnolia*			cS,lrW	cS	fS,cT,lrW
Cape May Warbler *Dendroica tigrina*			ifS,rW	ifS,xW	lifS,fT,rW

	Hawaii	Alaska	Yukon Terr.	Northwest Terr.	British Columbia	Alberta	Saskatchewan	Manitoba	Ontario
Hutton's Vireo					luP				
Warbling Vireo		luS	lrS	luS	cS	cS	cS	cS	cS
Philadelphia Vireo		xV		xS*,xV	luS,xV	uS	uS	uS,fT	fS
Red-eyed Vireo		xS*,rV		luS	cS	cS	cS	cS	cS
Black-whiskered Vireo									
Yucatan Vireo									

Family Emberizidae: Emberizids
Subfamily Parulinae: Wood-Warblers

	Hawaii	Alaska	Yukon Terr.	Northwest Terr.	British Columbia	Alberta	Saskatchewan	Manitoba	Ontario
Bachman's Warbler									
Blue-winged Warbler							xV		luS
Golden-winged Warbler							xV	lrS	luS
Tennessee Warbler		lrS	uS	cS	fS	fS	cS	cS	cS
Orange-crowned Warbler		cS	fS	fS	cS,rW	fS,cT	fS,cT	fS,cT	uS
Nashville Warbler		xV-q			luS,rT	lrS,xV	uS†	cS	cS
Virginia's Warbler									xV
Colima Warbler									
Lucy's Warbler									
Northern Parula						xS*,xV	rV	luS	uS
Tropical Parula									
Crescent-chested Warbler									
Yellow Warbler		cS	cS	cS	cS	cS	cS	cS	cS,xW
Chestnut-sided Warbler		xV-q			xS*,xV	luS	fS	fS	cS
Magnolia Warbler		rV		uS	fS	uS	fS	fS	cS
Cape May Warbler		xV	xS	liuS	liuS	iuS	iuS†	iuS	ifS

	Québec	Newfoundland	New Brunswick	Prince Edward I.	Nova Scotia	Washington	Oregon	California	Nevada	Idaho
Hutton's Vireo						fP	fP	fP	xV	
Warbling Vireo	lfS	xV	uS		rV	cS	cS	cS,xW	cS	cS
Philadelphia Vireo	fS	rS	uS	rS*,rT	rT			rV,xW	xV	
Red-eyed Vireo	cS	luS	cS	cS	cS	fS	uS	rV	rV	fS
Black-whiskered Vireo										
Yucatan Vireo										

Family Emberizidae: Emberizids
Subfamily Parulinae: Wood-Warblers

	Québec	Newfoundland	New Brunswick	Prince Edward I.	Nova Scotia	Washington	Oregon	California	Nevada	Idaho
Bachman's Warbler										
Blue-winged Warbler	xV	xV	xV		rV			xV		
Golden-winged Warbler	lrS		xV		xV		rV	rV		xV
Tennessee Warbler	cS	fS	cS	fS	fS	xV	rV	uV,rW	rV	xV
Orange-crowned Warbler	uS	uS	rT		rT,xW	cS,rW	cS,rW	cS,fW	fS,cT,rW	fS,cT,rW
Nashville Warbler	cS	lrS,rT	cS,xW	uS†	fS	fS,xW	fS,xW	fS,rW	luS,uT	uS
Virginia's Warbler							xV	luS,rV,xW	fS	luS
Colima Warbler										
Lucy's Warbler								luS,rV,xW	lfS	
Northern Parula	uS	rS*,rV	cS	fS	fS	xV	xS*,xV	xS,rV,rW	rV	
Tropical Parula										
Crescent-chested Warbler										
Yellow Warbler	cS	cS	cS	cS	cS	cS	cS	cS,rW	cS	cS
Chestnut-sided Warbler	cS	xV	fS	fS	cS	xV	rV	rV,xW	rV	xV
Magnolia Warbler	cS	fS	cS	cS	cS	xV	rV	rV,xW	xV	xV
Cape May Warbler	lfS	rS*,rV	lfS	iuS	iuS,fT,xW	xV	xV	rV,xW	xV	xV

	Montana	Wyoming	Utah	Colorado	Arizona	New Mexico	North Dakota	South Dakota	Nebraska	Kansas	Oklahoma
Hutton's Vireo					fP	luS.lrW					
Warbling Vireo	cS	cS	cS	cS	cS.xW	cS	cS	cS	cS	cS	fS
Philadelphia Vireo	xV	rV		rV	rV	xV	lrS.rT	rT	rT	rT	rT
Red-eyed Vireo	cS	fS	rV	uS	xS*.rV	uV	cS	cS	cS	cS	cS
Black-whiskered Vireo											
Yucatan Vireo											

Family Emberizidae: Emberizids
Subfamily Parulinae: Wood-Warblers

	Montana	Wyoming	Utah	Colorado	Arizona	New Mexico	North Dakota	South Dakota	Nebraska	Kansas	Oklahoma
Bachman's Warbler											exV-q
Blue-winged Warbler			xV-q	rV	xV	xV	xV	rV	xS*.rT	rT	xS.rT
Golden-winged Warbler				rV	xS*.xV	xV	lrS	rT	rT	rT	rT
Tennessee Warbler	lrS.uT	uT	rV	xS*.uT	rV	rV	cT	cT	cT	cT	fT
Orange-crowned Warbler	fS.cT	fS.cT	fS.cT.rW	uS.cT.xW	uS.cT.fW	uS.cT.rW	lrSt.cT	cT	cT.xW	cT.rW	cT.uW
Nashville Warbler	luS.rT	rT	uT	uT	fT.xW	uT	uT	fT	fT	cT.xW	cT
Virginia's Warbler		luS.rV	fS	fS	cS	cS			xV	xV	lrT
Colima Warbler											
Lucy's Warbler			lfS.xV	exS	cS	fS					
Northern Parula	xV	rV		rV	xS*.rV.xW	xS.rV	lrSt.rT	uT	uT	lfS.fT	fS
Tropical Parula					xS*						
Crescent-chested Warbler					xS.xV						
Yellow Warbler	cS	cS	cS	cS	cS.rW	cS	cS	cS	cS	fS.cT	fS.cT
Chestnut-sided Warbler	xV	rV	xV-q	xS.rV	rV.xW	rV	lrS.fT	fT	xS.uT	uT	uT
Magnolia Warbler	rV	rV	xV	rV	rV.xW	rV	fT	fT	uT	uT	uT
Cape May Warbler	xV	xV		rV	xV.xW	xV	uT	rT	rT	rT	rT

Vireonidae

	Texas	Minnesota	Iowa	Missouri	Arkansas	Louisiana	Wisconsin	Michigan	Illinois	Indiana	Ohio
Hutton's Vireo	lfS,luW										
Warbling Vireo	uS,cT,xW	cS	cS	cS	uS	uS,fT	cS	cS	cS	fS	fS
Philadelphia Vireo	uT,xW	luS,uT	uT	uT	uT	fT,xW	uT	rS,uT	fT	fT	uT
Red-eyed Vireo	fS,cT	cS	cS	cS	cS	cS	cS	cS	cS	cS	cS
Black-whiskered Vireo	xV					xS*,xV					
Yucatan Vireo	xV										

Family Emberizidae: Emberizids
Subfamily Parulinae: Wood-Warblers

	Texas	Minnesota	Iowa	Missouri	Arkansas	Louisiana	Wisconsin	Michigan	Illinois	Indiana	Ohio
Bachman's Warbler				eS	eS	eS*,xT				exV	
Blue-winged Warbler	fT	luS,uT	uS	uS	luS,fT	fT	uS	uS	uS	fS	fS
Golden-winged Warbler	uT	fS	eS,uT	uT	uT	uT	fS	uS	lrS,uT	lrS,uT	rS,uT
Tennessee Warbler	cT,rW	fS,cT	cT	cT	cT	cT	lrS,cT	luS,cT	cT	cT	cT
Orange-crowned Warbler	luS,cW	xS*,fT	fT	fT,xW	fT,rW	cW	fT	fT,xW	fT,xW	fT,xW	uT,xW
Nashville Warbler	cT,uW	cS	cT	cT,xW	cT	fT	cS	fS,cT	xS,cT,xW	cT	exS,cT
Virginia's Warbler	lrS,uT								xV		
Colima Warbler	lfS,xV										
Lucy's Warbler	lrS,xV					xV					
Northern Parula	cS,rW	fS	lrS,uT	cS	cS	cS,xW	uS	uS	fS,xW	fS	uS
Tropical Parula	lrP					xV					
Crescent-chested Warbler	xV-q										
Yellow Warbler	fS,cT,xW	cS	cS	fS,cT	uS,cT	cT,xW	cS	cS	fS,cT	fS,cT	fS,cT
Chestnut-sided Warbler	cT,xW	cS	lrS,cT	xS,cT	cT	cT	cS	fS,cT	lrS,cT	lrS,cT	rS,cT
Magnolia Warbler	cT,xW	fS,cT	cT	cT	fT	cT,xW	uS,cT	fS,cT	cT	cT	lrS,cT
Cape May Warbler	rT,xW	ifS,fT	rT	rT,xW	rT	rT	iuS,fT	iuS,fT,xW	uT,xW	fT,xW	fT

	West Virginia	Kentucky	Tennessee	Mississippi	Alabama	Maine	New Hampshire	Vermont	Massachusetts	Rhode Island	Connecticut
Hutton's Vireo											
Warbling Vireo	fS	fS	uS	uS,fT	lrS,rT	fS	fS	fS	fS	uS	fS
Philadelphia Vireo	uT	fT	fT	fT	uT	uS	uS	rS,uT	uT	rT	rT
Red-eyed Vireo	cS	cS	cS	cS	cS	cS	cS	cS	cS	cS	cS
Black-whiskered Vireo				xV	rV						
Yucatan Vireo											

Family Emberizidae: Emberizids
Subfamily Parulinae: Wood-Warblers

	West Virginia	Kentucky	Tennessee	Mississippi	Alabama	Maine	New Hampshire	Vermont	Massachusetts	Rhode Island	Connecticut
Bachman's Warbler		eS		eS*,xT	eS,xT						
Blue-winged Warbler	fS	uS,fT	uS,fT	fT	uS	rS	rS	rS	uS	fS	fS
Golden-winged Warbler	fS	xS,uT	luS,uT	uT	uT	xS*,rV	rS	uS	rS	eS,rT	lrS,rT
Tennessee Warbler	cT	cT	cT,xW	cT	cT	cS	uS,cT	rS,cT	fT	uT	fT
Orange-crowned Warbler	uT	uT,xW	uT,rW	fW	uW	rT	rT	rT	rW	rT,xW	rW
Nashville Warbler	lrS,cT	cT,xW	cT	fT	uT	cS	fS	fS	uS,fT	luS,uT	rS,fT
Virginia's Warbler											
Colima Warbler											
Lucy's Warbler									xV		
Northern Parula	uS,fT	uS,fT	fS	cS	cS,xW	cS	fS	uS	rS,fT	eS,fT	uS,fT
Tropical Parula											
Crescent-chested Warbler											
Yellow Warbler	cS	fS,cT	uS,cT	cT	uS,cT	cS	cS	cS	fS,cT	fS	cS
Chestnut-sided Warbler	fS,cT	lfS,cT	lfS,cT	cT,xW	xS*,cT	cS	cS	cS	cS	fS	fS
Magnolia Warbler	fS	cT	cT	cT,xW	cT	cS	fS,cT	fS,cT	fS,cT	fT	rS,fT
Cape May Warbler	fT,xW	fT	fT,xW	rT	uT	ifS	iuS,fT	lrS,fT	fT	fT	fT

Vireonidae • 307

	New York	Pennsylvania	New Jersey	Delaware	Maryland	Dist. of Columbia	Virginia	North Carolina	South Carolina	Georgia	Florida
Hutton's Vireo											
Warbling Vireo	fS	fS	fS	rS	uS	uS	uS	lrS,rT	xT	rT	rT
Philadelphia Vireo	lrS,uT	uT	uT	uT	uT	rT	rT	rT	rT	rT	rT
Red-eyed Vireo	cS	cS	cS	cS	cS	cS	cS	cS	cS	cS	fS,cT
Black-whiskered Vireo								xV			cS
Yucatan Vireo											

Family Emberizidae: Emberizids
Subfamily Parulinae: Wood-Warblers

	New York	Pennsylvania	New Jersey	Delaware	Maryland	Dist. of Columbia	Virginia	North Carolina	South Carolina	Georgia	Florida
Bachman's Warbler						xS*,xV	exV	eS,lrS*,xT	eS,xT		xT,exW
Blue-winged Warbler	fS,xW	fS	fS	lfS,fT	uS,fT	fT	luS,fT	luS,uT	xS*,uT	luS,uT	uT,xW
Golden-winged Warbler	uS	uS	lrS,rT	rT	lfS,uT	rT	lfS,uT	lfS,uT	eS,uT	luS,uT	rT
Tennessee Warbler	luS,cT,xW	cT	cT	uT	fT,xW	cT	fT	fT,xW	fT	fT	uT,rW
Orange-crowned Warbler	uT,rW	uT,xW	rW	rT,xW	rW	rT	rW	uW	uW	uW	fW
Nashville Warbler	fS,cT,xW	uS,cT,xW	lrS,uT	uT	luS,fT	fT	lrS*,fT,xW	uT	rT	uT	uT,rW
Virginia's Warbler			xV								
Colima Warbler											
Lucy's Warbler											
Northern Parula	uS,fT	fS	uS,fT	fS	fS,cT	fT	cS,xW	cS,xW	cS,xW	cS,rW	cS,fW
Tropical Parula											
Crescent-chested Warbler											
Yellow Warbler	cS	cS	cS	fS	cS	uS,fT	cS	cS	uS,cT	uS,cT	lfS,cT,uW
Chestnut-sided Warbler	cS	fS,cT	uS,fT	xS*,uT	fS,cT	fT	fS,cT	lcS,fT	lrS,fT	lfS,fT	uT,rW
Magnolia Warbler	fS,cT	fS,cT	lrS,cT	fT	lfS,cT	fT	lfS,cT	xS*,cT	fT	fT	uT,rW
Cape May Warbler	lrS,fT,xW	fT,xW	fT	fT	fT,xW	fT	fT,xW	fT,xW	fT,xW	fT	fT,rW

Emberizidae • 309

		Date	Location	Cont. North America	Canada	Lower 48
Black-throated Blue Warbler *Dendroica caerulescens*				fS,lrW	fS	fS,lrW
Yellow-rumped Warbler *Dendroica coronata*				cP	cS,rW	cP
Black-throated Gray Warbler *Dendroica nigrescens*				fS,luW	lfS,xS*,rV,xW	fS,luW
Townsend's Warbler *Dendroica townsendi*				cS,lfW	cS,lrW	lcS,cT,lfW
Hermit Warbler *Dendroica occidentalis*				lcS,rV,lrW	xV	lcS,fT,lrW
Black-throated Green Warbler *Dendroica virens*				cS,lrW	cS	fS,cT,lrW
Golden-cheeked Warbler *Dendroica chrysoparia*				lfS,xV		lfS,xV
Blackburnian Warbler *Dendroica fusca*				cS,xW	cS,xW	fS,cT,xW
Yellow-throated Warbler *Dendroica dominica*				cS,lfW	rV	cS,lfW
Grace's Warbler *Dendroica graciae*				lcS,xS*,xV,xW		lcS,xS*,xV,xW
Pine Warbler *Dendroica pinus*				cS,fW	luS,xS*,rV,lrW	cP
Kirtland's Warbler *Dendroica kirtlandi*				luS,rT	xS*,lrT	luS,rT
Prairie Warbler *Dendroica discolor*				fS,lfW	luS,rV	cS,lfW
Palm Warbler *Dendroica palmarum*				fS,cT,fW	fS,lrW	lfS,cT,fW
Bay-breasted Warbler *Dendroica castanea*				ifS,fT,xW	ifS	lifS,fT,xW
Blackpoll Warbler *Dendroica striata*				cS	cS	lfS,cT
Cerulean Warbler *Dendroica cerulea*				uS	luS,xV	fS
Black-and-white Warbler *Mniotilta varia*				fS,cT,lfW	cS,xW	fS,cT,uW
American Redstart *Setophaga ruticilla*				cS,luW	cS	cS,luW
Prothonotary Warbler *Protonotaria citrea*				fS,lrW	luS,rV	cS,lrW
Worm-eating Warbler *Helmitheros vermivorus*				uS,lrW	rV	uS,lrW
Swainson's Warbler *Limnothlypis swainsonii*				uS,xW	xV	uS,xW
Ovenbird *Seiurus aurocapillus*				cS,uW	cS	cS,uW
Northern Waterthrush *Seiurus noveboracensis*				cS,rW	cS,xW	fS,cT,rW

	Hawaii	Alaska	Yukon Terr.	Northwest Terr.	British Columbia	Alberta	Saskatchewan	Manitoba	Ontario
Black-thr. Blue Warbler				xV	xV	xV	xS*,rV	rV	fS
Yellow-rumped Warbler		cS,xW	cS	cS	cS,uW	cS	cS,xW	cS	cS,rW
Black-thr. Gray Warbler					lfS,fT	xS*,xV	xV		xV,xW
Townsend's Warbler		fS	uS		cS,rW	luS,rT	xS,xV-q		xV
Hermit Warbler		xV-q							xV
Black-thr. Green Warbler		xV		xS*	lrS	uS	fS†	fS	cS
Golden-cheeked Warbler									
Blackburnian Warbler					xV	lrS	fS	cS	cS,xW
Yellow-throated Warbler							xV-q		rV
Grace's Warbler									
Pine Warbler						xS*,xV	rV	luS	uS,rW
Kirtland's Warbler									xS*,lrT
Prairie Warbler									luS
Palm Warbler		xV-q	xV	lcS	luS,rV,xW	uS	cS	fS	uS,xW
Bay-breasted Warbler		xV		liuS	lrS†	iuS	iuS	iuS	ifS
Blackpoll Warbler		cS	cS	cS	fS	fS	fS,cT	cS	fS,cT
Cerulean Warbler								exV	luS
Black-and-white Warbler		xV		lfS	luS,xV	fS	fS	fS	cS,xW
American Redstart		luS	lrS†	lfS	cS	cS	cS	cS	cS
Prothonotary Warbler							xV-q		luS
Worm-eating Warbler							xV-q		rV
Swainson's Warbler									
Ovenbird		xV		lfS	uS	fS	cS	cS	cS
Northern Waterthrush		fS	fS	fS	fS,xW	fS	fS	fS	cS

Emberizidae • 311

	Québec	Newfoundland	New Brunswick	Prince Edward I.	Nova Scotia	Washington	Oregon	California	Nevada	Idaho
Black-thr. Blue Warbler	fS	xV	fS	uS	uS		xS*,rV	rV,xW	rV,xW	xV
Yellow-rumped Warbler	cS,rW	cS,rW	cS,rW	cS	cS,rW	cS,fW	cP	cP	cS,uW	cS,rW
Black-thr. Gray Warbler	xV				xV	cS	cS,xW	fS,cT,rW	fS	lfS
Townsend's Warbler		xV			xV	cS,rW	uS,cT,uW	cT,fW	fT	fS
Hermit Warbler	xV				xV	lfS	cS,xW	cS,rW	lrS,uT	
Black-thr. Green Warbler	cS	cS	cS	cS	cS	xV	xV	xS*,rV,xW	xV	
Golden-cheeked Warbler								xV		
Blackburnian Warbler	cS	rS	cS	fS	uS	xV		rV	xV	
Yellow-throated Warbler	xV	xV	xV	xV	rV			xS,rV,xW	xV	xV
Grace's Warbler								xS*,xV,xW	luS	
Pine Warbler	luS,xW	xV	rV,xW	xV	rV,rW			xV,xW	xV	
Kirtland's Warbler	xS*									
Prairie Warbler	xV	xV	rV		rV		xV	xS*,rV,xW		
Palm Warbler	uS	uS,xW	fS	uS	uS,cT,rW	rV,rW	rV,rW	uV,rW	xV	xV
Bay-breasted Warbler	ifS	rS†	ifS	iuS	iuS,fT		xS*,xV	rV,xW	xV	xV
Blackpoll Warbler	cS	cS	fS,cT	rS*,cT	uS,cT	xV-q	xS,rV	uV	rV	xV
Cerulean Warbler	lrS		xV		xV			rV	xV	
Black-and-white Warbler	cS	fS,xW	cS	fS	cS	rV,xW	rV,xW	xS*,uV,rW	rV	xV
American Redstart	cS	fS	cS	cS	cS	fS	lrS,rT,xW	xS,uT,rW	uT	uS
Prothonotary Warbler	xV	xV	xV		rV	xV	xV	rV,xW	xV	
Worm-eating Warbler	xV		xV		rV			xS*,rV,xW	xV	
Swainson's Warbler					xV					
Ovenbird	cS	fS	cS	cS	fS	xV	xV	rV,xW	rV	xV
Northern Waterthrush	cS	cS	cS	uS†	cS	luS,rT	lrS,rT	uT,rW	rT	luS,rT

	Montana	Wyoming	Utah	Colorado	Arizona	New Mexico	North Dakota	South Dakota	Nebraska	Kansas	Oklahoma
Black-thr. Blue Warbler	xV	rV	xV	rV	rV,xW	rV	rV	rV	rV	rV	rV
Yellow-rumped Warbler	cS,xW	cS,xW	cS,rW	cS,rW	cP	cS,fW	luS,cT	lfS,cT,xW	xS,cT,xW	cT,rW	cT,fW
Black-thr. Gray Warbler	xV	fS	fS	fS	cS,uW	fS	xV-q	xV	rV	rV	lrT
Townsend's Warbler	fS	exS,rS*,uT	uT	uT	cT,rW	fT	xV	xV	rV	rV	lrT,xV
Hermit Warbler				xV	xV	cT,xW	rT			xV	xV
Black-thr. Green Warbler	xV	xV		rV	rV,xW	rV	uT	uT	uT	uT	uT
Golden-cheeked Warbler											
Blackburnian Warbler	xV	rV		rV	rV	xV	uT	uT	uT	uT	uT
Yellow-throated Warbler	xW	xV	xV	rV	xV,xW	xV			xV	rV	lrS,rT	uS
Grace's Warbler			uS	lfS	cS	fS					
Pine Warbler	xV			rV		xV	rV	rV	rT	rT	lfS,luW
Kirtland's Warbler											
Prairie Warbler	xV			xV	xV,xW	xV		xV	xS*,xV	eS,rT	uS
Palm Warbler	rV	xV	xV	rV	rV,xW	rV	fT	fT	uT	rT	rT
Bay-breasted Warbler	xV	xV	xV	xS,rV	rV	rV	uT	uT	uT	rT	rT
Blackpoll Warbler	uT	uT	xV	uT	rV	rV	cT	fT	fT	fT	uT
Cerulean Warbler				xV	xV		xS*,xV	xV	lrS,rT	xS,rT	lrS,uT
Black-and-white Warbler	lrS,rT	uT	rT	uT	xS*,rT,rW	uT	uS,fT	rS,fT	rS,fT	uS,fT	fS,cT
American Redstart	fS	fS	rS	fS	lrS,uT,rW	xS*,uT	fS,cT	fS	uS,fT	uS,fT	lrS,fT
Prothonotary Warbler		xV		rV	rV	rV	xV	eS†,rV	lrS	luS,rT	uS
Worm-eating Warbler		xV		rV	rV,xW	rV	xV	xV	xS*,rT	exS*,rT	lrS,rT
Swainson's Warbler				xV	xV				xV	xV	lrS
Ovenbird	uS	fS	xV	uS	rV,xW	rT	uS,fT	uS,fT	uS	luS,uT	luS,uT
Northern Waterthrush	fS	xS*,uT	rT	uT	rT,xW	uT,xW	lfS,fT	fT	xS*,uT	uT	uT

Emberizidae • 313

	Texas	Minnesota	Iowa	Missouri	Arkansas	Louisiana	Wisconsin	Michigan	Illinois	Indiana	Ohio
Black-thr. Blue Warbler	rV,xW	uS	rT	rT	rT	rT	uS	uS,fT	uT	fT,xW	exS,fT
Yellow-rumped Warbler	lcS,cW	cS,xW	cT,rW	cT,uW	cW	cW	fS,cT,rW	fS,cT,rW	cT,uW	cT,uW	cT,uW
Black-thr. Gray Warbler	xS*,uT,rW	xV	xV			rV,xW	xV	xV	xV	xV-q	xV
Townsend's Warbler	lfT,rV,rW	xV	xV			xV			xV	xV-q	xV
Hermit Warbler	lrT,xV,xW	xV		xV		xV	xV				
Black-thr. Green Warbler	cT,rW	fS,cT	cT	cT	cT	cT	fS,cT	fS,cT	rS*,cT,xW	xS,cT	uS,cT
Golden-cheeked Warbler	lfS,rT										
Blackburnian Warbler	fT	cS	fT	fT	fT	fT	fS,cT	fS,cT	cT	cT	lrS,cT
Yellow-throated Warbler	fS,uW	xV	lrS,rT	fS	cS	cS,rW	xS*,rV	lrS,rV	uS	uS	uS,xW
Grace's Warbler	lrS,xV										
Pine Warbler	cP	uS	rT	luS,rT,xW	cP	cP	uS,xW	uS,xW	lrS,rT,xW	lrS,rT	rS,xW
Kirtland's Warbler		xV		xV			xS*,xV	luS	xV	xT	rT
Prairie Warbler	luS,uT,xW	xV	xS*,rT	uS	fS	fS,xW	lrS	rS	uS	fS	uS
Palm Warbler	uW	lfS,cT	cT	fT,xW	fT,rW	fW	lrS,cT	luS,cT	cT,xW	cT,rW	fT,xW
Bay-breasted Warbler	fT,xW	iuS,fT	fT	uT	uT	fT	fT	lrS,fT	cT	cT	cT
Blackpoll Warbler	uT	cT	cT	cT	fT	fT	cT	xS*,cT	cT	cT	cT
Cerulean Warbler	luS,uT	uS	uS	uS	uS	uS,fT	uS	uS	fS	fS	fS
Black-and-white Warbler	fS,cT,uW	fS,cT	rS,cT	uS,cT	fS,cT	uS,cT,rW	fS,cT	fS,cT	rS,cT	uS,cT	uS,cT
American Redstart	luS,cT,rW	cS	fS,cT	fS,cT	fS,cT	fS,cT,xW	cS	cS	fS,cT	fS,cT	fS,cT
Prothonotary Warbler	uS,fT	luS,rT	uS	fS	fS	cS,xW	uS	uS	fS,xW	fS	uS
Worm-eating Warbler	lrS,uT	rV	lrS	uS	uS	rS,uT	xS,rV	lrS*,rV	uS	uS	uS
Swainson's Warbler	lrS,uT			lrS	uS	fS			lrS,xV		xS*,xV
Ovenbird	cT,rW	cS	fS,cT	fS	fS	cT,xW	cS,xW	cS	fS,cT,xW	fS,cT	fS,cT,xW
Northern Waterthrush	cT,rW	fS	fT	fT	uT	cT,rW	uS,fT,xW	fS	fT	xS,fT	lrS,fT

	West Virginia	Kentucky	Tennessee	Mississippi	Alabama	Maine	New Hampshire	Vermont	Massachusetts	Rhode Island	Connecticut
Black-thr. Blue Warbler	fS	lfS,uT,xW	lfS,uT	rT	rT	fS	fS	fS	uS,fT	luS,fT	uS,fT
Yellow-rumped Warbler	lrS,cT,uW	cT,fW	cT,fW	cW	cW	cS,rW	cS,rW	fS,cT,rW	uS,cT,fW	rS,cT,fW	lrS,cT,uW
Black-thr. Gray Warbler			xV	xV	xV	xV-q	xV-q		xV	xS*,xV	xV-q
Townsend's Warbler				xV			xV		xV		
Hermit Warbler									xV		xV-q
Black-thr. Green Warbler	fS,cT	uS,cT	uS,cT	cT	uS,cT	cS	fS,cT	fS,cT	fS	uS,fT	fS
Golden-cheeked Warbler											
Blackburnian Warbler	fS,cT	luS,fT	luS,fT	cT	xS*,cT	cS	cS	fS	fS	lrS,uT	uS,fT
Yellow-throated Warbler	uS	fS	fS	cS,lrW	cS,lrW	xV	xV,xW	xV	rV	xS*,rV	xS*,rV
Grace's Warbler											
Pine Warbler	uS,rW	uS,rW	fS,uW	cP	cP	fS,xW	fS	uS	fS,rW	fS,rW	uS,fT,xW
Kirtland's Warbler	xT	xT			xV-q						
Prairie Warbler	uS	fS	fS	fS,xW	cS,xW	luS,rV	uS	luS	fS	fS	fS
Palm Warbler	fT	cT,rW	cT,uW	fT,uW	cT,fW	fS,xW	xS,fT,xW	uT	fT,rW	fT,rW	fT,rW
Bay-breasted Warbler	xS,cT,xW	fT	fT	fT	fT	ifS	iuS,fT	rS,fT	fT	uT	fT
Blackpoll Warbler	cT	cT	cT	cT	cT	fS,cT	fS,cT	fS,cT	lrS,cT	cT	cT
Cerulean Warbler	fS	fS	fS	rS†,fT	uS	rV	xV	lrS	xS*,rT	lrS*	rS
Black-and-white Warbler	fS,cT	fS,cT	fS,cT	uS,cT,rW	uS,cT,rW	cS	cS	fS,cT	fS,cT	fS,cT	fS,cT,xW
American Redstart	fS,cT	fS,cT,xW	fS,cT	fS,cT,xW	fS,cT	cS	cS	cS	cS	fS,cT	fS,cT
Prothonotary Warbler	lrS,rT	fS	fS	cS	cS	rV	xV	xV	xS,rV	rV	exS,rV
Worm-eating Warbler	fS	fS	uS	uS	uS	xS*,xV	xV	xV	rS	rS	uS
Swainson's Warbler	uS	uS	uS	uS	uS				xV		xV-q
Ovenbird	cS	fS,cT,xW	cS,xW	luS,cT	fS,cT	cS,xW	cS	cS,xW	cS	cS	cS
Northern Waterthrush	fS	fT	fT	cT	cT	cS	fS	fS	uS,cT	uS,fT	luS,cT,xW

Emberizidae • 315

	New York	Pennsylvania	New Jersey	Delaware	Maryland	Dist. of Columbia	Virginia	North Carolina	South Carolina	Georgia	Florida
Black-thr. Blue Warbler	fS.xW	fS	lrS.fT	fT	lfS.fT	fT	lcS.fT	lcS.fT	luS.fT	lfS.fT	fT.rW
Yellow-rumped Warbler	cS.uW	rS.cT.uW	lrS.cT.fW	cT.fW	xS.cW	cT.uW	cW	cW	cW	cW	cW
Black-thr. Gray Warbler	rV	xV	xV.xW				xV.xW		xV	xV	rV.xW
Townsend's Warbler	xV	exV	xV.xW					xV-q			xV
Hermit Warbler	xV-q										
Black-thr. Green Warbler	fS.cT.xW	fS.cT	uS.fT	uT	uS.fT	fT	fS	fS	fS	uS.fT	uT.rW
Golden-cheeked Warbler											xV
Blackburnian Warbler	fS.cT	fS.cT	lrS.fT	uT	lrS.fT	uT	luS.fT	luS.fT	xS*.fT	luS.fT	uT.xW
Yellow-throated Warbler	xS.rS*.rV	lrS.rT	luS.rT	uS	fS.xW	rT	cS	cS.lrW	cS.luW	cS.uW	cS.fW
Grace's Warbler											
Pine Warbler	uS.rW	uS.xW	cS.rW	cS.xW	cS.uW	uT	cS.uW	cS.fW	cP	cP	cP
Kirtland's Warbler		xT			xT-q		xT	xT-q	xT	xT	rT
Prairie Warbler	uS.fT	fS	cS	fS	cS	fT	cS	cS.rW	cS.rW	cS.uW	cS.fW
Palm Warbler	xS.fT.rW	fT.xW	fT.rW	fT.xW	fT.uW	fT.xW	fW	cT.fW	cT.fW	cT.fW	cW
Bay-breasted Warbler	lrS.fT	fT	fT	uT	fT	fT	fT	uT	uT	uT	rT.xW
Blackpoll Warbler	lfS.cT	cT	cT	cT	cT	cT	cT	cT	cT	cT	cT
Cerulean Warbler	uS	fS	uS	luS.rT	uS	uT	uS	lrS.uT	rT	rS.uT	rT
Black-and-white Warbler	fS.cT.xW	fS.cT	fS.cT	uS.cT	fS.cT.xW	cT	fS.cT.xW	fS.cT.rW	uS.cT.uW	uS.cT.rW	cT.fW
American Redstart	cS	fS.cT.xW	fS.cT	fS.cT	fS.cT	rS.cT	fS.cT	fS.cT	uS.cT	fS.cT	cT.uW
Prothonotary Warbler	lrS.rT	luS.rT	uS	fS	fS	rS	fS	cS	cS	cS	cS.rW
Worm-eating Warbler	uS	uS	uS	fS	fS	rS.uT	fS	uS	luS.uT	uS	lrS.uT.rW
Swainson's Warbler	rV	xS*.xV	xV	xS	lrS		uS	uS	uS	uS	uS.xW
Ovenbird	cS.xW	cS.xW	cS.xW	fS	cS.xW	fS	cS	cS.rW	fS.cT.rW	fS.cT.rW	cT.fW
Northern Waterthrush	cS.xW	fS.cT	uS.fT	fT.xW	lfS.cT.xW	fT	lrS*.cT	exS*.cT.xW	cT	cT.rW	cT.uW

	Date	Location	Cont. North America	Canada	Lower 48
Louisiana Waterthrush *Seiurus motacilla*			fS.xW	lrS.xS*.rV	fS.xW
Kentucky Warbler *Oporornis formosus*			fS.lrW	xS*.rV	cS.lrW
Connecticut Warbler *Oporornis agilis*			uS	uS	luS.rT
Mourning Warbler *Oporornis philadelphia*			fS.xW	cS	uS.xW
MacGillivray's Warbler *Oporornis tolmiei*			cS.lrW	cS	cS.lrW
Common Yellowthroat *Geothlypis trichas*			cS.fW	cS.xW	cP
Bahama Yellowthroat *Geothlypis rostrata*			xV		xV
Gray-crowned Yellowthroat *Geothlypis poliocephala*			eP.xV.xW		eP.xV.xW
Hooded Warbler *Wilsonia citrina*			cS.lrW	lrS.rV	cS.lrW
Wilson's Warbler *Wilsonia pusilla*			cS.luW	cS.xW	fS.cT.rW
Canada Warbler *Wilsonia canadensis*			fS	fS	fS
Red-faced Warbler *Cardellina rubrifrons*			lfS.xS*.rV.xW		lfS.xS*.rV.xW
Painted Redstart *Myioborus pictus*			lcS.xS.rV.lrW	xV	lcS.xS.rV.lrW
Slate-throated Redstart *Myioborus miniatus*			xV		xV
Fan-tailed Warbler *Euthlypis lachrymosa*			xV		xV
Golden-crowned Warbler *Basileuterus culicivorus*			xV.xW		xV.xW
Rufous-capped Warbler *Basileuterus rufifrons*			xS.xP*.xV.xW		xS.xP*.xV.xW
Yellow-breasted Chat *Icteria virens*			cS.rW	luS.xS*.rV.xW	cS.rW
Olive Warbler *Peucedramus taeniatus*			lfS.xV.luW		lfS.xV.luW

Subfamily Coerebinae: Bananaquits

	Date	Location	Cont. North America	Canada	Lower 48
Bananaquit *Coereba flaveola*			rV.rW		rV.rW

Subfamily Thraupinae: Tanagers

	Date	Location	Cont. North America	Canada	Lower 48
Stripe-headed Tanager *Spindalis zena*			rV.xW		rV.xW
Hepatic Tanager *Piranga flava*			lcS.rV.lrW		lcS.rV.lrW
Summer Tanager *Piranga rubra*			cS.lrW	exS*.rV	cS.lrW

Distributional Checklist of North American Birds

	Hawaii	Alaska	Yukon Terr.	Northwest Terr.	British Columbia	Alberta	Saskatch-ewan	Manitoba	Ontario
Louisiana Waterthrush									lrS
Kentucky Warbler		xV					xV-q		xS*,rV
Connecticut Warbler					lrS	uS	uS	fS	uS
Mourning Warbler				xS*	lfS†	fS	cS	cS	cS
MacGillivray's Warbler		lcS,xV	luS		cS	fS	lfS		xV
Common Yellowthroat		lfS,xV	lcS	luS†	cS,xW	cS	cS	cS	cS,xW
Bahama Yellowthroat									
Gray-crowned Yellowthroat									
Hooded Warbler								xV	lrS
Wilson's Warbler		cS	cS	cS	cS,xW	fS	fS	uS,fT	fS,xW
Canada Warbler		xV			lrS	uS	uS	uS	fS
Red-faced Warbler									
Painted Redstart					xV				xV
Slate-throated Redstart									
Fan-tailed Warbler									
Golden-crowned Warbler									
Rufous-capped Warbler									
Yellow-breasted Chat					luS	luS	luS	xV	lrS,xW
Olive Warbler									

Subfamily Coerebinae: Bananaquits

	Hawaii	Alaska	Yukon Terr.	Northwest Terr.	British Columbia	Alberta	Saskatch-ewan	Manitoba	Ontario
Bananaquit									

Subfamily Thraupinae: Tanagers

	Hawaii	Alaska	Yukon Terr.	Northwest Terr.	British Columbia	Alberta	Saskatch-ewan	Manitoba	Ontario
Stripe-headed Tanager									
Hepatic Tanager									
Summer Tanager							xV	xV	rV

	Québec	Newfound-land	New Brunswick	Prince Edward I.	Nova Scotia	Washington	Oregon	California	Nevada	Idaho
Louisiana Waterthrush	xS*				rV			exV		
Kentucky Warbler	xV	xV	xV		rV			rV,xW	xV	
Connecticut Warbler	luS		xT		rT		xV	rV	xV	
Mourning Warbler	fS	fS	fS	uS	uS,fT		xV	rV,xW		
MacGillivray's Warbler						cS	cS	cS,rW	cS	cS
Common Yellowthroat	cS	fS	cS	cS	cS	cS,xW	cS,rW	cP	cS,xW	fS,cT
Bahama Yellowthroat										
Gray-crowned Yellowthroat										
Hooded Warbler	xV	xV	xV		rV	xW	xV	rV,xW	xV	
Wilson's Warbler	fS	fS	uS,fT	rS*,fT	uS,fT	cS,xW	cS,xW	cS,rW	fS,cT	fS,cT
Canada Warbler	fS	rS*,rV	fS	uS	fS		xV	rV	xV	
Red-faced Warbler								xS*,xV	xV	
Painted Redstart								xS,rV,rW	lrS	
Slate-throated Redstart										
Fan-tailed Warbler										
Golden-crowned Warbler										
Rufous-capped Warbler										
Yellow-breasted Chat	rV	rV,xW	xS*,rV,xW	xV	rV,xW	fS	fS	uS,xW	fS	fS
Olive Warbler										

Subfamily Coerebinae: Bananaquits

	Québec	Newfound-land	New Brunswick	Prince Edward I.	Nova Scotia	Washington	Oregon	California	Nevada	Idaho
Bananaquit										

Subfamily Thraupinae: Tanagers

	Québec	Newfound-land	New Brunswick	Prince Edward I.	Nova Scotia	Washington	Oregon	California	Nevada	Idaho
Stripe-headed Tanager										
Hepatic Tanager									lrS,xV,rW	lrS*,xW
Summer Tanager	xV	xV	exS*,rV		rV		xV	luS,rV,rW	luS	

	Montana	Wyoming	Utah	Colorado	Arizona	New Mexico	North Dakota	South Dakota	Nebraska	Kansas	Oklahoma
Louisiana Waterthrush				xV	xV,xW	xV	xV	xV	lrS,rT	luS,uT	uS
Kentucky Warbler	xV	xV		xV	rV	xV	xV	xV	luS,rT	lfS,uT	fS
Connecticut Warbler	xV		xV	xV	xV		rT	rT	rV	xV	rV
Mourning Warbler	xV			xV	xV	xV	lfS,uT	uT	uT	uT	uT
MacGillivray's Warbler	cS	cS	cS	cS	fS,cT,xW	fS,cT	rV	lrS,rV	xS*,rT	rT	luT
Common Yellowthroat	cS	cS	cS	cS	cS,fW	fS,cT,rW	cS	cS	cS	fS,cT,xW	fS,cT,uW
Bahama Yellowthroat											
Gray-crowned Yellowthroat											
Hooded Warbler		xV	xV-q	rV	xS*,rV	rV	xV	xV	exS,rT	lrS,rT	luS,rT
Wilson's Warbler	fS,cT	fS,cT	fS,cT	fS,cT	cT,rW	luS,cT	fT	fT	fT	fT	fT
Canada Warbler	xV	xV	xV	rV	xV	xV	lrSt,uT	uT	rT	rT	rT
Red-faced Warbler					fS,xW	luS,rV					
Painted Redstart			xV	xV	cS,rW	fS					
Slate-throated Redstart					xV	xV					
Fan-tailed Warbler					xV						
Golden-crowned Warbler											
Rufous-capped Warbler					xS,xV						
Yellow-breasted Chat	fS	fS	fS	fS	cS	fS	uS	fS	fS	uS	fS
Olive Warbler					fS,uW	luS					

Subfamily Coerebinae: Bananaquits

Bananaquit											

Subfamily Thraupinae: Tanagers

	Montana	Wyoming	Utah	Colorado	Arizona	New Mexico	North Dakota	South Dakota	Nebraska	Kansas	Oklahoma
Stripe-headed Tanager											
Hepatic Tanager			xV		lrS,xV	cS,rW	fS				
Summer Tanager	xV	xV	uS	rV	cS,rW	fS	xV	xV	lfS	lfS,fT	cS

Emberizidae • 321

	Texas	Minnesota	Iowa	Missouri	Arkansas	Louisiana	Wisconsin	Michigan	Illinois	Indiana	Ohio
Louisiana Waterthrush	luS,fT	luS,rV	uS	fS	fS	fS	uS	uS	uS	uS	fS
Kentucky Warbler	fS,cT	xS*,rV	uS	fS	cS	cS	lrS,rV	lrS,rV	fS	fS	fS
Connecticut Warbler	rV	uS	rT	rT	xV	xV-q	uS	uS	rT	rT	rT
Mourning Warbler	uT	fS	uT	uT	uT	uT	fS	fS	lrS,uT	uT	xS,uT
MacGillivray's Warbler	fT	xV		xV		xV					
Common Yellowthroat	fS,cW	cS	cS	cS,xW	cS,uW	cP	cS,xW	cS,rW	cS,rW	cS,rW	cS,rW
Bahama Yellowthroat											
Gray-crowned Yellowthroat	eP,xV,xW										
Hooded Warbler	fS,cT,xW	xS,rV	rS	uS	cS	cS,xW	lrS,rV	uS	uS	uS	fS
Wilson's Warbler	fT,rW	xS,lrS*,fT	fT	fT	fT	fT,rW	fT	xS*,fT	fT	fT	fT
Canada Warbler	fT	fS	fT	uT	uT	fT	fS	fS	xS,fT	fT	lrS,fT
Red-faced Warbler	xS*,lrT,xV										
Painted Redstart	luS,xV				xV	xV-q	xV				xV
Slate-throated Redstart											
Fan-tailed Warbler											
Golden-crowned Warbler	xV,xW										
Rufous-capped Warbler	xP*,xS*,xV,xW										
Yellow-breasted Chat	cS,rW	rS	rS	fS	cS	cS,xW	rS	uS,xW	fS,xW	fS	fS
Olive Warbler	xV-q										

Subfamily Coerebinae: Bananaquits

Bananaquit											

Subfamily Thraupinae: Tanagers

Stripe-headed Tanager											
Hepatic Tanager	luS,xV,xW					xV		xV			
Summer Tanager	cS,rW	rV	lrS	cS	cS	cS,rW	exS,rV	lrS*,rV	fS	fS	uS

	West Virginia	Kentucky	Tennessee	Mississippi	Alabama	Maine	New Hampshire	Vermont	Massachusetts	Rhode Island	Connecticut
Louisiana Waterthrush	fS	fS	fS	fS	fS	luS	uS	uS	uS	uS	fS
Kentucky Warbler	fS	cS	cS	cS	cS	rV	xV	xV	xS*,rV	xS*,rV	lrS
Connecticut Warbler	rT	rT	rT	xV	rT	rT	rT	rT	rT	rT	rT
Mourning Warbler	lfS,uT	uT	uT	uT	uT	fS	uS	uS	lrS,uT	rT	rT
MacGillivray's Warbler									xV		xV
Common Yellowthroat	cS,xW	cS,rW	cS,rW	cS,fW	cS,fW	cS	cS	cS,xW	cS,rW	cS,rW	cS,rW
Bahama Yellowthroat											
Gray-crowned Yellowthroat											
Hooded Warbler	cS	fS	cS	cS,xW	cS	rV	xV	xV	eS,rV	rS	uS
Wilson's Warbler	fT	fT,xW	fT	fT,rW	uS,fT	luS,fT	lrS,fT	fT	uT	fT	
Canada Warbler	fS	lfS,fT	lfS,fT	fT	uT	fS	fS	fS	fS	uS,fT	uS,fT
Red-faced Warbler											
Painted Redstart					xV-q				xV		
Slate-throated Redstart											
Fan-tailed Warbler											
Golden-crowned Warbler											
Rufous-capped Warbler											
Yellow-breasted Chat	cS	cS	cS	cS,xW	cS,xW	rV,xW	eS,rV,xW	exS,rV	rS,uT,rW	rS,uT,rW	uS,rW
Olive Warbler											

Subfamily Coerebinae: Bananaquits

Bananaquit											

Subfamily Thraupinae: Tanagers

	West Virginia	Kentucky	Tennessee	Mississippi	Alabama	Maine	New Hampshire	Vermont	Massachusetts	Rhode Island	Connecticut
Stripe-headed Tanager											
Hepatic Tanager											
Summer Tanager	fS	cS	cS	cS,xW	cS,xW	rV	xV		rV	xS*,rV	xS*,rV

Emberizidae • 323

	New York	Pennsylvania	New Jersey	Delaware	Maryland	Dist. of Columbia	Virginia	North Carolina	South Carolina	Georgia	Florida
Louisiana Waterthrush	fS	fS	fS	uS	fS	fS	fS	fS	fS	fS	lfS,fT,xW
Kentucky Warbler	luS,rV	uS	uS	uS	fS	rS	fS	fS	fS	fS	luS,uT,rW
Connecticut Warbler	uT	uT	uT	rT	uT	uT	rT	rT	rT	rT	uT
Mourning Warbler	uS	uS	uT	rT	lrS,uT	uT	lrS,rT	xS*,rT	xT	rT	rT
MacGillivray's Warbler											
Common Yellowthroat	cS,rW	cS,rW	cS,rW	cS,uW	cS,uW	cS,rW	cS,uW	cS,fW	cS,fW	cP	cP
Bahama Yellowthroat											xV
Gray-crowned Yellowthroat											
Hooded Warbler	uS	fS	uS	uS	fS	rS,fT	cS	cS	cS	cS	fS,rW
Wilson's Warbler	lrS,fT	fT	uT	uT	uT,xW	uT	uT,xW	uT	uT,xW	uT,xW	rW
Canada Warbler	fS	uS,fT	luS,fT	uT	luS,fT	fT	lfS,fT	lfS,uT	xS*,uT	luS,uT	rT
Red-faced Warbler											
Painted Redstart	xW									xV	
Slate-throated Redstart											
Fan-tailed Warbler											
Golden-crowned Warbler											
Rufous-capped Warbler											
Yellow-breasted Chat	uS,rW	fS,xW	fS,rW	fS,xW	cS,xW	rS	cS,rW	cS,rW	cS,rW	cS,rW	uS,rW
Olive Warbler											

Subfamily Coerebinae: Bananaquits

	New York	Pennsylvania	New Jersey	Delaware	Maryland	Dist. of Columbia	Virginia	North Carolina	South Carolina	Georgia	Florida
Bananaquit											rV,rW

Subfamily Thraupinae: Tanagers

	New York	Pennsylvania	New Jersey	Delaware	Maryland	Dist. of Columbia	Virginia	North Carolina	South Carolina	Georgia	Florida
Stripe-headed Tanager											rV,xW
Hepatic Tanager											
Summer Tanager	lrS*,rV	luS	uS,xW	uS	fS	uT	cS	cS	cS,xW	cS,xW	cS,rW

	Date	Location	Cont. North America	Canada	Lower 48
Scarlet Tanager *Piranga olivacea*			fS	fS	cS
Western Tanager *Piranga ludoviciana*			cS,rW	fS	cS,rW

Subfamily Cardinalinae: Cardinals, Grosbeaks and Allies

	Date	Location	Cont. North America	Canada	Lower 48
Crimson-collared Grosbeak *Rhodothraupis celaeno*			xV		xV
Northern Cardinal *Cardinalis cardinalis*			cP	lfP,xP*,rV,xW	cP
Pyrrhuloxia *Cardinalis sinuatus*			lcP,xS,rV,xW		lcP,xS,rV,xW
Yellow Grosbeak *Pheucticus chrysopeplus*			xS*,xV		xS*,xV
Rose-breasted Grosbeak *Pheucticus ludovicianus*			cS,rW	cS,lrW	cS,rW
Black-headed Grosbeak *Pheucticus melanocephalus*			cS,rW	lfS,rV,xW	cS,rW
Blue Bunting *Cyanocompsa parellina*			xV,xW		xV,xW
Blue Grosbeak *Guiraca caerulea*			fS,lrW	rV	cS,rW
Lazuli Bunting *Passerina amoena*			fS,lrW	lfS,rV	cS,lrW
Indigo Bunting *Passerina cyanea*			cS,rW	fS	cS,rW
Varied Bunting *Passerina versicolor*			lfS,xV,xW		lfS,xV,xW
Painted Bunting *Passerina ciris*			lfS,rV,luW	xV	fS,rW
Dickcissel *Spiza americana*			icS,rW	lirS,xS*,rV,lrW	icS,rW

Subfamily Emberizinae: Emberizines

	Date	Location	Cont. North America	Canada	Lower 48
Olive Sparrow *Arremonops rufivirgatus*			lcP		lcP
Green-tailed Towhee *Pipilo chlorurus*			fS,uW	rV,xW	fS,uW
Rufous-sided Towhee *Pipilo erythrophthalmus*			cP	fS,lfW	cP
Brown Towhee *Pipilo fuscus*			lcP,xV		cP
Abert's Towhee *Pipilo aberti*			lcP		lcP
White-collared Seedeater *Sporophila torqueola*			eP,lrP*		eP,lrP*
Black-faced Grassquit *Tiaris bicolor*			xV		xV

Species	Hawaii	Alaska	Yukon Terr.	Northwest Terr.	British Columbia	Alberta	Saskatchewan	Manitoba	Ontario
Scarlet Tanager		xV			exV	xV	rS	uS	fS
Western Tanager		luS,xV	xV	luS	cS	uS	uS	xS*,rV	rV

Subfamily Cardinalinae: Cardinals, Grosbeaks and Allies

Species	Hawaii	Alaska	Yukon Terr.	Northwest Terr.	British Columbia	Alberta	Saskatchewan	Manitoba	Ontario
Crimson-collared Grosbeak									
Northern Cardinal							xP*,xV,xW	lrP,rV,rW	fP
Pyrrhuloxia									
Yellow Grosbeak									
Rose-breasted Grosbeak					luS	luS,xV	uS	cS	cS	cS,xW
Black-headed Grosbeak		xV-q			xV	fS	lrS,xV	lrS,xW	rV	xV,xW
Blue Bunting									
Blue Grosbeak							xV-q	xV-q	rV
Lazuli Bunting					exV	fS	uS	luS	rV	xV
Indigo Bunting		xV-q			rV	xS*,xV	xS,rS*,rV	lfS	cS
Varied Bunting									
Painted Bunting									
Dickcissel					xV,xW	xV	lirS	lirS	lirS,xW

Subfamily Emberizinae: Emberizines

Species	Hawaii	Alaska	Yukon Terr.	Northwest Terr.	British Columbia	Alberta	Saskatchewan	Manitoba	Ontario
Olive Sparrow									
Green-tailed Towhee					xW		xV	xV,xW	xV
Rufous-sided Towhee		xV			lcS,lfW	uS	fS,xW	uS,xW	cS,rW
Brown Towhee									
Abert's Towhee									
White-collared Seedeater									
Black-faced Grassquit									

Emberizidae • 327

	Québec	Newfound-land	New Brunswick	Prince Edward I.	Nova Scotia	Washington	Oregon	California	Nevada	Idaho
Scarlet Tanager	lfS	rV	uS	rV	rT		xV	rV	xV	
Western Tanager	xV		xV		xV	cS	cS.xW	cS.rW	cS	cS

Subfamily Cardinalinae: Cardinals, Grosbeaks and Allies

	Québec	Newfound-land	New Brunswick	Prince Edward I.	Nova Scotia	Washington	Oregon	California	Nevada	Idaho
Crimson-collared Grosbeak										
Northern Cardinal	luP	xV.xW	lrP	xV.xW	rP			lrP	xV	
Pyrrhuloxia								xS.xV.xW	xV	
Yellow Grosbeak										
Rose-breasted Grosbeak	cS.xW	rS.xW	cS	fS	fS	xV	xS*.rV	xS.rS*.uV.rW	uV	rV
Black-headed Grosbeak			xV		xV	cS	cS.xW	cS.rW	cS	fS
Blue Bunting										
Blue Grosbeak	xV	xV	rV		rV		xW	fS.xW	fS	lrS
Lazuli Bunting						fS	fS	fS.xW	cS	cS
Indigo Bunting	fS	rV	rS	xV	xS*.rV	xV	rV.xW	rS.uV.xW	rS*.uV	rV
Varied Bunting							xV.exW			
Painted Bunting			xV		xV-q		xV	rV	xV	
Dickcissel	xS*.rV	rV.xW	rV.rW	xV	rV.xW	xV.xW	xV	rV.xW	rV	

Subfamily Emberizinae: Emberizines

	Québec	Newfound-land	New Brunswick	Prince Edward I.	Nova Scotia	Washington	Oregon	California	Nevada	Idaho
Olive Sparrow										
Green-tailed Towhee	xV				xV	lrS.xW	uS	fS.rW	fS.xW	fS
Rufous-sided Towhee	luS.lrW	xV.xW	rV.xW	xV.xW	rV	cP	cP	cP	cS.fW	fS.rW
Brown Towhee							lfP	cP		
Abert's Towhee									lfP	lfP
White-collared Seedeater										
Black-faced Grassquit										

328 • *Distributional Checklist of North American Birds*

	Montana	Wyoming	Utah	Colorado	Arizona	New Mexico	North Dakota	South Dakota	Nebraska	Kansas	Oklahoma
Scarlet Tanager	xV	xV	xV	rV	rV	rV	fS	uS	uS	uS	uS
Western Tanager	cS	cS	cS	cS	cS,rW	cS	lrS†,rV	lcS,uT	lfS,uT	uT	luT

Subfamily Cardinalinae: Cardinals, Grosbeaks and Allies

	Montana	Wyoming	Utah	Colorado	Arizona	New Mexico	North Dakota	South Dakota	Nebraska	Kansas	Oklahoma
Crimson-collared Grosbeak											
Northern Cardinal		xV	xV	lrP,rP*	cP	lfP,rV,xW	lrP,rV,xW	fP	fP	cP	cP
Pyrrhuloxia					fP	fP					xV,xW-q
Yellow Grosbeak					xS*,xV						
Rose-breasted Grosbeak	rT	xS,uT	rV	xS*,uT	rV,xW	rT	fS	fS	fS	uS	rS,uT
Black-headed Grosbeak	fS,xW	fS	cS,xW	fS,xW	cS,rW	cS	fS	fS	fS	uS	xS,lrS*,uT
Blue Bunting											
Blue Grosbeak	xS*,xV	rS	fS	fS	cS,rW	cS	lrS,rV	uS	uS	fS	cS
Lazuli Bunting	fS	cS	cS	cS	uS,fT,rW	uS,fT	fS	fS	fS	rS,uT	uS
Indigo Bunting	rS*,rV	uS†	rS,rV	uS	rS,uV,xW	uS	fS	fS	fS	cS	cS
Varied Bunting					lfS,xV	luS,xV					
Painted Bunting		xV		xV	rV,xW	luS,rV			xV	luS	cS
Dickcissel	irS	irS	xV	irS	rV,xW	xS*,rT	ifS	ifS	icS,xW	icS	icS,xW

Subfamily Emberizinae: Emberizines

	Montana	Wyoming	Utah	Colorado	Arizona	New Mexico	North Dakota	South Dakota	Nebraska	Kansas	Oklahoma
Olive Sparrow											
Green-tailed Towhee	uS	fS	fS	fS,xW	fP	fS,luW	xV		lrT,xW	luT,xW	luT,xW
Rufous-sided Towhee	fS,xW	fS,xW	cS,fW	fS,uW	cP	cP	fS,xW	fS,rW	fS,uW	uP	xS,fW
Brown Towhee					fP	cP	cP		xV	xV	lfP
Abert's Towhee			lfP		cP	luP					
White-collared Seedeater											
Black-faced Grassquit											

	Texas	Minnesota	Iowa	Missouri	Arkansas	Louisiana	Wisconsin	Michigan	Illinois	Indiana	Ohio
Scarlet Tanager	fT	cS	fS	fS	fS	fT	cS	cS	fS	fS	fS
Western Tanager	lfS.fT.rW	rV	xV	xV	xV	rV.rW	exS.xV	xV-q	xV	xV-q	xV.xW

Subfamily Cardinalinae: Cardinals, Grosbeaks and Allies

	Texas	Minnesota	Iowa	Missouri	Arkansas	Louisiana	Wisconsin	Michigan	Illinois	Indiana	Ohio
Crimson-collared Grosbeak	xV										
Northern Cardinal	cP	cP	cP	cP	cP	cP	cP	cP	cP	cP	cP
Pyrrhuloxia	cP										
Yellow Grosbeak											
Rose-breasted Grosbeak	cT.rW	cS.xW	cS.xW	fS.cT.xW	xS*.cT	cT.xW	cS.xW	cS.xW	fS.cT.xW	fS.cT.xW	fS.cT.xW
Black-headed Grosbeak	lcS.fT.rW	xS*.xV	xV	exS.rV	rV.xW	rV.rW	xV.xW	xV.xW	xV.xW	xV.xW-q	xV.xW
Blue Bunting	xV.xW					xV					
Blue Grosbeak	cS.xW	luS.xV	uS	fS	cS	fS.cT.xW	xS.rV		uS.xW	uS	lrS
Lazuli Bunting	lrS.uT.xW	xV	rV	exS.xV	xV	xV	xV		xV	xW-q	
Indigo Bunting	cS.rW	cS	cS	cS.xW	cS	cS.rW	cS	cS.xW	cS.xW	cS.xW	cS
Varied Bunting	luS.xV.xW										
Painted Bunting	cS.rW	xV		luS.rV	fS	cS.rW	xV	xV	xV	xV	
Dickcissel	icS.rW	icS	icS	icS.xW	icS.rW	icS.rW	ifS.xW	iuS	icS.xW	ifS.xW	irS.xW

Subfamily Emberizinae: Emberizines

	Texas	Minnesota	Iowa	Missouri	Arkansas	Louisiana	Wisconsin	Michigan	Illinois	Indiana	Ohio
Olive Sparrow	lcP										
Green-tailed Towhee	lrS.uW	xW	xV	xV.xW	xV	xV.xW	xV.xW	xV.xW	xV.xW	xV.xW-q	xV.xW
Rufous-sided Towhee	lcS.cW	fS.rW	fS.rW	cS.uW	fS.cW	fS.cW	cS.rW	cS.rW	cS.uW	cS.uW	cS.uW
Brown Towhee	cP										
Abert's Towhee											
White-collared Seedeater	eP.lrP*										
Black-faced Grassquit											

	West Virginia	Kentucky	Tennessee	Mississippi	Alabama	Maine	New Hampshire	Vermont	Massachusetts	Rhode Island	Connecticut
Scarlet Tanager	cS	fS	fS	IrS,fT	fS	fS	fS	fS	fS	fS	cS
Western Tanager		xV		rV,xW	rV,xW	rV,xW	xV	xV-q	rV,rW	xV	rV,xW

Subfamily Cardinalinae: Cardinals, Grosbeaks and Allies

	West Virginia	Kentucky	Tennessee	Mississippi	Alabama	Maine	New Hampshire	Vermont	Massachusetts	Rhode Island	Connecticut
Crimson-collared Grosbeak											
Northern Cardinal	cP	cP	cP	cP	cP	uP	fP	fP	cP	cP	cP
Pyrrhuloxia											
Yellow Grosbeak											
Rose-breasted Grosbeak	fS,cT,xW	IfS,cT,xW	IfS,cT,xW	cT,xW	cT,xW	cS,xW	cS,xW	cS	fS,xW	fS	fS,xW
Black-headed Grosbeak		xV	xV,xW	rV,rW	rV,rW	xV,xW	xV	xV-q	rW	xV,xW	xV,xW
Blue Bunting											
Blue Grosbeak	rS	rS	uS	fS	fS,xW	fS,xW	rV,xW	xV	xV-q	rV,xW	rV,xW	xS*,rV
Lazuli Bunting						xV					
Indigo Bunting	cS	cS,xW	cS,xW	cS,xW	cS,xW	fS	fS	fS	fS	uS	cS
Varied Bunting											
Painted Bunting			IrS	fS	IrS,uT,xW	xV	xV-q		xV,xW	xV	xV
Dickcissel	irS,xW	iuS,xW	ifS,rW	ifS,rW	iuS,rW	rV,xW	rV,xW	xS*,rV,xW	eS,rV,rW	rV,rW	eS,rV,rW

Subfamily Emberizinae: Emberizines

	West Virginia	Kentucky	Tennessee	Mississippi	Alabama	Maine	New Hampshire	Vermont	Massachusetts	Rhode Island	Connecticut
Olive Sparrow											
Green-tailed Towhee	xW		xV	xV	xV,xW	xW	xV		xV,xW		xV-q
Rufous-sided Towhee	cS,uW	cS,fW	cP	cP	cP	cS,rW	cS,rW	cS,xW	cS,uW	cS,uW	cS,uW
Brown Towhee											
Abert's Towhee											
White-collared Seedeater											
Black-faced Grassquit											

	New York	Pennsylvania	New Jersey	Delaware	Maryland	Dist. of Columbia	Virginia	North Carolina	South Carolina	Georgia	Florida
Scarlet Tanager	cS	cS	cS	fS	cS	fS	fS	fS	lfS,uT	fS	uT
Western Tanager	rV,xW	xV,xW	rV,xW		xV		xV,xW	rV,rW	rV,rW	xV,xW	rV,rW

Subfamily Cardinalinae: Cardinals, Grosbeaks and Allies

	New York	Pennsylvania	New Jersey	Delaware	Maryland	Dist. of Columbia	Virginia	North Carolina	South Carolina	Georgia	Florida
Crimson-collared Grosbeak											
Northern Cardinal	cP	cP	cP	cP	cP	cP	cP	cP	cP	cP	cP
Pyrrhuloxia											
Yellow Grosbeak											
Rose-breasted Grosbeak	cS,xW	fS,cT,xW	fS,xW	uT	fS,cT,xW	fT	fS,xW	lfS,fT,xW	uT,xW	luS,uT,xW	fT,rW
Black-headed Grosbeak	rV,rW	xV,xW	rV,xW	xV	xV,xW	xV,xW	rV,xW	rV,xW	xV,xW	xV,xW	xV,xW
Blue Bunting											
Blue Grosbeak	xS,rV	uS	fS	fS	fS	rS	fS,xW	fS,xW	fS,xW	fS,xW	fS,rW
Lazuli Bunting		xW			xV,xW		xV,xW		xW		xV
Indigo Bunting	cS	cS,xW	cS,xW	cS	cS,xW	cS	cS,xW	cS,xW	cS,xW	cS,rW	cS,uW
Varied Bunting											
Painted Bunting	rV	xV,xW	rV,xW		xV,xW		rV,xW	lfS,xW	lcS,xW	lfS,rW	lfS,uW
Dickcissel	eS,rV,rW	irS,rT,xW	irS,rW	rT,xW	irS,rT,xW	xT	irS,rW	irS,rW	irS,rW	irS,rT,xW	uT,rW

Subfamily Emberizinae: Emberizines

	New York	Pennsylvania	New Jersey	Delaware	Maryland	Dist. of Columbia	Virginia	North Carolina	South Carolina	Georgia	Florida
Olive Sparrow											
Green-tailed Towhee			xV,xW	xV			xV,xW		xW	xV	
Rufous-sided Towhee	cS,uW	cS,uW	cS,uW	cS,uW	cS,fW	fP	cP	cP	cP	cP	cP
Brown Towhee											
Abert's Towhee											
White-collared Seedeater											
Black-faced Grassquit											xV

Emberizidae • 333

	Date	Location	Cont. North America	Canada	Lower 48
Greater Antillean Bullfinch *Loxigilla violacea*			xV		xV
Bachman's Sparrow *Aimophila aestivalis*			uS,lfW	xV	uP
Botteri's Sparrow *Aimophila botterii*			lfS,lrW		lfS,lrW
Cassin's Sparrow *Aimophila cassinii*			lcS,xS*,rV,luW	xV	fS,luW
Rufous-winged Sparrow *Aimophila carpalis*			lfP		lfP
Rufous-crowned Sparrow *Aimophila ruficeps*			lcP,xS*,rV,xW		fP
American Tree Sparrow *Spizella arborea*			cP	cS,uW	cW
Chipping Sparrow *Spizella passerina*			cS,fW	cS,lrW	cP
Clay-colored Sparrow *Spizella pallida*			fS,uW	cS,xW	fS,uW
Brewer's Sparrow *Spizella breweri*			cS,lcW	lfS	cS,lcW
Field Sparrow *Spizella pusilla*			cP	lfS,rV,lrW	cP
Worthen's Sparrow *Spizella wortheni*			exS*		exS*
Black-chinned Sparrow *Spizella atrogularis*			lfS,xS*,xV,luW		lfS,xS*,xV,luW
Vesper Sparrow *Pooecetes gramineus*			cS,fW	cS,lrW	cS,fW
Lark Sparrow *Chondestes grammacus*			cS,fW	lfS,rV	cS,fW
Black-throated Sparrow *Amphispiza bilineata*			lcP,xS*,rV,xW	xV	cS,lcW
Sage Sparrow *Amphispiza belli*			fS,lfW	exV	fP
Five-striped Sparrow *Amphispiza quinquestriata*			luS,xW		luS,xW
Lark Bunting *Calamospiza melanocorys*			ifS,fW	lifS,rV	cS,fW
Savannah Sparrow *Passerculus sandwichensis*			cP	cS,luW	cP
Baird's Sparrow *Ammodramus bairdii*			lfS,xS*,rT,lrW	lfS,xV	lfS,xS*,rT,lrW
Grasshopper Sparrow *Ammodramus savannarum*			fS,uW	luS,rV,xW	cS,uW
Henslow's Sparrow *Ammodramus henslowii*			rP	lrS,xV	uP
Le Conte's Sparrow *Ammodramus leconteii*			fS,uW	fS	lfS,uW

	Hawaii	Alaska	Yukon Terr.	Northwest Terr.	British Columbia	Alberta	Saskatchewan	Manitoba	Ontario
Gr. Antillean Bullfinch									
Bachman's Sparrow									xV
Botteri's Sparrow									
Cassin's Sparrow									xV
Rufous-winged Sparrow									
Rufous-crowned Sparrow									
American Tree Sparrow		cS,rW	cS,xW	cS	luS,fT,uW	cT,uW	lfS,cT,uW	cS,rW	lcS,cT,fW
Chipping Sparrow		uS	fS	fS	cS	cS	cS,xW	cS,xW	cS,xW
Clay-colored Sparrow		xV	lrS*	luS	fS,xW	cS	cS	cS	uS
Brewer's Sparrow			luS		fS	lfS	lfS		
Field Sparrow							xV	xS,rV	lfS,lrW
Worthen's Sparrow									
Black-chinned Sparrow									
Vesper Sparrow				luS	fS	cS	cS,xW	cS	fS,rW
Lark Sparrow					lfS,xV	lfS,xV	fS	luS,xV	lrS,xV
Black-throated Sparrow					xV	xV			
Sage Sparrow					exV				
Five-striped Sparrow									
Lark Bunting					xV	liuS	ifS	liuS	rV
Savannah Sparrow	xV	cS,xW	cS,xW	cS	cS,uW	cS	cS	cS	cS,rW
Baird's Sparrow					xV	uS	fS	luS	
Grasshopper Sparrow					lrS	luS	uS	luS	luS
Henslow's Sparrow									lrS
Le Conte's Sparrow			xS*	lfS	lfS	fS	fS	fS	uS

	Québec	Newfoundland	New Brunswick	Prince Edward I.	Nova Scotia	Washington	Oregon	California	Nevada	Idaho
Gr. Antillean Bullfinch										
Bachman's Sparrow										
Botteri's Sparrow										
Cassin's Sparrow					xV			xS*,xV	exV	
Rufous-winged Sparrow										
Rufous-crowned Sparrow								uP	rV	
American Tree Sparrow	fS,cT,luW	fS,xW	cT,fW	uT,rW	fT,uW	uW	uW	irW	uW	uW
Chipping Sparrow	cS,xW	luS,xV	cS,xW	cS	cS,xW	cS	cS,rW	cS,uW	cS,rW	cS,xW
Clay-colored Sparrow	lrS	xV,xW	xV		rV	xS*,rV,xW	rV,xW	rV,xW	rV	rV
Brewer's Sparrow						cS	cS	cS,fW	cS	cS
Field Sparrow	luS,xV,xW	xV	rS,xW		rV,xW			xS*	xV	
Worthen's Sparrow										
Black-chinned Sparrow							xS*	fS,xW	luS	
Vesper Sparrow	fS	xV,xW	uS	uS†	uS,rW	cS	cS,xW	luS,uW	cS,uW	cS
Lark Sparrow	xV	rV	rV	xV	rV	fS	cS,luW	cS,fW	cS	fS
Black-throated Sparrow						xS*,xV	uS	cS,uW	cS	rS
Sage Sparrow						uS	fS	fP	fP	uS
Five-striped Sparrow										
Lark Bunting	xV	xV	xV		xV	xV	xV,xW	xS,rV,rW	rV	liuS,xV,xW
Savannah Sparrow	cS,xW	cS,rW	cS,rW	cS	cS,rW	cS,uW	cS,fW	cP	fS,cT,rW	fS,cT,xW
Baird's Sparrow								xV		
Grasshopper Sparrow	lrS	rV	rV	xV	rV,xW	uS	uS,xW	uS,rW	rS	rS
Henslow's Sparrow	xS,xV				xV-q					
Le Conte's Sparrow	rS	xV			xV	xV	xV	xV	xV	exV

336 • Distributional Checklist of North American Birds

	Montana	Wyoming	Utah	Colorado	Arizona	New Mexico	North Dakota	South Dakota	Nebraska	Kansas	Oklahoma
Gr. Antillean Bullfinch											
Bachman's Sparrow										xV	lrS,xV
Botteri's Sparrow					luS	xV					
Cassin's Sparrow		xV		fS	cS,uW	cS,xW		xV	lrS	fS	fS
Rufous-winged Sparrow					lfP						
Rufous-crowned Sparrow			lrP†	luS,lrW	cP	fP				xS*,xW	fP
American Tree Sparrow	cT,fW	cT,fW	uW	icW	irW	iuW	cT,fW	cT,fW	cW	cW	icW
Chipping Sparrow	cS,xW	cS	cS	cS,xW	cP	cS,fW	cS	cS,xW	cS	fS	fS,uW
Clay-colored Sparrow	fS	uS,fT	xV	xS*,fT,xW	rT,xW	uT,xW	cS	fS	xS,fT	fT	fT
Brewer's Sparrow	cS	cS	cS,xW	cS,xW	lcS,xS*,cW	lcS,lfW	luS	luS,uT	luS,uT	lrS,uT	xS,luT,xW
Field Sparrow	uS	rS*		rP*	xV,xW	xV,lrW	fS	fS	cS,rW	cS,uW	cS,fW
Worthen's Sparrow						exS*					
Black-chinned Sparrow			luS		fS,uW	fS,rW					
Vesper Sparrow	cS	cS	cS,xW	cS,xW	fS,cW	fS,cW	cS,xW	cS	fS,cT	xS*,cT,xW	cT,uW
Lark Sparrow	fS	cS	cS	cS	fS,cW	cS,luW	fS	fS	cS	cS,xW	cS,rW
Black-throated Sparrow	xV	lrS†,xV	cS,xW	fS,xW	cP	cP		xV	xV	xV	luS,xW
Sage Sparrow	xS,xV	fS	fS,uW	fS	fP	fP				xV,xW	xW-q
Five-striped Sparrow					luS,xW						
Lark Bunting	ifS	cS	lrS,rT	cS,xW	xS,cW	iuS,cT,fW	cS	cS	cS	ifS,cT,rW	iuS,fT,rW
Savannah Sparrow	cS	fS,cT	cS,rW	fS,cT	luS,cW	uS,cW	cS	fS,cT	uS,cT	cT,rW	cT,fW
Baird's Sparrow	uS	xS*,rT		rT	xV,lrW	rT,lrW	fS	rS	rT	rT	xT
Grasshopper Sparrow	fS	fS	rS	uS	lcS,fW	xS*,rT,xW	cS	cS	cS	cS	fS,xW
Henslow's Sparrow							xS*,xV	eS†,xS*,rV	lrS,rT	lrS,rT	xS*,xT
Le Conte's Sparrow	lrS,xV	xV	xV	xV	xV	rV,xW	fS	xS†,uT	uT	uT,rW	fT,uW

Emberizidae • 337

	Texas	Minnesota	Iowa	Missouri	Arkansas	Louisiana	Wisconsin	Michigan	Illinois	Indiana	Ohio
Gr. Antillean Bullfinch											
Bachman's Sparrow	uP			lrS	uS	fP		xV	lrS,xV	rS	eS,xS*,xV
Botteri's Sparrow	lfS,lrW										
Cassin's Sparrow	cS,uW								xV	xS*	
Rufous-winged Sparrow											
Rufous-crowned Sparrow	cP				lrP						
American Tree Sparrow	iuW	cT,fW	cW	cW	iuW	xV,xW	cT,fW	cT,fW	cW	cW	cW
Chipping Sparrow	fS,cW	cS,xW	cS	cS,xW	cS,uW	fS,cW	cS,xW	cS,xW	cS,xW	cS,xW	cS,xW
Clay-colored Sparrow	cT,fW	fS,xW	eS,xS*,uT	uT,xW	rT	rV,xW	fS	uS	xS,uT	xS*,uT	rV
Brewer's Sparrow	fW	xV				xV			xV		
Field Sparrow	fS,cW	cS,xW	cS,rW	cS,uW	cP	fS,cW	cS,rW	cS,rW	cS,uW	cS,uW	cS,uW
Worthen's Sparrow											
Black-chinned Sparrow	lfP,xV										
Vesper Sparrow	exS,cW	cS,xW	cS,xW	lrS,fT,rW	fW	cW	cS,xW	fS,rW	fS,rW	fS,rW	fS,rW
Lark Sparrow	cS,fW	uS	uS	fS	fS	fS,rW	uS	eS,rV	uS	rS	rS
Black-throated Sparrow	cP	xV				xV-q	xV,xW	xW	xV,xW		xV
Sage Sparrow	uW										
Five-striped Sparrow											
Lark Bunting	iuS,cW	eS,rV,xW	xS*,rV	xS,xV		xV	rV,xW	xS*,xV,xW	rV,xW	xV	xV,xW
Savannah Sparrow	cW	cS	fS,cT,xW	xS*,cT,rW	cW	cW	cS,xW	fS,cT,rW	fS,cT,rW	fS,cT,rW	fS,cT,rW
Baird's Sparrow	rW	eS,xS*,xV		xV			xS*,xV				xV
Grasshopper Sparrow	fS,uW	cS	cS	cS,xW	uS	lrS,uW	fS	uS	cS,xW	fS	uS,xW
Henslow's Sparrow	lrS,rW	lrS,rS*	rS†	rS	rW	fW	uS	uS	rS,exW	uS	uS
Le Conte's Sparrow	fW	fS	uT	fT,uW	fT,uW	fW	uS	luS,rT	eS,uT,rW	rT,xW	rT

	West Virginia	Kentucky	Tennessee	Mississippi	Alabama	Maine	New Hampshire	Vermont	Massachusetts	Rhode Island	Connecticut
Gr. Antillean Bullfinch											
Bachman's Sparrow	eS	rS	rS	uP	uP						
Botteri's Sparrow											
Cassin's Sparrow											
Rufous-winged Sparrow											
Rufous-crowned Sparrow											
American Tree Sparrow	fW	ifW	iuW	irW	irW	cT,fW	cT,fW	cT,fW	fW	fW	fW
Chipping Sparrow	cS,xW	cS,xW	cS,uW	fS,cW	fS,cW	cS,rW	cS,xW	cS,xW	cS,xW	cS,rW	cS,rW
Clay-colored Sparrow	xV	xV	xV-q	rV,xW	rV,xW	xS*,rV	rV	xV	rV,rW	rV	rV,xW
Brewer's Sparrow									exV		
Field Sparrow	cS,uW	cS,fW	cP	fS,cW	cP	uS,xW	uS,rW	fS,xW	fS,uW	fS,uW	cS,uW
Worthen's Sparrow											
Black-chinned Sparrow											
Vesper Sparrow	fS,rW	rS,fT,rW	lrS,fT,uW	fW	xS*,fW	uS	uS	uS	uS,rW	rP	uS,rW
Lark Sparrow	rS	rS	uS	uS,rW	lrS,uT,rW	rV	rV		rV,rW	rV,xW	rV,xW
Black-throated Sparrow						xV-q					
Sage Sparrow											
Five-striped Sparrow											
Lark Bunting		xV	xV	xV,xW	xV		xV	rV,xW	xV	xV,xW	
Savannah Sparrow	fS,cT,rW	rS,cT,uW	xS,cT,fW	cW	cW	cS,rW	fS,cT,rW	fS,cT,xW	fS,cT,rW	fS,cT,uW	fS,cT,uW
Baird's Sparrow											
Grasshopper Sparrow	uS	fS,xW	fS,rW	rS†,uW	uP	lrS,xW	rS	uS	uS	uS	uS
Henslow's Sparrow	rS	rS,xW	xS*,rT,xW	uW	uW	xV	eS,xS*,xV	eS,xS*,rV	lrS,rV,xW	eS,xV,xW	eS,rT
Le Conte's Sparrow	xV	rT,xW	uT,rW	uW	uW	xV			xV,xW		

Emberizidae • 339

	New York	Pennsylvania	New Jersey	Delaware	Maryland	Dist. of Columbia	Virginia	North Carolina	South Carolina	Georgia	Florida
Gr. Antillean Bullfinch											xV
Bachman's Sparrow	xV	eS	xV		eS	xV	eS	uS,lrW	uP	fS,uW	fP
Botteri's Sparrow											
Cassin's Sparrow			xV								
Rufous-winged Sparrow											
Rufous-crowned Sparrow											
American Tree Sparrow	cT,fW	cW	ifW	iuW	ifW	iuW	iuW	irW	xV,xW	xW	
Chipping Sparrow	cS,rW	cS,rW	cS,rW	cS,rW	cS,uW	rS,fT,rW	cS,uW	cS,fW	fS,cT,fW	fS,cW	luS,cW
Clay-colored Sparrow	lrS,rV	xS*,rV,xW	rV,xW	xV,xW	xV	xV	rV,xW	rV,xW	rV,xW	xV	rV,rW
Brewer's Sparrow											
Field Sparrow	cS,uW	cS,uW	fS,uW	fS,uW	cS,fW	rS,fW	cS,fW	cP	cP	cP	luS,fW
Worthen's Sparrow											
Black-chinned Sparrow											
Vesper Sparrow	fS,rW	fS,rW	rS,uT,rW	uS,rW	fS,uW	uT	uS,fT,uW	luS,fT,uW	fW	fW	fW
Lark Sparrow	rV,xW	eS,rV,xW	rV,xW	rV,xW	eS,rV	xV	xS,rV,xW	xS,rW	rT,xW	rT,xW	rW
Black-throated Sparrow			xV,xW				xW				xV
Sage Sparrow											
Five-striped Sparrow											
Lark Bunting	rV	rV,xW	xV	xV	xV		xV	xV	xV	rV,xW	xV,xW
Savannah Sparrow	cS,uW	fS,cT,uW	uS,cT,uW	cT,fW	uS,cT,fW	fW	lrS,cW	xS*,cW	cW	cW	cW
Baird's Sparrow	xV-q				xV						
Grasshopper Sparrow	uS	uS,xW	uS	fS	fS	uT	fS,xW	fS,rW	fS,uW	uP	luS,uW
Henslow's Sparrow	rS	uS	eS,xS*,rT	rS	rS,xW	xT	rS,xW	lrS,rW	xS,uW	uW	uW
Le Conte's Sparrow	rV	xV	xV,xW	xV,xW	xV,xW		rV	rT,xW	rW	uW	uW

Emberizidae • 341

	Date	Location	Cont. North America	Canada	Lower 48
Sharp-tailed Sparrow *Ammodramus caudacutus*			fP	uS.lrW	fP
Seaside Sparrow *Ammodramus maritimus*			fP	rV.xW	fP
Fox Sparrow *Passerella iliaca*			cS.fW	cS.uW	fP
Song Sparrow *Melospiza melodia*			cP	cS.fW	cP
Lincoln's Sparrow *Melospiza lincolnii*			cS.fW	cS.lrW	fS.cT.fW
Swamp Sparrow *Melospiza georgiana*			cP	cS.luW	fS.cW
White-throated Sparrow *Zonotrichia albicollis*			cP	cS.rW	fS.cW
Golden-crowned Sparrow *Zonotrichia atricapilla*			lcS.fW	cS.luW	xS.fW
White-crowned Sparrow *Zonotrichia leucophrys*			cP	cS.luW	cP
Harris' Sparrow *Zonotrichia querula*			lcS.fW	cS.rW	fW
Dark-eyed Junco *Junco hyemalis*			cP	cS.fW	cP
Yellow-eyed Junco *Junco phaeonotus*			lcP.xV.xW		lcP.xV.xW
McCown's Longspur *Calcarius mccownii*			lfS.uT.lfW	lfS.rV.xW	lfS.uW
Lapland Longspur *Calcarius lapponicus*			cS.fW	cS.rW	cT.fW
Smith's Longspur *Calcarius pictus*			lfS.uT.lfW	fS	uW
Chestnut-collared Longspur *Calcarius ornatus*			lcS.fT.lcW	lcS.rV	fS.cW
Little Bunting *Emberiza pusilla*			xV		
Rustic Bunting *Emberiza rustica*			lrT.xV.xW	xV.xW	xV.xW
Yellow-breasted Bunting *Emberiza aureola*			xV		
Gray Bunting *Emberiza variabilis*			xV		
Pallas' Reed-Bunting *Emberiza pallasi*			xV		
Common Reed-Bunting *Emberiza schoeniclus*			xV		
Snow Bunting *Plectrophenax nivalis*			cS.ifW	cS.ifW	cT.ifW
McKay's Bunting *Plectrophenax hyperboreus*			lfS.luW	xW	xW

	Hawaii	Alaska	Yukon Terr.	Northwest Terr.	British Columbia	Alberta	Saskatchewan	Manitoba	Ontario
Sharp-tailed Sparrow				lrS	luS	uS	uS	uS	uS
Seaside Sparrow									
Fox Sparrow		cS,lrW	cS	cS	cS,lfW	fS	uS,xW	cS,xW	uS,rW
Song Sparrow		cP	luS	lfS	cP	cS	cS,rW	cS,xW	cS,uW
Lincoln's Sparrow		cS,xW	cS	cS	cS,rW	fS	fS	fS	fS,xW
Swamp Sparrow		xV	lrS	fS	luS,rV,xW	uS	fS	cS	cS,uW
White-throated Sparrow		xS*,rV,xW	luS	fS	fS,rW	cS,xW	cS,rW	cS,rW	cS,uW
Golden-crowned Sparrow		cS,rW	cS	luS,xV	cS,uW	luS,rV	rV	xV	xV,xW
White-crowned Sparrow		cS,rW	cS	cS	cS,uW	cS	cS,xW	cS	lfS,cT,rW
Harris' Sparrow		rV,rW	xS*	cS	rV,rW	uT	luS,cT,rW	fS,cT,xW	lrS,uT,rW
Dark-eyed Junco		cS,uW	cS,rW	cS	cP	cS,uW	cS,uW	cS,rW	cS,fW
Yellow-eyed Junco									
McCown's Longspur					exV	uS	fS,xW	rV	
Lapland Longspur		cS,rW							
Smith's Longspur		fS	lcS,cT,xW	cS	uT,rW	cT,rW	cT,rW	lfS,cT,rW	lfS,fT,uW
Chestnut-coll. Longspur		xV-q	luS	fS	lfS,rT	uT	uT	lfS,fT	luS,rT
Little Bunting		xV			xV	fS	cS	lcS,xV	xV
Rustic Bunting		lrT,xV			xV,xW				
Yellow-breasted Bunting		xV-q							
Gray Bunting		xV							
Pallas' Reed-Bunting		xV							
Common Reed-Bunting		xV							
Snow Bunting	xV	cS,fW	lcS,cT,uW	cS,rW	lrS,uW	cT,icW	cT,ifW	cT,ifW	cT,icW
McKay's Bunting		lfS,luW			xW				

Emberizidae • 343

Species	Québec	Newfoundland	New Brunswick	Prince Edward I.	Nova Scotia	Washington	Oregon	California	Nevada	Idaho
Sharp-tailed Sparrow	uS		fS	uS	fS,rW			xV,rW		
Seaside Sparrow			rV		rV,xW					
Fox Sparrow	cS,xW	cS,rW	fS,rW	uT	luS,fT,rW	fS,cW	fS,cW	fS,cW	fS,rW	fS,xW
Song Sparrow	cS,rW	luS,rW	cS,uW	cS,rW	cS,uW	cP	cP	cP	cS,fW	cS,fW
Lincoln's Sparrow	fS,xW	fS,xW	fS	fS	uS	fS,cT,uW	fS,cT,uW	fS,cT,fW	fS,cT,rW	fS,xW
Swamp Sparrow	cS,xW	cS,xW	cS,rW	fS	fS,rW	xV,xW	rV,xW	rV,rW	rV,xW	xV
White-throated Sparrow	cS,rW	cS,rW	cS,uW	cS,rW	cS,uW	rW	rW	uW	rW	rW
Golden-crowned Sparrow					xV	xS,cT,fW	cT,fW	cW	luT,rV,rW	rT,xW
White-crowned Sparrow	fS,rW	fS,xW	uT,xW	uT	uT,xW	cS,fW	cS,fW	cP	luS,cW	cS,fW
Harris' Sparrow	xV		xV-q		xV,xW	xV,rW	rV,rW	rV,rW	rV,rW	rV,rW
Dark-eyed Junco	cS,uW	cS,fW	cS,fW	cS,fW	cS,fW	cP	cP	cP	cP	cP
Yellow-eyed Junco										
McCown's Longspur							xV,xW	rV,rW	xV	xV
Lapland Longspur	lfS,uT,rW	luS,uT,rW	uT,rW	uT,rW	uW	uT,rW	uW	uW	rW	rW
Smith's Longspur										
Chestnut-coll. Longspur		xV	xV		xV	xV	xV	rV,rW	rV	
Little Bunting										
Rustic Bunting							xV	xW		
Yellow-breasted Bunting										
Gray Bunting										
Pallas' Reed-Bunting										
Common Reed-Bunting										
Snow Bunting	lfS,cT,uW	lfS,fW	cT,fW	fW	cT,fW	iuW	iuW	rV,xW	xW	ifW
McKay's Bunting						xW	xW			

344 • *Distributional Checklist of North American Birds*

	Montana	Wyoming	Utah	Colorado	Arizona	New Mexico	North Dakota	South Dakota	Nebraska	Kansas	Oklahoma
Sharp-tailed Sparrow	xS*,xV			xV			uS	xS*,rT	rT	rT	rT
Seaside Sparrow											
Fox Sparrow	fS,xW	fS,xW	uS	uS,rW	uW	xS*,uW	uT,xW	uT,xW	uT,rW	fT,rW	fW
Song Sparrow	cS,uW	cS,fW	cS,fW	cS,fW	cP	uS,cW	cS,rW	cS,uW	cS,fW	lrS,cW	cW
Lincoln's Sparrow	fS	fS	fS,rW	fS,xW	luS,cW	lfS,cW	cT	cT	cT	cT,rW	cT,uW
Swamp Sparrow	xT,xW	xT	rV,xW	uW	rV,rW	uW	uS,xW	uS	luS,uT,rW	fT,uW	fW
White-throated Sparrow	uT,rW	uT,rW	rW	uW	uW	uW	luS,cT,rW	cT,rW	fT,rW	fT,uW	fW
Golden-crowned Sparrow	xV		xV,xW	xV,xW	rV,rW	rV,rW	xV		xV	xV	
White-crowned Sparrow	cS,rW	cS,uW	cP	cP	lrS,cW	lfS,cW	cT,rW	cT,rW	cT,uW	cT,fW	cT,fW
Harris' Sparrow	uT,rW	uW	rV,rW	uW	rV,rW	uW	cT,rW	cT,uW	cT,fW	cW	cW
Dark-eyed Junco	cS,fW	cP	cP	cP	cP	cP	xS*,cT,uW	lfS,cT,fW	luS,cW	cW	cW
Yellow-eyed Junco					cP	lfP					
McCown's Longspur	fS	fS	xV,xW	lfS,uT	rW	rW	uS	eS,uT	lrS,uT	uT,rW	eS,uW
Lapland Longspur	cT,uW	cT,fW	uW	cW	rV,rW	xV,xW	cT,uW	cT,fW	cT,fW	cW	cW
Smith's Longspur	xT				xV		uT	uT	uT,rW	uT,rW	fW
Chestnut-coll. Longspur	fS	fS	xV	lfS,fT,rW	cW	cW	cS	cS	fS,cT,rW	eS,fT,uW	cT,fW
Little Bunting											
Rustic Bunting											
Yellow-breasted Bunting											
Gray Bunting											
Pallas' Reed-Bunting											
Common Reed-Bunting											
Snow Bunting	cT,ifW	iuW	iuW	iuW	xV	exV	cT,icW	icW	ifW	irW	xV
McKay's Bunting											

Emberizidae • 345

	Texas	Minnesota	Iowa	Missouri	Arkansas	Louisiana	Wisconsin	Michigan	Illinois	Indiana	Ohio
Sharp-tailed Sparrow	fW	luS,rT	rT	rT	rT	cW	rT	rT	rT	rT	rT
Seaside Sparrow	fP					cP					
Fox Sparrow	fW	fT,rW	fT,uW	fT,uW	fW	fW	fT,uW	fT,uW	fT,uW	fT,uW	fT,uW
Song Sparrow	cW	cS,rW	cP	fS,cW	cW	cW	cS,uW	cS,uW	cP	cP	cP
Lincoln's Sparrow	cW	uS,fT,xW	fT,rW	fT,rW	fT,uW	fW	uS,fT,xW	uS,fT,xW	exS,fT,rW	fT	uT,xW
Swamp Sparrow	fW	cS,rW	fS,cT,uW	exS,cT,fW	cT,fW	cW	cS,rW	fS,cT,uW	uS,cT,fW	uS,cT,uW	uS,cT,uW
White-throated Sparrow	cW	cS,rW	cT,uW	cT,fW	xS*,cW	cW	fS,cT,uW	fS,cT,uW	cT,fW	cT,fW	eS,cT,fW
Golden-crowned Sparrow	rV,rW		xV			xV,xW	exV	xW	xV		
White-crowned Sparrow	cW	cT,xW	cT,uW	cT,fW	fW	fW	fT,rW	fT,rW	fT,uW	fT,uW	fT,uW
Harris' Sparrow	cW	fT,rW	fT,uW	fW	uW	rW	uT,rW	rT,xW	uT,rW	rV,xW	rV,rW
Dark-eyed Junco	lcS,cW	fS,cW	cW	cW	cW	fW	uS,cW	fS,cW	cW	cW	lrS,cW
Yellow-eyed Junco	xV,xW-q										
McCown's Longspur	fW	eS,xV		xV,xW		xV		xV		xV-q	
Lapland Longspur	fW	cT,uW	cT,fW	cT,fW	fW	rW	cT,uW	fT,uW	cT,fW	fT,uW	uW
Smith's Longspur	uW	rT	rT,xW	uT,rW	uW	rW	xT	xV	uT	rV,xW	rV,xW
Chestnut-coll. Longspur	cW	lfS,rV	xV	xV,xW	xV,xW	xV,xW	xV	xV-q	xV		
Little Bunting											
Rustic Bunting											
Yellow-breasted Bunting											
Gray Bunting											
Pallas' Reed-Bunting											
Common Reed-Bunting											
Snow Bunting	xV,xW	cT,ifW	ifW	irW	xW		cT,ifW	cT,ifW	ifW	ifW	ifW
McKay's Bunting											

	West Virginia	Kentucky	Tennessee	Mississippi	Alabama	Maine	New Hampshire	Vermont	Massachusetts	Rhode Island	Connecticut
Sharp-tailed Sparrow	xT	xT	rT	fW	fW	fS	uS,xW	xV	fS,rW	fS,xW	fS,rW
Seaside Sparrow				fP	fP	rV	xS*,xV,xW		luS,rW	uS,rW	uS,rW
Fox Sparrow	fT,uW	fT,uW	fW	fW	fW	lrS,fT,rW	fT,rW	fT,xW	fT,rW	fT,uW	fT,uW
Song Sparrow	cP	cP	fS,cW	cW	luS,cW	cS,uW	cS,uW	cS,uW	cP	cS,fW	cP
Lincoln's Sparrow	uT	fT,xW	fT,xW	uT,rW	uT,rW	fS,xW	uS	uS,fT,xW	lrS,uT,xW	uT	uT,xW
Swamp Sparrow	uS,cT,uW	cT,fW	cW	cW	cW	cS,rW	cS,xW	fS,cT,xW	fS,cT,uW	fS,uW	fS,cT,uW
White-throated Sparrow	xS,cW	cW	cW	cW	cW	cS,uW	cS,uW	cS,uW	fS,cT,fW	xS,cT,fW	luS,cT,fW
Golden-crowned Sparrow						xW			xV,xW		
White-crowned Sparrow	fT,uW	fW	fW	uW	uW	fT,rW	fT,xW	fT,xW	uT,rW	uT,rW	uT,rW
Harris' Sparrow	xV,xW	xV,xW	rV,xW	xV	xV,xW	xV	xV,xW	xV,xW	rV,rW	xV,xW	xV,xW
Dark-eyed Junco	cP	lfS,cW	lcS,cW	cW	cW	cS,fW	cS,fW	cS,fW	fS,cW	luS,cW	uS,cW
Yellow-eyed Junco											
McCown's Longspur										xW	
Lapland Longspur	rW	uW	uW	rW	rW	uT,rW	uW	uT,rW	uW	uW	uW
Smith's Longspur			xV,lrW	xV,lrW	xV,xW	xW		xV-q	xV	xV	xV
Chestnut-coll. Longspur						exV			xV,xW		xV
Little Bunting											
Rustic Bunting											
Yellow-breasted Bunting											
Gray Bunting											
Pallas' Reed-Bunting											
Common Reed-Bunting											
Snow Bunting	irW	irW	irW	xV		cT,fW	cT,fW	fW	cT,fW	fW	cT,fW
McKay's Bunting											

Emberizidae • 347

	New York	Pennsylvania	New Jersey	Delaware	Maryland	Dist. of Columbia	Virginia	North Carolina	South Carolina	Georgia	Florida
Sharp-tailed Sparrow	fS,rW	rT	fS,rW	uS,rW	fS,uW	exT	lfS,cT,uW	xS*,cW	cW	fW	fW
Seaside Sparrow	uS,rW	xV	fS,rW	fS,rW	cS,rW		cS,uW	cP	fS,cW	fP	fP
Fox Sparrow	fT,uW	fT,uW	fT,uW	fT,rW	fT,uW	uT,rW	fW	fW	fW	fW	uW
Song Sparrow	cS,fW	cP	cP	cP	cP	cP	cP	cP	luS,cW	luS,cW	cW
Lincoln's Sparrow	lrS,fT,xW	uT,xW	uT,xW	uT	uT,xW	uT	uT,rW	uT,rW	rW	rW	rW
Swamp Sparrow	fS,cT,uW	fS,cT,fW	fS,cT,uW	fS,cT,fW	fS,cW	fT,uW	lrS,cW	cW	cW	cW	cW
White-throated Sparrow	fS,cT,fW	luS,cT,fW	lrS,cT,fW	cW	lrS*,cW	cW	xS*,cW	cW	cW	cW	cW
Golden-crowned Sparrow	xV,xW	xV	xV,xW								
White-crowned Sparrow	fT,rW	fT,rW	fT,uW	uW	fT,uW	uT,rW	uW	uW	uW	uW	uW
Harris' Sparrow	rV,xW	rV,xW	rV,xW	xV	xV,xW		xV,xW	xV,xW	xV,xW	xV,xW	xV,xW
Dark-eyed Junco	cP	fS,cW	lrS,cW	cW	lrS,cW	cW	lfS,cW	lcS,cW	lrS,cW	luS,cW	fW
Yellow-eyed Junco											
McCown's Longspur											
Lapland Longspur	uW	uW	rW	rW	rW	xT	rW	rW	xV,rW	rV,rW	rV,xW
Smith's Longspur	xV				xV,xW			xV,xW	exV,exW		
Chestnut-coll. Longspur	xV,xW		xV,xW		xV		xV				xV
Little Bunting											
Rustic Bunting											
Yellow-breasted Bunting											
Gray Bunting											
Pallas' Reed-Bunting											
Common Reed-Bunting											
Snow Bunting	cT,fW	ifW	cT,fW	ifW	iuW	irW	iuW	irW	rV,rW	xV,xW	rV,rW
McKay's Bunting											

Emberizidae • 349

Subfamily Icterinae: Icterines

	Date	Location	Cont. North America	Canada	Lower 48
Bobolink *Dolichonyx oryzivorus*			fS	cS	fS,cT
Red-winged Blackbird *Agelaius phoeniceus*			cP	cS,uW	cP
Tricolored Blackbird *Agelaius tricolor*			lcP		lcP
Tawny-shouldered Blackbird *Agelaius humeralis*			xV		xV
Eastern Meadowlark *Sturnella magna*			cP	lcS,xS*,rV,lrW	cP
Western Meadowlark *Sturnella neglecta*			cP	cS,rW	cP
Yellow-headed Blackbird *Xanthocephalus xanthocephalus*			cS,fW	cS,lrW	cS,fW
Rusty Blackbird *Euphagus carolinus*			fP	fS,rW	luS,fW
Brewer's Blackbird *Euphagus cyanocephalus*			cS,fW	cS,uW	cP
Great-tailed Grackle *Quiscalus mexicanus*			fS,lcW	xV,xW	cP
Boat-tailed Grackle *Quiscalus major*			lcP,xV		cP
Common Grackle *Quiscalus quiscula*			cP	cS,rW	cP
Bronzed Cowbird *Molothrus aeneus*			lcS,xS*,rV,lfW		lcS,xS*,rV,lfW
Brown-headed Cowbird *Molothrus ater*			cP	cS,rW	cP
Black-cowled Oriole *Icterus dominicensis*			xV	xV	
Black-vented Oriole *Icterus wagleri*			xS*,xV		xS*,xV
Orchard Oriole *Icterus spurius*			cS,lrW	luS,rV	cS,lrW
Hooded Oriole *Icterus cucullatus*			lcS,xV,lrW		lcS,xV,lrW
Streak-backed Oriole *Icterus pustulatus*			xV,xW		xV,xW
Altamira Oriole *Icterus gularis*			lfP		lfP
Audubon's Oriole *Icterus graduacauda*			lrP		lrP
Northern Oriole *Icterus galbula*			cS,rW	cS,lrW	cS,rW
Scott's Oriole *Icterus parisorum*			lfS,xS*,xV,lrW	xV	uS,lrW

Subfamily Icterinae: Icterines

	Hawaii	Alaska	Yukon Terr.	Northwest Terr.	British Columbia	Alberta	Saskatchewan	Manitoba	Ontario
Bobolink								xS*,xV	cS,rW
Red-winged Blackbird		xV	xV	xV	luS,xV	uS	fS	cS	cS
Tricolored Blackbird									
Tawny-should. Blackbird									
Eastern Meadowlark									cS,rW
Western Meadowlark									
Yellow-headed Blackbird		xV,xW		xV	cS,uW	cS,rW	cS,rW	cS,rW	uS,xW
Rusty Blackbird		rV	xV	xV	fS,rW	fS	cS	cS,xW	luS,rV,xW
Brewer's Blackbird		fS,rW	fS	fS	uS,rW	uS,rW	fS,rW	fS,cT,rW	fS,cT,rW
Great-tailed Grackle		xV	xV	lfS,xV	cS,fW	cS,rW	cS,rW	cS,xW	uS,rW
Boat-tailed Grackle					xV				
Common Grackle		xV		luS	luS,xV	fS	cS,rW	cS,rW	cS,uW
Bronzed Cowbird									
Brown-headed Cowbird		rSt,xW	lrSt	lfS	cS,rW	cS,xW	cS,xW	cS	cS,uW
Black-cowled Oriole									
Black-vented Oriole									
Orchard Oriole							rS	luS,xV	luS
Hooded Oriole									
Streak-backed Oriole									
Altamira Oriole									
Audubon's Oriole									
Northern Oriole		xV	xV		fS	fS	cS,xW	cS	cS,rW
Scott's Oriole									xV

Subfamily Icterinae: Icterines

	Québec	Newfoundland	New Brunswick	Prince Edward I.	Nova Scotia	Washington	Oregon	California	Nevada	Idaho
Bobolink	fS	luS,rV	cS	cS	fS	uS	luS,xV	eS†,rV	luS,rV	uS
Red-winged Blackbird	cS,rW	luS,rV,xW	cS,rW	cS	cS,rW	cS,fW	cP	cP	cP	cS,fW
Tricolored Blackbird							lfS,lrW	cP	lrW	
Tawny-should. Blackbird										
Eastern Meadowlark	lcS,xV,xW	rV,xW	uS,xW	xS*,xV	lrS,rW					
Western Meadowlark	lrS				xV-q	cS,fW	cS,fW	cP	cP	cS,uW
Yellow-headed Blackbird	xS*,rV,xW	xV,xW	rV		rV,xW	cS,rW	cS,rW	fP	cS,rW	cS,rW
Rusty Blackbird	fS,rW	fS,xW	uS,fT,rW	uS,fT	uS,fT,rW	rV,xW	xV	rV,rW	rV	xV
Brewer's Blackbird	xV				xV,xW	cS,fW	cP	cP	cS,fW	cS,fW
Great-tailed Grackle					xV-sp,xW		xV	fP	uS,luW	
Boat-tailed Grackle										
Common Grackle	cS,rW	luS,rW	cS,uW	cS,rW	cS,uW	xV,xW	xV	rV,xW	rV	lrS,rV,xW
Bronzed Cowbird								lrS,xS*		
Brown-headed Cowbird	cS,rW	uS,rW	cS,uW	fS,uW	fS,uW	cS,rW	cS,uW	cS,fW	cS,rW	cS,xW
Black-cowled Oriole					xV-q					
Black-vented Oriole										
Orchard Oriole	rV		rV	xV	rV		xV	rV,rW	xV	
Hooded Oriole							xV,xW	fS,rW	luS,xW	
Streak-backed Oriole								xV,xW		
Altamira Oriole										
Audubon's Oriole										
Northern Oriole	fS	rV,xW	fS,rW	rS	uS,rW	fS,xW	cS,xW	cS,rW	cS,xW	fS
Scott's Oriole							xW		uS,rW	uS	xS,xV

Emberizidae • 351

Subfamily Icterinae: Icterines

	Montana	Wyoming	Utah	Colorado	Arizona	New Mexico	North Dakota	South Dakota	Nebraska	Kansas	Oklahoma
Bobolink	fS	uS	rS	rS	lrS,rV	xS*,rV	fS	fS	fS	luS,fT	uT
Red-winged Blackbird	cS,uW	cS,uW	cP	cP	cP	cP	cS,rW	cS,uW	cS,fW	cP	cP
Tricolored Blackbird											
Tawny-should. Blackbird											
Eastern Meadowlark											
Western Meadowlark	cS,uW	cS,uW	cP	cS,fW	cP	cP	cS,rW	cS,uW	cS,fW	cP	fS,cW
Yellow-headed Blackbird	cS,xW	cS	cS,xW	cS	fS,cW	fS,cT,fW	cS,rW	cS,xW	cS,xW	fS,cT,xW	exS,lrS*,cT,xW
Rusty Blackbird	uT,xW	uT,xW	xV	rW	rV,rW	rT,xW	fT,rW	fT,uW	fT,uW	fT,uW	fW
Brewer's Blackbird	cS,uW	cS,uW	cS,fW	cS,fW	fS,cW	fS,cW	cS,rW	cS,rW	lfS,fT,rW	fT,uW	exS,xS*,fW
Great-tailed Grackle			uS,xW	rS,xW	cP	cP			luS	fS,lfW	cS,fW
Boat-tailed Grackle											
Common Grackle	fS,rW	cS,rW	lrS,rV	cS,xW	xW	fS,uW	cS,rW	cS,uW	cS,uW	cS,uW	cS,fW
Bronzed Cowbird					cS,uW	luS,xV					
Brown-headed Cowbird	cS,xW	cS	cS,rW	cS,rW	cP	cP	cS,xW	cS,rW	cS,uW	cS,fW	cP
Black-cowled Oriole											
Black-vented Oriole											
Orchard Oriole	uS	fS†		fS	rV,xW	luS,uT	fS	fS	fS	fS	cS
Hooded Oriole			luS		cS,rW	uS					
Streak-backed Oriole					xV,xW						
Altamira Oriole											
Audubon's Oriole											
Northern Oriole	fS	cS	cS	cS,xW	cS,rW	cS,xW	fS	fS,xW	cS	cS,xW	cS,xW
Scott's Oriole		lrS	uS	lrS,xV	fS,rW	fS,xW			xV	xV	

(Eastern Meadowlark row values, positioned under Utah through Oklahoma: lrS† | fP | fS,uW | xS*,xV | lrS,uT | fS,uW | cP | cP)

Subfamily Icterinae: Icterines

	Texas	Minnesota	Iowa	Missouri	Arkansas	Louisiana	Wisconsin	Michigan	Illinois	Indiana	Ohio
Bobolink	uT	cS	fS	luS,fT	fT	fT	fS	fS	uS,fT	uS,fT	uS,fT
Red-winged Blackbird	cP	cS,uW	cS,uW	cP	cP	cP	cS,uW	cS,uW	cS,fW	cS,fW	cS,fW
Tricolored Blackbird											
Tawny-should. Blackbird											
Eastern Meadowlark	cP	cS,rW	cS,xW	cS,fW	cP	cP	cS,rW	cS,rW	cS,fW	cS,uW	cS,uW
Western Meadowlark	uS,cW	cS,rW	cS,uW	uP	xS,uW	lrS,uW	fS,rW	uS,rW	fS,rW	uS†,rW	rS
Yellow-headed Blackbird	lrS,cT,uW	cS,xW	fS,xW	luS,uT,rW	uT,xW	uT,xW	uS,xW	rS	luS,rT,xW	lrS,rT,xW	lrS,rV,xW
Rusty Blackbird	fW	lrS,cT,rW	fT,uW	fT,uW	fW	fW	cT,rW	xS,cT,rW	fT,uW	fT,uW	fT,rW
Brewer's Blackbird	luS,cW	fS,xW	xS*,uT,rW	uW	fW	fW	fS,rW	fS,xW	luS,uT,rW	luS,uT,rW	rT,xW
Great-tailed Grackle	cP	xV-sp	xS	lrP	lrP	uP			xV		
Boat-tailed Grackle	lfP					lcP					
Common Grackle	cP	cS,uW	cS,uW	cS,fW	cP	cP	cS,uW	cS,uW	cS,fW	cS,fW	cS,fW
Bronzed Cowbird	cS,fW			xW		luP,xV,xW					
Brown-headed Cowbird	cP	cS,rW	cS,uW	cS,fW	cP	cP	cS,rW	cS,uW	cS,fW	cS,fW	cS,fW
Black-cowled Oriole											
Black-vented Oriole	xS*,xV										
Orchard Oriole	fS,cT,xW	fS	fS	cS	cS	cS,xW	uS	uS	fS	fS	fS
Hooded Oriole	uS,lrW										
Streak-backed Oriole											
Altamira Oriole	lfP										
Audubon's Oriole	lrP										
Northern Oriole	fS,cT,rW	cS,xW	cS,xW	cS,xW	cS,xW	fS,cT,rW	cS,xW	cS,xW	cS,xW	cS	cS,xW
Scott's Oriole	fS,xW	xS*				xV,xW					

Subfamily Icterinae: Icterines

	West Virginia	Kentucky	Tennessee	Mississippi	Alabama	Maine	New Hampshire	Vermont	Massachusetts	Rhode Island	Connecticut
Bobolink	uS.fT	lrS.fT	xS.fT	fT	xS*.fT	cS	cS	fS	fS.cT	uS.cT	uS.cT
Red-winged Blackbird	cS.fW	cS.fW	cP	cP	cP	cS.rW	cS.rW	cS.rW	cS.rW	cS.uW	cS.uW
Tricolored Blackbird											
Tawny-should. Blackbird											
Eastern Meadowlark	cS.uW	cS.fW	cP	cP	cP	fS.rW	fS.rW	fS.rW	fS.uW	fS.uW	cS.uW
Western Meadowlark		xS*,xT.xW	lrS.rW	xT.xW	rW	xS*,xV	xV		rV	xV	xS*-q
Yellow-headed Blackbird	xV	xV.xW	xV.xW	rV.xW	rV.xW	rV	xV	xV	rV.xW	rV.xW	rV.rW
Rusty Blackbird	fT.uW	fW	fW	fW	fW	uS.fT.rW	uS.fT.rW	uS.fT.rW	lrS.fT.rW	fT.uW	fT.rW
Brewer's Blackbird	rV	uT.rW	uT.rW	fW	fW	xV			rV.xW	xV.xW	xV-q
Great-tailed Grackle											
Boat-tailed Grackle				lcP	lcP						
Common Grackle	cS.fW	cP	cP	cP	cP	cS.uW	cS.uW	cS.rW	cS.uW	cS.uW	cS.fW
Bronzed Cowbird				xV.xW	xV						
Brown-headed Cowbird	cS.fW	cS.fW	cP	cP	cP	cS.uW	cS.uW	cS.uW	cS.uW	cS.uW	cS.uW
Black-cowled Oriole											
Black-vented Oriole											
Orchard Oriole	fS	cS	cS	cS	cS.xW	lrS.rV	lrS	lrS	rS	rS	rS
Hooded Oriole											
Streak-backed Oriole											
Altamira Oriole											
Audubon's Oriole											
Northern Oriole	cS.xW	fS.cT.xW	uS.cT.xW	fS.cT.rW	uS.fT.rW	fS.rW	fS.rW	fS.rW	fS.rW	cS.rW	cS.rW
Scott's Oriole											

Subfamily Icterinae: Icterines

	New York	Pennsylvania	New Jersey	Delaware	Maryland	Dist. of Columbia	Virginia	North Carolina	South Carolina	Georgia	Florida
Bobolink	cS	fS	uS,cT	fT	lfS,fT	uT	lrS,cT	xS,cT	cT	cT	cT
Red-winged Blackbird	cS,uW	cS,fW	cS,fW	cP	cP	fS,cW	cP	cP	cP	cP	cP
Tricolored Blackbird											
Tawny-should. Blackbird											xV
Eastern Meadowlark	cS,uW	cS,uW	fS,uW	fP	cP	rS,uW	cP	cP	cP	cP	cP
Western Meadowlark	lrS,rV	xS*,rV	xV					xV,xW-q	xV	xV,xW	lrW
Yellow-headed Blackbird	rV,rW	rV,xW	rV,rW	rV,xW	rV,xW	xV,xW	rV,xW	rV,xW	rV,xW	rV,rW	rV,rW
Rusty Blackbird	lrS,fT,rW	fT,uW	fT,uW	fT,uW	fT,uW	fT,uW	fW	fW	fW	fW	uW
Brewer's Blackbird	xS*,rV	rV,xW	xV	rV,rW	rV,rW	xV,xW-q	rV,xW	rT,xW	uW	uW	uW
Great-tailed Grackle											
Boat-tailed Grackle	lrS,xW	xV	lfS,luW	lfS,luW	lcS,lfW		lcP	lcP	lcP	lcP	cP
Common Grackle	cS,uW	cS,fW	cS,fW	cP	cP	cP	cP	cP	cP	cP	cP
Bronzed Cowbird											xV,rW
Brown-headed Cowbird	cS,uW	cS,fW	cS,uW	cP	cP	cP	cP	cP	fS,cW	fS,cW	uS,cW
Black-cowled Oriole											
Black-vented Oriole											
Orchard Oriole	rS	uS	fS	fS	fS	uS,fT	fS	cS,xW	cS	cS	fS,cT,rW
Hooded Oriole											
Streak-backed Oriole											
Altamira Oriole											
Audubon's Oriole											
Northern Oriole	cS,rW	cS,rW	cS,rW	fS,xW	cS,rW	uS,fT,rW	cS,rW	fS,uW	xS,fT,uW	uS,fT,uW	fT,uW
Scott's Oriole											

Family Fringillidae: Fringilline and Cardueline Finches and Allies
Subfamily Fringillinae: Fringilline Finches

	Date	Location	Cont. North America	Canada	Lower 48
Common Chaffinch *Fringilla coelebs*			xV,xW	xW	xV
Brambling *Fringilla montifringilla*			luT,rV,rW	xV,xW	xV,rW

Subfamily Carduelinae: Cardueline Finches

	Date	Location	Cont. North America	Canada	Lower 48
Rosy Finch *Leucosticte arctoa*			fP	fS,iuW	uS,fW
Pine Grosbeak *Pinicola enucleator*			fS,ifW	fS,ifW	uS,ifW
Common Rosefinch *Carpodacus erythrinus*			rV		
Purple Finch *Carpodacus purpureus*			fS,ifW	cS,iuW	fS,cT,icW
Cassin's Finch *Carpodacus cassinii*			fP	lfS,xV,lrW	cS,fW
House Finch *Carpodacus mexicanus*			cP	lcS,xS*,rV,lfW	cP
Red Crossbill *Loxia curvirostra*			ifP	ifP	ifP
White-winged Crossbill *Loxia leucoptera*			ifP	ifP	liuS,iuW
Common Redpoll *Carduelis flammea*			cS,icW	cS,icW	icW
Hoary Redpoll *Carduelis hornemanni*			fS,ifW	fS,ifW	irW
Eurasian Siskin *Carduelis spinus*			xV	xV	xV
Pine Siskin *Carduelis pinus*			cP	icS,ifW	cP
Lesser Goldfinch *Carduelis psaltria*			fS,lcW	xV	fP
Lawrence's Goldfinch *Carduelis lawrencei*			luS,xV,lifW		luS,xV,lifW
American Goldfinch *Carduelis tristis*			cP	cS,ifW	cP
Oriental Greenfinch *Carduelis sinica*			rV		
European Greenfinch *Carduelis chloris*			xV	xV	
Eurasian Bullfinch *Pyrrhula pyrrhula*			xV,xW		
Evening Grosbeak *Coccothraustes vespertinus*			fS,icW	fS,icW	fS,icW
Hawfinch *Coccothraustes coccothraustes*			rV		

Family Fringillidae: Fringilline and Cardueline Finches and Allies
Subfamily Fringillinae: Fringilline Finches

	Hawaii	Alaska	Yukon Terr.	Northwest Terr.	British Columbia	Alberta	Saskatchewan	Manitoba	Ontario
Common Chaffinch									
Brambling		luT,rV,xW			xV,xW			xV	xV

Subfamily Carduelinae: Cardueline Finches

	Hawaii	Alaska	Yukon Terr.	Northwest Terr.	British Columbia	Alberta	Saskatchewan	Manitoba	Ontario
Rosy Finch		fS,uW	fS,xW	luS*	fS,uW	lfS,iuW	iuW	xV,xW	xV,xW
Pine Grosbeak		cS,fW	cS,fW	fS,uW	fS,ifW	lfS,ifW	luS,ifW	fS,ifW	fS,ifW
Common Rosefinch		rV							
Purple Finch		xV,xW	luS	luS	fS,ifW	uS	fS,rW	cS,rW	cS,iuW
Cassin's Finch					fS,rW	lrS,xV			
House Finch					cS,fW	xS*,rV,xW	xV,xW-q	xV	
Red Crossbill		ifP	ifS,iuW	liuS,irW	ifP	ifP	ifP	ifP	ifP
White-winged Crossbill		ifP	icP	ifS,iuW	ifP	ifP	ifP	ifP	ifP
Common Redpoll	xV	cP	cS,fW	cS,fW	luS,ifW	xS,icW	uS,icW	fS,icW	uS,icW
Hoary Redpoll		fP	lfS,uW	fP	iuW	ifW	ifW	luS,iuW	iuW
Eurasian Siskin		xV-q							
Pine Siskin		icP	icS,xW	ifS	cP	icS,iuW	icS,iuW	icS,iuW	ifP
Lesser Goldfinch					xV				xV
Lawrence's Goldfinch									
American Goldfinch		xV-q	xV		cS,uW	cS,xW	cS,irW	cS,iuW	cS,ifW
Oriental Greenfinch		rV							
European Greenfinch									
Eurasian Bullfinch		xV,xW							
Evening Grosbeak		xV,xW	xV	lrS*	fS,icW	fS,icW	fS,icW	fS,icW	fS,icW
Hawfinch		rV							

Family Fringillidae: Fringilline and Cardueline Finches and Allies
Subfamily Fringillinae: Fringilline Finches

	Québec	Newfoundland	New Brunswick	Prince Edward I.	Nova Scotia	Washington	Oregon	California	Nevada	Idaho
Common Chaffinch		xW								
Brambling					xV	xW	xW	xW	xV	

Subfamily Carduelinae: Cardueline Finches

	Québec	Newfoundland	New Brunswick	Prince Edward I.	Nova Scotia	Washington	Oregon	California	Nevada	Idaho
Rosy Finch						uP	uP	fP	uP	uS,fW
Pine Grosbeak	fS,ifW	cS,fW	uS,ifW	rS†,ifW	uS,ifW	rS,iuW	lrS,iuW	luP	luP	uS,ifW
Common Rosefinch										
Purple Finch	cS,iuW	fS,iuW	cS,iuW	cS,iuW	cS,iuW	cS,ifW	cP	cP	xV,xW	xV
Cassin's Finch						cS,rW	cS,uW	cS,fW	cS,fW	fS,uW
House Finch						cP	cP	cP	cP	fP
Red Crossbill	ifP	ifS,iuW	iuP	iuP†	iuP	ifP	ifP	ifP	ifP	ifP
White-winged Crossbill	ifP	ifP	ifP	ifP†	ifP	irS,iuW	xS,irW	xV	xV	xS*,irW
Common Redpoll	fS,ifW	fP	icW	ifW	icW	iuW	irW	xV,eW	irW	iuW
Hoary Redpoll	luS,iuW	lrS*,iuW	irW		irW	xW			xV	xW
Eurasian Siskin		xV								
Pine Siskin	ifP	ifP	ifP	iuS†,ifW	icP	cP	cP	cP	cP	cP
Lesser Goldfinch						lrS	uP	cP	fS,uW	xS*,xV
Lawrence's Goldfinch								uS,iuW	xV	
American Goldfinch	cS,liuW	luS,xW	cS,ifW	fS,ifW	fS,ifW	cS,fW	cS,fW	fS,cW	fS,ifW	fS,ifW
Oriental Greenfinch										
European Greenfinch				xV-q						
Eurasian Bullfinch										
Evening Grosbeak	fP	uS,cW	fS,cW	uS,cW	uS,cW	fS,icW	fS,icW	iuS,ifW	liuS,ifW	fS,icW
Hawfinch										

Family Fringillidae: Fringilline and Cardueline Finches and Allies
Subfamily Fringillinae: Fringilline Finches

	Montana	Wyoming	Utah	Colorado	Arizona	New Mexico	North Dakota	South Dakota	Nebraska	Kansas	Oklahoma
Common Chaffinch											
Brambling	xV		xV	xV,xW			xW				

Subfamily Carduelinae: Cardueline Finches

	Montana	Wyoming	Utah	Colorado	Arizona	New Mexico	North Dakota	South Dakota	Nebraska	Kansas	Oklahoma
Rosy Finch	fS,ifW	uS,fW	uS,fW	fS,cW	xV,rW	luS,uW	iuW	irW	irW		xW-q
Pine Grosbeak	uS,ifW	uS,ifW	uS,ifW	uS,ifW	luS,irW	luS,iuW	ifW	irW	irW	irW	xV,xW-q
Common Rosefinch											
Purple Finch	rV,rW	rV,rW		rV,rW	rV,rW	xV,xW	lrS,uT,rW	uT,iuW	uT,iuW	ifW	ifW
Cassin's Finch	fS,uW	cS,uW	cS,fW	cS,fW	lfS,cW	fS,cW		xS*,luW	lrW	xV,xW	lrW
House Finch	fS,uW	cS,fW	cP	cP	cP	cP	xV,xW	xV,xW	luS,uW	lfS,fW	lfP
Red Crossbill	ifP	ifP	ifP	ifP	iuS,ifW	iuS,ifW	irS,ifW	liuS,ifW	liuS,ifW	xS,ifW	irW
White-winged Crossbill	irS†,iuW	irS*,iuW	xS,irW	xS*,irW		xS*,xV,xW	xS*,ifW	xS*,iuW	iuW	irW	xV,xW
Common Redpoll	icW	iuW	irW	irW		xV,xW	icW	ifW	iuW	irW	xV,xW
Hoary Redpoll	irW	xV,xW					irW	irW	xW		
Eurasian Siskin											
Pine Siskin	cS,ifW	cP	cP	cP	cP	cP	iuS,fT,ifW	ifS,icW	iuS,icW	iuS,icW	exS,xS*,icW
Lesser Goldfinch		rV	fS,uW	fS,rW	cP	cS,uW	xS	xV	xV	xV,xW	luP
Lawrence's Goldfinch					lrS,ifW	lirW					
American Goldfinch	cS,iuW	fS,ifW	fS,ifW	fS,icW	xS,fW	lrS*,fW	cS,iuW	cS,ifW	cS,fW	cP	fS,cW
Oriental Greenfinch											
European Greenfinch											
Eurasian Bullfinch											
Evening Grosbeak	fS,icW	fS,icW	iuS,ifW	fS,icW	iuP	iuS,ifW	ifW	lrS,ifW	ifW	iuW	iuW
Hawfinch											

Family Fringillidae: Fringilline and Cardueline Finches and Allies
Subfamily Fringillinae: Fringilline Finches

	Texas	Minnesota	Iowa	Missouri	Arkansas	Louisiana	Wisconsin	Michigan	Illinois	Indiana	Ohio
Common Chaffinch											
Brambling		xW									

Subfamily Carduelinae: Cardueline Finches

	Texas	Minnesota	Iowa	Missouri	Arkansas	Louisiana	Wisconsin	Michigan	Illinois	Indiana	Ohio
Rosy Finch		xV,xW	xV				xW	xV,xW			xV,xW
Pine Grosbeak	xV	ifW	irW	irW	xW		iuW	xS,ifW	irW	irW	irW
Common Rosefinch											
Purple Finch	ifW	fS,cT,ifW	cT,ifW	ifW	icW	ifW	fS,cT,ifW	fS,cT,ifW	exS,cT,ifW	cT,ifW	lrS,cT,ifW
Cassin's Finch	xS*,rW										
House Finch	cP										
Red Crossbill	lirS,irW	iuS,ifW	xS,iuW	iuW	irW	xV,xW	iuS,ifW	iuS,ifW	xS,iuW	iuW	xS,iuW
White-winged Crossbill	xV,xW	lirS†,ifW	irW	irW	xV,xW		lirS,iuW	lirS,iuW	iuW	irW	irW
Common Redpoll	xV,xW	icW	ifW	iuW	xV,xW		icW	icW	iuW	iuW	iuW
Hoary Redpoll		irW	xW				irW	irW	xV,xW	xW	xW
Eurasian Siskin											
Pine Siskin	IuS,ifW	ifS,cT,ifW	irS,ifW	xS,ifW	ifW	iuW	iuS,cT,ifW	ifS,cT,ifW	xS,ifW	xS,ifW	irS,ifW
Lesser Goldfinch	fP			xV		xV,xW					
Lawrence's Goldfinch	lirW										
American Goldfinch	lrS,cW	cS,iuW	cP	cP	fS,cW	lrS,cW	cS,ifW	cS,ifW	cP	cS,fW	cS,fW
Oriental Greenfinch											
European Greenfinch											
Eurasian Bullfinch											
Evening Grosbeak	iuW	fS,icW	ifW	iuW	iuW	iuW	lrS,icW	fS,icW	ifW	ifW	ifW
Hawfinch											

Family Fringillidae: Fringilline and Cardueline Finches and Allies
Subfamily Fringillinae: Fringilline Finches

	West Virginia	Kentucky	Tennessee	Mississippi	Alabama	Maine	New Hampshire	Vermont	Massachusetts	Rhode Island	Connecticut
Common Chaffinch						xV			xV		
Brambling									xW		

Subfamily Carduelinae: Cardueline Finches

	West Virginia	Kentucky	Tennessee	Mississippi	Alabama	Maine	New Hampshire	Vermont	Massachusetts	Rhode Island	Connecticut
Rosy Finch						xW					
Pine Grosbeak	irW	xV,exW				uS,ifW	eS,xS*,ifW	xS*,ifW	iuW	irW	iuW
Common Rosefinch											
Purple Finch	uS,cT,icW	icW	icW	icW	icW	cS,iuW	fS,iuW	fS,iuW	fS,ifW	uS,ifW	uS,ifW
Cassin's Finch											
House Finch											
Red Crossbill	irS,ifW	iuW	lirS,irW	xS,xV	xS*,irW	iuP	iuS,ifW	irS,ifW	irS,ifW	iuW	irS*,ifW
White-winged Crossbill	iuW	irW	irW			iuS,ifW	iuS,ifW	irS,ifW	ifW	iuW	iuW
Common Redpoll	iuW	irW	xV		xV,xW	icW	icW	icW	icW	ifW	ifW
Hoary Redpoll						irW	irW	irW-q	irW	irW	irW
Eurasian Siskin						xV-q			xV		
Pine Siskin	irS,ifW	xS,ifW	lirS*,ifW	ifW	ifW	ifP	iuS,icW	iuS,icW	irS,icW	ifW	lirS,icW
Lesser Goldfinch		xV									
Lawrence's Goldfinch											
American Goldfinch	cS,fW	cP	fS,cW	uS,cW	uS,cW	cS,ifW	cS,ifW	cS,ifW	cS,fW	fS,cT,fW	cS,fW
Oriental Greenfinch											
European Greenfinch											
Eurasian Bullfinch											
Evening Grosbeak	icW	iuW	iuW	iuW	iuW	fS,cW	uS,cW	uS,cW	xS,cW	xS,cW	xS,cW
Hawfinch											

Family Fringillidae: Fringilline and Cardueline Finches and Allies
Subfamily Fringillinae: Fringilline Finches

	New York	Pennsylvania	New Jersey	Delaware	Maryland	Dist. of Columbia	Virginia	North Carolina	South Carolina	Georgia	Florida
Common Chaffinch											
Brambling	xW	xW	xV								

Subfamily Carduelinae: Cardueline Finches

	New York	Pennsylvania	New Jersey	Delaware	Maryland	Dist. of Columbia	Virginia	North Carolina	South Carolina	Georgia	Florida
Rosy Finch											
Pine Grosbeak	ifW	iuW	iuW	xV	irW		irW	xV,xW	xV,xW		
Common Rosefinch											
Purple Finch	fS,cT,ifW	fS,cT,ifW	iuS,cT,ifW	ifW	iuS,ifW	ifW	lrS,icW	icW	ifW	xS*,ifW	iuW
Cassin's Finch											
House Finch											
Red Crossbill	iuS,ifW	irS,ifW	irS,ifW	iuW	lirS*,ifW	iuW	lirS,iuW	lirS,irW	irW	xS*,irW	xV
White-winged Crossbill	xS,lirS*,ifW	iuW	iuW	irW	irW	irW	irW	irW			xV
Common Redpoll	icW	ifW	ifW	iuW	iuW	xV,xW	irW	irW	xV,xW	xV,xW	
Hoary Redpoll	irW	xW	xV,xW		xW						
Eurasian Siskin											
Pine Siskin	iuS,icW	irS,icW	lirS,icW	ifW	icW	ifW	lirS*,ifW	lirS*,ifW	ifW	ifW	iuW
Lesser Goldfinch		xW									
Lawrence's Goldfinch											
American Goldfinch	cS,ifW	cS,fW	cP	cP	cP	cP	cP	fS,cW	uS,cW	uS,cW	cW
Oriental Greenfinch											
European Greenfinch											
Eurasian Bullfinch											
Evening Grosbeak	uS,icW	icW	xS,icW	icW	ifW	ifW	ifW	ifW	iuW	iuW	irW
Hawfinch											

Subfamily Drepanidinae: Hawaiian Honeycreepers

	Date	Location	Hawaii
Laysan Finch *Telespyza cantans*			lfp
Nihoa Finch *Telespyza ultima*			lfP
Ou *Psittirostra psittacea*			rP†
Palila *Loxioides bailleui*			luP
Lesser Koa-Finch *Rhodacanthis flaviceps*			E†
Greater Koa-Finch *Rhodacanthis palmeri*			E†
Kona Grosbeak *Chloridops kona*			E†
Maui Parrotbill *Pseudonestor xanthophrys*			luP
Common Amakihi *Hemignathus virens*			cP
Anianiau *Hemignathus parvus*			lcP
Greater Amakihi *Hemignathus sagittirostris*			E†
Hawaiian Akialoa *Hemignathus obscurus*			E†
Kauai Akialoa *Hemignathus procerus*			lrP†
Nukupuu *Hemignathus lucidus*			rP†
Akiapolaau *Hemignathus munroi*			luP
Kauai Creeper *Oreomystis bairdi*			lfP
Hawaii Creeper *Oreomystis mana*			luP
Maui Creeper *Paroreomyza montana*			lcP
Molokai Creeper *Paroreomyza flammea*			lrP†
Oahu Creeper *Paroreomyza maculata*			lrP†
Akepa *Loxops coccineus*			uP
Ula-ai-hawane *Ciridops anna*			E†
Iiwi *Vestiaria coccinea*			fP
Hawaii Mamo *Drepanis pacifica*			E†

Fringillidae • 367

		Date	Location	Cont. North America	Canada	Lower 48
Black Mamo 　*Drepanis funerea*						
Crested Honeycreeper 　*Palmeria dolei*						
Apapane 　*Himatione sanguinea*						
Poo-uli 　*Melamprosops phaeosoma*						

Additional species

Native species counts

	North America			
Total species	920	859	586	789
Breeding species	717	650	416	548
Wintering species	728	664	331	651

	Hawaii
Black Mamo	E†
Crested Honeycreeper	IfP
Apapane	cP
Poo-uli	IrP†

Additional species

Native species counts

	Hawaii	Alaska	Yukon Terr.	Northwest Terr.	British Columbia	Alberta	Saskatchewan	Manitoba	Ontario
Total	217	435	248	290	431	354	367	362	422
Breeding	76	253	180	225	284	260	251	269	278
Wintering	151	177	59	47	256	111	139	102	212

Fringillidae • 369

	Québec	Newfoundland	New Brunswick	Prince Edward I.	Nova Scotia
Black Mamo					
Crested Honeycreeper					
Apapane					
Poo-uli					

	Washington	Oregon	California	Nevada	Idaho

Additional species

Native species counts

	Québec	Newfoundland	New Brunswick	Prince Edward I.	Nova Scotia
Total	380	340	362	273	398
Breeding	256	164	187	141	174
Wintering	159	158	160	95	176

	Washington	Oregon	California	Nevada	Idaho
Total	409	431	558	418	348
Breeding	242	252	308	232	221
Wintering	268	289	457	224	170

	Montana	Wyoming	Utah	Colorado	Arizona	New Mexico	North Dakota	South Dakota	Nebraska	Kansas	Oklahoma
Black Mamo											
Crested Honeycreeper											
Apapane											
Poo-uli											

Additional species

Native species counts

	Montana	Wyoming	Utah	Colorado	Arizona	New Mexico	North Dakota	South Dakota	Nebraska	Kansas	Oklahoma
Total	374	378	370	433	494	467	361	375	412	412	436
Breeding	236	226	230	256	273	267	214	218	216	202	210
Wintering	169	138	201	198	355	270	120	139	158	187	235

Fringillidae • 371

	Texas	Minnesota	Iowa	Missouri	Arkansas	Louisiana	Wisconsin	Michigan	Illinois	Indiana	Ohio
Black Mamo											
Crested Honeycreeper											
Apapane											
Poo-uli											

Additional species

Native species counts

	Texas	Minnesota	Iowa	Missouri	Arkansas	Louisiana	Wisconsin	Michigan	Illinois	Indiana	Ohio
Total	583	389	365	380	356	422	392	381	391	374	376
Breeding	329	247	193	177	154	170	231	224	203	181	198
Wintering	464	174	156	205	189	307	182	191	212	186	194

372 • *Distributional Checklist of North American Birds*

	West Virginia	Kentucky	Tennessee	Mississippi	Alabama	Maine	New Hampshire	Vermont	Massachusetts	Rhode Island	Connecticut
Black Mamo											
Crested Honeycreeper											
Apapane											
Poo-uli											

Additional species

Native species counts

	West Virginia	Kentucky	Tennessee	Mississippi	Alabama	Maine	New Hampshire	Vermont	Massachusetts	Rhode Island	Connecticut
Total	297	331	340	368	385	401	364	333	441	382	385
Breeding	173	160	173	148	172	201	184	187	207	167	182
Wintering	140	184	181	248	279	178	166	128	245	210	205

Fringillidae • 373

	New York	Pennsylvania	New Jersey	Delaware	Maryland	Dist. of Columbia	Virginia	North Carolina	South Carolina	Georgia	Florida
Black Mamo											
Crested Honeycreeper											
Apapane											
Poo-uli											

Additional species

Native species counts

	New York	Pennsylvania	New Jersey	Delaware	Maryland	Dist. of Columbia	Virginia	North Carolina	South Carolina	Georgia	Florida
Total	426	394	416	360	384	299	406	405	384	378	452
Breeding	230	190	200	150	200	92	203	194	167	169	163
Wintering	254	208	252	203	242	136	270	271	269	274	350

Part II

Introduced Populations

Order Ciconiiformes: Herons, Ibises, Storks and Allies
Family Ardeidae: Bitterns and Herons

	Date	Location	Cont. North America	Canada	Lower 48
Cattle Egret *Bubulcus ibis*					

Order Anseriformes: Screamers, Swans, Geese and Ducks
Family Anatidae: Swans, Geese and Ducks
Subfamily Anserinae: Whistling-Ducks, Swans and Geese

Mute Swan *Cygnus olor*			IfP,rV,xW	IuP,xV	fP
Canada Goose *Branta canadensis*			fP		fP

Subfamily Anatinae: Ducks

American Black Duck *Anas rubripes*			IrP	IrP	IrP
Mottled Duck *Anas fulvigula*			IrP		IrP
Mallard *Anas platyrhynchos*			IrP		rP

Order Galliformes: Gallinaceous Birds
Family Cracidae: Curassows and Guans

Plain Chachalaca *Ortalis vetula*			IrP		IrP

Family Phasianidae: Partridges, Grouse, Turkeys and Quail
Subfamily Phasianinae: Partridges and Pheasants

Gray Partridge *Perdix perdix*			fP	fP	fP
Black Francolin *Francolinus francolinus*			IrP		IrP
Gray Francolin *Francolinus pondicerianus*					
Erckel's Francolin *Francolinus erckelii*					
Chukar *Alectoris chukar*			uP	IuP	fP
Japanese Quail *Coturnix japonicus*					
Kalij Pheasant *Lophura leucomelana*					
Red Junglefowl *Gallus gallus*					

Order Ciconiiformes: Herons, Ibises, Storks and Allies
Family Ardeidae: Bitterns and Herons

	Hawaii	Alaska	Yukon Terr.	Northwest Terr.	British Columbia	Alberta	Saskatchewan	Manitoba	Ontario
Cattle Egret	cP								

Order Anseriformes: Screamers, Swans, Geese and Ducks
Family Anatidae: Swans, Geese and Ducks
Subfamily Anserinae: Whistling-Ducks, Swans and Geese

	Hawaii	Alaska	Yukon Terr.	Northwest Terr.	British Columbia	Alberta	Saskatchewan	Manitoba	Ontario
Mute Swan									
Canada Goose					luP	eP			luP

Subfamily Anatinae: Ducks

	Hawaii	Alaska	Yukon Terr.	Northwest Terr.	British Columbia	Alberta	Saskatchewan	Manitoba	Ontario
American Black Duck									
Mottled Duck					lrP				
Mallard	lfP								

Order Galliformes: Gallinaceous Birds
Family Cracidae: Curassows and Guans

	Hawaii	Alaska	Yukon Terr.	Northwest Terr.	British Columbia	Alberta	Saskatchewan	Manitoba	Ontario
Plain Chachalaca									

Family Phasianidae: Partridges, Grouse, Turkeys and Quail
Subfamily Phasianinae: Partridges and Pheasants

	Hawaii	Alaska	Yukon Terr.	Northwest Terr.	British Columbia	Alberta	Saskatchewan	Manitoba	Ontario
Gray Partridge					lfP	fP	cP	fP	fP
Black Francolin	fP								
Gray Francolin	fP								
Erckel's Francolin	fP								
Chukar	fP				luP	eP			
Japanese Quail	rP								
Kalij Pheasant	fP								
Red Junglefowl	lfP								

Order Ciconiiformes: Herons, Ibises, Storks and Allies
Family Ardeidae: Bitterns and Herons

	Québec	Newfoundland	New Brunswick	Prince Edward I.	Nova Scotia
Cattle Egret					

	Washington	Oregon	California	Nevada	Idaho

Order Anseriformes: Screamers, Swans, Geese and Ducks
Family Anatidae: Swans, Geese and Ducks
Subfamily Anserinae: Whistling-Ducks, Swans and Geese

	Québec	Newfoundland	New Brunswick	Prince Edward I.	Nova Scotia
Mute Swan	xV				
Canada Goose					

	Washington	Oregon	California	Nevada	Idaho
Mute Swan	xV				
Canada Goose					

Subfamily Anatinae: Ducks

	Québec	Newfoundland	New Brunswick	Prince Edward I.	Nova Scotia
American Black Duck					
Mottled Duck					
Mallard					

	Washington	Oregon	California	Nevada	Idaho
American Black Duck	IrP				
Mottled Duck					
Mallard					

Order Galliformes: Gallinaceous Birds
Family Cracidae: Currassows and Guans

	Québec	Newfoundland	New Brunswick	Prince Edward I.	Nova Scotia
Plain Chachalaca					

	Washington	Oregon	California	Nevada	Idaho

Family Phasianidae: Partridges, Grouse, Turkeys and Quail
Subfamily Phasianinae: Partridges and Pheasants

	Québec	Newfoundland	New Brunswick	Prince Edward I.	Nova Scotia
Gray Partridge	IrP		IrP	fP	IuP
Black Francolin					
Gray Francolin					
Erckel's Francolin					
Chukar					
Japanese Quail					
Kalij Pheasant					
Red Junglefowl					

	Washington	Oregon	California	Nevada	Idaho
Gray Partridge	fP	uP		uP	uP
Black Francolin					
Gray Francolin					
Erckel's Francolin					
Chukar	fP	fP	fP	fP	fP
Japanese Quail					
Kalij Pheasant					
Red Junglefowl					

Order Ciconiiformes: Herons, Ibises, Storks and Allies
Family Ardeidae: Bitterns and Herons

	Montana	Wyoming	Utah	Colorado	Arizona	New Mexico	North Dakota	South Dakota	Nebraska	Kansas	Oklahoma
Cattle Egret											

Order Anseriformes: Screamers, Swans, Geese and Ducks
Family Anatidae: Swans, Geese and Ducks
Subfamily Anserinae: Whistling-Ducks, Swans and Geese

	Montana	Wyoming	Utah	Colorado	Arizona	New Mexico	North Dakota	South Dakota	Nebraska	Kansas	Oklahoma
Mute Swan	IrP,xV										xV-q
Canada Goose				luP	luP						

Subfamily Anatinae: Ducks

	Montana	Wyoming	Utah	Colorado	Arizona	New Mexico	North Dakota	South Dakota	Nebraska	Kansas	Oklahoma
American Black Duck											
Mottled Duck											
Mallard											

Order Galliformes: Gallinaceous Birds
Family Cracidae: Curassows and Guans

	Montana	Wyoming	Utah	Colorado	Arizona	New Mexico	North Dakota	South Dakota	Nebraska	Kansas	Oklahoma
Plain Chachalaca											

Family Phasianidae: Partridges, Grouse, Turkeys and Quail
Subfamily Phasianinae: Partridges and Pheasants

	Montana	Wyoming	Utah	Colorado	Arizona	New Mexico	North Dakota	South Dakota	Nebraska	Kansas	Oklahoma
Gray Partridge	fP	uP	uP				cP	fP	luP		
Black Francolin											
Gray Francolin											
Erckel's Francolin											
Chukar	uP	fP	fP	uP	luP	luP		eP			
Japanese Quail											
Kalij Pheasant											
Red Junglefowl											

Order Ciconiiformes: Herons, Ibises, Storks and Allies
Family Ardeidae: Bitterns and Herons

	Texas	Minnesota	Iowa	Missouri	Arkansas	Louisiana	Wisconsin	Michigan	Illinois	Indiana	Ohio
Cattle Egret											

Order Anseriformes: Screamers, Swans, Geese and Ducks
Family Anatidae: Swans, Geese and Ducks
Subfamily Anserinae: Whistling-Ducks, Swans and Geese

	Texas	Minnesota	Iowa	Missouri	Arkansas	Louisiana	Wisconsin	Michigan	Illinois	Indiana	Ohio
Mute Swan		rV	xS,rW	lrP	xV		uP	fP	luP	uP	lrS,uW
Canada Goose						luP					

Subfamily Anatinae: Ducks

	Texas	Minnesota	Iowa	Missouri	Arkansas	Louisiana	Wisconsin	Michigan	Illinois	Indiana	Ohio
American Black Duck											
Mottled Duck											
Mallard						rP					

Order Galliformes: Gallinaceous Birds
Family Cracidae: Curassows and Guans

	Texas	Minnesota	Iowa	Missouri	Arkansas	Louisiana	Wisconsin	Michigan	Illinois	Indiana	Ohio
Plain Chachalaca											

Family Phasianidae: Partridges, Grouse, Turkeys and Quail
Subfamily Phasianinae: Partridges and Pheasants

	Texas	Minnesota	Iowa	Missouri	Arkansas	Louisiana	Wisconsin	Michigan	Illinois	Indiana	Ohio
Gray Partridge		cP	fP				fP	lrP	luP	uP	eP
Black Francolin						lrP-q					
Gray Francolin											
Erckel's Francolin											
Chukar	eP-q	lrP									
Japanese Quail											
Kalij Pheasant											
Red Junglefowl											

Order Ciconiiformes: Herons, Ibises, Storks and Allies
Family Ardeidae: Bitterns and Herons

	West Virginia	Kentucky	Tennessee	Mississippi	Alabama	Maine	New Hampshire	Vermont	Massachusetts	Rhode Island	Connecticut
Cattle Egret											

Order Anseriformes: Screamers, Swans, Geese and Ducks
Family Anatidae: Swans, Geese and Ducks
Subfamily Anserinae: Whistling-Ducks, Swans and Geese

	West Virginia	Kentucky	Tennessee	Mississippi	Alabama	Maine	New Hampshire	Vermont	Massachusetts	Rhode Island	Connecticut
Mute Swan	rV	xV,xW			lrP	lrW	luP	xV	fP	cP	cP
Canada Goose	lfP		uP	uP		uP		uP		fP	fP

Subfamily Anatinae: Ducks

	West Virginia	Kentucky	Tennessee	Mississippi	Alabama	Maine	New Hampshire	Vermont	Massachusetts	Rhode Island	Connecticut
American Black Duck											
Mottled Duck											
Mallard			rP	rP	rP						

Order Galliformes: Gallinaceous Birds
Family Cracidae: Curassows and Guans

	West Virginia	Kentucky	Tennessee	Mississippi	Alabama	Maine	New Hampshire	Vermont	Massachusetts	Rhode Island	Connecticut
Plain Chachalaca											

Family Phasianidae: Partridges, Grouse, Turkeys and Quail
Subfamily Phasianinae: Partridges and Pheasants

	West Virginia	Kentucky	Tennessee	Mississippi	Alabama	Maine	New Hampshire	Vermont	Massachusetts	Rhode Island	Connecticut
Gray Partridge								luP			eP
Black Francolin											
Gray Francolin											
Erckel's Francolin											
Chukar											
Japanese Quail											
Kalij Pheasant											
Red Junglefowl											

Order Ciconiiformes: Herons, Ibises, Storks and Allies
Family Ardeidae: Bitterns and Herons

	New York	Pennsylvania	New Jersey	Delaware	Maryland	Dist. of Columbia	Virginia	North Carolina	South Carolina	Georgia	Florida
Cattle Egret											

Order Anseriformes: Screamers, Swans, Geese and Ducks
Family Anatidae: Swans, Geese and Ducks
Subfamily Anserinae: Whistling-Ducks, Swans and Geese

	New York	Pennsylvania	New Jersey	Delaware	Maryland	Dist. of Columbia	Virginia	North Carolina	South Carolina	Georgia	Florida
Mute Swan	lcP	luP	fP	uP	uP		luP	xV	xV		
Canada Goose	cP	cP	fP	rP	uP	uP	fP	rP		lrP	rP

Subfamily Anatinae: Ducks

	New York	Pennsylvania	New Jersey	Delaware	Maryland	Dist. of Columbia	Virginia	North Carolina	South Carolina	Georgia	Florida
American Black Duck											
Mottled Duck									lrP		
Mallard								rP	rP	rP	rP

Order Galliformes: Gallinaceous Birds
Family Cracidae: Curassows and Guans

	New York	Pennsylvania	New Jersey	Delaware	Maryland	Dist. of Columbia	Virginia	North Carolina	South Carolina	Georgia	Florida
Plain Chachalaca										lrP	

Family Phasianidae: Partridges, Grouse, Turkeys and Quail
Subfamily Phasianinae: Partridges and Pheasants

	New York	Pennsylvania	New Jersey	Delaware	Maryland	Dist. of Columbia	Virginia	North Carolina	South Carolina	Georgia	Florida
Gray Partridge	luP	eP									
Black Francolin											lrP
Gray Francolin											
Erckel's Francolin											
Chukar											
Japanese Quail											
Kalij Pheasant											
Red Junglefowl											

	Date	Location	Cont. North America	Canada	Lower 48
Ring-necked Pheasant *Phasianus colchicus*			cP	fP	cP
Common Peafowl *Pavo cristatus*					

Subfamily Tetraoninae: Grouse

Willow Ptarmigan *Lagopus lagopus*			luP	luP	
White-tailed Ptarmigan *Lagopus leucurus*			luP		luP
Ruffed Grouse *Bonasa umbellus*			lrP		lrP

Subfamily Meleagridinae: Turkeys

Wild Turkey *Meleagris gallopavo*			uP	luP,xV	uP

Subfamily Odontophorinae: Quail

Northern Bobwhite *Colinus virginianus*			luP,xV	lrP,xV	luP
Scaled Quail *Callipepla squamata*			lrP		lrP
Gambel's Quail *Callipepla gambelii*			lrP		lrP
California Quail *Callipepla californica*			lcP	lcP	lcP
Mountain Quail *Oreortyx pictus*			lrP	lrP	

Order Gruiformes: Cranes, Rails and Allies
Family Gruidae: Cranes
Subfamily Gruinae: Typical Cranes

Whooping Crane *Grus americana*			lrP*		lrP*

Order Columbiformes: Sandgrouse, Pigeons and Doves
Family Pteroclididae: Sandgrouse

Chestnut-bellied Sandgrouse *Pterocles exustus*					

Family Columbidae: Pigeons and Doves

Rock Dove *Columba livia*			cP	cP	cP
Ringed Turtle-Dove *Streptopelia risoria*			luP		luP

Distributional Checklist of North American Birds

Species	Hawaii	Alaska	Yukon Terr.	Northwest Terr.	British Columbia	Alberta	Saskatchewan	Manitoba	Ontario
Ring-necked Pheasant	fP				lfP	fP	fP	lfP	fP
Common Peafowl	luP								

Subfamily Tetraoninae: Grouse

Species	Hawaii	Alaska	Yukon Terr.	Northwest Terr.	British Columbia	Alberta	Saskatchewan	Manitoba	Ontario
Willow Ptarmigan									
White-tailed Ptarmigan									
Ruffed Grouse									

Subfamily Meleagridinae: Turkeys

Species	Hawaii	Alaska	Yukon Terr.	Northwest Terr.	British Columbia	Alberta	Saskatchewan	Manitoba	Ontario
Wild Turkey	lfP					lrP	lrP	lrP	luP

Subfamily Odontophorinae: Quail

Species	Hawaii	Alaska	Yukon Terr.	Northwest Terr.	British Columbia	Alberta	Saskatchewan	Manitoba	Ontario
Northern Bobwhite					lrP				
Scaled Quail									
Gambel's Quail	lfP								
California Quail	fP				lcP				
Mountain Quail					lrP				

Order Gruiformes: Cranes, Rails and Allies
Family Gruidae: Cranes
Subfamily Gruinae: Typical Cranes

Species	Hawaii	Alaska	Yukon Terr.	Northwest Terr.	British Columbia	Alberta	Saskatchewan	Manitoba	Ontario
Whooping Crane									

Order Columbiformes: Sandgrouse, Pigeons and Doves
Family Pteroclididae: Sandgrouse

Species	Hawaii	Alaska	Yukon Terr.	Northwest Terr.	British Columbia	Alberta	Saskatchewan	Manitoba	Ontario
Chestnut-bellied Sandgrouse	luP†								

Family Columbidae: Pigeons and Doves

Species	Hawaii	Alaska	Yukon Terr.	Northwest Terr.	British Columbia	Alberta	Saskatchewan	Manitoba	Ontario
Rock Dove	cP	luP	luP	luP	cP	cP	cP	cP	cP
Ringed Turtle-Dove									

Introduced Phasianidae • 387

	Québec	Newfoundland	New Brunswick	Prince Edward I.	Nova Scotia	Washington	Oregon	California	Nevada	Idaho
Ring-necked Pheasant	lrP	lrP	uP	uP	fP	cP	fP	fP	fP	cP
Common Peafowl										

Subfamily Tetraoninae: Grouse

	Québec	Newfoundland	New Brunswick	Prince Edward I.	Nova Scotia	Washington	Oregon	California	Nevada	Idaho
Willow Ptarmigan					luP					
White-tailed Ptarmigan							lrP	luP-q		
Ruffed Grouse									lrP	

Subfamily Meleagridinae: Turkeys

	Québec	Newfoundland	New Brunswick	Prince Edward I.	Nova Scotia	Washington	Oregon	California	Nevada	Idaho
Wild Turkey	lrP					luP	luP	uP	luP	rP

Subfamily Odontophorinae: Quail

	Québec	Newfoundland	New Brunswick	Prince Edward I.	Nova Scotia	Washington	Oregon	California	Nevada	Idaho
Northern Bobwhite	xV					uP	lrP			lrP
Scaled Quail						lrP			lrP	
Gambel's Quail										lrP
California Quail						cP			fP	lfP
Mountain Quail										

Order Gruiformes: Cranes, Rails and Allies
Family Gruidae: Cranes
Subfamily Gruinae: Typical Cranes

	Québec	Newfoundland	New Brunswick	Prince Edward I.	Nova Scotia	Washington	Oregon	California	Nevada	Idaho
Whooping Crane										lrS*

Order Columbiformes: Sandgrouse, Pigeons and Doves
Family Pteroclididae: Sandgrouse

	Québec	Newfoundland	New Brunswick	Prince Edward I.	Nova Scotia	Washington	Oregon	California	Nevada	Idaho
Chestnut-bellied Sandgrouse										

Family Columbidae: Pigeons and Doves

	Québec	Newfoundland	New Brunswick	Prince Edward I.	Nova Scotia	Washington	Oregon	California	Nevada	Idaho
Rock Dove	cP	cP	cP	cP	cP	cP	cP	cP	cP	cP
Ringed Turtle-Dove								lrP-q		

	Montana	Wyoming	Utah	Colorado	Arizona	New Mexico	North Dakota	South Dakota	Nebraska	Kansas	Oklahoma
Ring-necked Pheasant	cP	cP	cP	fP	rP	lfP	cP	cP	cP	cP	lfP
Common Peafowl											

Subfamily Tetraoninae: Grouse

	Montana	Wyoming	Utah	Colorado	Arizona	New Mexico	North Dakota	South Dakota	Nebraska	Kansas	Oklahoma
Willow Ptarmigan											
White-tailed Ptarmigan			luP								
Ruffed Grouse											

Subfamily Meleagridinae: Turkeys

	Montana	Wyoming	Utah	Colorado	Arizona	New Mexico	North Dakota	South Dakota	Nebraska	Kansas	Oklahoma
Wild Turkey	uP	fP	uP					luP			

Subfamily Odontophorinae: Quail

	Montana	Wyoming	Utah	Colorado	Arizona	New Mexico	North Dakota	South Dakota	Nebraska	Kansas	Oklahoma
Northern Bobwhite	eP										
Scaled Quail											
Gambel's Quail											
California Quail			fP								
Mountain Quail											

Order Gruiformes: Cranes, Rails and Allies
Family Gruidae: Cranes
Subfamily Gruinae: Typical Cranes

	Montana	Wyoming	Utah	Colorado	Arizona	New Mexico	North Dakota	South Dakota	Nebraska	Kansas	Oklahoma
Whooping Crane	xS*	lrS*	xS*,rT	rT	xT-q	lrW					

Order Columbiformes: Sandgrouse, Pigeons and Doves
Family Pteroclididae: Sandgrouse

	Montana	Wyoming	Utah	Colorado	Arizona	New Mexico	North Dakota	South Dakota	Nebraska	Kansas	Oklahoma
Chestnut-bellied Sandgrouse											

Family Columbidae: Pigeons and Doves

	Montana	Wyoming	Utah	Colorado	Arizona	New Mexico	North Dakota	South Dakota	Nebraska	Kansas	Oklahoma
Rock Dove	cP	cP	cP	cP	cP	cP	cP	cP	cP	cP	cP
Ringed Turtle-Dove						lrP-q					

	Texas	Minnesota	Iowa	Missouri	Arkansas	Louisiana	Wisconsin	Michigan	Illinois	Indiana	Ohio
Ring-necked Pheasant	luP	cP	cP	lfP			cP	fP	cP	cP	fP
Common Peafowl											

Subfamily Tetraoninae: Grouse

Willow Ptarmigan											
White-tailed Ptarmigan											
Ruffed Grouse											

Subfamily Meleagridinae: Turkeys

Wild Turkey		luP									

Subfamily Odontophorinae: Quail

Northern Bobwhite											
Scaled Quail											
Gambel's Quail											
California Quail											
Mountain Quail											

Order Gruiformes: Cranes, Rails and Allies
Family Gruidae: Cranes
Subfamily Gruinae: Typical Cranes

Whooping Crane											

Order Columbiformes: Sandgrouse, Pigeons and Doves
Family Pteroclididae: Sandgrouse

Chestnut-bellied Sandgrouse											

Family Columbidae: Pigeons and Doves

Rock Dove	cP	cP	cP	cP	cP	cP	cP	cP	cP	cP	cP
Ringed Turtle-Dove	lrP-q										

Distributional Checklist of North American Birds

	West Virginia	Kentucky	Tennessee	Mississippi	Alabama	Maine	New Hampshire	Vermont	Massachusetts	Rhode Island	Connecticut
Ring-necked Pheasant	luP		lrP			uP	fP	lrP	fP	fP	fP
Common Peafowl											

Subfamily Tetraoninae: Grouse

Willow Ptarmigan											
White-tailed Ptarmigan											
Ruffed Grouse											

Subfamily Meleagridinae: Turkeys

Wild Turkey											

Subfamily Odontophorinae: Quail

Northern Bobwhite											
Scaled Quail											
Gambel's Quail											
California Quail											
Mountain Quail											

Order Gruiformes: Cranes, Rails and Allies
Family Gruidae: Cranes
Subfamily Gruinae: Typical Cranes

Whooping Crane											

Order Columbiformes: Sandgrouse, Pigeons and Doves
Family Pteroclididae: Sandgrouse

Chestnut-bellied Sandgrouse											

Family Columbidae: Pigeons and Doves

	West Virginia	Kentucky	Tennessee	Mississippi	Alabama	Maine	New Hampshire	Vermont	Massachusetts	Rhode Island	Connecticut
Rock Dove	cP	cP	cP	cP	cP	cP	cP	cP	cP	cP	cP
Ringed Turtle-Dove						luP					

	New York	Pennsyl-vania	New Jersey	Delaware	Maryland	Dist. of Columbia	Virginia	North Carolina	South Carolina	Georgia	Florida
Ring-necked Pheasant	fP	fP	fP	fP	fP		IuP	IuP			
Common Peafowl											

Subfamily Tetraoninae: Grouse

Willow Ptarmigan											
White-tailed Ptarmigan											
Ruffed Grouse											

Subfamily Meleagridinae: Turkeys

Wild Turkey											

Subfamily Odontophorinae: Quail

Northern Bobwhite											
Scaled Quail											
Gambel's Quail											
California Quail											
Mountain Quail											

Order Gruiformes: Cranes, Rails and Allies
Family Gruidae: Cranes
Subfamily Gruinae: Typical Cranes

Whooping Crane											

Order Columbiformes: Sandgrouse, Pigeons and Doves
Family Pteroclididae: Sandgrouse

Chestnut-bellied Sandgrouse											

Family Columbidae: Pigeons and Doves

	New York	Pennsyl-vania	New Jersey	Delaware	Maryland	Dist. of Columbia	Virginia	North Carolina	South Carolina	Georgia	Florida
Rock Dove	cP	cP	cP	cP	cP	cP	cP	cP	cP	cP	cP
Ringed Turtle-Dove											IuP

Introduced Columbidae • 393

	Date	Location	Cont. North America	Canada	Lower 48
Spotted Dove *Streptopelia chinensis*			IcP		IcP
Zebra Dove *Geopelia striata*					
White-winged Dove *Zenaida asiatica*			IfP		IfP
Mourning Dove *Zenaida macroura*					

Order Psittaciformes: Parrots and Allies
Family Psittacidae: Lories, Parakeets, Macaws and Parrots
Subfamily Platycercinae: Australian Parakeets and Rosellas

Budgerigar *Melopsittaculus undulatus*			IcP		IcP

Subfamily Psittacinae: Typical Parrots

Rose-ringed Parakeet *Psittacula krameri*			IuP		IuP

Subfamily Arinae: New World Parakeets, Macaws and Parrots

Monk Parakeet *Myiopsitta monachus*			IuP		IuP
Canary-winged Parakeet *Brotogeris versicolurus*			IfP		IfP
Red-crowned Parrot *Amazona viridigenalis*			IfP		IfP
Lilac-crowned Parrot *Amazona finschi*			IrP		IrP
Yellow-headed Parrot *Amazona oratrix*			IrP		IrP

Order Strigiformes: Owls
Family Tytonidae: Barn-Owls

Common Barn-Owl *Tyto alba*					

Order Apodiformes: Swifts and Hummingbirds
Family Apodidae: Swifts
Subfamily Chaeturinae: Chaeturine Swifts

Gray Swiftlet *Aerodramus vanikorensis*					

Order Passeriformes: Passerine Birds
Family Alaudidae: Larks

Eurasian Skylark *Alauda arvensis*			IuP	IuP	IuP

	Hawaii	Alaska	Yukon Terr.	Northwest Terr.	British Columbia	Alberta	Saskatchewan	Manitoba	Ontario
Spotted Dove	cP								
Zebra Dove	cP								
White-winged Dove									
Mourning Dove	IrP†								

Order Psittaciformes: Parrots and Allies
Family Psittacidae: Lories, Parakeets, Macaws and Parrots
Subfamily Platycercinae: Australian Parakeets and Rosellas

Budgerigar									

Subfamily Psittacinae: Typical Parrots

Rose-ringed Parakeet	IrP								

Subfamily Arinae: New World Parakeets, Macaws and Parrots

Monk Parakeet									
Canary-winged Parakeet									
Red-crowned Parrot									
Lilac-crowned Parrot									
Yellow-headed Parrot									

Order Strigiformes: Owls
Family Tytonidae: Barn-Owls

Common Barn-Owl	uP								

Order Apodiformes: Swifts and Hummingbirds
Family Apodidae: Swifts
Subfamily Chaeturinae: Chaeturine Swifts

Gray Swiftlet	IrP								

Order Passeriformes: Passerine Birds
Family Alaudidae: Larks

Eurasian Skylark	fP			IuP					

Introduced Columbidae • 395

	Québec	Newfoundland	New Brunswick	Prince Edward I.	Nova Scotia	Washington	Oregon	California	Nevada	Idaho
Spotted Dove								IcP		
Zebra Dove										
White-winged Dove										
Mourning Dove										

Order Psittaciformes: Parrots and Allies
Family Psittacidae: Lories, Parakeets, Macaws and Parrots
Subfamily Platycercinae: Australian Parakeets and Rosellas

Budgerigar										

Subfamily Psittacinae: Typical Parrots

Rose-ringed Parakeet										

Subfamily Arinae: New World Parakeets, Macaws and Parrots

Monk Parakeet										
Canary-winged Parakeet								IrP-q		
Red-crowned Parrot								IrP-q		
Lilac-crowned Parrot								IrP-q		
Yellow-headed Parrot								IrP-q		

Order Strigiformes: Owls
Family Tytonidae: Barn-Owls

Common Barn-Owl										

Order Apodiformes: Swifts and Hummingbirds
Family Apodidae: Swifts
Subfamily Chaeturinae: Chaeturine Swifts

Gray Swiftlet										

Order Passeriformes: Passerine Birds
Family Alaudidae: Larks

Eurasian Skylark						IuP				

396 • *Distributional Checklist of North American Birds*

	Montana	Wyoming	Utah	Colorado	Arizona	New Mexico	North Dakota	South Dakota	Nebraska	Kansas	Oklahoma
Spotted Dove											
Zebra Dove											
White-winged Dove											
Mourning Dove											

Order Psittaciformes: Parrots and Allies
Family Psittacidae: Lories, Parakeets, Macaws and Parrots
Subfamily Platycercinae: Australian Parakeets and Rosellas

Budgerigar											

Subfamily Psittacinae: Typical Parrots

Rose-ringed Parakeet											

Subfamily Arinae: New World Parakeets, Macaws and Parrots

Monk Parakeet											
Canary-winged Parakeet											
Red-crowned Parrot											
Lilac-crowned Parrot											
Yellow-headed Parrot											

Order Strigiformes: Owls
Family Tytonidae: Barn-Owls

Common Barn-Owl											

Order Apodiformes: Swifts and Hummingbirds
Family Apodidae: Swifts
Subfamily Chaeturinae: Chaeturine Swifts

Gray Swiftlet												

Order Passeriformes: Passerine Birds
Family Alaudidae: Larks

Eurasian Skylark											

	Texas	Minnesota	Iowa	Missouri	Arkansas	Louisiana	Wisconsin	Michigan	Illinois	Indiana	Ohio
Spotted Dove											
Zebra Dove											
White-winged Dove											
Mourning Dove											

Order Psittaciformes: Parrots and Allies
Family Psittacidae: Lories, Parakeets, Macaws and Parrots
Subfamily Platycercinae: Australian Parakeets and Rosellas

Budgerigar											

Subfamily Psittacinae: Typical Parrots

Rose-ringed Parakeet											

Subfamily Arinae: New World Parakeets, Macaws and Parrots

Monk Parakeet											
Canary-winged Parakeet											
Red-crowned Parrot											
Lilac-crowned Parrot											
Yellow-headed Parrot											

Order Strigiformes: Owls
Family Tytonidae: Barn-Owls

Common Barn-Owl											

Order Apodiformes: Swifts and Hummingbirds
Family Apodidae: Swifts
Subfamily Chaeturinae: Chaeturine Swifts

Gray Swiftlet											

Order Passeriformes: Passerine Birds
Family Alaudidae: Larks

Eurasian Skylark											

	West Virginia	Kentucky	Tennessee	Mississippi	Alabama	Maine	New Hampshire	Vermont	Massachusetts	Rhode Island	Connecticut
Spotted Dove											
Zebra Dove											
White-winged Dove											
Mourning Dove											

Order Psittaciformes: Parrots and Allies
Family Psittacidae: Lories, Parakeets, Macaws and Parrots
Subfamily Platycercinae: Australian Parakeets and Rosellas

Budgerigar											

Subfamily Psittacinae: Typical Parrots

Rose-ringed Parakeet											

Subfamily Arinae: New World Parakeets, Macaws and Parrots

	West Virginia	Kentucky	Tennessee	Mississippi	Alabama	Maine	New Hampshire	Vermont	Massachusetts	Rhode Island	Connecticut
Monk Parakeet											
Canary-winged Parakeet										IrP-q	IrP
Red-crowned Parrot											
Lilac-crowned Parrot											
Yellow-headed Parrot											

Order Strigiformes: Owls
Family Tytonidae: Barn-Owls

Common Barn-Owl											

Order Apodiformes: Swifts and Hummingbirds
Family Apodidae: Swifts
Subfamily Chaeturinae: Chaeturine Swifts

Gray Swiftlet											

Order Passeriformes: Passerine Birds
Family Alaudidae: Larks

Eurasian Skylark											

Introduced Columbidae • 399

	New York	Pennsylvania	New Jersey	Delaware	Maryland	Dist. of Columbia	Virginia	North Carolina	South Carolina	Georgia	Florida
Spotted Dove											
Zebra Dove											
White-winged Dove												IfP
Mourning Dove											

Order Psittaciformes: Parrots and Allies
Family Psittacidae: Lories, Parakeets, Macaws and Parrots
Subfamily Platycercinae: Australian Parakeets and Rosellas

Budgerigar											IcP

Subfamily Psittacinae: Typical Parrots

Rose-ringed Parakeet											IuP

Subfamily Arinae: New World Parakeets, Macaws and Parrots

Monk Parakeet	IrP	IrP	IrP								IuP
Canary-winged Parakeet											IfP
Red-crowned Parrot											IfP
Lilac-crowned Parrot											
Yellow-headed Parrot											

Order Strigiformes: Owls
Family Tytonidae: Barn-Owls

Common Barn-Owl											

Order Apodiformes: Swifts and Hummingbirds
Family Apodidae: Swifts
Subfamily Chaeturinae: Chaeturine Swifts

Gray Swiftlet											

Order Passeriformes: Passerine Birds
Family Alaudidae: Larks

Eurasian Skylark											

Family Paridae: Titmice

		Date	Location	Cont. North America	Canada	Lower 48
Varied Tit *Parus varius*						

Family Pycnonotidae: Bulbuls

Red-vented Bulbul *Pycnonotus cafer*						
Red-whiskered Bulbul *Pycnonotus jocosus*				IfP		IfP

Family Muscicapidae: Muscicapids
Subfamily Sylviinae: Old World Warblers, Kinglets and Gnatcatchers

Japanese Bush-Warbler *Cettia diphone*						

Subfamily Turdinae: Solitaires, Thrushes and Allies

White-rumped Shama *Copsychus malabaricus*						

Subfamily Timaliinae: Babblers

Greater Necklaced Laughing-thrush *Garrulax pectoralis*						
Gray-sided Laughing-thrush *Garrulax caerulatus*						
Melodious Laughing-thrush *Garrulax canorus*						
Red-billed Leiothrix *Leiothrix lutea*						

Family Mimidae: Mockingbirds, Thrashers and Allies

Northern Mockingbird *Mimus polyglottos*						

Family Sturnidae: Starlings and Allies
Subfamily Sturninae: Starlings

European Starling *Sturnus vulgaris*				cP	cP	cP
Common Myna *Acridotheres tristis*						
Crested Myna *Acridotheres cristatellus*				IfP	IfP	
Hill Myna *Gracula religiosa*				IuP		IuP

Family Paridae: Titmice

	Hawaii	Alaska	Yukon Terr.	Northwest Terr.	British Columbia	Alberta	Saskatchewan	Manitoba	Ontario
Varied Tit	ePt†								

Family Pycnonotidae: Bulbuls

Red-vented Bulbul	cP								
Red-whiskered Bulbul	lcP								

Family Muscicapidae: Muscicapids
Subfamily Sylviinae: Old World Warblers, Kinglets and Gnatcatchers

Japanese Bush-Warbler	fP								

Subfamily Turdinae: Solitaires, Thrushes and Allies

White-rumped Shama	cP								

Subfamily Timaliinae: Babblers

Gr. Necklaced Laugh.-thrush	lrP†								
Gray-sided Laugh.-thrush	lrP†								
Melodious Laugh.-thrush	fP								
Red-billed Leiothrix	fP								

Family Mimidae: Mockingbirds, Thrashers and Allies

Northern Mockingbird	fP								

Family Sturnidae: Starlings and Allies
Subfamily Sturninae: Starlings

			Yukon Terr.	Northwest Terr.	British Columbia	Alberta	Saskatchewan	Manitoba	Ontario
European Starling	xV	luP,xV	rS,xW	lcS,xV	cP	cS,uW	cS,fW	cS,fW	cP
Common Myna	cP								
Crested Myna					lfP				
Hill Myna									

Family Paridae: Titmice

	Québec	Newfound-land	New Brunswick	Prince Edward I.	Nova Scotia		Washing-ton	Oregon	California	Nevada	Idaho
Varied Tit											

Family Pycnonotidae: Bulbuls

Red-vented Bulbul											
Red-whiskered Bulbul											

Family Muscicapidae: Muscicapids
Subfamily Sylviinae: Old World Warblers, Kinglets and Gnatcatchers

Japanese Bush-Warbler											

Subfamily Turdinae: Solitaires, Thrushes and Allies

White-rumped Shama											

Subfamily Timaliinae: Babblers

Gr. Necklaced Laugh.-thrush											
Gray-sided Laugh.-thrush											
Melodious Laugh.-thrush											
Red-billed Leiothrix											

Family Mimidae: Mockingbirds, Thrashers and Allies

Northern Mockingbird											

Family Sturnidae: Starlings and Allies
Subfamily Sturninae: Starlings

European Starling	cS.fW	cP	cP	cP	cP		cP	cP	cP	cP	cP
Common Myna											
Crested Myna											
Hill Myna											

Family Paridae: Titmice

	Montana	Wyoming	Utah	Colorado	Arizona	New Mexico	North Dakota	South Dakota	Nebraska	Kansas	Oklahoma
Varied Tit											

Family Pycnonotidae: Bulbuls

Red-vented Bulbul											
Red-whiskered Bulbul											

Family Muscicapidae: Muscicapids
Subfamily Sylviinae: Old World Warblers, Kinglets and Gnatcatchers

Japanese Bush-Warbler											

Subfamily Turdinae: Solitaires, Thrushes and Allies

White-rumped Shama											

Subfamily Timaliinae: Babblers

Gr. Necklaced Laugh.-thrush											
Gray-sided Laugh.-thrush											
Melodious Laugh.-thrush											
Red-billed Leiothrix											

Family Mimidae: Mockingbirds, Thrashers and Allies

Northern Mockingbird											

Family Sturnidae: Starlings and Allies
Subfamily Sturninae: Starlings

European Starling	cP	cP	cP	cP	cP	cP	cP	cP	cP	cP	cP
Common Myna											
Crested Myna											
Hill Myna											

Family Paridae: Titmice

	Texas	Minnesota	Iowa	Missouri	Arkansas	Louisiana	Wisconsin	Michigan	Illinois	Indiana	Ohio
Varied Tit											

Family Pycnonotidae: Bulbuls

Red-vented Bulbul											
Red-whiskered Bulbul											

Family Muscicapidae: Muscicapids
Subfamily Sylviinae: Old World Warblers, Kinglets and Gnatcatchers

Japanese Bush-Warbler											

Subfamily Turdinae: Solitaires, Thrushes and Allies

White-rumped Shama											

Subfamily Timaliinae: Babblers

Gr. Necklaced Laugh.-thrush											
Gray-sided Laugh.-thrush											
Melodious Laugh.-thrush											
Red-billed Leiothrix											

Family Mimidae: Mockingbirds, Thrashers and Allies

Northern Mockingbird											

Family Sturnidae: Starlings and Allies
Subfamily Sturninae: Starlings

European Starling	cP	cP	cP	cP	cP	cP	cP	cP	cP	cP	cP
Common Myna											
Crested Myna											
Hill Myna											

Family Paridae: Titmice

	West Virginia	Kentucky	Tennessee	Mississippi	Alabama	Maine	New Hampshire	Vermont	Massachusetts	Rhode Island	Connecticut
Varied Tit											

Family Pycnonotidae: Bulbuls

Red-vented Bulbul											
Red-whiskered Bulbul											

Family Muscicapidae: Muscicapids
Subfamily Sylviinae: Old World Warblers, Kinglets and Gnatcatchers

Japanese Bush-Warbler											

Subfamily Turdinae: Solitaires, Thrushes and Allies

White-rumped Shama											

Subfamily Timaliinae: Babblers

Gr. Necklaced Laugh.-thrush											
Gray-sided Laugh.-thrush											
Melodious Laugh.-thrush											
Red-billed Leiothrix											

Family Mimidae: Mockingbirds, Thrashers and Allies

Northern Mockingbird											

Family Sturnidae: Starlings and Allies
Subfamily Sturninae: Starlings

European Starling	cP	cP	cP	cP	cP	cP	cP	cP	cP	cP	cP
Common Myna											
Crested Myna											
Hill Myna											

Family Paridae: Titmice

	New York	Pennsylvania	New Jersey	Delaware	Maryland	Dist. of Columbia	Virginia	North Carolina	South Carolina	Georgia	Florida
Varied Tit											

Family Pycnonotidae: Bulbuls

	New York	Pennsylvania	New Jersey	Delaware	Maryland	Dist. of Columbia	Virginia	North Carolina	South Carolina	Georgia	Florida
Red-vented Bulbul											
Red-whiskered Bulbul											IfP

Family Muscicapidae: Muscicapids
Subfamily Sylviinae: Old World Warblers, Kinglets and Gnatcatchers

	New York	Pennsylvania	New Jersey	Delaware	Maryland	Dist. of Columbia	Virginia	North Carolina	South Carolina	Georgia	Florida
Japanese Bush-Warbler											

Subfamily Turdinae: Solitaires, Thrushes and Allies

	New York	Pennsylvania	New Jersey	Delaware	Maryland	Dist. of Columbia	Virginia	North Carolina	South Carolina	Georgia	Florida
White-rumped Shama											

Subfamily Timaliinae: Babblers

	New York	Pennsylvania	New Jersey	Delaware	Maryland	Dist. of Columbia	Virginia	North Carolina	South Carolina	Georgia	Florida
Gr. Necklaced Laugh.-thrush											
Gray-sided Laugh.-thrush											
Melodious Laugh.-thrush											
Red-billed Leiothrix											

Family Mimidae: Mockingbirds, Thrashers and Allies

	New York	Pennsylvania	New Jersey	Delaware	Maryland	Dist. of Columbia	Virginia	North Carolina	South Carolina	Georgia	Florida
Northern Mockingbird											

Family Sturnidae: Starlings and Allies
Subfamily Sturninae: Starlings

	New York	Pennsylvania	New Jersey	Delaware	Maryland	Dist. of Columbia	Virginia	North Carolina	South Carolina	Georgia	Florida
European Starling	cP	cP	cP	cP	cP	cP	cP	cP	cP	cP	cP
Common Myna											
Crested Myna											
Hill Myna											IuP

Family Zosteropidae: White-eyes

		Date	Location	Cont. North America	Canada	Lower 48
Japanese White-eye *Zosterops japonicus*						

Family Emberizidae: Emberizids
Subfamily Cardinalinae: Cardinals, Grosbeaks and Allies

Northern Cardinal *Cardinalis cardinalis*				IrP		IrP

Subfamily Emberizinae: Emberizines

Red-crested Cardinal *Paroaria coronata*						
Yellow-billed Cardinal *Paroaria capitata*						
Yellow-faced Grassquit *Tiaris olivacea*						
Saffron Finch *Sicalis flaveola*						

Subfamily Icterinae: Icterines

Western Meadowlark *Sturnella neglecta*						
Spot-breasted Oriole *Icterus pectoralis*				IuP		IuP

Family Fringillidae: Fringilline and Cardueline Finches and Allies
Subfamily Carduelinae: Cardueline Finches

House Finch *Carpodacus mexicanus*				fP	IfP,xS*,rV,xW	cP
European Goldfinch *Carduelis carduelis*				eP		eP
Yellow-fronted Canary *Serinus mozambicus*						
Common Canary *Serinus canaria*						

Family Passeridae: Old World Sparrows

House Sparrow *Passer domesticus*				cP	cP	cP
Eurasian Tree Sparrow *Passer montanus*				IfP,xV,xW		IfP,xV,xW

Family Estrildidae: Estrildid Finches
Subfamily Estrildinae: Estrildine Finches

Red-cheeked Cordonbleu *Uraeginthus bengalus*						
Lavender Waxbill *Estrilda caerulescens*						

Family Zosteropidae: White-eyes

	Hawaii	Alaska	Yukon Terr.	Northwest Terr.	British Columbia	Alberta	Saskatchewan	Manitoba	Ontario
Japanese White-eye	cP								

Family Emberizidae: Emberizids
Subfamily Cardinalinae: Cardinals, Grosbeaks and Allies

Northern Cardinal	cP								

Subfamily Emberizinae: Emberizines

Red-crested Cardinal	cP								
Yellow-billed Cardinal	IfP								
Yellow-faced Grassquit	IuP†								
Saffron Finch	IfP								

Subfamily Icterinae: Icterines

Western Meadowlark	IfP								
Spot-breasted Oriole									

Family Fringillidae: Fringilline and Cardueline Finches and Allies
Subfamily Carduelinae: Cardueline Finches

House Finch	cP								IfP
European Goldfinch									
Yellow-fronted Canary	IfP								
Common Canary	IuP								

Family Passeridae: Old World Sparrows

House Sparrow	cP	xV-q	xW	IfS,IuW	cP	cP	cP	cP	cP
Eurasian Tree Sparrow									

Family Estrildidae: Estrildid Finches
Subfamily Estrildinae: Estrildine Finches

Red-cheeked Cordonbleu	IrP†								
Lavender Waxbill	IrP†								

Family Zosteropidae: White-eyes

	Québec	Newfound-land	New Brunswick	Prince Edward I.	Nova Scotia		Washington	Oregon	California	Nevada	Idaho
Japanese White-eye											

Family Emberizidae: Emberizids
Subfamily Cardinalinae: Cardinals, Grosbeaks and Allies

Northern Cardinal									IrP		

Subfamily Emberizinae: Emberizines

Red-crested Cardinal											
Yellow-billed Cardinal											
Yellow-faced Grassquit											
Saffron Finch											

Subfamily Icterinae: Icterines

Western Meadowlark											
Spot-breasted Oriole											

Family Fringillidae: Fringilline and Cardueline Finches and Allies
Subfamily Carduelinae: Cardueline Finches

House Finch	IrP		xS*,rV,xW		xS*,rV						
European Goldfinch											
Yellow-fronted Canary											
Common Canary											

Family Passeridae: Old World Sparrows

House Sparrow	cP	cP	cP	cP	cP		cP	cP	cP	cP	cP
Eurasian Tree Sparrow											

Family Estrildidae: Estrildid Finches
Subfamily Estrildinae: Estrildine Finches

Red-cheeked Cordonbleu											
Lavender Waxbill											

Family Zosteropidae: White-eyes

	Montana	Wyoming	Utah	Colorado	Arizona	New Mexico	North Dakota	South Dakota	Nebraska	Kansas	Oklahoma
Japanese White-eye											

Family Emberizidae: Emberizids
Subfamily Cardinalinae: Cardinals, Grosbeaks and Allies

Northern Cardinal											

Subfamily Emberizinae: Emberizines

Red-crested Cardinal											
Yellow-billed Cardinal											
Yellow-faced Grassquit											
Saffron Finch											

Subfamily Icterinae: Icterines

Western Meadowlark											
Spot-breasted Oriole											

Family Fringillidae: Fringilline and Cardueline Finches and Allies
Subfamily Carduelinae: Cardueline Finches

House Finch											
European Goldfinch											
Yellow-fronted Canary											
Common Canary											

Family Passeridae: Old World Sparrows

House Sparrow	cP	cP	cP	cP	cP	cP	cP	cP	cP	cP	cP
Eurasian Tree Sparrow											

Family Estrildidae: Estrildid Finches
Subfamily Estrildinae: Estrildine Finches

Red-cheeked Cordonbleu											
Lavender Waxbill											

Family Zosteropidae: White-eyes

	Texas	Minnesota	Iowa	Missouri	Arkansas	Louisiana	Wisconsin	Michigan	Illinois	Indiana	Ohio
Japanese White-eye											

Family Emberizidae: Emberizids
Subfamily Cardinalinae: Cardinals, Grosbeaks and Allies

Northern Cardinal											

Subfamily Emberizinae: Emberizines

Red-crested Cardinal											
Yellow-billed Cardinal											
Yellow-faced Grassquit											
Saffron Finch											

Subfamily Icterinae: Icterines

Western Meadowlark											
Spot-breasted Oriole											

Family Fringillidae: Fringilline and Carduelinae Finches and Allies
Subfamily Carduelinae: Carduelinae Finches

	Texas	Minnesota	Iowa	Missouri	Arkansas	Louisiana	Wisconsin	Michigan	Illinois	Indiana	Ohio
House Finch		xS*,xV	xV	xP	xV,xW	xV,xW	xV,xW-q	uP	IrP,rV,rW	uP	fP
European Goldfinch											
Yellow-fronted Canary											
Common Canary											

Family Passeridae: Old World Sparrows

	Texas	Minnesota	Iowa	Missouri	Arkansas	Louisiana	Wisconsin	Michigan	Illinois	Indiana	Ohio
House Sparrow	cP	cP	cP	cP	cP	cP	cP	cP	cP	cP	cP
Eurasian Tree Sparrow				IfP				xV		IfP	

Family Estrildidae: Estrildid Finches
Subfamily Estrildinae: Estrildine Finches

Red-cheeked Cordonbleu											
Lavender Waxbill											

Family Zosteropidae: White-eyes

	West Virginia	Kentucky	Tennessee	Mississippi	Alabama	Maine	New Hampshire	Vermont	Massachusetts	Rhode Island	Connecticut
Japanese White-eye											

Family Emberizidae: Emberizids
Subfamily Cardinalinae: Cardinals, Grosbeaks and Allies

	West Virginia	Kentucky	Tennessee	Mississippi	Alabama	Maine	New Hampshire	Vermont	Massachusetts	Rhode Island	Connecticut
Northern Cardinal											

Subfamily Emberizinae: Emberizines

	West Virginia	Kentucky	Tennessee	Mississippi	Alabama	Maine	New Hampshire	Vermont	Massachusetts	Rhode Island	Connecticut
Red-crested Cardinal											
Yellow-billed Cardinal											
Yellow-faced Grassquit											
Saffron Finch											

Subfamily Icterinae: Icterines

	West Virginia	Kentucky	Tennessee	Mississippi	Alabama	Maine	New Hampshire	Vermont	Massachusetts	Rhode Island	Connecticut
Western Meadowlark											
Spot-breasted Oriole											

Family Fringillidae: Fringilline and Cardueline Finches and Allies
Subfamily Carduelinae: Cardueline Finches

	West Virginia	Kentucky	Tennessee	Mississippi	Alabama	Maine	New Hampshire	Vermont	Massachusetts	Rhode Island	Connecticut
House Finch	fP	uS,fW	uP	xV,xW	uP	fP	fP	fP	fP	cP	cP
European Goldfinch											
Yellow-fronted Canary											
Common Canary											

Family Passeridae: Old World Sparrows

	West Virginia	Kentucky	Tennessee	Mississippi	Alabama	Maine	New Hampshire	Vermont	Massachusetts	Rhode Island	Connecticut
House Sparrow	cP	cP	cP	cP	cP	cP	cP	cP	cP	cP	cP
Eurasian Tree Sparrow		xW									

Family Estrildidae: Estrildid Finches
Subfamily Estrildinae: Estrildine Finches

	West Virginia	Kentucky	Tennessee	Mississippi	Alabama	Maine	New Hampshire	Vermont	Massachusetts	Rhode Island	Connecticut
Red-cheeked Cordonbleu											
Lavender Waxbill											

Family Zosteropidae: White-eyes

	New York	Pennsylvania	New Jersey	Delaware	Maryland	Dist. of Columbia	Virginia	North Carolina	South Carolina	Georgia	Florida
Japanese White-eye											

Family Emberizidae: Emberizids
Subfamily Cardinalinae: Cardinals, Grosbeaks and Allies

Northern Cardinal											

Subfamily Emberizinae: Emberizines

Red-crested Cardinal											
Yellow-billed Cardinal											
Yellow-faced Grassquit											
Saffron Finch											

Subfamily Icterinae: Icterines

Western Meadowlark											
Spot-breasted Oriole												IuP

Family Fringillidae: Fringilline and Cardueline Finches and Allies
Subfamily Carduelinae: Cardueline Finches

	New York	Pennsylvania	New Jersey	Delaware	Maryland	Dist. of Columbia	Virginia	North Carolina	South Carolina	Georgia	Florida
House Finch	cP	cP	cP	cP	cP	cP	cP	uS,fW	IrS,uW	uP	xV
European Goldfinch	eP										
Yellow-fronted Canary											
Common Canary											

Family Passeridae: Old World Sparrows

House Sparrow	cP	cP	cP	cP	cP	cP	cP	cP	cP	cP	cP
Eurasian Tree Sparrow											

Family Estrildidae: Estrildid Finches
Subfamily Estrildinae: Estrildine Finches

Red-cheeked Cordonbleu											
Lavender Waxbill											

	Date	Location	Cont. North America	Canada	Lower 48
Orange-cheeked Waxbill *Estrilda melpoda*					
Black-rumped Waxbill *Estrilda troglodytes*					
Common Waxbill *Estrilda astrild*					
Red Avadavat *Amandava amandava*					
Warbling Silverbill *Lonchura malabarica*					
Nutmeg Mannikin *Lonchura punctulata*					
Chestnut Mannikin *Lonchura malacca*					
Java Sparrow *Padda oryzivora*					

Additional species

Native and introduced species counts

	North America			
Total species	975	879	596	809
Breeding species	776	674	427	571
Wintering species	784	685	342	671

418 • Distributional Checklist of North American Birds

	Hawaii
Orange-cheeked Waxbill	IuP†
Black-rumped Waxbill	IrP†
Common Waxbill	IfP
Red Avadavat	IfP
Warbling Silverbill	fP
Nutmeg Mannikin	cP
Chestnut Mannikin	IcP
Java Sparrow	IuP

Additional species

Native and introduced species counts

	Hawaii	Alaska	Yukon Terr.	Northwest Terr.	British Columbia	Alberta	Saskatchewan	Manitoba	Ontario
Total	271	438	251	293	445	360	375	368	429
Breeding	131	255	182	228	298	266	259	275	285
Wintering	205	179	62	49	270	117	147	108	219

Introduced Estrildidae • 419

	Québec	Newfoundland	New Brunswick	Prince Edward I.	Nova Scotia
Orange-cheeked Waxbill					
Black-rumped Waxbill					
Common Waxbill					
Red Avadavat					
Warbling Silverbill					
Nutmeg Mannikin					
Chestnut Mannikin					
Java Sparrow					

	Washington	Oregon	California	Nevada	Idaho
Orange-cheeked Waxbill					
Black-rumped Waxbill					
Common Waxbill					
Red Avadavat					
Warbling Silverbill					
Nutmeg Mannikin					
Chestnut Mannikin					
Java Sparrow					

Additional species

Native and introduced species counts

	Québec	Newfoundland	New Brunswick	Prince Edward I.	Nova Scotia
Total	389	343	368	278	404
Breeding	263	168	192	146	180
Wintering	166	162	166	100	182

	Washington	Oregon	California	Nevada	Idaho
Total	422	440	571	428	358
Breeding	254	261	321	242	231
Wintering	280	298	470	234	180

	Montana	Wyoming	Utah	Colorado	Arizona	New Mexico	North Dakota	South Dakota	Nebraska	Kansas	Oklahoma
Orange-cheeked Waxbill											
Black-rumped Waxbill											
Common Waxbill											
Red Avadavat											
Warbling Silverbill											
Nutmeg Mannikin											
Chestnut Mannikin											
Java Sparrow											

Additional species

Native and introduced species counts

	Montana	Wyoming	Utah	Colorado	Arizona	New Mexico	North Dakota	South Dakota	Nebraska	Kansas	Oklahoma
Total	383	385	380	438	501	472	367	381	417	416	441
Breeding	245	233	239	261	280	273	220	224	221	206	214
Wintering	178	145	210	203	361	276	126	145	163	191	239

Introduced Estrildidae • 421

	Texas	Minnesota	Iowa	Missouri	Arkansas	Louisiana	Wisconsin	Michigan	Illinois	Indiana	Ohio
Orange-cheeked Waxbill											
Black-rumped Waxbill											
Common Waxbill											
Red Avadavat											
Warbling Silverbill											
Nutmeg Mannikin											
Chestnut Mannikin											
Java Sparrow											

Additional species

Native and introduced species counts

	Texas	Minnesota	Iowa	Missouri	Arkansas	Louisiana	Wisconsin	Michigan	Illinois	Indiana	Ohio
Total	589	398	372	387	361	427	400	388	399	381	383
Breeding	335	254	199	184	157	176	237	231	211	188	205
Wintering	470	181	162	212	193	312	189	198	220	193	201

	West Virginia	Kentucky	Tennessee	Mississippi	Alabama	Maine	New Hampshire	Vermont	Massachusetts	Rhode Island	Connecticut
Orange-cheeked Waxbill											
Black-rumped Waxbill											
Common Waxbill											
Red Avadavat											
Warbling Silverbill											
Nutmeg Mannikin											
Chestnut Mannikin											
Java Sparrow											

Additional species

Native and introduced species counts

	West Virginia	Kentucky	Tennessee	Mississippi	Alabama	Maine	New Hampshire	Vermont	Massachusetts	Rhode Island	Connecticut
Total	303	337	345	372	391	407	370	340	447	389	393
Breeding	179	164	179	153	180	206	191	194	213	175	191
Wintering	145	190	186	252	285	184	172	134	251	217	213

	New York	Pennsylvania	New Jersey	Delaware	Maryland	Dist. of Columbia	Virginia	North Carolina	South Carolina	Georgia	Florida
Orange-cheeked Waxbill											
Black-rumped Waxbill											
Common Waxbill											
Red Avadavat											
Warbling Silverbill											
Nutmeg Mannikin											
Chestnut Mannikin											
Java Sparrow											

Additional species

	New York	Pennsylvania	New Jersey	Delaware	Maryland	Dist. of Columbia	Virginia	North Carolina	South Carolina	Georgia	Florida

Native and introduced species counts

	New York	Pennsylvania	New Jersey	Delaware	Maryland	Dist. of Columbia	Virginia	North Carolina	South Carolina	Georgia	Florida
Total	435	402	423	366	390	303	412	411	390	383	466
Breeding	240	199	208	157	207	97	210	201	173	176	179
Wintering	263	216	259	209	248	140	276	276	274	279	363

Bibliography

The following references pertain in whole or part to the distribution of the birds of North America:

American Ornithologists' Union. 1931. *Check-list of North American birds*, 4th ed. Amer. Ornith. Union, Lancaster, PA. 526 pp.

American Ornithologists' Union. 1957. *Check-list of North American birds*, 5th ed. Amer. Ornith. Union, Baltimore, MD. 691 pp.

American Ornithologists' Union. 1982. Thirty-fourth supplement to the American Ornithologists' Union check-list of North American Birds. Supplement to *The Auk* **99**: 1cc-16cc.

American Ornithologists' Union. 1983. *Check-list of North American birds*, 6th ed. Amer. Ornith. Union, Washington, D.C. 877 pp.

American Ornithologists' Union. 1985. Thirty-fifth supplement to the American Ornithologists' Union check-list of North American birds. *Auk* **102**: 680–686.

Flint, V. E., R. L. Boehme, Y. V. Kostin and A. A. Kuznetsov. 1984. *A field guide to the birds of the USSR*. Princeton Univ. Press, Princeton, NJ. 353 pp.

Godfrey, W. E. 1966. *The birds of Canada*. National Museums of Canada, Bull. No. 203. Biological Series No. 73. Ottawa, Ontario. 428 pp.

National Geographic Society. 1983. *Field guide to the birds of North America*. National Geographic Soc., Washington, D.C. 464 pp.

Palmer, R. S. (ed.). 1962. *Handbook of North American birds, Vol. 1, Loons through Flamingos*. Yale Univ. Press, New Haven, CT. 567 pp.

Palmer, R. S. (ed.). 1976. *Handbook of North American birds, Vol. 2, Waterfowl (Part 1)*. Yale Univ. Press, New Haven, CT. 521 pp.

Palmer, R. S. (ed.). 1976. *Handbook of North American birds, Vol. 3, Waterfowl (Part 2)*. Yale Univ. Press, New Haven, CT. 560 pp.

Peterson, R. T. 1980. *A field guide to the birds*. Houghton Mifflin, Boston. 384 pp.

Robbins, C. S., B. Bruun and H. S. Zim. 1983. *A guide to field identification: birds of North America*. Golden Press, New York. 360 pp.

Roberson, D. 1980. *Rare birds of the West Coast of North America*. Woodcock Publications, Pacific Grove, CA. 496 pp.

The following references pertain in whole or in part to the birds of individual provinces and territories of Canada:

ALBERTA

Salt, W. R. and J. R. Salt. 1976. *The birds of Alberta with their ranges in Saskatchewan and Manitoba*. Hurtig Pubs., Edmonton, Alberta. 498 pp.

Stepney, P. H. R. 1981. *Checklist of Alberta birds*, 4th ed. Prov. Museum of Alberta, Edmonton. 9 pp.

BRITISH COLUMBIA

Campbell, R. W. 1984. *Checklist of British Columbia Birds*. British Columbia Prov. Museum, Victoria. 812 pp.

MANITOBA

Anonymous. 1979. *Manitoba birds: field checklist*. Manitoba Museum of Man and Nature, Winnipeg. 6 pp.

Cleveland, N. J., G. D. Grieef, G. E. Holland, P. A. Horch, R. W. Knapton, R. F. Koes and W. D. Kyle. 1978. *Field check-list of the birds of south-eastern Manitoba*. Manitoba Naturalists' Society, Winnipeg. 8 pp.

Lane, J. A. and B. Chartier. 1983. *A birder's guide to Churchill*. L & P Press, Denver, CO.

NEW BRUNSWICK

Anonymous. 1985. *Checklist of New Brunswick Birds*. New Brunswick Federation of Naturalists and New Brunswick Museum, Saint John. 5 pp.

Squires, W. A. 1976. *The birds of New Brunswick*, 2nd ed. Museum Monograph No. 7. New Brunswick Museum, Saint John. 221 pp.

NEWFOUNDLAND (including Labrador and Saint-Pierre et Miquelon)

Etcheberry, R. and M. Borotra. 1982. *Les oiseaux de Saint-Pierre et Miquelon*. R. Etcheberry, Saint-Pierre. 78 pp.

Maunder, J. E. and W. A. Montevecchi. 1982. *Field check-list of the birds of insular Newfoundland*. Newfoundland Natural History Society, St. John's. 2 pp.

Montevecchi, W. A. and L. M. Tuck. In press. *Newfoundland birds: an historical survey*. Bull. Nuttall Ornith. Club, Cambridge, MA.

Todd, W. E. C. 1963. *Birds of Labrador Peninsula and adjacent areas*. Carnegie Museum and Univ. of Toronto Press, Toronto, Ontario.

NORTHWEST TERRITORIES

Gollop, J. B. and B. W. Johns. 1978. *Birds of the Northwest Territories*, preliminary checklist. Canadian Wildlife Service, Saskatoon, Sask. 2 pp.

Scotter, G. W., L. N. Carbyn, W. P. Neily and J. D. Henry. 1985. *Birds of Nahanni National Park, Northwest Territories*. Saskatchewan Natural History Society Special Pub. No. 15, Regina, Sask. 74 pp.

NOVA SCOTIA

Allen, C. R. K., P. R. Dobson, B. J. Smith, G. D. Perry, R. B. Dickie and J. S. Cohrs. 1984. *Birding Nova Scotia*. Nova Scotia Bird Society, Halifax. 31 pp.

Tufts, R. W. 1973. *The birds of Nova Scotia*, 2nd ed. Nova Scotia Museum, Halifax. 532 pp.

ONTARIO

Goodwin, C. E. 1982. *A bird finding guide to Ontario*. Univ. of Toronto Press, Toronto, Ontario.

James, R. D., P. D. McLaren and J. C. Barlow. 1976. *Annotated checklist of the birds of Ontario*. Royal Ontario Museum, Toronto. 75 pp.

Peck, G. K. and R. D. James. 1983. *Breeding birds of Ontario: Vol. 1, Non-passerines*. Royal Ontario Museum, Toronto. 321 pp.

Speirs, J. M. 1985. *Birds of Ontario*. Natural Heritage/Natural History Inc., Toronto, Ontario. 1524 pp.

Wormington, A. and R. D. James. 1984. Ontario Bird Records Committee checklist of the birds of Ontario. *Ontario Birds* **2**: 13–23.

PRINCE EDWARD ISLAND

Dept. of Tourism, Parks and Conservation. 1978. *Field checklist of birds, Prince Edward Island, Atlantic Canada*. P. E. I. Government, Charlottetown.

Martin, K. and W. Cairns. 1979. *Avifaunal survey of Prince Edward Island National Park*. Canadian Wildlife Serv., Charlottetown, P. E. I. 231 pp.

QUÉBEC

David, N. 1980. *Status and distribution of the birds of southern Québec*. Club des Ornithologues du Québec, Sainte-Foy. 213 pp.

SASKATCHEWAN

Kreba, R. 1983. *Field checklist of Saskatchewan birds*, 6th ed. Saskatchewan Museum of Natural History, Regina. 6 pp.

Mitchell, H. H. 1924. Birds of Saskatchewan. *Canadian Field-Naturalist* **38**: 101–120.

YUKON TERRITORY

Game Branch, Yukon Territorial Government. 1970. *Field checklist of the birds of the Yukon Territory*. Yukon Dept. of Renewable Resources and Yukon Conservation Society, Whitehorse. 1 p.

Grünberg, H. 1984. *Field checklist of the birds of the Yukon Territory*. Yukon Conservation Society, Whitehorse. 4 pp.

The following references pertain in whole or in part to the birds of the individual states (and District of Columbia) of the United States:

ALABAMA

Imhof, T. A. 1976. *Alabama's birds*, 2nd ed. Univ. of Alabama Press, Univ. of Alabama. 445 pp.

Imhof, T. A. 1985. *Occurrence of Alabama's birds by season and region*. T. A. Imhof, Birmingham, AL. 12 pp.

Imhof, T. A. In press. *Annotated checklist of Alabama birds*. Dept. of Conservation & Natural Resources, State of Alabama, Montgomery.

ALASKA

Armstrong, R. H. 1980. *A guide to the birds of Alaska*. Alaska Northwest Publ. Co., Anchorage. 309 pp.

Gabrielson, I. N. and F. C. Lincoln. 1959. *The birds of Alaska*. Stackpole Co., Harrisburg, PA. and Wildl. Mgmt. Inst., Washington, D.C. 922 pp.

Gibson, D. D. 1983. *Checklist of Alaska birds*. Univ. Alaska Museum, Fairbanks. 8 pp.

Kessel, B. and D. D. Gibson. 1978. Status and distribution of Alaska birds. *Stud. Avian Biology* **1**: 1–100.

ARIZONA

Arizona Bird Committee. 1984. *Checklist of the birds of Arizona*. Arizona Bird Committee, Phoenix. 8 pp.

Monson, G. and A. R. Phillips. 1981. *Annotated checklist of the birds of Arizona*. Univ. of Arizona Press, Tucson. 240 pp.

ARKANSAS

Anonymous. 1980. *Arkansas Audubon Society field list*. Arkansas Audubon Soc., Wilton. 4 pp.

James, D. 1982. *Checklist of the birds sighted in Arkansas*. Ark. Acad. of Sci., Ark. Biota Checklist No. 33. Univ. of Arkansas Press, Fayetteville. 9 pp.

James, D. and J. C. Neal. In press. *Arkansas birds—their distribution and abundance*. Univ. of Arkansas Press, Fayetteville.

CALIFORNIA

Jones, L., K. Garrett and A. Small. 1981. Checklist of the birds of California. *Western Birds* **12**: 57–72.

Garrett, K. and J. Dunn. 1981. *Birds of southern California, status and distribution*. Los Angeles Audubon Soc., Los Angeles. 408 pp.

Grinnell, J. and A. H. Miller. 1944. *The distribution of the birds of California*. Pacific Coast Avifauna No. 27. Cooper Ornithological Soc., Berkeley, CA. 608 pp.

McCaskie, G. 1984. *Field list of the birds of California*. San Diego Field Ornithologists, San Diego, CA. 16 pp.

McCaskie, G., P. De Benedictis, R. Erickson and J. Morlan. 1979. *Birds of northern California, an annotated field list*, 2nd ed. Golden Gate Audubon Soc., Berkeley, CA. 84 pp.

COLORADO

Andrews, R. A. 1980. The C.F.O. checklist of Colorado Birds. *Colorado Field Ornithologists' Journal* **14**: 82–87.

Bailey, A. M. and R. J. Niedrach. 1967. *Pictorial checklist of Colorado birds*. Denver Museum of Nat. Hist., Denver, CO. 168 pp.

Chase, C. A., III, S. J. Bissell, H. E. Kingery, W. D. Graul and M. B. Dillon, eds. 1982. *Colorado bird distribution latilong study*. Colorado Field Ornithologists, Denver. 78 pp.

Colorado Field Ornithologists. 1984. *Field checklist of Colorado birds*. Colorado Field Ornithologists, Denver. 6 pp.

CONNECTICUT

Proctor, N. S. and F. C. Sibley. 1978. *Preliminary checklist of the birds of Connecticut*. Noble S. Proctor, Branford, CT. 6 pp.

Delaware
Hess, G. K. and M. V. Barnhill III. 1984. Delmarva Ornithological Society Records Committee report. *Delmarva Ornithologist* **16**: 14–16.

District of Columbia
Czaplak, D. In press. Checklist of the birds of the District of Columbia. *Atlantic Naturalist*.

Florida
Sprunt, A., Jr. 1954. *Florida bird life*. Coward-McCann, Inc. and National Audubon Society, New York. 527 pp.

Georgia
Denton, J. F., W. W. Baker, L. B. Davenport Jr., M. N. Hopkins and C. S. Robbins. 1977. *Annotated checklist of Georgia birds*. Occasional Pub. No. 6. Georgia Ornithological Soc. 57 pp.

Hawaii
Berger, A. J. 1981. *Hawaiian Birdlife*, 2nd ed. Univ. Press of Hawaii, Honolulu. 260 pp.

Pyle, R. L. 1983. Checklist of the birds of Hawaii. *Elepaio* **44**: 47–58.

Idaho
Burleigh, T. D. 1971. *Birds of Idaho*. Caxton Printers, Caldwell, ID.

Stephens, D. A. and T. D. Reynolds. 1983. Birds of southwestern Idaho. *Great Basin Naturalist* **43**: 728–738.

Illinois
Bohlen, H. D. 1978. *An annotated check-list of the birds of Illinois*. Popular Science Series, Vol. IX. Illinois State Museum, Springfield. 156 pp.

Indiana
Indiana Ornithological Records Committee. 1980. Indiana Audubon Society checklist of Indiana birds. *Indiana Audubon Quarterly* **58**: 132–138.

Keller, C. E., S. A. Keller and T. C. Keller. 1979. *Indiana birds and their haunts*. Indiana Univ. Press, Bloomington. 224 pp.

Mumford, R. E. and C. E. Keller. 1984. *Birds of Indiana*. Indiana Univ. Press, Bloomington. 400 pp.

Iowa
Dinsmore, J. J., T. H. Kent, D. Koenig, P. C. Peterson and D. M. Roosa. 1984. *Iowa birds*. Iowa State Univ. Press, Ames. 356 pp.

Iowa Ornithologists' Union. 1982. Official checklist of Iowa birds. *Iowa Bird Life*, Sept. 1982: 67–77.

Kansas
Ely, C. A. and M. Thompson. In press. *Birds of Kansas*. Kansas Regency Press, Lawrence.

Johnston, R. F. 1965. *A directory to the birds of Kansas*. Misc. Pub. No. 41. Museum of Nat. Hist., Univ. of Kansas, Lawrence. 67 pp.

Kansas Ornithological Society. 1982. *Check list: birds of Kansas*. Kansas Ornithological Society, Winfield. 4 pp.

Kentucky
Mengel, R. M. 1965. *The birds of Kentucky*. Ornithological Monograph No. 3. American Ornithologists' Union.

Monroe, B. L., Jr. 1969. *Summary of occurrence of birds of Kentucky*. Kentucky Ornithological Soc., Louisville. 10 pp.

Louisiana
Lowrey, G. H., Jr. 1974. *Louisiana Birds*, 3rd ed. Louisiana State Univ. Press, Baton Rouge. 651 pp.

Maine
Vickery, P. D. 1978. *Annotated checklist of Maine birds*. Maine Audubon Soc., Falmouth. 20 pp.

Vickery, P. D. and J. Despres. 1984. Checklist of the birds of Maine. *Maine Birdlife* **5**: 53–61.

Maryland
Maryland Ornithological Society. 1978. *Checklist of Maryland birds*. Maryland Ornithological Soc., Baltimore. 4 pp.

Robbins, C. S. and D. Bystrak. 1977. *Field list of the birds of Maryland*, 2nd ed. Maryland Ornithological Soc., Baltimore. 45 pp.

Stewart, R. E and C. S. Robbins. 1958. *Birds of Maryland and the District of Columbia*. North America Fauna No. 62. U. S. Fish & Wildlife Serv., Washington, D.C. 401 pp.

Massachusetts
Blodget, B. G. 1983. *Massachusetts bird list*. Massachusetts Div. of Fisheries & Wildlife, Boston. 24 pp.

Griscom, L. and D. Snyder. 1955. *The birds of Massachusetts*. Peabody Museum, Salem, MA.

Michigan
Payne, R. B. 1983. *A distributional checklist of the birds of Michigan*. Misc. Publ. 164. Univ. of Michigan Museum of Zoology, Ann Arbor. 71 pp.

Minnesota
Eckert, K. R. 1983. *A birder's guide to Minnesota*. K. R. Eckert, Duluth, MN.

Green, J. C. and R. B. Janssen. 1975. *Minnesota birds*. Univ. of Minnesota Press, Minneapolis. 217 pp.

Minnesota Ornithological Records Committee. 1983. *Checklist of Minnesota Birds*. Minnesota Ornithologists' Union. 13 pp.

Mississippi
Mississippi Ornithological Society Records Committee. 1985. *Birds of Mississippi, field checklist*. Mississippi Ornithological Soc., Jackson. 8 pp.

Toups, J. 1984. *Birds of the Mississippi Coast*. Mississippi Coast Audubon Soc., Jackson. 8 pp.

Missouri
Easterla, D. A. and R. A. Anderson. 1979. *Checklist of Missouri birds*. Audubon Soc. of Missouri, St. Louis. 4 pp.

Montana

Hays, R., R. L. Eng and C. V. Davis. 1984. *A list of Montana birds*. Montana Dept. of Fish, Wildlife and Parks, Helena. 8 pp.

Skaar, D., D. Flath and L. S. Thompson. 1985. *P. D. Skaar's Montana bird distribution*, 3rd ed. Proc. Montana Acad. Sciences 44 (suppl.): Monograph No. 3. 70 pp.

Nebraska

Johnsgard, P. A. 1979. *Birds of the Great Plains: breeding species and their distribution*. Univ. of Nebraska Press, Lincoln. 539 pp.

Johnsgard, P. A. 1980. *A revised list of the birds of Nebraska and adjacent states*. Occasional Papers No. 6. Nebraska Ornithologists' Union. 154 pp.

Rosche, R. C. 1982. *Birds of northwestern Nebraska and southwestern South Dakota: an annotated checklist*. R. C. Rosche, Chadron, NE.

Nevada

Lawson, C. S. 1977. *Nevada State Museum field list of the birds of Nevada*. Nevada State Museum, Carson City. 16 pp.

Ryser, F. 1976. *Checklist of the birds of Nevada*. Univ. of Nevada Museum of Biology, Reno. 22 pp.

New Hampshire

Elkins, K. C. 1982. *A checklist of the birds of New Hampshire*. Audubon Soc. of New Hampshire, Concord. 32 pp.

New Jersey

Leck, C. F. 1984. *The status and distribution of New Jersey's birds*. Rutgers Univ. Press, New Brunswick, NJ. 214 pp.

New Mexico

Hubbard, J. P. 1970. *Checklist of the birds of New Mexico*. New Mexico Ornithological Society, Albuquerque. 103 pp.

Hubbard, J. P. 1978. *Revised checklist of the birds of New Mexico*. New Mexico Ornithological Society, Albuquerque. 110 pp.

Huntington, D. and S. Huntington. 1983. *Rare and unusual birds of New Mexico*. New Mexico Ornithological Society, Albuquerque. 110 pp.

New York

Bull, J. 1974. *Birds of New York State*. Doubleday / Natural History Press, Garden City, NY. 655 pp.

Bull, J. 1976. *Supplement to birds of New York State*. Federation of N. Y. State Bird Clubs, Inc. 49 pp.

North Carolina

Lee, D. S. 1980. Supplement to the 1978 Checklist of North Carolina's birds. *Chat* **44**: 59–61.

North Carolina Records Committee. 1978. *Checklist of North Carolina's Birds*. Carolina Bird Club and North Carolina State Museum of Nat. Hist., Raleigh. 37 pp.

Pearson, T. G., C. S. Brimley and H. H. Brimley. 1959. *Birds of North Carolina*. Revised ed. by D. L. Wrey and H. T. Davis. North Carolina Dept. of Agriculture, Raleigh.

Potter, E. F., J. F. Parnell and R. P. Teulings. 1980. *Birds of the Carolinas*. Univ. of North Carolina Press, Chapel Hill. 408 pp.

North Dakota

Faanes, C. A. and R. E. Stewart. 1982. Revised checklist of North Dakota birds. *The Prairie Naturalist* **14**: 81–92.

Stewart, R. E. 1975. *Breeding birds of North Dakota*. Tri-College Env. Center, Fargo, ND. 295 pp.

Oklahoma

Sutton, G. M. 1974. *A check-list of Oklahoma birds*. Univ. of Oklahoma, Norman. 48 pp.

Wood, D. S. and G. D. Schnell. 1984. *Distributions of Oklahoma birds*. Stovall Museum, Univ. of Oklahoma, Norman. 209 pp.

Ohio

Thompson, T. 1983. *Birding in Ohio*. Indiana Univ. Press, Bloomington, IN. 256 pp.

Trautman, M. B. and M. A. Trautman. 1968. Annotated list of the birds of Ohio. *Ohio Journ. Sci.* **68**: 257–332.

Oregon

Crabtree, T. J. and H. B. Nehls. 1981. A checklist of the birds of Oregon. *Western Birds* **12**: 145–156.

Gabrielson, I. N. and S. G. Jewett. 1940. *Birds of Oregon*. Oregon State College, Corvallis. 650 pp.

Gordon, S. C. 1981. *Field checklist of the birds of Oregon*. Spec. Pub. No. 2. Oregon Field Ornithologists, Eugene. 16 pp.

Oregon Bird Records Committee. 1985. *Revised list of Oregon birds*. Oregon Field Ornithologists, Eugene. 9 pp.

Ramsey, F. L. 1978. *Birding Oregon*. Audubon Soc. of Corvallis, Corvallis, OR. 176 pp.

Pennsylvania

Wood, M. 1979. *Birds of Pennsylvania*. Pennsylvania State Univ., University Park. 133 pp.

Wood, M. 1983. *Birds of central Pennsylvania*, 3rd ed. Pennsylvania State Univ., University Park. 82 pp.

Rhode Island

Conway, R. A. 1979. *A field checklist of Rhode Island birds*. R. I. Ornithological Club Bulletin No. 1. Audubon Soc. of Rhode Island, Providence. 42 pp.

Rhode Island Ornithological Club. 1983. *Check-list of Rhode Island birds 1900–1982*. Audubon Soc. of Rhode Island, Providence. 6 pp.

South Carolina

Chamberlain, E. B. 1978. *Field card of South Carolina birds*. Charleston Nat. Hist. Soc., Charleston, SC. 10 pp.

Potter, E. F., J. F. Parnell and R. P. Teulings. 1980. *Birds of the Carolinas*. Univ. of North Carolina Press, Chapel Hill, NC. 408 pp.

Sprunt, A., Jr. and E. B. Chamberlain. 1970. *South Carolina bird life*. Revised ed. with a supplement by E. M. Burton. Kingsport Press, Kingsport, TN. 655 pp.

SOUTH DAKOTA
Whitney, N. R., Jr., B. E. Harrell, B. K. Harris, N. J. Holden, J. W. Johnson, B. J. Ross and P. F. Springer. 1978. *The birds of South Dakota*. South Dakota Ornithologists' Union, Vermillion. 311 pp.

TENNESSEE
Bierly, M. L. 1980. *Bird finding in Tennessee*. M. L. Bierly, Nashville, TN. 238 pp.

TEXAS
Bird Records Committee of the Texas Ornithological Society. 1984. *Checklist of the birds of Texas* (K. A. Arnold, ed.). Texas Ornithological Society, Austin. 147 pp.

Bryan, K., T. Gallucci and D. H. Riskind. 1984. *A checklist of Texas birds*. Texas Parks & Wildlife Dept., Austin. 36 pp.

Oberholser, H. C. 1974. *The bird life of Texas* (E. B. Kinkaid Jr., ed.). Univ. of Texas Press, Austin. 1069 pp.

UTAH
Behle, W. H. and M. L. Perry. 1975. *Field check-list of the birds of Utah*. Utah Museum of Nat. Hist., Salt Lake City. 4 pp.

Behle, W. H. and M. L. Perry. 1975. *Utah birds: checklist, seasonal and ecological occurrence charts and guides to bird finding*. Utah Museum of Nat. Hist., Salt Lake City. 143 pp.

Behle, W. H., E. D. Sorensen and C. M. White. In press. *Utah birds: a revised checklist*. Utah Museum of Nat. Hist., Salt Lake City.

Walters, R. E. and E. Sorensen, eds. 1983. *Utah bird distribution: latilong study*. Utah Div. of Wildlife Resources Pub. 83-10. Salt Lake City. 97 pp.

VERMONT
Ellison, W. G. 1981. *A guide to bird finding in Vermont*. Vermont Inst. of Nat. Sci., Woodstock.

Laughlin, S. B. and D. P. Kibbe (eds.). 1985. *The atlas of breeding birds of Vermont*. Univ. Press of New England, Hanover, NH. 456 pp.

Spear, R. N., Jr. 1976. *Birds of Vermont*. Green Mt. Audubon Soc., Burlington, VT. 86 pp.

VIRGINIA
Virginia Society of Ornithology Checklist Committee. 1979. *Virginia's birdlife—an annotated checklist*. Virginia Avifauna No. 2. Virginia Soc. of Ornithology, Lynchburg. 118 pp.

WASHINGTON
Jewitt, S. G., W. P. Taylor, W. T. Shaw and J. W. Aldrich. 1953. *Birds of Washington State*. Univ. of Washington Press, Seattle. 767 pp.

Mattocks, P., G. Hunn, D. Paulson and A. Richards. 1984. *Checklist of Washington birds*. Seattle Audubon Soc., Seattle, WA. 4 pp.

Mattocks, P. W., E. Hunn and T. R. Wahl. 1976. A checklist of the birds of Washington State, with recent changes annotated. *Western Birds* **7**: 1–24.

WEST VIRGINIA
Hall, G. A. 1983. *West Virginia birds*. Spec. Pubs. No. 7. Carnegie Museum of Nat. Hist., Pittsburgh, PA. 190 pp.

WISCONSIN
Barger, N. R., R. H. Lound and S. D. Robbins. 1975. *Wisconsin Birds—a checklist with migration graphs*. Wisconsin Society for Ornithology, Madison. 36 pp.

Robbins, S. D. In press. *Wisconsin Birdlife*. Univ. of Wisconsin Press, Madison.

WYOMING
Oakleaf, B., H. Downing, B. Raynes, M. Raynes and O. K. Scott. 1982. *Wyoming avian atlas*. Wyoming Game & Fish Dept., Lander. 87 pp.

Scott, O. K. 1983. *Check list—birds of Wyoming*. Oliver K. Scott, Casper, WY. 4 pp.

Biographical sketches

David DeSante

David DeSante was born in Akron, Ohio, in 1942. He became interested in birds at a very early age, and cannot remember a time when he was not chasing birds. Dave began his professional career as an engineer but, in 1968, changed fields into biology, earning his Ph.D. in Biological Sciences from Stanford University in 1973. His dissertation research concerned "mirror-image" misorientation in wood warblers. After teaching ecology and population biology at Stanford University and Reed College, Dave joined the staff of Point Reyes Bird Observatory in 1978 where he is now Senior Research Biologist. His current projects include long-term studies of the stability and dynamics of a Sierran subalpine breeding bird community, the population dynamics of landbirds in coastal central California and the migration of landbirds on the Farallon Islands and the adjacent mainland California coast.

Peter Pyle

Born in Seattle in 1957, Peter Pyle developed a childhood interest in birds while assisting his parents at Maryland and Hawaii banding stations. At the age of 19, he began eight years of seasonal work with the Fish and Wildlife Service, censusing the endangered birds and plants of Hawaii and Micronesia. Between seasons he earned a B.A. in Biology from Swarthmore College (1979) and picked up odd jobs while birding and traveling extensively through Eurasia, Mexico and Central America. Peter is currently a Research Associate and part-time biologist for Point Reyes Bird Observatory, dividing his time between the Farallon Islands; the tropics, where he leads cultural and wildlife tours; and mainland California, where he is assembling an identification, ageing, and sexing guide for North American banders.

F. P. Bennett, Jr.

F. P. (Tony) Bennett, Jr. was born in 1948 and was raised in the small west Texas town of Marfa where his childhood interest in birds first developed along the barrel of a BB gun. Fortunately, after a family move to tropical southern Texas, the BB gun was replaced by paints, brushes and binoculars, and a life-long desire to paint tropical birds. While pursuing his B.S. in Commercial Art, Tony was commissioned to paint the 48 color plates for L. Irby Davis' *A field guide to the birds of Mexico and Central America*. Tony's paintings have been exhibited in numerous shows around the country including the prestigious Leigh Yawky Woodson Art Museum "Birds in art" exhibition. Currently he is working with two other artists on illustrating the almost 1700 species for *The birds of Peru*, a work in progress by personnel of Louisiana State University.

Keith Hansen

Keith Hansen's first interest in nature and birdlife started in the woodlands of eastern Maryland, although he was born in Beeville, Texas, in 1958. When Keith was twelve, he and his family moved to California where his passion for birding grew rapidly. During the past ten years Keith has spent several fall seasons studying bird migration on the Farallon Islands as well as pursuing avian interests in Canada, Mexico and Central America. Coming from a family of artists, Keith began at an early age to take an interest in the faithful depiction of birds in their natural environs. His work has regularly appeared in a number of ornithological journals and he has recently designed and illustrated *Birds of the Sierra—coloring book* and completed most of the artwork in *Discovering Sierra birds*.

Addenda

In this section we list new records we are aware of that have occurred since March 1, 1985 in the area covered by this checklist. We cannot vouch for the authenticity of any of the records in this section, nor do we claim that they necessarily represent natural occurrences. We also do not claim that these lists are comprehensive. Many records are still under review by the appropriate state or province records committees.

The first list gives nine species entirely new to the checklist. In addition to the species' English and scientific names we provide the appropriate codes. We suggest that readers add these species to the body of the work in the spaces provided on the last pages of Part I, Native Populations, as soon as they are accepted on the North American list.

Oriental Pratincole, *Glareola maldivarum*: Continental North America and Alaska—*xV*.

Swallow-tailed Gull, *Creagrus furcatus*: Continental North America, lower 48 states and California—*xV*.

Little Tern, *Sterna albifrons*: Hawaii—*xV* (from *xV-sp* listed under Least Tern).

Mugimaki Flycatcher, *Ficedula mugimaki*: Continental North America and Alaska—*xV*.

Brown Flycatcher, *Muscicapa latirostris*: Continental North America and Alaska—*xV*.

Siberian Blue Robin, *Luscinia cyane*: Continental North America and Alaska—*xV*.

Gray Silky-flycatcher, *Ptilogonys cinereus*: Continental North America, lower 48 states and Texas—*xV*.

Flame-colored Tanager, *Piranga bidentata*: Continental North America, lower 48 states and Arizona—*xS*.

Shiny Cowbird, *Molothrus bonariensis*: Continental North America, lower 48 states and Florida—*xS**.

The second list presents new state or province records, along with appropriate codes.

Eared Grebe: Québec—*xV*.
Western Grebe: Ontario—*rV* (from *rV-sp*).
Northern Fulmar: Pennsylvania—*xV*.
Black-capped Petrel: Rhode Island—*xV*.
Murphy's Petrel: California—*xV*.
Sooty Shearwater: Mississippi—*xV*.
Townsend's Shearwater: Continental North America, lower 48 states and California—*xV*.
Band-rumped Storm-Petrel: Louisiana—*xV*.
White-tailed Tropicbird: New Jersey—*xV*.
Red-billed Tropicbird: Texas—*xV*.
Olivaceous Cormorant: South Dakota—*xS**.
Magnificent Frigatebird: Alaska—*xV* (from *xV-sp*) and Colorado—*xV*.
Little Blue Heron: Oregon—*xV*.
White Ibis: Colorado—*xV*.
Black-bellied Whistling-Duck: Mississippi—*xV*.
Garganey: Texas—*xV*.
Common Goldeneye: Hawaii—*xW*.
Mississippi Kite: Saskatchewan—*xV*.
Common Black-Hawk: California—*xV*.
Short-tailed Hawk: Arizona—*xV*.
Ferruginous Hawk: Alabama—*xW*.
Virginia Rail: Alaska—*xW*.
Wilson's Plover: Arkansas—*xV*.
Northern Jacana: Arizona—*xP**.
Wood Sandpiper: Lower 48 states and California—*xV*.
Long-billed Curlew: Tennessee—*xV*.
Rufous-necked Stint: New York—*xV*.
Little Stint: New Jersey—*xV*.
Curlew Sandpiper: Newfoundland—*xV* and Maryland—*xV*.
Stilt Sandpiper: Newfoundland—*xV*.
Buff-breasted Sandpiper: Nevada—*xV*.
Long-tailed Jaeger: Hawaii—*xV*.
Little Gull: Alberta—*xV* and Arkansas—*xV*.
Heermann's Gull: Utah—*xV*.
California Gull: Louisiana—*xV*.
Slaty-backed Gull: Yukon Territory—*xV*.
Great Black-backed Gull: Utah—*xV*.
Sabine's Gull: South Carolina—*xT*.
Gull-billed Tern: Ontario—*xV*.
Royal Tern: Wisconsin—*xV*, Arkansas—*xV* and Illinois—*xV*.
Roseate Tern: Ontario—*xV* and Georgia—*xT*.
Forster's Tern: Vermont—*xT*.
Bridled Tern: Arkansas—*xV* and Connecticut—*xV*.
White-winged Tern: Québec—*xS*.
Black Guillemot: Virginia—*xV*.
Kittlitz's Murrelet: Canada and British Columbia—*xW*.
Ancient Murrelet: New Mexico—*xV*.
White-winged Dove: Minnesota—*xV*.
Western Screech-Owl: Kansas—*xV*.
Broad-billed Hummingbird: Nevada—*xV* and South Carolina—*xV*.
Anna's Hummingbird: Utah—*xV*.
Rufous Hummingbird: Newfoundland—*xV*, Ohio—*xV*, Tennessee—*xV* and North Carolina—*xV* (from *xV-sp*).
Acorn Woodpecker: Utah—*xV*.

Williamson's Sapsucker: Illinois—*xV*.
Three-toed Woodpecker: California—*xV*.
Alder Flycatcher: California—*xV*.
Say's Phoebe: Vermont—*xV*.
Ash-throated Flycatcher: New Brunswick—*xV*.
Couch's Kingbird: New Mexico—*xV*.
Fork-tailed Flycatcher: Rhode Island—*xV* and Delaware—*xV*.
Jackdaw: Ontario—*xV*, Maine—*xV* and Pennsylvania—*xS*.
Pygmy Nuthatch: North Dakota—*xV*.
Mountain Bluebird: Arkansas—*xV*.
Fieldfare: Massachusetts—*xV*.
Sage Thrasher: Delaware—*xV*.
Yellow Wagtail: British Columbia—*xV*.
White Wagtail: Arizona—*xV-sp* and Michigan—*xV*.
Red-throated Pipit: British Columbia—*xV*.
Bell's Vireo: South Carolina—*xV*.
Yellow-throated Vireo: Idaho—*xV*.
Philadelphia Vireo: Washington–*xV*.
Golden-winged Warbler: Alberta—*xV* and Wyoming—*xV*.
Yellow-throated Warbler: Oregon—*xV*.
Kentucky Warbler: Utah—*xV*.
Mourning Warbler: Utah—*xV*.
Hooded Warbler: Saskatchewan—*xV*.
Lazuli Bunting: Alaska—*xV-q*.
Brewer's Sparrow: New Jersey—*xV*.
Henslow's Sparrow: Colorado—*xV*.
Smith's Longspur: Idaho—*xV*.
Great-tailed Grackle: Idaho—*xV* and Ohio—*xV*.
Boat-tailed Grackle: Massachusetts—*xV*, Rhode Island—*xV* and Connecticut—*xV*.
Orchard Oriole: Newfoundland—*xV*.
Brambling: Wyoming—*xV* and Indiana—*xV*.
Lesser Goldfinch: North Carolina—*xV*.

The third list presents new breeding records for species that were previously included as non-breeders on the list for that particular state or province. We have again provided updated codes for these species.

Pied-billed Grebe: Hawaii—*xS,rV,xW*.
Double-crested Cormorant: South Carolina—*xS,fS*,cW*.
Little Blue Heron: Indiana—*xS,uS**.
Northern Shoveler: Maryland—*xS,fT,uW*.
Willet: Newfoundland—*xS,rV*.
Herring Gull: Indiana—*xS,fS*,cW*.
White-winged Tern: Continental North America—*xS,xS*,rV* and Canada—*xS,xS*,xV*.
Boreal Owl: Washington—*rP†*.
Buff-collared Nightjar: Continental North America, lower 48 states and Arizona—*lrS* (from *lrS†*).
White-eared Hummingbird: Continental North America and lower 48 states—*xS,lrS*,xV* and Arizona—*xS,lrS**.
Clark's Nutcracker: South Dakota—*xS,irW*.
Jackdaw: Continental North America—*xS,xP*,xV,xW* and lower 48 states—*xS,xP*,xV*.
Fish Crow: Maine—*xS, xV*.
Mountain Chickadee: Oklahoma—*xS,luT,xW*.
Brown Creeper: Missouri—*xS,cT,fW*.
Seaside Sparrow: New Hampshire—*xS,xS*,xV,xW*.
American Goldfinch: New Mexico—*xS,lrS*,fW*.
House Finch (introduced populations): Arkansas—*xS,xV,xW*.

Finally, just as this book went to press, it was discovered that the introduced turtle-doves in the Miami, Florida, area are actually Collared Turtle-Doves (*Streptopelia decaocto*) rather than Ringed Turtle-Dove (*S. risoria*), as presented above. The wild origin and natural range of the domestic *S. risoria*, however, is uncertain. The domestic stock, from which introductions were made elsewhere in North America, may have been derived from either *S. decaocto* of Eurasia or *S. roseogrisea* of Africa, these forms being considered conspecific by some authors (A.O.U. 1983).

Index

Boldfaced page numbers refer to illustrations.

— A —

Accentor, Siberian, 285
Accipiter cooperii, 93
　gentilis, 93
　striatus, 93
Accipitridae, 85
Accipitrinae, 85
Acridotheres cristatellus, 401
　tristis, 401
Acrocephalus familiaris, 261
Actitis hypoleucos, 133
　macularia, 133
Aechmophorus clarkii, 4, 21
　occidentalis, 21
Aegithalidae, 253
Aegolius acadicus, 197
　funereus, 197
Aerodramus vanikorensis, 393
Aeronautes saxatalis, 205
Aethia cristatella, 173
　pusilla, 173
　pygmaea, 173
Agelaius humeralis, 349
　phoeniceus, 349
　tricolor, 349
Aimophila aestivalis, 333
　botterii, 333
　carpalis, 333
　cassinii, 333
　ruficeps, 333
Aix sponsa, 69
Ajaia ajaja, 61
Akepa, 365
Akialoa, Hawaiian, 365
　Kauai, 8, 365
Akiapolaau, **364**, 365
Alauda arvensis, 237, 393
Alaudidae, 237, 393
Albatross, Black-browed, 12, 21
　Black-footed, 9, 11, 21
　Laysan, 11, 21
　Short-tailed, 21
　Shy, 21
　Wandering, 21
　Yellow-nosed, 12, 29
Alca torda, 165
Alcedinidae, 213
Alcidae, 165
Alectoris chukar, 377
Alle alle, 165
Amakihi, Common, 365
　Greater, 365
Amandava amandava, 417
Amaui, 4, 269
Amazilia beryllina, 205
　tzacatl, 205
　violiceps, 205
　yucatanensis, 205
Amazona finschi, 393
　oratrix, 181, 393
　viridigenalis, 181, 393
Ammodramus bairdii, 333
　caudacutus, 341
　henslowii, 333
　leconteii, 333
　maritimus, 341
　savannarum, 333

Amphispiza belli, 333
　bilineata, 333
　quinquestriata, 333
Anas acuta, 69
　americana, 77
　bahamensis, 69
　clypeata, 77
　crecca, 69
　cyanoptera, 77
　discors, 69
　falcata, 69
　formosa, 69
　fulvigula, 69, 377
　laysensis, 69
　penelope, 77
　platyrhynchos, 69, 377
　poecilorhyncha, 69
　querquedula, 69
　rubripes, 69, 377
　strepera, 77
　wyvilliana, 69
Anatidae, 61, 377
Anatinae, 69, 377
Anhinga, **52**, 53
Anhinga anhinga, 53
Anhingidae, 53
Ani, Groove-billed, 12, 189
　Smooth-billed, 12, 189
Anianiau, 365
Anous minutus, 165
　stolidus, 165
Anser albifrons, 69
　brachyrhynchus, 61
　erythropus, 6
　fabalis, 61
Anseriformes, 3, 61, 377
Anserinae, 61, 377
Anthus cervinus, 285
　gustavi, 285
　hodgsoni, 285
　spinoletta, 285
　spragueii, 285
　trivialis, 285
Apapane, 367
Aphelocoma coerulescens, 245
　ultramarina, 245
Aphriza virgata, 133
Apodidae, 197, 393
Apodiformes, 197, 393
Apodinae, 197
Apus apus, 197
　pacificus, 205
Aquila chrysaetos, 93
Aramidae, 117
Aramus guarauna, 117
Aratinga holochlora, 181
Archilochus alexandri, 205
　colubris, 205
Ardea herodias, 53
Ardeidae, 53, 377
Arenaria interpres, 133
　melanocephala, 133
Arinae, 181, 393
Arremonops rufivirgatus, 325
Asio flammeus, 189
　otus, 189
Athene cunicularia, 189

Atthis heloisa, 205
Auk, Great, 8, 165
Auklet, Cassin's, 173
　Crested, 173
　Least, 173
　Parakeet, 173
　Rhinoceros, 173
　Whiskered, 173
Auriparus flaviceps, 253
Avadavat, Red, 417
Avocet, American, **124**, 125
Aythya affinis, 77
　americana, 77
　collaris, 77
　ferina, 77
　fuligula, 77
　marila, 77
　valisineria, 77

— B —

Bananaquit, 317
Barn-Owl, Common, 189, 393
Bartramia longicauda, 133
Basileuterus culicivorus, 317
　rufifrons, 317
Beardless-Tyrannulet, Northern, 221
Becard, Rose-throated, 237
Bittern, American, 53
　Least, 53
Black-Hawk, Common, 6, 93, 433
Blackbird, Brewer's, 349
　Eurasian, 277
　Red-winged, 349
　Rusty, 349
　Tawny-shouldered, 349
　Tricolored, 349
　Yellow-headed, 349, **416**
Bluebird, Eastern, 269
　Mountain, 269, 434
　Western, 269
Bluetail, Red-flanked, 269
Bluethroat, **268**, 269
Bobolink, 349
Bobwhite, Northern, 109, 385
Bombycilla cedrorum, 285
　garrulus, 285
Bombycillidae, 285
Bonasa umbellus, 101, 385
Booby, Blue-footed, 45
　Brown, 45
　Masked, 45
　Red-footed, 45
Botaurus lentiginosus, 53
Brachyramphus brevirostris, 173
　marmoratus, 173
Brambling, 6, 357, 434
Brant, 69
Branta bernicla, 69
　canadensis, 69, 377
　leucopsis, 69
　ruficollis, 6
Brotogeris versicolurus, 393
Bubo virginianus, 189
Bubulcus ibis, 53, 377
Bucephala albeola, 85
　clangula, 77
　islandica, 77

Budgerigar, 393
Bufflehead, 85
Bulbul, Red-vented, 401
　Red-whiskered, 401
Bullfinch, Eurasian, 357
　Greater Antillean, 333
Bulweria bulwerii, 29
　fallax, 29
Bunting, Blue, 325
　Gray, 341
　Indigo, 325
　Lark, 333
　Lazuli, 325, 434
　Little, 341
　McKay's, 341
　Painted, 325
　Rustic, 341
　Snow, 341
　Varied, 325
　Yellow-breasted, 5, 341
Burhinidae, 117
Burhinus bistriatus, 117
Bush-Warbler, Japanese, 401
Bushtit, 253
Buteo albicaudatus, 93
　albonotatus, 93
　brachyurus, 93
　buteo, 93
　jamaicensis, 93
　lagopus, 93
　lineatus, 93
　magnirostris, 93
　nitidus, 93
　platypterus, 93
　regalis, 93
　solitarius, 93
　swainsoni, 93
Buteogallus anthracinus, 93
Butorides striatus, 53
Buzzard, Common, 5, 93

— C —

Cairina moschata, 69
Calamospiza melanocorys, 333
Calcarius lapponicus, 341
　mccownii, 341
　ornatus, 341
　pictus, 341
Calidris acuminata, 141
　alba, 133
　alpina, 141
　bairdii, 141
　canutus, 133
　ferruginea, 141
　fuscicollis, 141
　himantopus, 141
　maritima, 141
　mauri, 141
　melanotos, 141
　minuta, 141
　minutilla, 141
　ptilocnemis, 141
　pusilla, 141
　ruficollis, 141
　subminuta, 141
　temminckii, 141
　tenuirostris, 133
Callipepla californica, 109, 385

douglasii, 5
   gambelii, 109, 385
   squamata, 109, 385
Calliphlox evelynae, 205
Calocitta colliei, 6
Calonectris diomedea, 29
   leucomelas, 29
Calothorax lucifer, 205
Calypte anna, 205
   costae, 205
Campephilus principalis, 221
Camptorhynchus labradorius, 77
Camptostoma imberbe, 221
Campylorhynchus brunneicapillus, 261
Canary, Common, 409
   Yellow-fronted, 409
Canvasback, 77
Caprimulgidae, 197
Caprimulgiformes, 197
Caprimulginae, 197
Caprimulgus carolinensis, 197
   indicus, 197
   ridgwayi, 197
   vociferus, 197
Caracara, Crested, 6, 93
Cardellina rubrifrons, 317
Cardinal, Northern, 1, 7, 325, 409
   Red-crested, 409
   Yellow-billed, 409
Cardinalinae, 325, 409
Cardinalis cardinalis, 325, 409
   sinuatus, 325
Carduelinae, 357, 409
Carduelis carduelis, 409
   chloris, 357
   flammea, 357
   hornemanni, 4, 357
   lawrencei, 357
   pinus, 357
   psaltria, 357
   sinica, 357
   spinus, 357
   tristis, 357
Carpodacus cassinii, 357
   erythrinus, 357
   mexicanus, 357, 409
   purpureus, 357
Casmerodius albus, 53
Catbird, Gray, 9, 277
Catharacta maccormicki, 149
   skua, 149
Cathartes aura, 85
Cathartidae, 85
Catharus fuscescens, 277
   guttatus, 277
   minimus, 277
   ustulatus, 277
Catherpes mexicanus, 261
Catoptrophorus semipalmatus, 125
Centrocercus urophasianus, 101
Cepphus columba, 165
   grylle, 165
Cerorhinca monocerata, 173
Certhia americana, 261
Certhiidae, 261
Certhiinae, 261
Ceryle alcyon, 213
   torquata, 213
Cerylinae, 213
Cettia diphone, 401
Chachalaca, Plain, 101, 377
Chaetoptila angustipluma, 293

Chaetura pelagica, 197
   vauxi, 197
Chaeturinae, 197, 393
Chaffinch, Common, 357
Chamaea fasciata, 277
Charadriidae, 117
Charadriiformes, 3, 117
Charadriinae, 117
Charadrius alexandrinus, 117
   dubius, 117
   hiaticula, 117
   melodus, 117
   mongolus, 117
   montanus, 125
   morinellus, 125
   semipalmatus, 117
   vociferus, 125
   wilsonia, 117
Chasiempis sandwichensis, 269
Chat, Yellow-breasted, 317
Chen caerulescens, 69
   canagica, 69
   rossii, 69
Chickadee, Black-capped, **252**, 253
   Boreal, **252**, 253
   Carolina, 253
   Chestnut-backed, 253
   Mexican, 253
   Mountain, 253, 434
Chlidonias leucopterus, 165
   niger, 165
Chloridops kona, 365
Chloroceryle americana, 213
Chlorostilbon ricordii, 205
Chondestes grammacus, 333
Chondrohierax uncinatus, 85
Chordeiles acutipennis, 197
   gundlachii, 197
   minor, 197
Chordeilinae, 197
Chuck-will's-widow, 197
Chukar, **376**, 377
Ciconiidae, 61
Ciconiiformes, 9, 53, 377
Cinclidae, 261
Cinclus mexicanus, 261
Circus cyaneus, 93
Ciridops anna, 365
Cistothorus palustris, 261
   platensis, 261
Clangula hyemalis, 77
Coccothraustes coccothraustes, 357
   vespertinus, 357
Coccyzinae, 181
Coccyzus americanus, 181
   erythropthalmus, 181
   minor, 181
Coereba flaveola, 317
Coerebinae, 317
Colaptes auratus, 221
Colibri thalassinus, 205
Colinus virginianus, 109, 385
Columba fasciata, 173
   flavirostris, 173
   leucocephala, 173
   livia, 385
   squamosa, 173
Columbidae, 173, 385
Columbiformes, 173, 385
Columbina inca, 181
   passerina, 181
   talpacoti, 181

Condor, California, **84**, 85
Contopus borealis, 221
   pertinax, 221
   sordidulus, 229
   virens, 229
Conuropsis carolinensis, 181
Coot, American, 109
   Caribbean, 4, 109
   Eurasian, 109
Copsychus malabaricus, 401
Coraciiformes, 213
Coragyps atratus, 85
Cordonbleu, Red-cheeked, 409
Cormorant, Brandt's, 45
   Double-crested, 45, 434
   Great, 45
   Olivaceous, 45, 433
   Pelagic, 45
   Red-faced, 45
Corvidae, 245
Corvus brachyrhynchos, 245
   caurinus, 4, 245
   corax, 253
   cryptoleucus, 253
   hawaiiensis, 253
   imparatus, 245
   monedula, 245
   ossifragus, 253
Coturnicops noveboracensis, 109
Coturnix japonicus, 377
Cowbird, Bronzed, 349
   Brown-headed, 349
   Shiny, 433
Cracidae, 101, 377
Crake, Corn, 109
   Paint-billed, 109
Crane, Common, 117
   Sandhill, 117
   Whooping, 117, 385
Creagrus furcatus, 433
Creeper, Brown, 16, 261, 434
   Hawaii, 365
   Kauai, 365
   Maui, 365
   Molokai, 8, 365
   Oahu, 365
Crex crex, 109
Crossbill, Red, 357
   White-winged, 357
Crotophaga ani, 189
   sulcirostris, 189
Crotophaginae, 189
Crow, American, 245
   Fish, 253, 434
   Hawaiian, 253
   Mexican, 245
   Northwestern, 4, 245
Cuckoo, Black-billed, 181
   Common, 181
   Mangrove, 15, 181
   Oriental, 181
   Yellow-billed, 181
Cuculidae, 181
Cuculiformes, 181
Cuculinae, 181
Cuculus canorus, 181
   saturatus, 181
Curlew, Bristle-thighed, 133
   Eskimo, 14, 133
   Eurasian, 133
   Far Eastern, 133
   Little, 133
   Long-billed, 133, 433
   Slender-billed, 133

Cyanocitta cristata, 245
   stelleri, 245
Cyanocompsa parellina, 325
Cyanocorax morio, 245
   sanblasianus, 6
   yncas, 245
Cyclorrhynchus psittacula, 173
Cygnus buccinator, 61
   columbianus, 61
   cygnus, 61
   olor, 377
Cynanthus latirostris, 205
Cypseloides niger, 197
Cypseloidinae, 197
Cyrtonyx montezumae, 109

— D —

Daption capense, 5
Delichon urbica, 245
Dendragapus canadensis, 101
   obscurus, 101
Dendrocygna autumnalis, 61
   bicolor, 61
Dendroica caerulescens, 309
   castanea, 309
   cerulea, 309
   chrysoparia, 309
   coronata, 309
   discolor, 309
   dominica, 309
   fusca, 309
   graciae, 309
   kirtlandi, 309
   magnolia, 301
   nigrescens, 309
   occidentalis, 309
   palmarum, 309
   pensylvanica, 301
   petechia, 301
   pinus, 309
   striata, 309
   tigrina, 301
   townsendi, 309
   virens, 309
Dickcissel, **324**, 325
Diomedea albatrus, 21
   cauta, 21
   chlororhynchos, 29
   exulans, 21
   immutabilis, 21
   melanophris, 21
   nigripes, 21
Diomedeidae, 21
Dipper, American, 261
Dolichonyx oryzivorus, 349
Dotterel, Eurasian, 125
Dove, Inca, 181
   Mourning, 9, 173, 393
   Rock, **384**, 385
   Spotted, 393
   White-tipped, 181
   White-winged, 173, 393, 433
   Zebra, 393
   Zenaida, 173
Dovekie, 165
Dowitcher, Long-billed, 12, 141
   Short-billed, 12, 141
Drepanidinae, 365
Drepanis funerea, 367
   pacifica, 365
Dryocopus pileatus, 221
Duck, American Black, 6, 69, 377
   Harlequin, 77
   Hawaiian, 69
   Labrador, 8, 77

Laysan, 69
Masked, 85
Mottled, 69, 377
Muscovy, 69
Ring-necked, **76**, 77
Ruddy, 85
Spot-billed, 69
Tufted, 77
Wood, **19**, 69
Dumetella carolinensis, 277
Dunlin, 141

— E —
Eagle, Bald, 85
Golden, 9, 93
White-tailed, 85
Ectopistes migratorius, 181
Egret, Cattle, 1, 53, 377
Chinese, 53
Great, 53
Little, 53
Reddish, 53
Snowy, 53
Egretta caerulea, 53
eulophotes, 53
garzetta, 53
gularis, 53
rufescens, 53
thula, 53
tricolor, 53
Eider, Common, 77
King, 77
Spectacled, 77
Steller's, 77
Elaenia martinica, 221
Elaenia, Caribbean, 221
Greenish, 221
Elaeniinae, 221
Elanoides forficatus, 85
Elanus caeruleus, 85
Elepaio, 269
Emberiza aureola, 341
pallasi, 341
pusilla, 341
rustica, 341
schoeniclus, 341
variabilis, 341
Emberizidae, 301, 409
Emberizinae, 325, 409
Emerald, Cuban, 205
Empidonax alnorum, 229
difficilis, 229
flaviventris, 229
fulvifrons, 229
hammondii, 229
minimus, 229
oberholseri, 229
traillii, 229
virescens, 229
wrightii, 229
Empidonomus varius, 237
Eremophila alpestris, 237
Estrilda astrild, 417
caerulescens, 409
melpoda, 417
troglodytes, 417
Estrildidae, 409
Estrildinae, 409
Eudocimus albus, 61
ruber, 61
Eugenes fulgens, 205
Euphagus carolinus, 349
cyanocephalus, 349
Euptilotis neoxenus, 213
Eurynorhynchus pygmeus, 141

Euthlypis lachrymosa, 317

— F —
Falco columbarius, 101
femoralis, 101
mexicanus, 101
peregrinus, 101
rusticolus, 101
sparverius, 93
subbuteo, 101
tinnunculus, 93
Falcon, Aplomado, 101
Peregrine, 101
Prairie, **100**, 101
Falconidae, 93
Falconiformes, 85
Ficedula mugimaki, 433
parva, 269
Fieldfare, 277, 434
Finch, Cassin's, 357
House, 7, 357, **408**, 409, 434
Laysan, 365
Nihoa, 365
Purple, 357
Rosy, 15, 357
Saffron, 409
Flamingo, Greater, 6, 61
Flicker, Northern, 221
Fluvicolinae, 221
Flycatcher, Acadian, 229
Alder, 229, 434
Ash-throated, 12, 229, 434
Brown, 433
Brown-crested, 229
Buff-breasted, 229
Dusky, 229
Dusky-capped, 229
Fork-tailed, 237, 434
Gray, 13, 229
Gray-spotted, 269
Great Crested, 229
Hammond's, 229
La Sagra's, 229
Least, 1, 229
Mugimaki, 433
Nutting's, 12, 229
Olive-sided, 221
Red-breasted, 269
Scissor-tailed, 6, 16, **236**, 237
Siberian, 269
Sulphur-bellied, 237
Variegated, 237
Vermilion, 229
Western, 229
Willow, 14, 229
Yellow-bellied, 229
Francolin, Black, 377
Erckel's, 377
Gray, 377
Francolinus erckelii, 377
francolinus, 377
pondicerianus, 377
Fratercula arctica, 173
cirrhata, 173
corniculata, 173
Fregata ariel, 53
magnificens, 53
minor, 53
Fregatidae, 53
Frigatebird, Great, 12, 53
Lesser, 53
Magnificent, 12, 53, 433
Fringilla coelebs, 357
montifringilla, 357
Fringillidae, 357, 409

Fringillinae, 357
Fulica americana, 109
atra, 109
caribaea, 4, 109
Fulmar, Northern, 29, 433
Fulmarus glacialis, 29

— G —
Gadwall, 16, 77
Galliformes, 101, 377
Gallinago gallinago, 141
stenura, 149
Gallinula chloropus, 109
Gallinule, Purple, 109
Gallus gallus, 377
Gannet, Northern, 45
Garganey, 6, 69, 433
Garrulax caerulatus, 401
canorus, 401
pectoralis, 401
Gavia adamsii, 21
arctica, 21
immer, 21
pacifica, 4, 21
stellata, 21
Gaviidae, 21
Gaviiformes, 21
Geococcyx californianus, 181
Geopelia striata, 393
Geothlypis poliocephala, 317
rostrata, 317
trichas, 317
Geotrygon chrysia, 181
montana, 181
Giant-Petrel, Antarctic, 5
Glareola maldivarum, 433
Glaucidium brasilianum, 189
gnoma, 189
Gnatcatcher, Black-capped, 269
Black-tailed, 269
Blue-gray, 269
Godwit, Bar-tailed, 133
Black-tailed, 133
Hudsonian, 133
Marbled, 133
Golden-Plover, Greater, 117
Lesser, **116**, 117
Goldeneye, Barrow's, 77
Common, 77, 433
Goldfinch, American, 357, 434
European, 409
Lawrence's, **356**, 357
Lesser, 16, 357, 434
Goose, Barnacle, 6, 69
Bean, 61
Canada, 7, 69, 377
Emperor, **68**, 69
Greater White-fronted, 16, 69
Hawaiian, 69
Lesser White-fronted, 6
Pink-footed, 61
Red-breasted, 6
Ross', 69
Snow, 69
Goshawk, Northern, 93
Grackle, Boat-tailed, 12, 349, 434
Common, 349
Great-tailed, 1, 5, 12, 349, 434
Gracula religiosa, 401
Grasshopper-Warbler, Middendorff's, 261
Grassquit, Black-faced, 325
Yellow-faced, 409
Grebe, Clark's, 4, 12, 21

Eared, 21, 433
Horned, 21
Least, 21
Pied-billed, 21, 434
Red-necked, 21
Western, 12, 21, 433
Greenfinch, European, 5, 357
Oriental, 357
Greenshank, Common, 125
Grosbeak, Black-headed, 6, 325
Blue, 325
Crimson-collared, 325
Evening, 357
Kona, 365
Pine, 357
Rose-breasted, 325
Yellow, 6, 325
Ground-Dove, Common, 181
Ruddy, 181
Grouse, Blue, 101
Ruffed, 101, 385
Sage, **100**, 101
Sharp-tailed, 101
Spruce, 101
Gruidae, 117, 385
Gruiformes, 109, 385
Gruinae, 117, 385
Grus americana, 117, 385
canadensis, 117
grus, 117
Guillemot, Black, 165, 433
Pigeon, 165
Guineafowl, Helmeted, 5
Guiraca caerulea, 325
Gull, Band-tailed, 5
Black-tailed, 5, 149
Bonaparte's, 149
California, 157, 433
Common Black-headed, 149
Franklin's, 149
Glaucous, 157
Glaucous-winged, 157
Great Black-backed, **156**, 157, 433
Heermann's, 9, 149, 433
Herring, 157, 434
Iceland, 157
Ivory, 157
Laughing, 149
Lesser Black-backed, 157
Little, 149, 433
Mew, 149
Ring-billed, 149
Ross', 157
Sabine's, 157, 433
Slaty-backed, 157, 433
Swallow-tailed, 433
Thayer's, 157
Western, 157
Yellow-footed, 157
Gygis alba, 165
Gymnogyps californianus, 85
Gymnorhinus cyanocephalus, 245
Gyrfalcon, 16, 101

— H —
Haematopodidae, 125
Haematopus bachmani, 125
palliatus, 125
Haliaeetus albicilla, 85
leucocephalus, 85
pelagicus, 85
Harrier, Northern, 93
Hawfinch, 357
Hawk, Broad-winged, 93

Cooper's, 93
Ferruginous, 93, 433
Gray, 93
Harris', 93
Hawaiian, 93
Red-shouldered, **92**, 93
Red-tailed, 93
Roadside, 93
Rough-legged, 93
Sharp-shinned, 93
Short-tailed, 93, 433
Swainson's, 93
White-tailed, 93
Zone-tailed, 6, 93
Hawk-Owl, Northern, 16, 189
Heliomaster constantii, 205
Helmitheros vermivorus, 309
Hemignathus lucidus, 365
　　munroi, 365
　　obscurus, 365
　　parvus, 365
　　procerus, 365
　　sagittirostris, 365
　　virens, 365
Heron, Great Blue, 53
　　Green-backed, 53
　　Little Blue, 53, 433, 434
　　Tricolored, 53
Heteroscelus brevipes, 133
　　incanus, 133
Himantopus himantopus, 125
　　mexicanus, 125
Himatione sanguinea, 367
Hirundapus caudacutus, 197
Hirundinidae, 237
Hirundininae, 237
Hirundo fulva, 245
　　pyrrhonota, 245
　　rustica, 245
Histrionicus histrionicus, 77
Hobby, Northern, 5, 101
Honeycreeper, Crested, 367
Hoopoe, 213
House-Martin, Common, 245
Hummingbird, Allen's, 12, 213
　　Anna's, 9, 205, 433
　　Antillean Crested, 6
　　Berylline, 1, 205
　　Black-chinned, 205
　　Blue-throated, 6, **204**, 205
　　Broad-billed, 205, 433
　　Broad-tailed, 205
　　Buff-bellied, 205
　　Bumblebee, 205
　　Calliope, 205
　　Costa's, 205
　　Lucifer, 205
　　Magnificent, **204**, 205
　　Ruby-throated, 205
　　Rufous, 12, 213, 433
　　Rufous-tailed, 205
　　Violet-crowned, 1, 205
　　White-eared, **204**, 205, 434
Hydrobates pelagicus, 37
Hydrobatidae, 37
Hylocharis leucotis, 205
Hylocichla mustelina, 277

— I —
Ibis, Glossy, 1, 12, 61
　　Scarlet, 6, 61
　　White, **60**, 61, 433
　　White-faced, 12, 61
Icteria virens, 317
Icterinae, 349, 409

Icterus cucullatus, 349
　　dominicensis, 349
　　galbula, 349
　　graduacauda, 349
　　gularis, 349
　　parisorum, 349
　　pectoralis, 409
　　pustulatus, 349
　　spurius, 349
　　wagleri, 349
Ictinia mississippiensis, 85
Iiwi, **364**, 365
Ixobrychus exilis, 53
Ixoreus naevius, 277

— J —
Jabiru, 61
Jabiru mycteria, 61
Jacana spinosa, 125
Jacana, Northern, 125, 433
Jacanidae, 125
Jackdaw, 6, 245, 434
Jaeger, Long-tailed, 149, 433
　　Parasitic, 149
　　Pomarine, 149
Jay, Blue, 1, 8, 245
　　Brown, 245
　　Gray, **244**, 245
　　Gray-breasted, 245
　　Green, 245
　　Pinyon, 245
　　San Blas, 6
　　Scrub, 6, 245
　　Steller's, 6, 245
Junco hyemalis, 341
　　phaeonotus, 341
Junco, Dark-eyed, 341
　　Yellow-eyed, 341
Junglefowl, Red, 377
Jynginae, 213
Jynx torquilla, 213

— K —
Kamao, 4, 269
Kestrel, American, 93
　　Eurasian, 93
Killdeer, 125
Kingbird, Cassin's, 16, 237
　　Couch's, 12, 237, 434
　　Eastern, 237
　　Gray, 237
　　Loggerhead, 237
　　Thick-billed, 1, 237
　　Tropical, 12, 237
　　Western, 237
Kingfisher, Belted, 213
　　Green, **212**, 213
　　Ringed, 213
Kinglet, Golden-crowned, 269
　　Ruby-crowned, 269
Kioea, 293
Kiskadee, Great, 6, 16, 229
Kite, American Swallow-tailed, 85
　　Black-shouldered, 85
　　Hook-billed, 85
　　Mississippi, 85, 433
　　Snail, 85
Kittiwake, Black-legged, 157
　　Red-legged, 157
Knot, Great, 133
　　Red, 133
Koa-Finch, Greater, 365
　　Lesser, 365

— L —
Lagopus lagopus, 101, 385
　　leucurus, 101, 385
　　mutus, 101
Lampornis clemenciae, 205
Laniidae, 293
Laniinae, 293
Lanius cristatus, 293
　　excubitor, 293
　　ludovicianus, 293
Lapwing, Northern, 117
Laridae, 9, 149
Larinae, 149
Lark, Horned, 237
Larus argentatus, 157
　　atricilla, 149
　　belcheri, 5
　　californicus, 157
　　canus, 149
　　crassirostris, 149
　　delawarensis, 149
　　fuscus, 157
　　glaucescens, 157
　　glaucoides, 157
　　heermanni, 149
　　hyperboreus, 157
　　livens, 157
　　marinus, 157
　　minutus, 149
　　occidentalis, 157
　　philadelphia, 149
　　pipixcan, 149
　　ridibundus, 149
　　schistisagus, 157
　　thayeri, 157
Laterallus jamaicensis, 109
Laughing-thrush, Gray-sided, 5, 401
　　Greater Necklaced, 401
　　Melodious, 401
Leiothrix lutea, 401
Leiothrix, Red-billed, 401
Leptotila verreauxi, 181
Leucosticte arctoa, 357
Limicola falcinellus, 141
Limnodromus griseus, 141
　　scolopaceus, 141
Limnothlypis swainsonii, 309
Limosa fedoa, 133
　　haemastica, 133
　　lapponica, 133
　　limosa, 133
Limpkin, 117
Locustella lanceolata, 261
　　ochotensis, 261
Lonchura malabarica, 417
　　malacca, 417
　　punctulata, 417
Longspur, Chestnut-collared, 341
　　Lapland, 341
　　McCown's, 341
　　Smith's, 341, 434
Loon, Arctic, 12, 21
　　Common, 8, 21
　　Pacific, 4, 12, 21
　　Red-throated, **20**, 21
　　Yellow-billed, 21
Lophodytes cucullatus, 85
Lophura leucomelana, 377
Loxia curvirostra, 357
　　leucoptera, 357
Loxigilla violacea, 333
Loxioides bailleui, 365
Loxops coccineus, 365

Luscinia calliope, 269
　　cyane, 433
　　svecica, 269
Lymnocryptes minimus, 141

— M —
Macronectes giganteus, 5
Magpie, Black-billed, 13, 245
　　Yellow-billed, 245
Magpie-Jay, Black-throated, 6
Mallard, 7, 69, 377
Mamo, Black, 367
　　Hawaii, 365
Mannikin, Chestnut, 417
　　Nutmeg, 417
Martin, Brown-chested, 237
　　Cuban, 237
　　Gray-breasted, 237
　　Purple, 237
　　Southern, 237
Meadowlark, Eastern, 349
　　Western, 1, 349, 409
Melamprosops phaeosoma, 367
Melanerpes aurifrons, 213
　　carolinus, 213
　　erythrocephalus, 213
　　formicivorus, 213
　　lewis, 213
　　uropygialis, 213
Melanitta fusca, 77
　　nigra, 77
　　perspicillata, 77
Meleagridinae, 101, 385
Meleagris gallopavo, 101, 385
Meliphagidae, 293
Melopsittaculus undulatus, 393
Melospiza georgiana, 341
　　lincolnii, 341
　　melodia, 341
Merganser, Common, 85
　　Hooded, 85
　　Red-breasted, 85
Mergellus albellus, 85
Mergus merganser, 85
　　serrator, 85
Merlin, 101
Micrathene whitneyi, 189
Millerbird, 261
Mimidae, 277, 401
Mimus gundlachii, 277
　　polyglottos, 277, 401
Mniotilta varia, 309
Mockingbird, Bahama, 277
　　Northern, 277, 401
Moho apicalis, 293
　　bishopi, 293
　　braccatus, 293
　　nobilis, 293
Molothrus aeneus, 349
　　ater, 349
　　bonariensis, 433
Monarchinae, 269
Moorhen, Common, 109
Motacilla alba, 285
　　cinerea, 285
　　flava, 285
　　lugens, 285
Motacillidae, 285
Murre, Common, 12, 165
　　Thick-billed, 12, 165
Murrelet, Ancient, 173, 433
　　Craveri's, 173
　　Kittlitz's, 173, 433
　　Marbled, **172**, 173
　　Xantus', 173

Muscicapa griseisticta, 269
    latirostris, 433
    sibirica, 269
Muscicapidae, 261, 401
Muscicapinae, 269
Myadestes lanaiensis, 4, 269
    myadestinus, 4, 269
    oahensis, 4, 269
    obscurus, 277
    palmeri, 277
    townsendi, 269
Mycteria americana, 61
Myiarchus, 12
    cinerascens, 229
    crinitus, 229
    nuttingi, 229
    sagrae, 229
    tuberculifer, 229
    tyrannulus, 229
Myioborus miniatus, 317
    pictus, 317
Myiodynastes luteiventris, 237
Myiopagis viridicata, 221
Myiopsitta monachus, 393
Myna, Common, 401
    Crested, 401
    Hill, 401

— N —

Needletail, White-throated, 197
Neocrex erythrops, 109
Neomorphinae, 181
Nesochen sandvicensis, 69
Night-Heron, Black-crowned, 53
    Yellow-crowned, **52**, 53
Nighthawk, Antillean, 197
    Common, 197
    Lesser, 197
Nightjar, Buff-collared, 197, 434
    Jungle, 197
Noddy, Black, 165
    Blue-gray, 165
    Brown, 165
Nucifraga columbiana, 245
Nukupuu, 365
Numenius americanus, 133
    arquata, 133
    borealis, 133
    madagascariensis, 133
    minutus, 133
    phaeopus, 133
    tahitiensis, 133
    tenuirostris, 133
Numida meleagris, 5
Nutcracker, Clark's, 245, 434
Nuthatch, Brown-headed, 261
    Pygmy, 261, 434
    Red-breasted, 253
    White-breasted, 253
Nyctea scandiaca, 189
Nycticorax nycticorax, 53
    violaceus, 53
Nyctidromus albicollis, 197

— O —

Oceanites oceanicus, 37
Oceanodroma castro, 37
    furcata, 37
    homochroa, 37
    leucorhoa, 37
    melania, 37
    microsoma, 45
    tethys, 37
    tristrami, 37
Odontophorinae, 109, 385

Oenanthe oenanthe, 269
Oldsquaw, 77
Olomao, 4, 269
Omao, 277
Oo, Bishop's, 12, 293
    Hawaii, 293
    Kauai, 14, 293
    Oahu, 293
Oporornis agilis, 317
    formosus, 317
    philadelphia, 317
    tolmiei, 317
Oreomystis bairdi, 365
    mana, 365
Oreortyx pictus, 109, 385
Oreoscoptes montanus, 277
Oriole, Altamira, **348**, 349
    Audubon's, 349
    Black-cowled, 349
    Black-vented, 349
    Hooded, 349
    Northern, 349
    Orchard, 349, 434
    Scott's, 349
    Spot-breasted, 409
    Streak-backed, 349
Ortalis vetula, 101, 377
Orthorhyncus cristatus, 6
Osprey, 85
Otus asio, 189
    flammeolus, 189
    kennicottii, 189
    sunia, 189
    trichopsis, 189
Ou, 365
Ovenbird, 309
Owl, Barred, 1, 8, 189
    Boreal, 197, 434
    Burrowing, 189
    Elf, 189
    Flammulated, 189
    Great Gray, 189
    Great Horned, 9, **188**, 189
    Long-eared, 189
    Northern Saw-whet, 197
    Short-eared, 189
    Snowy, 189
    Spotted, 189
Oxyura dominica, 85
    jamaicensis, 85
Oystercatcher, American, 125
    Black, 125

— P —

Pachyramphus aglaiae, 237
Padda oryzivora, 417
Pagophila eburnea, 157
Palila, 365
Palmeria dolei, 367
Pandion haliaetus, 85
Pandioninae, 85
Parabuteo unicinctus, 93
Parakeet, Canary-winged, 393
    Carolina, 8, 181
    Green, 181
    Monk, 393
    Rose-ringed, 393
Pardirallus maculatus, 109
Paridae, 253, 401
Paroaria capitata, 409
    coronata, 409
Paroreomyza flammea, 365
    maculata, 365
    montana, 365
Parrot, Lilac-crowned, 393

    Red-crowned, 181, **392**, 393
    Thick-billed, 181
    Yellow-headed, 181, 393
Parrotbill, Maui, 365
Partridge, Gray, 377
Parula americana, 301
    pitiayumi, 301
    superciliosa, 301
Parula, Northern, **300**, 301
    Tropical, 301
Parulinae, 301
Parus atricapillus, 253
    bicolor, 253
    carolinensis, 253
    cinctus, 253
    gambeli, 253
    hudsonicus, 253
    inornatus, 253
    rufescens, 253
    sclateri, 253
    varius, 401
    wollweberi, 253
Passer domesticus, 409
    montanus, 409
Passerculus sandwichensis, 333
Passerella iliaca, 341
Passeridae, 409
Passeriformes, 221, 393
Passerina amoena, 325
    ciris, 325
    cyanea, 325
    versicolor, 325
Pauraque, Common, 197
Pavo cristatus, 385
Peafowl, Common, 385
Pelagodroma marina, 37
Pelecanidae, 45
Pelecaniformes, 9, 45
Pelecanus erythrorhynchos, 45
    occidentalis, 45
Pelican, American White, 45
    Brown, **44**, 45
Perdix perdix, 377
Perisoreus canadensis, 245
Petrel, Bermuda, 29
    Black-capped, **28**, 29, 433
    Black-winged, 29
    Bonin, 11, 29
    Bulwer's, 29
    Cape, 5
    Cook's, 29
    Dark-rumped, 29
    Herald, 12, 29
    Jouanin's, 29
    Kermadec, 12, 29
    Mottled, 29
    Murphy's, 29, 433
    Phoenix, 5, 12, 29
    Soft-plumaged, 5, 29
    Solander's, 29
    Stejneger's, 29
    Tahiti, 5, 12
    White-necked, 29
Peucedramus taeniatus, 317
Pewee, Greater, 221
Phaeoprogne tapera, 237
Phaethon aethereus, 45
    lepturus, 45
    rubricauda, 45
Phaethontidae, 45
Phaetusa simplex, 165
Phainopepla, 293
Phainopepla nitens, 293
Phalacrocoracidae, 45

Phalacrocorax auritus, 45
    carbo, 45
    olivaceus, 45
    pelagicus, 45
    penicillatus, 45
    urile, 45
Phalaenoptilus nuttallii, 197
Phalarope, Red, 149
    Red-necked, 149
    Wilson's, **148**, 149
Phalaropodinae, 149
Phalaropus fulicaria, 149
    lobatus, 149
    tricolor, 149
Phasianidae, 101, 377
Phasianinae, 377
Phasianus colchicus, 385
Pheasant, Kalij, 377
    Ring-necked, **375**, 385
Pheucticus chrysopeplus, 325
    ludovicianus, 325
    melanocephalus, 325
Philomachus pugnax, 141
Phoebe, Black, 229
    Eastern, 229
    Say's, **228**, 229, 434
Phoenicopteridae, 61
Phoenicopteriformes, 61
Phoenicopterus ruber, 61
Phylloscopus borealis, 269
    fuscatus, 261
    sibilatrix, 261
Pica nuttalli, 245
    pica, 245
Picidae, 213
Piciformes, 213
Picinae, 213
Picoides albolarvatus, 221
    arcticus, 221
    borealis, 221
    nuttallii, 221
    pubescens, 221
    scalaris, 221
    stricklandi, 221
    tridactylus, 221
    villosus, 221
Pigeon, Band-tailed, 173
    Passenger, 8, **180**, 181
    Red-billed, 173
    Scaly-naped, 173
    White-crowned, 173
Pinguinus impennis, 165
Pinicola enucleator, 357
Pintail, Northern, 69
    White-cheeked, 6, 69
Pipilo aberti, 325
    chlorurus, 325
    erythrophthalmus, 325
    fuscus, 325
Pipit, Pechora, 285
    Red-throated, 285, 434
    Sprague's, **284**, 285
    Water, 15, 285
Piranga bidentata, 433
    flava, 317
    ludoviciana, 325
    olivacea, 325
    rubra, 317
Pitangus sulphuratus, 229
Plataleinae, 61
Platycercinae, 393
Plectrophenax hyperboreus, 341
    nivalis, 341
Plegadis chihi, 61

falcinellus, 61
Plover, Black-bellied, 117
  Common Ringed, 117
  Little Ringed, 117
  Mongolian, 117
  Mountain, 125
  Piping, 117
  Semipalmated, 117
  Snowy, 117
  Wilson's, 117, 433
Pluvialis apricaria, 117
  dominica, 117
  squatarola, 117
Pochard, Common, 77
Podiceps auritus, 21
  grisegena, 21
  nigricollis, 21
Podicipedidae, 21
Podicipediformes, 21
Podilymbus podiceps, 21
Polioptila caerulea, 269
  melanura, 269
  nigriceps, 269
Polyborus plancus, 93
Polysticta stelleri, 77
Poo-uli, 367
Pooecetes gramineus, 333
Poorwill, Common, 197
Porphyrula martinica, 109
Porzana carolina, 109
  palmeri, 109
  sandwichensis, 109
Prairie-Chicken, Greater, 101
  Lesser, 101
Pratincole, Oriental, 433
Procellariidae, 29
Procellariiformes, 9, 11, 21
Procelsterna cerulea, 165
Progne chalybea, 237
  cryptoleuca, 237
  elegans, 237
  subis, 237
Protonotaria citrea, 309
Prunella montanella, 285
Prunellidae, 285
Psaltriparus minimus, 253
Pseudonestor xanthophrys, 365
Psittacidae, 181, 393
Psittaciformes, 181, 393
Psittacinae, 393
Psittacula krameri, 393
Psittirostra psittacea, 365
Ptarmigan, Rock, 101
  White-tailed, 15, 101, 385
  Willow, 101, 385
Pterocles exustus, 385
Pteroclididae, 385
Pterodroma alba, 5, 29
  arminjoniana, 29
  cahow, 29
  cookii, 29
  externa, 29
  hasitata, 29
  hypoleuca, 29
  inexpectata, 29
  longirostris, 29
  mollis, 29
  neglecta, 29
  nigripennis, 29
  phaeopygia, 29
  rostrata, 5
  solandri, 29
  ultima, 29
Ptilogonatidae, 293

Ptilogonys cinereus, 6, 433
Ptychoramphus aleuticus, 173
Puaiohi, 277
Puffin, Atlantic, 173
  Horned, 173
  Tufted, 173
Puffinus assimilis, 37
  auricularis, 37
  bulleri, 37
  carneipes, 37
  creatopus, 29
  gravis, 37
  griseus, 37
  lherminieri, 37
  nativitatis, 37
  opisthomelas, 37
  pacificus, 37
  puffinus, 37
  tenuirostris, 37
Pycnonotidae, 401
Pycnonotus cafer, 401
  jocosus, 401
Pygmy-Owl, Ferruginous, 189
  Northern, 189
Pyrocephalus rubinus, 229
Pyrrhula pyrrhula, 357
Pyrrhuloxia, 325

— Q —
Quail, California, 109, 385
  Elegant, 5
  Gambel's, 109, 385
  Japanese, 377
  Montezuma, 109
  Mountain, 109, 385
  Scaled, 109, 385
Quail-Dove, Key West, 181
  Ruddy, 181
Quiscalus major, 349
  mexicanus, 349
  quiscula, 349

— R —
Rail, Black, **108**, 109
  Clapper, 109
  Hawaiian, 109
  King, 109
  Laysan, 109
  Spotted, 109
  Virginia, 109, 433
  Yellow, 109
Rallidae, 109
Rallinae, 109
Rallus elegans, 109
  limicola, 109
  longirostris, 109
Raven, Chihuahuan, 253
  Common, 253
Razorbill, 165
Recurvirostra americana, 125
Recurvirostridae, 125
Redhead, 77
Redpoll, Common, 357
  Hoary, 4, 357
Redshank, Spotted, 125
Redstart, American, **308**, 309
  Painted, 1, **316**, 317
  Slate-throated, 317
Redwing, 277
Reed-Bunting, Common, 341
  Pallas', 341
Reef-Heron, Western, 53
Regulus calendula, 269
  satrapa, 269
Remizidae, 253

Rhodacanthis flaviceps, 365
  palmeri, 365
Rhodostethia rosea, 157
Rhodothraupis celaeno, 325
Rhynchopsitta pachyrhyncha, 181
Ridgwayia pinicola, 277
Riparia riparia, 245
Rissa brevirostris, 157
  tridactyla, 157
Roadrunner, Greater, 181
Robin, American, 8, 277
  Clay-colored, 277
  Rufous-backed, 277
  Siberian Blue, 433
Rosefinch, Common, 357
Rostrhamus sociabilis, 85
Rubythroat, Siberian, **268**, 269
Ruff, 141
Rynchopinae, 165
Rynchops niger, 165

— S —
Salpinctes obsoletus, 261
Sanderling, 133
Sandgrouse, Chestnut-bellied, 385
Sandpiper, Baird's, 141
  Broad-billed, 141
  Buff-breasted, 141, 433
  Common, 133
  Curlew, 141, 433
  Green, 125
  Least, 141
  Marsh, 125
  Pectoral, **140**, 141
  Purple, 141
  Rock, 141
  Semipalmated, 141
  Sharp-tailed, **140**, 141
  Solitary, 125
  Spoonbill, 141
  Spotted, **132**, 133
  Stilt, 141, 433
  Terek, 133
  Upland, 133
  Western, 141
  White-rumped, 141
  Wood, 125, 433
Sapsucker, Red-breasted, 221
  Red-naped, 4, 221
  Williamson's, 221, 434
  Yellow-bellied, 221
Saxicola torquata, 269
Sayornis nigricans, 229
  phoebe, 229
  saya, 229
Scaup, Greater, 77
  Lesser, 77
Scolopacidae, 125
Scolopacinae, 125
Scolopax minor, 149
  rusticola, 149
Scops-Owl, Oriental, 189
Scoter, Black, 77
  Surf, 77
  White-winged, 77
Screech-Owl, Eastern, 189
  Western, 189, 433
  Whiskered, 189
Sea-Eagle, Steller's, 85
Seedeater, White-collared, 325
Seiurus aurocapillus, 309
  motacilla, 317
  noveboracensis, 309
Selasphorus platycercus, 205
  rufus, 213

  sasin, 213
Serinus canaria, 409
  mozambicus, 409
Setophaga ruticilla, 309
Shama, White-rumped, 401
Shearwater, Audubon's, 37
  Black-vented, 12, 37
  Buller's, 9, **36**, 37
  Christmas, 37
  Cory's, **28**, 29
  Flesh-footed, 37
  Greater, 9, 37
  Little, 37
  Manx, 12, 37
  Pink-footed, 9, 29
  Short-tailed, 37
  Sooty, 9, 37, 433
  Streaked, 29
  Townsend's, 12, 37, 433
  Wedge-tailed, 37
Shelduck, Common, 6
  Ruddy, 6
Shoveler, Northern, 77, 434
Shrike, Brown, 293
  Loggerhead, 1, 14, 293
  Northern, **292**, 293
Sialia currucoides, 269
  mexicana, 269
  sialis, 269
Sicalis flaveola, 409
Silky-flycatcher, Gray, 6, 433
Silverbill, Warbling, 417
Siskin, Eurasian, 5, 357
  Pine, 357
Sitta canadensis, 253
  carolinensis, 253
  pusilla, 261
  pygmaea, 261
Sittidae, 253
Sittinae, 253
Skimmer, Black, 165
Skua, Great, 12, 149
  South Polar, 12, 149
Skylark, Eurasian, 237, 393
Smew, 85
Snipe, Common, 141
  Jack, 141
  Pin-tailed, 149
Solitaire, Townsend's, 10, 269
Somateria fischeri, 77
  mollissima, 77
  spectabilis, 77
Sora, 109
Sparrow, American Tree, 10, 333
  Bachman's, 1, 14, 333
  Baird's, 333
  Black-chinned, 333
  Black-throated, **332**, 333
  Botteri's, 333
  Brewer's, 333, 434
  Cassin's, 333
  Chipping, 16, 333
  Clay-colored, 1, 333
  Eurasian Tree, 409
  Field, 333
  Five-striped, 1, 333
  Fox, 341
  Golden-crowned, 341
  Grasshopper, 333
  Harris', 10, 341
  Henslow's, 1, 14, 333, 434
  House, **408**, 409
  Java, 417
  Lark, 333

Le Conte's, 333
Lincoln's, 341
Olive, 325
Rufous-crowned, 16, 333
Rufous-winged, 333
Sage, 11, 333
Savannah, 333
Seaside, 15, 341, 434
Sharp-tailed, 15, 341
Song, 341
Swamp, 9, 10, 341
Vesper, 333
White-crowned, **340**, 341
White-throated, 10, **340**, 341
Worthen's, 333
Sphyrapicus nuchalis, 4, 221
  ruber, 221
  thyroideus, 221
  varius, 221
Spindalis zena, 317
Spiza americana, 325
Spizella arborea, 333
  atrogularis, 333
  breweri, 333
  pallida, 333
  passerina, 333
  pusilla, 333
  wortheni, 333
Spoonbill, Roseate, **60**, 61
Sporophila torqueola, 325
Starling, European, 293, **400**, 401
Starthroat, Plain-capped, 205
Stelgidopteryx serripennis, 245
Stellula calliope, 205
Stercorariinae, 149
Stercorarius longicaudus, 149
  parasiticus, 149
  pomarinus, 149
Sterna albifrons, 12, 433
  aleutica, 165
  anaethetus, 165
  antillarum, 165
  caspia, 157
  dougallii, 157
  elegans, 157
  forsteri, 165
  fuscata, 165
  hirundo, 157
  lunata, 165
  maxima, 157
  nilotica, 157
  paradisaea, 165
  sandvicensis, 157
Sterninae, 157
Stilt, Black-necked, **124**, 125
  Black-winged, 125
Stint, Little, 141, 433
  Long-toed, 141
  Rufous-necked, 141, 433
  Temminck's, 141
Stonechat, 5, 269
Stork, Wood, **60**, 61
Storm-Petrel, Ashy, 37
  Band-rumped, 37, 433
  Black, 37
  British, 37
  Fork-tailed, **36**, 37
  Leach's, 37
  Least, 45
  Sooty, 11, 37
  Wedge-rumped, 37
  White-faced, 37
  Wilson's, 9, 37
Streptopelia chinensis, 393

  decaocto, 434
  risoria, 385, 434
  roseogrisea, 434
Streptoprocne zonaris, 197
Strigidae, 189
Strigiformes, 189, 393
Strix nebulosa, 189
  occidentalis, 189
  varia, 189
Sturnella magna, 349
  neglecta, 349, 409
Sturnidae, 293, 401
Sturninae, 293, 401
Sturnus vulgaris, 293, 401
Sula bassanus, 45
  dactylatra, 45
  leucogaster, 45
  nebouxii, 45
  sula, 45
Sulidae, 45
Surfbird, 133
Surnia ulula, 189
Swallow, Bahama, 245
  Bank, 245
  Barn, 245
  Cave, 245
  Cliff, 245
  Northern Rough-winged, 245
  Tree, iii, 237
  Violet-green, 245
Swan, Mute, 377
  Trumpeter, 61
  Tundra, 16, 61
  Whooper, 61
Swift, Antillean Palm, 205
  Black, 197
  Chimney, 197
  Common, 197
  Fork-tailed, 205
  Vaux's, 197
  White-collared, 197
  White-throated, 205
Swiftlet, Gray, 5, 393
Sylviinae, 261, 401
Synthliboramphus antiquus, 173
  craveri, 173
  hypoleucus, 173

— T —

Tachornis phoenicobia, 205
Tachybaptus dominicus, 21
Tachycineta bicolor, 237
  cyaneoviridis, 245
  thalassina, 245
Tadorna ferruginea, 6
  tadorna, 6
Tanager, Flame-colored, 433
  Hepatic, 1, 317
  Scarlet, 325
  Stripe-headed, 317
  Summer, 317
  Western, 325
Tarsiger cyanurus, 269
Tattler, Gray-tailed, 133
  Wandering, 133
Teal, Baikal, 69
  Blue-winged, 69
  Cinnamon, 6, 77
  Falcated, 6, 69
  Green-winged, 69
Telespyza cantans, 365
  ultima, 365
Tern, Aleutian, 165
  Arctic, 165
  Black, 165

  Bridled, 165, 433
  Caspian, 157
  Common, 157
  Elegant, 1, 6, 9, 157
  Forster's, 165, 433
  Gray-backed, 165
  Gull-billed, 157, 433
  Large-billed, 165
  Least, 12, 165
  Little, 12, 433
  Roseate, 157, 433
  Royal, 157, 433
  Sandwich, 157
  Sooty, 165
  White, **164**, 165
  White-winged, 165, 433, 434
Tetraoninae, 101, 385
Thick-knee, Double-striped, 117
Thrasher, Bendire's, 285
  Brown, 285
  California, 285
  Crissal, 285
  Curve-billed, 6, 11, 16, 285, **416**
  Le Conte's, 285
  Long-billed, 285
  Sage, 277, 434
Thraupinae, 317
Threskiornithidae, 61
Threskiornithinae, 61
Thrush, Aztec, 277
  Dusky, 277
  Eye-browed, 277
  Gray-cheeked, 15, 277
  Hermit, 277
  Swainson's, 277
  Varied, 10, 277
  Wood, **276**, 277
Thryomanes bewickii, 261
Thryothorus ludovicianus, 261
Tiaris bicolor, 325
  olivacea, 409
Timaliinae, 277, 401
Tit, Siberian, 253
  Varied, 401
Titmouse, Bridled, 253
  Plain, 253
  Tufted, 1, 253
Tityrinae, 237
Towhee, Abert's, 325
  Brown, 8, 325
  Green-tailed, 325
  Rufous-sided, 325
Toxostoma bendirei, 285
  crissale, 285
  curvirostre, 285
  lecontei, 285
  longirostre, 285
  redivivum, 285
  rufum, 285
Tree-Pipit, Brown, 285
  Olive, 285
Tringa erythropus, 125
  flavipes, 125
  glareola, 125
  melanoleuca, 125
  nebularia, 125
  ochropus, 125
  solitaria, 125
  stagnatilis, 125
Trochilidae, 205
Troglodytes aedon, 261
  troglodytes, 261
Troglodytidae, 261

Trogon elegans, 213
Trogon, Eared, 213
  Elegant, 213
Trogonidae, 213
Trogoniformes, 213
Tropicbird, Red-billed, 9, 45, 433
  Red-tailed, 45
  White-tailed, 45, 433
Tryngites subruficollis, 141
Turdinae, 269, 401
Turdus grayi, 277
  iliacus, 277
  merula, 277
  migratorius, 277
  naumanni, 277
  obscurus, 277
  pilaris, 277
  rufopalliatus, 277
Turkey, Wild, 101, 385, **416**
Turnstone, Black, 133
  Ruddy, 133
Turtle-Dove, Collared, 434
  Ringed, **384**, 385, 434
Tympanuchus cupido, 101
  pallidicinctus, 101
  phasianellus, 101
Tyrannidae, 221
Tyranninae, 229
Tyrannus caudifasciatus, 237
  couchii, 237
  crassirostris, 237
  dominicensis, 237
  forficatus, 237
  melancholicus, 237
  savana, 237
  tyrannus, 237
  verticalis, 237
  vociferans, 237
Tyto alba, 189, 393
Tytonidae, 189, 393

— U —

Ula-ai-hawane, 365
Upupa epops, 213
Upupidae, 213
Uraeginthus bengalus, 409
Uria aalge, 165
  lomvia, 165

— V —

Vanellinae, 117
Vanellus vanellus, 117
Veery, 277
Verdin, 253
Vermivora bachmani, 301
  celata, 301
  chrysoptera, 301
  crissalis, 301
  luciae, 301
  peregrina, 301
  pinus, 301
  ruficapilla, 301
  virginiae, 301
Vestiaria coccinea, 365
Violet-ear, Green, 6, 205
Vireo altiloquus, 301
  atricapillus, 293
  bellii, 293
  crassirostris, 293
  flavifrons, 293
  gilvus, 301
  griseus, 293
  huttoni, 301
  magister, 301
  olivaceus, 301

philadelphicus, 301
solitarius, 293
vicinior, 293
Vireo, Bell's, 293, 434
  Black-capped, 293
  Black-whiskered, 15, 301
  Gray, 293
  Hutton's, 301
  Philadelphia, 301, 434
  Red-eyed, 301, **416**
  Solitary, 293
  Thick-billed, 293
  Warbling, 301
  White-eyed, 293
  Yellow-throated, 293, 434
  Yucatan, 301
Vireonidae, 293
Vireoninae, 293
Vulture, Black, 6, 85
  Turkey, 85

— W —

Wagtail, Black-backed, 12, 285
  Gray, 285
  White, 12, 285, 434
  Yellow, 285, 434
Warbler, Arctic, 269
  Bachman's, 8, 14, 301
  Bay-breasted, 309
  Black-and-white, 309
  Black-throated Blue, **308**, 309
  Black-throated Gray, 309
  Black-throated Green, 309
  Blackburnian, 309
  Blackpoll, 15, 309
  Blue-winged, 301
  Canada, 317
  Cape May, 301
  Cerulean, 16, 309
  Chestnut-sided, 301
  Colima, 301
  Connecticut, 317
  Crescent-chested, 301
  Dusky, 261
  Fan-tailed, 317
  Golden-cheeked, 309
  Golden-crowned, 317
  Golden-winged, 301, 434
  Grace's, 1, 309
  Hermit, 309
  Hooded, 10, 317, 434
  Kentucky, 317, 434
  Kirtland's, 309
  Lanceolated, 261
  Lucy's, 301
  MacGillivray's, 317
  Magnolia, 301
  Mourning, 317, 434
  Nashville, 301
  Olive, **316**, 317
  Orange-crowned, 301
  Palm, 16, 309
  Pine, 309
  Prairie, 10, 309
  Prothonotary, 309
  Red-faced, **316**, 317
  Rufous-capped, 317
  Swainson's, 309
  Tennessee, 301
  Townsend's, 309
  Virginia's, 301
  Wilson's, 317
  Wood, 261
  Worm-eating, 309
  Yellow, 301
  Yellow-rumped, 8, 309, **416**
  Yellow-throated, 6, 11, 309, 434
Waterthrush, Louisiana, 317
  Northern, 309
Waxbill, Black-rumped, 417
  Common, 417
  Lavender, 409
  Orange-cheeked, 417
Waxwing, Bohemian, 285
  Cedar, 285
Wheatear, Northern, 269
Whimbrel, 133
Whip-poor-will, 1, **196**, 197
Whistling-Duck, Black-bellied, 61, 433
  Fulvous, 61
White-eye, Japanese, 409
Wigeon, American, 77
  Eurasian, 10, 77
Willet, 125, 434
Wilsonia canadensis, 317
  citrina, 317
  pusilla, 317
Wood-Pewee, Eastern, 229
  Western, 229
Woodcock, American, **148**, 149
  Eurasian, 149
Woodpecker, Acorn, 213, 433
  Black-backed, 221
  Downy, 221
  Gila, 213
  Golden-fronted, 213
  Hairy, 221
  Ivory-billed, 8, 221
  Ladder-backed, **220**, 221
  Lewis', 213
  Nuttall's, **220**, 221
  Pileated, 221
  Red-bellied, 1, 213
  Red-cockaded, 1, **220**, 221
  Red-headed, 213
  Strickland's, 221
  Three-toed, 221, 434
  White-headed, 221
Woodstar, Bahama, 205
Wren, Bewick's, 1, 14, 16, 261
  Cactus, 261
  Canyon, 261
  Carolina, 1, **260**, 261
  House, 261
  Marsh, 13, 261
  Rock, 261
  Sedge, 261
  Winter, 261
Wrentit, **276**, 277
Wryneck, Eurasian, 213

— X —

Xanthocephalus xanthocephalus, 349
Xema sabini, 157
Xenus cinereus, 133

— Y —

Yellowlegs, Greater, 125
  Lesser, 125
Yellowthroat, Bahama, 317
  Common, 317
  Gray-crowned, 317

— Z —

Zenaida asiatica, 173, 393
  aurita, 173
  macroura, 173, 393
Zonotrichia albicollis, 341
  atricapilla, 341
  leucophrys, 341
  querula, 341
Zosteropidae, 409
Zosterops japonicus, 409